THE OFFICIAL® GUIDE TO
ARTIFACTS OF
ANCIENT
CIVILIZATIONS

THE OFFICIAL® GUIDE TO ARTIFACTS OF ANCIENT CIVILIZATIONS

FIRST EDITION

by ALEX G. MALLOY

Foreword by HARMER JOHNSON

HOUSE OF COLLECTIBLES
THE BALLANTINE PUBLISHING GROUP · NEW YORK

Important Notice. All of the information, including valuations, in this book has been compiled from the most reliable sources, and every effort has been made to eliminate errors and questionable data. Nevertheless, the possibility of error, in a work of such immense scope, always exists. The publisher will not be held responsible for losses that may occur in the purchase, sale, or other transaction of items because of information contained herein. Readers who feel they have discovered errors are invited to *write* and inform us, so they may be corrected in subsequent editions. Those seeking further information on the topics covered in this book are advised to refer to the complete line of *Official Price Guides* published by the House of Collectibles.

 This is a registered trademark of Random House, Inc.

Published by: House of Collectibles
                 The Ballantine Publishing Group
                 201 East 50th Street
                 New York, NY 10022

Distributed by The Ballantine Publishing Group, a division of Random House, Inc., New York, and simultaneously in Canada by Random House of Canada Limited, Toronto.

http://www.randomhouse.com

Manufactured in the United States of America

ISBN: 0-676-60079-4
ISSN: 1096-2360

Cover design by Kristine V. Mills-Noble

Cover photo by George Kerrigan. By permission of David A.J. Liebert, The Time Machine Co., Queens, NY

Text and layout editor: Eric S. Percival

First Edition: November 1997

10 9 8 7 6 5 4 3 2 1

Thy word is a lamp unto my feet and a light unto my path.
Psalms 80:13

CONTENTS

ACKNOWLEDGMENTS

Over twenty-six years ago, Jerry Eisenberg encouraged me to establish an Ancient Gallery of Artifacts on Madison Avenue in New York, just one block from the Metropolitan Museum of Art. He guided me, consigned a multitude of fine items to me, and generally encouraged me in the field of selling ancient art and artifacts. The result for me was, in 1971, a fine catalogue of over 300 objects offered for sale. Thank you, Jerry.

During this period, many new colleagues guided and encouraged me. Among these are Peter Sharrer, the late Ed Smith, Helen Woodhull, and Harmer Johnson, then with Parke-Bernet Galleries, now director of Harmer Johnson Books. To Harmer, who has been so kind as to write the foreword to this book, a thank you.

During the early 1970s, while attending various auction sales in New York City, I met a dealer who has now been a friend for over twenty-five years. David Liebert assisted me in my gallery in the Fuller Building at 57th and Madison Ave., and today has a fine mail order auction business. Utilizing his vast knowledge of ancient art, David has now contributed some of the introductions to this publication.

At this same time, Joe Rose, with his vast stories, was the Director at Harmer Rooke. He kept us all laughing. His son, Howard Rose, has established a New York City auction house in his own right, Arte Primitivo. Howard has granted the use of his auction cataloguing for most of the Pre-Columbian section of this book, along with his fine Pre-Columbian photographs.

Over the years, many people have assisted me in cataloguing antiquities. Early members of this group include Judith A. Cox, Carl S. Berkowitz, Irene F. Preston, David Liebert, and Leslie A. Naughton. During the last ten years, the list has grown: Allen G. Berman, DeAnne E. Komlo, Alison James, Ruth Malloy, Camden W. Percival, David W. Sorenson, Ph.D., Christine Nash, and Arlen R. Percival have all worked on cataloguing.

The production of this book fell into the capable hands of Eric S. Percival, whose computer skills are surpassed only by his abilities in the theatre. Early assistance with the book was rendered by Kathleen F. Terkelsen.

A special thank you to Elaine, without whose support this book would not exist. Her tolerance of antiquities, games, and hostas has been highly appreciated. Special thanks to Rod, Cynthia, Clara and Cove Malloy, and Carey, Becky, and Abbey Hall.

Alex G. Malloy

FOREWORD

The collecting of antiquities is not a recent pursuit, though the considerable coverage it now receives in the international press might suggest otherwise. Collectors have been active for hundreds, indeed thousands, of years. The Romans, admiring the ancient Greeks, were passionate in their acquisition of Classical sculpture, and took this compliment a step further by making their own copies of early Greek marbles. In later centuries wealthy patrons and aristocrats of Europe amassed superb collections of marble and bronze statuary, and painted vases. Most have long since been sold and dispersed, and now form the core of the great museum collections of the world. Early Spanish explorers in the Americas acquired Pre-Columbian masterpieces that now lie in the museums of the Vatican, Vienna, and elsewhere in Western Europe. Increasing archaeological exploration and study fanned this fascination with the past, and the founding of public museums enabled the populace to see and appreciate these ancient treasures.

Dealers and auction houses have sold ancient art for hundreds of years, but it is only relatively recently that the public has been exposed to the collecting opportunity. This development was spurred by the international auction houses, primarily Sotheby's and Christie's, and the large number of dealers in Europe and the United States.

Major antiquities command prices commensurate with fine works of art in other fields. The public auction record for a Pre-Columbian work currently stands at $429,000, paid for an Olmec serpentine mask (Sotheby's, New York, 1991). The antiquity record is held by an Assyrian gypsum relief that sold for $11,860,310 (Christie's, London, 1994). However, the vast majority of objects are remarkably inexpensive, considering their great antiquity. This fact is little known by most people, and is therefore a significant factor in the slowness of the market's development.

The diversity of available and affordable material is almost endless. Finely worked Prehistoric flint implements from Africa and Asia, dating back more than 500,000 years, and palpable evidence of the beginnings of mankind, are easily acquired. Roman glass vessels, in a great variety of colors and perfectly preserved after two thousand years, can be bought for less than $300. Painted Greek vases, depicting mythological and domestic scenes, appear in auction house and dealers' catalogues. Ancient Egyptian sculptures, representing the myriad of deities in the pantheon, are readily obtainable. Stone, bronze, terracotta and wood statuary, vessels and utensils, some simple in their design, others highly complex with decorative and abstract forms, are plentiful. Even finely fashioned ancient gold and silver jewelry, set with precious and semi-precious stones, and wearable after thousands of years, appear with regularity in auctions and galleries.

In the Pre-Columbian world of Meso-America and South America, where the material cultures date back to before 2000 B.C., pottery and terracotta vessels and figures are in profusion and plentiful on the market, as are stone sculptures and multi-colored tunics and textiles, brilliant examples of the weaver's art that are more than 2,000 years old.

As in all collecting, the ancient field is beset by forgeries. This problem was accentuated by the rising prices of the 1970s and 1980s, though the basements of many museums contain examples of the early forgeries dating to the 19th century and earlier. All collectors, including the finest of museums, make mistakes, but this should not deter either the beginning or advanced buyer. A good relationship with other collectors, dealers and auction houses, where knowledge is readily proffered and shared, minimizes the inherent risks.

In the past three decades many countries have become more aware of their cultural heritage, particularly as the financial worth of art increased. This interest, and concern that too many objects are leaving their countries of origin, has resulted in a tightening of controls over what should and should not be legally exported. The UNESCO Convention on Cultural Property certainly dampened Pre-Columbian collecting enthusiasm in the 1970s, while currently proposed action in Europe is further challenging the free movement of property.

Fortunately, many hundreds of years of international collecting have resulted in a vast amount of ancient art coming into Western European and American collections. It is these objects that will continue to circulate amongst dealers and collectors, being added to existing collections as well as forming the bases for new collectors as they plunge into the exciting world of antiquities.

Harmer Johnson

PREFACE

A book on collecting antiquities, directed at the starting collector, has long been needed. There have been beginners' guides published in England, over ten years ago, which treated this collecting field in a basic introductory manner. This book was envisioned with the thought of bringing the potential collector into this vast field with confidence. It was considered important to give the reader the beginning knowledge on how to collect and what can be collected. Along with this, a general descriptive guide to objects offered and sold in the marketplace, with values, would be needed. Time charts were added to place each object into its time frame and establish its relationship to others around it. Various pictorial charts have been provided to assist the collector in identifying shapes and deities encountered. A glossary is provided to help the reader with the unique terms of the field, and a select bibliography provides a guide for further reading.

The scope of the book is ancient art and antiquities, from earliest man to the fall of Rome. Ancient Eastern Asia, including ancient China, Japan, and the western Pacific Rim are not addressed in this volume. Artifacts from the aboriginal Indians of North America north of the Rio Grande have also been excluded.

The intent of this book is to acquaint the reader with antiquities available for all pocketbooks, with the emphasis on ancient artifacts costing $300 or less. The more spectacular objects of ancient art are usually for the well-to-do connoisseur and the active museums, and are not the focus of this book. These pages reveal ancient objects which can be held and collected by everyone.

The values presented are for artifacts which have sold over a period of ten years. The values of the older objects sold have been updated to the current international market. The values of the objects one will encounter can be higher or lower, depending on condition, mounting, and other factors. These values are intended as a guide and can change. The prices are what a dealer in antiquities would ask, not what a dealer would pay.

THE OFFICIAL® GUIDE TO
ARTIFACTS OF
ANCIENT
CIVILIZATIONS

COLLECTING ANTIQUITIES

Antiquities are those objects made or fashioned by man in ancient times. These artifacts span a long period of time from the emergence of early man to the fall of Rome in 476 A.D., and in the New World before first contact with European man. These items range from a stone axehead made by Homo Habilis, to a clay tablet from Ur III in Mesopotamia written in cuneiform writing, to a Jewish lamp made in ancient Israel during the time of Moses, to a hand-crafted terracotta head of Hera modeled by an ancient Greek Athenian, to an iron Roman key from the 3rd century A.D., to a Peruvian head vessel. All these objects have long been viewed at museums throughout the world. They have been the subject of wonder and study. Now the general public is becoming aware that you can own an ancient Roman ring with a stone depicting Fortuna standing. Yes, you can own these items and collect them.

Most ancient artifacts found can be categorized as hard items such as stone, metal, clay and pottery, and glass, but sometimes wood, cloth and leather are encountered. These have survived hundreds and sometimes thousands of years. Wood and cloth will be found in specific environments and are available on a limited scale.

The collecting of antiquities has been pursued as long as man has been on the earth. The question arises, "What could I collect?" The answer is simple: "What do you like?" or "What are you fascinated with?" One could collect all objects from a certain people group like the Achaeminid Dynasty. These Persians were the foes of the Greeks and they produced metal weapons, stone seals, metal coins, terracotta figures and pottery. All of these would make a nice collection. Collecting a specific category within a large historic group, such as Egyptian amulets, is possible. Egyptian amulets were made in stone, metal, and mostly faience. These were objects that the Egyptians wore and they relate to the vast Egyptian culture and its religious beliefs. Today, this is a popular series to collect.

Some collectors specialize in collecting lamps. While most ancient lamps are made of terracotta, some are found in metal and even stone. Ancient lamps were made during three periods. These include Biblical, Greek, and Roman. Lamps will generally be reasonably priced, and as a result one can put together a representative collection. Each lamp can be purchased well below $250. If you have an unlimited or high budget you could consider collecting Roman marble sculpture. Your collection might rival the Boston Museum of Fine Arts or the Metropolitan Museum of Art, although for the most part this is not possible for the general collector of antiquities. These ideas should help you focus on how and what you can collect. If you can't focus on a specific area it is good to start by obtaining objects from each historical area, that is, a selection from Early Man, Western Asia, the Holy Land, etc.

After you have chosen a category or a pattern of collecting, the next step is to get your feet wet. Traditionally ancient artifacts can be purchased at auction or private sales. You can't just go down to the corner shop and purchase a Roman-Egyptian terracotta head; you need to contact an antiquity dealer or write for fixed priced or auction catalogues. A list of auction houses, mail bid dealers, or ancient art galleries is provided later on. Terminology can be intimidating, but that's why you bought this guide book of terms used and values encountered. Today there are knowledgeable dealers and auction houses throughout the United States and Europe. The expanding interest in collecting ancient art has resulted in newer knowledgeable dealers. Just thirty years ago antiquities in the United States could be found in New York City and the Los Angeles area only. Now one can travel to Boston, Chicago, San Francisco, Washington, Denver, and San Diego, as well as sites in New Jersey, Maryland, Connecticut, Florida, and Michigan, to view and purchase antiquities. One of the fine sources to find ancient art is Europe. London, Paris, Zurich, Basle, Rome, Milan, Amsterdam, and Munich, along with Israel and Egypt, are among the main areas to search for antiquities. A caveat warning regarding purchasing in the Middle East: know your dealer or ask yourself if you can return any object in six months or a year to this dealer for a refund if it is a fake.

BUYING ANTIQUITIES

Buying at auction. Buying antiquities at auction has long proven to be a satisfactory route. Public or mail bid auction houses provide well-documented catalogues of the items to be sold. All reputable houses and dealers guarantee each object or lot sold. Many have viewing times for inspection. The auctioneer will be glad to discuss any lot you might be interested in. You might want to know what color the patina on a Roman bronze figure of Jupiter is, and the quality of the surface and facial features. It is always advisable to carefully read the terms of sale and to follow them. Some sales will have lots with multiple objects. Feel free to inquire about specific details, as sometimes these lots will be overlooked by other bidders. It is good to understand the perimeters of the auction house reserve. The reserve is the price that the lot will not go under. This price is to protect the seller. The auction house has a responsibility to you, the buyer, and to the seller. Today a 10-15% buyer's fee will be added to the price. The seller also will receive 10-25% less to pay the auction house commission. These commissions sometimes will be more depending on the quality of the consignment. A potential bidder must read descriptions carefully, as some lots are sold as is, or they might say "in the style of" or just not even give a date. This can often mean that the quality is sub par or that there is question as to when the object was made, be it ancient or modern. Buying at auction has many advantages. You can research any object before the sale and determine what you are willing to pay. You can decide which items you want to go for and pursue them only. Some of the finer antiquities appear only at auction.

Buying from fixed price lists. This means of purchasing objects has many of the advantages of buying at auction. Researched catalogues provide the major advantage along with a usual return privilege. The price is set by the seller and you, the buyer, determine if it is worth it to you. There is no buyer's fee. The disadvantage is trying to buy it before someone else does. This requires the buyer to be aggressive and to contact the dealer directly via phone, fax or e-mail in a timely fashion.

Buying one on one. Buying from a dealer face to face has its disadvantages and advantages. You can view the object, study it, negotiate the price and purchase it in one sitting. Many collectors only wish to do business this way. The disadvantage is you can often get caught up in the pressure to make a final decision. You will not have the ability to check the object out further. This can be remedied by knowing your dealer and trusting his or her knowledge. This is usually not a problem with any antiquity dealer in the United States, Europe, or Australia; however, the problem can arise in other areas when trying to return objects, so be careful. It is always good advice to buy from specialists, because when you venture outside the specialist, you can get stung. I remember about twenty-five years ago I was shopping a flea market, and a dealer had a bronze Byzantine coin depicting the emperor Justin and his wife Sophia seated facing. I asked him how much it was. He then began to tell me this great story of the Spanish twins and the great rarity of this coin. His asking price was a special offer just for me – $100. I said no thank you. One year later I was in the same city where I had a table selling antiquities and ancient coins and this man came up to me. He did not remember me from the past and showed me this same coin and asked me what it was. I told him what it was and offered him $3 for it and he was happy with the offer.

VALUES

The values of antiquities can range from over one million dollars to as little as $25. With this vast range in prices, you must settle into the price range you wish to collect. Fine carved marble sculpture and fine painted Greek vases will put you into the class of competing with museums. Medium sized objects, that is, smaller than ten inches, will often run under $1000, but magnificent quality will push the price upwards. Gold and silver objects will usually start at $500 and up, while bronze and terracotta objects will generally be in a more affordable range. Interest in objects that exhibit ancient writing has spurred keen price increases, but such objects are still affordable to the general collector.

The collector must always keep in mind the quality of the object, or the original fineness with which it was made. A finely carved fragment of a marble hand can bring many thousands of dollars, while a small, crude marble hand can be purchased for under $100. Quality makes a great difference. Another main determiner of value is condition, or how well the object has stood the test of time and weathering. Low quality, rare Roman lamps sell for as little as ten for $150, while one of those same lamps in superb condition can bring in $150 by itself. A fibula in nice shape without the clasp pin can bring in $25, while the same fibula with the clasp pin can bring in $100 or more.

Generally the fine high end of the antiquities market, that is, the antiquities valued over $10,000, can see ups and downs predicated on external financial circumstances. A fast-rising stock market will see a lower value antique market. Collectors must always remember that the museums will always be after the finest objects, and this fact keeps the overall values fluctuating at a less dramatic swing. The lower priced antiquities' values have resulted in a different pattern over the last thirty years. There has come to be a larger discrepancy of values between finer and less fine objects. The old adage of supply and demand is more at work with antiquities valued under $300 than ever before. If these objects were being found at a lesser rate, like the high end antiquities, it would result in a fast increase in prices. Middle and lower quality antiquities are still being found in good quantities, especially in Eastern Europe, and this results in a steady state, or slightly rising values. As these sources dry up, so will the value increase. Today there are a large number of new collectors in the market. This number keeps growing each year, and the values will also ease upward as a result.

GRADING ANCIENT ART

The process of grading ancient objects is generally a logical process. One must imagine the object as it was new, then take into account what has happened to it with time. Wear and weathering of thousands of years has changed the object. Organic materials will tend not to survive, like wood, cloth, bone, baskets, sandals, etc. These can be found in dry climates like Egypt. Organic materials are more prone to deterioration, and will do so at a faster rate than other antiquities. If you do not protect these objects, the clock will keep ticking, and the destruction cycle will continue.

ANTIQUITY GRADING GUIDE

While antiquity grading has not reached the degree of uniformity that has been achieved in the numismatic industry, it is important to establish some means by which the bidder can reasonably understand the state of preservation of the items on which he is bidding. To this end we have provided the definitions below for the grading terms we have employed in this and our other antiquity catalogues. It should be understood that the terms used herein are descriptions only of that item as described in the catalogue. When a fragment is being offered, the grading is for just that portion present.

Reconstructed:	An item or section of an item reassembled exclusively of its original fragments.
Restored:	An absent portion of the item has been filled in with a modern replacement (either in the original or a "patch" color) in order to better convey the original form or shape of the item.
Superb:	A completely intact piece with original surfaces and glaze or patina. None but the most minute chipping or corrosion. A museum quality piece.
Choice:	An essentially intact piece with much of the original surfaces or patina. Minor chipping or corrosion will be present, not affecting over-all form. It is in this grade that most antiquities are collected.
Average:	The majority of the piece is present although it may be reconstructed. The surfaces may be subject to wear, abrasion or encrustation. Much excavated material is found in this grade.

Metal will show different rates of destruction. Gold, the noble metal, will not deteriorate, but many ancient gold items are electrum, which is a natural gold and silver alloy, and electrum does weather. Silver can crystallize and break. Oxides can form on silver, creating horn silver deposits, and this can obscure the fineness. Bronze is susceptible to oxides that can result in badly corroded pieces. Bronze disease is the dreaded foe of bronze. It is an oxide that eats into the bronze, and causes the surface to deteriorate. It can be spotted by its light green powder appearance, starting with little pin head spots and growing to cover the entire object. Fine, hard green patina will enhance the look and value of a bronze figure, but only if it is non-active; the active green spots caused by bronze disease will only lessen the object's beauty and value. Of the metals, bronze is the most prevalent found in metal antiquities. Many weapons and tools of iron were made during the Iron Age and later. However, fewer objects of iron have reached us today because iron deteriorates quickly once subjected to the air as it comes out of the ground. It is not uncommon to see small flakes of iron drop off a fine sword blade right before your own eyes. Treatment is essential to help preserve these antiquities.

Another factor in grading is what was worn or broken off during the years. An object could be worn or broken in antiquity, or it could have been broken in modern times. Patinas will usually tell the tale of when the damage occurred. Determining how much restoration has been performed on an object is of prime importance in grading and valuing an antiquity. Restoration has been done from ancient time up to today. Modern restoration is done to enhance the look and value of an object. There are three types of restoration. One is to restore and to add to minor parts missing, and made to hide traces of restoration. This would include such things as adding a small missing piece to a broken vase. The second is to add to minor parts missing, but not intended to make the restoration concealed. For example, if the missing piece of the vase were in the middle of a painting, the reconstruction might involve filling in the space, but leaving that part of the picture blank. These two types of restoration are generally acceptable, but will result in a lower value. The third type of restoration is to add to or make major areas present again, such as taking a statue of which only the legs remain, and adding on the full upper body. This is unacceptable to most collectors, as it is intended to create a new object that many consider close to a fake. To further illustrate these three types of restoration, let us apply each to an imagined terracotta figure of a standing ram, originally covered with a white slip, and some details in black and red. The first type of restoration would add a broken leg, or add to some chipped areas of the body only. The second type would do the same, and then add the white slip and finer details. The third type would add 3/4 of the front with head, legs, and paint-on details. In this case you would have started with only the body and back legs as genuine. This would not be acceptable to collectors.

Reconstruction is common in antiquities, especially in objects that are likely to break, such as pottery, terracottas, glass, lamps, jewelry, and wood objects. It involves taking a broken antiquity and putting the pieces back together, usually without adding any new ones. An example would be taking a shattered vase and gluing the pieces back together. This practice is certainly acceptable, but reconstruction can detract from the value if poorly done. However, reconstruction does not necessarily mean that an object will have a low value; in fact, the great multi-million dollar Euphoronos Greek vase of the Metropolitan Museum of Art was reconstructed.

CARE AND PRESERVATION OF ANTIQUITIES

There is no substitute for a professional restorer when dealing with a fine work of ancient art. While it is true that some simple procedures can be performed by the amateur collector, extensive repair, restoration, or cleaning of ancient art should best be placed in the hands of an expert restorer. The fee the restorer will charge is more than outweighed by the ability to safeguard against the loss and distress that could potentially be caused by inadvertently damaging or destroying a unique and irreplaceable object. Therefore, the following remarks on repair, conservation, and display are meant to enable the amateur to appreciate the problems involved. Under no circumstances should they be considered a "Do it yourself" guide to the repair and restoration of antiquities, as this should always be referred to a competent professional.

We should first consider a matter that should always be in the mind of anyone entrusted with the care of an ancient artifact. Antiquities, like fine machines, benefit greatly from what might be called preventative maintenance. One of the chief enemies of ancient art is excessive humidity, particularly during the summer months. Any visitor to a museum may have noticed the elaborate measures undertaken to control humidity and temperature. Wherever possible, it is wise to keep antiquities enclosed, usually in a glass fronted vitrine, cabinet, or case. Such a storage place should be provided with a small open container of silica gel desiccating crystals, obtainable from any chemical supply house. Silica gel is a blue crystal that turns pink when saturated. The crystals should be changed as soon as their color has changed. They may be reused when dried out in an ordinary oven at moderate heat. The color will turn back to blue. I find that the plastic caps of large drug store pill containers or jars make excellent receptacles for silica gel. Organic materials require some humidity, since they become brittle when overly dry. In excessively dry situations, they may require the use of a humidifier. It is recommended that a professional be consulted if there is any doubt. The use of a desiccant is essential for the prevention of bronze disease, a condition which causes the patina of an ancient bronze to break out into unsightly green spots. These spots will spread not only on the piece itself, but also to other nearby objects. The condition is caused by a chemical change in the cuprous chloride of a bronze. Cuprous chloride gives the green color often found in ancient bronze patina, but when diseased, it becomes cupric chloride. The metal then becomes soft and sheds a fine whitish powder which is a deadly poison if swallowed, inhaled, or allowed to penetrate the skin. A bronze affected with bronze disease should be isolated immediately, and treated by a trained professional.

Antiquities generally are not so fragile that they need to be handled with anything beyond normal caution, although bronzes should be handled as little as possible. Still, care should always be exercised in handling an ancient object. Pieces should not be moved by grasping extremities such as heads, arms, handles, rims, etc. Always handle an antiquity with both hands, and make sure it is firmly supported before movement is effected. Remember to only handle one piece at a time.

Needless to say, antiquities should rest firmly on a solid support even when stored. Space should be left between objects so that one object will not be inadvertently damaged when moving another. It is also unwise to place antiquities underneath any object which might accidentally fall on them. I will never forget the time, years ago, when I hung a picture over an open shelf of antiquities. For some reason I have never quite understood, after a few days the picture fell off the wall, shattering a fine South Italian kylix. If you must place your antiquities or any other valuable, breakable objects in open display, it should be your cardinal rule to allow them plenty of room in all directions. It is also possible to purchase glass or lucite display cases of varying sizes, which will give added beauty and protection to your collection. Lighting is also a factor. Organic materials such as textiles may suffer from exposure to strong light. In general, diffuse lighting placed at a distance is best.

Small objects such as scarabs and amulets may be stored in several ways. I find that the most efficient is to purchase velvet lined, divided trays from a jewelry supply house. These trays come in fitted cases. A coin dealer might also be able to supply you with a special cabinet designed for the storage and display of coins. Such cabinets are also good for small, relatively flat antiquities. Some dealers and collectors keep small objects in plastic bags or envelopes. This is usually safe enough if the object is not too delicate, but it is not very pleasing as a display method. If you cannot obtain jewelry trays, a fair substitute can be made from a compartmentalized plastic box, available in any hardware store. Just fill the compartments with cotton to provide a nest for your objects. If you plan to move your objects frequently, it is wise to purchase the special foam pads which fit over the jewelry trays mentioned above. This will prevent the objects from being damaged when the whole case is carried from one place to another. Particular care should be exercised when moving pieces stored in cabinets, in order to avoid striking the object on the shelf above. This precaution is especially important with ancient glass and pottery. When selecting a display site, it is also important to remember that children, pets, and admiring friends and relatives can spell the destruction of your prized possessions if the objects are not safely out of reach.

Ancient artifacts should be mounted for display in such a way as to show their characteristics properly. There are many types of mounts possible, depending on the size, condition, and nature of the antiquity. A large stone sculpture obviously requires different handling from a fragile, small piece of glass. Ancient Egyptian jewelry can often be mounted so that it may safely be worn today. Such mounting, however, should be done with taste and sympathy for the piece's value as an antiquity. I have, for example, seen jewelers mount scarabs so that the inscription cannot be seen. Larger objects may be mounted on bases made of various materials. Wood, marble, and lucite are quite popular for this purpose. Textiles, papyri, and other relatively flat objects may be framed for shelf display or hanging. Once again, it cannot be overemphasized that such mounting is best done by a trained professional. This is particularly true when pieces are already mounted in unsightly old mountings, since removal from the old mount can be disastrous if not done properly. I have known instances when well-meaning people damaged a fine piece in an overly hasty attempt to remove it from an unsightly setting. It is not essential that each piece in a collection be mounted, but it is essential that any mounted piece be properly done. Such proper mounting requires artistic taste, knowledge of materials, manual skill, and patience. While the skilled collector may save some money by doing it alone, it is best left to those who have spent their lives acquiring this ability.

If this is true of mounting, it is equally true of cleaning. When properly stored in a closed environment, antiquities should not need cleaning. The old story of the upstairs maid shattering an ancient vase with her carelessly wielded feather duster is not very far from reality. Collectors have been known to do irreparable damage to valuable objects in a misguided attempt to clean them. For example, the most frequently used cleaning method for ancient bronze requires a tedious and extremely exacting mechanical process of removal with special tools, often taking weeks and months. Over-cleaning by as much as a hundredth of a millimeter may destroy the surface. The restorer must know exactly how much of the patina may safely be removed, yet collectors have been known to immerse bronzes in solvents and even acids, in the mistaken belief that this is an effective method of cleaning them. While it is true that such materials are at times used by professional restorers, their use by the amateur is likely to result in severe damage. In fact, the collector should be wary of purchasing an overly cleaned piece, as damage may take many years to manifest itself. If there is some question regarding the condition of a piece, a competent restorer or reputable dealer should be consulted.

Condition is always important in determining the value of an object. Once again, the only sure protection for the collector is to buy from a reputable dealer who will point out any repairs or restoration done to the object. Such repairs and restorations, if done properly, are by their nature difficult to detect. This creates a great danger when buying at auction, since catalogue descriptions may be inaccurate, incomplete, or misleading. It is necessary for prospective buyers to examine pieces closely for condition prior to the sale, for they are frequently less than they appear to be from a distance. Such an examination will best be conducted with the aid of a good color-corrected magnifying glass, which will often reveal details that are difficult or impossible to discern with the naked eye. A strong pocket flashlight is also an invaluable tool in inspecting ancient art, as repairs and restorations are even harder to detect in poor or average light. When we consider that dealers and museums often must resort to sophisticated scientific techniques such as the use of ultraviolet light, x-rays, carbon-14, and thermoluminescence tests in order to detect forgeries, repairs, and restorations, it becomes clear that the guidance and security obtained by dealing with reputable professionals is of utmost importance. There are no hard and fast instant rules for detecting repairs and restorations. It is an ability that comes from prolonged study of both intact and repaired or restored antiquities. You must train your eye to detect anomalies in the physical composition of the object. You need to search for areas of discoloration, uneven surfaces with no apparent explanation, cracks which completely circle an object or part of an object, and areas which seem to make no sense stylistically in an otherwise stylistically sound piece. It is not uncommon to find what is called a "marriage" or a "pastiche." This is an object composed of two or more ancient parts not originally belonging to each other. For example, the base of one vessel found without its neck may be joined to the neck of another piece – either similar, or, at times, vastly inappropriate – found without its base. This is frequently done with ancient glass objects. The resulting whole, of course, appears to be an item of considerably greater value than the actual combined values of the component parts.

This is not to say that repair and restoration are evil in and of themselves. They can enhance the appreciation of a damaged or fragmentary work of ancient art. Many a wooden piece, as has been noted in the chapter on wood, has benefited from proper restoration. However, the buyer should be aware of such repair and restoration. The sales price should also reflect it. Should a piece be damaged while in your possession, or be in need of repair or restoration when acquired, a competent restorer should be contacted to handle the job.

The reader may well ask at this point, "How does one find a competent restorer?" One good way is to consult other collectors in your area. Alternatively, you might get in touch with your local museum curator. He will usually be able to refer you. In fact, some major museums with large conservation departments will accept private commissions. If you are in touch with a reputable dealer, he will also probably be able to recommend a reputable restorer. In major urban centers, it can often be as easy as consulting the phone book. A word to the wise, however: ancient artifacts should only be entrusted to restorers who have had extensive experience in the care of such objects. This may necessitate shipping the object to a distant city. New York, for example, is the home of many of the world's most respected restorers of antiquities.

Museums take elaborate care in the shipping of antiquities, and, as a general rule, do so only when absolutely necessary. The collector should be no less cautious. If shipping an antiquity any distance, an expert should be consulted regarding packaging, and the shipment should always be sent insured for its full value.

Anyone who examines the surface of objects left in the open air will immediately see the detrimental effects of corrosive fumes and chemicals in our modern atmosphere. Their effects have become an increasing concern of art historians, governments, museums, and others concerned with the conservation of our cultural heritage. Some of the causes of this atmospheric pollution can be found in abundance in the average home. Cooking fumes, household cleaning agents, dust, fireplaces, etc. can all have a detrimental effect, as well as fumes seeping in from out of doors. The surface of a fine Roman head once in my possession was marred by a former owner who "kept it for years on his mantelpiece." It will now have to undergo proper cleaning by a restorer. If your objects cannot be kept in an enclosed space as previously recommended, at least place them in an interior room, away from wide variations of heat and cold. Excessive vibrations should also be avoided. I once had the misfortune of seeing an unfired brick I had found near Jericho begin to disintegrate because I had placed it near a wall adjacent to an elevator shaft.

While we are discussing protective measures, some thought should be given to providing adequate protection against fire and theft. The collector would also do well to consult his insurance broker or agent yearly in order to make sure that the collection is adequately covered. Antiquity values can change rapidly, and coverage should keep up with such changes. Given even a minimum of proper thought and care, there is no reason why an antiquity should not last indefinitely, giving the collector pleasure for a lifetime, and being passed on to future generations for their enjoyment. After all, these objects have already survived for hundreds, and often thousands, of years.

WHERE TO FIND ANTIQUITIES

MAGAZINES ON ANTIQUITIES

The Bead Journal
A Quarterly Publication of Ancient,
Ethnic, and Contemporary Jewelry
P.O. Box 24C47
Los Angeles, CA 90024

Biblical Archaeology Review
P.O. Box 7026
Red Oak, IA 51591
for subscription call 1 (800) 678-5555

The Celator
Journal of Ancient
and Medieval Artifacts
142 Lodi St.
Lodi, WI 53555
Tel: (608) 592-4684

Prehistoric Antiquities Quarterly
7045 East State, Route 245
North Lewisburg, OH, 43060

Minerva
The International Review of Ancient Art
and Archaeology
by Aurora Publications, Ltd.
14 Old Bond St.
London, W1X 3DB, U.K.
Tel: (0171) 495-2590

SOURCES FOR BOOKS ON ANTIQUITIES

Archaeologia
707 Carlston Ave.
Oakland, CA 94610

George Fredrick Kolbe
P.O. Drawer 3100
Crestline, CA 92325

Harmer Johnson Books
21 East 65th St.
New York, NY 10021
Tel: (212) 535-9118

John F. Bergman
4223 Iroquois Ave.
Lakewood, CA 90713
Tel: (310) 421-0171

Michael Graves-Johnston
P.O. Box 532
#54 Stockwell Park Rd.
London, SW9 OD4, UK
Tel: (0171) 254-2069

Papyrus Books
34372 Dunhill Dr.
Fremont, CA 94555

ANTIQUITY AUTHENTICATORS

Alex G. Malloy
Alex G. Malloy, Inc.
15 Danbury Rd.
Ridgefield, CT 06877
Tel: (203) 438-0396
Fax: (203) 438-6744
e-mail: alexmalloy@aol.com

Howard Rose
Arte Primivito
3 East 65th St., Suite 2
New York, NY 10021
Tel: (212) 570-6999
Fax: (212) 570-1899
e-mail: arteprim@mail.iidt.net

Jerome Eisenberg
Royal Athena Galleries
9478 West Olympic Blvd.,
Suite 304
Beverly Hills, CA 90212
Tel: (310) 277-0133
Fax: (310) 277-0616
e-mail: ancientart@aol.com

David Liebert
The Time Machine Co.
P.O. Box 282
Queens, NY 11367
Tel: (718) 544-2708
Fax: (718) 261-0767

Harmer Johnson
Harmer Johnson Books
21 East 65th St.
New York, NY 10021
Tel: (212) 535-9118

Richard Kersey
Sotheby's
1334 York Ave.
New York, NY 10021
Tel: (212) 606-7000

J. Max Bernheimer
Christie's
502 Park Ave.
New York, NY 10022
Tel: (212) 546-1000

Major museums and universities are also a good source for advice concerning the authentication of various antiquities.

FINDING ANTIQUITIES TO BUY AND SELL

It is recommended that you choose dealers and auction houses that have several years invested in the antiquities market. They will have maintained a customer loyalty over the years, and years of experience will contribute to a dealer's knowledge of antiquities. Addresses and phone numbers of dealers and auction houses can be found in the magazines listed above. Feel free to call them and request to be put on their mailing list. If you find a dealer near you, call and make an appointment to see what they might have for sale or show what you might have to sell them. Whether you deal person-to-person or via mail order, it is important to establish a good working relationship with whomever you are working with. Never be afraid to ask questions. A good dealer will be happy to answer them.

WEAPONS AND TOOLS

Collecting ancient weapons and tools is rapidly increasing in popularity. The books and research in this field of collecting has long been overlooked. Now the volume of information gathered and objects found has grown, with an increased emphasis on dating and origins of weapons. Petrie paved the way close to a hundred years ago with his studies on tools and weapons. Now, with closer studies on the published archaeological finds, the chronological dating is becoming more clear.

The earliest known tools and weapons are stone hand axes. These stone implements were crafted in Africa, the cradle of mankind. The migration of early man has resulted in stone artifacts being found at thousands of sites throughout the world. These stone artifacts trace the story of mankind down to the emergence of the Copper and Bronze Ages and the technological changes. From this period, change came rapidly with the development of metal, especially in the use of weapons such as daggers, metal arrowheads, swords, and axes.

THE ANCIENT METAL ARROWHEAD

The metal arrowhead is the natural evolution of the Neolithic and Copper Age flint arrowheads. The earliest metal arrowheads came from the Western Anatolian tradition and spread to Susa-Iranian and Egyptian areas. The Beaker Culture (2250-2000 B.C.) of the Spanish peninsula was the first to develop metallurgy in Europe, and specifically the arrowhead in Europe. They produced arrowheads extensively: the early copper arrowhead known as the Palmela type has been found at fifty-five sites throughout Spain.

In approaching the study of the metal arrowheads, their purpose must be explored. The elements used by the archer are the bow, an arrow consisting of arrowhead, shaft and feathers, and later the quiver. The earliest shafts were reeds: naturally straight, somewhat stiff, and light in weight. These were ideal for use with an arrowhead with a tang. The socketed arrowhead would be used with slender wooden shafts. The arrowhead is a ballistic device; its weight must be considered in relation to the "weight" of the bow (the force necessary to draw the bow). The weight of the arrowhead must be in a 1:7 ratio to the total weight of the arrow (the sum of the arrowhead, shaft, feathers, and binding material). Scholars have contended that the weight of an arrowhead could be no heavier than 10 gm, even taking into consideration longer arrows and big bows. Heads heavier than 10 gm. must belong to the javelin class. The Neo-Assyrians had javelin throwers in their army along with bowmen. Each Roman soldier had a javelin as part of his accoutrement.

The next consideration is the purpose of the arrow. This can be determined only with the arrowhead. Wide-bladed arrowheads were used for attacking flesh; the barbed arrowhead made the arrows hard to remove from flesh. The narrower forms were ideal for penetrating armor, leather, and clothing. The heavy arrowhead could be used for up-close attacks. Lighter, trimmer arrowheads were good at a distance. During the Mongol invasion, each horseman would have several quivers, each containing thirty or more of a specialized type of arrow.

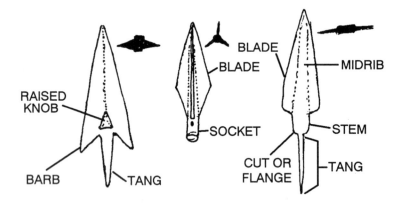

ELEMENTS OF THE ARROWHEAD

The earliest forms of metal arrowheads are of hammered copper; we can find early copper arrowheads in Susa, Anatolia, Egypt of the XI Dynasty, and Spain in Europe. Each dates to the 3rd millenium B.C., with Susa and Anatolia being the earliest. Each arrowhead has a long tang and hammered blade and edges. The workmanship is much cruder than their predecessors.

The copper types quickly gave way to the bronze arrowheads. Bronze was commonly used from 2500 B.C. through the Parthian and Roman periods. Bronze's properties made it excellent for casting and filing by the soldiers. The Romans did, however, have arrowsmiths who probably worked in iron for arrows and small javelin heads.

The earliest bronze types were hammered flat using rounded leaf-shaped heads; this slowly changed to cast arrowheads with various midribs, some with flanged tangs. The Anatolian type was a flat, broad midrib, while the Fertile Crescent saw a single ridge rib; later the midrib became rounded and socketed. From the later 2nd millenium, the number of arrowheads made increased along with various new types. The rhombic and barbed arrowhead from Egypt was used and is found in iron in sites from Israel; this was popular in the late 2nd to early 1st millenia B.C. By the 9th century B.C. most prominent ancient centers were using the barbed type. Iron leaf arrowheads were also used extensively in the Levant. Many sited from ancient Israel report this type dating from 1200 to 800 B.C.

The varieties of shapes changed vastly from area to area. Petrie classsified the arrowheads in thirteen categories of shapes, which can be found in most bronze types:

A: Flat Bladed
B: Rib Bladed
C: Trilobate Bladed
D: Trilobate Solid
E: Flat Barbed
F: Wide Barbed
G: Rhombic
H: Spur
I: Lances
J: Square Heads
K: Cones
L: Single Barbs
M: Splayed

The Scythians were members of a trans-Caucasian nomadic culture which began its conquest of southern central and western Asia in the 8th century B.C. As they advanced they pushed the Cimmarians before them, each causing havoc in Asia Minor. For a period of twenty-eight years, the Scythians held sway in Asia Minor, western Persia, and Syria. Even Egypt felt this nomadic power in the 7th century B.C. The Greek historian Herodotus spoke of them initially as a barbaric people who drank blood and used the skulls of their foes as drinking cups. By the 6th century the Greeks had developed good rapport with the Scythians, resulting in the Greek colonies of Pontapacum and Olbia in the Euxone region. The Scythians actually protected these Greek colonies; in this region of the northern Black Sea even some Scythian kings were half-Greek.

The controversy over the socketed trilobate arrowheads is wide; the archaeologists have for the most part not seriously addressed the so-called Scythian arrowheads. Many American antiquities dealers rarely know what they are actually selling and arbitrarily call all trilobate arrowheads Roman. The academic world is now finding many answers not known to Petrie and other archaeological pioneers. In an important study, Sulimirski stated in 1954 that the trilobate arrowheads were introduced about 750 B.C. His later studies published in 1978 pushed the date even earlier, as did Boehmer in 1972. By 690-680 B.C., the time of the neo-Assyrian annals of Sargon II and Assarhaddon, the Scythian invaders swept southward and attacked the Assyrian kingdom. The impact of their warfare was profound. The Scythian bowmen became legend with their newly adapted weapon which could fly longer and pierce armor, and which was light to carry. The trilobate arrows truly changed history.

The difficulty is to ascertain the subtle differences in the arrowheads in preceding cultures and centuries. The trilobate arrowhead was copied by various peoples down to the 3rd century A.D. We can find Greek, Achaeminid, Medean, and Parthian counterparts. Muscarella states that the trilobate arrowheads became neutral in battle "...as it no longer was used by one or the other in battle, but by both." After close scrutiny of many hundreds of trilobate arrowheads which have passed through our hands, and a special observation of actual site information, I have devised a chart of the idiosyncrasies of various types.

The earliest trilobate arrowheads have a tendency to elongation and medium sockets. Those excavated at Karmir-Blur, now in the Hermitage Museum, attest to these early Scythian types.

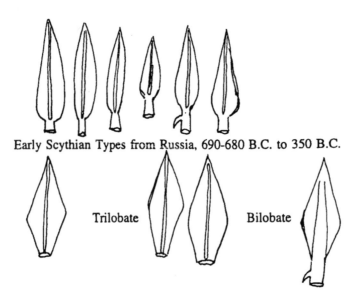

Early Scythian Types from Russia, 690-680 B.C. to 350 B.C.

Trilobate   Bilobate

Achaemenid Trilobate Arrowheads 550-350 B.C.

The Persian types will tend to have broad, more angular deltoid blades and almost no socket shaft. Similar rounded blades were also used. This arrowhead was standard equipment for forces in the Persian army. Schmidt discovered over 3600 examples at the treasury in Persepolis.

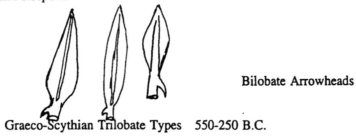

Bilobate Arrowheads

Graeco-Scythian Trilobate Types   550-250 B.C.

The spur was popular in the Graeco-Scythian types; many non-spur types were also used. The Scythian bowman's rig: the pointed cap, bow-case, patterned track-suit, and the trilobate arrows were introduced to Athens in the second half of the 6th century B.C.

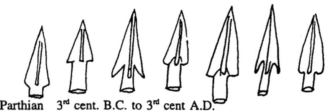

Parthian   3rd cent. B.C. to 3rd cent A.D.

During the Parthian period the barbed types emerged. Non-barbed trilobate arrowheads were also used. These barbed and non-barbed arrowheads are found at Dura-Europus from the Parthian-Roman struggles and through the Parthian occupation. The arrowheads are not Roman, but Parthian. They are rarely found in Roman cities in the Levant, and are not found at all in the African or European Roman world. It must be remembered that each new generation of trilobate arrowhead did not totally supersede the earlier types.

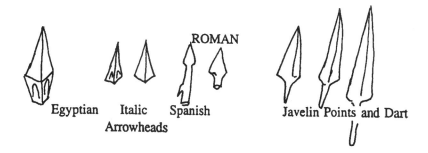

Roman Republican arrowheads vary widely as to place of origin: the Italic arrowheads were more diminutive than their counterparts in the East. The trilobate arrowheads are flat-sided with triangular sockets. The western Republican bilobate arrowhead used a small point and long shaft with spur. This was copied after a popular type of the Greeks. We also see some small iron heads trilobate, either barred or not. We find a limited number of Roman arrowheads in Roman cities.

It must be understood that purely Roman Imperial arrowheads are rare. The Roman legionary preferred hand-to-hand over distance fighting. His main weapons were the short sword, gladius, throwing spear, pilum, and javelin. The javelin point with a tang two to three feet long ended in a solid square point of iron. These are rarely found with the tang intact. The basic reason was that the iron head was hammered hard while the tang was not. The relative softness of the tang made it bend upon penetration and rendered it difficult to remove. The British Museum has no complete javelins. Today these javelin points are often confused with arrowheads.

Another object used by the Roman legions was the catapult dart or bolt; these were socketed and of larger size. Each legion would have sixty catapults to be employed in sieges; these used the catapult darts.

The Romans did utilize auxiliary troops to augment their powerful legions. During the Republican period slingers were often used along with bowmen. These auxiliaries were often dependent or semi-dependent client kingdom troops with special military skills. Caesar employed archers against Ptolemy in the great Imperatorial struggles in Spain. Germanicus used Gallic and German bowmen in victories in 14 A.D. Septimius Severus used an auxiliary of mounted archers from Osrhoene in Mesopotamia in his many Eastern exploits; Maximus used Syrian bowmen in his eastern Roman army. The Syrians were known for their great skill in archery. The eastern auxiliaries used the same trilobate arrowhead as was employed by the Parthians.

Iron became the standard metal used in arrowheads with the advent of the Dark Ages. The arrows became heavier and heavier, especially with the use of the longbow and crossbow, and with the great skill of the Mongols.

POTTERY

The development of pottery over the millennia has resulted in so vast an array of pottery types that it would be difficult for the large museums to have a large, comprehensive collection. Seven types of pottery decoration can be found: 1) painted glaze and fired, 2) painted non-glaze, 3) two or more colors of clay fired, giving a multi-color pattern, 4) stamped incuse pattern applied to the vessel, 5) a repossé pattern applied to the vessel, 6) incised decoration, and 7) hand molded with finger-induced design. Two types of plain ware are identified: 1) a plain ware with no slip, and 2) a plain ware with colored slip applied over part or all of vessel. One or more of these types can be found on any vessel.

The soils and clays help us to identify the various locations of manufacture. The earliest pottery was hand molded. This procedure finally gave way to the pottery wheel. The Greeks produced pottery vessels of high quality. The greater potters even signed their names along with the Greek vase painters.

The earliest evidence of pottery occurs during the 6th millennium B.C., during the Neolithic period — sites from Anatolia and the Middle East revealed early forms of pottery. The most spectacular finds are from Hacilar in southwest Turkey, and at Catal Hüyük. These 6000 B.C. communities of town-size proportion saw the early emergence of civilization with an agrarian and hunting lifestyle. Clay vessels were made during the Pottery Neolithic A period in the Middle East during the 6th-5th millennium B.C. Also, all of the great civilizations of the Near East produced pottery. Plain ware and painted ware were manufactured, and by the close of the 3rd millennium B.C. pottery was made throughout the Western Asiatic region. During this period, the proliferation of the wheel made pottery much easier to create, and it soon became accessible to everyone.

Pottery from the Fertile Crescent, the Holy Land, Persia, Anatolia, and early Europe used simple decoration techniques. They used slip over the vessel, incision design, and painted geometric patterns. The shapes, for the most part, are simple but sometimes include tall necks, flair rims, elongated spouts, strap handles, and many times, rounded bases.

Pre-dynastic pottery is one of the most interesting of the Egyptian types. Black top jars and crimson buffware are among the more sought after of the potteries. The Egyptians manufactured, along with the plainer pottery vessels, fine carved stone vessels and brightly colored blue faience.

Greek pottery, in all its many places and periods, is the most sought after. It is a most satisfying area to collect. The earliest dates are from around the 2nd millennium B.C. The potter's wheel was introduced as a means of achieving finer manufacture. The vibrant black and red colors of Greek pottery were a result of the slips and paints which contained iron. This resulted in firing to cause a chemical reaction to the conditions in the kiln. They used a three-step firing cycle. The first stage was letting oxygen in the kiln, producing the red-orange color. In the next step, no oxygen was let in, and the firing procedure would begin, using green wood. This produced the black colors. The last step was the reissuing of oxygen. Here the ferrous oxide turns back to red. Whites and purples were added before firing. This produced some of the most beautiful ancient objects known.

The categories of Greek pottery are Minoan, Mycenian, Proto-Geometric, Geometric, Corinthian, East Greek, Athens (Attic black figure, Attic red figure), South Italian (Apulian, Campanian, Lucanian, Sicilian), Hellenistic (Gnathian, Calen, and Megarian), Etruscan (Bucchero, Etrusco-Corinthian, Standard Etruscan), and Cypriot.

Not only whole Greek vases are collected. Vase fragments are highly cherished. The fine artwork of the vase paintings are revealed even on fragments.

Roman pottery can vary greatly as to the area and period of manufacture – it was produced all over the Roman world. Roman pottery consisted mostly of undecorated table ware. There are three main categories of Roman pottery. The first is red-gloss wares, first produced during the Arretium period of Augustus. Various other areas, such as Gaul, East Greek, and later North Africa, produced a lesser terra-sigilatta. This type consisted mostly of dishes, bowls, and cups. Relief mold designs consisting of human, animal, or plant motifs were used on a bright red-orange ware. The second group is the lead glazed vessels, usually bowls and cups, with various color glaze. This originated in the Eastern Roman Empire during the 1st century B.C. The third group is the coarse wares, used in various areas of the empire. Among these vessels are Egyptian red slip ware, Italian thin-walled ware, Bobastis ware, Fayoum red and brown slip wares, upper Egyptian coarse painted ware, various Egyptian brown ware, Barbotine ware, Menas flasks, and Palestinian ware. The Roman shapes, fabrics, and uses could vary greatly.

TERRACOTTAS

Pottery terracotta figures were made during the same period as the pottery vessels. They were generally produced with religious overtones. The early Northern Syrian and Mesopotamian terracotta figures were depictions of the "mother goddess," with large breasts. Dated from 5000-4500 B.C., fertility gods were popular in the Middle East. Many areas produced idol figures, including Canaan, Anatonia, North Syria, Cyprus, Egypt, Amlash, Uratu, Northern Pakistan, and India. The goddess Astarte was worshipped in Canaan in the late Bronze Age. Terracotta figures are prevalent in this period. The terracottas from the Mesopotamian areas were widely manufactured. At most periods, plaques may be found which feature a nude goddess with her arms raised to her breasts. These terracottas usually had a flat back like a plaque.

Early Greece produced the "mother goddess" from Thessaly, and Mycenae, Boeotia, and even the Vinca culture of Yugoslavia produced early idol figures. Greek terracottas are the finest made in ancient times. The periods of Greek terracotta range from: 1) Prehistoric: 2000-1100 B.C. Crete (Minoan-Mycenae); 2) Dark Ages: 1100-650 B.C. Geometric, Cyprus, Crete; 3) Archaic: 650-500 B.C. Rhodes, East Greece, Boeotia, Cyprus; 4) Classical: 500-330 B.C. Rhodes, Boeotia, Attica, Corinth, South Italy, Sicily, Crete, Melos; 5) Hellenistic: c. 330 B.C.-100 A.D. Attic-Boeotia (Tanagra), Alexandria, South Italy, Myrina, Smyrna.

Terracottas were initially hand molded. Later came the development of the clay mold, with which the artisan could push the soft clay into the mold, and produce a fine terracotta on the spot. This was certainly one of the first examples of mass production. This mold could provide a limited number of copies before it lost definition. The results were beautiful. The Greek terracotta craftsman was called *coroplats*, which is Greek for "dollmaker." These terracottas were mass produced, and anyone in the society could afford them. Their use was twofold: they could be used either for religious purposes, as tools for the veneration of the gods and goddesses, or for secular purposes, as toys for the living and gifts from friends for the departed.

Full figures or heads are widely collected today. Here we have the Archaic, Classical, and Hellenistic sculpture of Greek art in the round at affordable prices. Nice Hellenistic terracotta Greek heads can be purchased for somewhere between $75-$150.

Roman terracottas are comparatively harder to find, except those manufactured in Egypt. The Egyptian terracottas produced are of Egyptian and Greek deities. The quality is cruder than the Hellenistic period, but often attractive. These terracottas were manufactured with a light red-brown clay.

METAL WORK

Copper has been worked since the beginning of the prehistoric period. We have found a variety of pins, arrowheads, and small personal accouterments from this time, and it was not long until these gave way to chisels, axes, needles, and larger tools. The copper was shaped by hammering.

During the Bronze Age an expansion was made to making vessels and statues of deities. Bronze was found in Egypt during the 3rd Dynasty. Beautiful bronze animals, pins, and finials from Luristan and Amlash in the 8th century B.C. can be found in the marketplace. Bronze kouros and animals are among the archaic bronzes made in Greece. From the 6th-4th century B.C., Etruscan bronzes were made in the forms of various figures, including warriors, gods, and goddesses. The Greco-Roman vessels were beautiful, and a fine degree of artistic ability is revealed in these works. Roman bronze figures are highly sought after, and can fetch handsome prices for top quality.

The vast pantheon of Egyptian gods and goddesses were made during the Late Dynastic period. All were cast by the "lost wax" process. These bronzes were carefully detailed, and often have traces of gilding. Osiris, Harpokrates, and Isis were among the popular subjects. Cats, Apis bulls, hawks, ibises, and pharaohs were also widely made.

Smaller bronze artifacts were also made. Bronze clothing ornaments, arrowheads, swords, daggers, buckles, fibulas, hair ornaments, and amulets were all among the items manufactured from Europe to Western Asia and Egypt in the early Bronze Age and down through the Roman period. These utilitarian objects were made by casting or hammering.

Lead was used only sparingly, but was utilized in Greco-Roman times for weights, seal impressions, and sling bullets. Iron was used from the Iron Age on, but has come down to us sparingly. Iron deteriorates when exposed to air, and we therefore find little of it today. Iron was mainly used to make weapons and tools.

STONE WORK

The larger stone work was usually made for the community rather than individuals. In Egypt, limestone was the main material of the land, and was found in the Eocene cliffs around the Nile Valley along 400 miles. Red granite, quartzite sandstone, colored marble, syenite, basalt, and obsidian were used. The great monuments of Egyptian antiquity are not available, but smaller objects, and fragments of sculpture and reliefs, are.

The Greeks used only white marble gained from quarries in Mount Pentelkon, near Athens. This deep honey-color marble had a fine grain. The marbles from Naxos, Paros, and Thasos were more crystalline. These marbles were used more in the Archaic period. These statues that have come to us today were from temples, sanctuaries, and tombs, or were a kind of limestone sculpture primarily used for architectural decorations. These items rarely appear for the collector, and the prices are only for the wealthy connoisseur. Cyprot limestone figures are the most affordable today.

Small statues from the Cyclades in the 3rd millennium B.C. now command very high prices today. Smaller Hellenistic sculpture is available today, and will bring strong prices. Many art historians believe this was the pinnacle of art achievement.

Roman sculpture is available, and generally it is very much the same as Greek sculpture. While the quality is less, the Romans copied the Greek originals down to the 1st century B.C. Marble sculpture was produced all through the Roman Empire. Notable centers of sculpture making were Palmyra, Alexandria, and Aphrodisias in the province of Asia. The stone used for Roman sculpture was from the region of Carrara. A fine white marble with gray veins was also used. The high point of Roman sculpture was reached during the reigns of Antoninus Pius through Marcus Aurelius. The 3rd century A.D. saw a decline to the stylized art of the Constantine period.

Small stone work is among man's earliest expressions of art and utility. The earliest examples are stone chipped axeheads, scrapers, and arrowheads. The tools are found in northeast Africa, and later in all Africa, Asia, and Europe.

At the dawn of civilization, small stone amulets, stamp seals, and beads started to be made, revealing information about art, myth, and ritual of the civilizations in and around the Tigris-Euphrates.

The earliest prehistoric stone work was produced around the 7th-5th millennium B.C. in the form of simply carved stamp seals with a carved flat surface, and pierced for suspension. By the early ceramic phase they become more numerous, and begin to take on more defined shapes, such as oval hemispheroids, gable hemispheroids, high and low gables, pyramids, and loop with square base, pyramid base, and oval base. The carved designs on the base can be varied mostly with geometric and animal motifs. Throughout this period, up to 800 B.C., various animal stamp seals were produced, along with simple animal amulets. These seals have been viewed as having amuletic powers, and providing protection and good fortune to the owner.

The cylinder seal began during the Uruk period, around 3200 B.C., in southern Mesopotamia. The cylinder seals continued to be made through the Neo-Assyrian period, in the 7th century B.C. At the end of this period, the Neo-Babylonian stamp seal became in vogue.

The cylinder seal has been widely collected throughout the centuries. Five collections have been put together during the last seventy-five years, and today it remains a popular collecting field.   Certain stones were used at different periods. Agates, steatite, calcite, serpentine, quartz, limestone, and lapis lazuli were used in the earlier periods.   During the turn of the 2nd millennium B.C., hematite was used extensively, especially during the Old Babylonian period.   During the later periods, we also find fine chalcedony, carnelian, and crystal, along with faience cylinder seals.

The imagery engraved on the seals express the beliefs of these early empires.   The seals remain our most complete expression of visual art.   The fineness of the engraver's art is expressed, especially during the Assyrian through the Old Babylonian periods.

The process of making a cylinder seal was as follows: first, shaping the seal, then drilling the hole (from each end), and then engraving the design.   The first seals were drilled by hand, but by the 18th century B.C., the bow drill was used.   We can tell what tool was used from the style of the seal.   The simplest tool was a graver, often flint, used for soft stone.   It had a beveled tip that created lines of thickness and depth.   Ball and tubular drills made circular patterns.   Harder stones were made with use of metal tools, and abrasives using quartz sand and emery.   The images on these seals could be geometric, horned animals, heroes and beasts in combat, presentation scenes, daily life scenes, and various deities.

The Greeks and Etruscans engraved hard, fine stones into intaglio gems.   They reveal exceptional art in miniature. The Romans continued this practice.   During the Roman Republic period, glass intaglios were widely used.   In the 2nd-3rd century A.D., stone was most widely used for intaglios.   Carved cameos were also finely made.

ANCIENT GLASS

Ancient glass making spans a period from 1500 B.C. to 500 A.D., and Egypt and the Mesopotamian region had workshops from the beginning of this period.   Important manufacturers rose to prominence in the period from 1400-800 B.C. The exceptional glass production during the Egyptian XVIII Dynasty is classified as magnificent.   Vases, flasks, amphoriskoi, goblets, and jugs are among the types of multi-colored vessels made.   Beads and inlays were used on King Tutankhamon's mask. This is one of the high points of glass making in ancient times.

Achaemenid glass production was elaborate, with amphoriskoi, alabastra, and glass beads being made during the 6th century B.C. on the Syrian coast.

The Augustian age of the Roman empire starts the beginning of glass production in the modern sense.   The invention of the blowpipe in Sidonian Phoenicia marks this turning point in glass production.   Output could be increased a thousandfold with the introduction of new, exciting shapes.   This technique quickly spread to Italy, and then throughout the empire.   Roman glass was so popular that most Romans owned glass objects of some kind, and therefore much of it has survived to be available today at reasonable prices.   Roman glass tear vials in relatively nice quality are valued at $100 to $150 apiece.

In collecting glass objects the collector should be aware how glass was made.   The earliest vessels were called core vessels.   These were produced by pouring melted glass into a clay core, which was in the shape of the desired vessel.   Hot threads of contrasting color were wrapped around the vessel, pressed, and combed to create a wavy pattern.   Finally the clay core was removed after cooling.

The technique for producing molded vessels and amulets was primarily used up to the 1st century B.C.   This process used a mold, or a process called the lost wax process, also used in making metal objects.

In the blowpipe process, still used today, hot glass is gathered at the end of a hollow tube through which air is blown. This produces the various shapes found today.   Using this simple procedure, 100 vessels can be made in an hour.

Cut design was produced on cooling vessels by cutting designs into the still pliable glass.   Only master craftsmen could perform this difficult process.

Mold-blown glass is manufactured by heating glass, and blowing it into a mold with a pipe.

Cameo glass is made by a process in which one white, opaque color layers a design on another opaque surface.   The artisan would then cut away the upper portion to create a design.

Millefiori and mosaic glass process is accomplished by pounding long threads of glass of contrasting design and color, creating a cross section design, often with floral, geometric, or animal motifs.   After heating, this bundle is called a cane.   It is then sliced and used as inlays.   These could be used in outer designs of vessels, beads, or inlays.

Glass bead production was extensive throughout this period.   The glass beads were popular, and were worn by all of society.   Clear glass, eye beads (produced by the Phoenicians), Millefiori, mold-made pendants, confetti beads, gold flake beads, and many polychrome-surfaced glass beads were widely made; these are popular collectibles today.

Alabastrons, balsam vials, columnar and ritual vials.—4th B.C., *a, b*—XVIIIth dynasty and later, *c, d, e*—4th century A.D., *f, h*.

Phial, drinking cups, patella and patera bowls, 1st century B.C.—2d century B.C. Ptolemaic silver, *d*—probably "simplum" cup, *e*—Lower row, 1st and 3d A.D.

Measure and drinking cups.—1st, *a, b*—2d, *c, d*—2d to 3d,   Beakers 3d to 4th, *a*—1st to 2d, *b, c*—3d, *d, e*—1st, *f*—6th

Cinerary urns, storage urns, jars—1st A.D., *a, c*—2d A.D., *d* to *h*.

Stamnium or cylinder flasks.—1st, *a, d*—2d, *e, m*—3d century A.D., *n* to *q*.

Droppers; amuletic or Temple series, *d*—Processional, *e, f*—Mercury, *g, h*.

ANCIENT GLASS

Ampulla or ball flasks.—1st, *a*—2d, *b*, *c*—3d, *e*, *f*—4th,

Ampulla jars.—Aryballos jar, sprinkler, canteens, 1st century A.D., *e*, *g*, *h*.

Unguent tubes, 1st to 4th century.—1st century, *a*, *f*—2d century A.D., *g*, *i*—3d century, *j*, *k*—4th A.D., *l*.

Ampulla bottles, 1st to 2d century A.D.—1st, *a*, *c*—2d century A.D., Syria and Europe, *d*, *h*.

Glass vessels from Pompeii, Naples Museum. VII, Various kinds of jugs; VIII, Lagonaria or water jugs; IX, Bottles and tubes—Lacrymaria or tear bottles—oil vials; X, Urns and plates.

ANCIENT GLASS

LAMPS

The earliest lamp other than a bowl with a wick is the saucer lamp. This lamp is a pinched rim bowl. It appeared with the introduction of wheel-made pottery. It had four pinched corners, used with four wick holes. The one-pinched corner lamp, or cocked-hat lamp, became the standard for about 2000 years.

The first Greek lamps were the cocked-hat type, made in Athens during the 7th century B.C. The transition to the bridged nozzle lamp occurred in Asia Minor. Athens then produced high-quality lamps from the 6th to the 4th century B.C. These new types were exported throughout the Mediterranean. They were wheel made, with a closed in shoulder and a distinct nozzle. They were glazed with the fine black glaze used in Athens. These lamps were used down to the 3rd century B.C. All areas of the Greek world eventually copied these for local use. During the Hellenistic period, molded lamps began to be produced; these became the standard throughout the Roman period. The early molded lamps were simple, but by the 2nd century B.C., designs appeared on the shoulders.

The Roman lamp in the 1st century A.D. had reached a high state of quality. These lamps from workshops in Rome became very popular throughout the Empire. They were eventually copied in local workshops. The type had a closed in body with geometric, animal, and human designs in relief on the discus, or central portion. They typically had a short, flat nozzle, and handles at the back. The early workshops all signed the lamps with stamped names or symbols at the base. Designed and ornamented shoulders were used in the Palestinian area, and the frog lamp from Roman Egypt became a standard type. This oval lamp originally had the frog relief image. The design changed later to palms incised at the shoulders. Various other designs were used.

The major use of the ancient lamp was illumination of domestic, commercial, and public buildings. At religious festivals and games, lamps were used on a large scale. Thousands of lamps were used during the secular games in 248 A.D. presented by Philip I. At Pompeii, around 500 lamps were used on a commercial street to light the shops. Lamps were used in large quantities as votive offerings to the gods in temples. Many lamps are found in tombs, where they were intended to light the way of the departed.

The ancient lamp is a highly collected artifact. The values are generally all under $200, and an attractive historical collection can be acquired for a reasonable amount of money.

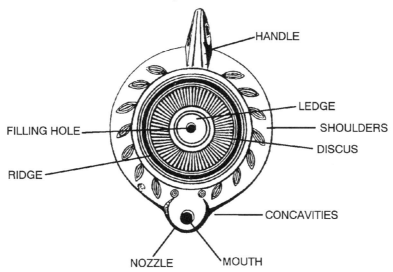

JEWELRY

Jewelry started to be made with the discovery of metal working. Copper and gold were worked into small ornaments and pins. In the Mesopotamia area around 3500 B.C., copper was cast into implements. The pieces of jewelry represent the beginning of the advanced metal-working process. At Tepe Gawra in the Jamdat Nasr period, gold rosette appliqués and studs were found, together with electrum and gold beads. The city of Ur produced a wealth of exceptionally fine pieces of gold and silver jewelry. Not long afterward, the Egyptians also started producing fine stone, metal, and carved ivory jewelry. The vast trade networks resulted in amulets, beads, and other ornaments being made throughout the Egyptian and Western Asiatic regions.

The Sumerians produced fine jewelry objects in gold, silver, copper, and semi-precious stones. Precious stones were thought to have specific properties. Gold was associated with the sun, and silver with the moon. The Mesopotamian Early

Dynastic period produced headdresses, earrings, hair rings, diadems, necklaces, gold and silver beads, pendants, amulets, and pins. Schools of jewelry working spread to Anatolia from 2500-2000 B.C. Especially fine were the objects from Troy. Gold jewelry was produced in Cyprus beginning around 2100-2000 B.C. Jewelry from Phoenicia, Syria, and Palestine were introduced by Egypt, Mesopotamia, and Cyprus.

To make the jewelry, gold was hammered from sheets, cast gold and gold wire were drawn, and molds were used in casting and stamping. Casting was usually done by the lost wax process. Chisels were used for piercing and cutting, although bead-makers used bow-drills.

Egyptian jewelry manufacturing reached a high pinnacle during the Early Dynastic period, resulting in fine bracelets, finger rings, collars, and necklaces. The inlay work for pectorals, girdles, earrings, and bracelets were unsurpassed during the New Kingdom. Much of Egyptian jewelry had magical significance. The decorations on Egyptian jewelry are limited to hieroglyphic signs, the scarab, and floral patterns such as the papyrus of lower Egypt and the lotus of Upper Egypt. Birds appeared more than animals, and humans were rarely used.

The earliest Greek jewelry was from the Minoans from the 17th century B.C., and later from Mycenae. The mainland Greek offshoot of the Minoan culture produced fine jewelry into the 14th and 15th century B.C. Rings, earrings, stamped appliqués and pendants were made. During the Archaic and Classical periods, jewelry was scarce due to conflict with the Persians. It was in the period between the defeats of the Persians and the rise of Alexander the Great that some of the finest jewelry of all time was produced. These masterpieces rank with the best gold work. Hellenistic jewelry was also in a high state of artistic merit, and is more available to the collector today. Earrings, necklaces, and pendants with animal heads depicting dolphins, bulls, goats, lions, lynxes, and gazelles are beautiful. By the end of the period, brightly colored stone and glass beads added to the decoration.

Etruscan jewelry is characterized by its technical perfection and variety. The use of granulation was unsurpassed. The fibula was made in a wide assortment of varieties.

Roman jewelry can be said to have started in 27 B.C. with the accession of Augustus to the title of Caesar. During the Republican period, jewelry was under official disapproval, and all surviving examples are copies from the Etruscans and the Greeks. Roman jewelry takes various forms. Ball earrings and earrings with hoops were popular, and are available today for the collector. Finger rings were extremely popular during the Empire. They were worn by male and female alike. The satirist Martial reported that there were some men who wore six rings on each finger. The fibula was extensively used by the Romans to fasten their garments. These fibula were re-introduced into Rome by the Celts. The most common was the crossbow type. Many collectors find it quite rewarding to collect these fibula, in all their many designs.

FIBULA DIAGRAM

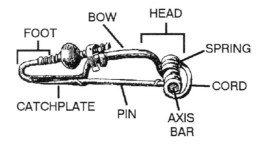

WRITING

The written word, the most important means of communication, has always been the main aspect by which a people establishes itself as a civilization. By inventing a writing system, a people could progress from a simple agrarian group to a more complex society which has the ability to form governmental systems, and to educate its members. Writing, as the tool of mankind, has enabled men to become learned scholars, brought separate cultures within each other's reach, and preserved historical events and happenings for posterity.

CUNEIFORM

Cuneiform, probably the oldest system of writing, was employed by the Sumerians, Akkadians, Babylonians, and Assyrians over 2000 years before Christ. At first, this wedge-shaped writing represented, in pictorial form, a few animate and inanimate objects. These signs then arose to depict phonetic values. Therefore, before long, cuneiform developed into a clearly defined linear script which could be used consistently and easily by Western Asiatic scribes.

HIEROGLYPHIC WRITING

This ancient script, called by the Egyptians "the speech of the Gods," was used mainly for inscriptional writing. Even as early as 3000 B.C., hieroglyphic writing was a highly developed pictorial and ideographic system. Strangely enough, although this formal style was to last over 3000 years, it never flourished, nor, indeed, spread past the borders of Egypt. Subsequently, with the rise of the incoming Greek and Latin languages, this beautiful script died along with the great dynasties of the pharaohs of ancient Egypt.

HIERATIC WRITING

When writing on papyrus and ostraca for business purposes, the ancient Egyptian scribe turned from hieroglyphic script to hieratic, which was a cursive derivative. Not only was hieratic used for business and religious texts, it was, in contrast, also used for profane writing. Hieratic was not utilized instead of hieroglyphic writing, but rather in conjunction with it – a quicker, "shorthand" script of a sometimes laborious hieroglyphic script.

ARAMAIC

Not to be confused with Jewish-Aramaic, Aramaic was often called Syriac by the Jews. It was a script used by the heathen neighbors of the Jews – the Aramaeans. The Aramaeans were wandering tribesmen who eventually settled in modern-day Syria around the 11th or 12th century B.C. Their script was alphabetic rather than pictorial, and from its conception progressed into a rather cursive script. By the 7th century B.C., Aramaic had become not only prominent, but the official language of the Near East, particularly of the Persian Empire.

HEBREW

Originally an offshoot of the Canaanite language, Hebrew began to become distinct around the 11th century B.C. Its use continued for 500 years, until somewhere around the 6th century B.C. For a long time, samples of early Hebrew writing were scarce, but over the past century hundreds of inscriptions have been found, and are an important source of information about the language and period of the Old Testament.

EDESSAN SYRIAC

Edessa, in northwest Mesopotamia, was one of the first centers of Christianity in the Syriac-speaking world. It was an island in a primarily Greek-speaking area. Edessan Syriac was a branch of Aramaic which became the most important language in the Eastern Roman Empire after Greek. The language gradually died out, except for some liturgical passages, because of the conquering foreigners – first the Persians and then the Arabs.

GREEK

One can never underestimate the importance of the Greek language, because most of the European languages are related to ancient Greek. The Greeks attributed the invention of their alphabet to the Phoenicians, from whom they learned the ability to write in approximately the 11th century B.C. At first written from right to left, Greek then progressed into being written alternatively from either right to left or left to right. However, it was only after 800 B.C. that it became commonplace to write from left to right.

COPTIC

The Coptic language is the only offshoot of the Greek which developed into a non-European language. Up until the 20th century, Coptic liturgical verses were still spoken in the Christian villages of Upper Egypt. Consisting mainly of Greek letters, Coptic does contain a part of its Egyptian heritage by using seven letters of the Demotic language or script. Demotic script was used in the Late period of ancient Egypt.

CLASSICAL LATIN

The Latin language was spread by Roman legionaries throughout most of the Roman Empire. It is the ancestor and basis of the Romance languages, for example, French or Spanish, and has influenced the majority of all the European languages. Today, it is thought that Latin originates from both the Greek and Etruscan alphabets, not purely from the Greek language, as was previously believed. An accurate date for the beginning of Latin is unobtainable; however, it was probably created approximately in the 7th century B.C.

SCARABS

Along with the pyramids, sphinxes, and mummies, the scarab amulet is probably the most familiar object representing Egypt. Although scarabs have been collected for centuries, and with particular interest in the 19th and early 20th centuries, this has not been true since the period before the Second World War.

The meaning of Kheper or Scarab is becoming, being, metamorphosing, generation, new life, virility, and resurrection. Certainly this is an essential symbol in Egyptian art. Although there is some disagreement as to when the scarab amulet was first made, it is generally accepted that with the beginning of the Middle Kingdom, the form was being used.

Of the literature available on scarabs, the majority has been published between the last quarter of the 19th century through the period just before the Second World War. As a general introduction, one could select from any of a number of works from this period, but I think part of the first paragraph from W.M.F. Petrie's classic work *Scarabs and Cylinders with Names*, published in 1917, serves this purpose admirably.

The little amulets of beetle form, which are the most usual production of Egyptian art, have fascinated the amateur collector for a century past, but have not yet fully received the scientific attention which is due them. The most obviously interesting classes of scarab are those with names of kings, of the royal family, and of officials. These carry with them in most cases a dating, which fixes their historical position. They therefore stand to Egyptian history much as coins stand in relation to Western history. They often add historical matter which is otherwise lost to us, and the style of their art and manufacture serves as an index to the changes which went on in the civilization.

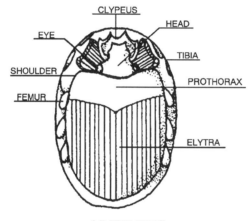

AMULETS

The amulet is a talisman or charm that is worn by an individual, and is believed to have magical powers. Three of the four Egyptian words for amulet come from a word meaning "to guard or protect." The Egyptians made amulets with the intention that the magical powers would last forever. The initial purpose was to protect the individual in this life, but it also had the additional purpose of offering protection in the afterlife.

Egyptian amulets are the most collected and available of ancient amulets. They were produced from the Pre-Dynastic period through Roman times, a period of about 4500 years. Shell and ivory Pre-Dynastic amulets were made depicting hippopotami, antelope heads, lions, dogs, and bulls. By the end of this period, stone amulets were commonly adorned. From the Old Kingdom on, a vast array of amulets of gods, goddesses, and sacred animals were produced in many media, including faience. Examples of amulets of protection were in inanimate forms such as the Ujat, or eye of the falcon-head Horus. The eye had been plucked out in a battle with Seth, and was healed by Thoth. This Ujat was used to ward off evil, and was even used for healing. Amulets of assimilation were produced to help the wearer take on qualities that the amulet represented. For example, a hare amulet would confer swiftness of movement and keenness of senses. Amulets of power were inanimate objects that conveyed royal and divine powers, and cosmic associations. The Red Crown of Lower Egypt, depicting a crown with a tall spike at the back and a curling spiral to the front, is an example of a symbol which was imbued with authority and power. The amulets of offerings, possessions, and property were to act as the substitutes for the wearer in the afterlife.

Mesopotamian amulets were carved in stone, and were in the forms of animals, usually recumbent. Often the bases were used as stamp seals. Luristan and Amlash produced bronze amuletic animals in the 9th-7th century B.C.

Roman amulets are found in bronze. They depict gods, goddesses, and the erotic phallus, a symbol of fertility worn by the military for good luck. Faience amulets were produced in Roman Egypt and Roman Syria as well. Parthian bronze gazelle amulets were found in the excavations at Dura Europus.

EARLY MAN – PALEOLITHIC

Homo, or man, first used stone tools as an extension of himself, to change other parts of his environment. In this way Paleolithic technology started and evolved. The earliest known stone tools are dated to the Oldowan period about 2.4 million years ago. They are found in Ethiopia, and belong to the sites known as the Oldowan industry. These are all based on Mary Leakey's excavations at the Olduvai Gorge in Tanzania. Homo Habilus is commonly thought to have made the Oldowan tools in East Africa. The tools were used for chipping and scraping. Hammer stones and axeheads were also made about 1.4 million years ago.

During the Acheulean period, heavy, sharp-edged tools were produced. Homo Erectus and later Homo Neanderthalensis produced these tools, along with Homo Sapiens.[*] These tools were flaked on both sides, and made of quartzite, lava, chert, and flint. This technological similarity lasted for over a million years, starting in Africa and spreading to Europe, Western Asia, and India. At the early Acheulean sites, we find hand axes and cleavers in Eastern Africa only. However, other sites dating 200,000 years ago reveal tools as far away as Swanscombe, England. By 1 million years ago, the dominating tool was more slim, biface, and sometimes lanceolate hand axes.

The Mousterian, or Middle Stone Age, was the period in which Homo Sapiens prospered technologically. Man's modern capacity for culture started in and around 50,000 years ago. The tools found include notched flakes, denticulates or flakes with a serrated edge, Leallois flakes, and Aterian points.

The Upper Paleolithic period exemplifies the early artifacts of Homo Sapiens. The tool functions became more apparent, punch-struck blades were introduced, and a refined bifacial technique was used. Approximately between 40,000 to 10,000 years ago, technology flourished at different times in different areas. Various diverse industries came about: the Aurignacian, the Chatel Perronian, the Gravettian, the Solutrean, and the Magdalenian. This was the period in which man first began to learn the use of fire, make clothing, build shelters, bury the dead, and create art.

The Mesolithic Period was a transition between the later Paleolithic and the beginning of the Neolithic. This period saw man change from a solely hunter society to the civilized Neolithic peoples.

The Neolithic and Copper Ages saw the final stages of the conversion of man from nomadic hunter to the farmer existence in villages. The stone artifacts continued to be made, but the purposes changed. Axes were now used for felling trees and shaping timber for the building of houses and huts. Denmark was widely populated, and exceptional thin-butted axe heads, gouges, chisels, battle-axes, and daggers were produced. Many of these axe heads were finely polished. Western Neolithic polished axes were produced with fine craftsmanship. The first Neolithic farmers to reach Italy and Central Europe were coming from the east and originally from Turkey. Domestic pottery was their gift, as well as their techniques of farming. Corrugated, incised, painted pottery of many types were made throughout Europe during this period. With pottery vessels came terracotta dolls and figurines. The Copper Age began around 7000 B.C. in Southeastern Turkey at Diyar Bakir. We know this because small copper pins have been excavated there, which date to about that time. The Copper Age came to various regions and areas at different times. The earliest working metal was a natural, unalloyed copper. The objects were cast in single piece molds.

The Bronze Age arrived in Europe in stages: in Crete, 3300-2100 B.C., in Greece, 2500-1700 B.C., in Coastal Italy, 2500-1850 B.C., in Inland Italy, 1850-1625 B.C., in Spain, 2500-2000 B.C., in Middle Europe, 2500-1900 B.C., in Western Europe, 1900-1600 B.C., in Northern Europe, 2500-1600 B.C. The objects reflect a barbarian society, concerned with warfare, weapons, and social status through ornamented pins, jewelry, finger and arm rings, and bracelets. By 2000 B.C., bronze work was widespread in Europe. Most bronze swords, brooches, knives, pins, and ornaments were made by casting copper ores and tin. These were not common in Europe, so with the Bronze Age came power struggles and warfare. A warlike society thrived in Europe from 2700-700 B.C.

The Iron Age came to Europe with a quick change in society. The use of iron for weapons and tools released the bronze workers to concentrate on producing luxury items and beautiful decorative objects. This period is known for its exceptional bronze work on jewelry, ornaments, and horse harness decorations. The fibula, or brooch, was worn by all society. By the second half of the Iron Age, the Celts (also known as the Gauls, Galli, or Gallatae) had swept through Central and Western Europe, where they settled, and extended their influence for about five centuries. The Celts were barbarians who had a common language that was spoken, but not generally written. Most of what we know of the Celts comes from Greek and Roman writers, as well as the rich treasure of artifacts the Celts left behind. By the 2nd century B.C., Celtic tribes had reached across to the Black Sea, and certain tribes had even swept into parts of Asia Minor. The Celtic period in Europe is the La Tène period.

---

[*] Homo Sapiens is first identified with the Dali site in China, dating c. 200,000 years ago. During the period from 200,000 to 40,000 years ago, Homo Sapiens and Neanderthalensis migrated from Africa.

This period is divided into three phases: I (Early), II (Middle), and III (Late). It lasts to the Roman period of the 1st century B.C.

EARLY MAN c. 2,000,000–10,000 B.C.		
PERIOD	**INDUSTRIES**	**EARLY HOMO**

PERIOD	INDUSTRIES	EARLY HOMO			
2 million years ago		•**Homo Habilis** Olduvai Gorge	•**Homo Rudolfensis** Kenya	•**Homo Ergaster** Kenya	Stone simple flake choppers
1.5 million years ago		**OLDOWAN**		•Kenya •So. Africa	
1 million years ago	Early or Old Acheulian	•**Homo Erectus** Java	•**Homo Heidelbergensis** Ethiopia		Stone hand axes and cleavers
500,000		•Java		•Java	
400,000	Middle Acheulean	•Peking	•Germany and France		
300,000			•Greece and Germany		
200,000			•Spain and Zambia	•**Homo Sapiens**	
150,000	Upper Acheulean			China	
100,000		•**Homo Neanderthalensis** Croatia and Italy		•Ethiopia	
90,000				•Israel	
80,000					
70,000	Mousterian	•Uzbekistan			
60,000		•Israel			
50,000		•Israel and France			
40,000		•Germany and France			
30,000				•**Cro-Magnon**	
20,000	Upper Paleolithic			France	
10,000				•Australia	

EARLY MAN
PALEOLITHIC TO IRON AGE

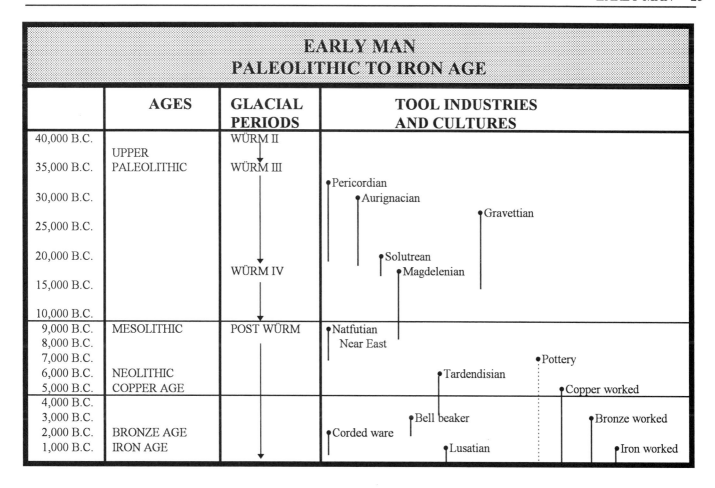

	AGES	GLACIAL PERIODS	TOOL INDUSTRIES AND CULTURES
40,000 B.C.	UPPER PALEOLITHIC	WÜRM II	
35,000 B.C.		WÜRM III	
30,000 B.C.			•Pericordian •Aurignacian
25,000 B.C.			•Gravettian
20,000 B.C.		WÜRM IV	•Solutrean
15,000 B.C.			•Magdelenian
10,000 B.C.			
9,000 B.C.	MESOLITHIC	POST WÜRM	•Natfutian Near East
8,000 B.C.			
7,000 B.C.			•Pottery
6,000 B.C.	NEOLITHIC		•Tardendisian
5,000 B.C.	COPPER AGE		•Copper worked
4,000 B.C.			
3,000 B.C.			•Bell beaker •Bronze worked
2,000 B.C.	BRONZE AGE		•Corded ware
1,000 B.C.	IRON AGE		•Lusatian •Iron worked

IRON AGE

	IRON AGE	NORTHERN EUROPE	CENTRAL EUROPE	SOUTHERN EUROPE	EASTERN EUROPE	WESTERN ASIA
1000 B.C.	Early Hallstatt	•Urn Field Culture	•Urn Field Culture	•Urn Field Culture	•Greek Migration	
900 B.C.						
800 B.C.	Middle Hallstatt			•Villanovan		•Greek
700 B.C.				•Etruscan	•Greek City-States	
600 B.C.	Late Hallstatt					•Achaemenid
500 B.C.	Early La Tène					
400 B.C.		Celtic Influence	Celtic		•Greek	•Parthian
300 B.C.	Middle La Tène			•Roman	•Roman	
200 B.C.						•Roman
100 B.C.	Late La Tène	•Roman	•Roman			

ROMAN EMPIRE

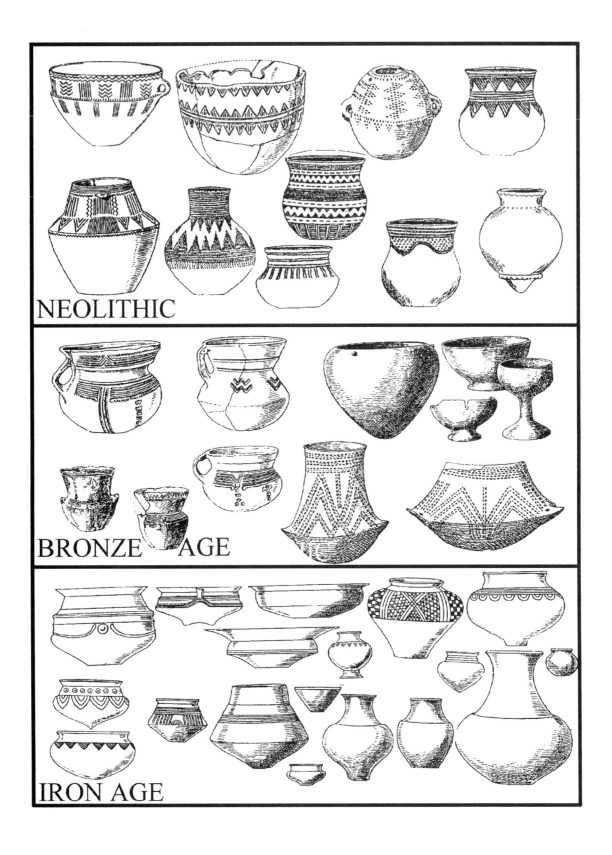

NEOLITHIC

BRONZE   AGE

IRON AGE

EARLY MAN

STONE

1. **HAND AXE. Homo Habilis. 1.8 Million B.C.** Grey rough lava hand axe with select chipping. Measures 12 x 8 cm. Cf. D. Johnson & J. Shreve, *Lucy's Child*, Pl. 4. Cf. Malloy, *Weapons* #1. Found in the Olduvai region of the Rift Valley, this tool is typical of the Olduvan stone tool industry and is one of the oldest tools of the earliest hominids.   It exemplifies the primitive early tool...........**CHOICE 600.00**

2. **HAND AXE. Homo Erectus. 1 Million-400,000 B.C.** Beige-grey rough lava hand axe.   Finely worked to biface shape. Measures 13 x 8 cm. Cf. Johnson & Shreve, pp. 148-150. Cf. Malloy, *Weapons* #2. These fine hand axes were found in the Rift Valley of Ethiopia. ....**CHOICE 300.00**

3. **HAND AXE. Homo Erectus. 1 Million-400,000 B.C.** Beige-grey rough lava hand axe, finely worked to biface shape. Measures 16.7 x 9.5 cm. Cf. Johnson & Shreve, pp. 148-150; Cf. Malloy, *Weapons* #2.   A very large example of the Homo Erectus hand axe of the Rift Valley.   Heavy grey patina..**CHOICE 350.00**

4. **OBSIDIAN KNIFE. Homo Erectus. 700,000-400,000 B.C.** Black obsidian rounded knife or scraper.   Length 8 cm. Cf. Malloy, *Weapons* #7.   Found in the Rift Valley of Ethiopia. Heavy grey patina.   The hand fits easily into shallow grooves A   chip   at   the   end   reveals   the   black   obsidian. ....**CHOICE 200.00**

5. **FLINT KNIFE. Mesolithic Campigny Period. 700,000-400,000 B.C.**   Thick flint biface, some cortex remaining. The edge forming a knife. Measures 7 x 4.5 cm. Found at Fleurac-Dordgne. The Mesolithic culture of northern France reflects   the   final   stage   of   the   Late   Paleolithic period..**CHOICE 125.00**

6. **HAND AXE. Homo Erectus. 700,000-400,000 B.C.** Black obsidian with two worked edges. Measures 12.7 x 6.2 cm. Cf. Malloy, *Weapons*.. ....**CHOICE 50.00**

7. **SCRAPER OR KNIFE. Homo Erectus. 700,000-400,000 B.C.** Black obsidian oval scraper or knife. Measures 6 x 3.5 cm.   Found   in   the   Rift   Valley   of   Ethiopia. ....**CHOICE 150.00**

8. **QUARTZ ARROWHEAD. Azerbeijan. Neolithic: 10,000 B.C.** White quartz arrowhead. Length 2.4 cm. Cf. Malloy, *Weapons* #14...**CHOICE 50.00**

9. **CALCITITE ARROWHEAD. Natufian Culture of the Levant. 10,000-8,000 B.C.** Grey-olive calcite arrowhead. Oval sides. Measures 3.9 x 1 cm. Cf. Giarod, Bate 437. ....**CHOICE 35.00**

10. **CHALCEDONY ARROWHEAD. Natufian. Mesolithic: 10,000-8,000 B.C.** Grey chalcedony "D"-shaped arrowhead. Measures 3.5 x 1.3 cm. Cf. J. Bescancon, *Tableaux de Prehistoric Libanaisa in Paleorient,* Vol. 3, 1975-77, p. 45, Cf. Malloy, *Weapons* #16...........................**CHOICE 35.00**

11. **STEATITE AXE/ADZE HEAD. Egypt: Neolithic.** Small black polished steatite axe or adze head. Thick rounded handle end, blade end wider and flattened. A similar blade was found at the oasis of El Khargeh in the Libyan Desert. Length 4.5 cm, width at blade 4.0 cm. Petrie, *Prehistoric Egypt* Pl. XXVII #2; Cf. Hayes fig. 4..........**SUPERB 150.00**

12. **FLINT KNIFE. Egypt: Pre-Dynastic.** Bi-convex light brown flint. Leaf-shaped with left edge more finely worked than right. 8 x 1.8 cm. Cf. Petrie, Brunton, and Murray, *Lahun II,* Pl. XXXVII, fig. 12, Cf. Malloy, *Weapons,* #9. ....**CHOICE 75.00**

13. **FLINT HAND AXE. Late Paleolithic- c. 5000-4000 B.C.** Pointed flint hand axe. Of brown flint patinated rose/cream. Symmetrical outline.   Probably worked in soft hammer technique.   12.3 cm long, 7.6 cm at widest point.   Cf. *Lord McAlpine Collection*, p. 52, fig. 1.4.   Some light brown flint color visible. ....**SUPERB 650.00**

14. **GRANITE MACE HEAD. Late 4th-3rd Millennium B.C.** Variegated brown and cream granite mace head. Oblate and pierced.   Diameter 6.2 cm. Cf. Sotheby's NY 10/25/87, #357, Cf. Malloy, *Weapons,* #26. Chip at one end of central hole...**SUPERB 125.00**

15. **FLINT AXE. Nordic Neolithic. 4000-2000 B.C.** Thick–butted with squared side, convex faces and broad butt. Polished. 20 x 5.5 x 4 cm.   Provenance of Denmark. Cf. *McAlpine Collection* 4.42.   A lovely and large example. ....**SUPERB 650.00**

16. **AXE HEAD. Western Neolithic. 4000-2000 B.C.** Black polished axe.   Pointed butt and rounded end, sharp curved sides.   Length 50 mm. Cf. *McAlpine Collection* 5.23. A gem. ....**SUPERB 135.00**

17. **STONE AXE. Hamangian Culture, Middle Neolithic: 3500-2700 B.C.** Grey-black granite axe.   Quadrangular with rounded base. Measures 85 x 42 mm. Cf. Birciu, *Romania,* Pl. 2 #9. Two chips to point......................**CHOICE 125.00**

18. **FLINT SCRAPER. Egypt, Early Dynastic.**   Unifacial scraper of brown flint. Rough workmanship. Body slightly curved. Basically oval-shaped, slightly pointed ends. 9.2 cm long x 5.8 cm wide. Cf. Spencer, fig. 742y; *Malloy,* #12. ....**CHOICE 150.00**

19. **KNIFE BLADE. Neolithic. 3200-1800 B.C.** Cream flint knife blade. With fine outline and greatest width toward point. Unpolished symmetrically shaped. Blunt end. 12 cm long, 3.7 cm wide (at widest point). Cf. *Lord McAlpine Collection*, p. 76, fig. 4.191 for similar shape and workmanship..**SUPERB 650.00**

20. **FLINT HAND BORER. British Paleolithic: Before 2000 B.C.** Cream-grey flint nose borer. Nicely flaked; grooved to fit comfortably in right hand. Length 9.7 cm, width 7.3 cm. Provenance: East Preston. Excavated in 1898. Ex: Bonhams 9/93. Cf. *Lord McAlpine Collection*, p. 53. ....**SUPERB 200.00**

21. **FLINT HAND SCRAPER. British Paleolithic. Before 2000 B.C.** Black flint scraper with section of cortex remaining on one side. Cortex is trimmed to make comfortable thumb hold; opposite side shaped for easy grip. Measures 5.6 x 5.1 cm. Provenance: Storrington Down, Sussex. Excavated in 1917. Ex: Bonhams 9/93. Cf. *Lord McAlpine Collection*, p. 53. A special little piece which gives the feel of the people who used it......**SUPERB 175.00**

22. **FLINT SCRAPER. British Paleolithic. Before 2000 B.C.** Black-grey scraper, with grooves for comfortable fit in right hand. Length 11.2 cm, width 4.6 cm. Provenance: Ightham. Ex: Bonhams 9/93. Cf. *Lord McAlpine Collection*, p. 53. ....**CHOICE 150.00**

23. **FLINT PICK. Mesolithic Campigny Period.** Found in the region of New Haven, France. This stone implement fits the hand perfectly. The Mesolithic culture of Northern France reflects the final stage of the Late Paleolithic period. 15.5 cm long, 5.2 cm wide....................**CHOICE 150.00**

24. **FLINT SCRAPER. France. Neolithic.** Honey-colored cherty flint. 8 cm long, 7.3 cm wide. Found on Surface LeGrande Pressigny, France, 1937. Cf. British Museum, *Guide to Antiquities of the Stone Age.* Case 137. ....**CHOICE 125.00**

25. **FLINT SAW BLADE. Paleolithic Period.** Yellow-brown flint saw blade; the type is known as a flint sickle. Length 9.3 cm, width 1.7 cm. Cf. Hayes, fig. 19. Nice color. ....**CHOICE 60.00**

26. **FLINT SCRAPER KNIFE. Neolithic Period.** Brown and black flint scraper-knife. Length 5 cm, width 3.1 cm. Cf. Hayes, fig. 4.3. ....**CHOICE 90.00**

27. **AMBER RIBBED BEAD. Italic. 8th-6th Century B.C.** Amber, in this period, was a highly prized commodity. It was attractive, pleasant to smell and touch and had a reputation for magical qualities. Similar beads were found at Picenum. Cf. Strong, *Catalogue of Carved Amber in the BM.* Pl. XXXI, 100..**CHOICE 65.00**

METAL

28. **COPPER ARROWHEAD. Ancient Spain: The Beaker Culture. 2250-2000 B.C.** Pointed leaf-shape, with tang. Known as the Palmela type. Length 5.5 cm. Malloy #80, Cf. Savory Fig. 61, Montilla fig. 60b. Found in Cordoba, Spain. The Bell-Beaker culture of Spain distributed copper arrowheads as far away as Britain. These are among the first metal arrowheads of Europe. ....**CHOICE 150.00**

29. **BRONZE SPIRAL FINGER RING. Central Europe. Bell-Beaker Culture: 2000-1800 B.C.** Flexible bronze spiral ring of eleven swirls. Length 26 mm, diameter 21 mm. Cf. Piggot, *Ancient Europe,* fig. 56. Nice green patina. Actually wearable even today. ....**CHOICE 125.00**

30. **BRONZE DRESS PIN. 2000-600 B.C.** Dress pin with bi-conical head. Tapering pin. Length 7.5 cm. Cf. Ashmolean Museum, *Antiquities from Europe and the Near East*, 13.8, p. 114..**CHOICE 125.00**

31. **COPPER STUD. Central Europe. Early Bronze Age: 1600-1400 B.C.** Conical copper stud. Hollow-domed up to spiked point. Straight angular crossbar at rear. Length 30 mm, diameter 28 mm. *McAlpine* 9.4............**CHOICE 40.00**

32. **BRONZE BRACELET. Italic. Bronze Age. 1600-1200 B.C.** Bronze coiled bracelet worked with two ridges. Diameter 41 mm. Cf. *McAlpine* 16.35 var. Ex: Villa Julia Collection..**CHOICE 125.00**

33. **BRONZE HAIR PIN. Central Europe. Bronze Age. 1600-1000 B.C.** Bronze pin with rounded end. Pierced bulbous protrusion quarter of the way down. Length 10.5 cm. Cf. Kimming-Hell, *Vorzeit an Rein und Donau*, #55. Fine green patina..**CHOICE 100.00**

34. **BRONZE HAIR PIN. Thrace. 1400-1000 B.C.** Bronze pin with terminal of oval disk with two large holes (as eyes). Decorated with concentric lines to short shoulder. Length 12 cm. ....**SUPERB 150.00**

35. **BRONZE BRACELET. Villanovian. 13th-11th Centuries B.C.** Bronze spear bracelet with undulating ends. Diameter 46 mm. Cf. Hencken, *Tarquinia and Etruscan Origins*, Pl. 73. Ex: Villa Julia Collection De-accession. One fourth missing..**CHOICE 75.00**

36. **BRONZE HAIR PIN. Scoglio del Tonno. Late Bronze Age: 1200-1000 B.C.** Bronze pin terminating in two spiral eyes. Trump, *Central and South Italy*, figs. 42 and 43. Ex: Villa Julia Collection. Characteristic of the Terramarra type. Green patina. ....**SUPERB 150.00**

37. **BRONZE PALSTAVE AXE HEAD. Celtic Middle Bronze Age. 1200-900 B.C.** Looped, with trident pattern. 15 x 3.8 cm This form of hand axe was developed about the same time throughout Central and Northwestern Europe. Cf. Nicholson, Merseyside County Museum, 15, 1. Cf. Savory, National Museum of Wales, 163, 168, 263. Intact with green patina......**CHOICE 400.00**

38. **TWO BRONZE BOSSE APPLIQUÉS. Halstat. Iron Age: 1000-800 B.C.** Two bronze raised ridge bosse disks, hammered pellet design. Diameter 15 mm. Hencken, Pl. 68......**CHOICE 60.00**

39. **BRONZE BOAT-SHAPED FIBULA. Villanovian. IIB. 800 B.C.** Hollow with incised lines lengthwise and widthwise. Larger than usual. 6.4 cm long. Cf. Sotheby's, Zinna Sale, 1962, #178. Sundwall, *Die Alteren Italischen Fibelin*, #178-287. End of pin missing. Nice large size. A very early bronze geometric work of art exemplifying man's early artistic expression in Europe. Encrusted patina......**CHOICE 500.00**

40. **BRONZE FIBULA. Villanovian. 800 B.C.** Bronze fibula, leech-shaped with attractive incised geometric pattern. 5 cm long. Cf. Sotheby's Zinna Sale, 1962, #178. Lovely green patina. Pin missing. Nice geometric rendering. ......**CHOICE 225.00**

41. **BRONZE FIBULA. Villanovian IIB: Early Iron Age. 800 B.C.** Fibula with hollow bow. Upper surface decorated with geometric design and hatching. Integral point formed by 2½ turn twist of metal. Length 6.0 cm. Cf. *Bronzes*, Boston MFA, #345, 346. Some encrustation......**CHOICE 250.00**

42. **BRONZE BRACELET. Villanovian. 800-700 B.C.** Bronze twisted wire bracelet. Diameter 34 mm. Cf. Nicholson, *Prehistoric Metalwork*, Merseyside Co. Museums, #345. Ex: Villa Julia Collection......**CHOICE 65.00**

43. **BRONZE SPIRAL BROOCH. Villanovian. 800-700 B.C.** Brooch formed of spiral with eight turns. Pin missing. Could be part of spectacle (two spirals). Diameter 4 cm. Cf. Nicholson, #302; Cf. Trump fig. 57k; *McAlpine* 16:14. Ex: Villa Julia Collection......**CHOICE 125.00**

44. **BRONZE LEECH FIBULA. Italic. 8th-6th Century B.C.** Geometric period. Solid leech semi-elliptical bow, with eleven bands of multi-incised line decoration. 6.3 cm. Fine green patina. Part of pin is broken. Hattat, 199. ......**SUPERB 200.00**

45. **LEECH TYPE FIBULA. Italic. 8th-6th Century B.C.** Very nice leech fibula with traditional incised geometric patterns, encircling lines in between herringbone pattern. Small catch plate and three-turned coil spring. 4.1 cm long. Ex: Villa Julia Collection. Hattat, #198, 199. Superb light green patina. Pin missing. Nice example of early Italic fibula. ......**SUPERB 300.00**

46. **BRONZE FIBULA. Italic. 800-500 B.C.** Solid bronze fibula with leech-type bow with pair of bosses protruding either side in center of bow. Also boss on end of long foot. No spring but a simple bonding of wire to make pin which is missing. Cf. Comstock & Vermeule #332 for similar shape. Dark green patina. Pin missing......**CHOICE 150.00**

47. **BRONZE SPINDLE BEAD. Villanovian. Period II: 750-700 B.C.** Bronze spindle-shaped bead formed of spiral wire. Length 5.3 cm. Hencken, Pl. 136; Cf. *McAlpine* 16:29. These occur at sites in Etruria, especially at Tarquinia. ......**CHOICE 55.00**

48. **BRONZE FIBULA. Italic. 700-500 B.C.** Bronze fibula in thin leech shape. Bow has incised encircling lines all over. Three-coil spring with pin mostly broken off. Catch plate has been bent back, maybe intentionally so that it lies side by side to bow. 3.5 cm long. Ex: MacGruder Collection, no. X 1570. Cf. Hattat, 198 for similar type shape. Most of pin missing. Green patina. ......**CHOICE 150.00**

49. **BRONZE FIBULA. Italic. 600-500 B.C.** Bronze fibula with high, solid bow, three-coil spring and long gulter-type catch plate. Small square protrusion at end of foot. Very simple design and workmanship. 4.7 cm long. Ex: Villa Julia Collection. Similar to nos. 204 and 205 in Hattat. Pin missing. Green patina. ......**CHOICE 150.00**

50. **BRONZE BROOCH. 1st Century B.C.** Bronze brooch in the shape of a warrior astride a galloping horse. The horse has a very dished face. Both the mane and the rider's hair are roached. The horse's body is enameled in blue, the rider's in red. Length 3.7 cm, height 2.7 cm. Cf. Richard Hattatt, *Ancient and Romano-British Brooches*, fig. 68, #160. Spring and catchplate at back, but pin missing. A charming piece. ......**CHOICE 600.00**

EARLY MAN

PLATE 1

EARLY MAN

PLATE 2

WESTERN ASIATIC

The Neolithic period in Western Asia can be traced to Anatolia, and the substantial population that inhabited Çatal Hüyük on the Konya plain. Along with Jericho and the Nafutian culture, and Hacilar farther west, this Anatolian site formed agricultural communities that depended on hunting for their diet. These were the first cities, and they lasted until the historic period. These Anatolian communities made pottery, and used it extensively. Goddess shrines were decorated with mythological bulls' heads, and huge birds of prey. Sculptures of hard stone and terracotta figures were also molded. Climate changes caused these communities to disappear by 5650 B.C.

The Neolithic period arrived somewhat later in Mesopotamia and Iran. The pottery found from this period reflects a similar daily life in these villages in and around the Middle Tigris and Euphrates and at the Samarra Region at the foot of the Zagros Mountains. Early characteristics include pottery, building houses out of clay, and the domestication of animals.

MESOPOTAMIA

Tell Halaf, an important site on the Khabur River in Syria, is the name given for the period from the late 6th to 5th millennium B.C. The Halaf period and culture produced the finest, most beautiful pottery in ancient Mesopotamia. Many cities produced this fine Halaf-type pottery. It was this culture that moved into the Chalcolithic Age, from 4300-3100 B.C.

The Ubaid period is named for the site of Tell Al-Ubaid, just four miles northwest of Ur. It covers the period that produced the painted pottery of the deepest levels of Ur. The Ubaid culture extended its influence far beyond its frontiers in Mesopotamia. The most interesting artifacts other than pottery are the terracotta elongated standing "mother-goddesses."

The city of Uruk, also known as Warka, marked the beginning of urban development.   These unprecedented developments of art and architecture manifested themselves through many different kinds of technology and metallurgy. The temples and public buildings drew attention to the decorated facades of polychrome mosaics. During the Uruk period, the city of Kish produced the first pictographic tablets. The earliest collection of writing on clay tablets known as cuneiform script was found at Uruk. It is from this point that the transition was made from prehistoric to historic man. Stamp seals are also found at Uruk, as they were at Tepe Gawra in the Ubaid period, but now the cylinder seal and sealings also appear. Sculpture on a large scale came into its own. In the north, almost contemporary with Uruk, is the Gawra period.

The Early Bronze Age, from 3100-2100 B.C., starts in Mesopotamia with the Jemdet Nasr period, from 3100-2900 B.C. Wheel-made pottery was distinctive to the period, with painted geometric and naturalistic patterns. The cylinder seals are much more common than in the Uruk period. The designs, however, are more limited to simple coarse linear patterns. This was the result of the expanded popularity of the use of the seal by more of the populace. The appearance of bronze objects is the beginning of the Bronze Age. During this period, it is felt that a new people came into this area of Lower Mesopotamia. They are identified as the Sumerians. They dominated society up to the Early Dynastic period. The Sumerian literature tells of the goddess Inana. Accounts of creation are found in the epic of Marduk, and the flood in the epics of Atrahasis and Gilgamesh. A similar literary pattern is found in the first eleven chapters of the Book of Genesis.

The Early Dynastic period, from 2900-2371, saw each city as a center, or kingdom.   They were ruled by kings mentioned in the Sumerian king list. The typical city-state in this period had a population of 10,000-20,000 inhabitants. Kish, Uruk (Eanna), Ur, Awan, Hamazi, Lagash, Abab, Mari, and Akshak are among the cities. The first dynasty at Kish had no less that 23 kings.

Sargon of Akkad, the founder of the Akkadian dynasty, was the first great conqueror named in history. His conquests became legends of later Babylonians. He first established himself in Akkad, and then Sumer, after which he moved to the east and defeated Elam Amurru in the west, and Subartu in the north. He gained control of Mari, and an area extending as far as what is now Lebanon, and the Taurus Mountains in Turkey. His son Naram-Sin conquered and destroyed Ebla, a city of 260,000 citizens, and the center of a kingdom that held Syria and Palestine in 2400-2250 B.C.

Art excelled during the Akkadian dynasty. A new, vigorous rendering of the anatomy is revealed in stelae, monuments in the round.

The Ur III dynasty of 2100-2006 B.C. is also known as the Neo-Sumerian period. This began with the Gotian invasion, which caused the collapse of the Akkadian dynasty. The invaders were quickly repulsed, and a new dynasty was established under King Ur-Nammu. The buildings and city were restored 1400 years later, and we can now see the grand design of Ur as excavated by Woolley. The magnificent ziggurat of Ur-Nammu measured 61 x 46 meters at the base. Other structures like the mausoleum and the temples were also built on a grand scale. During this period of over 140 years, five kings ruled over the vast empire. All were great builders. The authority of the state grew with a hierarchy of civil servants. The vast economic records have come to us in the form of cuneiform tablets. These tablets are available to the collector today.

By the turn of the 2nd millennium B.C., the center of power was shifting. Isin, Larsa, and Eshuna gained power, and several new dynasties arose. The Babylonian dynasty was established in 2004 B.C., and eleven rulers reigned in this great empire until 1595 B.C., a period of 409 years. This was known as the Old Babylonian period. During this period, the great ruler Hammurabi reigned for forty-three years, from 1792-1750 B.C. During his tenure, the Hammurabi code of laws was formed, touching commercial, social, and domestic life. He conquered many of the remaining cities of Mesopotamia.

It is during this Babylonian period that the Biblical figure Abraham appears, and leaves Ur and Haran on his journey with God.

Art continued to excel, with relief carvings and fine hard stone sculpture. The cylinder seals were of fine workmanship, but were static in composition with presentation scenes.

The Kassite period is a period of decline, after the Hittite raid on Babylon in 1595 B.C. By the mid-15th century B.C., the Kassites had gained control of Lower Mesopotamia. They had trade contact with Egypt, and later Assyria.

The early 1500s B.C. saw the Mitannians, who were Indo-Aryan, establish a small empire by bringing together the states of Northern Mesopotamia. At its zenith, from 1500-1350 B.C., their empire stretched from the Mediterranean to the Zagros Mountains. For 200 years, they had political influence on Egypt and the Hittites.

With the weakening of Mitannian influence and strength, Assyria began to rise as an independent power and state. Ashur-Oballit I (1365-1330 B.C.) changed the city of Ashur from a trade city to the capital of the Assyrian empire. Assyria was put into a recession after the reign of Tukulti-Ninurta I (1244-1208 B.C.). This continued for the most part until the 9th century B.C., when its power was unsurpassed. From the period of 200 years from then to the 7th century B.C., Assyria was by far the most dominant power in Western Asia. Under Esarhaddon (680-669 B.C.), this empire controlled Elam, Babylonia, Eastern Anatolia, Palestine, Syria, and even Egypt. The Assyrian national god was Ashur, often represented among wings, and sometimes as a symbol of a winged rosette. The carving of cylinder seals caused a new upsurge in interest. Some of the monumental sculptures created during this period include giant guardian figures of winged human-headed bulls and lions. This relief sculpture from the palace is amazing.

A revolt in Babylon resulted in the fall of Ashur and Nineveh in 612 B.C. After this, a new power emerged, the Chaldeans. With this shift in power began the Neo-Babylonian period. In 539 B.C., the Persian ruler Cyrus II, or the Great, defeated the Babylonians. The Achaemenid empire became one of the largest of the ancient world. At its greatest point, the Achaemenid empire contained Mesopotamia, Syria, Egypt, Asia Minor, Thrace, Iran, and parts of India.

ANATOLIA

The Assyrian Colony period in Anatolia took place from 1920-1740 B.C. These colonies were trading partners with Ashur. They received tin and textiles, and they exported gold and silver.

The history of the Hittite kingdom starts in the Late Bronze Age (1600-1200 B.C.), or the Hittite Old Kingdom, and progresses to the Hittite empire of 1450-1180 B.C. The Hittites, under their king Hattusilis I, swept in and conquered Aleppo, and then conducted the famous raid on Babylon in 1595 B.C. The rich centers of the empire in the southeast were Tarsus, Carchemish, and Insupia (Ugarit). The Hittites were great charioteers, from the time of the Old Kingdom conquests on. Monumental rock reliefs at Yazilikaya display the gods of the Hittites. The so-called Neo-Hittite Art period took from the old tradition and blended it with Syrian, Hurrian, Assyrian, and some Aramaic techniques.

IRAN

The Village period saw food-producing villages by the 7th millennium. Small clusters of village appeared at the plains of Den Luran, Susiana, Mahidasht, Hulailan, and Solduz. This period on the Susiana Plain (Susa A) lasted until the 4th millennium B.C.

During the Uruk period in Susa, efforts began to be made to bring the whole plain under a central administration. The result was the development of a state organization. Population increased substantially as the villages were abandoned.

The Proto-Elamite period, beginning around 2700 B.C., is when the southwest area of Iran emerged as Elam. The Elamite state was later controlled by the Akkadians. They shared control with the Simasaki during the Old Elamite period (2500-1500 B.C.).

The kings of Maitani, or the Mitannians, created a small empire. These people of Indo-Aryan origin settled and brought together the Hurrian states of Northern Mesopotamia. Their political influence was strong, rivaling Egypt and Anatolia from 1500-1350 B.C.

Elam was the center area of Susania, with its capital city at Susa. The Middle Elamite period spanned the 13th and 12th centuries. Military victories at Babylon and farther north resulted in a period of prosperity and strength. Nebuchadnezzar I, the king of Babylon, ended all this late in the 12th century.

Luristan was located in the western region of Iran in an open area of plains intersected by the Zagros Mountains. The Lurs were known for their bronze industry, and their society was closely connected to the use of the horse. The period of Luristan influence spanned from the 12th to the 7th century B.C. The period of greatest bronze output and prosperity can be dated to the last two centuries of their influence. For many years, all bronze artifacts coming from Iran were thought to be from Luristan, but today the differences have become more clear with modern excavations and studies. Luristan showed an independent and creative flair in their bronze workshops.

TOOLS AND WEAPONS

One of the most collected areas of antiquity is Western Asiatic weapons. The vast finds of Sythian-Achaemenid and Parthian arrowheads have been a stepping stone into this field. The prices for these have been very reasonable for years. Now the prices are easing upward. The wonderful array of bronze weapons from Iran, and especially Luristan, has excited collectors and scholars alike. Bronze shaft-hole axes, adzes, and pick-axes are found in Luristan and the southwest Caspian area. A wide range of daggers, dirks, and swords are also widely available, along with the occasional iron sword. Arrowheads and spearheads dominate this market, including some inscribed with cuneiform writing. Maceheads are found in bronze, and in fine carved stone marble, hematite, chalcedony, and serpentine. Collectors must be careful to know all the bronze objects offered. In the past, there has been a tendency for dealers to lump all Western Asiatic bronze weapons as Luristan. This misrepresentation is changing now, and the way was paved with the aid of fine published collections and new scholarship by Dr. P. R. S. Moorey at the Ashmolean Museum in Oxford.

POTTERY

The wealth of ancient pottery found in Western Asia is vast, to say the least. The very early pottery from Hacilar, in Turkey, during the Chalcolithic period, is highly sought after. The collector should be warned that many fakes of this pottery have been found on the marketplace in the past. Pottery from Mesopotamia is not widely offered for sale. The fine painted examples from the Halaf period are widely sought, but not found. Pottery found in Iran and Syria have been more available to the collector, but this has changed with the uncertainty in the political climate today. Generally speaking, plain ware, when found, can be purchased at very favorable prices. The only problem lies in finding it. Painted pottery is more attractive and more available to the collector, but is also more expensive. This area of collecting has been neglected in the past.

TERRACOTTA FIGURES

Terracotta figures are a widely collected field in Western Asiatic art. The early mother goddess and primitive idol figures have been the subjects of special shows in Paris, London, and New York. The appreciation of these early expressions of emerging man has been popular. The bizarre Sypo-Hittite terracotta heads have long been an interesting type of collectible. A warning to the collector: full standing figures are, much more often than not, highly restored. The heads usually are fine, but the rest of the figures are fully new restorations. Most of these terracottas were votive in nature, and the heads were broken off at a shrine and offered to the gods. They are usually not found complete. Along with the humanesque heads, terracotta animals are also collected. Babylonian and other Mesopotamian terracotta plaques are available along with the later Parthian man-on-horse terracottas.

METAL

Bronze objects other than weapons and tools are widely available. A wealth of objects costing $50 and up is available to the collector. The finer cast bronze Mesopotamian figures are found at the higher end of the market. Anatolia bull figures are attractive, and can be purchased at under $1000, while the Phrygian fibula can be found at around $250. Bronze objects from Iran have been found extensively. Snake head bracelets and bracelets with knobbed decorations have been found, as have bells and other bronze horse accoutrements. The horse cheek pieces display the artist's craft and style, and are found throughout Iran. The wonderful animal amulets and figures have been available and popular with collectors for 50 years. They are from the Caspian region, including Luristan and Amlash. The wealth of Luristan bronzes include animal head pins, the heraldic animal bronze finials, animal head bracelets, and disk head pins executed in repoussé. In the 8th century, arm fibulas were fashioned throughout Western Asia, and they are widely available to the collector today.

STONE

Among the most popular Western Asiatic collectibles are seals. They can exemplify the culture represented in fine detail in the miniature. The stamp seals are the most reasonably priced, but are simple in design. The amuletic animal seals are often found in fine quality. The cylinder seals are the best examples of Western Asiatic art. Care must be taken to know the process of manufacture and the styles within the cultures, if one is to avoid purchasing fakes. A series of serpentine cylinder seals with erotic scenes has appeared on the market in the last five years, and they are all false. Finding re-cut seals is not uncommon. This practice was done from dynasty to dynasty. The difficulty lies in identifying modern re-cutting practices. Newly cut stone will usually have a sharpness to it, and will lack apparent wear to the material cut.

A guide to the collector on the Glyptic art found on cylinder and stamp seals, with stylistic development, can be found below:

Prehistoric:	1) Animal, 2) Geometric patterns
Uruk Period:	1) Animal rows, 2) Pigtail figures, 3) Geometric patterns
Late Uruk Period:	1) Animal rows, 2) Patterns including geometric cross-hatching zig-zags and herringbones
Jamdat Nasr:	1) Animal rows, 2) Geometric patterns
Early Dynastic:	1) Animal rows, 2) Figures with animals, 3) Combat scenes, 4) Ritual banquets, 5) Decorative animal motifs
Akkadian:	1) Combat scenes, 2) Mythological scenes with sun and water gods, 3) Worship scenes and banquets
Ur III:	1) Presentations to a deity, 2) Presentations to a king
Old Babylonian:	1) Presentation scenes, 2) Sun god and scimitar god, 3) Figure with mace, 4) Water god, 5) God with crook, 6) Suppliant goddess, 7) Nude female facing, 8) Combat scenes
Kassite:	1) Presentations
Middle Assyrian:	1) Combat scenes, 2) Animal scenes, 3) Ritual scenes
Neo-Assyrian and	
Neo-Babylonian:	1) Contest scenes, 2) Real animals, 3) Imaginary animals, 4) Hunting scenes, 5) Banquet scenes, 6) Worship of deities, 7) Deities in combat, 8) Worship of symbols, 9) War scenes: a) linear style, b) cut style, c) drill style, d) modeled style
Achaemenid:	1) Kneeling archer, 2) Royal hero, 3) Animal scenes
Syrian (Early):	1) Working figures, 2) Animals, 3) Patterns
Syrian (Middle):	1) Banquet, 2) Human figures with animals
Syrian (Late):	1) Figures with round cap, 2) Seated figures, 3) Deity scenes, 4) Mesopotamian deities, 5) Egyptian deities, 6) Heroes against animals and demons, 7) Rituals, 8) Decorative
Mitannian:	1) Ritual, 2) Deities and figures, 3) Deities with humans, 4) Winged sun disc, 5) Animals
Elamite:	1) Geometric

JEWELRY

The word "goldsmith," or jeweler, appeared in Akkadian cuneiform texts. The word for jewelry in Assyrian cuneiform was "dumaqu." Jewelry was used by individuals throughout society, in both secular and religious contexts.

The Prehistoric use of jewelry was sporadic, but by the Early Dynastic period, various areas were providing gold, silver, and bronze jewelry. Semi-precious stones were used in context as inlays, or parts of the jewelry.

Early Ur produced headdresses, gold earrings, gold wire hair rings, diadems, necklaces, and gold and silver beads of various shapes and sizes. In the Akkadian period, Ur produced hair rings, earrings, pendants, beads, and pins in copper. Gold pins were produced in Anatolia along with necklaces and beads. Some of the Western Anatolian gold earrings produced in 2500-200 B.C. are solid gold. Crescent and disc gold earrings are from Babylonia. Assyrian pendants are ornate gold, and there is some use of cloisonné. More use of disc pendants and geometric pendants along with rings, buttons, and beads can be found in objects from Urartu. Gold animal rondels, bracelets, earring fibulae, and rings can be found from Western Iran in the 8th century B.C. By the Neo-Assyrian period, the level of jewelry making had grown to a high level of ornate workmanship. Work in the round of heads of the goddess Ishtar, figures of nude goddesses, ram's head finials, and animal head gold bracelets are all magnificent. Gold jewelry is relatively expensive. An Achaemenid gold ring dating to the 5th century B.C. with spiral form and bovine terminal heads brought $4000 at auction.

Marduk-Gilgamesh: Assyrian

Adad with stars

Zirbanit: Babylonian

Ramman-Martu: Babylonian

Marduk

Etana

Eabani: Babylonian

Tiamat: The Dragon, Babyonian

Enlil: Babylonian

Belit: God with dragon

Ishtar with stars

Adad: Assyrian

Shamash: over mountain

Ishtar: Babylonian

Ninkigal: Goddess of Hades

Nusku: Ur goddess

Ningishzida: Sumerian and Babylonian

Shamash

Shamash

Gilgamesh

Siru: Serpent god, Babylonian

Elam: Goddess of winged gate/bull

Bau-Gula: seated goddess

Bau-Gula: Agricultural goddess

Ea: Water god, Babylonian

Ningursu: Agricultural god

Eagle of Lagash

Akkadian: Naked goddess stormy rains

Ea: Water god, Assyrian

Assyrian dragon

Assyrian: Bel and the dragon

Bau: Babylonian

Nergal: Attacking enemy

Ishkara: Naked goddess

Aaor Shala: Vested consort

Nergal: Lion-head god

Sandu: Babylonian-Hittite

Syrian: Two-headed god

Sharruma: Divine son, Hittite

Hepat: Great Goddess, Hittite

Teshub: Storm god of sky, Hittite

Astarte: Phoenecian-Hittite

Tarhundas: God of storms, Hittite

WESTERN ASIATIC GODS AND GODDESSES

STONES USED IN STAMP AND CYLINDER SEALS

Prehistoric:
clay
limestone
marble
mica-shist
*serpentine
shist
*steatite

Uruk:
calcite
limestone
*marble
rock crystal
serpentine
talc

Jemdet Nasr:
agate
alabaster
basalt
bone
calcite
chalk
chert
composition
limestone
*marble
mica-shist
*serpentine
shell
steatite
travertine

Early Dynastic:
alabaster
chalcite
chalk
chert
composition
*limestone
*marble
serpentine
travertine

Akkadian:
agate
calcite
composition

Akkadian (cont.):
diorite
hematite
lapis lazuli
limestone
marble
nephrite
quartz
rock crystal
*serpentine
shell

Ur III:
diorite
hematite
jasper
limestone
marble
nephrite
rock crystal
*serpentine
shell
*steatite

Old Babylonian:
agate
alabaster
carnelian
composition
diorite
*hematite
jasper
lapis lazuli
limestone
limonite
obsidian
rock crystal
serpentine
steatite

Kassite:
agate
amazon stone
chalcite
chert
composition
jasper
lapis lazuli
serpentine

Middle Assyrian:
agate
carnelian
limestone
marble
mica-shist
sardonyx
serpentine
talc

Neo-Assyrian:
agate
calcite
carnelian
*chalcedony
*chert
*composition (faience)
flint
jasper
lapis lazuli
*limestone
*marble
obsidian
pyrophyllite
sard
sardonyx
*serpentine
travertine
tuff

Cappadocia:
*hematite
jasper
limonite
serpentine

Achaemenid:
*agate
carnelian
composition
chalcedony
chert
glass
jasper
lapis lazuli
*limestone
marble
serpentine

Syrian:
bone
hematite
limestone
marble
*serpentine
steatite

Old Assyrian Colony:
fossil coral
*hematite
marble
serpentine

Mitannian:
agate
carnelian
chalcedony
*chert
*composition (faience)
*hematite
limonite
marble
steatite

Cypriot:
carnelian
cuprous sulfide
hematite
marble
serpentine
*steatite

Leventine:
bronze
chert
composition (faience)
glass
hematite
limestone
marble
pyrophyllite
schist
*serpentine
*steatite

Middle Elamite:
composition (faience)
serpentine

*stone commonly used in the period

WESTERN ASIATIC

	SYRIA	ANATOLIA	NORTHERN MESOPOTAMIA	CENTRAL MESOPOTAMIA	NORTHERN AND CENTRAL IRAN	WESTERN IRAN AND LURISTAN	SUSIANA	LOWER MESOPOTAMIA
9000	Mureybet (Mesolithic)	Belbasi Beldibi	Zawi Chemi Shanidar		Cave of Belt			
8500						Ganj Dareh (Pre-Pottery)		
8000						Tell Asiab near Kermanshah (Pre-Pottery)		
7500		Cayonu (Pre-Pottery, Neolithic)						
7000		Hacilar (Pre-Pottery)	Jarmo (Pre-Pottery)			Ganj Dareh (Pottery)		
6500	Ugarit V-C (Pre-Pottery, Neolithic)	Catal Hüyük X (Pottery)	Jarmo (Pottery, Neolithic) II	Tell Es-Sawwan		Tepe Guran (Pre-Pottery)		
6000	Ugarit V-B (Pottery, Neolithic, V-A)		Hassuna I a, b, c II	Periods of Jarmo I and Hasuna II		Tepe Guran (Pottery)		
5500	Ugarit IV-C	**Hacilar** (Pottery, Neolithic)	Hassuna III Samarra period	Samarra period III IV	Tepe Sialk I		Jaffarabad 4-6	Eridu XIX, XV

WESTERN ASIATIC

	SYRIA	ANATOLIA	NORTHERN MESOPOTAMIA	CENTRAL MESOPOTAMIA	NORTHERN AND CENTRAL IRAN	WESTERN IRAN AND LURISTAN	SUSIANA	LOWER MESOPOTAMIA
5000	Ugarit IV-B **Tell Halaf period**		Hassuna VI **Halaf period** Tepe Gawra	**Tell Halaf period V**	I		Jaffarabad 3^{m-n}	Eridu XIV XIII (workshop)
4500	IV-A		**Gawra Ubaid period**		II	First necropolises of Luristan: Hakalan		Eridu XII **Ubaid period** VIII
4000	Ugarit III-C (transition)		Gawra Late Ubaid XII		III		Jaffarabad 1-3 Susa I, 27 25 23	VII VI XV
3500			Gawra XI		IV		Susa 22-18 Susa 17 **Proto-Urban**	Eridu V-II **URUK PERIOD** Uruk XIV Uruk IV
3000	Ugarit III-B "Ubaid"		Gawra VIII-C, B, A Gawra VII		Proto-Elamite	Large caves of Luristan	Susa 16-13 **Proto-Elamite**	**Jemdet Nasr period** Uruk III
2500							**Early Dynastic** Susa Painted ceramics	Uruk II-I Early Dynastic period

WESTERN ASIATIC

	IRAN	NORTHERN MESOPOTAMIA	SOUTHERN MESOPOTAMIA	ANATOLIA
2800	Hissar II and Tureng Tepe II: appearance of gray ceramics	Nineveh V	**Early Dynastic I**	Troy II 2800-2300
2700	**Early Dynastic Civilization at Susa** Large caves of Luristan	Temple H of Ishtar at Assur	**Early Dynastic II**: "Square Temple" of Eshnunna "Temple Oval" of Khafaje	
2600	Second style painted ceramics (Yahya IV-B) (Giyan IV)		**Early Dynastic III**: Mesi-Lim, king of Kish Royal tombs of Ur	
2500			Ur-Nanshe at Lagash Palace of Mari	
2400	(Hissar III-A)		Eannatum at Lagash	"Royal tombs" of Alaja Hüyük
2350	── Awan Dynasty ── **Akkadian Empire**	**Akkadian Empire**	**Akkadian Empire**, Sargon, c. 2340	
2300		Temple G of Ishtar at Assur	Rimush, Manishtusu, Narim-Sin, Sharkalisharri	
2250	Puzur Inshushinak			
2200		(Gawra VI)	Guti invasion	Hattusas V
2150	(Yahya IV-A)		Gudea at Lagash	
2100			**Third Dynasty of Ur** 2111-2003	
2000	── Simashki Dynasty ── (Giyan III)	**Assyrian** Temple E of Ishtar at Assur	Isin and Larsa dynasties	
1900		**Assyrian Kingdom**		**Assyrian Colonies**
1800	Sukkalmahhu period Eclipse of civilizations of Luristan and Turkmenistan	Shamshi-Adad I 1814-1782	**First Dynasty of Babylon** 1894-1595 Hammurabi 1792-1750	Destruction of karum II of Kanish Restoration of karum I-b of Kanish **Old Syrian Period** Restoration of karum I-b of Kanish

WESTERN ASIATIC

	IRAN	NORTHERN MESOPOTAMIA	SOUTHERN MESOPOTAMIA	ANATOLIA
1750	(Giyan III)		**Old Babylonian Period** Samsu-iluna 1749-1712	
1700	Kutir-Nahhunte I Tan-Uli		Abi-eshuh 1711-1694	
1650			Samsu-ditana 1625-1595	**Old Hittite Empire** 1650-1500 Mursilis I takes Aleppo and Babylon
1600	(Giyan II)		1595 Babylon taken by the Hittites **Kassite Dynasty** 1595-1155	
1550				Telepinus 1525-1500
1500		**Mitannian Empire** Saustatar Apogee of Nuzi		
1450			Karaindash (1445-1427) Kurigalzu I	Tudhaliyas III
1400		Decline of Mitanni **Middle Assyrian Empire** Assur-uballit I 1366-1330		Suppiluliumas 1380-1346
1350				
1300	**Middle-Elamite Period** Untash-Napirisha (Tombs of Marlik)			Tudhaliyas IV 1265-1235
1250		Tukulti-Ninurta I 1244-1208	Adad-shum-usur 1218-1189	
1200	Shutruk-Nahhunte 1185-1155 Kutir-Nahhunte 1155-1150 Shilhak-Inshushinak 1150-1120 (Iron I necropolises in Luristan) Eclipse of Elam (Hasanlu V)	Assur-dan I 1179-1134 Tiglath-pileser I 1117-1077	Melishipak II End of Kassites **Second Isin Dynasty** Nebuchadnezzar I 1126-1105	End of Hittite Empire Phrygians in Anatolia, under the name of Mushki

WESTERN ASIATIC

	IRAN	NORTHERN MESOPOTAMIA	SOUTHERN MESOPOTAMIA	ANATOLIA
1050		Assurnasirpal I 1050-1032	Second Dynasty "Of the Land of the Sea"	
1000	Citadel of Hasanlu IV		**Elamite Dynasty**	Kingdom of Malatya (Milid)
950	Iron II necropolises in Luristan			
		Assur-dan II 934-912		
900	Necropolis B of Sialk	**Neo-Assyrian** Assurnasirpal II 883-859 Shalmaneser III 858-824	Nabu-alpa-addina 888-855	
850	Fortress of Baba Jan in Luristan Destruction of Hasanlu IV	Adad-Nirari III 810-783		Sardur in Urartu 832-825
800				Manua 805-788
750		Tigath pileser III 744-727		Sardur III 765-733
	Neo-Elamite Period Shutruk Nahhunte II 717-699	Shalmaneser V 726-722 Sargon II 721-705	Merodach-Baladan II 721-710 and 704-703	Rusas 730-714 Midas in Phrygia Cimmerian invasion
700	Defeat of Elamites at Til Tuba (653)	Sennacherib 704-681 Esarhaddon 680-669 Assurbanipal 668-c. 630	Capture and annexation of Babylon by Sennacherib	
650	Susa taken by Assurbanipal (646) **Achaemenid Dynasty** Cyrus I, king of Anshan	Civil War after 627 End of Assyria (612)	Destruction of Babylon by Assurbanipal (648) Neo-Babylonian Dynasty	Alyattes in Lydia
600	Cyaxares, king of Medes End of Luristan civilization **Mede Empire** Astyages 585-550 **Achaemenid Dynasty**		Nabopolassar 626-605 Nebuchadnezzar II 604-562	609-560 Destruction of Urartu Croesus 560-546
550	Cyrus II, "the Great" Death of Cyrus II Cambyses II 529-522 Darius I 522-486		Nabonidus 555-539 Capture of Babylon by Cyrus (539), Achaemenid Dynasty	
500			Revolt and capture of Babylon (484)	Revolt of Ionia Persian Wars
	Xerxes I 485-465 Artaxerxes I 464-424			
450	Darius II 424-405 Artaxerxes II 404-359			
400				
350	Artaxerxes III 359-337 Darius III Codoman 335-330		Capture of Babylon	

WESTERN ASIATIC

WEAPONS AND TOOLS
Stone
Arrowheads
51. **BONE ARROWHEAD. Neo-Elamite. 1200-800 B.C.** Long tapering blade and longish tang. Length 6.3 cm. Similar types in bronze were found at Marlik. This rare arrowhead was probably used for hunting animals. Cf. Moorey #80 (for bronze type). Very rare...............................**CHOICE 125.00**

Mace, Axe, and Adze Heads
52. **MACE HEAD. Late 4th-3rd Millennium B.C.** Variegated black and grey granite mace head. Oblate and pierced through top and bottom. Diameter 5 cm. Cf. Sotheby's NY 10/25/87, #357. Some minor chips.............**CHOICE 175.00**

53. **MACE HEAD. North Syrian. 3200-2200 B.C.** Black chlorite pointed and pear shaped. 7.5 x 5.5 cm. Cf. Petrie, XXVI, 62, Cf. Muscarella, *Bronze & Iron MMA*, #540. Restoration to back of head. Found in Anatolia. ....**CHOICE 175.00**

54. **MACE HEAD. Susa. 3500-2500 B.C.** Black steatite head with three large globes. 4 cm diameter. Cf. Petrie, *Prehistoric Egypt*, XXII, 65...........................**CHOICE 200.00**

55. **MACE HEAD. Susa. 3500-2500 B.C.** Hard white limestone with four knobs. 7 cm in diameter, 5.4 cm height. Cf. Petrie, *Prehistoric Egypt*, Mace, p. 23. ......**CHOICE 125.00**

56. **MACE HEAD. Sumerian. 3rd Millennium B.C.** Marble three headed, all with eyes composed of concentric circles. Measures 35 mm x 35 mm. Scarce type. Sotheby & Co. Catalogue of Egyptian Seals, p. 52, photo 226. April 1975. ....**CHOICE 85.00**

57. **MACE HEAD. Assyrian. 2500-2000 B.C.** White marble carved mace head. 4.5 cm high, 1.5 cm diameter opening. Van-Boren, *Symbols of Gods*, p. 166. Found in the Tigris and Euphrates region................................**CHOICE 150.00**

Metal
Swords, Daggers, and Blades
58. **COPPER DAGGER BLADE. Early Anatolian. Copper Age Stratum I, 3500-2200 B.C.** Flat blade with wide tang pierced at end. Length 10.5 cm. Malloy #58; Schmidt fig. 137b. ....**SUPERB 250.00**

59. **COPPER DAGGER BLADE. Sumerian. 3000 B.C.** Blade cut from sheet. No midrib. End has three rivet holes. Length 37.3 cm. Malloy #58a; MacKay Pl. LXII:17. Similar to the blades excavated at the "A" cemetery at Kish. Restoration to blade. Rare. ....**CHOICE 375.00**

60. **BRONZE DAGGER. Mesopotamian. Late 3rd Millennium B.C. Jemdet Nasr.** Made from hammered sheet. Very wide blade tapering to a rounded end. Slightly sloping shoulders. Thick, flat tapering tang with splayed end, emulating hilt. Length 29 cm including handle. Width 5.7 cm. Malloy 451. Cf. Moorey, #44 for similar sheet metal replicas of weapons for tombs.....................**CHOICE 500.00**

61. **BRONZE DAGGER. Ur III. Susa. 2000-1800 B.C.** Miniature. Bronze, midrib, double-edged blade with very small barbs near the square shoulders, pommel. 7.5 cm long, 1.5 cm wide. Possibly used as a toy. Cf. Moorey (44) fig. 12, p. 66.....................................**CHOICE 75.00**

62. **BRONZE DIRK. Northwest Persian. 2nd Millennium B.C.** Solid cast bronze; hilt cast into blade. Flat flare pommel, central rib decoration. Length 27 cm. Nice patina. ....**CHOICE 350.00**

63. **BRONZE SWORD. Amlash or Afghanistan. Late 2nd-Early 1st Millennium B.C.** Bronze cast sword with round pommel and protruding knob at guard. Leaf-shaped blade with central rib. Length 39 cm. Moorey-, Frankfort-. Restoration to part of blade.......................**CHOICE 375.00**

64. **BRONZE SWORD. Luristan. 1200-1000 B.C.** Complete sword with bronze handle with complete flanges in lower part of hilt, rivet hole near hilt. 39.7 cm long, 3 cm wide. Blade slightly bent. The hilt at one time had an inlay of bone or wood. Moorey 48 var...........................**CHOICE 325.00**

65. **BRONZE SWORD. Northern Persia. 1200-1000 B.C.** Long shaft and midrib. 56.8 x 3.7 cm. Moorey, Pl. 5, 42 var. ....**CHOICE 350.00**

66. **BRONZE SWORD BLADE. 1200-800 B.C.** Central shaft with tang. 22 cm long. 4.7 cm wide. Green patina. Moorey #40...**CHOICE 125.00**

67. **BRONZE DIRK. Elamite. 1200-800 B.C.** Solid cast bronze dirk. Blade cast separately from hilt. Double-edged blade with wide midrib, tapering down to rounded end. Rectangular guard with pinched sides on flanged hilt, splaying out to end. No inlay remaining. Length 30.8 cm including handle. Muscarella #391. Moorey #47-50. Cf. Malloy, *Weapons*, #54..............................**CHOICE 350.00**

68. **BRONZE SWORD BLADE. Northwest Iranian. Late Bronze: 1200-800 B.C.** Large cast blade with broad flat tang with hole at end. Blade has broad flat midrib ending at shoulder. Rounded shoulders. Double-edged blade ends in sharp point. End of tang bent. Length 47.5 cm including tang. Cf. Berghe Abb4 (lintis). Cf. Malloy, *Weapons*, #62. ....**SUPERB 300.00**

69. **BRONZE SPEARHEAD. Middle Elamite. 1200-800 B.C.** Ovate blade with low midrib. Folded socket with rivet hole at base with rivet of iron present. 26.6 x 3.7 cm. 2 cm diameter opening. Similar types were found through Caucasia and Western Persia. Cf. Gimbutas, *Bronze Age Culture in Central and Eastern Europe*, Pl. 95, TLI. Cf. Moorey, 87. ....**CHOICE 200.00**

70. **BRONZE DAGGER BLADE. 1200-800 B.C.** Deltoid with midrib and tapering tang. 14.6 x 3.5 cm. Moorey 64. ....**CHOICE 100.00**

71. **BRONZE DIRK. Luristan. 1200-800 B.C.** Bronze cast dirk with thin double-edged tapering to rounded end. Wide slightly protruding midrib making blade convex on both sides. Flanged hilt with no wood or ivory remaining. Rectangular guard, hilt tapering down to splayed end. Length 37 cm including handle. Malloy #53; Cf. Moorey #47-50. Very utilitarian piece. Some nicks in blade. ....**CHOICE 350.00**

72. **BRONZE DAGGER BLADE OR SPEARHEAD. Northern Persian. 1200-700 B.C.** Ribbed blade has medium tang with flattened, curved end. Length 11.2 cm. Cf. Moorey 71, 73.............................**CHOICE 100.00**

73. **BRONZE DAGGER BLADE. Luristan. 11th-9th Century B.C.** Broad circular edges. Three rivet holes with two rivets. 15.7 x 3.5 cm. Cf. Moorey, 46 (blade). ....**SUPERB 150.00**

74. **BRONZE DAGGER. Amlash. Early 1st Millennium B.C.** Cast bronze dagger with thick tapering blade. Slight midrib. Blade tapers down to triangular point. Thick rectangular guard with two ridges, tapering toward blade. Flanged cylindrical hilt with wood remaining in inlay. Hilt splays out on either side. Separately cast pommel missing. Length 26 cm. Malloy #51; Cf. Frankfurt-am-Main pp. 62-66, nos. 66-70. Small piece missing from handle. Wood remaining in inlay. ....**CHOICE 400.00**

75. **BRONZE DAGGER. Early 1st Millennium B.C.** Bronze dagger blade. Shaft with one rivet hole. 15.2 x 2.6 cm. This form copies the Hittite (Anatolian) wide midrib. Cf. Muscarella, *Bronze & Iron MMA*, 392. ....**CHOICE 85.00**

76. **COPPER SWORD BLADE. Iron II A-B: 1000-800 B.C.** Copper blade with midrib, flat tang. Four holes at base for attaching to handle. Length 27.3 cm (10¼"). Cf. Hancock 49 H1. From the time of Saul and David. Tip twisted at slight angle.......................................**CHOICE 250.00**

77. **BRONZE SWORD BLADE. 1000-700 B.C.** Flat tang with hole at end, rounded shoulders, straight-sided double-edge sword. High midrib. 38.8 cm long, 4.5 cm wide. Long blade example. Moorey 39.......................**CHOICE 150.00**

78. **IRON KNIFE. Iron Age. 1000-586 B.C.** Sharp, one-sided blade, brown with some encrustation. Two rivets remaining at top. Found in Israel. 19.7 cm long. Petrie, 210-211 (XXVIII-XXIX Dynasty). Encrusted...........**CHOICE 250.00**

79. **BRONZE DAGGER BLADE. Luristan. 9th-8th Century B.C.** Blade with short tang, raised central ridge. Length 13.8 cm including tang. Cf. Moorey #38, Cf. Malloy, *Weapons*.....................................**CHOICE 85.00**

80. **BRONZE SWORD. Northwest Persia. Luristan. 850-700 B.C.** Part of hilt, raised midrib with blood ridges. The hilt has a decoration of dogs' heads, two rivets at hilt. 22 x 4.6 cm, 2 cm diameter opening. Cf. Moorey, Pl. 7, 58. ....**CHOICE 250.00**

81. **DAGGER BLADE. Luristan. 800-700 B.C.** Tapering triangular with tang and midrib. 21.5 x 4 cm. Cf. *Tepe Giyan, Level I and Tepe Sialk Plateau and Tepe Guran Graves*. Moorey 38. Green patina.............**CHOICE 150.00**

82. **BRONZE SWORD BLADE. Neo-Elamite. 800-700 B.C.** Tapering triangular blade with high midrib, short tang and two rivet holes at shoulder. 33.2 x 5.4 cm. Muscarella-. Goddard-. Moorey-. Green patina.............**CHOICE 400.00**

83. **BRONZE CEREMONIAL DAGGER. Caspian. 8th-7th Century B.C.** Ram head hilt with loop, three lines with triangular hole at guard. 21.9 x 1.6 cm. This type appears unknown in animal pendants with similar animal heads. Cf. Boisgirard-Heeckeren Collection X, 1980, #128. Goddard-. Moorey-Muscarella-. Rare........................**CHOICE 400.00**

Spear and Javelin Points

84. **BRONZE JAVELIN. Ur III. Late 3rd Millennium B.C.** Square tapering to point. Socket with holes for rivet. 18.8 cm long, 1.8 cm diameter. Cf. Excavations in Ur, Assur and Carchmish. Cf. Muscarella, MMS #519. Muscarella suggests that the socket type is, in fact, a spear butt. Rare. ....**CHOICE 200.00**

85. **BRONZE SPEAR BUTT. Northwest Iran. 2nd Millennium B.C.** Hollow cast spear butt with cylindrical handle and rectangular body tapering to a point. Hole through handle. Conical end attached, separately cast. Delicate suspension hole in top, single hole near end of handle. Length 45.5 cm. Malloy #77; Cf. Muscarella #163, 518/19. Very tip of point broken off. ....**SUPERB 600.00**

86. **BRONZE SPEAR BUTT. Northwest Iran. 2nd Millennium B.C.** Cast spear butt with solid square section tapering down to blunt small end. Cylindrical hilt with two holes through. Pyramidal cone-shaped pommel with open work decoration. Large suspension hole intact. Length 33 cm. Malloy #78; Cf. Muscarella #163, 518/19 for similar open work and bronze treatment. Broken off at end. ....**CHOICE 450.00**

87.   **BRONZE SPEARHEAD. Luristan, Northeast Iran. Early Bronze Age.** Head with flat blade, two edges. Blade tapers to point. Rounded shoulders and tapering tang. Length 21.8 cm including tang. Malloy #69; Cf. Muscarella #174 for same shape but smaller. Nicks to both edges. ....**CHOICE 200.00**

88.   **BRONZE SPEAR POINT. Kassite. 1600-1100 B.C.** Bronze point with high rib, long tang, curved barbs. Length 9.3 cm. The Kassites conquered Elam and Babylon with these characteristic weapons. De Morgan fig. 575, Goddard, *Les Bronzes de Luristan*, Pl. XIII: 32:4. Small chip on blade. ....**CHOICE 200.00**

89.   **BRONZE SPEARHEAD. Caucasian Western Persia. 1200-800 B.C.** Leaf blade with rounded midrib with folded socket and rivet hole. Incised herringbone pattern on midrib at shoulder. More incised design around socket. This type is found throughout the Caspian Sea area. Nice incised pattern. Cf. Moorey 87.............................**SUPERB 150.00**

90.   **BRONZE SPEAR POINT. Neo-Elamite. 1200-800 B.C.** Cast deltoid blade with long tapering tang. Length 12.1 cm. Found over western Iran and eastern Iraq. Moorey 64. ....**CHOICE 100.00**

91.   **IRON JAVELIN HEAD. Western Persia. 1200-700 B.C.** Rhomboid head tapering, pyramidal form, long tapering tang. 12.8 cm long. General type used for piercing leather and scale armor. Cf. Moorey, 77 var................**CHOICE 125.00**

92.   **BRONZE SPEARHEAD BLADE. Northern Persia. Neo-Elamite. 1000-600 B.C.** Barbs and high midrib with long shaft. 11.2 cm. Cf. Muscarella, *MMA* 401..**CHOICE 75.00**

93.   **BRONZE SPEARHEAD. Neo-Elamite. 800-700 B.C.** Triangular tapering blade, straight shoulders, socketed pronounced midrib, incised palm design on socket. 20 x 1.3 cm diameter opening. Cf. Moorey #88 var. Green patina. ....**CHOICE 150.00**

94.   **BRONZE SPEAR POINT. Neo-Elamite. 800-700 B.C.** Triangular, straight, tapering socketed high midrib. Incised horizontal palm design with some geometric design on blade. 19 x 2.2 cm, 1.4 cm diameter opening. Cf. Moorey 88 var. For designed spearhead. Very jagged edges. Rare. ....**AVERAGE 125.00**

95.   **BRONZE SPEAR POINT. Neo-Elamite. 750-600 B.C.** Deltoid barbed blade with high rib and cut down tang. Total length 15 cm. Cf. Malloy, *Weapons*, #72. Chips to edges, one barb...**CHOICE 75.00**

96.   **BRONZE SPEARHEAD. Egypt. 6th-2nd Century B.C.** Head with central ridge. Length 16 cm including tang. Malloy #74; Cf. Petrie #192. Chips on edge. ....**CHOICE 125.00**

97.   **BRONZE SPEARHEAD. Achaemenid. 539-331 B.C.** Socketed head. Rhombic shape with barbs at each corner. Length 7.5 cm. Malloy #75; Cf. Koldewey Pl. 184a. Very rare..**CHOICE 200.00**

98.   **BRONZE SPEARHEAD. Achaemenid. 539-331 B.C.** Hollow with hole shaft opening at bottom until ¾ way up shaft. Rhombic head with barbs at each corner. 7.5 cm long, 1.5 cm wide. Very rare. Cf. Koldewey, *Das Wieder Eerstehende Babylon*, Pl. 184a.................**CHOICE 175.00**

Arrowheads

99.   **BRONZE ARROWHEAD. Ur II. Susa. Late 3rd Millennium B.C.** Hammered flat and cut from sheet. With barbs and wide flat tang. Measures 5 x 2 cm. Cf. Comments Moorey, *Ancient Persian Bronzes in the Ashmolean Museum*, #44. Minor corrosion and small chip to edge. ....**CHOICE 80.00**

100. **BRONZE ARROWHEAD. Mesopotamia. Ur III. Susa. Late 3rd Millennium B.C.** Hammered flat and cut from sheet. Slightly curved barbs, medium tang. Length 8.2 cm. Cf. Moorey #44, Cf. Malloy, *Weapons*, #83. ....**CHOICE 100.00**

101. **BRONZE ARROWHEAD. Ur III. Susa. Later 3rd Millennium B.C.** Hammered flat and cut from sheet. Elongated with barbs. 5 x 2 cm. Cf. Comments Moorey #44. Green patina. Chip at edge. Scarce.............**CHOICE 80.00**

102. **BRONZE ARROWHEAD. Ur III. Susa.** Hammered flat and cut from sheet. Barbs. 3.3 x 1.8 cm. Cf. Comments Moorey #44. Green patina. Scarce. ....**CHOICE 100.00**

103. **BRONZE ARROWHEAD. Sumerian. Susa. 2000 B.C.** Flat blade. 4.9 x 1.5 cm. Petrie 20..............**CHOICE 45.00**

104. **BRONZE ARROWHEAD. Sumerian. Susa. 2000 B.C.** Flat. Susa type with slight ridge. 7.3 cm long, 1.7 cm wide. Light green patina. ....**CHOICE 55.00**

105. **FLAT BRONZE BLADE. Sumerian. Susa. 2000 B.C.** Susa type. 9.7 cm long, 2 cm wide. Cf. Petrie 20. ....**CHOICE 45.00**

106. **BRONZE BLADE. Hissar III. c. 2000 B.C.** Long blade with large midrib with stem and tang. Arrowhead. 11.5 cm long, 1.7 cm wide. Tepe Hissar region is in the Elburz Mountains southeast of the Caspian Sea. A finely worked bronze arrowhead. Cf. *Trade with Caspian.* Mallowan, *Early Mesopotamia and Iran.* Fig. 190................**CHOICE 85.00**

107. **BRONZE ARROWHEAD. Elamite. 1800-1600 B.C.** Incised herringbone pattern on rib. Bronze flat blade with short flat tang. 8.5 cm long, 2 cm wide. Green patina. Scarce with incised design. Moorey-. Cf. Petrie 20. Goddard-...**CHOICE 60.00**

108. **BRONZE ARROWHEAD.** Old Babylonian to Old Elamite. 1800-1500 B.C. Flat blade with slight midstem, flat tang. 8.8 x 1.8 cm. Petrie-. Cf. Pl. XLI, 2, 22. Green patina..**CHOICE 55.00**

109. **BRONZE ARROWHEAD.** Old Babylonian to Old Elamite. 1800-1500 B.C. Flat-shaped blade with slight midrib. 7 x 1 cm. Cf. Petrie-. Pl. XLI, 2, 22..**CHOICE 45.00**

110. **BRONZE BLADE.** Old Babylonian to Old Elamite. 1800-1500 B.C. Flat diamond shafted blade, slight midstem, encrustation on tip of arrowhead. 6.5 cm long, 1.5 cm wide. Petrie-. Similar copies on Pl. XLI 2, 22........**CHOICE 45.00**

111. **BRONZE ARROWHEAD. Kassite. 1600-1100 B.C.** High rib and long tang. Curved inward barbs. 6.5 x 2.1 cm. The Kassites conquered Elam and Babylonia with this type of weapon. Goddard 32-34. Cf. De Morgan fig. 575. ....**CHOICE 75.00**

112. **BRONZE ARROWHEAD. Kassite. 1600-1100 B.C.** High rib and long tang and curved barbs. 7.5 cm long, 3 cm wide. The Kassites conquered Elam and Babylonia with these characteristic weapons that represented one of the most attractive arrowheads made by man. Cf. De Morgan, fig. 575. Goddard, *Les Bronzes du Luristan*, p. xiii, 32, 34. ....**SUPERB 100.00**

113. **BRONZE ARROWHEAD. Old Babylonian—Neo-Elamite. 1500-1000 B.C.** Hammered leaf-shaped blade with short tang. Length 5.1 cm. Cf. Petrie, *Tools and Weapons*, #20 for type..**CHOICE 75.00**

114. **BRONZE ARROWHEAD. Old Babylonian—Neo-Elamite. 1500-1000 B.C.** Hammered flat from cut sheet. Long tang. Length 6.7 cm. Malloy #86; Petrie 2-4 ....**CHOICE 60.00**

115. **BRONZE ARROWHEAD. Hittite. 14th-13th Century B.C.** Long barbs, only one remaining, thick midstem, long tang, quite heavy. 12 cm long, 2.3 cm wide. Chip off one barb. Cf. C.W. Ceram, *The Secret of the Hittites*, p. 203. Rare ....**CHOICE 100.00**

116. **BRONZE BLADE. Hittite. 14th-13th Century B.C.** Triangular in shape with protruding midstem. Shaft hole. 3.5 cm long, 1.23 cm wide. Found with the preceding arrowhead. Unusual and possibly unpublished type. Green patina. Petrie-. Palestine Exploration Fund-. Moorey-. ....**CHOICE 125.00**

117. **BRONZE ARROWHEAD. Hittite. 1400-1200 B.C.** Long barbs, thick midstem and long tang. 6.7 x 1.8 cm. Ceram, *Secret of Hittites*, p. 203 var. A lovely surface and a beautifully styled shape. Rare...................**SUPERB 200.00**

118. **BRONZE ARROWHEAD. Northern Persia. 1200-800 B.C.** Deltoid winged blades, prominent midrib tang. 5.5 x 1.5 cm. Koldewey, *Das Wieder Ersthende Babylon*, fig. 184, b. Muscarella, *Bronze & Iron MMA*, 409. ..**CHOICE 55.00**

119. **BRONZE ARROWHEAD. Elamite Middle Period. 1200-800 B.C.** Deltoid has long tang with shaft cut. Length 10.7 cm. Muscarella #412, Cf. Malloy, #93........**CHOICE 50.00**

120. **BRONZE ARROWHEAD. Elamite Middle Period. 1200-800 B.C.** Elongated leaf design, long tang, central midrib. Length 8.2 cm. Moorey 69-70, Cf. Malloy #94. ....**CHOICE 45.00**

121. **BRONZE ARROWHEAD. Elamite Middle Period. 1200-800 B.C.** Elongated leaf design. Long tang, central midrib. Length 9.0 cm. Moorey 69-70, Cf. Malloy #95. ....**CHOICE 50.00**

122. **BRONZE ARROWHEAD. Assyrian. 1200-800 B.C.** Rhombic head, no barbs. 6 cm long, 2.5 cm wide. Scarce. These types of rhombic head arrowheads were widely used by the Egyptians and found usually with barbs. This type dates to the same time frame but was found in northern Mesopotamia.....................................**CHOICE 75.00**

123. **BRONZE ARROWHEAD. Elamite Middle Period. 1200-800 B.C.** Central midrib with tang. 7 cm long, 1.7 cm wide. Cf. Moorey p. 85, fig. 17, #69-70. ......**CHOICE 35.00**

124. **ARROWHEAD. Neo Elamite. 1200-800 B.C.** Long tapering blade and longish tang. Length 6.3 cm. Similar types in bronze were found at Marlik.. This rare arrowhead was probably used for hunting animals. Cf. Moorey, #80 (for bronze type). Very rare......................**CHOICE 125.00**

125. **BRONZE ARROWHEAD. Middle Elamite Period. 1200-800 B.C.** Elongated leaf design, medium tang, central midrib. Length 10 cm. Malloy, *Weapons* #94; Moorey 69-70. ....**CHOICE 55.00**

126. **BRONZE ARROWHEAD. Elamite Middle Period. 1200-800 B.C.** Rounded head with thick tang and central midrib. Length 6.5 cm. Malloy #96; Cf. Moorey 69-70. ....**CHOICE 70.00**

127. **BRONZE ARROWHEAD. 1200-700 B.C.** With midrib and short tang. Length 64 mm. Moorey p. 85, fig. 17, #72. ....**CHOICE 50.00**

128. **BRONZE ARROWHEAD. Northern Persia. 1200-700 B.C.** Midrib and long tang. 10.5 cm long, 2.5 cm wide. Green patina. Moorey p. 85, fig. 17, #72. ....**CH-SUP 40.00**

129. **BRONZE ARROWHEAD. Northern Persia. 1200-700 B.C.** Midrib and long tang. 8 x 1.5 cm. Moorey, p.85, fig. 17, #72. ....**CHOICE 40.00**

130. **BRONZE ARROWHEAD. Central Persia and Luristan. 1000 B.C.** Long thin bladed head with stem and long tang. 12.8 cm long, 1.4 cm wide. Scarce type. Cf. Moorey 75. ....**SUPERB 45.00**

131. **BRONZE ARROWHEAD. Central Persia and Luristan. 1000 B.C.** Blade with flat midrib. Square sectioned tang tapering to point. 11 x 1.8 cm. Bumford #16. Moorey #74. ....**CHOICE 50.00**

132. **BRONZE ARROWHEAD. Neo-Assyrian. Nineveh. 800 B.C.** Ribbed blade with midstem and shaft hole. 3.7 cm long, 1.3 cm wide. Chip to tip. Malachite patina. Cf. Petrie, Pl. XLI 32................................**CHOICE 55.00**

133. **BRONZE ARROWHEAD. Neo-Assyrian. Nineveh. 800 B.C.** Ribbed blade with wide stem and shaft hole. 3.6 x 1.4 cm. Encrusted with blue-green malcite patina. Petrie Pl. XLI 32..**CHOICE 75.00**

134. **BRONZE ARROWHEAD. Neo-Assyrian. Nineveh. 800 B.C.** Ribbed blade with wide stem and socket. Length 3.4 cm. Petrie Pl. XLI 32, Cf. Malloy #101. Light green patina. ....**CHOICE 75.00**

135. **BRONZE ARROWHEAD. Neo-Assyrian. Nineveh. 800 B.C.** Ribbed blade with wide stem and socket. Length 3.4 cm. Malloy #101; Petrie Pl. XLI 32. Light green patina. ....**CHOICE 50.00**

136. **BRONZE ARROWHEAD. Scythian. 8th-7th Century B.C.** Bi-blade leaf-shaped socketed head. Length 4.2 cm. Malloy #106; Cf. Azarpay Pl. 8...................**SUPERB 45.00**

137. **BRONZE ARROWHEAD. Scythian 8th-7th Century B.C.** Elongated tri-blade head, short socket. Length 4 cm. Malloy #107; Cf. Azarpay Pl. 8. This blade was found in eastern Turkey. Similar types in the Hermitage Museum are from Karmir-Blur..**CHOICE 40.00**

138. **BRONZE ARROWHEAD. Scythian. 8th-7th Century B.C.** Trilobate leaf-shaped blade with tang. Length 3.1 cm. Most unusual with tang..............................**CHOICE 100.00**

139. **BRONZE ARROWHEAD. 7th-6th Century B.C.** Trilobate head with elongated narrow blades, short socket. Length 38 mm...**CHOICE 30.00**

140. **COPPER ARROWHEAD. XXVI Dynasty: 661-525 B.C.** Triangular head with barbs. Midstem thick at shoulder, tapering to point. Pointed tang. Measures 5.2 x 1.5 cm. Cf. Petrie 131. Some azurite patina.................**CHOICE 135.00**

141. **BRONZE ARROWHEAD. 600 B.C.** Deltoid blade with central ridge, shortened point with long sloping edge to base. Length 5.2 cm. Similar blades were found at Memphis palace at the introduction of the Persian period.....**CHOICE 125.00**

142. **IRON ARROWHEAD. Neo-Assyrian. Achaemenid. 600-400 B.C.** Trilobate with small barbs and long shaft. 48 x 7 mm. This style is similar to socketed spear heads of this period found between the Tigris and Euphrates Rivers region. Petrie-. A rare type. ....**CHOICE 100.00**

143. **BRONZE ARROWHEAD. Achaemenid. 6th-4th Century B.C.** Trilobate head with broad angular deltoid blades, short socket. Length 2.5 cm. Muscarella 322, Cf. Tushingham fig. 69, 20 var., Cf. Malloy #109. ....**CHOICE 50.00**

144. **BRONZE ARROWHEAD. Persia. Achaemenid. 6th-4th Century B.C.** Triangular blade with long tang. 6.6 x 2.2 cm. Similar arrowheads found in Egypt during the 27th Dynasty commonly called the "Persian Dynasty." Petrie, 121, 122, 136.......................................**CHOICE 50.00**

145. **BRONZE ARROWHEAD. Persia. Achaemenid. 6th-4th Century B.C.** Triangular blade with long tang. Protruding barbs. Similar arrowhead found in Egypt during the 27th Dynasty, which was called the "Persian Dynasty." Chips to end of barbs. Cf. Petrie 96.........................**CHOICE 45.00**

146. **BRONZE ARROWHEAD. Medo-Persian. 600-300 B.C.** Socketed bi-blade head with long spur. Length 4.6 cm. Cf. Malloy, *Weapons*, #114...............................**CHOICE 75.00**

147. **BRONZE ARROWHEAD. 600-300 B.C.** Trilobate head with broad angular deltoid blades. Short socket. Length 32 mm (from the Persian-style arrowheads). Found in Egypt. Light green patina.....................................**CHOICE 25.00**

148. **BRONZE ARROWHEAD. Achaemenid. 539-331 B.C.** Barbed with shaft. 4 cm long, 1.3 cm wide. This type was used throughout the known civilized world at this time. Green patina. Chip at shaft. ....**SUPERB 55.00**

149. **BRONZE TRI-BLADE. Achaemenid. 539-331 B.C.** Barbed, no shaft. 3.4 cm long, 1.5 cm wide. A scarcer type with no shaft. Green patina.........................**CHOICE 45.00**

150. **BRONZE ARROWHEAD. Achaemenid. 539-331 B.C.** With rounded tri-blade. Spur on shaft. 3 cm long, 7 mm wide. Type developed from Sythian types. Cf. Karmir, Blur, Hermitage Museum. Chip to shaft...............**CHOICE 40.00**

151. **BRONZE ARROWHEAD. Achaemenid. 539-331 B.C.** Triangular with shaft hole, no barbs. 3.7 cm long, 1.3 cm wide. Petrie 246 var...................................**CHOICE 40.00**

152. **BRONZE ARROWHEAD. Achaemenid. 539-331 B.C.** Rounded tri-blade. Spur on shaft. 30 x 8 mm. Type developed from Scythian types. Cf. Karmir, Blur, Hermitage Museum...**CHOICE 25.00**

153. **BRONZE BLADE. Achaemenid. 5th-4th Century B.C.** Triangular barbed with long shaft. 2.7 x 1 cm. A gem arrowhead..**SUPERB 75.00**

154. **IRON ARROWHEAD. Sythian. 5th-4th Century B.C.** Triangular. Hole in shaft with look of indented barbs on each plane. 2.7 cm long, 1 cm wide. For other earlier Sythian arrowheads Cf. #50-51. Cf. Minns, *Kiev District Tombs*, fig. 82.35. ....**SUPERB 45.00**

155. **BRONZE ARROWHEAD. Syrian. 4th-3rd Century B.C.** Trilobate head. Sharp blades, no shaft, sharp barbs protruding behind shaft. Length 38 mm. Malloy-. A rare example of a transitional type from Achaemenid to Parthian. ....**SUPERB 125.00**

156. **BRONZE ARROWHEAD. Ptolemaic Period. 400-100 B.C.** Bilobate head, short shaft, leaf shape with central rib. Length 46 mm. Encrusted with heavy patina. ....**CHOICE 65.00**

157. **BRONZE ARROWHEAD. 3rd Century B.C.-2nd A.D.** Trilobate socketed head with barbs. Length 30 mm. Malloy 116; Petrie 69-71; Muscarella 180................**CHOICE 55.00**

158. **BRONZE ARROWHEAD. Parthian. 3rd Century B.C.-2nd Century A.D.** Socketed trilobate head, with barbs. Length 3.3 cm. Petrie 69-71, Muscarella 180, Cf. Malloy 116..**CHOICE 45.00**

159. **BRONZE ARROWHEAD. Parthian. 3rd Century B.C.-2nd Century A.D.** Socketed trilobate head with barbs. Length 2.3 cm. Petrie 69, Muscarella 180, Cf. Malloy 116. ....**CHOICE 45.00**

160. **IRON BLADE. 2nd Century B.C.-1st Century A.D.** Flat diamond-shaped blade, flanged at base. 7.6 cm x 2.8 cm. Cf. Petrie XLII, 193, 194. Chip on blade............**CHOICE 55.00**

Mace, Axe, and Adze Heads

161. **BRONZE AXE HEAD. Proto-Dynastic to Ur III. 3000-2750 B.C.** Cut from sheet. End curled, rivet hole in center. Length 14.3 cm. DeShayes #1960, Pl. XXXII:9; Malloy #30a. Similar axe heads were found at Ur II Levels at Ur excavations..**CHOICE 325.00**

162. **BRONZE AXE HEAD. Mesopotamia. 3000-2500 B.C. Jemdet Nasr (Proto-Elamite).** Early type of axe head. Simple socket type with ribbing. Cast blade flares out. Edge of blade blunted as if by a very heavy object. Socket hole rather large. Very heavy with somewhat crude workmanship. Length 11 cm. Malloy #31. Cf. Moorey, #21, Cf. Muscarella, p.391, fig. 517 for similar but earlier type. Muscarella suggests that this type was used as a tool rather than as a weapon......................................**SUPERB 500.00**

163. **BRONZE ADZE HEAD. Early Dynastic. 2600-2400 B.C.** Tall, narrow shaft with whole blade widening at cutting edge. 13.6 cm. x 6 cm. Bomford #9. Moorey 30....**CH-SUP 400.00**

164. **BRONZE ADZE-AXE HEAD. Persia-Northeastern Iran. 2200-1500 B.C.** Short shaft hole. Axe blade has expanding sides, adze blade is rounded. Length 14.5 cm. Similar adze-axes were found at Tepe Hissar Level III. DeShayes, XXXVIII:1, #2221; Malloy, *Weapons* #43. A heavy weapon. ....**CHOICE 500.00**

165. **BRONZE SHAFT HOLE AXE HEAD. Old Babylonian. 2nd Millennium B.C.** Tall narrow short-hole with rib band at top and bottom. Close cross-hatching on shaft, blade straight and curves down to cutting edge. Blade was not ground for use. 9 cm high, 8 cm long. Similar design on a mural in the Old Babylonian palace at Mari. The origin of this would place it to eastern Iraq or western Iran. For basic style without back protuberance. Cf. Moorey #7. ....**SUPERB 550.00**

166. **BRONZE AXE HEAD. Caucasus. 2000-1500 B.C.** Bronze axe head with expanding blade. Central ridge from shaft onto blade. Top of blade at right angle to shaft. Shaft starts halfway from blade. Length 14.4 cm. Malloy 34; Cf. DeShayes #1652, Pl. XXVI, 13. Cf. *Axes of Pilenkovo*, also #1421. Very rare....................................**CHOICE 750.00**

167. **BRONZE AXE HEAD. Old Babylonian. 2000-1500 B.C.** Cast spike-butted axe head with short oval shaft hole. Cast with three raised moldings ending in three downward pointing spur-like terminals. Blade rises above top of shaft and curves down. Blade thick and crude. Cf. Terminals. Length 12.8 cm. Malloy 35; Cf. Moorey, Ash. #2; DeShayes 1447 var. An unusually heavy cast with oxidation. ....**CHOICE 350.00**

168. **BRONZE AXE HEAD. Canaanite. 18th-17th Century B.C.** Long narrow blade with hole shaft at end. Ridge below. 12 x 2 cm. Cf. Bulletin Pr. Musee de Beyrouth, II (1933), Pl. 28; p. 34 (fig. 51c). Kafer-Garra Site. Cf. DeShayes, *Les Qurils de Bronze, de Indus au Danube*, #1508 (Pl. LVIII, 7). Rare. Green patina.....**CHOICE 500.00**

169. **BRONZE MACE HEAD. Elamite. 1500-1000 B.C.** Tube domed over at one end with five protruding rhomboids at rim of dome. Five holes at base of mace. Green patina. Cf. for shape, Moorey 99....................................**CHOICE 250.00**

170. **BRONZE MACE HEAD FRAGMENT. Hasanlu. 800-500 B.C.** Spiked. Three spikes with four ridges to bottom. 7.6 cm long. Cf. *Hasanlu Excavations*, Period IV. Cf. Muscarella, *MMA* 70.................................**SUPERB 150.00**

171. **IRON MACE HEAD. Parthian-Sassanian. 500-800 A.D.** Round eight-sided globe, knob at top. 6.2 x 6 cm. Moorey-. Petrie-. Iraq Museum-.................................**CHOICE 150.00**

Tools

172. **BRONZE RAZOR. Old Babylonian–Neo-Elamite. 1800-500 B.C.** Fan shaped with tine. Length 5.5 cm, width 3.5 cm. Cf. Petrie for similar type, Pl. X, 51-55. Found in the northern region of Mesopotamia. ....**CH-SUP 75.00**

173. **BRONZE SHIELD BOSS. Neo-Elamite–Achaemenid. 1000-400 B.C.** Circular sheet with plain umbo pierced in center. Five spearheads in repoussé, row of dots at edge. The Dailaman discs were dated late Achaemedian to Parthian period and were intended as cymbals. These shield bosses were used over a long period of time and were applied to wooden shields. The spearhead repoussé suggests shield boss, not cymbal. Cf. Dailaman. Cf. Moorey 468. ....**CHOICE 125.00**

174. **BRONZE SHIELD BOSS. Neo-Elamite–Achaemenid. 1000-400 B.C.** Circular sheet with plain umbo pierced in center. Nine pellet-rendered rosettes around. 14.2 cm diameter. The shield boss was used over a long period of time and was applied to wooden shields. Moorey, 481. Flan crack. ....**CHOICE 150.00**

175. **BRONZE RAZOR. Caspian. 8th-7th Century B.C.** Ram's head handle. 10.6 x 1.4 cm. Unusual and very rare. Similar to dagger above. Moorey-. Goddard-. Muscarella-. Green patination. ....**CHOICE 300.00**

POTTERY

176. **KERMAN. Southeastern Iran. 4200-3500 B.C.** Buff pottery bowl. Red slip at outer and inner rim. Black design of water in wavy lines and V design. This item was reportedly found in Kerman. Cf. Amiet, *Art Ancient Near East*, #182 (shape). Cf. Schmidt, *Tepe Hissar*, Shape Pl. III, 3439, inner design Pl. 111, 4243...............**CHOICE 225.00**

177. **KERMAN. Southeastern Iran. 4200-3500 B.C.** Grey pottery bowl with black design in quartered bands. Amiet, *ANE*-. Schmidt, *Tepe Hissar*......................**CHOICE 200.00**

178. **JEMDET NASR. 3500-2900 B.C.** Buff polychrome pottery vessel. Squat swelling center and small pedestal base. Shoulder black painted with a ferruginous glaze, with a cross-hatch design making a five-pointed star. In each angle of the star is a ferrous red design of two fish, rosette, snake, and plant or flower bud. Height 8 cm diameter 9 cm. Cf. Mackay Pl. LXXVII, fig. 1 var. A nice early polychrome vessel. Intact..............................**CHOICE 750.00**

179. **TEPE GIHAN. 1st Millennium B.C.** Buff cup with dark brown-red painted bands. Paint on rim of handle. Height 7.5 cm, diameter 8 cm. Intact..........................**CHOICE 300.00**

180. **PARTHIAN. 3rd Century A.D.** Round ceramic vessel with four pointed legs. Glazed ware. ....**CHOICE 400.00**

181. **PARTHIAN. 3rd Century A.D.** Rhomboid ceramic vessel with side lugs pierced and four pointed legs. Yellow and brown glaze ware. A very early glazed ware with lovely angular Geometric style. Intact and rare....**CHOICE 500.00**

TERRACOTTA

182. **TERRACOTTA VENUS. Western Azerbaijan. Neolithic Hajji Firuz. 6200-5500 B.C.** Grey, baked burnished with pinched head and two eyes, pierced breasts and dot pattern in pubic area. 5.4 cm. Cf. University of Penn. Hasanlu Project 1968. The Neolithic villages of this area had free-standing square houses usually of mud brick and clay floors. An expressive primitive human figure. Repaired at neck. ....**CHOICE 250.00**

183. **TERRACOTTA CERAMIC TOKEN. Susa. 5500 B.C.** Buff. Length 35 mm. This terracotta token representing metal was fired for permanency and was used in trade as an archaic recording system. This "ultimately led to the invention of writing" as per Schmandt-Besserat. Cf. Schmandt-Besserat p. 26. Rare.................**CHOICE 500.00**

184. **TERRACOTTA FEMALE FIGURE. Northern Mesopotamia. Iran. Ubaid 1, 5000-4000 B.C.** Light brown. Elongated nude female figure, arms, head, and left leg at knee missing, heavy white slip over all figure, traces of black design "J" at neck area. Cf. *Clay Figures of Al' Ubaid I*. Woolley, *Development of Sumerian Art*, Pl I. 6.9. Very rare type. Broken and repaired at waist...........**CHOICE 400.00**

185. **TERRACOTTA LEOPARD. Ubaid Period. 4400-3600 B.C.** White wash and black dots over entire body. A very similar example was found at Tepe Gawra in the Ubaid period. Cf. Goff, fig. 212 ....**CHOICE 750.00**

186. **TERRACOTTA ZEBU. Tepe Gawra. Ninevite Period: 4000-3000 B.C.** Figure of a zebu with a hump on its back. Length 3.9 cm, height 2 cm. Cf. Goff, fig. 641. ....**CHOICE 100.00**

187. **TERRACOTTA BUST. Mesopotamia. Early Dynastic II. 2800-2600 B.C.** Male god. Pinched nose dab and pierced eyes. Beard and incised turban headdress. Muscarella, *Ladders*. Cf. Van Buren, fig. 10 var. A scarce type. ....**CHOICE 200.00**

188. **TERRACOTTA HEAD OF FEMALE. North Syria. Early Dynastic II Period. 2750-2600 B.C.** High headdress, pierced eyes with necklace. Muscarella, *Ladders*, 193. Chip at top. ....**CHOICE 50.00**

189. **TERRACOTTA PLAQUE. Early Dynastic. 2600-2500 B.C.** Male figure standing right with left arm raised behind bent human figure facing right, engaged in sexual act. 7.5 x 7 cm. Ex. Bernard Greltner Collection, Alsace, French Ambassador to Iraq, 1969-1974. The depiction of this sexual act is one of the earliest known. Cf. Van Buren, *Clay Figurines of Babylonia and Assyria*, fig. 207 for bull mastiff and similar rendering of man behind. Cf. for bent figure, Amiet, *GS*, #613-14. Rare......................**CHOICE 1200.00**

190. **TERRACOTTA OX HEAD. Anatolian. Alishar II 2300-1800 B.C.** Grey-beige. The eyes are roundly modeled and circled, the muzzle is beautifully chiseled. Solid. 46 mm. Cf. Habib Anavian Coll. 23. Cf. Schmidt, *Alishar Mound*, 1927-29, fig. 128. These ox heads were among the finest styled objects to come from Period II at Alishar-Huyuk. This period was known by Schmidt as "Alien Peoples." ....**CHOICE 125.00**

191. **BUFF TERRACOTTA BULL. Neo-Sumerian. Early Bronze Age. c. 2200 B.C.** Somewhat coarsely modeled with curved horns. Length 46 mm, height 31 mm. Cf. Parrot, *Tello*, Pl. 51a. Cf. Field Museum of Natural History, *Anthropology*, Vol. 1, Pl. XLVII, 2471. The Field Museum example is a ram of similar design. It was described by Mackay as a child's toy in his Excavations at Kish in Mesopotamia 1929. Parrot identifies similar terracotta figures as Neo-Sumerian. Chip on left hindquarters. ....**CHOICE 200.00**

192. **TERRACOTTA MONKEY IDOL. Susa. 2112-1763 B.C.** Grey with one leg and arms missing. Finely detailed face with pellet eyes. 40 mm x 80 mm. These were found in levels of Ur III and the epoch of Isin Larsa. Cf. Barrelet, *Figurines et Reliefs en Terre Cuite de la Mesopotamie Antique*, #I 1. ....**CHOICE 200.00**

193. **TERRACOTTA HEAD. Mesopotamia. 2000-1500 B.C.** Humbaba, grotesque devil's head with ridges above eyes, cheeks and nose, no headdress. Humbaba was the demon defeated by Gilgamesh. Later in style than the Ur, Dig Deqqeh and Thureau-Dangin examples. Height 3.2 cm. Cf. Van Buren, *Clay Figurines of Babylonia and Assyria*, LVII, 270 var...**CHOICE 800.00**

194. **TERRACOTTA HEAD. North Syrian. 1900-1750 B.C.** Two eyes on one side. 2.2 x 3 cm. The stylization of the eyes and facial features place this head to similar sites of Hama level H, Alalakh level V, and Ebla. Cf. Muscarella, *Ladders to Heaven*, #201 ....**CHOICE 50.00**

195. **TERRACOTTA BUST WITH HEADDRESS.** With pierced pellet eyes. Height 43 mm, width 18 mm. Cf. Muscarella, *Ladders* #199. Other type figurines were found in Northern Mesopotamia and Syria. Broken at waist and arms missing..**CHOICE 65.00**

196. **TERRACOTTA FRAGMENTARY PLAQUE. Old Babylonian. 1st Dynasty of Babylon. c. 1890-1590 B.C.** Half figure of Ishtar. Pointed cap and triangular face. Right arm folding across chest. 6.3 cm high, 4.7 cm wide. Ex. Bernard Grettner Collection, Alsace, French Ambassador to Iraq, 1969-1974. Cf. Barrelet, Pl. XXXIII, #334. Cf. Van Buren, *Clay Figures of Babylonia and Assyria*, fig. 132. ....**AVERAGE-CHOICE 225.00**

197. **BUFF TERRACOTTA FIGURE OF ISHTAR. Old Babylonian. 1800 B.C.** As the mother goddess, facing, hands clasped at waist, nude, wearing three-rowed choker necklace with central round pendant, hair rolled up at forehead. 4" high. Cf. Barrelet, *Figurine et Reliefs en Terre Cuite de la Mesopotamie Antique*, #395. Cf. Van Buren, *Clay Figurines of Babylonia and Assyria*, #91. Ishtar was one of the major deities of the Babylonians as can be seen from the preponderance of her image on cylinder seals. Small restored section at ankle. Nice example..................**CHOICE 450.00**

198. **TERRACOTTA FERTILITY FIGURE. Ardebil. West Caspian Sea Region. 1500 B.C.** Very crude pinched head. Doll or fertility figure. 25 mm x 70 mm. Upper fragment. Left arm missing. Unusual ....**CHOICE 150.00**

199. **TERRACOTTA HORSE HEAD.** Arched head with pellet eye and stylized mane. 4 cm x 3.7 cm. For similar arched back horse head but in bronze. Cf. *Urartian Art and Artifacts*, Azarday, Pl. 27, dated 713-685 B.C. Head fragment..**CHOICE 65.00**

200. **TERRACOTTA BUST OF ASTARTE. Neo-Hittite. 1000 B.C.** Terracotta bust of the fertility goddess with almond eyes. Hair tied at side and flaring out. Hands to breast at front. Van Buren 187. Measures 55 x 27 mm. The Neo-Hittite civilization is a period of Dark Ages from 1200-900 B.C. in Anatolia. Upper half of plaque present. ....**CHOICE 175.00**

201. **TERRACOTTA RAM RHYTON AMLASH. 10th-7th Century B.C.** Grey. Head of ram with curled horns, back handle to open spout. Three-legged base. Height 13 cm, length 15 cm. Cf. Gabus & Jund, *Amlash Art*, Pl. VII. Repaired foot and neck, chip off spout and one horn. ....**CHOICE 475.00**

202. **BAS RELIEF TERRACOTTA FRAGMENT. Neo-Babylonian. c. 612-539 B.C.** Nude female half figure. Stylized facial features, straight hair. Arms held straight at sides. Body broken off at hips. 7.3 cm high, 3.8 cm wide. Ex. Bernard Grettner Collection, Alsace, French Ambassador to Iraq, 1969-74. Cf. Barrelet, Pl. XX, #212. Chip to lower right shoulder...**CHOICE 200.00**

203. **TERRACOTTA BAS RELIEF PLAQUE HEAD. Seleucid. 4th-2nd Century B.C.** Female head with headdress and hair at cheeks. Similar to Tello Excavation types found. 33 x 36 mm. Cf. Barrelet, *Figurines et Reliefs*, p. xlv, 494 var. Terracotta plaques were made from old Babylonian times to the Parthian period. The Seleucid type is rare..**CHOICE 150.00**

204. **TERRACOTTA MOLD. Parthian. 3rd-2nd Century B.C.**
Two male figures, one playing the lyre, the second, on the left, leaning over other's shoulder. Heads somewhat cocked together. Wearing himation over lower portion of left figure's body. The right figure is fully clothed with Phrygian trousers and Parthian bashlyk. Ex. Bernard Grettner Collection, Alsace. French Ambassador to Iraq 1969-1974. Rare.
....**CHOICE 1200.00**

205. **TERRACOTTA FIGURE. Parthian. 3rd-2nd Century B.C.** Female standing, head cowered slightly left. Left arm raised to chest. Long hair knotted in back. Ex. Bernard Grettner Collection, Alsace. French Ambassador to Iraq,1969-74..**AVERAGE 280.00**

206. **TERRACOTTA PLAQUE BAS RELIEF. Parthian. 247 B.C.-224 A.D.** Couple standing with pleated garments. Left figure playing flute, right figure playing drum. Traces of red slip on garments. 9.8 x 4.2 cm. Ex. Bernard Grettner Collection, Alsace. French Ambassador to Iraq, 1969-1974. Cf. Rostovtzeff, Yale Studies, 185, fig. 22..**CHOICE 200.00**

207. **TERRACOTTA BAS RELIEF SECTION. Parthian. c. 247 B.C.-224 A.D.** Bearded head of man to right. Full cheeks, fat nose and thick lips. 9.5 cm high, 6.2 cm wide, 4 cm thick. Ex. Bernard Grettner Collection, Alsace. French Ambassador to Iraq, 1969- 74. ....**CHOICE 500.00**

208. **GLAZED POTTERY HEAD. Parthian. 2nd Century B.C.–2nd Century A.D.** Dark green, bearded head with headdress and pellet eyes. Height 42 mm, width 30 mm. For early glazed Parthian objects, Cf. Pope Pl. 185:A, B, 183. It was in the Parthian period that glazes first came into general use, even though glazing was known and practiced in Egypt for centuries. ....**CHOICE 150.00**

209. **TERRACOTTA BUST. Parthian. 2nd Century B.C.-2nd Century A.D.** Parthian horseman. Head from pushed in mold, bearded head with flap cap, Aryan features. Traces of red slip. Legrain, *Nippur*, Pl. XLVII, 245....**CHOICE 75.00**

210. **TERRACOTTA HEAD. Parthian. 2nd Century B.C.-2nd Century A.D.** Parthian horseman. Head made from mold. Bearded head with peaked cap with top turned over flap. Aryan features with thick eyebrows. The Roman writer, Justin, XII, 3, states that the Parthians nearly spent their lives on horseback. Cf. Legrain, *Terracotta From Nippur*, Pl. XLVIII, 248...**SUPERB 100.00**

211. **TERRACOTTA HEAD OF DEITY. Parthian. c. 1st –2nd Century A.D.** Perhaps a sun god. Large, almond-shaped eyes and small mouth. Long, straight nose. Headdress. 5.1 cm x 3.4 cm. *Porous*. Ex. Bernard Grettner Collection, Alsace. French Ambassador to Iraq, 1969-74. Cf. Barrelet, Pl. LXVII, #500. ....**CHOICE 275.00**

212. **TERRACOTTA HORSEMAN. 1st-2nd Century A.D.** Bearded with tiara.   Forepart only. 10 x 7.5 cm. Cf. Koldewey, *Das Wieder Erstehende* Babylon, ABB 150. Minor chips...**CHOICE 80.00**

213. **TERRACOTTA HEAD. Parthian. 1st –3rd Century A.D.** Male horseman with top of horse present.   Seleucia manufacture. Colledge, *The Parthians*, Pl. 20 a & b. ....**CHOICE 100.00**

214. **TERRACOTTA HEAD. Parthian. 1st-3rd Century A.D.** Head of male horseman. Seleucia manufacture. Colledge, *The Parthians*, Pl. 20 a & b. ....**CHOICE 100.00**

METAL

215. **OLD BABYLONIAN. c. 2100-2000 B.C.** Bronze head of priest. 15 mm.   For similar style and workmanship Cf. *Bronze Foundation Cones of Goudea and Isin Larsa*...**CHOICE 250.00**

216. **OLD BABYLONIAN. c. 2100-2000 B.C.** Bronze finial. Kneeling figure of a bald priest holding a serpent. 41 mm. For similar style and workmanship Cf. *Bronze Foundation Cones of Goudea and Isin Larsa*.   Very rare. ....**CHOICE 1500.00**

217. **ANATOLIA. c. 2000-1800 B.C.** Bronze bull standing with horns. Cf. Kozloff, *Mildenberg Collection* #11. Right horn tip missing. Green-brown patina. ....**CHOICE 450.00**

218. **ANATOLIA. 2000-1800 B.C.** Bronze bull standing with horns. Cf. Kozloff, *Mildenberg Collection* #11. Larger than previous example. Bold, with more definition. No chips. Green patina. ....**CHOICE 650.00**

219. **TURKMENIAN. 2000-1600 B.C.** Bronze pin. Probably for clothing. Design of swastika with curled ends on head. Measures 7.6 cm x 3 cm. Head of pin 1.5 cm square. Nice patina..**CHOICE 125.00**

220. **ANATOLIA. 2nd Millennium B.C.** Bronze dog figure with long neck, short legs, and lovely stylized elongated body design. Pierced eyes. Length 4 cm. Reminiscent of the modern dachshund. Tail chipped off. Green-black patina. Superb style and a rare type......................**SUPERB 500.00**

221. **ANATOLIA. 2nd Millennium B.C.** Bronze bull with pellet eyes, straight horns, and tail. 20 mm x 40 mm. Cf. Kozloff, *Mildenberg Coll.* #11. Cf. Muscarella, *Ladders* 125. Rare...**CHOICE 500.00**

222. **NORTH SYRIAN. 1500-1000 B.C.** Bronze figure of man. Height 29 mm. Nice patina. Legs missing..**CHOICE 135.00**

223. **ASSYRIAN. 15th-10th Century B.C.** Collar plaque. Bronze zoomorphic horse collar plaque with hang-braided terminal ending in bull's head. Green patina. 11.8 cm long. Similar to Assyrian reliefs at Tepe Sialk. Sialk, Pl. LVI. End of bull's left horn is chipped.   Very rare. ....**CHOICE 300.00**

224. **·ELAMITE. 1200-900 B.C.** Bronze openwork rattle bell. Cruciform style, loop at top. Length 7.5 cm. Cf. Muscarella, *MMA* 337 for basic type..............................**CHOICE 65.00**

225. **NORTHWESTERN IRAN. Hasan Lu. Period IV: 1200-800 B.C.** Bronze openwork rattle bell. Height 3.8 cm. Muscarella, *MMA* 96-101. ....**CHOICE 65.00**

226. **WESTERN IRAN. Late 2nd-Early 1st Millennium B.C.** Bronze cast pin with conical head. Decorated with incised bands encircling pin. Length 22 cm. Cf. Moorey 268. ....**CHOICE 75.00**

227. **IRANIAN. Late 2nd-1st Millennium B.C.** Double-headed pendant, one side goat or sheep, other side ram or antelope. Bronze. Hole in center. Two solid elongated round weights hang below animals. Perhaps used as a weight on clothing. 36 x 27 mm. Cf. Sotheby's Catalogue of Ancient Iranian Bronzes, Nov. 1975.....................**CHOICE 100.00**

228. **IRANIAN c.1000 B.C.** Pin of human forearm. With pin crossing wrist, hand extends, hinge at shoulder. Two squared sections make upper and lower arms, while a thinner, rounded, bent section is the elbow. Circular disks above and below square sections. Hand relatively flat, this probably held the pin in place. 3.2 cm pin, 3.1 cm lower arm, 2.2 cm upper arm. Goddard, *Bronzes du Luristan*, Pl. XXIX, fig. 101, p. 75. Intact. Pin remains, but is immovable. ....**CHOICE 150.00**

229. **IRANIAN. Early 1st Millennium B.C.** Bronze bell with double horse finial, pattern around rim of bell. 25 mm. Iron clapper missing as usual. Green patina........**CHOICE 45.00**

230. **IRANIAN. Early 1st Millennium B.C.** Bronze bell with horse finial. 40 mm. Corroded iron clapper inside. Green patina..**CHOICE 55.00**

231. **IRANIAN. 1st Millennium B.C.** Bronze addorsed ram's finial. Eyes defined, protruding ears. It is suggested that similar types date from a Hellenistic date as there are Greek examples of this form. Muscarella, *MMA*, 363 var. ....**CHOICE 100.00**

232. **IRANIAN. 1st Millennium B.C.** Bronze harness ring. Globular knob on one end and bird's head on the other end with bulging eye.   Muscarella, *MMA*, 360, fig. 25. ....**CHOICE 75.00**

233. **KERMAN.   1st Millennium B.C.** Bronze zebu (bull) elongated body, detail on face of animal. Length 40 mm, height 35 mm. This bronze zebu was found in the region of Seistan near Kerman and near the site of Tal-i-iblis. ....**CHOICE 175.00**

234. **LURISTAN. 1000-800 B.C.** Bronze goat amulet passant. Back leg missing.   Moorey 422.   Green patina and encrustation...................................**CHOICE 90.00**

235. **LURISTAN. 10th-7th Century B.C.** Antelope head in bronze cast, top of pin. No pin stem. 33 mm. Pins similar to those found at Sialk (Sialk, 11, Pl. XXIX, 1, top) and at Marlik (Marlik, fig. 31). Cf. Moorey p. 193, #312-13. Cf. Frankfurt #33.................................**CHOICE 60.00**

236. **LURISTAN.   9th-8th Century B.C.** Bronze finial in the form of the head of a serpent with protruding eyes. 25 mm x 40 mm. These eyes are a stylistic feature of Luristan art. ....**CHOICE 95.00**

237. **ANATOLIA.   9th-8th Century B.C.** Geometric bronze horse in a magnificent simple style. 1.5 cm x 3.3 cm. A little gem..................................**SUPERB 500.00**

238. **LURISTAN. Group IV-Later: 9th-8th Century B.C.** Bronze horse's cheek pieces. Twin birds facing outward to other bird heads. Leaf design between. Birds have large protruding eyes. All in square with each side 7 cm. The bird is intended to be a cock. For dating, Cf. Moorey, *Iran*, Vol. 9 (1971), p. 123. Muscarella-, Moorey-. Bottom quarter section missing....................................**CHOICE 250.00**

239. **LURISTAN. 900-700 B.C.** Plain bronze/copper mix pin with very long tapered shank. Top of shank is hammered out to form a large flat disk with small perforations at top (now folded back). Edge of disk serrated, otherwise plain. 33 cm long. Cf. Moorey, *Ancient Bronzes From Luristan*, Pl. XV, a and b. Intact but edge slightly eroded. Some blue patina or paint on disk................................**CHOICE 80.00**

240. **LURISTAN. 900-700 B.C.** Bronze pair of bar-shaped cheek pieces of a bit for horse's bridle with loops at each end and in center.   Each approx. 13 cm long. Cf. Moorey, *Ancient Bronzes From Luristan*, Pl.. 15b.   The bar-shaped cheek pieces usually hold a jointed mouthpiece rather than the straight bar snaffles with very ornate cheek pieces. ....**CHOICE 350.00**

241. **NORTHWEST IRAN. 9th-7th Century B.C.** Bronze bell with addorsed bird heads. Cf. Christie's, Mar. 1970, #145. For basic type, Cf. Muscarella, *MMA* 150....**CHOICE 60.00**

242. **LURISTAN. c. 800 B.C.** Pendant. Cast bronze. A number of model situlae have been reported from Luristan though the actual examples from the region do not normally have loop handles. 35 mm x 28 mm. Cf. Moorey, Pl. 65.412. ....**CHOICE 35.00**

243. **LURISTAN. 800 B.C.** Bronze bracelet. Pattern probably deriving from an earlier bead prototype. 58 mm. Luristan "peoples" lived east of the Tigris and Euphrates in the Zagros Mountains. Green patina ....**CHOICE 45.00**

244. **LURISTAN. 8th Century B.C.** Bronze human figure. Standing male figure with arms akimbo. Suspension loop. Height 42 mm. Cf. Moorey #430 Dark patina. ....**CHOICE 225.00**

245. **LURISTAN. 8th Century B.C.** Bronze human figure. Standing male figure with arms to head as in worship. Height 43 mm. Cf. Moorey p. 234, VII; Sialk II, Pl. XXVII, 2. Mounted....................................**CHOICE 150.00**

246. **LURISTAN. 8th Century B.C.** Bronze horse collar appliqué. Length 9.5 cm. Assyrian reliefs at Tepe Sialk show this horse collar appliqué. Moorey 152........**CHOICE 85.00**

247. **WESTERN ASIATIC. 8th-Early 7th Century B.C.** Miniature bronze vessel, three feet, ovoid body below wide cylindrical neck with pronounced lip. Pierced for suspension. 30 mm x 15 mm. Rare...............................**CHOICE 125.00**

248. **IRAN. 8th-7th Century B.C.** Bronze zoomorphic tri-headed pendant finial. Top has three bird heads, below, three facing bull heads, loop above. This basic type is not represented in most Luristan collections. Berghe, Staatssammlung Munchen-. Cf. Goddard 190 var. Moorey-. Muscarella, *MMA*-. Sotheby's Adam Collection, for style. Encrusted green patina..**CHOICE 250.00**

249. **IRAN. 8th-7th Century B.C.** Bronze stamp seal with double bird's head. Pierced at neck for suspension. Double cross incised on seal. Length 42 cm. Moorey #465. Green patina. ....**CHOICE 225.00**

250. **KERMAN. 8th-7th Century B.C.** Bronze horse figure with reins and harness. 27 x 40 mm. Cf. Malloy, 1973 Vol. 1, 15c. Muscarella, *MMA*-. Moorey.-.............**CHOICE 200.00**

251. **WESTERN ASIATIC. 8th-Early 7th Century B.C.** Bronze miniature vessel with straight neck and bulbous body. Three small legs. Suspension hole on either side of neck for hanging. Height 3.4 cm. Rare....................**CHOICE 100.00**

252. **SCYTHIAN. 7th Century B.C.** Bronze migratory bird in flight. Wings spread, head arched, eye, beak and wings defined with incisions. Found in northeastern Turkey. Cf. Kozloff, *Mildenberg Collection*, #35. Green patina. ....**CHOICE 500.00**

253. **LURISTAN. 7th-5th Century B.C.** Bronze hollow cast finial or standard support. Mount with tubular neck and bell-shaped body and flat base. Decorated with incised horizontal bands on base. In two pieces: break at body and neck joint. Height 14.3 cm. Base diameter 3.2 cm. Cf. Moorey, *Bronzes du Luristan*. Pl. 39, 196, 197, 208, 209. Green patina. ....**CHOICE 125.00**

254. **ACHAEMENID. 425-420 B.C.** Bronze ram's head terminal fragment. Side of head of ram with defined eye and ram's horn. Length 4.1 cm. Probably used as a torque finial. Cf. Moorey, *Ashmolean*. Pl. XXV.B. Superb craftsmanship ....**CHOICE 150.00**

255. **PARTHIAN. 400-200 B.C.** Bronze plaque depicting two pegasi rearing facing each other. Measures 6.9 cm x 6.8 cm. Cf. for similar style, Musée du Louvre, *L'Orient Musilman*, p. 14......................................**SUPERB 1200.00**

256. **PARTHIAN. 400-200 B.C.** Bronze plaque depicting two pegasi rearing facing each other. Measures 6.9 cm. by 6.8 cm. Cf. for similar style, Musée du Louvre, *L'Orient Musilman*, p. 14. ....**CHOICE 750.00**

257. **PARTHIAN. c. 1st-2nd Century A.D.** Solid bronze head with vertical hole running through. Stylized features, pointed top of head, and short neck. 3.2 cm high. Red, green and gold patina over smooth bronze..................**CHOICE 150.00**

STONE

258. **STEATITE FIGURE. Jemdet Nasr. 3200-2900 B.C.** Black bull with horns. Length 1.0 cm. For workmanship, Cf. Mackay, *Jemdet Nasr* #3304........................**CHOICE 80.00**

259. **LIMESTONE CARVED BULL. Jemdet Nasr. 3200-2900 B.C.** Light brown, reclining, full face. Length 30 mm. Cf. Yale 124..**CHOICE 175.00**

260. **LIMESTONE QUADRUPED. Early Proto-Elamite Period, 3000-2900 B.C.** White, standing with head down. Pierced for suspension at withers. Slight indication of eyes. 31 mm long. For similar shape, Cf. Habib Avanian, 1977,#32. Early Proto-Elamite. Cf. Amiet, *Elam* #63. ....**CHOICE 125.00**

261. **STEATITE COSMETIC BOTTLE. Pre-Sargonid Early Dynastic. 3000-2500 B.C.** Dark grey. Linear pattern on shouldered vessel with button base and flare rim. Height 5.5 cm, diameter 3.6 cm. Cf. Lamberg-Karlovsky Excavations at Tepe Yahya #82, 83. Two chips at rim.......**SUPERB 400.00**

262. **STEATITE COSMETIC BOTTLE. Pre-Sargonid. Early Dynastic. 3000-2500 B.C.** Dark grey. Linear pattern on shouldered vessel with button base and flair rim. 55 mm high, 36 mm dia. Carved vessels of steatite with animal and geometric motifs were used in the Temple of Sin in the Diyala region and the Temple of Inanna in Kerman. Tepe Yahya and its environs were a center of raw steatite and manufacture of vessels, a main export to Mesopotamia and Persia. Lamberg-Karlovsky recovered over 1000 vase fragments from Tepe Yahya. Lamberg-Karlovsky, *Excavations at Tepe Yahya*. Museum fur Kunst, Hamburg #82.83. Two chips at rim..........................**SUPERB 400.00**

263. **ALABASTER BOWL. Sumerian-Kish. 2950-2750 B.C.** Rather deep and convex sides, slightly flattened at base. Slightly carinated rim. 110 mm diameter. The quality of this bowl is of similar workmanship to those stone vessels found at Kish. Mackay suggests that at this period of time the stone bowl industry was a dying industry at the fourth Kingdom of Kish (2943-2753 B.C.). Mackay, *Sumerian Palace and the "A" Cemetery at Kish*, Part II, Pl. LV.6. ....**SUPERB 350.00**

264. **ALABASTER BOWL. Sumeria-Kish. 2950-2750 B.C.** Deep and convex sides, carinated rim, with rim pedestal base. The quality of this vessel is of similar workmanship to those stone vessels found at Kish. Mackay, *Sumerian Palace and the "A" Cemetery at Kish*, Part 11, Pl. LV. 6. Yellow beige patina and encrustation ....**SUPERB 450.00**

265. **HEMATITE CARVED LION. Old Babylonian. 1894-1595 B.C.** Black, seated with its head turned left. Length 2.2 cm. Hematite was the most commonly used stone during this dynasty. Goff-, MacKay-...........................**CHOICE 125.00**

266. **CLOTHING APPLIQUÉ. Northern Mesopotamia-Iran. Hissar III. 1500-1200 B.C.** Shell disc with four small lugs on perimeter. Decoration of concentric circles. Pierced at the center and small holes through two opposing lugs. Measures 4.5 cm x 4.3 cm. Cf. for similar circle-and-dot pattern, *Tepe Hissar*, Hissar III level. ....**CHOICE 75.00**

267. **NORTH SYRIAN. 9th–8th Century B.C.** Black steatite offering spoon. Short hollow tube joined to a shallow bowl at the base. Hatched rim. Length 8.5 cm. Used in temple rituals for offerings and libations throughout the Middle East, in Assyria, Palestine, Anatolia and Iran. Scholars agree that these bowls were manufactured at Chatal Huyuk and exported throughout the known world. Muscarella, *Ladders to Heaven*, 232. Rare...............................**CHOICE 250.00**

268. **BONE GODDESS FIGURE. Seleucid-Syrian. Hellenistic Period. 3rd-2nd Century B.C.** Standing with arms at breast. Wearing long chiton. Hair tied up in bow on top of head. Chip to left of lower drapery. Repaired at neck and knees. ....**CHOICE 150.00**

269. **LIMESTONE MALE BUST. Parthian. 1st Century B.C.-1st Century A.D.** Figure with hair band. Hand to breast, draped in himation. An excellent representation of the dual character of Parthian art as a contest between and the fusion of the two diverse aesthetic tendencies: the foreign Hellenistic tradition and the native Oriental style. Syrian manufacture. Cf. Pope, *A Survey of Persian Art*, Vol. VII, Pl. 5. 131c, 134b. Colledge-. Basmachi ....**CH-SUP 1250.00**

270. **MARBLE CARVED BUST. Parthian. 2nd-4th Century A.D.** White, larger than life size, modeled in the round. Semetic bearded bust of curly, short-haired man. Both arms drawn up to breast with hands clasping, broad drapery over shoulders. The modeling and style is highly influenced by the portrait busts of Palmyra. This bust does not have the fine polishing characteristic of Palmyran workmanship. A cruder head, currently at Yale, was found at Dura cut in Eastern style of gypsum. It was set in plaster and probably set on a shelf or pedestal like the heads of the Great Hall at Hatra. Cf. *Dura-Europus, 1931-32*, Rostovtzeff, Pl. XVI, 1. ....**CHOICE 8500.00**

STAMP SEALS

271. **BLACK STEATITE SEAL. Early Man. Pre-Pottery Level. 7th Millennium B.C**, Truncated, partial pyramidal. Random criss-cross at base, criss-cross at side panel. Very crude design and workmanship. An example of man's earliest expression in amuletic seals from the North Mesopotamia Syrian region. Cf. Buchanan, *Ash.* 11. ....**CHOICE 150.00**

272. **DROP STAMP SEAL. Syro-Mesopotamia. Amug B. 6th Millennium B.C.** Grey steatite. Rays from central drilled hole. Pierced at top for suspension. Slightly irregular shape. 10 x 10 mm. Buchanan, *Ash.* II....................**CHOICE 65.00**

273. **STEATITE STAMP SEAL PENDANT. Syria. Amug B. 6th Millennium B.C.** Black. Irregular flat oval with an irregular criss-cross design. Drilled through the center. Measures 30 x 24 mm. Buchanan, Ash. II-...**CHOICE 50.00**

274. **STEATITE SEAL BOSS. Syrian. Amug Period: 6th Millennium B.C.** Grey. On high sloping oval base. Four planes of alternating parallel lines. Length 18 mm. For design, Cf. Buchanan/Moorey, *Ashmolean* #19-20. ....**CHOICE SUPERB 125.00**

275. **NORTH SYRIA. 6th-4th Millennium B.C.** Black serpentine loop-handled seal. Line filled cross. Cf. Buchanan, *Ash.* 11, 20 for design. ....**CHOICE 75.00**

276. **MARBLE RECTANGULAR SEAL. North Syria. 6th-4th Millennium B.C.** White-orange loop-handled. Crosshatch design. 30 x 23 mm. Buchanan-. Amiet-. Chip on edge. ....**CHOICE 100.00**

277. **PYRAMID SEAL. North Syria. Amug G Period, 5000 B.C.** Black serpentine, truncated and crudely shaped. Crossed-line pattern. 2 cm x 1.4 cm. Buchanan, YBC-3, Amug A, OIP 61, fig.37.1, 3.5. ....**SUPERB 125.00**

278. **PYRAMID SEAL. North Syria. Amug G Period, 5000 B.C.** Hemispheroid stamp seal. Black-gray serpentine. Lightly carved lines of four-lined crosslet, dot in center. Radial lines in quads. 2.2 cm diameter. Cf. Goff. fig. 179. ....**CHOICE 65.00**

279. **PYRAMID SEAL. North Syria. Amug G Period, 5000 B.C.** Pyramid seal. Black steatite, tail truncated. Pierced for suspension. X on base, on walls. 8 mm x 7 mm. Chip at top. ....**CHOICE 35.00**

280. **PYRAMID SEAL. North Syria. Amug G Period, 5000 B.C.** Steatite tabloid seal. Black house with door in linear design. 1.5 cm x 1.2 cm. Amiet *GS-*, Buchanan *YBC-*.For style, Cf. Buchanan *YBC*-109. ....**SUPERB 80.00**

281. **STEATITE HEMISPHEROID SEAL. North Mesopotamian 5th–4th Millennium B.C.** Black, with angle-filled cross. Diameter 40 mm. Cf. Buchanan, Yale 34-35; Cf. Buchanan/Moorey, *Ashmolean* #30. Very large stamp seal. Chip on edge. 1/3 of edge design chipped off. ....**CHOICE 250.00**

282. **BLACK STEATITE SEAL. Mesopotamia/Syria. Old Hassuna-Halaf Tradition. 5000-4000 B.C.** Low pierced ridge. Geometric I pattern. Amiet, *GMA*, 132 var. Buchanan, *Yale-*. For shape, Cf. Buchanan, *Ash*. 11, 75. ....**CHOICE 100.00**

283. **HEMISPHEROID SEAL. Anatolia-North Syria. Amug E Period. 5000-4000 B.C.** Black-grey serpentine. Lightly curved lines of four-lined crosslet, dot in center, radial lines in quads. Diameter 2.2 cm. Cf. Goff, fig. 179. ....**CHOICE 65.00**

284. **AMULETIC SEAL PENDANT. Mesopotamia. Halaf Period. 4500-4000 B.C.** Grey-black linear design. Cf. Goff, fig. 110...**CHOICE 100.00**

285. **STEATITE AMULETIC SEAL. Mesopotamia. Halaf Period. 4500-4000 B.C.** Black, seated animal. Similar pendants were found at Arpachiyah. Cf. Goff, fig. 110, Cf. Basmachi, Iraq Museum, 10, 18 ....**SUPERB 120.00**

286. **BLACK STEATITE SEAL. North Syrian. Halaf Period. 4500-4000 B.C.** Hemispheroid. Linear hatched section. On each side two middle lines. Attempt at piercing. Early crude design. Cf. Buchanan, *Yale* #39 for design variation. ....**CHOICE 80.00**

287. **STEATITE SEAL.. North Syrian. Amug Valley. 4000 B.C.** Black, truncated pyramid. Irregular grooves of crossed lines. Measures 18 x 16 cm. Cf. Buchanan, *Yale* #2. ....**CHOICE 65.00**

288. **STEATITE SEAL. Mesopotamia or North Syria. 4000 B.C.** Carved black square with ridge handle. Design is cross with parallels. Measures 15 x 15 mm. *Ashmolean Museum* II, 19..**CHOICE 65.00**

289. **STEATITE GABLE SEAL North Syrian and Anatolian. Late Prehistoric: First Half of 4th Millennium B.C.** Black. Design of standing quadruped (horse?). Measures 27 x 25 mm. Typical gable seals were made until the late 4th millennium B.C. Cf. Buchanan/Moorey, *Ashmolean* 82-132 (gable seals)...**CHOICE 150.00**

290. **STEATITE SEAL. Syria. 4th Millennium B.C.** Black, oval shape with pierced back loop. Design of angle-filled cross with two central lines. Measures 19 x 17 mm. Buchanan, *Ash* 22. ....**CHOICE 75.00**

291. **WESTERN ASIATIC. Susa A. c. 3500 B.C.** Black steatite pendant seal. Gate. 14 x 9 mm. Amiet.........**CHOICE 50.00**

292. **STEATITE SEAL. Susa. Susa A. c. 3500 B.C.** Black semi-lenticlaroid. Linear pattern, possibly an edifice. Reverse quartered with possible characters. Measures 25 x 12 mm. Amiet-. Broken and repaired......................**CHOICE 75.00**

293. **HEMISPHEROID STAMP SEAL. Western Iran. Susa A Period. c. 3500 B.C.** Black steatite low oval. Antelope seated. with long curved horn. Triangular headed serpent in field, plant below, and arrowhead before 40 mm x 38 mm. A large and rare impressive stamp seal. Cf. Noveck, *Mark of Ancient Man* #3. Cf. Amiet, *G.S.* #190. ......**SUPERB 300.00**

294. **HEMISPHEROID STAMP SEAL. Western Iran. Susa A Period. c. 3500 B.C.** Black steatite low oval. Human figure with both arms raised before four-legged animal facing away with head turned back. Arrowhead below. Four drill holes below, with three drills in field. 38 x 32 mm. Drill marks are found on similar seals in Amiet *G.S. 143*. Human representation is very rare on early stamp seals. ....**CHOICE 180.00**

295. **STAMP SEAL. Northern Mesopotamia-Iran. Proto-Urban Period. 3500-3100 B.C.** Black-gray steatite hemispheroid. Angle filled crosslet. 18 mm diameter. Fine quality seal. Buchanan *YBC* 34. Amiet, *G.S.* 246. ....**SUPERB 90.00**

296. **STAMP SEAL-AMULET. Northern Mesopotamia-Iran. Proto-Urban Period. 3500-3100 B.C.** Black steatite. Triangular, looped for suspension. Linear tree design. 30 x 25 mm. Cf. von Aulock 345......................**SUPERB 135.00**

297. **HEMISPHEROID STAMP SEAL. Northern Mesopotamia. Late Gawra Period. 3500-3000 B.C.** Black steatite. Goat advancing. 19 mm. Buchanan, *AMII*, 57. Buchanan, *YBC* 80. Gawra 1, Level VIII....................**CHOICE 125.00**

298. **STEATITE GABLE SEAL. North Syria. Late Prehistoric Period. Gawra XIII. 3500-3000 B.C.** Black linear animal grazing. Cf. Buchanan, *Ash*. II, 101-104. Amiet. ....**CHOICE 75.00**

299. **STEATITE TRIANGULAR SEAL. North Syria. 3500-3000 B.C.** Grey-black, with a loop-handled. Antelope running to right, small animal in field. Buchanan, *Ash.* ....**CHOICE 100.00**

300. **STEATITE GABLE SEAL. North Syria. 3500-3000 B.C.** Black. Bird standing. Buchanan, *Ash.* II-. Buchanan, *Yale.* ....**CHOICE 65.00**

301. **STEATITE HEMISPHEROID SEAL. North Syria. 3500-3000 B.C.** Black. Divided in three compartments with crescent in two. Goff, fig. 507. Buchanan, *Ash.* II-. Buchanan, *Yale* ....**CHOICE 65.00**

302. **MARBLE TABLOID SEAL. Mesopotamian. Late Prehistoric Period. 3500-3000 B.C.** Beige. Lion advancing, drill marks below. Mallowan's excavations at Tell Brak revealed several tabloids like this specimen. Cf. Buchanan, *Ash.* 11, 161 var. Chipped.........................**CHOICE 125.00**

303. **STEATITE HEMISPHEROID SEAL. Mesopotamia/Syria. Late Prehistoric Period. 3500-3000 B.C.** Black. Irregular criss-cross. Cf. Buchanan, *Yale*, 22 var. ....**CHOICE 60.00**

304. **STEATITE HEMISPHEROID SEAL. Mesopotamia/Syria. Late Prehistoric Period. 3500-3000 B.C.** Black geometric pattern. Cf. Buchanan, *Yale* 18. Buchanan, *Ash.* ....**CHOICE 75.00**

305. **STAMP BUTTON. Sussania. Susa A. 3500-3000 B.C.** Dark grey serpentine. Cross-hatching random. 17 mm. Amiet *G.S.* 21. ....**CHOICE 65.00**

306. **STEATITE GABLE STAMP SEAL. North Syria. Amug G Period. 3500-3000 B.C.** Black. Depicts three graduated arrowheads facing inward. 2.7 cm x 2.2 cm. Cf. for style, Buchanan, *YC*, p. 44-60. Gabled seals were predominantly from the North Syrian Prehistoric period. This seal with arrowhead depiction was a magical amulet for the hunt. ....**SUPERB 200.00**

307. **STEATITE GABLE SEAL. North Syrian. Late Prehistoric Period. Gawra XIII. 3500-3000 B.C.** Black. Antelope with arrow point before. The gable seals are prevalent in the late Prehistoric period in Anatolia and North Syria. Buchanan, *Ash.* II, # 104 var............**CHOICE 125.00**

308. **STEATITE HEMISPHEROID SEAL. Mesopotamia/Syria. Late Prehistoric Period. 3500-3000 B.C.** Black. Irregular criss-cross. Cf. Buchanan, *Yale*, 22 var. ....**CHOICE 60.00**

309. **GABLE SEAL. 3500-3000 B.C.** Red serpentine, crude animal with long tail. Two marks before. 2.4 cm x 1.6 cm. Seal shows wear. Cf. Buchanan *YBC* 53.....**CHOICE 60.00**

310. **STEATITE STAMP SEAL. Anatolia. Early-Middle Bronze Age. 3500-3000 B.C.** Black stalk with stem handle. Mostly black. 2 cm x 1.7 cm diameter, 2.3 cm long handle. Cf. Buchanan, *AMII*, 1-22............................**CHOICE 25.00**

311. **STEATITE LOOP SEAL. Syria. Late Prehistoric. 3500-3000 B.C.** Black on thick oval base. Linear design may represent an antelope. Diameter 16 mm. Cf. Buchanan, *Yale* 86 and 88. Linear style. Chip at base..........**CHOICE 100.00**

312. **MARBLE HEMISPHEROID SEAL. Mesopotamia. Late Prehistoric Period. 3500-3000 B.C.** White. Design of two ibexes reversed and opposed. Drill style. Diameter 44 mm, height 15 mm. Cf. Buchanan, *Yale* 102. Large size. One drill hole in design goes through to suspension hole. Chip on edge...**CHOICE 450.00**

313. **HEMISPHEROIDAL SEAL. Uruk Period. 3400-3200 B.C.** Black steatite. Design of human walking, with palm branch before. Diameter 28 mm. Similar seals were found at Tepe Gawra. Cf. Homes-Fredericq 109. Crude carving. ....**CHOICE 250.00**

314. **BUTTON SEAL. Susa B. c. 3300 B.C.** Black steatite. Quartered linear. 17 mm. Amiet, *G.S.* 248...**CHOICE 85.00**

315. **HEMISPHEROID SEAL. Uruk. Jemdet Nasr Period. 3300-3000 B.C.** Red marble colored. Depicts two reclining bulls with two small objects on each side. Drill style. Suspension hole through. Measures 28 x 22 mm. Cf. Amiet *GMA* 159; Cf. Buchanan, *Yale* 117 for style. Nice color. Finely burnished. Very attractive seal ....**CH-SUP 300.00**

316. **AMULET SEAL. Uruk. Jemdet Nasr Period. 3300-3000. B.C.** Pale aragonite streaked white, beige, orange, and grey-green. Amulet in shape of a seated bovine with curved legs, pierced eyes. Pierced for suspension. The seal depicts five stylized animals. Measures 38 x 24 mm. Cf. von Aulock, Von Der Osten Pl. 2, 24; Cf. Collection Arnold Trampitsch, Adertajen 5/14/92, #210 and 208 for seal design. A gem amulet-seal..**SUPERB 1200.00**

317. **STEATITE STAMP SEAL. Mesopotamia. Susa B Period: 3200-3000 B.C.** Black in quartered section with arcs. Suspension hole through middle. High domed back. 2.1 cm in diameter. Cf. Amiet *GS*, #246. Some minor chipping. ....**CHOICE 100.00**

318. **AMULET SEAL. Mesopotamia. 3200-3000 B.C.** Brown steatite lying lion amulet, pierced horizontally. Seal in bottom depicts horse galloping, palm behind and bush with three sprigs before. 2 cm long. Cf. Eisen, Moore-. Buchanan, *Yale*-. Buchanan, *Ashmolean*-. Very unusual. Chip to one corner of seal ....**CHOICE 90.00**

319. **QUARTZ HEMISPHEROID SEAL. South Mesopotamia and Sussania. Uruk Period. 3200-3000 B.C.** Opaque. Line-filled cross. Buchanan, *Yale*-..............**CHOICE 80.00**

320. **STEATITE SEAL. North Mesopotamia. Ninevite Period. 3200-2800 B.C.** Grey loop handled. Stylized round face. This cult symbol using the eye symbol. The eye symbol was used in the eye-temple at Brak in Mallowan excavations. This cult symbol was also found at Tepe Gawra. Cf. Amiet, *GMA.* 103-4 for larger type seal. Buchanan, *Yale-*. Buchanan, *Ash.-* Rare.................................**CHOICE 250.00**

321. **MARBLE SEAL. Mesopotamia. Ninevite Period. 3200-2800 B.C.** Grey, loop-handled. Flower design with eight petals. Cf. Goff, fig. 684 for stone rosette from the eye-temple with floral design with eight petals with veins, center pierced. Cf. Goff, fig. 631, 4 var. Chip to end of two petals. ....**CHOICE 120.00**

322. **STAMP SEAL. Hissar II Period. c. 3000 B.C.** Black steatite oval with loop. Antelope standing with two arrow-heads and two pellets above. Projectiles. Tree before. 29 mm x 22 mm. Seals of this shape are rare. Cf. Buchanan, *YBC* 88. Cf. Museum Journal 23 (1933), Pl. 107A. ....**SUPERB 275.00**

323. **STEATITE BUTTON SEAL. Proto-Elamite. 3000-2500 B.C.** Black with linear and drilling geometric design. Diameter 11 cm. For type, Cf. Amiet *GS*, 317. ....**CHOICE 65.00**

324. **HEMISPHEROID STAMP SEAL. North Mesopotamia. Gawra VIII Period. 3000-2500 B.C.** Black steatite of two schematic animals. 3.1 cm. Cf. Buchanan, *Ash* 118, Cf. Tepe Gawra, Speiser 1935, 33 Level VIII. Nice size. ....**CHOICE 125.00**

325. **BUTTON SEAL. Anatolian. 3rd Millennium B.C.** Red porphyry. Irregular human figure running, arms out. Measures 15 x 13 mm. Buchanan, *Ash-*.....**CHOICE 100.00**

326. **STEATITE STAMP SEAL. Tepe Hissar. Hissar III Period. 2900-1800 B.C.** Black. Rectangular. Irregular geometric pattern. 26 x 21 mm. Used for impressing and sealing containers. Cf. Univ. of Pa. Tepe Hissar, 1932. ....**SUPERB 135.00**

327. **STEATITE BUTTON SEAL. Proto-Elamite. 3000-2500 B.C.** Black with linear and drilling geometric design. Diameter 1.1 cm. For type, Cf. Amiet *GS*, 317. ....**CHOICE 50.00**

328. **STEATITE SEAL. Early Dynastic. 2800-2600 B.C.** Black-grey, loop-handled. Criss-cross pattern. Cf. Mallowan, 1936, Pl. 18, fig. 7.5. Cf. Buchanan, *Ash*. II, #136. ....**CHOICE 75.00**

329. **STAMP SEAL. Turkmenistan-Eastern Iran. Hissar II-B Period. 2650-2450 B.C.** Bronze long stalk handled. Quartered circle design, each quad filled with rounded chevrons. 47 mm diameter, 33 mm handle. Cf. Porada, *Corpus 9*.................**SUPERB 250.00**

330. **BRONZE STAMP SEAL Southern Turkmenia. Margiana and Bactrian Bronze Age. 2100-1500 B.C.** Compartmental stylized animal. 20 mm x 20 mm. Similar seals were found at Altyn-Depe where the society had attained a very high level of development. Cf. Masson & Kiiatkina. For similar seal, Cf. Pitman, *AAM* 38. Cf. Masson and Kiiatkina, *Man at the Dawn of Civilization,* fig. 2. ....**CHOICE 125.00**

331. **STEATITE OVOID SEAL. Early Iranian. Later Prehistoric. Early 2nd Millennium B.C.** Black and thin. Convex face, parallel designs from edge. Horizontal perforation. Length 29 mm. Buchanan/Moorey, *Ashmolean* #239 var.; Cf. Tepe Giyan, Ghirshman 1935, Pl. 38, 43. Worn seal design.....................................**CHOICE 125.00**

332. **LIMESTONE STAMP SEAL. Southern Turkmenistan. Proto-Indian Type. 2nd Millennium B.C.** Square with stalk. Linear pattern with dot and circles. 33 mm x 38 mm, 1 mm stalk. This seal is similar to the types found at the site Altyn-Depe. Amiet. *G.S.-*. Cf. Kohl, *Bronze Age Civilization of Central Asia*, Masson p. 151, fig. 1 and 2. ....**SUPERB 225.00**

333. **CARNELIAN AMULET OR SEAL. Hittite. 2nd Millennium B.C.** Lozenge and dot pattern. Dots through entire thickness. 1.9 cm. x 2.2 cm. Rare......**CHOICE 80.00**

334. **STEATITE BUTTON SEAL. Syrian. c. 1850-1750 B.C.** Black seal with depiction of a gazelle leaping and pellets above. Measures 1.3 cm x 1 cm. Cf. Von Der Osten, *A.S.,* #107. ....**CHOICE 80.00**

335. **STAMP SEAL. Margiana. Namazga VIB. Togolok Stage. 1800-1500 B.C.** Bronze, round with stalk and compartmental design. Dividing line transected by serpent, chevron in opposing angles. 23 mm diameter, 15 mm stalk. For a similar seal, Cf. Pitman, *AAM* 38. Cf. Saruanidi, *Margiana*, fig. 4..**CHOICE-SUPERB 135.00**

336. **BRONZE STAMP SEAL. Margiana. Namazga VIB. Togolok Stage. 1800-1500 B.C.** Square with rounded corners with two snake-like figures. Button loop for suspension. The Bronze Age Namazaga civilization ranged from southern Turkmenistan-Iranian plateau, northern Afghanistan and Pakistan from 3600-1500 B.C. Green patina. Cf. Saruanidi, *Margiana in The Bronze Age*, fig. 4, pp. 165-193. In *Bronze Age Civilization of Central Asia-Recent Soviet Discoveries*.........................**CHOICE 125.00**

337. **COPPER SEAL. Margiana. 1800-1500 B.C. Bronze Age (Togolok Stage).** Compartmented of dog with tail over back. These peoples were located in what is now Turkmenistan. Saruanidi, *Margiana* fig. 4. Green patina..**CHOICE 150.00**

338. **HEMISPHEROID SEAL. North Mesopotamian. 1500 B.C.** Bluish composition with central pellet and radial lines from center. Diameter 13 mm. Cf. Buchanan, *Yale*, 28. ....**CHOICE 75.00**

339. **HEMISPHEROID STAMP SEAL. Mitannian. 1500-1300 B.C.** Grey serpentine oval. Horse standing, tail above, holding wheat in mouth. This style with drilled muzzle and head, and brisket and hind with lineal legs and tail certainly of Mitannian manufacture. Chip on top. Superb deep carving. A gem impression. Buchanan, *YBC*-. Buchanan, *AM* Von Der Osten, *Newell*-. Von Der Osten, *Brett*. ....**SUPERB 150.00**

340. **CHALCEDONY SEAL. Hittite. 1400-1200 B.C.** Red, cylindrical shape with stamp at each end. Designs: human shape, gazelle. Length 12 mm, diameter 8 mm. Buchanan calls these types "degenerate Mitannian style." Cf. Buchanan 1016. Found in Anatolia...........................**CHOICE 150.00**

341. **HEMISPHEROID STAMP SEAL. Hittite. 1400-1200 B.C.** Red and cream chalcedony. Horseman galloping holding sword. Diameter 1.7 cm. Cf. Buchanan, *Ash.* #1016. Scarce. ....**CHOICE 150.00**

342. **ANATOLIAN. c. 1000 B.C.** Black steatite amulet seal. Irregular shape as cross, with cross-hatching. Measures 1.8 x 1.7 cm. Cf. Von Der Osten *A.S.* #349.........**CHOICE 125.00**

343. **STEATITE TABLOID SEAL. Neo-Hittite. Early 1st Millennium B.C.** Black with robed figure with sword on obverse, horse on reverse. Cut in linear style. Measures 1.4 x 1.5 cm. For style, Cf. Muscarella, *Ladder to Heaven,* #238. ....**CHOICE 75.00**

344. **BRONZE SEAL. Anatolian. 1st Millennium B.C.** Rectangular with loop. 8 x 5 mm wide, 15 mm high. Winged griffin........................**AVERAGE 50.00**

345. **GABLE STAMP SEAL. Syrian. 1st Millennium B.C.** Black serpentine. At base, scorpion. X on each rise. 12 x 22 mm.Chip at top corner of base...................**CHOICE 125.00**

346. **SCARABOID SEAL. 1st Millennium B.C** Red feldspar. Two crescents separated by abstract linear pattern. 18 mm x 23 mm ....**FINE 100.00**

347. **CHALCEDONY SEAL. Neo-Assyrian. 900-700 B.C.** Creamy with design of crescent and moon with rays. Diameter 15 mm...........................**CHOICE 80.00**

348. **OVAL STAMP SEAL. Neo-Assyrian. 900-700 B.C.** Black serpentine. Winged griffin. Measures 2.2 cm x 1.8 cm. Bold style. Rare type...........................**CHOICE 150.00**

349. **SCARABOID. Phoenicia. 8th-7th Century B.C.** Bluish-black glass paste. Deity seated in high back throne with arm raised in act of adoration. 1.7 cm x 1.3 cm. Cf. for style, Pitman *AAM* 83. Very scarce. Phoenician glass scaraboids are not often found. ....**CHOICE 250.00**

350. **STEATITE TABLOID SEAL. Uratu. 8th-7th Century B.C.** Black and linear in style. O: Pegasus flying right, crescent above, bush before. R: Antelope advancing, bush before, crescent above. Measures 2.3 x 2.1 cm. For style, Cf. Pitman *AAM* #92. The Archaic Greek influence is apparent. ....**CHOICE 250.00**

351. **BLACK STEATITE DISCOID. Uratu. 8th-7th Century B.C.** Sphinx seated, wing outstretched, A behind, plant before. 16 x 18 mm. Cf. Pitman, *Ancient Art in Miniature* 87. Cf. *NCBS* 379. Newell identifies this type as Hittite. ....**AVERAGE 100.00**

352. **PYRAMID-SHAPED SEAL. Neo-Babylonian. 625-539 B.C.** Creamy marble. Drill style depicting Ishtar standing with wings or rays emanating from center. Height 26 mm. Seal measures 19 x 13 mm. Legrain-. Rare type. ....**CHOICE 200.00**

353. **CHALCEDONY STAMP SEAL. Neo-Babylonian. 625-500 B.C.** Milky with worshipper before an altar. Pale blue in color. Chip on edge. 20 mm. Cf. *Newell Coll*, Osten, #486. ....**CHOICE 145.00**

354. **STEATITE SCARABOID. Achaemenid. Over Palestine. 6th-5th Century B.C.** Brown. Winged disk above seated figure with palm and staff at each side. Measures 16 x 13 mm. Found in Israel...............................**AVERAGE 80.00**

355. **FELDSPAR SCARABOID. Achaemenid. 6th-5th Century B.C.** Green. Crescent on long staff above altar. Palm each side. Attendant at one side below, diminutive figure of sphinx on altar. 18 x 14 mm. Nice color stone. Von Der Osten, *Newell*-. Pitman-. Von Der Osten, *Brett*-. Rowe. ....**AVERAGE 80.00**

356. **STEATITE ROUND SEAL. Achaemenid. 539-331 B.C.** Buff. Winged disc, crescent. Height 1.7 cm. ....**AVERAGE 80.00**

357. **CONOID STAMP SEAL. Late Parthian or Early Sassanian. 200-300 A.D.** Banded calcite. Lion recumbent, head turned back, tail above. 13 x 11 mm diameter, 16 mm long. Cf. Göbl. 430b. Cf. Von Der Osten, *Newell*, 557. ....**SUPERB 80.00**

358. **SEAL INTAGLIO. Sassanian. 250-500 A.D.** Amethyst domed. Panther advancing. 13 x 11 mm. A lovely precious stone. Göbl. 44a.........................**SUPERB 125.00**

359. **STAMP SEAL. Sassanian. 224-642 A.D.** Quartz with man's head. 11 mm x 9 mm. Göbl 7a........**CHOICE 75.00**

360. **HEMATITE SEAL. Sassanian. 224-642 A.D.** Stage seated, crescents. 15 mm. Göbl 51a............**SUPERB 75.00**

361. **ELLIPSOID SEAL. Sassanian. 224-642 A.D.** Rock crystal, with raven. 12 mm. Rock crystal was highly sought after among the ancient peoples. Göbl. 36a. ......**CHOICE 100.00**

362. **ONYX ELLIPSOID SEAL. Sassanian. 3rd Century A.D.** Brown and cream. Depicts a man worshipping with raised arms before a lighted altar, with a star above and inscription behind. Measures 18 x 12 mm. Göbl 4b. A lovely seal..**SUPERB 250.00**

363. **ORANGE CARNELIAN INTAGLIO. 3rd Century A.D.** Winged zebu with hump. Göbl 70 var. A superb carving and in fine style. Some small chips..................**SUPERB 350.00**

364. **CHALCEDONY INTAGLIO. Parthian-Sassanian. 3rd-4th Century A.D.** White. Bust of bearded male in cap. Palm to left and right. Measures 1 cm. x 0.8 cm..**CHOICE 125.00**

365. **HEMATITE ELLIPSOID SEAL. Sassanian. 3rd-5th Century A.D.** Black, with image of scorpion. Measures 10 x 5 mm. Göbl 20a. Pierced for suspension. ....**SUPERB 85.00**

366. **HEMATITE STAMP SEAL. Sassanian. 3rd-7th Century A.D.** Horse prancing. High domed shape with suspension hole through. Diameter 1.4 cm. Ex. Malloy Sale XIX, March 1984. Cf. Göbl 48a....................................**CHOICE 80.00**

367. **ELLIPSOID STAMP SEAL. Sassanian. 3rd-7th Century A.D.** Milky translucent chalcedony. Suspension hole through center. Portrays fish. Measures 1.3 cm. x 1 cm. Göbl 23a. ....**CHOICE AVERAGE 65.00**

368. **CHALCEDONY STAMP SEAL. Sassanian. 3rd-7th Century A.D.** Very large, white translucent. Bearded head; sun and moon each side, wings monogram below. Measures 2.5 cm x 2 cm. Göbl 7a............................**CHOICE 150.00**

369. **CHALCEDONY STAMP SEAL. Sassanian. 3rd-7th Century A.D.** Light brown chalcedony ring-shaped seal with flower bud very clearly depicted. Measures 1.5 cm x 1.1 cm. Göbl 956....................................**CHOICE 65.00**

370. **CHALCEDONY STAMP SEAL. Sassanian. 3rd-7th Century A.D.** White/milky. Star pattern. Slim donut seal with central suspension hole. Measures 1.2 cm x 1.4 cm. Göbl 101a. Some minor chipping..................**CHOICE 60.00**

371. **JADE STAMP SEAL. Sassanian. 3rd-7th Century A.D.** Green with depiction of a zebu. Suspension hole in middle; high dome other side of seal. Diameter 1.1 cm. Göbl 53. ....**SUPERB 150.00**

372. **HEMATITE STAMP SEAL. Sassanian. 3rd-7th Century A.D.** Schematic representation of a gazelle. Measures 1.4 cm by 1.3 cm. Cf. Göbl 52a. ....**CHOICE 125.00**

373. **ORANGE CARNELIAN ELLIPSOID SEAL. 4th-5th Century A.D.** Stag standing. Göbl 51..........**SUPERB 85.00**

374. **CHALCEDONY STAMP SEAL. 4th-5th century A.D.** Eagle. Göbl 79i ....**CHOICE 60.00**

375. **CARNELIAN STAMP SEAL. 4th-5th Century A.D.** Eagle with wings open. Decorated geometric back. Scarce. ....**CHOICE 100.00**

376. **CARNELIAN STAMP SEAL. 4th-5th Century A.D.** Winged ram bust forepart. Göbl 55. ....**SUPERB 150.00**

377. **AGATE STAMP SEAL. 4th-5th century A.D.** Spider. Creamy White. Göbl-. ....**CHOICE 100.00**

378. No entry.

379. **AGATE STAMP SEAL. 4th-5th century A.D.** Lighted altar. Göbl 98a var. Unusual shape. Crude design. ....**CHOICE 150.00**

380 **ELLIPSOID SEAL. Sassanian. 5th Century A.D.** Victory "winged" figure to right holding diadem before. Very small. Measures 0.9 cm x 0.8 cm. Göbl 2a; BM Bk 1-4. Chip to one side, does not affect depiction. ....**CHOICE 125.00**

381. **STAMP SEAL. 500 A.D..** Chalcedony with lion advancing. 18 x 12 mm. Göbl 43a................................**CHOICE 75.00**

GLASS

382. **GLASS SCARABOID. Achaemenid. 6th-5th Century B.C.** Green. Depicts crescent on long staff above altar, palm each side. Below is a diminutive figure of sphinx on an altar. Measures 1.8 cm x 1.4 cm. Cf. Pitman-; Rowe-; Von Der Osten, *Newell*--. Nice color stone and very rare. ....**AVERAGE 150.00**

383. **GLASS PASTE CYLINDER SEAL. Parthian. 300 B.C.-200 A.D.** Blue-black with variegated grey-buff iridescence. Humans fighting rampant winged lions. Height 1.5 cm. Cf. Buchanan *AMI* 1049a for style. Cf. Buchanan 1048 for glass seal. Rare..**CHOICE 150.00**

384. **PERSIAN SATRAPS. c. 200 B.C.** Oval greenish yellow glass intaglio with figure on horseback brandishing sword. Pierced vertical for suspension. 23 x 16 mm. Rare. Cf. Waterman, *Tel Umar*, XIX, 3....................**CHOICE 125.00**

385. **GLASS INTAGLIO. c. 200 B.C.** Oval, clear yellow intaglio of young Satrap in tight tiara with flaps under chin. Pierced vertically for suspension. 24 x 18 mm Rare. For type glass intaglio Parthian, Cf. Waterman, *Excavations at Tel Umar, Iraq*, XIX, 3. For similar portrait see P. Bedoukian's article on Armenian Sophene and Commagen in Museum notes #23, p. 85 #18. The Zariadres portrait is similar in type. Zariadres was Satrap of Sophene located between the Tigris and Euphrates...............**CHOICE 175.00**

CYLINDER SEALS

386. **SYRIA. 3600-2900 B.C.** Brown-black limestone cylinder seal with loop at top. Linear design, rushing water with fish within. Cf. Buchanan, *Yale*, #204 var........**SUPERB 150.00**

387.   **PEDMONT JEMDET NASR. c. 3200-2900 B.C.** Clear calcite cylinder seal with lineal opposing triangles indicating mountains and valleys. Height 17 mm. Buchanan, *Yale* 203. Fine quality seal..**SUPERB 225.00**

388.   **JEMDET NASR. 3200-2900 B.C.** Dark grey terracotta cylinder seal. Linear design of tree on mound, building with two rounded door openings, rounded hut upside down. Height 20 mm. For style, Legrain, *UR Excavations*, Vol. III, 405. Buchanan, *AM*, 229 var......................**CHOICE 275.00**

389.   **PERIPHERAL JEMDET NASR.** Cream calcite cylinder seal. Depicts two leaves and cone. BMC.- Buchanan. Amiet. Height 13 mm. Very clear. ....**SUPERB 350.00**

390.   **URUK IV. Proto-Elamite. 3200-3100 B.C.** Blue frit cylinder seal. Three advancing figures carrying upright staffs. 18 mm. Very similar to pigtail figures identified by Porada. This type is not pigtailed and with larger heads. Pale grey faience cylinder seals with trace found in proto-literate levels at Diyala region. Frankfurt 162. This seal appears to be akin to Egyptian blue. Buchanan, *YBC* 155 without pigtails. Cf. Amiet, 745. ....**CHOICE 250.00**

391.   **PROTO-ELAMITE. 3200-3100 B.C. (Uratu IV).** Blue frit cylinder seal, three advancing figures with arms outstretched carrying something in hands. 2.3 cm high. Amiet *GS*, #745, Cf. Frankfurt, #162, Cf. Buchanan *YBC* #155. This blue frit cylinder seal is similar to proto-literative levels of frit cylinders found in the Diyala Region. ....**CHOICE 225.00**

392.   **JEMDET NASR. 3200-3000 B.C.** Buff seal. Linear design consisting of quatrafoil and crescents with circled dot design. Length 27 mm. Cf. BM, *Asiatic Seals*, Pl. 8a, #89843. ....**CHOICE 200.00**

393.   **JEMDET NASR. 3200-2900 B.C.** Black-grey terracotta cylinder seal. Linear design representing reeds and trees. Frankfurt, *Diyala* #157 var. Cf. Teissier-. Amiet, *GMA*-. Buchanan, *Yale*-..**CHOICE 150.00**

394.   **PEDMONT JEMDET NASR. 3200-2900 B.C.** Clear calcite cylinder seal with linear opposing triangles. Cf. Buchanan, *Yale* 203. Fine quality seal ....**SUPERB 165.00**

395.   **JEMDET NASR. 3200-2900 B.C.** Dark gray terracotta cylinder seal. Linear design of tree on mound. Building with two rounded door openings. Rounded hut upside down. 20 mm. For style, Cf. Legrain, *Ur Excavations* Vol. III, #405. Cf. Buchanan, *AM* 229 var. ....**CHOICE 225.00**

396.   **URUK IV-JEMDET NASR. 3200-2900 B.C.** White limestone cylinder seal. Crude drilling of animal with pellets in field. 14 mm. Primitive and crude. Cf. Amiet 65, 762. Buchanan, *YBC* 1429......................**AVERAGE 50.00**

397.   **URUK IV-JEMDET NASR. 3100-2900 B.C.** Grey limestone cylinder seal. Horizontal lizard. 18 mm. Cf. Frankfurt, *Diyala Region*, 461 var..........................**AVERAGE 120.00**

398.   **URUK IV-JEMDET NASR. 3100-2900 B.C.** Cream calcite cylinder seal. Geometric lozenge fish in geometric rippled water. 19 mm. Cf. Frankfurt, *Diyala Region*, 171. ....**CHOICE 125.00**

399.   **PRE-DYNASTIC. 3000-2750 B.C.** Grey beige sard cylinder seal. Advancing quadruped, palm downward. Fara type. Height 2.0 cm. Cf. Amiet *GMA*, 731 var. 20% of top of seal missing. Bold carving...............................**CHOICE 150.00**

400.   **PROTO-ELAMITE DIVERSE. 3000-2500 B.C.** Black steatite. Boar to left, tree above. 19 mm. Amiet, *GS* 103-32..**CHOICE 150.00**

401.   **PROTO-ELAMITE DIVERSE. 3000-2500 B.C.** White steatite. Linear design of figure before tree and another smaller figure. Length 32 mm. Cf. for style, Amiet *GS*, 1357..**CHOICE 200.00**

402.   **PROTO-ELAMITE MESOPOTAMIAN STYLE. 3000-2500 B.C.** White grey marble. Linear design. Length 18 mm, diameter 12 mm. ....**CHOICE 135.00**

403.   **PROTO-ELAMITE. Early Dynastic. 3000-2500 B.C.** White chalk cylinder seal. Linear design with tower and ladder, tree. 30 mm. Crude. ....**CHOICE 150.00**

404.   **PROTO-ELAMITE DIVERSE. 3000-2500 B.C.** Black steatite cylinder seal with two horses walking, line and drill pattern. 2.2 cm high. Amiet, *GS*, #B19 ......**CHOICE 125.00**

405.   **PROTO-ELAMITE DIVERSE. 3000-2500 B.C.** Black steatite cylinder seal depicting a boar running left with a tree above. Cf. Amiet, *GS* 103-32......................**CHOICE 100.00**

406.   **JEMDET NASR–PROTO-ELAMITE. 3000-2500 B.C.** Mesopotamian style white marble cylinder seal with two gazelles running left, pellets in field. Height 21 mm. Amiet *GS* 913, Buchanan, *Yale* 174-5..................**CHOICE 250.00**

407.   **PROTO-ELAMITE DIVERSE. c. 3000-2500 B.C.** Black steatite seal. Depicts two animals within two trees-linear design. Height 23 mm. Amiet, 1028-1029. Style combines both the drill and linear designs. ....**CHOICE 300.00**

408.   **PROTO-ELAMITE DIVERSE. 3000-2500 B.C.** Black steatite. Portrays a human builder and a bull in a very crude linear design. Height 22 mm. Amiet *GS*, figs. 1351-58. ....**CHOICE 150.00**

409.   **PROTO-ELAMITE DIVERSE. 3000-2500 B.C.** Black steatite seal depicting two calves advancing, bush before each. Height 13 mm. Amiet *GS*, 1054-60..**CHOICE 150.00**

410. **PROTO-ELAMITE DIVERSE. 3000-2500 B.C.** Black steatite. Human right with sword. Bull butting downwards. Another animal right 22 mm. For style, Cf. Amiet 1028. ....**CHOICE 140.00**

411. **PROTO-ELAMITE. 3000-2500 B.C.** White marble cylinder seal. Lozenge fish in stylized water ripples. 21 mm. Quality stone. Cf. Amiet, *GS* 886................**SUPERB 150.00**

412. **PROTO-ELAMITE. 3000-2500 B.C.** Grey serpentine. Irregular lines as vegetation. 8 mm. Cf. Amiet, *GS* 842-3 ....**CHOICE 75.00**

413. **PROTO-ELAMITE. 3000-2500 B.C.** Mesopotamian style. White marble cylinder seal. Two gazelles running left, pots in field. 21 mm. Cf. Amiet, *GS* 913. Buchanan, *Yale* 174-5..............................**CHOICE 150.00**

414. **PROTO-ELAMITE. 3000-2500 B.C.** White marble cylinder seal, linear design. Cf. Frankfurt, *Diyala*, #408. Amiet, *GS-*, Buchanan, *Yale*......................**CHOICE 125.00**

415. **JEMDET NASR. 3rd Millennium B.C.** Buff agate seal. Six seated pigtailed figures before one seated figure facing them. Three vases below. Length 14 mm. Cf. Buchanan 17 var. Nice style................................**CHOICE 650.00**

416. **PROTO-ELAMITE. CLASSIC. 2900-2700 B.C.** Black steatite cylinder seal. X in squares, occasional pellets. 25 mm. Amiet, *GS*. ....**CHOICE 150.00**

417. **PROTO-ELAMITE. 2900-2700 B.C.** White marble cylinder seal with linear pattern of alternating directions. 1.9 cm high. Cf. Amiet, *GS*, #1231-2, 1287. Chip and repair, otherwise choice........................**CHOICE 125.00**

418. **SYRIA. 2900-2200 B.C.** Black serpentine cylinder seal. Hero standing behind lion with arms outstretched, gazelle behind. 17 mm. Cf. Amiet, *GMA* 85.d. Frankfurt, XXXIX var. Cf. Buchanan, *Yale-*. Buchanan, *Ash.-*. Teissier, *Marcopoli* 323-3......................**CHOICE 250.00**

419. **SYRIA. 2900-2200 B.C.** Black metallic cylinder seal. Animal (gazelle?) standing, two figures before. Cf. Buchanan, *Yale*, Teissier. Crude design.....**CHOICE 150.00**

420. **EARLY DYNASTIC. Old Sumerian. 2750-2650 B.C.** Black steatite cylinder seal. Shrine vertical with side door. Two horizontal trees. Ram seated and small quadruped behind. 27 mm. This representation was used at Jemdet Nasr sights with animals at shrine. This style indicates a slightly later period, post-Jemdet Nasr. Seal broken and repaired. Amiet 65, 1029, 1054 for Proto-Elamite (c. 3000 B.C.). Cf. Buchanan, *AM* 120 for style ....**CHOICE 250.00**

421. **EARLY DYNASTIC. Old Sumerian. 2750-2650 B.C.** Terracotta cylinder seal. Traces of blue wash. Female fig. with pigtail. Tree to right. Vegetation similar to Jemdet Nasr styles. 29 mm. The type is reminiscent of the pigtail figures but with a linear style. Terracotta cylinder seals were found in the Diyala region in early dynastic find spots. Cf. Frankfurt, *Diyala*, 262 for TC seal..............**CHOICE 150.00**

422. **MESOPOTAMIA-EARLY DYNASTIC. 2750-2500 B.C.** Terracotta seal with traces of blue wash. Female figure with a pigtail, tree to right. Vegetation similar to Jemdet Nasr styles. Height 2.9 cm. Frankfurt, *Diyala* 262 for terracotta seal. ....**CHOICE 150.00**

423. **EARLY DYNASTIC III. 2750-2350 B.C.** 1st Phase. Black marble cylinder seal. Hero standing with spear stabbing lion which is attacking ram, which in turn is standing with head looking back. Arrow point above ram. 40 mm. Buchanan, *Yale* 290 and 292. A worn seal but large and rare. ....**AVERAGE 175.00.**

424. **EARLY DYNASTIC. 2750-2350 B.C.** White opaque chalcedony cylinder seal. Linear schematic winged animal with bird wings open. Cf. Buchanan, *Ash.* I, 219. ....**CHOICE 250.00**

425. **EARLY DYNASTIC II. 2700 B.C.** White chalcite cylinder seal. Seated figure before animals in combat (one a lion); human figure behind. Height 2.5 cm. Cf. Buchanan, *Yale* for combatant animals and seated figure 243. Chips to top of cylinder....................................**CHOICE 225.00**

426. **EARLY DYNASTIC II. c. 2700 B.C.** White and pink marble cylinder seal. Standing figure, small quadruped at feet, building behind. Bird flying in upper field, area of corrosion Possible inscription. Cf. Teissier-. Buchanan, *Ash.-*, Buchanan, *Yale* 243........................**CHOICE 250.00**

427. **EARLY DYNASTIC II. c. 2700 B.C.** Black serpentine cylinder seal with nude hero standing fighting an upright lion with open mouth, also another upright lion attacking a rampant goat with head right. Height 22 mm. Buchanan, *Yale* 250 and 247. A gem cylinder seal. Finely carved. ....**SUPERB 1000.00**

428. **EARLY DYNASTIC II. 2700 B.C.** Grey limestone cylinder seal with florid stylized floral design. Unfinished seal with drill holes. Cf. Von Der Osten, *Newell-*. Amiet, *GS-*. Teissier-. Amiet, *GMA*, 965-70 for style. Buchanan, *Ash*, Buchanan, *Yale*......................................**CHOICE 150.00**

429. **EARLY DYNASTIC II. 2700-2600 B.C.** Creamy marble mottled brown cylinder seal. Hero standing., arm raised between crossed upright lion and bull. Goat and lion behind. Three goats standing upright before. Star in field. 28 mm. Some pitting to surface. Cf. Buchanan, *YBC* 248. ....**CHOICE 400.00**

430. **MESOPOTAMIA. Early Dynastic II. 2750-2350 B.C.** Creamy marble, mottled brown. Hero standing, arm raised between crossed upright lion and bull, three goats standing upright before star in field. 28 mm. Buchanan, *YBC* 248. A bold depiction of this early scene...............**CHOICE 500.00**

431. **EARLY DYNASTIC II. 2600-2334 B.C.** Yellow-cream marble cylinder seal. Two standing supplicants before altar. Winged animal behind. 28 mm. Cf. Teissier, *Marcopoli Collection* 62 var. for style.........................**SUPERB 400.00**

432. **EARLY DYNASTIC III. 2600-2500 B.C.** White marble cylinder seal. Upper register contains two figures seated face to face drinking beer from straws. Lower register similar to above. Some wear. Frankfurt, *Diyala Region*, 334. Cf. Wiseman, *BMC* 1, Pl. 26, C. Upper register. ....**CHOICE 200.00**

433. **EARLY DYNASTIC III. 2600-2500 B.C.** White limestone. Hero fighting lion. Crossed upright animals. Ibex and panther behind (winged?). 15 mm x 33 mm. 30 mm long. Chips and scratches. Cf. Buchanan, *YBC* 316 var. Buchanan, *AM* 175 var. ....**AVERAGE 150.00**

434. **EARLY DYNASTIC III. 2600-2500 B.C.** Yellow-cream alabaster. Irregular tree pattern. Ram standing with head back. 29 mm. Ram worn. Cruder design than Buchanan, *AM*, 215 but ibex is similar in head treatment and attitude. ....**NEAR CHOICE 175.00**

435. **SARGONIC.** Brownish-gray calcite cylinder seal. Bearded hero, nude, in conflict with a lion, water buffalo in conflict with bearded hero in short skirt. 25 mm. Cf. Collon, *BMC* 11, 78 var. Buchanan, *BMC*, 406. Scarce. ..**CHOICE 600.00**

436. **EARLY AKKADIAN. 2334-2260 B.C.** White marble cylinder seal. Two crossed lions attacking two antelopes. 22 mm. Worn. Cf. Teissier, *Marcopoli*, 69...**AVERAGE 50.00**

437. **EARLY AKKADIAN. 2334-2154 B.C.** White marble cylinder seal. Two-panel representation of god of vegetation. Seated god before shrine. Seated figure before rope border. Separation below seated figures. Areas worn or weathered. Cf. Canes 263-214. ....**CHOICE 175.00**

438. **EARLY AKKADIAN. 2334-2154 B.C.** Gray calcite (limestone) cylinder seal. Snake god seated, terminal gate, to back. Before, standing attendant in long garment. Traces of cuneiform inscription. 24 mm. Frankfurt considered the snake-god (Ningizida) the god of fertility. Figure worn. Cf. Collon, BMC II, 186 var. ....**CHOICE 300.00**

439. **EARLY AKKADIAN. 2334-2260 B.C.** White marble. Two lions attacking two horned animals rampant between. 16 mm. Teissier #66, Buchanan *Yale* #379. A sharp example of the rare early Akkadian.............**SUPERB 400.00**

440. **POST-AKKADIAN. 2200-2150 B.C.** Black serpentine. Standing figure before seated deity, tree behind. 14 mm. Buchanan, *Ash.* 396. Worn........................**CHOICE 125.00**

441. **POST-AKKADIAN. After 2154 B.C.** Shell cylinder seal. Presentation scene, with seated deity and two worshippers. Star in field. Height 2.7 cm. Collon, *BMC* II, 299. Strong wear, weathering to surface........................**CHOICE 175.00**

442. **EARLY DYNASTIC II. 2113-2006 B.C.** Black marble. Hero standing with spear, stabbing loins of lion, who is in turn attacking a ram which stands with its head looking back. Arrow point above the ram. 40 mm. Buchanan, *Yale* 290 and 292; Buchanan, *Ash.*-. A worn seal but large and rare. ....**AVERAGE 375.00**

443. **UR III. c. 2000 B.C.** White-beige chalcedony cylinder seal. Presentation scene, goddess leads one worshipper to throned deity. No crescent or inscription. Height 2.6 cm. Cf. Collon, *British Museum Cylinder Seals* II #398......**CHOICE 125.00**

444. **SYRIAN. 2000-1900 B.C.** Black and grey serpentine cylinder seal. Standing figure drawing bow before quadruped in crude linear design. 19 mm. Cf. Teissier, *Marcopoli Collection* 365 ....**CHOICE 125.00**

445. **OLD BABYLONIAN. Geoy Tepe in North Western Iran. Early Second Millennium B.C.** Alabaster cylinder carved in relief. Bearded king standing in long garment with crown and hair tufted, clasping spear-tipped column facing. Clasping column is bearded worshiper wearing flap headdress, also in long garment. 56 mm. Cf. Pittman, *AAM* fig. 16, MMA 1886, 86.11.1. Very Rare...**CHOICE 1000.00**

446. **OLD BABYLONIAN. Geoy Tepe in North Western Iran. Early Second Millennium B.C.** Alabaster cylinder carved in relief. Crowned and bearded king kneeling before undetermined figure. 33 mm. Cf. Pittman, *AAM* fig. 16. Very rare. ....**CHOICE 500.00**

447. **ELAMITE. 2000-1500 B.C.** Black steatite pierced through top. Design of king seated with two attendants. Length 27 mm. Worn..**CHOICE 75.00**

448. **ELAMITE. 2000-1500 B.C.** White composition cylinder seal. Faience gone white. Male figure brandishing sword at sphinx standing facing. Height 2.4 cm. Traces of light blue color remain. Cf. Amiet *GS* 1976 var.......**AVERAGE 150.00**

449. **LEVANTINE. 2nd Millennium B.C.** Grey steatite. Man hunting two animals. Gazelle, cat, and short dog below. Man has quiver over shoulder. 17 mm. Buchanan 1028 var. An unusual depiction................................**CHOICE 200.00**

450. **OLD ASSYRIAN COLONY. 1920-1840 B.C.** Black serpentine carved cylinder seal. Two workers advancing, first carrying wheat to waist high container, another carrying wheat from other direction. Example of workers making beer. 17 mm. This seal purchased by Burgess from N.E. Hornsy on April 12, 1911. N.E. Hornsy purchased cylinder in "1910 at Aleppo from a man who came from the country." With display card from Burgess stating "Hittite seal cylinder, intermediate square becoming rounded." Cf. Teissier, *Marcopoli Collection* 393 (style)...............**CHOICE 350.00**

451. **PROVINCIAL STYLE (CAPPADOCIAN). 1900-1800 B.C.** Black steatite cylinder seal. Long-garmented figure with high tiara seated on high backed chair, receiving vessel from suppliant, warrior behind with bow, and another warrior with spear wearing feather (?) headdress. 23 mm. For static figures see Canes 1092E (Cappadocian?). Vertical garment rendering is found on Buchanan, *YBC* 872. The tall headdress and the presentation of vessels are similar to the Old Babylonian cylinder seals. ....**CHOICE 375.00**

452. **OLD BABYLONIAN. 1900-1600 B.C.** Black hematite cylinder seal. Shamash, the sun god, standing left, foot on stool, two worshippers before with arms raised. 22 mm. Shamash was the god of justice and law who gave protection to the poor and wronged. Porada, Morgan LIB, 531var. Cf. Buchanan, *Yale-*. Teissier, *Marcopoli Collection*, 109 var. ....**CHOICE 350.00**

453. **OLD SYRIAN, MATURE. 1850-1720 B.C.** Cream-brown calcite cylinder seal. Presentation scene: Seated figure on cat (panther), holding scepter, star above, between solar disc, before stands suppliant. Goddess holding three-pronged flail, behind standing figure 22 mm. Cf. Teissier 434-458 for style. Classical style with lovely delineation, molded and rounded forms ....**CHOICE 300.00**

454. **OLD SYRIAN, MATURE. 1850-1720 B.C. (AMORITE).** Green faience carved cylinder seal. Facing radiate figure with arms raised in long garment, winged disc above, kneeling supplicant with arms raised on each side, ram recumbent with head back. 18 mm. Teissier, *Marcopoli Collection*, for rendering of style 535. The Old Syrian style is associated with the Amorite Kingdoms in Northern Syria. This seal is of linear style dating later in the period...**SUPERB 400.00**

455. **OLD BABYLONIAN. 1844-1712 B.C.** Black hematite. The moon goddess Sin seated with animal offering before, king behind. Robed worshipper with hands clasped, and two figures behind. 22 mm. Worn on one side...**CHOICE 400.00**

456. **SYRIAN. 1850-1620 B.C.** Black hematite cylinder seal of two registers. Upper register: two seated figures facing each other; vase with straws for drinking beer, two attendants behind each figure, two kneeling figures before winged goddess. Lower register: Two bearded males facing and holding ornate column, monkey standing behind, Egyptian god Anubis standing holding ibex, winged figure walking facing, Hathor standing behind holding ibex. Teissier, banquet scene. Cf. Teissier, *Marcopoli Collection* 533 for winged deity, Anubis Cf. Teissier 513.......**SUPERB 1000.00**

457. **OLD BABYLONIAN. 1822-1750 B.C.** Black hematite cylinder seal. The king with a mace facing suppliant goddess behind is facing nude goddess. 18 mm. This nude goddess was first introduced in Mesopotamia during the reign of Apil-Sin in 1822 B.C. and remained popular for 70 years ending with the culmination of Hammurabi's reign in 1750 B.C. Collon, *BMC* III, 283..................**CHOICE 450.00**

458. **OLD BABYLONIAN. 1800-1650 B.C.** Banded agate cylinder seal. Standard presentation scene, with seated deity and two worshippers standing. 21 mm. Seated figure worn. Cf. Collon, *BMC* III, 8...............................**CHOICE 300.00**

459. **OLD BABYLONIAN. 1800-1650 B.C.** Black geothite cylinder seal. Presentation scene with seated deity. Cuneiform legend, (Samas)-AYA. Sun god and his consort. One third chip off seal surface. Cf. Collon, *BMC* III, 10. ....**CHOICE 225.00**

460. **OLD BABYLONIAN. 1800-1650 B.C.** Black hematite cylinder seal. Warrior god holding double lion headed mace with foot on lion's head. Before, suppliant goddess with arms raised with king before with raised arm. Cuneiform inscription name UTU Samas. Inscription *BMC* 551. Cf. Collon, *BMC* III, 386 var............................**CHOICE 400.00**

461. **LATE OLD BABYLONIAN. 1730-1600 B.C.** Black serpentine cylinder seal. Combat scene with warrior stabbing lion, similar rendering upside down. 24 mm. From the years of the ruler Samsuiluna, down to the last Babylonian monarch Samsuditana, this stylized design continued. These unusual glyptic styles of drilling and linear design were revived in the Neo-Assyrian types. In the Southern Turkumenia area this crude pattern was also used in the 2nd millennium. Buchanan, *YBC* 1072, Cf. Teissier, *Marcopoli Collection* 131 var. ....**CHOICE 350.00**

462. **UGARIT.   Recent 1, 1550-1450 B.C.** Grey limestone cylinder seal. Crossed rampant gazelles, large spear garlanded. 18 mm. Ras Shamra, 11. 194. Chip at top. ....**CHOICE 250.00**

463. **MITANNIAN. 1550-1350 B.C.** Faience composition cylinder seal with greenish glaze. Figure holding gazelles upright; two rampant gazelles facing; two standing figures facing tree of life; gazelles grazing below. Height 2.4 cm. Cf. Teissier: for figure standing before rampant gazelle #577; for supplicants and gazelles #573. Some wear to seal. ....**CHOICE 150.00**

464. **MITANNIAN. 1500-1350 B.C.** Elaborate style black serpentine cylinder seal. Funnel-shaped head gods standing with raised arms before star, one on each side, standing on animals, antelope standing below star. 27 mm. Canes 1 1022 var. This seal is typical of Elamite elements and represents the cut Mitannian style of North Eastern Iran. The figure standing on his characteristic animal can be seen in the bas-relief of Maltaya...**CHOICE 300.00**

465. **MITANNIAN. 1550-1350 B.C.** White faience composition cylinder rhyolite seal. Two worshippers standing facing sacred tree, behind, two rampant lions facing. A ritual scene of worship and prayer. Cf. Tessier, *Marcopoli Collection*, #573. A worn seal...........................**NEAR CHOICE 150.00**

466. **MIDDLE ASSYRIAN–KASSITE. 1500-1300 B.C.** Blue-green glass paste cylinder seal. Centaur feeding goat from basket, star of Ishtar above, rhomb below. 21 mm. For centaurs, Cf. Ward, 631-33. For human torso centaur, Cf. Frankfort XXXI, f. identified as late Kassite. Cf. Collon, *BMC* 386. This pastoral scene is quite unusual as most centaurs in this period are in a warrior attitude. ....**SUPERB 450.00**

467. **MIDDLE ELAMITE. 1500-1200 B.C.** Blue-green faience cylinder seal. Linear seal with asymmetrical patterns. 20 mm. Cf. Amiet *GS* 2106. ....**CHOICE-SUPERB 80.00**

468. **MIDDLE ELAMITE. 1500-1100 B.C.** Grey faience cylinder seal. Herringbone pattern around seal, very light. 29 mm. Cf. Amiet *GS* 2097. ....**AVERAGE 50.00**

469. **MITANNIAN. 14th-13th Century B.C.** Buff frit seal. Design of birds in a row with geometric design below. Length 16 mm. Cf. Buchanan 950 var........**CHOICE 150.00**

470. **LEVANTINE or NEO-HITTITE. 1400-1100 B.C.** Black steatite cylinder seal. Crude design with two elongated stick figures seated, sipping beer from straw. This region encompassed Palestine and the Syrian coastal area. Teissier, *Marcopoli Collection*, 672 var. Cf. Buchanan, *Ash.* #1036 var. ....**CHOICE 300.00**

471. **LEVANTINE. 13th Century B.C.** Black steatite cylinder seal. Crude linear animal group. Goat standing (vertical animal) or seated goat herd. Height 1.9 cm. Buchanan, *AM*, 1019 var. Made during the "Dark Age" upheavals during the 1200s B.C...**CHOICE 300.00**

472. **MIDDLE ASSYRIAN. 1300-1200 B.C.** Agate cylinder seal. Horse upright being tamed by human figure, nonsensical cuneiform legend. 31 mm. For horse, Cf. Teissier, *Marcopoli Collection*, 141. Middle Syrian seals are very scarce. Broken off at base. ....**CHOICE 250.00**

473. **NEO-ASSYRIAN. 900-800 B.C.** Linear style. Black serpentine cylinder seal. Worshipper standing, facing either side of sacred tree, above which is winged sun disc, crescent in sky with star, plant below. The winged disc was a symbol of the Assyrian national god, Ashur. Teissier, *Marcopoli Collection*, #226. Upper two thirds of register present. ....**CHOICE 200.00**

474. **NEO-ASSYRIAN.** Early drilled style. Black steatite cylinder seal with bronze knob at top and traces of copper encasement to bottom. Two winged genii worshiping Sin, crescent on staff and pedestal, the emblem of Marduk, spade on staff and pedestal behind. 31 mm. Cf. Buchanan, *AM* 636 var. Cf. Canes 705 var...............................**CHOICE 550.00**

475. **NEO-ASSYRIAN. 9th Century B.C.** Black steatite. Linear style. Attendant standing before table with bull's head atop. Seated deity to other side. Length 32 mm. Buchanan 592. Worn seal. ....**CHOICE 285.00**

476. **NEO-ASSYRIAN. 900-800 B.C.** Red-pink chalcedony seal. Hero running and brandishing a spear at an antelope, also a griffin leaping toward him. Star and crescent above. Height 28 mm. For similar subject but archer, Teissier, *Marcopoli Collection*, #264. Newell-; Porada-. Highest quality and lovely color seal. ....**SUPERB 600.00**

477. **NEO-ASSYRIAN. 900-800 B.C.** Pink chalcedony seal. Two griffins leaping with wings open, crescent and 8-pointed star above, plant below. Height 32 mm. Buchanan, *Yale-*; Etude Tajan 10/13/95 #109. The execution and composition of this high animation is extremely rare during this epoch. Beautiful color and style. ....**SUPERB 650.00**

478. **NEO-ASSYRIAN. 900-750 B.C.** Light green-grey steatite. Design of ram walking with head turned back. Sacred tree before, crescent above. Length 28 mm. Buchanan, *Ashmolean* 588-9......................................**CHOICE 125.00**

479. **KASSITE–NEO-ELAMITE. 9th-8th Century B.C.** Faience linear cylinder seal with brown color on inscriptions. Two birds confronting each other, above them a crescent. Similar to several in Buchanan. Quite stylized. 22mm. Cf. Buchanan Pl. 41, 619, 620 var...................**CHOICE 150.00**

480. **KASSITE–NEO-ELAMITE. 9th-8th Century B.C.** Green-blue faience cylinder seal. Two birds, wings spread facing left, linear border, perhaps dots but worn. 24 mm. Similar types, Cf. Buchanan, *Ancient Near Eastern Seals*, p. 112, p. 141:619-21. ....**AVERAGE 50.00**

481. **KASSITE–NEO-ELAMITE. 9th-8th Century B.C.** Blue faience cylinder seal.   Hunting contests, hunter with a scimitar (?) running toward an animal (antelope). Animal has head turned behind him.   There is a star between them, which usually symbolizes a sacred tree.   A very popular theme in Neo-Assyrian art. 23 mm. Pierpont Morgan Library Collection, vol. 1, Pl. LXXXVIII, LXXXIX XC 610-622 var. ....**AVERAGE 75.00**

482. **KASSITE–NEO-ELAMITE. 9th-8th Century B.C.** Linear style, orange marble cylinder seal. Hero shooting arrow at ibex rampant, ram running below. 24 mm. Cf. Canes, 620 var. Nice color stone. ....**AVERAGE 125.00**

483. **KASSITE–NEO-ELAMITE. 9th-8th Century B.C.** Creamy white and green chalcedony cylinder seal, with bronze pin in top. Hero in running attitude shooting arrow at antelope running, head turned back. 25 mm. Cf. Teissier, *Marcopoli Collection*, 148. Buchanan, *AM* 574. Canes 617 var. ....**CHOICE 250.00**

484. **KASSITE–NEO-ELAMITE. 9th-8th Century B.C.** Black steatite cylinder seal. Winged hero running holding knife, ram leaping before him. 28 mm. Cf. Buchanan, *AM* 582. ....**CHOICE 275.00**

485. **NEO-ASSYRIAN. 9th-8th Century B.C.** Green-blue faience cylinder seal. Two birds with wings spread facing left. Linear border perhaps dots but worn. Height 2.4 cm. For similar types, Cf. Buchanan, *Ancient Near Eastern Seals* p.112, Pl. 41: 619, 621...........................**AVERAGE 100.00**

486. **MITANNIAN. 9th-8th Century B.C.**   Faience linear cylinder seal. With blown color on inscriptions. Two birds confronting each other; above and between them, a crescent. Height 2.2 cm. Buchanan, Pl. 41, 619, 620 var. Similar to several in Buchanan. Stylized. ....**CHOICE 150.00**

487. **NEO-ASSYRIAN. 900-700 B.C.** Green-blue glazed faience cylinder seal. Two bird-men confronting each other. Tessier, *Marcopoli Collection*, 182. Nice color but pitting to surface. ....**CHOICE 125.00**

488. **NEO-ASSYRIAN. 900-700 B.C.**   Faience cylinder seal. Geometric pattern. 2 cm. Teissier...............**CHOICE 75.00**

489. **KASSITE–NEO-ELAMITE. 900-700 B.C.** Black serpentine cylinder seal. Ibex and goat rampant, facing tree, star behind. Cuneiform inscription in field. 25 mm. Novack, *MAM* 36. Cf. Canes 591 var. ....**CHOICE 325.00**

490. **NEO-ASSYRIAN. 900-700 B.C.** Buff faience cylinder seal. Archer standing shooting an arrow at a gazelle. A crescent in the field.   Height 27 mm.   Buchanan 617. ....**CHOICE 150.00**

491. **NEO-ASSYRIAN. 900-700 B.C.**   Buff faience linear cylinder seal. With blown color on inscriptions. Two birds advancing with wings up. Height 27 mm. Buchanan, *Ash.* 623. ....**CHOICE-SUPERB 165.00**

492. **NEO-ELAMITE. 900-700 B.C.** Black steatite cylinder seal. Ram standing, crescent above. 11 mm. Unfinished seal with central hole started but not completed. Cf. Amiet, *GS* 2189. ....**CHOICE 125.00**

493. **NEO-ELAMITE. 900-700 B.C.** Agate cylinder seal. Hero standing holding lion by paw and tail, star and crescent above, bush below. As in the Novack seal, the hero's limbs cross over and overlap creating a continuous band of relief. This is contemporary while the star and crescent indicate Neo-Assyrian affinities; the flattened headdress of the hero and the style put this seal in the Neo-Elamite period and region.   Novack, *MAM*, 37. Cf. Canes, 826 var. Cf. Buchanan, *AM* 674 var. 25 mm. ....**AVERAGE 85.00**

494. **NEO-ASSYRIAN. 900-700 B.C.** Black marble cylinder seal. Standing goddess, Ishtar, in nimbus of stars, raised before altar, above which is seven stars of the Pleadies, crescent above. 18 mm. Ishtar was the principal goddess of the Assyrians. She was worshipped as an astrological deity. The seven stars (Pleadies) represent the heavens.   Cf. Teissier, *Marcopoli Coll.*, 210-14 var. ....**CHOICE 350.00**

495. **NEO-ASSYRIAN. 900-700 B.C.** Black pyro-phyllite. Worshipper before seated deity, crescent above, bird between, scorpion above quadruped. Height 25 mm. ....**CHOICE 450.00**

496. **NEO-ASSYRIAN. 883-612 B.C.** Black serpentine cylinder seal. Linear style. Three worshipers: one standing with staff, figure behind with arm raised, before is figure with arm raised and holding bow. Height 2.5 cm. Cf. Buchanan *Yale*; Buchanan *Ash.* 599 var.; Teissier-. Worn....**CHOICE 150.00**

497. **NEO-ASSYRIAN. 800-700 B.C.** Linear style.   White marble cylinder seal. Two standing supplicants, arms raised, before seated deity, bull behind with crescent on head, winged sun disc above. Porada, Morgan-. Buchanan, *Yale*-Teissier, *Marcopoli Collection*-.   Von Der Osten, *Newell*. ....**CHOICE 300.00**

498. **KASSITE–NEO-ELAMITE. 800-700 B.C.** Linear style. Black serpentine cylinder seal. Archer on one knee aiming at griffin, plant between, crescent above, traces of inscription or border above. 24 mm. Cf. Teissier, *Marcopoli Collection*, 147. ....**CHOICE 250.00**

499. **NEO-ASSYRIAN. 800-700 B.C.** Linear style.   Black serpentine cylinder seal. Archer running, dispatching arrow at running goat with head facing back, star in field. Cf. Eisen, Moore-. Buchanan, *Ash.*-. Teissier, *Marcopoli Collection* 156 var. Porada.....................**SUPERB 450.00**

500.   **NEO-BABYLONIAN. 8th-7th Century B.C.** Cream marble cylinder seal. Male hero restraining rampant sphinx and ostrich; rhomb in lower field. Height 1.9 cm. Cf. Buchanan, *Ash.* 661 var.; Cf. Canes 670 and 673 var. Weathered surface. Scarce............**PARTS CHOICE 125.00**

501.   **KASSITE—NEO-ELAMITE. 8th-7th Century B.C.** Green faience cylinder seal. Archer standing in long garment, drawing bow, sphinx standing, crescent in field, plant between. 8 mm x 25 mm. Cf. Canes 611-615. This rendering is dated to about 800 B.C. ....**CHOICE 200.00**

502.   **NEO-BABYLONIAN. 8th-7th Century B.C.** Cream marble cylinder seal. Modeled style of male hero restraining rampant sphinx and ostrich, rhomb in lower field. 19 mm. Cf. Buchanan, *AM* 661 var. Cf. Canes 760, 763 var. Scarce. Weathered surface parts...............**CHOICE 80.00**

503.   **NEO-ASSYRIAN. 800-600 B.C.** Blue-green glazed frit cylinder seal. Two panels of left-facing chevrons. Height 3.4 cm. Small chip at top. ....**CHOICE 100.00**

504.   **NEO-ASSYRIAN. 800-600 B.C.** Grey faience cylinder seal. Linear design of birds walking. 26 mm. Buchanan 623. ....**CHOICE 125.00**

505.   **NEO-BABYLONIAN. 700-600 B.C.** Brown-olive chalcedony marble seal with large suspension hole. Lion with one paw on back of another animal. Neo-Babylonian cut style. 20 mm long, c.10 mm diameter. Buchanan, *Ash.* 651 for style. Scarce...................**CHOICE 275.00**

506.   **NEO-BABYLONIAN. 625-539 B.C.** Creamy chalcedony pyramid-shaped seal. Worshipper before altar with arms raised in drilled style. This drilled style was prominent during the Neo-Babylonian period. Von Der Osten, *Newell Collection*, 482...........................**SUPERB 200.00**

507.   **LATE NEO-ASSYRIAN. 600 B.C.** Yellow orange chert cylinder seal. Depicts an archer in a pointed cap, kneeling and drawing a bow at an ibex rampant. Height 1.6 cm. Ravn, *Danish*, 156. Canes, 813 var............**CHOICE 350.00**

508.   **ACHAEMENID PERIOD. 522-424 B.C.** Yellow-orange chert cylinder seal. Archer in pointed cap, kneeling, drawing bow at ibex rampant. Aramaic inscription "WAZA." 16 mm. Ravn, *Danish*, 156. Cf. Canes, 813 var. .....**CHOICE 350.00**

509.   **PARTHIAN. 300 B.C.-200 A.D.** Blue-black glass paste cylinder seal. Variegated grey-buff iridescence. Humans fighting rampant winged lions. 15 mm. For style, Cf. Buchanan, *AMI*, 1049a. For glass seal, Cf. Buchanan 1048. Rare. ....**CHOICE 175.00**

WRITING

510.   **SUMERIAN. 3000-2500 B.C.** Cuneiform tablet. Administrative text. Sara type. Lists names and numbers in two columns of six and four lines. Reverse uninscribed. 53 x 55 mm. Provenance uncertain. Sumerian cuneiform tablets are quite scarce.................................**CHOICE 750.00**

511.   **SARGONIC. 24th-23rd Century B.C.** Buff terracotta cuneiform tablet. Economic account of sale of sheep. A simple test listing fields and their crops: Thus 30 less 3 (fat-tailed) sheep field/26 lambs field/20 less two/20 less 1 reeds. Measures 37 x 36 mm. Half of tablet. Very rare..**CHOICE 850.00**

512.   **UR III. 2113-2006 B.C.** Cuneiform tablet. Receipt of cattle. Obverse: One young gazelle/for the fattening shed/delivery by Ilallum/ur-Ban was the overseer. Reverse: On the 20th day/from Abbasaga/withdrawn/on the 17th month/the year when the high priestess of the sacred hall of Inanna was installed. ....**SUPERB 275.00**

513.   **UR III. 2113-2006 B.C. Reign of Ibbi-Sin.** Dark grey-black terracotta cuneiform tablet. Economic account of a transaction of cattle stating 37 cows, 44 oxen, 8 cows, 17 cows. Dated to the first year of Ibbi-Sin, seventh month. From the city of Umma. Measures 51 x 35 mm. Quarter of tablet present. Writing superb. ....**SUPERB 300.00**

514.   **UR III. 2113-2006 B.C.** Grey-black cuneiform tablet. Economic account of expenditure of barley. Sealed with cylinder seal with partial name. From the city of Umma. Measures 52 x 40 mm. Half of one side of tablet. ....**CHOICE 200.00**

515.   **UR III. 2113-2006 B.C.** Grey-black cuneiform tablet. Economic account. Sealed with a cylinder seal. From Umma. Measures 43 x 29mm. Half of tablet present. ....**CHOICE 200.00**

516.   **UR III. 2113-2006 B.C.** Brown terracotta cuneiform tablet. Account of offering of grain and one grass-fed bull for the house of (temple). From the city of Umma. Measures 46 x 40 mm. Half of tablet. One side very nice.......**CHOICE 250.00**

517.   **UR III. 2113-2006 B.C. Su-Sin Year 4.** Dark grey terracotta cuneiform tablet. Dated to the fourth year of the reign of Su-Sin. Sealing with name present on cylinder seal. From Umma. Measures 39 x 36 mm. Half of tablet. ....**AVERAGE-CHOICE 150.00**

518. **UR III. 2113-2006 B.C. Amar-Sin. 2046-2038 B.C.** Cuneiform tablet dated 2038 B.C. Economic document receipt of domestic animals. Obverse refers to 1 ox, 4 sheep, 1 male goat, on the 17th day from Abbasaga Ahuwer. Reverse: Accepting them on the 12th month, the year when Huhnuri was destroyed. Amar-Sin, King of Ur, divided the priorities of his reign between military expeditions and temple building. The private sector in business and private property grew during his reign. Minor hairline cracks. ....**SUPERB 275.00**

519. **UR III. Reign of Amar-Sin. 2046-2038 B.C.** Cuneiform tablet with sealing dated 2040 B.C. from Niovur. Inscription reads: Obverse: 2 cross beams mats/their size is...sar each/30 traveling baskets of 30 sila each broken. Reverse: From (official) Lu ... seal of Ur-D-Shul-Pa-E./contribution of [broken]/1st month) of Nippur (month)/the year when Shash Rom (year) was destroyed. Cylinder seal impression with name of Ur-D-Shul-Pa-E and seated figure. 41 x 46 mm. Baked for preservation. Chip to reverse ....**CHOICE 325.00**

520. **UR III. Amar-Sin Year 4: 2043 B.C.** Light red-brown terracotta cuneiform tablet. Economic text. Dated to the fourth year of Amar-Sin. Trace of sealing with the name present. From the city of Umma. 40 x 43 mm. Flaking. One-third of tablet. Writing choice...................**CHOICE 250.00**

521. **UR III. Reign of Amar-Sin. Dated 2043 B.C.** Dark grey terracotta tablet. Dated "Year after the throne of Enlil was built." Measures 34 x 34 mm. Fraction of tablet resulting in four large chips..**CHOICE 250.00**

522. **UR III. Reign of Amar-Sin. Dated 2037 B.C.** Buff terracotta tablet of economic food rations. Interesting listings such as 1 woven basket, oil, onions, seasonings, and beer. Dated day, month, and year: 10th month, 12th day and 8th year of the reign of Amar-Sin. Measures 25 x 20 mm. Similar to Sinst tab. I-740 or I-713. Cuneiform writing superb. ....**CHOICE 300.00**

523. **UR III. Reign of Su-Sin. Dated 2033 B.C.** Dark grey surface cuneiform tablet fragment with year formula present. 45 x 42 mm. Rough, flaked clay ....**AVERAGE 100.00**

524. **UR III. Reign of Su-Sin. Dated 2033 B.C.** Dark grey terracotta cuneiform tablet. Economic account of sale of animals at the city of Umma. Listed animals are: 1 barley fed sheep, 1 barley-fed sheep and two lambs, 2 goats, 3 lambs, 1 goat. Received from an individual named Gu-Nammu. Dated fourth month of the fifth year of the reign of Su-Sin. Measures 31 x 24 mm. One-half fragment present, but contains superb cuneiform writing.............**CHOICE 275.00**

525. **EARLY OLD BABYLONIAN. 1934-1924 B.C.** Clay cone tablet of King Lipit-Ishtar of Isin. Commemorates the building of a courthouse in Isin. In Sumerian language. Measures 9.5 cm x 4.5 cm (at widest point) Cf. Hallo, *Bibliotheca Orientalis* 18. Half fragment...**CHOICE 300.00**

526. **OLD BABYLONIAN. 1894-1595 B.C.** Terracotta cuneiform tablet fragment. Includes part of date formula. 3½ lines present. 3.2 cm x 2.3 cm. ....**CHOICE 150.00**

527. **OLD BABYLONIAN. 1894-1595 B.C.** Terracotta cuneiform tablet. Grain account includes 30 gin of grain and 3½ gin 2 mina. Five lines. Measures 3.5 cm. x 3.2 cm. Bottom and back obliterated......................**CHOICE 300.00**

528. **MARI ON THE EUPHRATES. 18th Century B.C.** Terracotta cuneiform tablet. Dated during the reign of King Zimri-Lim. Five lines of writing dated year E, month 3. Record of economic exchange. Sealed with elements of design of heifer and calf suckling. Rare. ....**CHOICE 450.00**

529. **OLD BABYLONIAN. 1792-1600 B.C.** Cuneiform tablet. Economic receipt for several animals. Measures 2.6 x 2.8 cm. From the time of Hammurabi. Rough, but restored. ....**AVERAGE 300.00**

530. **NEO-BABYLONIAN. c. 604-562 B.C.** Brick fragment. Inscribed in cuneiform. Measures 5.5 x 3 cm. Probably from the time of Nebuchadnezzer...................**AVERAGE 400.00**

531. **NEO-BABYLONIAN. Nebuchadnezzar II. 604-562 B.C.** Terracotta brick fragment. Measures 75 x 55 mm, 45 mm wide. Partial cuneiform inscription of the whole text which reads: "Nebuchadnezzar, King of Babylon, provider of the temples Esangil and Ezida, foremost heir of Nabopolassar, King of Babylon." Nebuchadnezzar was celebrated for the splendor of his rebuilt city, Babylon, his military might and his important role in Biblical history. Although he conquered Jerusalem 586 B.C., Nebuchadnezzar is seen in Jewish tradition in a favorable light. Straw was used to make the bricks and in this particular fragment, impressions of the straw can still be seen. Cf. Langdon, *Die NeuBabylonischen Konigsinschriften*, Leipzig, 191 1, p. 202. .**CHOICE 450.00**

532. **NEO-ASSYRIAN. 600 B.C.** Clay tablet of an administrative text with witness names. From the site of Assur. Measures 50 x 26 mm. ....**SUPERB 250.00**

WESTERN ASIATIC

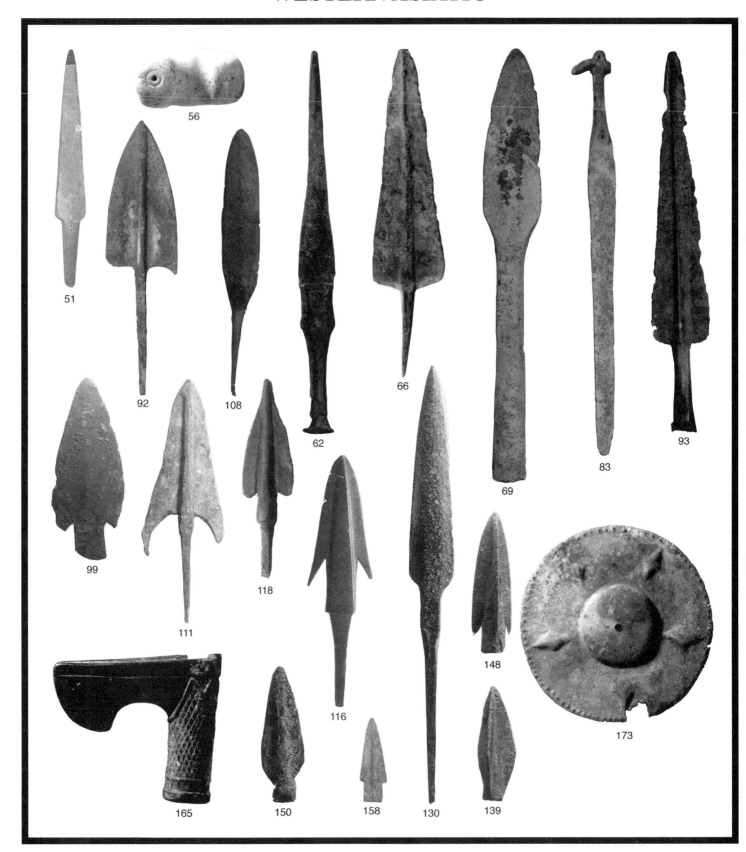

51

56

92

108

62

66

69

83

93

99

111

118

148

116

173

165

150

158

130

139

PLATE 3

183

194

191

182

206

197

203

216

208

252

178

232

233

254

267

218

263

262

518

PLATE 4

WESTERN ASIATIC

271

275

282

285

295

299

339

293

360

320

353

418

395

393

394

387

PLATE 5

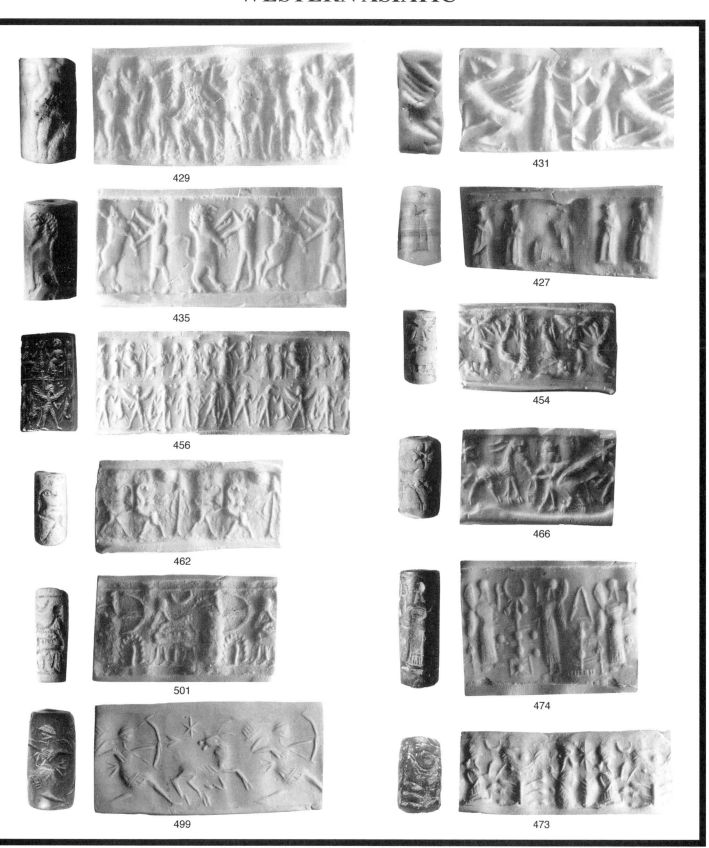

429

431

435

427

456

454

462

466

501

474

499

473

PLATE 6

ANCIENT HOLY LAND

The term "Holy Land" has been used rather loosely by scholars and laymen alike. It is often used to refer to the modern state of Israel, e.g., "visit the Holy Land on El Al airlines." In addition to this usage, the area of Syria and Palestine known in Biblical times as the land of Canaan is sometimes called by Biblical scholars "the Holy Land." For this reason in Jewish and Christian popular usage, this land of Canaan is also known as the Holy Land or the Promised Land. In the art world today the term Holy Land most often today refers to an area which encompasses in whole or in part the modern countries of Syria, Lebanon, Jordan, the Sinai area of Egypt, and Israel. This area is referred to as the Holy Land by students of ancient art because most of the major events of the Judaeo-Christian Bible occurred within its borders and it is thus the focus of Biblical archaeology. For example, the Kingdom of Israel under David and Solomon when it reached its greatest extent included most of this area.

As we noted above the Bible sometimes refers to the area or various parts of it as the land of Canaan. In Biblical times, Canaan was usually defined as the part of Syria and Palestine lying between the Mediterranean Sea and the Jordan River where Israel arose c. 1200 B.C. The name is probably derived from a term meaning "maker or dealer in purple-dyed goods." In the Bible, Canaanite sometimes has the technical meaning of "merchant" (see Isaiah 23:8 for example). It was inhabited by a number of different peoples and tribes mostly of Semitic origin. The Bible mentions the Jebusites, Hivites, Amorites, and Hittites, among others. The culture of these "Canaanites" extended back to at least the Neolithic period as excavations have shown. Important Biblical sites such as Beersheba were established as early as the Chalcolithic period. Canaanite culture was, by no means, as uniform as Egyptian culture. Canaanite art was eclectic in nature. Although many of the ornaments are Egyptian, the figures wear Asiatic dress, and the many depictions of lions found are a feature of Assyrian or Hittite art. The famed Megiddo ivories dating from the 13th century B.C. are a good example. They reflect the same mixture of styles, plus a strong Aegean influence as well. Canaanite civilization for the most part did not produce great monuments like those found in Egypt and Mesopotamia, but its physical remains, pottery, bronzes, jewelry, etc., shed much illumination on the life of its people. It reached its height in the Bronze Age when the mythic epics of the Canaanite deities such as Baal, Astarte, and local deities such as Melquarth formed the basis of the synchristic religion of the people throughout the area. Political power was for the most part vested in city states such as Jericho and Megiddo, but the Israelite conquest in the Late Bronze Age bought with it a new cultural identity, although much of the material artifacts showed little change. This was probably because Canaanite culture, including the material culture and art forms, its Semitic language, and literary forms, as well as some religious ideas and practices, were shared by the concurring Israelites. Other aspects of the Canaanite culture were anathema, such as sacred prostitution and human sacrifice. For this reason the Bible tells us that the Lord commanded the Israelites to destroy the Canaanites. According to the Biblical narrative, following the conquest the great Canaanite city states lay in ruins and the belief in monotheism, which was at the core of the Hebrew religion, gradually took a firm hold on the people. Soon after Israel's emergence in Canaan, three new terms tended to replace Canaan in general usage: Israel for the interior highlands, the stronghold of the Israelites; Phoenicia for the northern coast which maintained its "Canaanite" character; and Philistia for the southern coast which had been conquered by the "Sea Peoples," the Philistines of the Bible.

The Kingdom of Israel was the name both of the United Kingdom of the Israelites under Kings Saul, David, and Solomon (c. 1020-c. 922 B.C.) and of the political unit formed by the ten northernmost Israelite tribes (Asher, Dan, Ephraim, Gad, Issachar, Manasseh, Naphtali, Reuben, Simeon, and Zebulun) when they revolted against the Davidic dynasty after the death of Solomon. The territory of the latter included what was left of the Davidic dynasty's holdings east of the Jordan River and extended south to a few kilometers north of Jerusalem, the capital of Judah, where the Davidic dynasty still held power. The Northern Kingdom's own capital moved several times until King Omri finally established it permanently at Samaria c. 875 B.C.

The first king of Israel, the Northern Kingdom, was Jeroboam but he failed to establish a firm dynasty. Throughout its short history Israel was continually rocked by bloody dynastic changes. The small nation was constantly harassed by strong enemies and experienced only two brief periods of expansion in the 9th and 8th centuries before it was destroyed by Assyria in 722-721 B.C.

When King Solomon died in 922 B.C., ancient Israel was divided into the Southern Kingdom of Judah and the Northern Kingdom of Israel. Comprising the tribes of Benjamin and Judah, the Southern Kingdom outlasted its Northern rival, perhaps because of the strength of its capital, Jerusalem. Judah collapsed in 587 B.C. when it was overrun by the Babylonians.

Although the Israelite kingdoms of the Biblical period left little in the way of great archaeological art (almost nothing remains of Solomon's temple, for example), their cultural and religious legacy was great.

Phoenicia was the ancient Greek name for the area extending from Mount Carmel north to the Eleutherus River in Syria. The Phoenicians were linguistically and culturally related to the Canaanites.

Already inhabited in Paleolithic times, Phoenicia developed into a manufacturing and trading center early in Near Eastern history. Cedars from its mountainous hinterland were imported by the Old Kingdom Egyptians c. 2800-c. 2200 B.C. By the 2nd millennium B.C. a number of Phoenician and Syrian cities achieved preeminence as seaports and vigorously traded in purple dyes and dyestuffs, glass, cedar wood, wine, weapons, and metal and ivory artifacts.

Divided by the Lebanon Mountains into small, loosely leagued city-states, Phoenicia was never politically strong. During Phoenicia's period of independence, individual Phoenician cities interacted with the rising state of Israel. In the 10th century B.C., King Solomon employed men and materials supplied by Hiram of Tyre to build his temple at Jerusalem. He joined with Hiram in sending sailing expeditions into the Red Sea and possibly also into the Mediterranean. The Bible also records personal and political contacts between the kings of the Northern Kingdom of Israel and Phoenician rulers.

During the early years of the 1st millennium B.C., Phoenicians explored the Mediterranean and perhaps even farther. During this period the Phoenician culture reached its peak. The Phoenician alphabet, devised in the 2nd millennium B.C. and adapted by the Greeks about 800 B.C. or earlier, was subsequently transmitted to Western Europe through Rome.

Phoenician art represents a direct extension of pre-existing Canaanite traditions and, as such, displays much eclecticism, drawing forms and motifs from the art of contemporary civilizations. This blending of motifs of diverse origins to create original and aesthetically unified art objects is a basic characteristic of all Phoenician art. The art of the Phoenicians in the west shows a similar blending, with an admixture of local ideas. Skilled in most media, Phoenician artists excelled in glass making, ivory carving, metal engraving, ornamental sculpture, and gold jewelry, as well as pottery and terracotta sculpture. Much material finds its way into the art market from modern Lebanon, and Phoenician art is sought after by many astute collectors today.

In the Hellenistic, Roman and Byzantine periods the art of the Holy Land reflected the tastes generally prevalent in the times. As a somewhat provincial area, however, they are often not in the highest style. The crafts were, however, highly developed; for example, some of the finest glass in the Roman Empire has been found in the Holy Land.

As can readily be seen, the art of the Holy Land, both in the pre-Biblical and Biblical periods, and even in the post-Biblical periods, often does not exhibit the technical sophistication and grander of the art of other ancient cultures. It does, however, have a special historical and cultural significance. Many of the "great" finds of Biblical archaeology, like the Dead Sea Scrolls, are noted more for their historic value than their artistic merit. The material remains which do survive, however, particularly those of the common people of the Holy Land, provide endless fascination for the scholar and collector alike.

AMULETS, SEALS AND SCARABS

Seals, scarabs and other small amulets are some of the most interesting items frequently found in Holy Land excavations. Most amulets are of stone and often represent various animals. They are often highly stylized but realistic types are found as well. Amulets in other materials such as faience are found with some regularity. Seals are usually of the stamp variety often in steatite or other soft stones, but other stones and materials are also found. Cylinder seals in various materials are found with some frequency as well. Many of the scarabs and scaraboids from the Holy Land date, not surprisingly, to the Hycksos period and are usually made of steatite; in fact, some of the finest Hycksos scarabs known were found in the Holy Land. Scarabs and scaraboids of other periods, some of which exhibit local peculiarities in various materials, are also fairly common.

TOOLS AND WEAPONS

Stone tools and weapons, such as arrow and mace heads, weights, celts and the like, were in use from the Neolithic period onward. Metal arrowheads and other weapons are found in large numbers from the Bronze Age onward and can be easily dated by style and workmanship.

POTTERY

Pottery finds in all periods from the Chalcolithic on are usually extensive, and pottery is the tool archaeologists use most in the Holy Land to date finds. Much work was done by archaeologists to establish the dating of Holy Land pottery and it is now very well established. Although the pottery was often rather simply decorated, sometimes with a nice slip or incised geometric pattern, some periods, such as the bichrome period in the Bronze Age, saw the production of beautifully painted pottery.

TERRACOTTA

Terracotta sculpture, although not as varied as in other areas, was quite popular in the Holy Land, particularly in the Bronze Age and Greco-Roman Periods. The Bronze Age sculptures are usually rather stylized but the later sculptures are realistic in the Greco-Roman manner. Most represent various deities as usual.

STONE AND GLASS

Stone objects are many and varied from Holy Land excavations, ranging from beautifully decorated ossuaries and sarcophagi to finely modeled stone vessels. Stone sculpture was also common in many periods. Softer stones such as limestone and alabaster seem to have been preferred and local volcanic stones were also in use. Some of the finest glass from the Greco-Roman period comes from the Holy Land. Some of the glass makers were so famous they signed their works much as painters do today.

LAMPS

The use of oil lamps in the funerary ritual was an important part of funerary practice in the Holy Land from very early times. Thus literally tens of thousands of lamps were preserved in sealed tombs and graves. For this reason we have a better record of the development of the oil lamp from the Holy Land than we do from many other areas. Lamps were usually of clay; the early ones were in the shape of shallow dishes or shells. By the Greek period, lamps became closed vessels, and in Roman times they were highly decorated with molded scenes. We can learn much about religious beliefs, both pagan and Judaeo-Christian, from the decoration on these lamps. Holy Land oil lamps are much in demand, both by lamp collectors and collectors of antiquities in general.

WRITING

Some of the most important antiquities found in the Holy Land were the written records. This is because any written records from the area might shed some light on the Bible. This is true of a name found on a seal as much as it is of a Dead Sea Biblical scroll. Many different languages and forms of writing were in use during various periods and in various parts of the Holy Land. Texts have been found written on leather, papyrus, and other materials including various metals in a number of languages and scripts, written on clay tablets in cuneiform script, inscribed in ink on pottery shreds (ostraca), stamped as seal impressions (bulae), or inscribed on the seals themselves, inscribed on objects of various materials particularly metal and glass, carved on stone monuments, and painted on walls and other objects. Since the Holy Land was one of the major crossroads of trade and travel in antiquity, almost every type of writing in use in the Mediterranean area at one time or another is found. Languages range the gamut from native languages such as Hebrew, Aramaic, Canaanite, and Phoenician to international languages such as Greek and Latin. Needless to say, any written object is highly desirable to most collectors.

JEWELRY

Jewelry, made both of precious metals and base metals, is often found in Holy Land excavations, particularly graves, since it was the custom to bury the deceased with his or her finery. Grave robbing was not the millennia-long industry it was in Egypt, perhaps because there was no centralized burial ground for royalty like the Valley of the Kings to constantly inspire tomb robbers with visions of untold wealth. Many intact and relatively intact burials have been found, albeit mostly of ordinary people rather than nobility, but even common people had some form of personal adornment in most periods of antiquity.

HOLY LAND POTTERY I

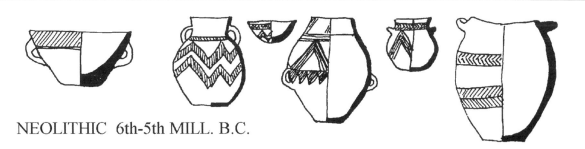

NEOLITHIC 6th-5th MILL. B.C.

CHALCOLITHIC 4th MILL. B.C.

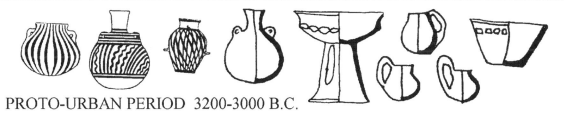

PROTO-URBAN PERIOD 3200-3000 B.C.

EARLY BRONZE AGE I 3000-2900 B.C.

EARLY BRONZE AGE II 2900-2650 B.C.

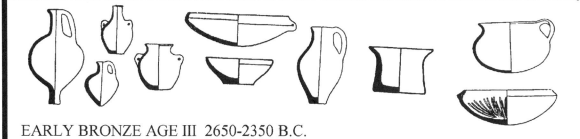

EARLY BRONZE AGE III 2650-2350 B.C.

HOLY LAND POTTERY II

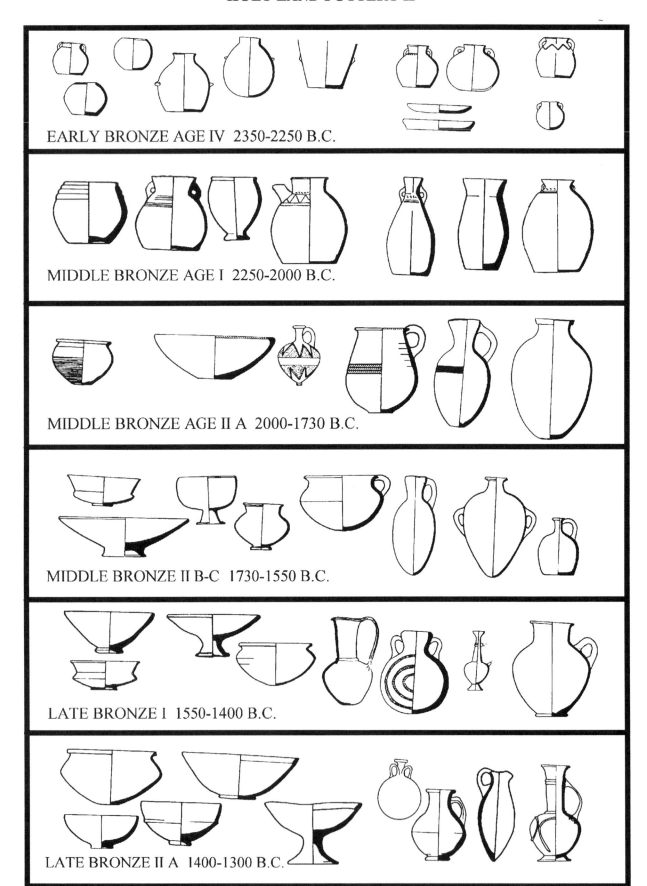

EARLY BRONZE AGE IV 2350-2250 B.C.

MIDDLE BRONZE AGE I 2250-2000 B.C.

MIDDLE BRONZE AGE II A 2000-1730 B.C.

MIDDLE BRONZE II B-C 1730-1550 B.C.

LATE BRONZE I 1550-1400 B.C.

LATE BRONZE II A 1400-1300 B.C.

HOLY LAND POTTERY III

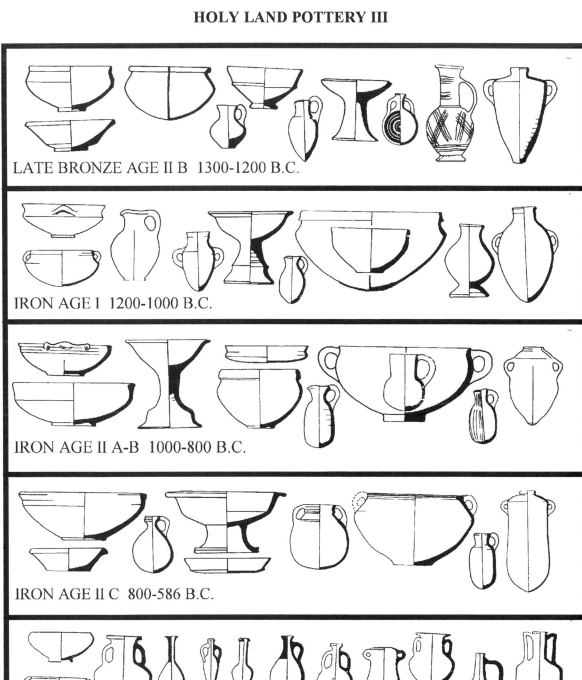

LATE BRONZE AGE II B 1300-1200 B.C.

IRON AGE I 1200-1000 B.C.

IRON AGE II A-B 1000-800 B.C.

IRON AGE II C 800-586 B.C.

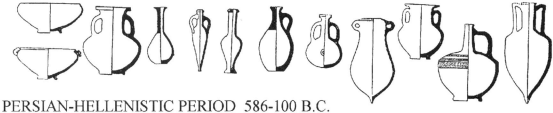

PERSIAN-HELLENISTIC PERIOD 586-100 B.C.

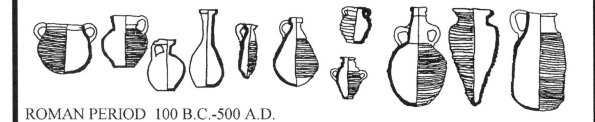

ROMAN PERIOD 100 B.C.-500 A.D.

HOLY LAND
c. 6000 B.C.-500 A.D.

DATES	HISTORICAL PERIOD	BIBLICAL PERIOD	BIBLICAL PEOPLE AND EVENTS	BIBLICAL BOOKS
6th Mill.B.C.	Neolithic Age	Period of Adam to Noah		Genesis
5th Mill.B.C.	Chalcolithic Age			
4000				
3000	Early Bronze Age			
		Period of Babal		
2000	Middle Bronze Age		• Abraham	
1900		Period of Patriarchs	• Isaac	
1800			• Jacob	
1700			• Joseph	
1600				
1500	Late Bronze Age	Israel in Egypt		
1400				
1300			• Moses	▌Exodus
1200	Iron Age	Exodus	• Fall of Jericho	
1100		Judges	• Samuel	▌Judges
			• Samson	▌Samuels
1000		Monarchy	• Saul	
900			• David • Solomon	▌Psalms
		Divided Kingdom	• 1st Temple Built	Kings Proverbs
800			• Ahab	
			• Elisha	
			• Uziah	
700	Persian Period		• Isaiah	▌Prophets
600		Exile	• Hezemiah	
			• Jeremiah	▌Daniel
500	2nd Temple Period		• 2nd Temple	
400		Return	• Nehemiah	▌Ezra
300				▌Malachi
200		Maccabees		▌Maccabees
100				
		Herod the Great		
1 B.C.				
1 A.D.	Roman Period	Life of Christ		▌Gospels
		Missionary Journeys	• Paul's Journeys	▌Paul Letters
100			• Destruction of Temple	▌Revelations
200		Post-Biblical Period		
300				
400			• Council of Nicaea	
500				

HOLY LAND

WEAPONS

Stone

533. **CALCITE ARROWHEAD. Judaea. Neolithic B Period. 7000-6000 B.C.** Grey. 2.4 x 1.2 cm. From excavation of the Biblical city of Jericho. Jericho is one of the oldest cities of mankind. Kenyon, *Archaeology in the Holy Land*, Pl. 18. ....**SUPERB 50.00**

534. **CALCITE ARROWHEAD. Judaea. Neolithic B Period. 7000-6000 B.C.** Grey. 18 x 18 mm. From excavations of the Biblical city of Jericho. Kenyon, *Archaeology in the Holy Land*, Pl. 18...............................**SUPERB 35.00**

535. **HEMATITE MACE HEAD. Early Canaanite-Western Asiatic. Late 4th-3rd Millennium B.C. Early Bronze Age-Chalcolithic Period.** Black hematite mace head, oblate and pierced. One end flatter; central hole larger at one end. Diam. 5 cm Cf. Sotheby's NY, 10/25/87 #357. Cf. American-Israel Culture House, Exhibit 1968, #16. Cf. Malloy, *Weapons*, #23. Similar hematite mace heads are found in many early Bronze Age sites.......................................**SUPERB 175.00**

536. **CHALCEDONY ARROWHEAD. Jericho. 2nd Millennium B.C.** Beige chalcedony arrowhead with barbs and tang. Length 2.2 cm. Petrie-. Cf. Malloy, *Weapons*, #22. ....**SUPERB 75.00**

Metal

Swords, Daggers, and Blades

537. **COPPER SWORD. Israel. 2000 B.C.** Curved sword. One side blunt with three rivet holes. 25.7 x 2.2 cm. From the time of Abraham, Isaac and Jacob. Cf. Hancock, fig. 49, 18 var. Green patina and light encrustation. ...**SUPERB 300.00**

538. **COPPER SWORD BLADE. Israel. 2000-1950 B.C. Middle Bronze Age I.** Long blade with midrib at base. Four rivet holes. 20.7 x 2.5 cm. From the time of Abraham. Maxwell-Hyslop, 1946, type 18. *McAlpine*. Cf. Ben-Tor, Azor, 1971, Qedem I, Pl. 22, 1 (dated to Proto-Urban Period). A lovely example.........................**SUPERB 500.00**

539. **COPPER DAGGER. Israel. 2000-1600 B.C. Middle Bronze Age.** Triangular-shaped blade with midrib and three rivets at base. 12.5 x 4 cm. From the time of Abraham to Joseph. Maxwell-Hyslop 1946, types 20-21. *McAlpine Collection* 17, 2. Cf. Ben-Tor, *Azor*, 1971, Qedem 1, Pl. 22, 2. ....**CHOICE 350.00**

540. **COPPER DAGGER BLADE. Israel. Middle Bronze Age: 2000-1600 B.C.** From the time of Abraham and Joseph. Triangular blade with notches between blade and handle. May have had rivet hole for handle. Length 13.6 cm. Width 2.3 cm. Cf. Ben-Tor, Pl. 22:2, Maxwell Hyslop 1946, type 20-21, *McAlpine Coll.* 17:21. Cf. Malloy, *Weapons*, #60. ....**CHOICE 300.00**

541. **BRONZE DAGGER. Israel. 1900-1550 B.C. Middle Bronze Age II.** Two edges. Short tang with two rivets. 19.8 x 5 cm. *"...And Ehund made for himself a dagger with two edges..."* Judges 3:16. For similar shape but elaborate design, Cf. Kozloff, *Ratner Collection*, fig. 15. Hancock, fig. 47, 6 and 22, 23 var............................**CHOICE 500.00**

542. **COPPER DAGGER BLADE. Israel, Iron II A-B: 1000-800 B.C.** From the time of Saul and David. Slightly corroded. Flat tang. Four holes at base for attaching to handle. Length 19 cm. Malloy #63; Hancock 49 H 1. ....**CHOICE 200.00**

Spear and Javelin Points

543. **IRON SPEARHEAD. Israel. 1000-586 B.C. Iron 11-A-C.** Midrib spear head with folded socket. 9.5 cm long, 1.5 cm wide. Slightly irregular and chip at socket, Cf. Ackerman & Braunstein, Jewish Museum NY 63, Cf. *Lachish III*, Pl. 56:30...**CHOICE 55.00**

544. **BRONZE SPEARHEAD. Judaea. 1000-586 B.C. Iron Age.** Socketed with high central midrib. Incised lines. 17.8 x 3.1 cm. 1.8 cm diameter opening. Hancock, fig. 57,3. Green patina. Chips to edges. ....**CHOICE 150.00**

545. **BRONZE SPEAR POINT. Israel. Neo-Babylonian Period. 8th-6th Century B.C.** Deltoid blade with raised mid rib, socketed stem. 13.4 x 3 cm, 1.5 cm diam. opening. Cf. Yale Inventory 1981-62.40, Baghouz. .**CHOICE 200.00**

546. **IRON JAVELIN. Israel. 700-586 BC.** Bodkin shaped, square sectioned. 11.1 cm. Aharoni states in his Lachish studies that these types were armour piercing bolts and certainly javelins and not arrowhead due to weight. This type is not generally found out of Holy Land sites. 26 gms. Aharoni, *Lachish V*, Pl. 36, 13 var. Cf. *Lachish Stratum II*. ....**CHOICE 100.00**

Arrowheads

547. **IRON ARROWHEAD. Israel. Iron Age. 1300-900 B.C.** Elongated leaf design. First iron made in Israel. Made at the beginning of the Iron Age. 10 cm long. 1.8 cm wide. Iron oxide. Mackenzie, Palestine Exploration Fund 1912-13. Pl. XXVIIII-6. ....**CHOICE 55.00**

548. **IRON ARROWHEAD. Israel. Iron Age. 1300-900 B.C.** Leaf type 5.8 cm long, 1.6 cm wide. Iron oxide. Mackenzie, Palestine Exploration Fund. 1912-1913, Excavations at Beth Shemesh, Pl. XLIII-23...............................**CHOICE 45.00**

549. **IRON ARROWHEAD. Israel. 1200-800 B.C..** Deltoid blade with barbs and long shaft. 8.6 x 1.8 cm. Cf. for shape, Muscarella, *Bronze and Iron, MMA* #408. Chip to blade. ....**CHOICE 55.00**

550. **IRON ARROWHEAD. Israel. 1200-800 B.C**. Rhombic head with two tang projectors, knob on each side. 6.5 x 1.5 cm. This type was popular in Egypt in bronze. Cf. Petrie 200-01, 203. 13.4 gm..................................**CHOICE 90.00**

551. **IRON ARROWHEAD. Israel. 1000-700 B.C.** Leaf shaped with thin tang. Encrusted. 10.3 cm. long, 2.7 cm. wide. "You will not fear the terror of the night, nor the arrow that flies by day." Psalm 91:5. Encrusted iron oxide. Nice size. Mackenzie Palestine Exploration Fund 1912-1913, Excavations at Beth Shemesh, Pl. LIX, 8. ....**CHOICE 65.00**

552. **IRON ARROWHEAD. Israel. 950-900 BC**. Deltoid blade with shaft. 5 x 1.6 cm. Cf. Aharoni, *Lachish*, Pl. 36 I var. ....**CHOICE 50.00**

553. **IRON ARROWHEAD. Israel 800-700 B.C**. Bobkin-shaped, square-section head with long tapering tang. Length 6.8 cm. Malloy #104; Cf. Aharoni 36:9. The bobkin-shaped arrowhead appeared as early as the 2nd millennium B.C. and continued in different shapes as late as medieval England..**CHOICE 35.00**

554. **IRON ARROWHEAD. Israel. 800-700 B.C.**. Bobkin-shaped square-sectioned head with short tang. Length 10.5 cm. Malloy #105; Cf. Aharoni 36:9, Tufnel Pl. 54:48. Petrie identifies these arrowheads as "armor piercing bolts." This bobkin-shaped head is a distinct type, and is most efficient against metal armor......................................**CHOICE 35.00**

555. **IRON ARROWHEAD. Israel. 800-700 B.C.** Leaf shaped with long shaft. 9.5 x 2.3 cm. Aharoni, *Lachish V*. Pl. 36,6, Lachish Stratum III. Palestine Exploration Fund, Annual 1912-13, Pl. XLIII, 23.................................**CHOICE 60.00**

556. **IRON ARROWHEAD. Israel. 800-700 B.C.**. Deltoid blade with shaft. 7.1 x 4.1 cm. Aharoni, *Lachish*, Pl. 36, 7. Lachish Stratum III.....................................**CHOICE 55.00**

557. **IRON ARROWHEAD. Israel. 800-700 B.C.** Elongated leaf shaped blade with long shaft. 8.8 x 1.4 cm. Aharoni, *Lachish V*, Pl. 36,8. Lachish Stratum III. Palestine Exploration Fund, Annual 1912-13, Pl. XXVII, 1. ....**CHOICE 55.00**

558. **IRON ARROWHEAD. Israel. 600 B.C.** Leaf shaped with high central rib and long shaft. 3.8 x 1.2 cm. These types were made during the Persian invasion of Israel. Petrie 33 var. ....**CHOICE 55.00**

559. **CAUCASUS. Sarmatian. 2nd Century B.C.-1st Century AD.** Flanged head tanged type. 7.7 cm long, 3.4 cm. wide. These arrowheads were found at sites throughout Phoenicia and in Egypt. Petrie states these Sarmatian types not native to Egypt were left behind by the soldiers. Unusual shape. Cf. Petrie p. 193 var. ....**CHOICE-SUPERB 75.00**

560. **IRON ARROWHEAD.** Flat diamond-shaped blade, flange at base. Length 7.6 cm, width 2.8 cm. Cf. Petrie, Pl. XLII.193,194. Chip on blade......................**CHOICE 55.00**

561. **IRON ARROWHEAD.** Flat diamond-shaped blade with flange below head, long tang. Length 5 cm, width 1.7 cm. Cf. Petrie 193 var. ....**SUPERB 60.00**

562. **IRON ARROWHEAD.** Flat, diamond-shaped blade, long tang with flange at head. Length 5.7 cm, width 1.2 cm. Cf. Petrie 143.4...............................**CHOICE-SUPERB 55.00**

Axe, Adze, and Mace Heads

563. **MACE HEAD. Early Canaanite Western Asiatic. Late 4th-Early 3rd Millennium B.C.** Early Bronze Age. Black hematite mace head, oblate and pierced. Cf. Sotheby's NY 10/25/87, #357; American-Israel Culture House Exhibit #198-16; Malloy, *Weapons* 23. ....**SUPERB 200.00**

564. **EARLY CANAANITE. Early Bronze Age (Chalcolithic Period) c. 3100 B.C.** Black hematite mace head. Pear shaped. 4.2 cm diameter. America-Israel Culture House, Exhibit 1968, #16. Similar Hematite maces are found in many early Bronze Age sites ....**SUPERB 200.00**

565. No entry.

566. **BRONZE BLADE AXE OR ADZE. Judaea. 2500-1500 B.C.** 12.2 cm x 3.3 cm. Cf. Hancock, fig. 46-11. Petrie-. These are found in the Pre-Israelite strata at Jericho. ....**CHOICE 150.00**

567. **BRONZE AXE. Israel. Middle Bronze. 1950-1750 B.C.** Fenestrated axe (duck bill axe). Socketed, two pierced "eyes" and ridge down center. 9.5 x 4.1 cm. *McAlpine* 17, 13. America-Israel Culture House Exhibit #81. Cf. Haaretz Museum, Tel-Aviv (49562). Muscarella, *MMA* 511. From the time of Abraham, Isaac and Jacob........**CH-SUP 1200.00**

568. **BRONZE AXE HEAD Canaanite. 18th-17th Century B.C.** Long, narrow blade with shaft at end, depression at bottom. 11.8 x 2.3 cm. Cf. Bulletin Pr. Musee de Beyreuth, 11 (1933), p. 28. p. 34, fig. 51c. Cf. DeShayes, *Les Quirils de Bronze de Lindys au Danube*, #1505, (Pl. LVII,7). Rare. ....**CHOICE-SUPERB 800.00**

569. **BRONZE AXE HEAD. Canaanite. 18th-17th Century B.C.** Long narrow blade with shaft at end, depression at bottom. Measures 10.4 x 2 cm. Cf. Musee de Beyreuth, p. 28, p. 34, fig. 51c. Cf. De Shayes #1505, Pl. LVIII, 7. Cf. Malloy, *Weapons*, #37. ....**SUPERB 400.00**

570. **BRONZE AXE HEAD. Canaanite. 18th-17th Century B.C.** Long narrow blade with horizontal shaft at end. Cut out depression below. Length 13.0 cm. Musee de Beyreuth, Pl. 28 p 34, fig. 51c; Malloy 37.......**CHOICE-SUPERB 400.00**

571. **BRONZE AXE HEAD Israel. 1800-1500 B.C.** Socketed with four ridges. 9.7 x 5 cm. Beth Shemesh-. *Lachish*-. Hancock-. Petrie-. *McAlpine*-. BM, *Bronze Age*-. Found in Israel. A rare weapon. ....**CHOICE 600.00**

572. **BRONZE AXE HEAD. Judaea. 1500-1300 B.C. Late Bronze.** Perforated with curved blade, socketed back protrusion. 14 x 3.5 cm. From the time of Moses. BM, *Bronze Age*.-. Petrie-. Qedem-. Hancock-. Beth Shemesh-Very rare. ....**CHOICE 750.00**

573. **BRONZE AXE HEAD. Israel. 1300-1100 B.C. Iron I.** Socketed blade with midrib. Socket decorated with five ridges, hook at top of socket. Measures 15.2 x 2 cm. Cf. BM, *Bronze Age*, fig. 181. Cf. Petrie, 118 (Jerusalem BM). From the time of Samuel and Judges. Green patina. Rare. ....**SUPERB 1500.00**

574. **BRONZE AXE HEAD. Israel. 1300-1000 B.C. Iron I (Time of Samuel and Judges).** Bronze head with socketed blade with raised midrib. Socket decorated with five ridges with hook on either side of base of blade (one missing). 15.2 x 2 cm. Malloy 38; Cf. British Museum, *Bronze Age*, fig. 181, lower. Petrie, *Tools and Weapons,* fig. 118 (Jerusalem B.M.) var. A fine axe head. ....**SUPERB 800.00**

575. **IRON PICK-AXE HEAD. Israel. Early Bronze Age. 1200-900 BC.** Vertically placed cutting blade with widening towards end, pick blade horizontally placed and of consistent width, central hole for mounting on handle between. Length 19.7 cm, width 5 cm. Seller, Beth-zur fig. 64. Cf. Kozloff, *Ratner Collection.* fig. 23 (RC56). "Rehoboam built his cities for defense in Judaea and fortified them and supplied food, oil, wine, and spears and shields of iron." -2 Chron. 11.5-12. ....**CHOICE 300.00**

576. **IRON AXE HEAD. Israel. Iron Age IIC- Hellenistic. 7th-1st Century B.C.** Pick-axe head. Vertical placed cutting blade widening towards end. Socketed rhomboid shield. 20.3 x 4.5, 2.4 cm wide. Seller, Beth-Zur fig. 64. Kozloff, *Ratner Collection.* fig. 23 (RC 56). Cf. Jewish Museum, #66..**CHOICE 300.00**

Tools

577. **IRON SPADE. Israel. 1200-900 B.C.** Triangular blade with tang. 22.7 x 8.7.............................**CHOICE 300.00**

578. **IRON PLOW POINT. Israel. 1200-586 B.C.** Long, narrow blade with open socket. 32.5 x 4 cm. Beer-Sheba 1:43-46. Cf. *Lachish* 77. ....**CHOICE 350.00**

579. **IRON TWIN PLOW HEAD. Israel. 7th Century B.C.** Twin pronged fork head. 27.5 x 11 cm. The Babylonians attacked Israel in the 600s B.C. Cf. *Biblical Archaeology Review*, XVI #2, p. 39. ....**CHOICE 350.00**

580. **IRON PLOW HEAD. Israel. 7th Century B.C.** Triangular blade with open socket. 35 x 8.5 cm, 8.3 cm diam. Cf. *Biblical Archaeology Review*, XVI #2, Ekron p. 39. Long massive tool. ....**CHOICE 450.00**

POTTERY

581. **JUDAEAN GOBLET. From the time before Noah. Chalcolithic Period. 4th Millennium B.C.** Spindle-shaped goblet with flat, solid base and slightly everted rim. Ivory-buff ware. Height 6.4 cm. Probably Beersheba culture. Amiran 5:3. Rare. One repair...................**CHOICE 300.00**

582. **JUDAEAN AMPHORISKOS. From the time of Noah. Early Bronze 1. 3100-2900 B.C.** Hand-made amphoriskos with round ovoid body with everted neck and two small string-hole handles at intersection of body and neck. Slightly concave base. Dark red to red-brown burnished slip over exterior and upper interior of mouth. Orange-buff ware. Height 11.5 cm. Cf. Amiran, photo 27, Pl. 9:17, 26, 30. *Dayan Coll.*, pp. 76-77. ....**CHOICE 350.00**

583. **JUDAEAN JUGLET. From the time of Noah. Early Bronze 1. 3100-2900 B.C.** Large juglet with rounded upper portion and straight sides receding to flat base. Thin everted lip on very short neck. High arched handle descending to waist. Red slip over tan ware. Height 12 cm. Amiran photo 50. Original handle reattached.................**CHOICE 275.00**

584. **JUDAEAN JUGLET. From the time of Noah. Early Bronze 1. 3100-2900 B.C.** Wheel-turned juglet with rounded and slightly depressed bottom. Medium neck widening slightly at lip. Flat base. Band handle arching slightly over mouth and joining body at midpoint. Pink-orange ware. Brick red slip over neck and handle, diagonal line decoration to body. Height 9.5 cm. Amiran 11:13, 15. ....**CHOICE 300.00**

585. **JUDAEAN CUP. From the time of Noah. Early Bronze 1. 3100-2900 B.C.** Wheel-made cup with depressed globular body, conical neck and everted lip. Crude strap handle from below lip to midpoint. Flat base. Black and red burnished slip over pink-buff ware. Natural flaw. Height 6.6 cm. Amiran photo 30 (body). *Dayan Coll.*, pp. 74-77. ....**CHOICE 200.00**

586. **WHEEL-TURNED JUGLET. From the time of Noah. Early Bronze 1. 3100-2900 B.C.** Rounded bi-conical body with shoulder below midpoint. Short neck with wide mouth. High arched handle meeting body just above base, which is flat. Highly burnished brick red slip over orange-pink clay. 8.8 cm high. Amiran, photo 50. Hairline crack reinforced with glue on interior................................**CHOICE 300.00**

587. **JUDAEAN CHALICE. From the time of Noah and the decline to idol worship. Early Bronze I-II. 3100-2650 B.C.** Wheel-turned chalice with wide bowl, rounded, with depression at center. Wide mouth with fine, everted lip. Short foot widens at base which is string cut. Brown-beige slip over ware varying from beige to pale red. Height 7 cm. This piece in no way resembles the fine Iron Age chalices to which it would ultimately give rise (Amiran 68:1-21, P.E.F. 1912-13, XXI.-1-6, Qedem 20, photo 47) but rather seems an improvement upon the cruder Chalcolithic goblet (Amiran 5:3). Chip at foot......................................**CHOICE 200.00**

588.   **JUDAEAN CUP.   From the time of Noah and idol worship. Early Bronze I-III. 3100-2350 B.C.** Wheel-made cup with depressed globular body, concave neck and wide flaring mouth. Band handle from below lip to midpoint. Concave disc base. Brick-red burnished slip with black speckles over dark buff ware. Height 6.5 cm. Cf. *Dayan Coll.*, pp. 74-77. A more advanced form of Amiran photo 30 showing many later refinements................**CHOICE 200.00**

589.   **JUDAEAN JUGLET.   From the time of idol worship. Early Bronze II. 2900-2650 B.C.** Wheel-turned juglet with piriform body and wide flat bottom.   Cylindrical neck, widening slightly towards lip. Band handle arching from lip to waist.   Pink-orange ware with brick red slip, burnished vertically on body.   Interior reserved.   Height 7.3 cm. Identical types have been found with fish net burnishing. Amiran   pp.   55,   59.   Original   handle   reattached. ....**CHOICE-SUPERB 250.00**

590.   **WHEEL-TURNED JUGLET.   From the time of idol worship. Early Bronze II. 2900-2650 B.C.** Piriform body and wide flat bottom. Cylindrical neck with fine everted lip. Band handle arching from lip to waist. Pink-buff ware with brick red burnished slip to exterior.   Two recessions to interior indicate the juncture of handle and lip. Height 7.3 cm. Amiran pp. 55, 59. Identical types have been found with fishnet burnishing. ....**CHOICE 200.00**

591.   **JUDAEAN JUGLET.   From the time of idol worship. Early Bronze II. 2900-2650 B.C.** Wheel-turned juglet with piriform body and flat bottom.   Cylindrical neck with fine everted lip.   Band handle arching from lip to waist. Pink-buff ware with pale brick red slip to exterior.   Burnished fishnet design to body. Height 9.8 cm. Amiran, pp. 55, 59, Pl. 15:14..**CHOICE 300.00**

592.   **JUDAEAN JAR.   From the time of idol worship. Early Bronze III-IV. 2650-2200 B.C.** Wheel-made jar with high-waisted globular body, thin neck and wide flaring lip. Partially smoothed string-cut base.   Cream-pink slip over buff   ware.   Height   9.0   cm.   Cf.   Amiran 20:9,   14. ....**CHOICE 165.00**

593.   **JUDAEAN JAR.   From the time of idol worship. Early Bronze III-IV. 2650-2200 B.C.** Wheel-made jar with inverted piriform body and wide mouth with everted lip. Flat base. Drab orange ware. Height 7.2 cm. Qedem, 1-10:8, Pl. 19:3.....................................**AVERAGE-CHOICE 135.00**

594.   **JUDAEAN JAR. From the time of Abraham. Middle Bronze I. 2250-2000 B.C.** Drop-shaped jar, wheel turned with flat base. Two holes below subtly everted lip. Peach slip over thin dark-buff ware. Height 6.5 cm. *Dayan Coll.* p.116. Ancient hole at corner of base...................**CHOICE 135.00**

595.   **JUDAEAN FLASK. From the time of Abraham. Middle Bronze 1. 2250-2000 B.C.** Squat flask, hand formed with globular body and flat disc base. Narrows towards everted lip, which is pierced by two small string cut holes. Pink-buff slip over grey ware. Incised zig-zag decoration in two concentric circles around shoulder. Height 5.5 cm, width 6 cm. *Dayan Coll.* p.116.   Charming shoulder decoration. ....**CHOICE 300.00**

596.   **JUDAEAN BOWL. From the time of Abraham. Middle Bronze I. 2250-1950 B.C.** Small wheel-made bowl with straight sides and body receding to flat base from above midpoint.   Buff slip over grey-buff ware. Diameter 6.2 cm. Amiran 23:7-8, 24:15-16...........................**CHOICE 125.00**

597.   **JUDAEAN JAR.   From the time of Abraham. Middle Bronze I. 2250-1950 B.C.** Hand-formed barrel-shaped jar with large flat base.   Flaring wheel-made neck and mouth attached at discernible joint.   Orange buff self slip. Height 18 cm. Amiran 22:22-23. This form was most common in the south.   Scarce period. ....**CHOICE 350.00**

598.   **JUDAEAN GOBLET.   From the time of Abraham. Middle Bronze I. 2250-1950 B.C.** Wheel-turned goblet with fine ridge pattern on exterior and evidence of band construction on interiors. Recessed disc base. Yellow-beige to pink-buff ware with self slip. Height 11.5 cm. Dia. 9 cm. Amiran 24:6 (and 23:6). A lovely shape.......**CH-SUP 200.00**

599.   **JUDAEAN BOWL.   From the time of the Patriarchs. Middle Bronze IC/IIA. 2100-1730 B.C.** Tan-buff wheel-made bowl with spherical body, small flat base, and thin, slightly everted rim. The fact that this bowl is wheel made, not hand made, places it in Amiran's transitional "Megiddo Group" or one of its early MBII descendants. 10.2 cm diam. Amiran 23:7, photo 95, p. 81. Small rim chip, otherwise superb.. **SUPERB 150.00**

600.   **JUDAEAN JUG. From the time of Abraham, Isaac and Jacob. Middle Bronze IIA. 2000-1730 B.C.** Slender juglet with inverted ovoid body and softly sloping shoulders and ring base.   Thin neck widening towards mouth but with slightly inverted lip.   Band handle from below lip to shoulder. Tan-buff self slip. Height 9.6 cm. Amiran photo 56 (shape), Pl. 33ff (lip).   While this form most closely parallels those of EBII, the lip used was not used until MBIIA.   A   very   graceful   form.   Edge   chip. ....**CHOICE 200.00**

601.   **JUDAEAN JUG. From the time of Abraham, Isaac and Jacob. Middle Bronze IIA. 2000-1730 B.C.** Wheel-made jug with rounded body and shoulder above midpoint. Medium neck with everted lip. Dark, pale orange ware. Cf. Amiran 33:5-6. Chip to rim. ....**CHOICE 135.00**

602. **WHEEL-TURNED JAR.** From the time of Abraham, Isaac and Jacob. Middle Bronze IIA. c. 2000-1730 B.C. Rounded body and short neck with wide mouth and everted lip. Flat, string cut base. Small chalk grit void at base of neck. Dark white slip over pale orange-buff ware. Height 7.5 cm. Amiran 35:3 and 11. ....**SUPERB 200.00**

603. **WHEEL-MADE BOTTLE.** From the time of Abraham, Isaac and Jacob. Middle Bronze IIA. 2000-1730 B.C. Globular body and large string cut base. Thin neck with flaring lip. Drab orange ware. Height 8 cm. Cf. Amiran 33:8. ....**CHOICE 150.00**

604. **JUDAEAN GIANT GOBLET.** From the time of Abraham, Isaac and Jacob. Middle Bronze IIA. 2000-1730 B.C. Wheel-turned giant goblet with semi-ovoid body marked by low rounded carination. Wide mouth with everted lip, flat disc base. Handle from lip to above midpoint (absent). Interior shows evidence of coil manufacture. Pale orange slip over orange-buff ware. Amiran 28:1-4. An impressive vessel.....................**CHOICE 350.00**

605. **JUDAEAN JUG.** From the time of Abraham, Isaac and Jacob. Middle Bronze IIA. 2000-1730 B.C. Wheel-made jug with ovoid body and nearly flat base. Cylindrical neck, widening slightly at upper half, with sharply pinched lip. Handle of round cross section from just below lip to body near intersection with neck. Fine, mild ribbing to body. Drab orange ware. Amiran 33:1-3. Bottom reconstructed. ....**CHOICE 350.00**

606. **JUDAEAN BOWL.** From the time of Abraham, Isaac and Jacob. Middle Bronze IIA. 2000-1730 B.C. Wheel-made bowl with sharp carination at midpoint. Rounded, convex sides with fine everted lip and convex disc base. Red-orange ware. Amiran 27:1 var............**CHOICE 285.00**

607. **WHEEL MADE JUG.** From the time of Abraham, Isaac and Jacob. Middle Bronze IIA. 2000-1730 B.C. Ovoid body, medium neck and trefoil lip. Handle from lip to shoulder. Flat base. Drab orange ware. Height 8 cm. Amiran 33:4........................**CHOICE 175.00**

608. **WHEEL-MADE JAR.** From the time of Abraham, Isaac and Jacob. Middle Bronze IIA. 2000-1730 B.C. High rounded shoulder and straight sides receding sharply to string-cut base. Small, sharply everted lip. Beige to buff slip over light buff ware. Height 5.7 cm. Diameter 6.6 cm. Cf. Amiran 35:5.............................**CHOICE 125.00**

609. **WHEEL-MADE JAR.** From the time of Abraham, Isaac and Jacob. Middle Bronze IIA. 2000-1730 B.C. Inverted piriform body with short neck and wide mouth with mild everted lip. Flat base. Buff ware. Cf. Amiran 35:1, 5. ....**CHOICE-SUPERB 150.00**

610. **WHEEL TURNED JUGLET.** From the time of Joseph and slavery in Egypt. Middle Bronze IIA-B. 2000-1650 B.C. Rounded body receding abruptly above shoulder to tall thin neck widening to a funnel like mouth. Band handle from neck to shoulder. Flat disc base. Pale pink self slip. Height 10.5 cm. Amiran 34:12. ....**CHOICE-SUPERB 250.00**

611. From the time of the Patriarchs. Middle Bronze IIA-B. 2000-1650 B.C. Reddish buff wheel-turned bowl with sharp carination, everted rim and ring base. 14.5 cm dia. One minor chip at rim and base. Intact. Palestine Exploration Fund Annual 1912-13-XVII. 4 as LBIIA. Amiran: photo 94. ....**SUPERB 250.00**

612. **WHEEL-MADE JAR.** From the time of Joseph and slavery in Egypt. Middle Bronze II. 2000-1550 B.C. Depressed globular body, flat, slightly angled base. Medium neck set off by two incised lines. Neck widens to form trefoil lip. Handle absent. Buff to pink-buff ware. Height 11.3 cm. Kenyon, fig. 43-44, Amiran 34. ....**CHOICE 175.00**

613. **WHEEL-MADE JAR.** From the time of Joseph and slavery in Egypt. Middle Bronze II. 2000-1550 B.C. Rounded above shoulder, straight sides below receding to flat base. Cylindrical neck of medium width widening slightly towards mouth. Crude texture reminiscent of earlier hand-formed wares. Unusual white slip over red-buff ware. Height 6.8 cm. Amiran 27:22, 28:11 (white slip). ....**AVERAGE-CHOICE. 135.00**

614. **WHEEL TURNED BOWL.** From the time of Joseph and slavery in Egypt. Middle Bronze IIB-C. 1730-1550 B.C. Gentle rounded carination and vertical sides below everted lip. Ring base. Traces of dark red slip over pink-buff ware. Height 8.7 cm. Diameter 11.2 cm. Amiran 27:8. Fully intact but natural pressure cracks to side.............**CHOICE 145.00**

615. **WHEEL TURNED BOWL.** From the time of Joseph and slavery in Egypt. Middle Bronze IIB-C. 1730-1550 B.C. Low, mild carination, everted gutter rim. Flat-to-round base. Pink-buff slip over yellow-green ware. 10 cm diam. Amiran 27:5. Some encrustation.........**AVERAGE-CHOICE 125.00**

616. **CYLINDRICAL JUGLET.** From the time of Joseph and slavery in Egypt. Middle Bronze IIB-C. 1730-1550 B.C. Grey-brown with angular shoulder and nearly straight sides widening towards base. Thin neck with double strap handle from mid-shoulder to lip. Rounded bottom set off at sharp angle from body. Some chalk and traces of black burnished slip. Height 12 cm. Similar juglets were recovered at Jericho in levels dating to MBII phase V. Kenyon 47:3, 45:3-5. ....**CHOICE 225.00**

617. **WHEEL-TURNED BOWL.** From the time of slavery in Egypt. Middle Bronze IIB-C. 1730-1550 B.C. Wide flaring body and exaggerated S-shaped carination below. Simple thin lip slightly depressed before firing on one side. Heavy, well-formed ring base. Buff self slip. Diameter 16.8 cm. Amiran 27:10. A lovely shape.............**CHOICE 400.00**

618.   **WHEEL-MADE BOWL.** **From the time of slavery in Egypt. Middle Bronze IIB-C. 1730-1550 B.C.** Shallow open form with rounded sides, turned in to result in straight, vertical interior walls. Sharply distinguished disc base gently receding towards center. Three small knobs on one side, the central and largest being vertically pierced for hanging. Red-brown burnished slip over light buff ware. Height 23.5 cm. Amiran 26:3..**CHOICE 350.00**

619.   **WHEEL-TURNED BOWL.** **From the time of Joseph and slavery in Egypt. Middle Bronze IIB-C. 1730-1550 B.C.** Rounded middle above straight sides receding towards flat base. Recession below lip resulting in mildly everted rim. Flat base. Diameter 9.5 cm. Amiran 30:4-5. ....**SUPERB 175.00**

620.   **WHEEL-MADE BOWL.** **From the time of Joseph and slavery in Egypt. Middle Bronze IIB-C. 1730-1550 B.C.** Round deep body and string cut base. Offset everted lip. Dark buff ware. Diameter 6.2 cm. Amiran..**CHOICE 85.00**

621.   **CYLINDRICAL JUGLET.** **From the time of Joseph and slavery in Egypt. Middle Bronze IIB-C. 1730-1550 B.C.** Rounded shoulder and thin neck. Double strap handle and rounded lip. Burnished grey ware. Height 13.5 cm. Kenyon 47:4 ....**CHOICE 275.00**

622.   **WHEEL-MADE AMPHORA.** **From the time of Joseph and slavery in Egypt. Middle Bronze IIB-C. 1730-1550 B.C.** Ovoid body, concave neck and everted lip with stepped rim. Convex, nearly flat base. Two vertical handles attached at midpoint. Shoulder ornamented by three concentric series of incises of grooves. Buff to orange-buff ware. Height 42.7 cm. *Beth Shemesh* 696, 665. Amiran photos 103, 105. Very large size. This unpainted variety was intended for commercial rather than household use. ....**SUPERB 1,500.00**

623.   **WHEEL-MADE JUGLET.** **From the time of Joseph and slavery in Egypt. Middle Bronze IIB-C. 1730-1550 B.C.** Ovoid body with high shoulder, thin cylindrical neck and thick broad lip. Double loop handle arching from base of neck to shoulder. Miniature ring base. Red burnished slip over buff ware. Amiran 34:15-16. Reconstructed. ....**AVERAGE-CHOICE 125.00**

624.   **WHEEL-TURNED JAR.** **From the time of Joseph and slavery in Egypt. Middle Bronze IIB-C. 1730-1550 B.C.** Tall rounded body and wide mouth with flat everted rim. Narrower ring base. Traces of black slip over buff ware. Cf. Amiran 34:6. Height 8 cm..........................**CHOICE 135.00**

625.   **WHEEL-TURNED JUGLET.** **From the time of Joseph and slavery in Egypt. Middle Bronze IIB-C. 1730-1550 B.C.** Squat bi-conical body with narrow, cylindrical neck. Thick everted lip. Rounded bottom with no sign of base. Pink-beige slip over tan ware. Diameter 6.4 cm. Amiran 34:11 and p. 112. Charming shape..........**CHOICE 160.00**

626.   **JUGLET.** **From the time of slavery in Egypt. Middle Bronze IIB-C. 1730-1550 B.C.** Buff squat piriform juglet with pronounced shoulder at midpoint. Narrow neck with everted rim. Puncture design in form of concentric circles around upper portion of body. Recessed base. Excavated near the Sea of Galilee. Tel el-Yahudiyeh ware such as this has been traced to the Hyksos presence in Canaan and follows their expansion into Egypt. It has been theorized that Joseph's arrival in Egypt coincided with that of this Semitic people. 7.5 cm. Amiran Pl. 36:14. Handle not present. Rare type. ....**CHOICE 300.00**

627.   **WHEEL-TURNED AMPHORISKOS.** **From the time of slavery in Egypt. Middle Bronze IIC-Late Bronze I. 1650-1400 B.C.** Rounded body marked by midpoint carination. Tall concave neck with everted lip. Thick loop handles attached to upper portion of body. Ring base. Peach slip over buff ware. Height 20 cm. Amiran 49:10. ....**CHOICE 500.00**

628.   **WHEEL-TURNED POT** **From the time of slavery in Egypt. Late Bronze I. 1550-1400 B.C.** Bi-conical body and subtle base. Beige slip over grey ware. Mouth opening is in the form of a slightly irregular oval. Diameter 9.5 cm. *Beth Shemesh* 81, 318 (T.2). Amiran 42:1, 2. ......**CH-SUP 135.00**

629.   **WHEEL-TURNED AMPHORISKOS.** **From the time of Moses and Judges. Late Bronze. 1550-1200 B.C.** Tan-buff. Rounded bi-conical body with shoulder above midpoint, narrow neck, and sharply everted rim forming ledge. Single, pierced lug handle. Traces of red-slip horizontal design around middle. Flat base. 9 cm. Intact. Cf. Grant, *Beth Shemesh* p.141, 4.3. ....**CHOICE 150.00**

630.   **WHEEL-MADE JAR.** **From the time of Moses and Judges. Late Bronze I-II. 1550-1200 B.C.** Round bi-conical body, short neck and wide mouth with everted lip. Buff ware decorated with red-brown bands above shoulder. 6.2 cm. high. Amiran photos 125, 191, 202, Pl. 51, 11-15. ....**CHOICE 225.00**

631.   **WHEEL-TURNED BOWL.** **From the time of Moses and Judges. Late Bronze. 1550-1200 B.C.** High carination and offset everted lip. Sides curve towards ring base. Traces of black slip over yellow-buff ware. Diameter 13.5 cm. *Beth Shemesh*, p. 145:3 (T.2)............................**CHOICE 175.00**

632.   **WHEEL-MADE BOWL.** **From the time of Moses and Judges. Late Bronze. 1550-1200 B.C.** Small with spherical body, wide mouth and everted lip. Ledge off lip to exterior is pierced through before firing from top to interior junction of body and mouth. Round bottom. Traces of black slip over tan-buff ware. Height 6.3 cm. *Beth Shemesh* p. 195:219 (T.1) (shape). While vessels with appended spouts are known for periods ranging at least from EB through Iron, vessels from Judaea with integral spouts such as this seem to be virtually unknown. Rare..**CHOICE 350.00**

633. **WHEEL-MADE JAR. From the time of Moses and Judges. Late Bronze I-II. 1550-1200 B.C.** Round biconical body and cylindrical neck. Irregular straight lip. Flat base. Buff ware decorated with red-brown bands above shoulder and at lip. Height 5.7 cm. Amiran photos 125, 191, 202, Pl. 51:11-15....................................**CHOICE 195.00**

634. **WHEEL-MADE SAUCER LAMP. From the time of Moses and Judges. Late Bronze. 1550-1200 B.C.** One deeply pinched corner forming nozzle. Rounded bottom. Pink-buff ware. Some blackening at nozzle. Schloessinger 315-17....................................**CHOICE 200.00**

635. **CHALICE-BOWL. From the time of Moses and Judges. Late Bronze Period. 1550-1200 B.C.** Deep rounded shoulder above midpoint and high sharply everted rim. Rounded button within ring base. Pale-red ware with beige-cream slip to exterior and mouth. Diameter 11.2 cm. Found at Hebron. A similar piece was recovered at the second cemetery of Beth Shemesh in 1928. Grant, *Beth Shemesh*, 149:89. Cf. Amiran 27:14-15 for MBII antecedents. ....**CHOICE 285.00**

636. **WHEEL-MADE GOBLET. From the time of Moses and Judges. Late Bronze Period. 1550-1200 B.C.** Sharp carination, body deeply concave above, rounded below. Everted lip and ring base. Traces of coil manufacture visible in interior. Beige-buff ware, self slip. Height 9.7 cm. During this period the old carinated forms led to new and creative varieties. This extremely graceful form differs from but is related to those illustrated in Amiran 40:1-2, 10. Magnificent form. Repair to lip................**CHOICE 275.00**

637. **WHEEL-TURNED JAR. From the time of Moses and Judges. Late Bronze. 1550-1200 B.C.** High rounded shoulder and body receding to flat base. Narrow neck with wide everted lip of triangular cross section. Ivory grey slip over orange buff ware. Height 7.5 cm. *Beth Shemesh* p. 141:4c.....................................**CHOICE 150.00**

638. **WHEEL-MADE BOTTLE. From the time of Moses and Judges. Late Bronze I-II. 1550-1200 B.C.** Round biconical body, narrow neck and everted lip. Hat base with crude ridge on body just above. Pink buff ware with wide red-brown band above shoulder. Height 6 cm. Amiran photos 125, 191, 202, Pl. 51:11-15............**SUPERB 250.00**

639. **WHEEL-MADE BOTTLE. From the time of Moses and Judges. Late Bronze I-II. 1550-1200 B.C.** Globular body gradually forming into narrow neck with wide everted lip. Round bottom. Dark tan ware with orange-red decoration in the form of spiral descending from neck to midpoint. Cf. Amiran photos 125, 191, 202, Pl. 51:11-15. ....**SUPERB 350.00**

640. **WHEEL-TURNED BOWL. From the time of Moses. Late Bronze IIA. 1400-1300 B.C.** Convex body above vestigial midpoint carination. Straight lower sides receding to flat, string-cut base. Offset everted rim. Pink-beige slip over yellow-beige ware. Height 4.5 cm. Amiran 39:10-11. Rim chips. ....**CHOICE 125.00**

641. **WHEEL-TURNED BOWL. From the time of Moses. Late Bronze IIA. 1400-1300 B.C.** Small with slightly rounded sides and offset everted lip. Shallow ring base. Dark slip over buff ware. Diameter 6.6 cm. Amiran 38:13. Small bowls were frequently used for votive purposes. ....**CHOICE-SUPERB 145.00**

642. **MINIATURE WHEEL-MADE BOWL. From the time of Moses. Late Bronze IIA. 1400-1300 B.C.** Slightly rounded sides and minimally everted lip. Ring base. Pink buff ware. Related to Amiran 38:13. Such bowls were frequently used for votive purposes ....**CHOICE 125.00**

643. **WHEEL-TURNED DIPPER-JUGLET. From the time of Moses. Late Bronze IIA. 1400-1300 B.C.** Conical body tapering to chisel base, slight trefoil lip. Single handle descending from lip to shoulder. Buff to green buff slip over grey-buff core. Height 17.5 cm. Amiran 46:15. ....**CHOICE 175.00**

644. **GREY JUGLET. From the time of Moses. Late Bronze. 1400-1300 B.C.** Burnished, with no incisions. Plain handle. For shape Cf. Amiran Pl. 36:10; for plain type Cf. Amiran photo 109. ....**CHOICE 200.00**

645. **WHEEL-MADE BOWL. From the time of Moses. Late Bronze IIA. 1400-1300 B.C.** Small, with slightly rounded sides and offset everted lip. Ring base. White-buff ware. Diameter 6.2 cm. Amiran 38:13. Small bowls were frequently used for votive purposes. ....**SUPERB 145.00**

646. **WHEEL-TURNED BOWL. From the time of Moses. Late Bronze IIA. 1400-1300 B.C.** Light brown, with ridge at midpoint, disc base, and plain lip. Red slip trim to outer rim. 18.5 cm diam. The ridge on this specimen is actually a degeneration of the more pronounced carination on similar bowls of MBIIC and LBI. It also differs by the lack of thickening at the lip. Said to have been found at Hebrun. Intact. Amiran 39:8. ....**CHOICE-SUPERB 250.00**

647. **BILBIL JUGLET. From the time of Moses and Judges. Late Bronze II. 1400-1200 B.C.** Spindle-shaped with wide waist and narrow neck with thickening at rim. Flat base. Buff knife-share ware. Cypriot manufacture. North Israel provenance. Height 9.5 cm. Cf. Amiran 55:12, 14-15. Restored ....**CHOICE 65.00**

648. **WHEEL-TURNED JAR. From the time of Moses and Joshua. Late Bronze II. 1400-1200 B.C.** Inverted piriform jar and wide mouth atop very short vertical neck. String cut base. Beige-buff self slip. Height 7 cm. Cf. *Dayan Collection.*, pp. 90-91. This piece, probably of Southern origin, bears relation to other Judaean and Canaanite work intended to imitate Egyptian forms of pottery. Unusual. ....**CHOICE-SUPERB 175.00**

649. **WHEEL-TURNED HOLE-MOUTH JAR. From the time of Moses, Judges and Saul. Late Bronze II-Iron I. 1400-1000 B.C.** Rounded conical body and small flat base. Clear evidence of coil construction within and to a lesser extent on exterior. Buff ware. Height 12 cm. *Beth Shemesh* 334. Tushingham 7:17. Unusual type. ....**CHOICE 275.00**

650. **JUGLET. From the time of Joshua. Late Bronze IIB. 1300-1200 B.C.** Buff shaved ware juglet. Handmade, conical body tapering to button base, slightly trefoil lip. Single handle descending from lip, through shoulder, into interior. Probably of Cypriot manufacture after a Canaanite prototype. Height 15 cm. Amiran, p.173, Pl. 55:15. Cf. Ustinov UP5. ....**CHOICE 175.00**

651. **WHEEL-TURNED JUG. From the time of Joshua. Late Bronze IIB. 1300-1200 B.C.** Depressed rounded body and wide cylindrical neck. Band handle with exterior groove extends from thin lip to shoulder. Flat base. Height 9.5 cm. Amiran 46:17. Some chips at rim.. ....**CHOICE 250.00**

652. **WHEEL-TURNED BOWL. From the time of Joshua. Late Bronze II B. 1300-1200 B.C.** Pronounced ridge at midpoint, deep ring base and plain lip. Beige ware with self slip. Diameter 16 cm, height 9.3 cm. The ridge on this specimen is actually a degeneration of the more pronounced carination on similar bowls of MB IIC and LB I. Amiran 39:17 and photo 128; Hazor p. 53; *Beth Shemesh* #351 (T.2)..**CHOICE 250.00**

653. **BUFF JUGLET. From the time of Joshua. Late Bronze IIB. 1300-1200 B.C.** Pointed bottom, handle from shoulder to rim. Rim plain, slightly pinched spout. Cf. Ustinov UP5; Amiran Pl. 55:15. ....**CHOICE 200.00**

654. **WHEEL-TURNED BOWL. From the time of Samuel and Judges. Iron I. 1200-1000 B.C.** Grooves at midpoint and below lip. Body straight between grooves, slightly curved below lower groove from which it recedes to ring base. Dark red slip to interior over pale orange ware. Diameter 21 cm. Ustinov 181. ....**CHOICE-SUPERB 175.00**

655. **WHEEL-TURNED BOWL. From the time of Samuel, Saul and Judges. Iron I. 1200-1000 B.C.** Rounded body with thin subtly everted lip. Ring base and mound handle to one side of interior. Light brown self slip. Diameter 7.4 cm. Amiran 61:8. Beth Shan 49:21 (handle)....**CHOICE 125.00**

656. **WHEEL-TURNED BOWL. From the time of Samuel and Judges. Iron I. 1200-1000 B.C.** Shallow canal carination below inverted rim. Flattened ring base. Red slip over orange core. 21 cm dia. This unusual carination was particularly characteristic of the north. Intact. Amiran 60:1,4. ....**SUPERB 150.00**

657. **WHEEL TURNED BOWL. From the time of Samuel and Judges. Iron I. 1200-1000 B.C.** Coarse, rounded bowl with semi-cylindrical bar handle and slightly recessed base. Yellow-buff slip over orange core. 16.5 cm diam. Intact. Amiran 60:14, 61:11. ....**CHOICE-SUPERB 150.00**

658. **JAR. From the time of Samuel and Judges. Iron I. 1200-1000 B.C.** Small, reddish-orange jar with ovoid body. Handles at waist (one missing) and hollow ridged lip. 14.7 cm. This form was frequently used for larger storage jars. The hollow cavity within the lip permitted the controlled pouring of the contents. Amiran 78,2. Negev, *Archaeological Encyclopedia of the Holy Land*, p.252. One handle missing otherwise. ....**CHOICE 150.00**

659. **WHEEL TURNED PYXIS. From the time of Samuel and Judges. Iron I. 1200-1000 B.C.** Light red-brown with mild carination at shoulder. Sharper one below, mildly everted rim, pierced lug handles, circular base. Red slip horizontal decoration around middle. 9.5 cm. Intact except for chip on top of one lug. Amiran 96:11. ....**CHOICE-SUPERB 200.00**

660. **WHEEL-TURNED BOWL. From the time of Saul and David. Iron IA-IIC. c. 1100-600 B.C.** Roughly cylindrical body with exaggerated rim at midpoint. Beige-buff slip over dark grey ware. String cut base of irregular form. Diameter 6 cm. Jerusalem. Scarce.............................**CHOICE 225.00**

661. **CYLINDRICAL WHEEL-TURNED JAR. From the time of Saul and David. Iron IB-IIA-C. c. 1100-600 B.C.** Of heavy ware with two thick snake ornaments around body. Flat base. Beige slip over grey ware. Cf. Jerusalem 10: 17. Rare. ....**CHOICE 250.00**

662. **WHEEL-TURNED JUG From the time of Saul and David. Iron IIA. 1050-900 B.C.** Small jug with globular body, cylindrical neck and flared rim. Strap handle from rim to shoulder. Red-brown slip, burnished surface. Flat base. A similar jug was recovered in Tomb 2 of Beth Shemesh. Minor chips on lip. Bold orange color. Palestine Exploration Fund 1912-13:XXXVII. 13, pp. 37, 67. Tiny edge chip. ....**SUPERB 250.00**

663. **WHEEL-TURNED BOWL. From the time of Elijah and Jeremiah. Iron IIA-B. c. 1000-800 B.C.** Rounded body and shallow, wide groove setting off thick everted rim. Flat, disc base. Heavy buff ware. Diameter 9.7 cm. Qedem 20, 33:28...**CHOICE 125.00**

664. **ROOSTER FIGURINE. From the time of Elijah and Jeremiah. Iron IIA-C. 1000-700 B.C.** Hand formed with hollow bulbous body on short pillar base, small round aperture at back of neck. Puncture design representing feathers. Beige slip on light yellow-buff core. Height 5.8 cm. Cf. Acherman/ Braunstein 40. Ustinov-. Head and tail restored, otherwise intact. ....**CHOICE 150.00**

665. **WHEEL-TURNED BOWL. From the time of Elijah and Jeremiah. Iron IIA-C. 1000-600 B.C.** High rounded midpoint and straight sides sloping towards flat base. Slightly inverted lip. Pink slip to interior over ware varying from pink to tan. Diameter 16.5 cm. Ustinov UP 183, base as 192. ....**CHOICE 150.00**

666. **WHEEL-MADE JUGLET. From the time of Joel and the Divided Kingdom. Iron IIB. 900-800 B.C.** Small with squat globular body, narrow neck slightly widening towards rim. Roundish handle from shoulder to just above midneck. Slightly pointed base set off from body by rounded carination. Grey-black ware with self slip. Considered a transitional form, the distinctive shape of this piece permits its dating to be more specific than the normal "Iron IIA-B" which must be assigned to most juglets of the same period. Cf. Ustinov UP 89 and p. 67. Scarce.........**CHOICE 150.00**

667. **WHEEL-TURNED BOWL. From the time of Elijah and Jeremiah. Iron IIB-C. 900-586 B.C.** Shallow, with central well and flat base below coarse everted-type shoulder. Reddish slip on orange core. While this is a later Iron Age form, the ware is similar to that used as early as Iron L Intact. Cf. Amiran 63:3, 64:6-10. ....**CHOICE 150.00**

668. **OSTRACUM. From the time of division between Israel and Judah. Iron Age. c. 900-300 B.C.** Inscription incised in white and beige slip. Transliterates as (r. to l.) ... It ... / ... gybad ... / ... hthh(or k) ... / ...[?]... While this inscription is Semitic, it is quite possibly Punic or Phoenician rather than early Hebrew. Cf. Diringer, *The Alphabet*, pp. 237, 262. Horn & Ruger, *Die Numider*, p. 106. *Illustrated Bible Dictionary I*, pp. 660-1. ....**CHOICE 150.00**

669. **WHEEL-TURNED JAR. From the time of Joel and the Divided Kingdom. Iron II Late B/Early C. c. 825-790 B.C.** Slightly squat rounded body and rounded base. Slightly wide concave neck with broad everted flaring rim. Tan-buff ware with mixed black and white grits. An unintentional carination occurs where the neck joins the body. Cf. Tell es-Sa'idiyeh 5:3 (Stratum VII). ....**CHOICE 150.00**

670. **WHEEL-MADE BOWL. From the time of Isaiah and Jeremiah. Iron IIC. 800-586 B.C.** Straight converging sides, abruptly receding below low carination. Flat base. Light red slip with darker red spiral to interior and over entirety of exterior above carination. Pale red ware. Height 13.9 cm. Cf. Ustinov UP 193, 203. ....**CHOICE 175.00**

671. **WHEEL-MADE AMPHORISKOS. From the time of Isaiah and Jeremiah. Iron IIC. 800-586 B.C.** Globular body, long cylindrical neck and thick everted lip. Two small handles from shoulders to midneck at which point is a ring. Shallow ring base. Tan slip over buff ware. Height 10 cm. Contemp. Amiran 88:20, photos 260, 268. Repaired at neck. ....**CHOICE 175.00**

672. **WHEEL-TURNED JUGLET. From the time of Isaiah and Jeremiah. Iron IIC. 800-586 B.C.** Globular body and narrow neck flaring widely to rim. Handle attaches to neck below mild ridge and descends to point high on body. Mildly concave base. Light buff ware with thin dark ivory slip. Brown-black painted decoration consisting of four patterns of four concentric circles arranged on upper part of body and circles of varying thickness around the upper neck and mouth interior. Height 10 cm. This juglet is similar in almost every aspect except color to the contemporary imported Cypriot ware which it imitates. Amiran 98:6 (Cyp.), 98:9-12 (local). ....**SUPERB 400.00**

673. **WHEEL-MADE JUGLET. From the time of Isaiah and Jeremiah. Iron IIC. 800-586 B.C.** Small with globular body and narrow neck widening towards rim at which it is slightly inverted. Round handle from shoulder to neck just below lip. Round bottom. Grey-black ware with widely spaced vertical burnishing around body. Height 7.5 cm. Ustinov 109 and p. 62. Amiran 89:22. ......**CHOICE 125.00**

674. **WHEEL-MADE JUGLET. From the time of Isaiah and Jeremiah. Iron IIC. 800-586 B.C.** Globular body and long conical neck, thickening at lip and offset disc base. Handle from lip to shoulder. Orange-tan ware with traces of darker slip. Height 7.2 cm. *Beth Shemesh* 211:127. Amiran p. 272. This form derives from metal prototypes. It was easier to produce a conical neck than a cylindrical one when working in metal. ....**CHOICE 175.00**

675. **WHEEL-TURNED BOWL. From the time of Isaiah and Jeremiah. Iron IIC. c. 800-586 B.C.** Miniature bowl with diverging straight sides. Carinated below midpoint, everted rim, flat base. Pale red ware of coarse manufacture. 7 cm diam. Such bowls were frequently used for votive purposes. Cf. Ustinov UP213-4. Cf. Amiran 65:15. Yadin, *Mazor* p. 115. ....**CHOICE 50.00**

676. **DIPPER JUGLET. Time of Kings, when Elijah and Jeremiah were prophets. Iron IIC. 800-586 B.C.** Buff, ovoid, slightly pinched, unfinished flared rim, one double-strap handle to shoulder. 9 cm. Ustinov UP 58-62. ....**CHOICE 165.00**

677. **WHEEL-MADE BOWL. From the time of Isaiah and Jeremiah. Iron IIC. 800-526 B.C.** Diverging straight sides carinated below midpoint, sharply everted ledge rim and flat base. Tan-buff with red slip above carination and on interior. Wheel burnished. 19 cm diam. Intact. Minor chips to rim. Ackerman/Braunstein 20. Amiran 65:14. Ustinov UP203. ....**CHOICE-SUPERB 250.00**

678. **WHEEL-MADE MUG. From the time of Isaiah and Jeremiah. Iron IIC. 731-550 B.C.** Bi-form body. Above midpoint sides are straight with only the slightest evidence of being convex. Below, body bulges and is rounded, above straight sides receding to flat disc base. Band handle from middle of upper to middle of lower section. Dark buff ware. Height 6.6 cm. Amiran 101:12. By this period the Ammonites had fallen under Assyrian control. They had traced their origins to Benammi, a son of Lot by his own daughter. ....**CHOICE 200.00**

679. **WHEEL-TURNED CUP. Ammonite Kingdom. 731-550 B.C. Period of Assyrian domination.** Compressed, rounded body and large, slightly convex cylindrical neck. Handle of round cross-section descending from lip to shoulder. Shallow disc base. Pale orange ware with self slip. Height 7.5 cm. This form was derived from slightly earlier Iron Age Judaean ware. Amiran 101:12, photo 304, pp. 294-95. Scarce. ....**CHOICE 325.00**

680. **WHEEL-MADE FLASK. From the time of the rebuilding of the temple. Persian Period. c. 600-300 B.C.** Ovoid with distinct horizontal banding and almost rounded bottom. Short, narrow neck offset from body and widening to form everted lip. Self slip over hard light grey ware, wheel burnished. Tushingham p. 33, fig. 16:13 (ware). Height 9.5 cm. Probably Persian manufacture. North Israel provenance. Restoration at lip. ....**SUPERB 150.00**

681. **WHEEL-MADE JAR. From the time of the reconstruction of the temple. Persian Period. 586-300 B.C.** Depressed globular body and wide mouth with everted lip. Semi-ring base irregularly formed. Possible evidence of misfiring to section of side. Pale brown slip over pale tan brown ware. Height 6.5 cm. Tushingham-. (Cf. 16:13-19). ....**CHOICE 125.00**

682. **WHEEL-MADE BOTTLE. From the time of Nehemiah and rebuilding the temple. Persian Period. 586-300 B.C.** Inverted piriform body, narrow neck and flaring mouth. String-cut base. Traces of black slip over cream ware. Height 9 cm. Cf. Qedem 9-9:5...**CHOICE-SUPERB 175.00**

683. **WHEEL-MADE JAR. From the time of the Maccabees and Hasmonean Dynasty. Hellenistic Period. 3rd-1st Century B.C.** Bi-conical body curved below shoulder. Medium neck with flaring lip. Lip has two very small protuberances. Flat base. Peach-buff slip over tan buff ware. Height 8 cm. Tell es-Sa'idiyeh 19:20........**CHOICE 225.00**

684. **WHEEL-MADE JAR. From the time of the Maccabees and Hasmonean Dynasty. Hellenistic Period. c. 2nd-1st Century B.C.** Thick piriform body and wide neck with flattened everted lip. Very heavy peg base. Buff ware. Handle absent. Cf. Hayes, *ROM* 253.........**CHOICE 145.00**

685. **WHEEL-TURNED BOWL. From the period of the Maccabees and Hasmonean Dynasty. Hellenistic Period. 2nd Century B.C.-1st Century A.D.** Light-tan with inverted rim and ring base. Faint traces of yellowish slip around rim. 12.5 cm dia. This shape is based on an Attic prototype which was popularly imported during the previous century. Ustinov UP378-381................................**SUPERB 125.00**

686. **WHEEL-MADE BOWL. From the time of Christ. Hasmonean to Roman Periods. 1st Century B.C.-1st Century A.D.** Unglazed with inverted rim and string cut base. 10.5 cm diam. Ustinov UP379. ....**SUPERB 75.00**

687. **FLASK. Thin-walled ware. Nabatean. 1st Century B.C.-1st Century A.D.** Brown-orange with fine flare rim, flat base. Height 10.5 cm. Very scarce.............**SUPERB 200.00**

688. **JUG. Thin-walled ware. Nabatean. 1st Century B.C.-1st Century A.D.** Ovoid body. Flare rim, strap handle. Orange-red slip over cream pottery. Height 8.5 cm. Very scarce. ....**SUPERB 300.00**

689. **VASE. Thin-walled ware. Nabatean. 1st Century B.C.-1st Century A.D.** Small with ovoid body. Flare rim, flat base. Cream clay with light yellow-orange slip. Height 5 cm. Very scarce...**SUPERB 100.00**

690. **WHEEL-TURNED BOTTLE. From the time of Christ. Early Roman Period. 20 B.C.-70 A.D.** Piriform body and cylindrical neck having slight bulge at its midpoint. Rim flares outward and slopes down to meet neck at an angle. Flat, string-cut base. Orange-buff ware with red slip at rim. Height 15 cm. *Israel in Antiquity* 111. Some salt encrustation..**CHOICE 100.00**

691. **WHEEL-TURNED MUG. From the time of Christ. Roman Period. 1st Century A.D.** Rounded body, low belly and broad flat base. Wide flaring collar-like rim, concave on inside. Small handle from lip to midpoint, ridged on outside. Intermittent grey slip over orange ware. Height 6 cm. Hayes, *ROM* 278. ....**CHOICE 175.00**

692. **WHEEL-MADE FLAGON. From the time of Christ and the Apostles. Roman Period. 1st Century A.D.** Sagging body tapering above to a tubular neck. Wide band rim with flat sides. Ring base. Buff slip over brick-red ware. Height 8 cm. Hayes, *ROM* 316-317 (form), 281 (lip). Slight abrasion at lip. ....**CHOICE 75.00**

693. **WHEEL-MADE BOTTLE. From the time of Christ and the Apostles. Roman Period. 1st Century A.D.** Globular form, high rounded shoulder and ring base. Incised rings on body below thin neck. Mouth flaring with "steps" to exterior. Fine grey ware. Height 10 cm. Cf. Hayes, *ROM* 280-81. Cf. Tushingham 23:20. ....**CHOICE-SUPERB 175.00**

694. **WHEEL-MADE BOTTLE. From the time of Christ. Roman Judaea, 1st Century A.D.** Pottery bottle with depressed piriform body, cylindrical neck and wide flat rim. Flat base. Light brown slip over grey-tan core. Height 14.3 cm. Cf. Ackerman and Braunstein III var....**CHOICE 150.00**

695. **WHEEL-MADE BOTTLE From the time of Christ. Roman Period. 1st Century A.D.** Elongated ovoid body and cylindrical neck. Everted lip and flat bottom. Some irregularity at bottom. Buff ware. Height 11.7 cm. Hayes, *ROM* 345b. ....**CHOICE 95.00**

696. **WHEEL-MADE COOKING POT From the time of Christ and the Apostles. Early Roman Period. 1st-2nd Century A.D.** Globular body, very mild spiral ribbing, short cylindrical neck and rounded bottom. Flared rim with exterior ridge below. Band handles from rim to shoulder. Grey brown slip over red-grey ware. Height 15.2 cm. Israeli provenance. Ackerman and Braunstein 113. Some reconstruction and restoration. ....**CHOICE 150.00**

697. **UNGUENTARIUM. From the time of Christ. Roman Period. 1st-2nd Century A.D.** Buff with ovoid body. Smoothed with subtle ribbing. Orange-brown slip on upper portion of tubular neck with rolled rim. 14.5 cm. Ackerman/Braunstein, *Israel in Antiquity*. III. Hayes, *ROM* 156-7. A lovely example............................**SUPERB 90.00**

698. **UNGUENTARIUM. From the time of Christ. Roman Period. 1st-3nd Century A.D.** Thickish orange-red clay with ovoid body. Smoothed. Flat roughly-cut base to tubular neck. Height 10 cm. Cf. *ROM* 344. ....**CHOICE 50.00**

699. **WHEEL-MADE JUG. From the time of persecution. Roman Period. 2nd-3rd Century A.D.** Near globular body, short conical neck widening to mouth with vertical moulding ornamented by central ridge. Short strap handle, minimally pinched lip, and slightly concave base. Ribbed body with smoothed neck. Orange self slip. Height 15 cm. Cf. *ROM* 323..........................**CHOICE 500.00**

700. **WHEEL-MADE JUGLET. From the time of Constantine and the First Ecumenical (Nicene) Council. Late Roman. c. 3rd Century A.D.** High-bellied body tapering to a flat wire-cut base, wide neck and mouth. Band handle from mouth to shoulder. Heavy spiral wheel-ridging on body. Orange slip over orange-buff ware. Height 7 cm. *ROM* 313. ....**CHOICE 150.00**

701. **WHEEL-MADE JUGLET. From the time of Constantine and the First Ecumenical (Nicene) Council. Late Roman.** 3rd-4th Century A.D. Egg-shaped body tapering to a flat wire-cut base, narrow neck with everted rim. Band handle with shaved exterior from mouth to shoulder. Spiral wheel-ridging on body. Red-brown ware. Height 7 cm. *ROM* 312. Ustinov UP330 (Hellenistic). ....**CHOICE-SUPERB 135.00**

702. **WHEEL-MADE JUGLET. From the time of Constantine and the First Ecumenical (Nicene) Council. Late Roman. 3rd-4th Century A.D.** Egg-shaped body tapering to a flat wire-cut base, narrow neck with wide, everted rim. Heavy band handle from mouth to shoulder. Spiral wheel-ridging on body. Red-brown slip over dark grey-brown ware. Height 6 cm. *ROM* 312. ....**CHOICE 100.00**

703. **FLASK. From the time of the Council of Nicaea. Late Roman. 3rd-4th centuries A.D.** Pink-orange clay with spiral ribbing, flaring rim, flat bottom. 7.8 cm. Cf. Hayes, *ROM* 307-8. ....**SUPERB 80.00**

TERRACOTTA

704. **TERRACOTTA FEMALE HEAD Judaea. Late Bronze. 1550-1200 B.C.** Mold-made Astarte plaque. Cf. Beth Misim, Albright, #6. Cf. James, *Beth Shan*, fig. 115, 2. ....**CHOICE 200.00**

705. **TERRACOTTA HEAD OF ASTARTE PLAQUE. Judaea. Iron I. 1200-1000 B.C.** Head fragment with band in hair, large disc in forehead. Albright 27.10. A superb example of high relief. The finest example we have handled. ....**SUPERB 200.00**

706. **TERRACOTTA FEMALE FIGURE. Judaeo-Phoenician. 5th-3rd Century B.C.** With left arm to breast, hollow mold, brown ware. Upper half of figure. Bulletin Du Musee de Beyrouth II, Pl. II, VII, VIII (Sidon). James, *Beth Shan*, fig. 116, 4...**CHOICE 125.00**

707. **FRAGMENT OF A LEGIONARY TILE. Jerusalem. Roman Period. 1st-3rd Century A.D.** From the Tenth Legion. The letters "LE" and part of a third letter, probably an "X" can be read. Measures 7 cm x 5.8 cm. Cf. Tushingham, pp. 60-61, fig. 1-38 (p. 418), and 1-29 (p. 419). ....**AVERAGE 150.00**

708. **TENTH LEGION TILE FRAGMENT. 2nd Century A.D.** Brick red ware with white-pink slip. Rectangular stamp impression with raised inscription: LEX[FR]. 6.7 x 7.7 x 3 cm thick. Barag Type IId. Tushingham fig. 66.6. The camp of Legion X Fretensis was located by Titus adjacent to the ruins of Jerusalem.....................................**CHOICE 150.00**

STAMP SEALS

709. **PALESTINE-CANAANITE. 1500-1000 B.C.** Baked gray clay hemispheroid with loop on top. Two standing priests in long garments, one with right arm raised; small vertical dots at each side. 16 x 15 mm. A most unusual stamp seal. Rare. Found in Israel. Cf. Von Der Osten, *Newell*, 52. For parallel style, cf. Rowe SIII..................................**CHOICE 175.00**

710. **PALESTINE. Second Beth Shemesh Period. 1200-1100 B.C.** Cream-yellow steatite scaraboid stamp seal. Man standing with arm raised before horse with head turned back. 19 x 14 mm. Found in Israel. Some chips in field. Rowe S013-16 var. The Rowe example depicts a man with birds; this example is certainly of the same style...**CHOICE 150.00**

711. **ANCIENT ISRAEL. 1200-1000 B.C.** Beige carved steatite scaraboid. Seated human figure on chair with right arm raised. Left arm down, and winged object to left. 1.9 cm long. Typical of the line figures in Rowe, S013-16. Found in Israel. ....CHOICE 350.00

712. **PALESTINE. XXII-XXIII Dynasty. 950-750 B.C.** Cream steatite cowroid seal. Seated man in cart. 14 x 13 mm. Found in Israel. Cf. Rowe-SI04(A) var. The Rowe example was found in debris with ivories. ....CHOICE 125.00

713. **PHOENICIAN. 8th-7th Century B.C.** Bluish black. Glass paste scaraboid. Deity seated on high-back throne, arm raised, monkey before with raised arm, attendant behind with raised arm in act of adoration. 17 x 13 mm. Egyptianizing style with hatched throne and central figure is typical of Phoenician style. Scarce. See Rowe for glass scaraboid of similar date. Cf. for style, Pitman, *AAM* 83. ....CHOICE 200.00

714. **PHOENICIAN. 8th-7th Century B.C.** Aqua clear glass scaraboid. Sphinx recumbent, wings up. Serpent before. In ex. ANKH (The Emblem of Life). One serpent on each side. 18 mm x 13 mm. Rare. For style, Cf. Pitman, *AAM* 83 var. ....CHOICE 250.00

715. **ACHAEMENID OVER PALESTINE. 6th-5th Century B.C.** Brown steatite scaraboid. Winged disk above seated figure with palm and staff at each side. Measures 16 x 13 mm. Found in Israel. ....AVERAGE 80.00

CYLINDER SEALS

716. **STEATITE CYLINDER SEAL. Levantine. 2nd Millennium B.C.** Grey steatite. Man hunting two animals. Gazelle, cat, and short dog below. Man has quiver over shoulder. 17 mm. Buchanan 1028 var. An unusual depiction. ....CHOICE 200.00

717. **TERRACOTTA CYLINDER SEAL. Palestine. 2nd Millennium B.C.** Crude stick figure seated with arms raised, before walking figure with head looking back, another standing figure upside down. 3.1 cm. This seal can certainly be classified by its simplified design. Similarly designed seals were found in Gaza sites. Cf. Petrie 1930-33. For similar subject, Cf. Canes 1090. For similar style, Cf. Buchanan, *AM*, 839. Cf. Novgayroh CXVII, XXXIII. ....CHOICE 500.00

718. **BLACK STEATITE CYLINDER SEAL. Late 2nd Millennium B.C.** Two advancing figures before seated figure in long garment, shrine door behind, all in dentated borders. 25 mm. Cf. style of figures in Buchanan, *AAM* 996. Cf. Buchanan, AM *992* for dentated borders. ....CHOICE 325.00

719. **BLACK STEATITE CYLINDER SEAL. Levant (North Syrian-Palestine). 19th-13th Century B.C.** Crude linear animal group, goat standing (vertical animal) or seated goatherd. Length 19 mm. Cf. Buchanan, *AM* 1019 var. Made during the "Dark Age" upheavals during the 1200s B.C. ....CHOICE 250.00

GLASS

720. **GLASS SCARABOID. Phoenician. 7th Century B.C.** Aqua. Depicts a king standing with one arm raised holding a weapon, the other arm holding a lion, one foot also on lion. Part of inscription (?). Measures 17 x 15 mm. Cf. München 209 for type; Cf. Harden, *Phoenicians*, fig. 82 for subject. Very rare. ....CHOICE 400.00

721. **EYE BEAD. 7th-5th Century B.C.** Black wound glass bead with five applied eyes. Perforated for stringing. Diameter 1.4 cm. These beads were worn to protect the wearer against the evil eye. Cf. Dubin, *History of Beads,* pp. 307-313. Purchased in 1919; found in the Kalla tomb near Tyre. ....CHOICE 60.00

722. **AMULET. 4th Century A.D.** Early Christian glass amulet representing the blood of Jesus in the form of globule suspended from thick loop. Black glass. 16 mm. "...and from Jesus Christ the faithful witness, the first born of the dead, the ruler of kings on earth. To Him who loves us and has freed us from our sins by His blood..." Rev. 1:5. Cf. Eisen and Kouchakji, Pl. 129. ....CHOICE 75.00

723. **GLASS AMULET. 4th Century A.D.** Joseph of Arimathea flask of twisted blue glass with open work sides. 21 mm. It was Joseph of Arimathea who gave his tomb for the burial of Jesus. According to the early Christian Book of Melkin "...Joseph had with him in the [i.e. his own] sarcophagus two little vases, white and silver, filled with the blood of Jesus." Hence these flask amulets gained popularity among early Christians, particularly in the Levant. Eisen, Glass, fig. 226d. Top portion of amulet...................AVERAGE 50.00

724. **ASTARTE AMULET. Phoenician. 1st Century B.C.-1st Century A.D.** Black glass, mold-made amulet with figure of Astarte. 2.9 x 1.8 cm, 2 mm thick. Encrustation. Cf. *From the Lands of the Bible, Art and Artifacts,* #203. ....CHOICE 200.00

LAMPS

725. **OIL LAMP. Israel. 2200-1500 B.C.** Buff-grey clay with white grit. Plate with four pinched sides at corners. Measures 9.8 cm square. Schloessinger 311. Traces of carbon at each corner. This is among the earliest known lamps. ....SUPERB 200.00

726. **OIL LAMP. Israel. 1550-1200 B.C.** Buff clay "cocked hat" lamp, saucer pinched at one point. Traces of carbon deposits at nozzle. Round base. Diameter 15 cm. Schloessinger 316. From the time of Moses and Judges............SUPERB 150.00

727. **SAUCER OIL LAMP. From the time of Moses and Judges. Late Bronze. 1550-1200 B.C.** With medium pinched nozzle, subtle rim flattening and rounded bottom. Blackening at nozzle. Orange buff ware. 13 cm wide. Schloessinger 317 ....**CHOICE 150.00**

728. **SAUCER OIL LAMP. From the time of Saul, David and Solomon. Iron I-11. 1200-586 B.C.** with sharply pinched nozzle, no flattening to rim, and low disc base. Grey ware. Schloessinger 318-21. Amiran 100:13. Reconstructed. ....**CHOICE 125.00**

729. **SAUCER OIL LAMP. From the time of Isaiah and Jeremiah. Iron IIC. 800-586 B.C.** With sharply pinched nozzle, distinct rim flattening and wide flat base. Brown ware. 6 cm wide, 6.5 cm long. Schloessinger 318-32 1. Amiran p. 291. Scarce type. ....**CHOICE 165.00**

730. **HELLENISTIC OIL LAMP. Palestinian 2nd-1st Century B.C.** Brownish grey clay and slip. Radial ribbing. Small blunt knob at side. Length 8.4 cm. *ROM* 62. Some hard clay encrustation...**CHOICE 100.00**

731. **OIL LAMP. "Herodian." Early Roman/Judaean. 1st Century B.C.-1st Century A.D.** Mold-made lamp of reddish-brown clay with round body. Large filling hole with petal-like incised lines radiating out from center hole. Remains of handle. Handmade spatulated nozzle added later. Some knife paring to sides of nozzle. Length 8.3 cm. Cf. Qedem, Hebrew University of Jerusalem Monographs Vol. 8, p. 81, #331-334 for similar shapes. Small hole to side. Unusual. ....**CHOICE-SUPERB 200.00**

732. **WHEEL-MADE LAMP. Herodian. c. 25 B.C.-200 A.D. Probably 1st Century A.D.** With flat upper and lower body and slightly convex sides. Spatulated nozzle offset by two incised lines. Medium filling hole within ridge. Flat base. Blackening at large wick hole. 9.3 cm. Schloessinger 331, 334. *ROM* 53. ....**CHOICE-SUPERB 250.00**

733. **ROMAN OIL LAMP. 1st Century A.D.** Style and manufacture of Israel. Buff clay lamp with traces of red-orange slip. Fruit-on-vine design on shoulder. "S" maker's mark on base. Length 8.3 cm. *ROM*-; Schl.-; Warschaw-. Chips at nozzle hole. ....**CHOICE 150.00**

734. **MOLD-MADE LAMP. Late 1st-2nd Century A.D.** Round body and short beak nozzle. Small flat discus decorated with "chicken" head. Small filling hole. Grape bunches and leaves ornament shoulder. Small solid handle. Flat base impressed with leaf spray above horizontal line. Israeli provenance. *ROM* 436 (potter's mark). Schl. 364 (motif), Schl. 399 (contemp). Repaired. Scarce type. ....**CHOICE 200.00**

735. **JUDAEAN OIL LAMP. 1st-2nd Century A.D.** Herodian lamp, buff coloring with widening nozzle. Length 8.5 cm. *ROM* 53; Schl. 331-334; Warschaw Coll. IMJ #78. ....**CHOICE 200.00**

736. **ROMAN OIL LAMP. 1st-2nd Century A.D.** Mold-made oil lamp with ovoid body and bow end nozzle offset by semi-volutes. Recessed discus with rough filling hole, surrounded by ring. Small "conical" handle attached at back. Pronounced ring base. Drab red-buff ware. Length 7.9 cm. *ROM*-; Schl.-. Said to be of north Levantine manufacture...**CHOICE 75.00**

737. **ROMAN OIL LAMP MEDALLION. Late 1st-2nd Century A.D.** Mold-made discus depicting the helmeted head of Athena left. Two filling holes. Egg border. Tan ware. Diameter about 5.2 cm. Schl. 167 (contemp.); Szentieleky 94a (design)............................**CHOICE-SUPERB 100.00**

738. **NOZZLE OIL LAMP. Roman Judaean. 4th Century A.D.** Bow-shaped, mold made. Piriform body, pyramidal handle and large filling hole. Integral bow nozzle, "pinched" at sides. Herringbone pattern to shoulder, two pine cones at intersection with nozzle. Ring base with central pellet. Traces of red slip over orange-tan ware. Length 7.5 cm. Schl. 436-7, 439. Scarce....................**CHOICE-SUPERB 135.00**

739. **OIL LAMP. Roman Judaean. 4th Century A.D.** Bow-shaped nozzle type. Mold made with piriform body and bow nozzle with "pinched" sides. Large filling hole with double border. Pyramidal handle. Shoulder ornamented with grapes and vines. Inverted amphora on top of nozzle. Flat base. Pale pink ware. Blackening at wick hole. Length 8.8 cm. Contemp. Schl. 436-7, 438. Sharp details but chips. Scarce. ....**CHOICE 125.00**

740. **NOZZLE-TYPE LAMP Roman-Judaean. 4th Century A.D.** Bow-shaped. Mold made with piriform body and bow nozzle with "pinched" sides. Large filling hole with triple border. Short pyramidal handle. Shoulder ornamented with grapes and vines. Inverted amphora on top of nozzle. Shallow ring base. Pale orange ware. Blackening at wick hole. Contemp. Schl. 436-7, 438. Scarce.. .**CHOICE 125.00**

741. **NOZZLE-TYPE LAMP. Roman Judaean. 4th Century A.D.** Bow-shaped. Mold- made oil lamp with piriform body, pyramidal handle and large filling hole. Integral bow nozzle, "pinched" at sides. Herringbone pattern to shoulder, two pine cones at intersection with nozzle. Ring base with central pellet. Traces of red slip over orange tan ware. 7.5 cm. Schl. 436-7, 439. Scarce. ....**CHOICE-SUPERB 135.00**

742. **OIL LAMP. Roman Judaean. 4th-5th century A.D.** Bow-shaped nozzle type. Mold-made lamp with ovoid body, large filling hole with thick border, and pyramidal handle. Bow-shaped nozzle decorated with inverted amphora between two bunches of grapes. Herringbone to shoulder. Flat base. Dark buff ware. Length 9.2 cm. Schl. 439. Scarce type. ....**AVERAGE 75.00**

743. **BUFF CLAY LAMP. 4th -5th Century A.D.** Wide flat rim with eight raised rosettes, cross at wick hole. Scarce. Cf. Waage, Pl. X, 814 (4th century A.D.) Cf. Rosenthal-Sivan-Qedem, 575. *Schloessinger Collection*.........**CHOICE 75.00**

744.   **MOLD-MADE LAMP. 5th Century A.D.** Piriform body with flat top and sloping straight sides. Narrow band shoulder. Medium filling hole surrounded by wreath design disposed triangularly. Large wick hole. Deep whirl pattern impressed in base, groove to underside of short stump handle. Dark-red glaze over pink clay. 8.9 cm. Rare. Bailey, *BM*. Q14533EA. *ROM-*. Deneauve-. *Schloessinger Collection.* ....**CHOICE 150.00**

JEWELRY

745.   **SILVER EARRING. Judaea, Solomonic Period. 10th Century B.C.** Drop lunate type earring. Height 1.3 cm. Cf. Maxwell-Hyslop, Pl. 19. Horn silver.........**CHOICE 100.00**

746.   **BLACK SERPENTINE SCARABOID. 9th-8th Century B.C.** Two standing stick men with arms raised. Wheel with eight spokes before. The Tyre kingdoms, Lebanon and Phoenicia, are mentioned profusely in the Bible. The wood for the temple at Jerusalem was supplied from the cedars of Lebanon (Phoenicia). The two men are standing in an attitude of worship. Cf. Munich, Band I, Teil I, 103 for style and figure. A nice size and bold carving. A rare seal. ....**CHOICE 1000.00**

747.   **GLASS ASTARTE PLAQUE.   Phoenician.   Roman Period. 2nd Century B.C.- 1st Century A.D.** Blue-black. Linear design, oval head with patterned bust. 4 x 2 cm. Cf. *Lands of the Bible*, 203. A nice example of this votive Astarte. Found in Israel ....**CHOICE 100.00**

WRITING

748.   **THEATRE TICKET. Palmyra. 2nd-3rd Century A.D.** Dark brown terracotta theatre ticket or token, commonly called a tessera. Two citizens are shown reclining, each wearing a turreted headdress. Aramaic legend to the left. Same image on both sides. Measures 1.7 x 1.6 cm. Cf. Dubuisson, Pl. XIVII:32. Scarce. ....**CHOICE 80.00**

536

538

543

545

549

550

568

567

571

566

573

577

578

PLATE 7

582

583

585

593

594

591

598

606

608

PLATE 8

HOLY LAND

600

617

621

612

605

620

614

596

PLATE 9

HOLY LAND

622

645

627

631

636

635

625

632

PLATE 10

HOLY LAND

648

651

653

663

666

654

700

671

694

672

702

PLATE 11

HOLY LAND

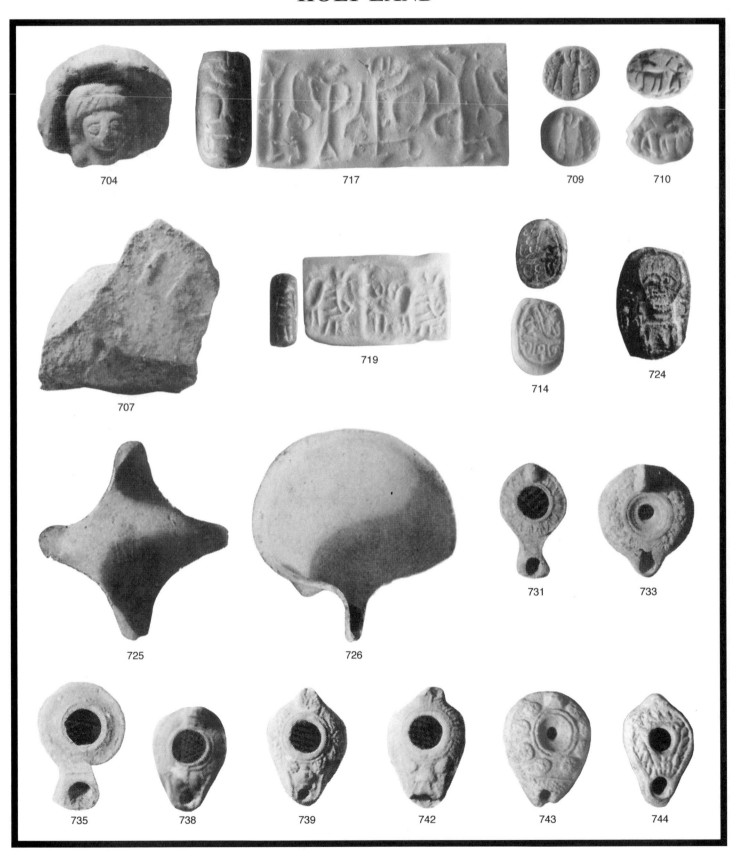

704

717

709

710

707

719

714

724

725

726

731

733

735

738

739

742

743

744

PLATE 12

CENTRAL ASIATIC

The area of Central Asia comprises parts or all of the modern states of India, Pakistan, Afghanistan and many of the newly independent former Soviet Republics on the southern border of Russia. It was an important area in antiquity because it was a meeting ground for the great eastern cultures of antiquity centered in Persia, Mesopotamia, India, and China. But it also developed important indigenous cultures. Some of them were nomadic, mostly to be found in the great central plains and grasslands of the region; others were settled civilizations mostly found in the western and southern fringes of the area. Both the nomads and the settled civilizations produced important works of art which are only gradually beginning to be understood through archaeological excavation.

One of the most important of the settled civilizations occupied the Indus Valley from about 2700 to 1750 B.C. Because its script remains undeciphered, the Indus civilization is known only from archaeological evidence. It is sometimes referred to as the Harappan civilization, named for the site of Harappa, one of its major centers. Geographically one of the most extensive early civilizations of the Old World, it stretched from north of the Hindu Kush down the entire length of the Indus and beyond into peninsular India. In the west, outposts that extended almost to the present-day Iranian-Pakistani border have been found along the inhospitable Makran coast. Excavations at the important site of Mehrgarh, at the foot of the Bolan Pass, indicate that large settlements may have existed in the area as early as the 7th millennium B.C. Two thousand or more years later sites in eastern Baluchistan and the Indus Valley were larger and more numerous. At some sites archaeologists have found various distinctive ceramic objects, such as terracotta toy carts. From this evidence archaeologists speculate that there took place an early, or pre-Harappan, spread of culture from the Punjab south to the Arabian Sea.

The famous cities of the mature Indus civilization were discovered accidentally in the mid-19th century during the construction of a railroad. Archaeological excavations were not begun until the 1920s. During that decade the so-called twin capitals of Indus civilization, Mohenjo-Daro and Harappa, were excavated under the direction of Sir John Marshall. Recent archaeological investigation has been concentrated on documenting the beginnings of urban life in the area. The civilization appears to have declined rapidly in the early 2nd millennium B.C. Some scholars have speculated about a final massacre, possibly by conquering Aryan peoples whose epics refer to their conquest of walled cities, but others have postulated an ecological disaster as the cause.

Archaeologists have long commented on the uniformity of the material remains of the Indus civilization. Pottery forms and designs were remarkably similar throughout the vast area encompassed by the Indus civilization. Few large works of art or pieces of statuary have been discovered, except for several notable examples from Mohenjo-Daro and Harappa. Spears, knives, and other objects of copper and bronze have been found, but most are of rather poor quality. The most developed craft appears to have been the carving and drilling of square stamp seals that depict various domestic animals, such as humped bulls, rhinoceroses, and elephants. These seals, numbering in the thousands, are the major source of writings in the pictographic Indus script. Attempts to decipher these symbols have so far been unsuccessful. Although not common on the art market, Indus Valley objects are highly sought after by collectors.

Another important early civilization in the area was centered in Bactria. Bactria was an ancient land on both sides of the upper Oxus River, today called the Amu Darya, in present-day northern Afghanistan and southern Tajikistan. Bactria was important for its strategic location between China, India, and the West. The prophet Zoroaster is said to have made his first converts in Bactria and to have died there. Bactria became an important province of the Achaemenid Empire, and after the conquests of Alexander III it became the center of an independent Greek kingdom whose rulers struck fine Greek-style coins. Many interesting artifacts have also been found including seals, stone vessels and figurines, and pottery. The kingdom lasted until 128 B.C., when northern nomads overran it. Bactria then became part of the Kushan empire and remained so until the 4th century A.D., when Sassanian governors became its rulers. The nomadic Hephthalites (White Huns) took control in the following century, ruling until the Arab conquest at the end of the 7th century. Much Bactrian art has come on the market in recent years, mostly from Afghanistan,

The Turkmen, or Turkoman, are a Central Asian ethnic group related to Anatolian Turks who are the principal nationality in Turkmenistan (Turkmenia). They probably arrived in the area about 600 A.D. They occupy a vast steppe which in antiquity was the home of nomadic peoples who, like the Lures of Persia and the Sythians of the Caspian area, created many interesting art objects. It was also an important link in the great silk caravan route to China. Now that the area is more accessible to western scholars, we will undoubtedly learn more about its art.

Gandhara was a semi-independent kingdom that flourished from the 3rd century B.C. to the 5th century in what is now northern Pakistan. It extended from present-day Rawalpindi through the Peshawar Valley to Kabul. The region was invaded by Persian rulers in the 6th century B.C. It came under Alexander the Great in 327 B.C., and was soon after captured by Chandragupta Maurya. Subsequently it fell to the Saka dynasty (Scythians) in 95 B.C., the Kushans in A.D. 48, and finally to the Muslims in the 7th to the 8th century. Its main city was Taxila. Gandharan art is principally known for its Greco-Buddhist school of sculpture, but lesser arts such as pottery and glass making were also practiced. Because of its affinity to classical sculpture, Gandharan sculpture is very popular among collectors today.

SEALS

Central Asian seals are found mainly from two of the cultures of the area. Perhaps the most interesting group comes from the Indus Valley culture where a large number of important seals were discovered. These may be a form of writing or may symbolize elaborate heraldic devices or standards that served to identify families and their properties from others. The other major group come from the Bactrian area where many bronze and stone seals have been found.

WEAPONS

Although weapons have been found in Central Asian excavations they are, with a few exceptions, mostly from the western area near Persia, and are usually of poor quality.

POTTERY AND TERRACOTTA

Pottery and terracotta sculptures from central Asia range from the many interesting examples of terracotta sculpture from the Indus Valley cultures, particularly figurines and chariot models, to the characteristic pottery and stucco sculpture of Gandara.

STONE, WRITING, AND JEWELRY

Some of the cultures of the Central Asian area were famous for their stone sculptures such as the Gandaran culture whose sculptures, mostly executed in shist, combined elements of Classical Art with native Indian art. Others produced beautiful jewelry such as the nomadic cultures of Turkmenistan. Writing records in general do not play an important role in most Central Asian cultures with the possible exception of the Indus Valley cultures where seal inscriptions and the like seem to point to an indigenous language. However, largely because no major inscriptions have been discovered, some scholars have surmised that the characters do not represent writing in the same sense that Sumerian cuneiform or Egyptian hieroglyphics were writing.

CENTRAL ASIATIC

WEAPONS
Stone
749. **QUARTZITE ARROWHEAD. Bronze Age. Margiana Culture (Central Asia) 2000-1500 B.C. (Middle Stage Gunur).** Light brown. 3.8 cm x 1.3 cm. Sarianidi, *Margiana in the Bronze Age*, fig. 12, 30. Found in Azerbajian. Tip missing.......................................**CHOICE-SUPERB 75.00**

Metal
Swords
750. **BRONZE SWORD. Afghanistan. 1200-800 B.C.** Hollow-cast bronze sword with disc pommel. Pommel separately cast, with three discs, one scalloped with annulet decoration. Round grip; thick guard with geometric design. Slight raised midrib. Blade separately cast. Length 40.8 cm. Cf. Muscarella, *Bronze and Iron*, p. 100, #166. Some erosion and chipping to blade. ....**CHOICE 400.00**

Axe Heads
751. **BRONZE AXE HEAD. Bactria. 1200-800 B.C.** Bronze axe head, socketed with knob at back. Round spoon-shaped blade with central ridge. Hole on either side of small shaft. 14 x 5.8 cm. Malloy 39; Talbot Rice-. A most unusual shape. Rare. ....**CHOICE 800.00**

752. **BRONZE AXE HEAD. Bactria. 1200-800 B.C.** Bronze axe head with socket in curve of blade. Pierced holes to each side. Curve ends in point behind socket. 10.5 x 4 cm. Malloy 40; Cf. Sotheby's, New York, 1986, #161; Talbot Rice. Green patina. ....**SUPERB 750.00**

Arrowheads
753. **BRONZE ARROWHEAD. North Central Asia. 6th-4th Century B.C.** Deltoid blade with small sharp barbs. 3.2 cm x 1.5 cm. Cf. Petrie 62. Scarce type. Hexagonal socket exterior.......................................**SUPERB 75.00**

TERRACOTTA
754. **TERRACOTTA FIGURE, Northern India. 2nd Millennium B.C.** A terracotta bird-faced fertility figure. Height 15.5 cm. ....**CHOICE 600.00**

755. **TERRACOTTA FIGURE, Northern India. 2nd Millennium B.C.** A terracotta conical-bottom figure with clasping hands. Height 11.5 cm. ....**CHOICE 300.00**

756. **FIGURINE. Archaic. 1st Millennium B.C.** Terracotta figurine, perhaps a monkey with circular eyes, full nose and mouth and pointed head to right. Right arm across chest, left arm bent with object underneath. Bottom half broken off. 6.4 cm x 6.4 cm. ....**CHOICE 350.00**

757. **MOUNTED INDIAN TERRACOTTA. 3rd-2nd Century B.C.** Male head. Height 6.5 cm. ....**CHOICE 100.00**

758. **MOUNTED INDIAN TERRACOTTA. 3rd-2nd Century B.C.** Yoked buffalo. Height 6.5 cm. ....**CHOICE 100.00**

759. **MOUNTED INDIAN TERRACOTTA. 3rd-2nd Century B.C.** Goatlike female. ....**CHOICE 150.00**

760. **MOUNTED INDIAN TERRACOTTA. 3rd-2nd Century B.C.** Bird...**CHOICE 100.00**

761. **MOUNTED INDIAN TERRACOTTA. 3rd-2nd Century B.C.** Bird head. ....**CHOICE 100.00**

762. **INDIAN TERRACOTTA HEAD. 2nd Century B.C.** Small reddish youth, Kasaumbi ....**CHOICE 250.00**

763. **TERRACOTTA FERTILITY FIGURINE. Shunga Period. 2nd-1st Century B.C.** Reddish clay with large slit eyes, angular forehead, and nose and small circular mouth. Large earrings with straight hair with deep vertical cuts through. Large necklace with linear design, protruding, pointed breasts, and arms broken off. 6.3 cm high, 4.7 cm wide. Ex: Richard E.S. Maxson Collection, 1925-1975, Amherst, MA. Cf. Barrelet, Pl. LXIV, #600. Cf. Wheeler, India and Pakistan, #55. ....**CHOICE 300.00**

764. **TERRACOTTA FIGURE. c. 100 B.C.-100 A.D.** Figure with small child. Child complete, figure gone from waist up. Height 9.8 cm. ....**CHOICE 200.00**

765. **TERRACOTTA HEAD. c. 100 B.C.-100 A.D.** Grey, bald with huge earlobes. Height 4.5 cm. ....**CHOICE 150.00**

766. **TERRACOTTA HEAD. c. 100 B.C.-100 A.D.** 7.8 cm head with ornate headdress. ....**CHOICE 150.00**

767. **TERRACOTTA HEAD. c. 100 B.C.-100 A.D.** 8.2 cm head with ornate headdress......................**CHOICE 150.00**

768. **TERRACOTTA BUST. c. 100 B.C.-100 A.D.** 6 cm headless bust. ....**CHOICE 100.00**

769. **TERRACOTTA HEAD FRAGMENT. Parthian Afghanistan. 1st Century B.C.-2nd Century A.D.** Found near Kabul. A handsome youth in long hair and wearing kausia. In especially nice Greco-Roman style. ....**CHOICE 100.00**

770. **TERRACOTTA HEAD FRAGMENT. Parthian Afghanistan. 1st Century B.C.-2nd Century A.D.** Found near Kabul. A bearded deity wearing wreathed polos. In especially nice Greco-Roman style. ....**CHOICE 100.00**

771. **TERRACOTTA HEAD FRAGMENT. Parthian Afghanistan. 1st Century B.C.-2nd Century A.D.** Found near Kabul. A veiled girl with prominent ears. ....**CHOICE 100.00**

772. **KUSHAN TERRACOTTA HEAD OF A KING. c. 1st-2nd Century A.D.** With incised moustache, headdress surmounted by fan-shaped crest. Uttar Pradesh, India, 7" (17.8 cm). ....**CHOICE-SUPERB 3000.00**

773. **INDIAN TERRACOTTA HEAD. 4th-5th Century A.D.** 11.4 cm laughing youth. Northern. India Ahichchhatra. ....**CHOICE 300.00**

METAL
774. **BACTRIAN COPPER ALLOY COSMETIC CONTAINER. Form of a Camel. Early 2nd Millennium B.C.** Western Central Asia, Middle Bronze Age, 7.9 cm. ....**CHOICE 10,000.00**

775. **BACTRIAN COPPER ALLOY COSMETIC CONTAINER. Form of a Mouflon. Early 2nd Millennium B.C.** With prominent dewlap. Western Central Asia, 9.2 cm. ....**CHOICE 7500.00**

776. **MARGIANA. 2nd Millennium B.C.** In copper, a stamp with triskeles base and stalk handle with loop top. Intact. Width 20.8 mm. ....**CHOICE 125.00**

777. **MARGIANA. 2nd Millennium B.C.** In faience, disc with "milled" edge and loop handle. Engraved on base an elegant rosette. Intact, with some of faience glaze remaining. Width 33 mm. ....**CHOICE 100.00**

778. **SARMATIAN BRONZE BELT PLAQUE. Horse. Late 1st Millennium B.C.** With left foreleg raised, bull head on its back; all within inverted lunate form. Height 9.9 cm. ....**CHOICE 7500.00**

779. **MARGIANA. c. 1500 B.C.** A bronze stamp seal, circular with loop handle. Design ornate six petalled rosette with circular border. Two minor edge chips. Diameter 5.6 cm. ....**CHOICE 125.00**

780. **MARGIANA. c. 1500 B.C.** Circular with starburst design. Loop worn through. Diam. 4.5 cm.............**CHOICE 75.00**

781. **MARGIANA. c. 1500 B.C.** Square with central cross. Diam. 3.3 cm. ....**CHOICE 75.00**

STONE
782. **TURKMENIAN. Bronze Pin. 2000-1600 B.C.** Long U-shaped pin with square head. Design of swastika with curled ends on head. Pin measures 7.6 x 3 cm, head 1.5 cm square. Nice patina..**CHOICE 100.00**

783. **MARGIANA. c. 1500 B.C.** Elephant amulet in stone. From Bactria in Afghanistan, in white calcite. A very well carved example. Pierced across the body for stringing. Length 18 mm. ....**CHOICE 150.00**

784. **MARGIANA. c. 1500 B.C.** Elephant amulet in stone. From Tel Brak in red brown steatite with dot and circle ornament. Pierced vertically. Length 16 mm. ....**CHOICE 150.00**

785. **MARGIANA. c. 1000 B.C.** A pyramidal stamp seal set in limestone. On base a winged, recumbent bull-sphinx with head turned back and wearing an Achaemenid-like crown. Height 16.3 mm. ....**CHOICE 100.00**

786. **MARGIANA. c. 1000 B.C.** From the Ordos, a bronze "button" shaped as the facing head of a fox. Height 23 mm. ....**CHOICE 100.00**

787. **MARGIANA. 4th-3rd Century B.C.** Greco-Persian type scaraboid in yellow and grey chalcedony. Carved in "a globolo" style is a running goat or ibex. Bored to take a thin wire to mount into a ring. Intact with very slight wear. Size: 15.4 x 20.4 mm. ....**CHOICE 300.00**

788. **MARGIANA. 4th-3rd Century B.C.** Greco-Persian type scaraboid of black to brown opaque sard. Carved in a "globolo" style is a recumbent winged bull in profile. Bored for stringing. Intact with only slight wear. Size: 15 x 16.6 mm. ....**CHOICE 200.00**

789. **STATUETTE OF BUDDHA. 2nd Century A.D.** Grey schist statuette of Buddha. Lovely carving of details of Buddha standing with hands holding flowers clasped to his chest. Hellenistic style draping of his clothes and also headdress, which looks Roman Egyptian. Facial features are stern, almost sad. 29 cm high. Cf. Talbot Rice, *Ancient Arts of Central Asia*, fig. 140. Buddhist art is said to have originated in Gandhara, and then spread toward Central Asia and China. Missing beneath thighs. ....**CHOICE 1750.00**

790. **HEAD OF BUDDHA. 2nd Century A.D.** Detailed head of Buddha in grey schist. Facial features indicate Asian influence. Wears headdress. Elongated earlobes with earrings and wearing large mustache. Eyes are staring, but face has withdrawn, quiet look. 15.7 cm high. Western influence can be seen in the work of the headdress. Cf. Talbot Rice, *Ancient Arts of Central Asia*. Missing below neck..**CHOICE 1600.00**

791. **SCHIST CARVING. 2nd Century A.D.** Female head. Height 1.8 cm. Gandharan. ....**AVERAGE 100.00**

792. **SCHIST CARVING. 2nd Century A.D.** Lion. Height 1.8 cm. Gandharan, ...**AVERAGE 100.00**

793. **SCHIST CARVING. 2nd Century A.D.** Man. Height 1.8 cm. Gandharan....................................**AVERAGE 100.00**

794. **SCHIST CARVING. 2nd Century A.D.** Donkey head. Height 1.8 cm. Gandharan.....................**AVERAGE 100.00**

795. **YAKSHI-MATHURA. 2nd Century A.D.** Indian stone goddess, 19.5 cm tall, mounted on wood. Generally exc. condition, though one breast is missing, plus a few other flaws. ....**CHOICE 300.00**

796. **FULL FIGURE. 2nd –3rd Century A.D.** Green/grey schist statuette of Buddha in traditional yoga or oriental pose. Buddha has childlike features, elongated earlobes, and hairstyle which is a mixture of Hellenistic, because of the curls, and Indian, because of the style worn. Drapery has lost some of the Hellenistic style and is more lineated in keeping with Indian art. Pose is relaxed and serene with detailed carving of hands clasped together in lap. 15 cm high. Cf. Talbot Rice, *Ancient Arts in Central Asia*, fig. 139. Intact and only very lightly worn. A lovely piece. ....**CHOICE 750.00**

797. **GANDHARAN FRIEZE FRAGMENT. 2nd-3rd Century A.D.** 22 x 7 cm section of grey schist carved with eight human figures and two trees. Well worn, though figures are clear. India. ....**CHOICE 300.00**

798. **GANDHARAN BUDDHA HEAD. 2nd-3rd Century A.D.** White stucco, molded head with serene facial detail, elongated earlobes, and short cropped hairdo with bun atop head. Light traces of red pigment on lips. Height 20.5 cm. Light pitting of surface, but intact and nice. Custom mount. ....**CHOICE 1000.00**

799. **GANDHARAN BUDDHA. c. 2nd-3rd Century A.D.** Grey schist carving of the seated deity, wearing multi-pleated garment and holding folded hands in lap as he meditates. Some chipping and roughness, but still quite exc. Height 17 cm. Custom base. ....**CHOICE 300.00**

800. **GANDHARA GREY SCHIST HEAD OF BUDDHA. 2nd-3rd Century A.D.** Hair flowing over large ushnisha. Pakistan. Height 22.2 cm. ....**SUPERB 6000.00**

801. **GANDHARA GREY SCHIST WINGED ATLAS. c. 3rd Century A.D.** Resting, grasping knee. Pakistan. Height 13.7 cm. ....**CHOICE 2000.00**

802. **GANDHARAN FRIEZE. c. 3rd Century A.D.** Gray schist stele fragment, 30.5 x 23.5 cm, with standing female dancing figure upon a pedestal, and another, smaller, to the side. Weathered but nice, though faces lack detail. India. ....**CHOICE 850.00**

803. **GANDHARA GREY SCHIST FRAGMENT. 3rd-4th Century A.D.** Portrays a turbaned bodhisattva head. ....**CHOICE 125.00**

804. **GANDHARA GREY SCHIST FRAGMENT. 3rd-4th Century A.D.** Buddha head, 17 cm. ....**CHOICE 150.00**

805. **GANDHARA GREY SCHIST FRAGMENT. 3rd-4th Century A.D.** Headless bust of Maitreya from a relief, with draped robe and hands in dharmacakra mudra. Height 22 cm. ....**CHOICE 125.00**

806. **GANDHARA GREY SCHIST FRAGMENT. 3rd-4th Century A.D.** Small headless figure of a richly dressed devotee. ....**CHOICE 125.00**

807. **GANDHARA GREY SCHIST FRAGMENT. 3rd-4th Century A.D.** Small headless figure of Vajrapani wearing short tunic and holding a vajra. Height 20 cm. ....**CHOICE 150.00**

808. **GANDHARA GREY SCHIST FRAGMENTARY RELIEF. 3rd-4th Century A.D.** The courtesan Amrapali presenting the Buddha with a mango grove. Seated on a draped throne with turned legs beneath the mango tree, his left hand holding a fold of his heavily pleated robe, two female attendants, holding a bowl and a vessel respectively, to the left, each wearing anklets, pantaloons, and tunic, a bust of Vajrapani (?) above them, with plain borders and acanthus frieze above, 41 cm. ....**CHOICE 750.00**

809. **GANDHARA GREY SCHIST FRAGMENT. 3rd-4th Century A.D.** Slightly concave form, with right hand raised in a recessed panel, ropework border. ....**CHOICE 300.00**

810. **GANDHARA GREY SCHIST FRAGMENT. 3rd-4th Century A.D.** Slightly convex form, carved with a lower register of three heavily draped figures separated by a column from a scene from the Great Departure with Siddharta bidding farewell to his horse Kanthaka and his groom Chandaka. ....**CHOICE 300.00**

811. **GANDHARA GREY SCHIST FRAGMENT. 3rd-4th Century A.D.** Depicts the birth of the Buddha, with the figure of Queen Maya standing beneath the *bodhi* tree at the left, her sister Mahaprajapati supporting her attended by a woman with a water vessel, each wearing jewelry and pleated robes. ....**CHOICE 300.00**

812. **GANDHARA GREY SCHIST OF BUDDHA. 3rd-4th Century A.D.** Meditative face with heavily lidded eyes, pouting lips and urna in relief, the hair and *usnisa* swept back in waves, from a relief, 18 cm. ....**CHOICE 750.00**

813. **GANDHARA GREY SCHIST HEADLESS MALE BODHISATTVA FIGURE. 3rd-4th Century A.D.** Standing on rectangular base with left hand on hip. 42 cm. ....**CHOICE 500.00**

814. **GANDHARA GREY SCHIST HEADLESS MALE BODHISATTVA FIGURE. 3rd-4th Century A.D.** Well modeled body, wearing jewelry, including amuletic necklaces. 27 cm. ....**CHOICE 500.00**

815. **GANDHARA GREY SCHIST RECTANGULAR PANEL. Buddha Enthroned. 3rd-4th Century A.D.** Right hand in abhaya, flanked by attendants. Pakistan. Height 31.8 cm. ....**SUPERB 4000.00**

CENTRAL ASIATIC

751

752

763

756

790

789

796

PLATE 13

EGYPTIAN ART AND ARCHAEOLOGY

The dawn of civilization in ancient Egypt is lost in the mists of prehistory. We know that the fertile Nile Valley attracted early man to its vicinity but experts differ as to when it happened. The archaeological record goes back in an uninterrupted progression at least to the Neolithic period c. 5000 B.C. and some scholars want to push it back even further.

Environment and geography strongly affected the history of ancient Egypt. In fact it is one of the classic examples used by proponents of geographic determinism. In a largely rainless climate, Egypt's high agricultural productivity depended on a long but very narrow flood plain formed by the Nile's annual inundation. Periodic, long-term decreases in its volume might create social stress and political and military conflict, while increases in volume increased food supplies and favored stability and centralized government. It was thus in the interest of the Egyptians to do everything in their power to regulate its flow from establishing a stable and powerful central government to propitiating the various deities they believed responsible for its rise and fall. Despite the shortage of arable land, Egypt was, for much of its history, in a protected and resource rich geographic environment. The deserts to the east and west had valuable stones and minerals and helped protect Egypt from much external attack or infiltration. To the south (northeast Africa) and northwest (Syria-Palestine), however, important kingdoms developed. Egypt traded with and exploited these kingdoms, but was also sometimes threatened by them as in the period of the Hyksos domination. Beyond Syria-Palestine, greater powers – in North Africa, Anatolia, Mesopotamia, and Iran – were alternately Egypt's allies and its rivals in Imperial expansion, but none was a direct threat before the 7th century B.C., so the Egyptians were able to enjoy thousands of years of development, for the most part, without foreign conquest. This goes a long way to explain the remarkable continuity of Egyptian culture over its long history. For example, once the Egyptian language was deciphered by the French scholar Jean Francois Champollion in the early 19th century (he was able to do this following the discovery some years earlier by Napoleon's forces in Egypt of the Rosetta stone, whose bilingual inscriptions in Greek and the ancient language of Egypt enabled him to make the decisive breakthrough in the decipherment of the hieroglyphic script), scholars could basically read texts from the Old Kingdom to the Roman period, a span of thousands of years, despite the inevitable changes in the language over time. While it is true that during its life of more than 3,000 years, the language underwent substantial changes in grammar, syntax, and vocabulary, as well as in the number and character of the hieroglyphic signs used in writing it, it remained basically the same language. From before 2650 B.C., scribes, when writing in ink, often adopted a cursive hand, known as hieratic, which developed until it bore little resemblance to the hieroglyphic script. Once the hieroglyphic script had been deciphered, however, it was possible to decipher the hieratic as well. An even more cursive script, called demotic, evolved from hieratic in about the 7th century B.C. and continued as late as the 5th century A.D. Scholars were able to read this as well.

The importance to Egyptology of this ability to read ancient Egyptian cannot be underestimated. Documents in these three scripts cover a wide variety of subjects, including religion, magic, practical wisdom, belles lettres, history, business, personal and legal matters, medicine, mathematics, and astronomy. Egyptologists of many nations have worked on these documents, publishing the texts with translations and commentaries, writing grammars, and compiling dictionaries. Although many of the original documents are damaged or incomplete, they have provided an invaluable insight into the mind of the ancient Egyptians. Try to read Chaucer in the original Middle English some time to get an idea of how the English language has changed over a far shorter period of time, and you will begin to understand the importance of linguistic continuity to ancient Egyptian culture. The archaeologist's spade has played an equally important role in understanding ancient Egypt. The number of monuments and the quantity of objects available for study are enormous, chiefly because of the long history and pre-history of the ancient Egyptians, the use from an early date of stone, the preservative effects of Egypt's dry climate, the rapid accumulation of wind-blown sand over edifices, and the burial of so much material of all kinds with the dead. The vast amount of material found in Egypt is certainly part of what makes Egypt such a magnet for the modern collector. To understand Egyptian art we must have some familiarity with Egyptian history. As noted, Egyptian civilization begins in the prehistoric period but scholars like to divide Egyptian history into periods roughly corresponding to the thirty dynasties of kings listed by Manetho, an Egyptian chronicler of the 3rd century B.C. The period before c. 3100 B.C., a time for which no written records exist and which is usually referred to as the prehistoric period in Egypt, is called the Pre-dynastic era. The process of Pre-dynastic cultural development is hard to follow in Egypt because major Pre-dynastic sites, on the flood plain, are inaccessible or destroyed and most data come from peripheral settlements and low-desert cemeteries. In northern Egypt, however, the development of Neolithic life can be traced at Merimdeh and in the Fayum sites which date back to at least 5000-4000 B.C. There and elsewhere in the North, the pervasive Northern culture emerged, characterized by monochrome pottery using incised and applied decoration. The earliest Neolithic phases of Southern Egypt are not yet identified, but two cultures existed there by c. 4000 B.C.: the Tasian, influenced by the North, and the Badarian, which originated in the Eastern desert. The former evolved into phases labeled Nakada I (also called the Amratian) and II (also called the Gerzean), representing a material culture very different from that of the North. In the South, among other differences, pottery is more varied in fabric, often has a black top, and favors painted decoration. This pottery is highly prized by collectors and a nice specimen can bring hundreds of dollars today.

According to later traditions, by late Pre-dynastic times, about 3300 B.C., chiefdoms had coalesced into two competitive kingdoms, Northern and Southern. Gradually, the characteristic material culture of the South had been spreading, and it replaced the once different one of northern Egypt in Nakada III. The Pre-dynastic Egyptians probably traded with Syria, Palestine, and northeast Africa throughout Pre-dynastic times. Mesopotamian-style cylinder seals, pottery, and artistic motifs have been found in Pre-dynastic sites but these may have come through intermediaries rather than by direct contact.

Pre-dynastic art was well developed but small scale. Figurines and statuettes of individual humans or animals, some modeled realistically, were made in mud, pottery, and ivory. Slate cosmetic palettes might be in bird or animal form, and painted designs on pottery placed humans, animals, and boats together in sometimes complex designs. All these are found in early Pre-dynastic graves. In later Pre-dynastic times, however, ivory knife handles and ceremonial palettes, perhaps dedicated to temples, bore scenes in relief, possibly including depictions of historical events, as did a wall painting in a chieftain's tomb at Hierakonpolis. Battles, hunts, and ceremonial scenes were favorite motifs. The conventions typical of historical art had their beginning in the Pre-dynastic period. Although Pre-dynastic Egyptian art is, in general, scarcer than Egyptian art of later periods, it is much in demand by collectors.

The two Pre-dynastic kingdoms of Upper and Lower Egypt were apparently unified by King Narmer. A famous ceremonial slate palette shows him surveying slaughtered prisoners, striking a Northern enemy, and wearing the regalia of both kingdoms. He and his immediate predecessors were buried at Abydos, at or near the Southern capital. Narmer's successors were the Pharaohs (kings) of the 1st and 2nd dynasties. Memphis became the new capital of United Egypt, and 1st dynasty tombs at nearby Saqqara are usually identified as the first royal tombs. Royal power had greatly increased by the 3rd dynasty, c. 2686-2613 B.C., when much larger royal tombs, now dominated by step pyramids in stone, were built at Saqqara. The best preserved is Zoser's step pyramid. Even more dramatic were the world famous pyramids of the 4th dynasty at Giza. Cheops's Giza pyramid was the largest ever built. Pyramids of the 5th and 6th dynasties at Abusir and Saqqara were smaller but still impressive. Many theories have been expounded regarding the pyramids and their use, but one thing is abundantly clear from the archaeological record – the materials, organization, and labor required by the pyramids, and the many estates supporting the cult and personnel of each, clearly reveal the king's firm control over Egypt and its resources.

Initially, the royal court with its adjacent cemeteries was the major center of intellectual, artistic, and architectural activity, but as towns began to develop in various parts of Egypt, they too shared in the cultural life of the time. Royal relatives and central officials were buried under Mastabas, rectangular superstructures of brick or stone. The Mastabas contained chapels and other rooms, increasing in number over time and opening up more wall space to be covered with reliefs and paintings. These depicted the funerary cult, and also the preparation of a multitude of foods, liquids, and objects for the benefit of the deceased. These Mastaba tombs were the prototypes for the Egyptian tombs of later periods. The Egyptian art which decorated their walls as all Egyptian art followed conventions which were established at an early date.

Centralized rule began to break down under the 7th dynasty. The ensuing chaotic period is known as the First Intermediate period c. 2181-2040 B.C. The Memphite monarchs were powerless to prevent provincial warlords from fighting each other over territory. Eventually two separate kingdoms emerged, one ruled by the 9th and 10th dynasties from Heracleopolis, the other by the 11th dynasty from Thebes. They tried to dominate each other but were mutually unsuccessful until the 20th century B.C., when the 11th dynasty kings conquered the North and rebuilt a centralized monarchy, inaugurating the Middle Kingdom which found its height in the 12th dynasty.

Amenemhet I founded the 12th dynasty in approximately 1991 B.C. He worked hard to restore royal prestige, seriously damaged by civil war and periodic famine in the First Intermediate Period. Its kings, living near Memphis, reduced provincial power and developed a loyal central elite. Funerary beliefs and rituals changed; the pyramid tombs of Old Kingdom royalty were redefined and new types of funerary furniture such as elaborate tomb models were introduced. The very rituals, once largely restricted to kings, now spread throughout all classes. The names of private individuals began to appear on scarabs and increasingly elaborate and private tombs of new designs, albeit often based on the Mastaba prototype, began to appear. Middle Kingdom art, although it follows the conventions common to all Egyptian art, is often seen today as more in tune with modern tastes for realism than the art of other periods and is thus highly regarded by most collectors.

Following the 12th dynasty a new period of decline set in called the Second Intermediate period c. 1786-1567 B.C. High officials became so powerful in the 13th dynasty that they manipulated and fought over the royal succession. Centralized power was disrupted and Egypt lay open to foreign domination. The Cushites of Upper Nubia occupied Lower Nubia, while Syro-Palestinians conquered Egypt itself and established the 15th dynasty. These Hyksos exploited Egyptian ideology but in many respects remained Syro-Palestinian in culture. Some Biblical scholars identify this period with the Biblical story of the

Patriarchs and the sojourn of the Hebrew people in Egypt. Eventually, Theban vassals of the 17th dynasty began a war of independence, resisted by an alliance of Hyksos and Cushites.

Art styles of the Second Intermediate Period are markedly different from the Middle Kingdom, not surprisingly, often showing a heavy Eastern influence. For example, Semitic names frequently appear on scarabs, and pottery, based on fertile crescent prototypes, appears. Egyptian influence continues to predominate, however, and the art of this period presents many interesting stylistic aspects for the collector and scholar alike.

Expelling the Hyksos, the Theban insurgents of the 17th dynasty founded the 18th dynasty, inaugurating ancient Egypt's most brilliant period, the New Kingdom 1570-1085 B.C. Its rulers included some of the greatest kings in Egyptian history: Hatshepsut, the woman who ruled as a man; Thutmose III, perhaps the greatest of all Pharaohs, whose very name was a magic amulet hundreds of years later; Akhenaten, the heretic, who tried to institute a form of monotheism; and the great king Ramses II who may have been the pharaoh of the Exodus. The New Kingdom was the "Golden Age" of ancient Egypt.

The art of ancient Egypt also reached its height in the New Kingdom. Although much did not survive the ravages of time, much did, such as the almost untouched treasures found in the tomb of a very minor pharaoh, Tutankhamen. What the funerary furniture of the great pharaohs such as Seti I and Ramses II was like, we can only guess. Not only royalty but middle-class peoples, who included many craftsmen, were well off, as can be seen from the prosperous village of Deir el Medinah, housing for 400 years the artisans who cut and decorated the royal tombs and is even now being excavated. Even minor arts were very well developed. Many of the less important finds unearthed in Tutankhamen's tomb such as Tutankhamen's thrones, weapons, and chairs were well crafted in exotic woods. Exquisite jewelry, amulets, scarabs, ushabtis, and other objects in stone, metal, and other materials are frequently found in Egyptian tombs and other archaeological sites.

Royal tombs in the New Kingdom show a radical change. The pyramids and mastabas of earlier generations were abandoned, to be taken over in a smaller scale by private tombs. Nearly all New Kingdom royal tombs are tunnels cut in the walls of the remote Valley of the Kings, their walls covered with a brightly painted underworld full of gods and demons. Royal funerary cult rites were performed in temples separate from the tombs and at the foot of the cliffs fronting the valley.

The New Kingdom was at its height in the 18th and 19th dynasties, but it began to decline in the 20th, and both the dynasty and the period ended in a civil war under Ramses XI. After 1085 B.C., Egypt split between a Northern 21st dynasty claiming national recognition and a line of Theban generals and high priests of Amun who actually controlled the South. Thus was the Third Intermediate Period ushered in. The 22nd dynasty rose from long-settled Libyan mercenaries and used a decentralized system, with kings based in the North and their sons ruling key centers elsewhere. Rivalries and sporadic civil wars resulted, and by the 8th century B.C. Egypt had divided into eleven autonomous states, their subjects dependent on congested, walled towns for security and exhibiting increased anxiety by adherence to local rather than national gods.

By the 25th dynasty the country once again fell into foreign hands. The Cushite rulers of the 25th dynasty brought limited unity and resisted Assyrian expansion into Syria-Palestine. Assyria occupied Egypt 617, 667-664 B.C., but a 26th dynasty regained independence and instituted an artistic revival which provides us with much of the Egyptian art on the market today. It did not last, however. The Persians ruled Egypt from 525 to 404 B.C., and again from 341 to 333 B.C. In the 4th century B.C., Egypt was wrested from Persia by Alexander the Great. Alexander's general Ptolemy I established a Macedonian dynasty that ruled the country for over 300 years. Although the Ptolemies supported traditional religion, native Egyptians resented the Greek officials and soldiers. A Roman takeover followed the death of Cleopatra VII, the last Ptolemaic ruler, in 30 B.C. For about two centuries, conditions were favorable under the Romans who respected Egyptian civilization, and who even adopted some of her deities into their pantheon. Although some distinctions between Hellenized and traditional Egyptians were broken down during the Ptolemaic and Roman periods, traditional life continued everywhere, Greek civilization being confined to Alexandria and a few other towns. Temples continued to be built in traditional form, but art had a hybrid quality. Wall scenes in tombs show a sometimes skillful but often clumsy mix of Egyptian and Hellenistic Greek styles and subjects. Later, emperors' faces in realistic Roman style were grafted incongruously onto traditional statues of the pharaoh, and realistic portraits, painted on wood, were integrated with Egyptian-style mummies and coffins. Sacred bird and animal cults were now especially popular, and many, sometimes striking, images were produced. This process continued into the Coptic period, the last to see a truly Egyptian art. During the independent Coptic period from the 4th to the 7th century A.D., which ended with the Arab conquest of 639-42 A.D., Christian images and religious practices gradually supplanted the ancient Egyptian culture.

Egyptian art has fascinated collectors and connoisseurs for millennia. Perhaps one reason is that, although it appears realistic, it followed certain conventions which remained dominant throughout its history. In painting and relief, human and animal figures are always drawn according to a set of fixed proportions, and reality is ignored so as to present the most characteristic aspects. Humans, for example, almost always have heads, legs, and feet in profile but eye and torso presented frontally. Figures were scaled according to their importance, and perspective is not depicted. Landscapes were sometimes depicted in schematic form, but architecture was rarely shown. Subject matter is also highly selective, for an idealized world is shown; aging, disease, injury, and death are usually omitted, except for inferior beings such as foreigners and animals.

Painting, relief, and sculpture were used mainly for temples and tombs, and consisted of representations of gods, kings, and deceased individuals. Complex compositions were avoided, although sometimes two or more figures might be shown side by side. Life-size statues were not uncommon, but most were smaller; colossal royal figures embellished temples. As in painting, set conventions were closely followed in statuary. Whether seated or standing, figures are always facing forward, with arms and legs in standardized positions.

Technically Egyptian sculpture and other art forms were often superb, although many clumsy works were also produced, but sculpture and other purported ancient art which ignores the major or minor conventions established by the Egyptians is often a tip-off for spotting a modern forgery. The vast richness of Egyptian art cannot begin to be done justice in this brief introduction, and the serious collector will make it a lifelong study.

TOOLS AND WEAPONS

As in many archaeological excavations, tools and weapons in iron, bronze and even precious metals are often found in Egyptian excavations of various periods. Many military items such as bows, arrowheads, swords, axes, spearheads and even whole chariots have been found in Egyptian tombs. Agricultural and domestic tools of various kinds–hoes, picks, hammers, builders tools, weavers implements–as well as personal implements such as tweezers, forks, spoons, knives, cosmetic applicators and the like, to name only a few, are often available to the collector. Nice Egyptian tools and many weapons can sometimes be acquired for under $200.

POTTERY

Pottery is quite plentiful in Egyptian excavations. Unfortunately, with the exception of the Pre-dynastic and New Kingdom and Roman periods, it is usually quite utilitarian and plain in nature. Roman period pottery from Egypt is rather distinctive and ranges from the simple to the elaborately painted. Often it is mold decorated with interesting designs in relief, for example, the highly decorated pilgrim flasks which occasionally appear on the market. Some Pre-dynastic, New Kingdom and Roman pottery found in Egypt is painted usually in a geometric style. Types of pottery, as usual, include domestic vessels of various wares, oil lamps often with relief decoration, most of which date to the Ptolemaic/Roman periods, some ritual vessels particularly in the New Kingdom, architectural elements such as tiles, and various types of pottery used in the extensive Egyptian funerary rites. Pottery coffins have been found in some excavations. Fine examples of Egyptian pottery from various periods can often be purchased by the astute collector for under $200.

TERRACOTTA

As has been noted elsewhere terracotta is a type of hard-baked clay, usually rendered brownish red in color. It was used extensively in ancient Egypt from the earliest times particularly for the production of sculptures of various sizes. Pottery sculpture on a small scale–statuettes, effigy vessels, figurines, and the like–was an important part of Roman-Egyptian daily life. Pottery sculpture representing deities, animals, objects, people, and even toys, is found in large quantities in Roman-Egyptian sites. Because of this, Roman period Egyptian sculpture is relatively cheap on the antiquities market. Pottery sculpture of earlier periods is rarer, although tomb models and other magical figures such as New Kingdom "concubine figures" appear with some regularity on the market. As with other Roman period pottery, a somewhat worn Roman-Egyptian head from a statuette, for example, might be purchased for as little as $10 while a superb example might go for several hundred. Earlier pottery sculptural pieces such as Middle Kingdom offering tables and New Kingdom "concubine figures" appear from time to time as well.

FAIENCE OBJECTS

Faience generally refers to a type of tin-glazed earthenware that became popular throughout Europe from the 16th century. This is confusing because the term is also used by archaeologists and art historians for a type of vitreous paste used, particularly in ancient Egypt, for the manufacture of small-scale sculptures and objects such as amulets, seals and ushabti figures (the ubiquitous Egyptian servants of the dead found in large numbers in most Egyptian burials). Faience came in many colors, blue and green being the most popular, but when found today it has often faded almost to white. Faience objects which retain their original color are thus highly prized by collectors. A true glass paste called "Egyptian Blue" which was also in widespread use in ancient Egypt is often confused with faience by the novice collector as is glazed steatite, a soft glazed stone often used by the ancient Egyptians for the same types of objects faience was. Amulets, ushabti figures and the like in faience are quite readily available to the collector of even very modest means.

METAL OBJECTS

Some Egyptian metalwork has survived from antiquity. Ranging from simple cooking pots to elaborate vessels made of precious metals, these objects can often be of great artistic merit, and some such as Tutankhamen's gold funerary mask are among the most famous of all Egyptian antiquities. The numerous metal sculptures which frequently appear on the market date to various periods but were particularly popular in the Late Period c. 600 B.C. These sculptures were often for religious use, representing the various deities of the Egyptian pantheon: Osiris, Isis, Horus, etc. Many sculptures were made for political use and/or public display. Small sculptures of animals sacred to the Egyptian deities – cats, ibises, fish and the like – are also quite common. While usually relatively expensive, good examples of Egyptian metalwork can sometimes be acquired for as little as $150.

WOOD AND CARTONAGE OBJECTS

Despite the fact that much of the wood used in ancient Egypt had to be imported from elsewhere, its extremely dry climate meant that materials such as wood and cartonage (a type of stucco sculpture made from plaster applied to a cloth or papyrus base and usually painted) have survived in Egypt in quantities not found elsewhere in the ancient world. The most common objects in cartonage were mummy masks and coffins, large numbers of which, particularly from later periods, have survived. Cartonage masks are in particular demand by collectors because they are often striking examples of Egyptian art. Wood was also in widespread use in all periods both for objects of mundane use, furniture and the like, and for objects of funerary and ritual use such as coffins, shrines, and other funerary furniture. Wood was used as well for sculpture, usually of a ritual or funerary nature. Examples are the various deities found most often sculpted in wood such as the Ptah seker Ausar figures of the Late Period, and the detailed tomb models of the Middle Kingdom. Small objects such as amulets and even scarabs were also made of wood on occasion. Even some utilitarian objects such as doors, boats, combs, etc., have been found in Egyptian excavations. For the collector interested in these perishable materials no place in the ancient world offers a more fertile prospect of forming a collection than Egypt.

STONE OBJECTS

Stone objects from Egypt are quite varied. Utilitarian objects such as stone vessels and cosmetic pallets are fairly common from the Pre-dynastic period to the Roman period. Much of ancient Egyptian architecture was in stone. Stone sculpture both in the round and in relief was in widespread use for the decoration of tombs, temples and residences throughout Egyptian history. Sculpture in stone, although formalized according to the conventions of ancient Egyptian art, often has a haunting beauty which has captured the imagination of its beholders throughout the ages. Perhaps because of this, Egyptian stone sculpture is among the most desirable of all collectable antiquities. Although great works of the Egyptian sculpture's art are beyond the scope of the average collector, many objects in stone can be had for relatively modest sums.

SCARABS

Scarabaeus sacer is the Latin name for the dung beetle. This particular variety, which was the type variety for the family Scarabaeidae, was sacred to the ancient Egyptians. They connected its habits of rolling balls of dung around their eggs with their concept of eternal life in the afterworld (actually several members of the family Scarabaeidae were venerated). Representations of this beetle were very common in Egyptian art and a whole class of seals and amulets were made in its image. These scarabs, as they are called today, were manufactured in a wide variety of materials including faience, stone, glass, and bone, from the Old Kingdom through the Roman period. They often bear various designs on their base including the names of various individuals both noble and common. The most interesting are those bearing the names of the pharaohs. The names of most of the royal Egyptian personages have been found on scarabs. The more popular pharaohs' names such as Thothmes III appear to have been used for hundreds of years after their demise. This was due to the fact that the very name of a great pharaoh was deemed to bring good luck to the bearer since the pharaoh was a deity in his own right. The names and/or the figures of other Egyptian deities are also quite common on these small seals. Egyptian scarabs are eminently collectable and many great collections have already been formed. Indeed so varied and numerous are they that scarab collecting might be considered a sub-field all by itself. Many antiquities dealers have issued catalogs entirely devoted to scarabs. Like ancient coins, scarabs can be purchased for prices ranging from a few dollars to many thousands depending on rarity, condition and the prevailing market.

AMULETS

The ancient Egyptians were great believers in magic, and the use of amulets for protection and benefit was an integral part of their religious belief and practice. The variety of amulets found in Egyptian excavations is mind boggling. Literally hundreds, if not thousands, of types have been identified by Egyptologists. The materials used in their manufacture are manifold—various stones, colored faience, wood, glass, bronze, silver, gold, ivory, and many other materials were all used. Each material undoubtedly had a special meaning to the Egyptians, as we know from surviving magical papyri. Amulets were fashioned in the shape of sacred animals such as the cat, or of deities such as Isis, or of symbols such as the eye of Horus. They might also take the shape of hieroglyphic signs or any number of other things. The modern collector often sees in Egyptian amulets a quaint assembly of animals, deities, and objets d' art, but to the ancient Egyptians they were a sacred chance to influence their lives. They were manufactured in vast quantities and many have survived. Since they are so numerous on the market the collector of almost any means can find amulets in his or her price range.

GLASS

Glass was in use in ancient Egypt from very early times. During the New Kingdom glass vessels made by the core form method were sometimes found in the tombs of the wealthy. Not much of this early glass has survived, however, and even a fragment can fetch a good price.

JEWELRY

Ancient Egyptian jewelry, like most ancient jewelry, can be of precious metal or base metal. Many stones and beads of faience and other materials were also used in the making of jewelry. Personal ornament was widespread among both men and women in all periods of ancient Egypt. Much jewelry has survived due to the Egyptian practice of burying the deceased with all of his or her finery. Pins, rings, bracelets, earrings, and necklaces are all found as are some purely Egyptian forms such as golden toe covers. Many amulets and seals were also worn as jewelry both by the living and the deceased. Although gold and silver objects are usually high priced, faience jewelry is within the reach of most collectors.

WRITING

Written records exist from most periods of Egyptian history, although they could only be read in relatively modern times. They have fascinated scholars for millennia. The hieroglyphic and hieratic scripts were in use from the Old Kingdom onward and the demotic script was in widespread use in later times. During the Ptolemaic and later Roman period, Greek and Latin were in common use. It was the finding of the Rosetta stone inscribed in hieroglyphics and Greek which allowed for the decipherment of the ancient Egyptian language. Inscriptions often appear on objects of stone, metal, pottery, faience, wood, and cartonage. For example, short inscriptions were often written on pottery shards called ostraca or inscribed on faience objects such as ushabtis. Most of the written records were on papyrus, much of which has survived due to the climate. Of particular interest are the so-called Books of the Dead. Many public and private inscriptions were carved in stone, much of which has survived. For example, most funerary monuments, particularly sarcophagi and the walls of the tomb, were almost always inscribed. Many utilitarian objects such as mirrors, combs, et.c, also bore inscriptions. Seals, particularly scarabs, are also an important source for epigraphic knowledge. Many an interesting collection of Egyptian art has been devoted solely to Egyptian writing.

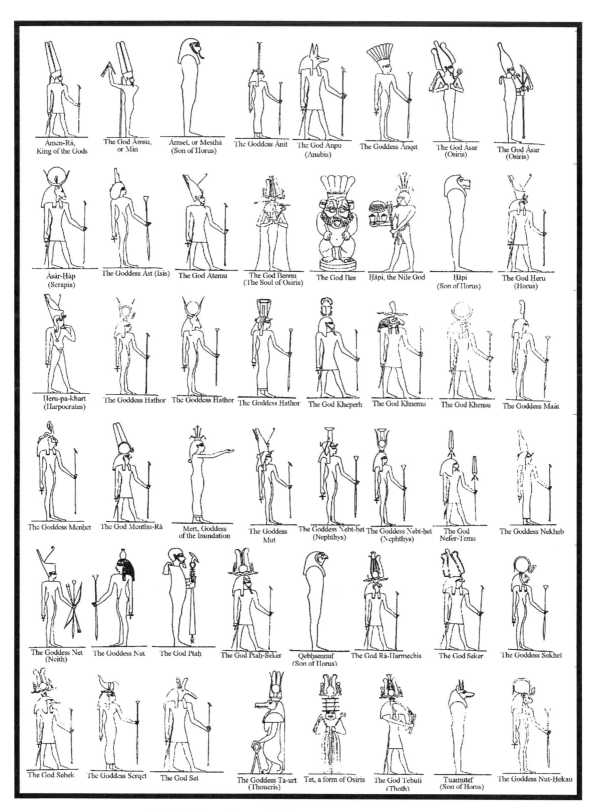

The following labels appear beneath the figures:

Amen-Râ, King of the Gods

The God Åmsu, or Min

Åmset, or Mesthå (Son of Horus)

The Goddess Anit

The God Anpu (Anubis)

The Goddess Ånqet

The God Åsar (Osiris)

The God Åsar (Osiris)

Åsår-Håp (Scrapis)

The Goddess Åst (Isis)

The God Atemu

The God Bennu (The Soul of Osiris)

The God Bes

Håpi, the Nile God

Håpi (Son of Horus)

The God Heru (Horus)

Heru-pa-khart (Harpocrates)

The Goddess Hathor

The Goddess Hathor

The Goddess Hathor

The God Kheperh

The God Khnemu

The God Khensu

The Goddess Maåt

The Goddess Menhet

The God Menthu-Rå

Mert, Goddess of the Inundation

The Goddess Mut

The Goddess Nebt-het (Nephthys)

The Goddess Nebt-het (Nephthys)

The God Nefer-Temu

The Goddess Nekheb

The Goddess Net (Neith)

The Goddess Nut

The God Ptah

The God Ptah-Seker

Qebhsennuf (Son of Horus)

The God Rå-Harmechis

The God Seker

The Goddess Sekhet

The God Sehek

The Goddess Serqet

The God Set

The Goddess Ta-urt (Thoueris)

Tet, a form of Osiris

The God Tehuti (Thoth)

Tuamutef (Son of Horus)

The Goddess Nut-Hekau

EGYPTIAN GODS AND GODDESSES

TIMELINE OF EGYPTIAN KINGS

EARLY DYNASTIC PERIOD
c. 3100-2613 B.C.
First Dynasty
c. 3100-2890 B.C.
Narmer (Menes)
Aha
Djer
Djet (Uadji)
Den (Udimu)
Anejib
Semerkhet
Qaa

Second Dynasty
c. 2890-2686 B.C.
Hotepsekhemwy
Raneb
Nynetjer
Peribsen
Khasekhem
Khasekhemwy

Third Dynasty
c. 2686-2613 B.C.
Sanakhte
Djoser
Sekhemkhet
Khaba
Huni

OLD KINGDOM
c. 2613-2133 B.C.
Fourth Dynasty
c. 2613-2494 B.C.
Sneferu
Cheops (Khufu)
Redjedef
Chephren (Khafre)
Mycerinus (Menkaure)
Shepseskaf

Fifth Dynasty
c. 2494-2345 B.C.
Userhaf
Sahure
Neferirkare Kakai
Shepseskare Isi
Neferefre
Nyuserre
Menkauhor Akauhor

Djedkare Isesi
Unas

Sixth Dynasty
c. 2345-2181 B.C.
Teti
Userkare
Meryre Phiops I (Pepi I)
Merenre Antyemsaf
Neferkare Phiops II (Pepi II)

FIRST INTERMEDIATE PERIOD
c. 2133-1991 B.C.
9th-11th Dynasty
c. 2133-1991 B.C.
Tepya Mentuhotpe I
Sehertowy Inyotef I
Wahankh Inyotef II
Nakhtnebtepnefer Inyotef III
Nebhepetre Mentuhotpe II
Sankhkare Mentuhotpe III
Nebtowyre Mentuhotpe IV

MIDDLE KINGDOM
c. 1991-1786 B.C.
12th Dynasty
c. 1991-1786 B.C.
Sehetepibre Ammenemes I, 1991-1962 B.C.
Kheperkare Sesostris I, 1971-1928 B.C.
Nubkaure Ammenemes II, 1929-1895 B.C.
Khakheperre Sesostris II, 1897-1878 B.C.
Khakaure Sesostris III, 1878-1843 B.C.
Nymare Ammenemes III, 1842-1797 B.C.
Makherure Ammenemes IV, 1798-1790 B.C.
Sobkkare Sobkneferu, 1789-1786 B.C.

SECOND INTERMEDIATE PERIOD
c. 1786-1567 B.C.
13th Dynasty
c. 1786-1633 B.C.
Sekhemre Sewadjtowy Sobkhotpe III
Khasekhemre Neferhotep
Meryankhre Mentuhotpe

15th Dynasty (Hyksos)
c. 1674-1567 B.C.
Mayebre Sheshi
Meruserre Yakubher
Seuserenre Khyan
Auserre Apophis I
Aqenenre Apophis II

17th Dynasty
c. 1650-1567 B.C.
Nubkheperre Inyotef VII
Seqenenre Tao I,"the Elder"
Seqenenre Tao II, "the Brave"
Wadjkheperre Kamose

NEW KINGDOM
c. 1567-1085 B.C.
18th Dynasty
c. 1567-1320 B.C.
Nebpehtyre Amosis, 1570-1546 B.C.
Djeserkare Amenophis I, 1546-1526 B.C.
Akheperkare Tuthmosis I, 1525-c.1512 B.C.
Akheperenre Tuthmosis II, c.1512-1504 B.C.
Makare Hatshepsut, 1503-1482 B.C.
Menkheperre Tuthmosis III, 1504-1450 B.C.
Akheprure Amenophis II, 1450-1425 B.C.
Menkheprure Tuthmosis IV, 1425-1417 B.C.
Nebmare Amenophis III, 1417-1379 B.C.
Neferkheprure Amenophis IV (Akhenaten), 1379-1362 B.C.
Ankhkheprure Smenkhkare, 1364-1361 B.C.
Nebkheprure Tutankhamun, 1361-1352 B.C.
Kheperkheprure Ay, 1352-1348 B.C.
Djeserkheprure Horemheb, 1348-1320 B.C.

19th Dynasty
c. 1320-1200 B.C.
Menpehtyre Ramesses I, 1320-1318 B.C.
Menmare Sethos I, 1318-1304 B.C.
Usermare Ramesses II, 1304-1237 B.C.
Baenre Merneptah, 1236-1223 B.C.
Menmire Amenmesses, 1222-1217 B.C.
Userkheprure Sethos II, 1216-1210 B.C.

20th Dynasty
c. 1200-1085 B.C.
Userkhaure Sethnakhte, 1200-1198 B.C.
Usermare-Meryamun, Ramesses III, 1198-1166 B.C.
Hiqmare Ramesses IV, 1166-1160 B.C.
Ramesses V-VIII, 1160-1142 B.C.
Neferkare Ramesses IX, 1142-1123 B.C.
Khepermare Ramesses X, 1123-1114 B.C.
Menmare Ramesses XI, 1114-1085 B.C.

THIRD INTERMEDIATE PERIOD
c. 1085-716 B.C.
21st Dynasty
c. 1085-935 B.C.

At Tanis
Nesbanebded (Smendes)
Psusennes I
Amenemope
Siamun
Psusennes II

At Thebes (Priest-Kings)
Herihor
Pinudjern I
Masaherta
Menkheperre
Pinudjem II

22nd Dynasty (Libyan or Bubastite)
c. 935-730 B.C.
Sheshonq I, c. 935-914 B.C.
Osorkon I, c. 914-874 B.C.
Takelothis I, c. 874-860 B.C.
Osorkon II, c. 860-837 B.C.
Sheshonq II, c. 837 B.C.
Takelothis II, c. 837-813 B.C.
Sheshonq III, c. 822-770 B.C.
Pami, c. 770-765 B.C.
Sheshonq IV, c. 765-725 B.C.

23rd Dynasty
c. 817(?)-730 B.C.
Petubastis

24th Dynasty
c. 730-709 B.C.
Tefnakhte
Bakenrenef (Bocchoris)

25th Dynasty (Nubian or Ethiopian)
c. 750-656 B.C.
Piankhi, c. 751-716 B.C.

LATE PERIOD
c. 712-332 B.C.
25th Dynasty (Nubian or Ethiopian), cont.
c. 750-656 B.C.
Shabaka, 716-695 B.C.
Shebitku, 695-690 B.C.
Taharqa, 689-664 B.C.
Tanutamun, 664-656 B.C.

26th Dynasty (Saite)
664-525 B.C.
Wahibre Psammetichus I, 664-610 B.C.
Wehemibre Necho II, 610-595 B.C.
Neferibre Psammetichus II, 595-589 B.C.
Apries, 589-570 B.C.
Amasis (Amosis II), 570-526 B.C.
Ankhkaenre Psamrnetichus III, 526-525 B.C.

27th Dynasty (Persian)
525-404 B.C.
Cambyses, 525-522 B.C.
Darius I, 521-486 B.C.
Xerxes, 486-466 B.C.
Artaxerxes, 465-424 B.C.
Darius II, 424-404 B.C.

28th and 29th Dynasties
404-378 B.C.
Achoris, 393-380 B.C.

30th Dynasty
380-343 B.C.
Nectanebes (Nectanebo I), 380-363 B.C.
Teos, 362-361 B.C.
Nectanebos (Nectanebo II), 360-343 B.C.

Second Persian Period
343-332 B.C.

HELLENISTIC PERIOD
c. 332-30 B.C.
Macedonian Kings
332-304 B.C.
Alexander the Great, 332-323 B.C.
Philip Arrhidacus, 323-316 B.C.
Alexander IV, 316-304 B.C.

The Ptolemies
304-30 B.C.
Ptolemy I Soter, 304-282 B.C.
Ptolemy II Philadelphus, 285-246 B.C.
Ptolemy III Euergetes, 246-221 B.C.
Ptolemy IV Philopator, 221-205 B.C.
Ptolemy V Epiphanes, 205- 180 B.C.
Ptolemy VI Philometor, 180-145 B.C.
Ptolemy VII Neos Philopator,145 B.C.
Ptolemy VIII Euergetes II, 170-116 B.C.
Ptolemy IX Soter II (Lathyros), 116-107 B.C.
Ptolemy X Alexander I, 107-88 B.C.
Ptolemy IX Soter II (restored), 88-81 B.C.
Ptolemy XI Alexander II, 80 B.C.
Ptolemy XII Neos Dionysos (Auletes), 80-51 B.C.
Cleopatra VII Philopator, 51-30 B.C.

Overlapping dates usually indicate co-regencies.

EGYPTIAN

WEAPONS

Stone

Swords, Daggers, and Blades

816. **BEIGE FLINT KNIFE. Neolithic Egypt.** One circular edge with one straight edge. Finely worked, leaf shape. 8.2 cm x 3.8 cm. Cf. Petrie, Lahun II, Pl. XXXIX, 84. ....**SUPERB 100.00**

817. **FLINT KNIFE. Egypt. 12th Dynasty. 2000-1800 B.C.** Opaque beige. 14.4 cm x 3.9 cm. Cf. Petrie, Illahun Kahun and Garob VII, 14. Similar types excavated at Kahun, a 12th dynasty site. Chip at edge. ....**CHOICE 125.00**

Arrowheads

818. **FLINT WINGED ARROWHEAD. Neolithic Egypt.** Light brown. 4.8 cm x 2.9 cm. Hayes, fig. 4.5. Nice example. Scarce.....................................**SUPERB 125.00**

Spear and Javelin Points

819. **FLINT SPEARHEAD. Neolithic Egypt.** Yellow-brown. 6.1 cm x 3.2 cm. Hayes, fig. 4.3. Finely worked. ....**SUPERB 100.00**

Metal

Swords, Daggers, and Blades

820. **IRON SWORD BLADE. Egyptian. 28th-29th Dynasty. 404-378 B.C.** Blade with straight back, single edge. Length 27.5 cm. Malloy #67; cf. Petrie 210-211. Slightly bent. Oxidation. ....**CHOICE 150.00**

Axe, Adze, and Mace Heads

821. **BRONZE ADZE HEAD. Egyptian. Early Dynastic. c. 3000 B.C.** Small bronze wedge-shaped adze head. Length 7.8 cm, width at blade end 2 cm, width at handle end 0.8 cm. Cf. Petrie, *Tools and Weapons,* Pl. XVI, #61. ....**CHOICE 125.00**

Arrowheads

822. **METAL ARROWHEAD. Egyptian. 11th Dynasty. 2134-2040 B.C.** Example of the earliest type used in Egypt with tine. 6.8 cm long, 1.5 cm wide. Dark green patina. Petrie 170-76.....................................**CHOICE 75.00**

823. **BRONZE ARROWHEAD. Egyptian. 19th Dynasty. 1329-64 B.C.** Triangular shaped arrowhead with short shaft and shaft hole. 3.5 cm long, 1.2 cm wide. A gem. Green patina. Petrie, *Tools and Weapons,* 131 var. ....**SUPERB 100.00**

824. **BRONZE ARROWHEAD. Egyptian. 19th Dynasty. 1329-64 B.C.** Similar to above. 2.5 cm long, 1.1 cm wide. Green patina. Petrie, *Tools and Weapons,* 131 var. ....**CHOICE 65.00**

825. **BRONZE ARROWHEAD. Egyptian. 19th-26th Dynasty. 1320-644 B.C.** Triangular, with medium expanding socket. Smooth side blades, slight barbs. Length 2.3 cm. Petrie, *T&W* #75, Cf. Malloy, *Weapons,* #88. Light green patina. ....**CHOICE 75.00**

826. **BRONZE ARROWHEAD. Egyptian. 19th-26th Dynasty. 1320-644 B.C.** Triangular-shaped with short shaft and shaft hole. 2.5 cm long. Petrie, *Tools and Weapons,* 131 var. Green patina. Attractive. ....**CHOICE-SUPERB 85.00**

827. **BRONZE ARROWHEAD. Egyptian. 20th-22nd Dynasty. 1200-800 B.C.** Rhombic head, deltoid midrib projection, elongated point. Shortened tang, two barbs. Length 3.4 cm. Petrie, *T&W* 201-2, Cf. Malloy, *Weapons,* #89. ....**CHOICE 75.00**

828. **IRON HEAD. Egyptian. 1200-800 B.C.** Rhombic. 7.4 cm long, 1.7 cm wide. Iron oxides. One barb chipped off. Very scarce. Cf. Petrie 202.............................**CHOICE 100.00**

829. **BRONZE ARROWHEAD. Egyptian. 1200-800 B.C.** Flat blade. Long shaft. Spur on side of shaft. 4.5 cm long, 1.4 cm wide. Traces of dried end of wooden shaft. Petrie 35. ....**SUPERB 60.00**

830. **BRONZE ARROWHEAD. Egyptian. 8th-4th Century B.C.** Triangled arrowhead with central shaft, shaft hole. 4.3 cm long, 1.2 cm wide. Patterned after Sythian style. Found in Egypt. Petrie reports similar arrowheads found at Memphis. Petrie XLI 246............................**CHOICE 70.00**

831. **COPPER ARROWHEAD. Egyptian. 26th Dynasty. 664-525 B.C.** Triangular-shaped arrowhead with barbs. Midstem wide at the shoulder, decreasing to tip, pointed tang. 5.2 cm long, 1.5 cm wide. Very scarce. Cf. Petrie, *Tools and Weapons* 131. ....**CHOICE 125.00**

832. **BRONZE ARROWHEAD. 26th-39th Dynasty. 664-200 B.C.** Leaf shaped with small tang and central shaft and small barb to blade. 6 cm long, 2 cm wide. Similar arrowheads were found at Memphis. Green patina encrustation. Cf. Petrie 42........................**CHOICE 60.00**

833. **IRON ARROWHEAD. 664-200 B.C.** Leaf shaped with protruding central stem, probably derived from the Asiatic arrowhead which is found at Minussinsk. 5.5 cm long, 2 cm wide. Petrie 41. ....**CHOICE 60.00**

834. **BRONZE ARROWHEAD. Egyptian. 6th-2nd Century B.C.** Elongated leaf-shaped head with wide central rib. Length 9.3 cm. Cf. Petrie 192, Malloy 74. Edge chipped. ....**CHOICE 50.00**

835. **COPPER ARROWHEAD. 27th Dynasty (Persian). 525-404 BC.** Diamond-shaped arrowhead. Flint tang ending in a point, attractive style. 7.5 cm long, 2 cm wide. The use of such form would be for cutting through leather garments, where the whole blow was wanted at once to make a single cut. A long tapering form would lose its force by wedging in the leather. Cf. Petrie 121,122, 136. ....**SUPERB 125.00**

836. **IRON STRAIGHT-BACKED BLADE. Egyptian. 28th-29th Dynasty. 404-378 B.C..** Slightly bent. 27.5 cm long, 3.2 cm wide. Iron oxide. Cf. Petrie 210-211. ....**CHOICE 175.00**

TOOLS

837. **IRON RAZOR. New Kingdom. 1567-1085 BC.** Paddle shaped. Length 12.3 cm, width 5.2 cm. Cf. Petrie 84. This razor was worked like a knife. Iron oxide deposits, some chips on edge. ....**CHOICE 135.00**

POTTERY

838. **BLACK-TOPPED POTTERY BOWL. Pre-Dynastic. 3300-3006 B.C.** Small bowl of red polished pottery with black top and inside. Surface quite uneven with some wearing. Bowl is round bottomed with rim curling in slightly. Chip in rim. Partly restored. 7 cm high, 10 cm diameter. Petrie, Nagada and Ballas, PL. XXII, #86. ....**CHOICE 500.00**

839. **DECORATED PAINTED BOWL. Pre-Dynastic. 3300-3006 B.C.** Orange-buff colored bowl which has red spirals decorated in red. Two crude tubular handles, horizontally attached. Above each handle, two wavy lines. Inverted neck with turned back flattened rim. Rounded bottom. 10.3 cm high, 11 cm in diameter This type of imported pottery not only came from the Mediterranean, but was only found at Nagada and nearby. In 3300 a new race had come into this area and took over from the Egyptians there. They used nothing Egyptian, and even went so far as to be very different in the productions of any made goods. This new race was thought to have been Lybians, the same people who would found the Amarite race in the Near East according to Quibell and Petrie. Cf. Petrie, Nagada and Ballas, Pl. XXXV, #67c. ....**CHOICE 1500.00**

840. **BLACK-TOPPED POTTERY VASE/JAR. Pre-Dynastic. 3300-3006 B.C.** Polished red pottery with highly polished black top. Sides of vase taper down to a point with a base which is very small. Neck flares slightly and rim has no lip. 22.3 cm high. 2 cm base, 9.3 cm diameter rim. Cf. Petrie, Nagada and Ballas, Pl. XIX, #376. ....**CHOICE 1000.00**

841. **ALABASTER VASE. Early Dynastic. 3100-2700 B.C.** Small white-buff alabaster vase with flare rim, ovoid body, and flat base. Height 4.5 cm. Cf. Noblecourt #42. Chips at rim..**CHOICE 185.00**

842. **POTTERY VESSEL. Old Kingdom.** Red burnished vessel of carinated form with pronounced rim. Height 8.5 cm, diameter 12.5 cm. Cf. Keramik Museum Westerwald, *Meisterwerke Altägyptixcher Keramik*, #144. Intact with some surface wear. Excavated by Flinders Petrie at Thebes. ....**CHOICE 500.00**

843. **ALABASTER VESSEL. Middle Kingdom. 2050-1786 B.C.** Small white-buff cylindrical alabaster vessel with slight flare rim. Height 8 cm. Cf. Noblecourt #75. Slight repair of one side. ....**CHOICE 400.00**

844. **TERRACOTTA VESSEL. Middle Kingdom. 2050-1786 B.C.** Reddish-beige with flair rim and round base with red slip. Burnished. 8 cm high, 3 cm wide rim. Ex. Garstang's Excavations of Abydos in 1908. #503 1 -Museum Accession 1935.5.32. Cf. Noblecourt, *Un Siecle Defouilles Francaises en Egypte* 1880-1980, #80.........................**CHOICE 350.00**

845. **POTTERY VESSEL. 18th Dynasty.** Small buff vessel with flat rim and long body which tapers to point. Two handles at sides (missing). Height 6.5 cm. For type of vessel Cf. Römer und Pelizäus Museum 185-188. Chipped at bottom; handles missing. ....**CHOICE 90.00**

846. **POTTERY JUGLET. 18th Dynasty.** Small light buff pottery juglet with ovoid body and flat base. Strap handle. Used as child's toy or perfume vessel. For ware, Cf. Römer und Pelizäus Museum 185-188.................**CHOICE 125.00**

847. **POTTERY SHERD. 18th Dynasty. Reign of Akhenaten. 1379-1362.** From Armarna. Sherd from piriform jar. 7 mm x 6.6 mm. Decorated with a band of blue outlined in black with outlines of petals in black over solid blue. Divided into sections in red. The lotus petals were characteristic of this type of pottery. That is known from the Palace of Amenphis III at Thebes. Boston, Museum of Fine Arts, *Egypt's Golden Age: The Art of Living in the New Kingdom 1558-1085 B.C.*, p. 93. Burlington Fine Arts Club 1922, p. 64, Pl. XXXV. ....**CHOICE 35.00**

848. **GLAZED POTTERY FRAGMENT. 18th Dynasty.** Bright blue-glazed fragment; portion of the rim of a bowl. Design in fine black on both sides; one side shows a row of triangles at the rim with a lotus flower below. Length along rim 8 cm, width 6 cm. Cf. British Museum, *Fourth Egyptian Room*, p. 259 #4790; Cf. Petrie, *Arts and Crafts of Ancient Egypt*, p. 110. Nice color. ....**CHOICE 225.00**

849. **TERRACOTTA JUGLET. 18th Dynasty.** Buff with three brown concentric bands. Wide shoulder and flair rim, rounded base. 6.5 cm high, 3 cm wide rim. Heick, *Agyptens Aufstieg Zur Weltmacht*, #145 var. ....**CHOICE 100.00**

850. **POTTERY JUGLET. 18th Dynasty.** Small light buff pottery juglet with ovoid body and flat base. Strap handle. Used as child's toy or perfume vessel. For ware, Cf. Römer und Pelizäus Museum 185-188.................**CHOICE 125.00**

851. **POTTERY VASE. Late 18th Dynasty.** Orange pottery vessel with cylindrical form tapering to rim, pointed base, red slip on rim.   Ex. Harry Houdini/Joseph Dunninger Collection. Cf. Peet-Loat, Abydos 111, Pl. VI, 26-7. Chip to rim. ....**SUPERB 500.00**

852. **POTTERY CUP. 20th Dynasty.** Small reddish-brown pottery cup with round body and handle. Length 7.5 cm, height 5 cm. Handle repaired. ....**CHOICE 150.00**

853. **ALABASTER PERFUME VESSEL. New Kingdom. 1546-1085 B.C.** Cream with horizontal bands, perfume jar in globule shape. Highly polished. Flat base with rounded sides tapering to neck. Small straight neck with straight lip. Walls of body quite thin; base fairly thick. Height 7.4 cm, diameter 7 cm. Some minor chipping around lip. ....**SUPERB 750.00**

854. **TERRACOTTA AMPHORA. New Kingdom. 1546-1085 B.C**. Red. Shaped vase. Handle and pointed base terminating in button. 15.5 cm high, 3.3 cm wide rim. Cf. Hilton Price Collection 3387. ....**SUPERB 450.00**

855. **PAINTED RED GLAZE VASE. New Kingdom. 1546-1085 B.C**. Red glazed vessel with flair rim with broad sloping shoulder terminating in sloping base. Black design on shoulder of radiating parallel lines of three, intersecting at three points. Cf. Kelly, *Pottery of Ancient Egypt*, Pl. 79, 139-141. Ex: Harry Houdini-Joseph Dunninger Collection. Some cracks in surface with some chips to glaze. Intact. ....**CHOICE 1000.00**

856. **ALABASTER VESSEL. Late Period.** Banded alabaster vessel: buff with white bands. Mottled grey at base. Lugs toward top. Thin walls (2 mm thick), becoming thicker toward base. Height 9.7 cm, outer diameter. 3.7 cm. Probably made during reign of the Nubian king Aspelta (c. 593-568 B.C.) Cf. Dunham, *Royal Cemeteries at Kush,* Vol. II, Nuri, Pl. XXIX, fig. 16-4-71g. ....**SUPERB 350.00**

857. **ALABASTER VASE. Late Period.** Small buff alabaster vessel with light bands in lower third. Teardrop shape. Smooth rim with no lip. Small lug on either side. Faint horizontal grooves above and below lugs. Height 5.3 cm. Similar alabaster vessels were found at Nuri in the tomb of Madiken, sister-wife of the Nubian king Anlamani (ruled 623-593 B.C.) Cf. Dunham 18-3-1013, Pl. LXXX, E27. Chip off rim. ....**CHOICE 150.00**

858. **POTTERY FLASK. Ptolemaic Period. c. 300 B.C.** Light buff pottery vessel. Flare rim and long ovoid body tapering to pedestal base. Height 8 cm. Cf. *Meisterwerke Altegyptischer Keramik* #368. ....**CHOICE-SUPERB 100.00**

859. **PORTION OF GLAZED POTTERY AMPHORA FLASK. Roman Period. 1st-2nd Century A.D.** Upper portion of dark buff amphora flask with brown glaze. Front side depicts two heads, probably the Dioscuri, side-by-side just below rim. Back side patterned. Handle to either side. Probably "Memphis" ware. Height 4.7 cm, width 5.0 cm. Mounted. For similar types, Cf. *Roman Pottery in the Ontario Museum* Pl. 21-22. ....**CHOICE 175.00**

860. **PORTION OF AMPHORA FLASK. Roman Egypt. 1st-2nd Century A.D.** Brown pottery. Upper part of the body of a flask with two handles. Depicts two heads, possibly the Dioscuri. Traces of reddish-brown slip. Probably Memphis ware. Measures 4.0 x 4.8 cm. Mounted. Cf. for similar types of ware, *Roman Pottery in the Ontario Museum*, Pl. 21-22. Petrie -; Hayes -..**CHOICE 150.00**

861. **BARBOTINE WARE CUP. Roman Period. 2nd Century A.D.** Orange-red slip over dark buff clay. White barbotine decoration as garlands. Inside, white slip. 9.8 cm high, 6.3 cm wide rim, 3.8 cm wide base. Superb and totally intact. Excavated in 1935. A gem cup. Cf. Hayes, *ROM* 244 var. ....**SUPERB 375.00**

METAL

862. **BRONZE FIGURE OF NEFERTEM. New Kingdom. 1546-1085 B.C.** Bronze walking Nefertem, arms at side, left foot advanced, royal kilt with middle piece and pleated. Wearing long wig with uraeus, pointed beard and tall headdress of lotus. Pendant loop at back. This important deity, Nefertem, was the son of Ptah and Sekhet. His title was "Protector" or "director of the two worlds." He represented the heat of fiery glory of the rising sun and his symbol was the lotus. Broken at knees. Ex. Harry Houdini Joseph Dunninger Collection. Steindorff, *Catalogue of the Egyptian Sculpture in the Walters Art Gallery*, LXXXIII, 514. ....**CHOICE 3500.00**

863. **BRONZE STATUETTE. Third Intermediate Period-Late Period.** Portrays Osiris carrying a long-handled crook and flail. Wears Atef crown with feather decoration. Uraeus missing. 14.6 cm high. Executed in a style similar to that of the New Kingdom. Cf. Zabem, *Ehtdeckungen-Agyptische Kunst in Suddeutschland*, #118. Worn with erosion. Encrusted patina. ....**AVERAGE-CHOICE 300.00**

864. **BRONZE OSIRIS STATUETTE. Third Intermediate Period-Late Period. 1085-334 B.C.** Probably 26th Dynasty. Bust and torso of bronze Osiris statuette. Wears Atef crown with feathers missing. Also wears false beard and Uraeus. Carrying crook and flail. 7.5 cm high. Cf. *Meisterwerk, Agyptische Keramik*, p. 186. Cat. No. 313. Very good modeling. Tang from waist. ....**SUPERB 1500.00**

865. **BRONZE STATUETTE.   Third Intermediate Period-Late Period**. Bronze statuette of the god, Osiris, carrying a crook and flail. The crook has a long handle. Wears Atef crown with feather decoration. Ureaus missing. 14.6 cm high. Executed in a style similar to that of the New Kingdom. Cf. Zabem, *Ehtdeckungen-Agyptische Kunst in Suddenstschland*, No. 118. Worn with erosion. Encrusted patina. ....**AVERAGE-CHOICE 400.00**

866. **BRONZE SITULA. Late Period**. Bronze bell-shaped situla vessel. Elongated with button base, dual loop handles. Measures 50 x 120 mm. Mounted on lucite stand. Vessels such as this had a ritual as well as domestic use. Cf. Petrie, *Stone & Metal Vases*, Pl. XLI, 71073. Excavated at Saqqara by the Egypt Exploration Society. De-accessioned from Oberlin College Museum Collection. Ex. Malloy, *Egyptian Art and Artifacts*, Summer 1980, #67. Vessel has cracked veins throughout but is very stable. Heavy green patination. One chip from lip and smaller hole at side of bottom edge. Encrusted with some sand-salt. ....**AVERAGE 450.00**

867. **STATUETTE OF BES.   Late Period. 1085-332 B.C.** Bronze tang at base for mounting. Bes plays a tambourine or drum, using both hands. Good detail, very unusual. Slight red oxide to crevices. 4 cm high. Cf. Bodil Hometnann, *Types of Ancient Egyptian Statuary*, p. 79. Hannover B.B. 227. Nice detail. Traces of red oxide. ....**CHOICE 400.00**

868. **AMULET OF BES. Late Period. 1085-332 B.C.** Bronze. Tang at base for mounting. Unusual. Bes seems to be playing a tambourine or drum, using both hands. Good detail. A little red oxide to crevices. Cf. Bodil Homemann, *Types of Ancient Egyptian Statuary*, p. 79. Cf. Hannover B.B. 227...**CHOICE 375.00**

869. **STATUETTE OF APIS. 25th Dynasty-Roman. 750 B.C.-1st Century A.D.** Bronze. Crude features. Legs missing, left leg advanced. Damage to neck. Sun-disk with Ureaus missing. Very elongated. Evidence of marks of saddle-cloth and triangle on forehead. 4.5 cm long, 1 cm wide. Apis was the holy bull, worshipped at the temple of Ptah in Memphis. When dead the Apis bull was buried and became a divinity. Green patina. Mounted on lucite. Cf. Steindorf, figures 635-640 var. ....**CHOICE 135.00**

870. **BRONZE OSIRIS STATUETTE. 26th Dynasty**. Bronze figure of Osiris standing holding crook and flail. Wears Atef crown, feathers missing. Uraeus on headdress. Hands not crossed. Tang for mounting. 15 cm high. Ex. Harry Houdini/Joseph Dunninger Collection. Cf. for similar shape and type. Sotheby's Auction, June 1967. Intact but some wearing and erosion. ....**CHOICE 1200.00**

871. **STATUETTE OF OSIRIS. 26th-30th Dynasty. 600-350 B.C.** Bronze figure of the god Osiris. Mummiform figure wearing the white Upper Egyptian crown and the divine ceremonial beard. Carrying the crook and flail in hands before him. Height 13.5 cm including mounting tang; figure height 11.5 cm. Mounted. Malloy Auction XXX #213. Cf. Röder, Pl. 136 p. 77. Ex. Harry Houdini/Joseph Dunninger Collection. ....**CHOICE 1700.00**

872. **STATUETTE OF OSIRIS. 26th Dynasty to Roman. 525 B.C.-1st Century A.D.** Bronze. Holding crook and flail. Wearing Atef crown. Heavy encrustation on upper half. Tang at base. 85 mm x 25 mm. Osiris is known as the chief god of Egypt, father of Horus and husband of Isis. Upper portion heavily encrusted. Petrie Pl. XXVIII, 157 var. ....**AVERAGE 50.00**

873. **OSIRIS.   Ptolemaic Period. 304-30 B.C.** Bronze. Dark green patina with short tang at base. Features rather crude. Holding crook in left hand, flail in right. Arms not crossed which is unusual. 74 mm. He is wearing the Atef crown and Uraeus. On top of crown is a solar disk. All in all a rather unusual little statuette. Dark green-brown patina. George Steindorf Walter's Art Gallery. Pl. LXVII, 375. ....**CHOICE 100.00**

STONE

874. **GNEISS ARM BRACELET.   Late Pre-Dynastic-4th Dynasty. 3200-2560 B.C.** Black and white stone Gneiss arm bracelet. Cf. Petrie, *Royal Tombs of Earliest Dynasties*, Vol. II, Pl. IX, 3, 4. Ex. Harry Houdini-Joseph Dunninger Collection. ....**SUPERB 400.00**

875. **ALABASTER VASE. Early Dynastic. 3100-2700 B.C.** Small white-buff alabaster vase with flare rim, ovoid body, and flat base. Height 4.5 cm. Cf. Noblecourt #42. Chips at rim. ....**CHOICE 185.00**

876. **ALABASTER JAR. Old Kingdom. 2686-2181 B.C.** Intact alabaster jar with flaring walls, flat base, flattened turned over rim. Cracked and repaired. Some pitting of the alabaster. 7.2 cm high. Ex. Harry Houdini-Joseph Dunninger Coll. Cf. Egyptian Art at Yale, p. 52. ....**CHOICE 700.00**

877. **ALABASTER JAR. First Intermediate Period. 2181-2050 B.C.** Small jar with flat base, wide shoulders and rounded neck. Rim broken off. 4 cm high, 4 cm diameter wide. Cf. *Mostegedda and the Tarion Culture*, Brunton, London, 1917, Pl. LXVIII, #23. ....**CHOICE 100.00**

878. **ALABASTER VASE. First Intermediate Period. 2181-1786 B.C.** Pink/white alabaster vase. Flaring sides to a slightly overturned rim. Base slightly convex. Very minor pitting. 13.6 cm high, 5.5 cm diameter rim. Ex. Harry Houdini-Joseph Dunninger Collection. Cf. Petrie, *Diospolis Parra, The Cemeteries of Abadiyeh and Hu*, Pl. XXIX var. ....**CHOICE 700.00**

879. **ALABASTER COSMETIC VESSEL. Middle Kingdom. c. 2050-c. 1786 B.C.** Remains of a thin lip around opening in top. Deep, but slim inside. Some chips to bottom. 3.9 cm in diameter. Cf. Harageh, Petrie, Pl. XLVII, # 43 var. Ex. Malloy Sale, May 1985 ....**CHOICE 150.00**

880. **ALABASTER VESSEL. Middle Kingdom.** Small white-buff cylindrical alabaster vessel with slight flare rim. Height 8 cm. Cf. Noblecourt #75. Slight repair of one side. ....**CHOICE 400.00**

881. **COBRA FRAGMENT. New Kingdom. 1650-1085 B.C.** White limestone fragment of wall carving of cobra, facing right. Evidence of orange color. Incised lines from eye. Measures 5 x 4.6 cm. Mounted. ....**CHOICE 150.00**

882. **CARVING FRAGMENT. New Kingdom.** Limestone torso and upper legs of Ptah. Head, lower legs, and arms broken off. Some brown slip remaining. Height 4.5 cm. ....**CHOICE 125.00**

883. **TORSO OF HORUS. New Kingdom.** Black steatite torso, nude and striding with left leg forward. Left arm held to side, right arm to breast. Height 56 mm. Mounted. Ex. Malloy Sale, May 1985. Carving in the round. Below knees, right hand, and head missing. A charming carving. ....**CHOICE 600.00**

884. **LIMESTONE SLAB. 18th Dynasty under Akhenaten. 1379-1362 B.C.** Stone slab with sunken relief carving of two half registers. Top half shows four feet walking left possibly depicting two people. Feet painted bright orange-red. Bottom half depicts a head from chin up. Perhaps a portrait of two of Akhenaten's priests. In front of head, also painted orange. Each head shows the left eye and nose, but one head is depicted behind another, therefore only first head shows left ear. In front of heads, three hieroglyphs in bas relief, not painted. 28.5 cm wide x 12.5 cm high. Cf. John D. Cooney, *Amarna Reliefs from Hermopolis in the American Collectibles* for similar carvings. ....**CHOICE 2500.00**

885. **LIMESTONE FRAGMENT. 18th Dynasty. 1373-1357 B.C.** Relief of Akhenaten wearing the crowns of Upper and Lower Egypt. Rays of the sun-disc to the upper left. Cartouches above. Traces of orange-red paint on pharaoh's face. Probably part of the temple at El-Armana. 22 cm x 21 cm. Cf. for similar relief, The Luxor Museum of Ancient Egyptian Art. ....**CHOICE 8000.00**

886. **STONE VASE. Sety I. 1318-1304 B.C.** Black marble vase with cartouche of Sety I. Vase is solid and was used as inlayed in stone tray. Ex. Harry Houdini-Joseph Dunninger. Used in the ceremony of "opening the mouth." Noblecourt, 1880-1980, #103. Naville, *Cemeteries of Abydos*, Pt. 1, 1909- 1910, Pl. IV, 206. Chips at rim and shoulder. Rare. ....**CHOICE 450.00**

887. **STONE HEAD OF HORUS. Late Period. Probably 26th Dynasty.** Grey schist head of Horus with hair in lock of youth at side of head. Some minor chips. Height 18 mm. Cf. Ddaressy, *Statues de Divinités*, 39280. A number of small grey schist statuettes of Isis and Horus were excavated in the area around Saqqara. ....**CHOICE 250.00**

888. **ALABASTER VASE. Late Period. 26th Dynasty.** Miniature alabaster vase with lug handles and rounded base. The inside walls flare rather wide at bottom. Horizontal veins running through. 5.5 cm x 2.4 cm diameter. Cf. Agyptische Kunst Auktion, April 1972, p. 22, #82. Cf. Petrie, 1937, Pl. 37. Chip at neck of vase...**CHOICE 200.00**

889. **RELIEF FRAGMENT. Late Period to Ptolemaic.** Limestone relief fragment of hand on knee. Fingernails delineated. Measures 80 x 110 mm. Mounted on lucite base. Excavated at Saqqara by the Egypt Exploration Fund #WS-2849. De-accessioned by Oberlin College Museum #5224. Ex. Malloy, *Egyptian Art and Artifacts*, Summer 1980, #114. ....**CHOICE 600.00**

890. **LIMESTONE FIGURINE. 850 B.C.** Limestone carved figurine in clumsy style. Figure is female with what looks like a cloak surrounding head and neck. Facial features clear but the rest not only unclear but strangely shaped. 7 cm high. Possibly figure of a Canaanite fertility goddess which promoted childbirth. Cf. for similar parallels, Petrie, Gerar, Pl. XXXV. Broken above waist.................**CHOICE 325.00**

891. **AMBER RIBBED BEAD. 8th-6th Century B.C.** Amber, to the European people of the Iron-Bronze Age, was a highly prized commodity. It was attractive, pleasant to smell and touch and had a reputation for magical qualities. Similar beads were found at Picenum. Cf. Strong, *Catalogue of Carved Amber in the British Museum*, Pl. XXXI, 100. ....**CHOICE 65.00**

892. **FIGURE OF APE. Ptolemaic-Roman. 350 B.C.-100 A.D.** Carved diorite. Squatting ape on base, tail curling around chest. 9.5 cm high, 4.7 x 4 cm base. Cf. Sotheby Park Bernet 12, 4, 78, #372. ....**CHOICE 1000.00**

893. **LIMESTONE RELIEF PLAQUE. Ptolemaic Period. 304-30 B.C.** 7.4 x 7.4 cm. Cf. Steindorff, 358a. The bird or quail chick represents the hieroglyphic letter "W." This piece was probably a sculptor's model....**AVERAGE 375.00**

894. **URAEUS FINIAL. Ptolemaic Period.** Bone carving finial of Uraeus. This is the top of a pin. Length 26 mm. ....**CHOICE 75.00**

895. **SLATE DISH. Roman-Egyptian Period. 1st-3rd Century A.D.** 8 cm diameter. Dish with four protrusions. Traces of design in ink, probably added in modern times. Intact except for chip. This may have been used as a cosmetic palette. Petrie, *Stone and Metal Vases*, 972. Ex. Malloy Auction Catalogue, Summer 1980 ....**CHOICE 150.00**

896. **MARBLE JEWELRY/PENDANT MOLD.** Roman Egyptian. 1st-4th Century A.D. Marble mold of bird standing on plinth. Above bird is oval ring probably for attachment to necklace. Mold appears to be used for making plaques out of thin sheet metal like gold or silver. Marble black. 4.9 cm x 3.6 cm x 2.1 cm. Makes a very good impression. Very unusual. Petrie-. Hayes...**CHOICE 150.00**

WOOD

897. **BOX WITH LID.** Roughly mummiform shape, "head" area held hinge rod by which lid pivoted. Lid decorated with design of St. Andrew's cross with bands above and below. Body of box undecorated. Pivot rod and some wood at rod connection are missing. Measures 18.3 x 7.0 cm. Cf. Michelowski, *Art of Ancient Egypt* #789 (cosmetic spoon) for pivot hinge; Cf. British Museum Guide, 3rd and 4th Egyptian Rooms, pp. 276, 277 for wooden boxes. ....**CHOICE 250.00**

898. **BOATMAN STATUE.** Middle Kingdom. 2050-1786 B.C. Wooden figure of a boatman, wearing black wig, having crude facial features. Arms and legs are missing. Traces of red and black paint over gesso, and white slip paint. Figure has been joined together at waist. Crude but charming workmanship. Measures 14.3 x 3.2 cm. Cf. Steindorf, *Walters Art Gallery,* 74-89 var. This boatman was probably one of the crew which stood at either bow or stern of a model boat. ....**AVERAGE-CHOICE 250.00**

899. **WOODEN STATUETTE.** Middle Kingdom. c. 2050-1786 B.C. Wooden statuette of servant figure standing with feet and arms missing. Painted details of eyes and eyebrows in black. Moderate carving. 34 cm high. Cf. Breasted, *Egyptian Servant Statues,* 4b var. Some splitting in wood. ....**CHOICE 2000.00**

900. **WOODEN VESSEL.** Middle Kingdom. 2050-1786 B.C. Wooden partially enclosed bowl with side pierced lugs, round bottom, shoulder with concentric circle design, in center a partial wooden divider. Hayes-. Petrie-. Reconstruction to central section. Broken off in central divider. Ex. Harry Houdini-Joseph Dunninger Collection. A rare piece ....**CHOICE 450.00**

901. **WOODEN VASE.** Middle Kingdom. 2050-1786 B.C. Nicely carved wooden vase or jar with tapering body. Base small and convex. Inverted neck with flaring rim and overturned lip. 10.5 cm high, 5 cm dia. rim. Although we have found no parallel for this piece, the shape and artwork of the wooden base is similar to Middle Kingdom artwork. Petrie-. Hayes-. Fine workmanship. Some cracking. ....**CHOICE 350.00**

902. **WOODEN USHABTI.** 19th Dynasty. 1320-1200 B.C. Figure in dark brown wood, with arms crossed and wearing bag wig. Finely carved face with ears defined. Height 20.5 cm. Mounted with flexo. Cf. Schneider 3.1.1.28. Paint missing. Some wood chips at shoulders. Some repair. A fine example of rare wood carved figure..........**CHOICE 900.00**

903. **WOODEN HEAD.** Middle Kingdom, 12th Dynasty. 1991-1786 B.C. Wooden head fragment of a servant figure. Traces of black hair paint. Hair in ridges on top. Nose and mouth in fine relief. Only the forepart of the head is present. Height 8.5 cm. Cf. Hilton-Price 3104a (The Hilton-Price objects are four seated squatting wooden servant figures.) Mounted on metal base. Right eye scratched. ....**CHOICE 800.00**

904. **WOODEN VESSEL.** New Kingdom. Small vessel with flat flare rim, ovoid body, and flat base. Used in wooden models found in tombs. Small chip at rim. Lovely little vessel. ....**CHOICE 200.00**

905. **WOODEN JACKAL FIGURE.** Late Period. 650-525 B.C. Wooden carved jackal represented as Anubis. Forelegs and ears missing. Traces of white under coating and black paint with red collar. Length 19 cm. Mounted on metal base. Berlin 863 var...**CHOICE 850.00**

906. **SARCOPHAGUS PANELS.** Late Period. In two pieces: the larger 47 cm x 21 cm, the smaller, 43 cm x 19 cm. There are four dowel holes on either edge of both wooden pieces. These pieces are the middle section of the sarcophagus. The picture depicted over both pieces is rather crude in workmanship, and executed in red, yellow, and blue paint over white ground. The goddess Mut, who was the sky goddess, has her wings outstretched to protect the owner within the coffin. Her body is painted in yellow, her wings in red and blue. Her facial features are very clear, but the solar disk on top of her head is very crudely drawn. The four sons of Horus, Auset-human-head, Hapy-baboon-head, Duatmutef-jackal-head, Kabhsenf-hawk-head, protect various parts of the mummy's body. The hieroglyphics are in horizontal section. Crude two panels. ....**CHOICE 600.00**

907. **KOHL POT.** Late Period. Wooden kohl pot with a wooden kohl stick. Bottle/pot shaped like an elongated cotton spool. Wrapped in three different cloths, white, green and outer cloth in blue. Also has yellow cord or thread. 10.5 cm long stick. 7 cm high pot. Petrie, *Objects of Daily Use,* PL XXII and XXIII. ....**CHOICE 275.00**

908. **WOODEN MUMMY MASK.** Ptolemaic Period. 306-30 B.C. Mask with traces of white and black outline around the eyes, eyebrow painted over gesso. 24 x 21.5 cm. Cf. Ede, Charles, Catalogue 97, Antiquities, #22. Crack over right eye. ....**CHOICE 350.00**

909. No entry.

910. **SECTION OF CARTONNAGE SARCOPHAGUS.** Ptolemaic Period. 304-30 B.C. Section of cartonnage showing a winged goddess, Isis, facing right. In front of her is an eye of Horus symbol. Behind her is her sister, Nephthys, whose properties included representing the sunset. Executed in blue, red, yellow and green paint with register of hieroglyphs at bottom. 16 cm x 9.5 cm. Cf. *Ancient Egyptian Art at Yale,* p. 160, for similar examples of cartonnage. ....**CHOICE 750.00**

911. **PIECE OF CARTONNAGE. Ptolemaic Period. 304-30 B.C.** Piece of cartonnage showing winged Isis facing figure of Osiris in mummiform with uraeus on headdress of Atef crown. The god, Thoth, is behind Isis. He is seen holding hand of deceased (missing). One register of hieroglyphs beneath Isis. Artwork executed in red, blue, green and yellow, slightly faded. 14.5 cm x 15 cm. Cf. *Ancient Egyptian Art at Yale*, p. 160, for similar example of cartonnage. ....**CHOICE 750.00**

912. **WOODEN FIGURE OF OSIRIS-SEKER-PTAH. Ptolemaic Period. 304-30 B.C.** Figure of Osiris-Seker-Ptah in mummiform. Head in bag wig. Coated with gesso and painted in colors. Traces of aegis. Black hair, red face, black eyes. Face finely delineated. Winged disc on top missing. Height 40 cm (15.5"). Zayed, *Egyptian Antiquities*, fig. 4. During and after the 26th dynasty, a composite funerary figure combining Osiris (the god of the dead) and Seker-Ptah (the creator god of Memphis) was used....**CHOICE 2750.00**

913. **LION FIGURE. Late Ptolemaic.** Large polychrome wooden bier support, in the shape of the forepart of a lion. The wood was carved, then painted in green, black, pink, white, and mustard. Height 36 cm, width 8.6 cm. Cf. Sotheby's, June 1989, #364; Cf. Gramm, *Kunst der Ptolemaer,* #40. Good color. ....**CHOICE 1200.00**

914. **URAEUS. Late Ptolemaic/Early Roman.** Small wooden uraeus with painted black eyes wearing pinkish-red sun disc. Back of figure painted mustard color. Body decorated with black, white, green, and pink diagonal and vertical lines. Height 9.5 cm. Rather crude. Attached to original mount of painted wood. ....**CHOICE 350.00**

915. **BUST OF HELIOS. Roman Period.** Wooden. Radiate crown headdress. Mounted. 72 mm high. Facial features very rough. Roman wood carved objects are rare even in Egypt. ....**CHOICE 250.00**

GLASS
916. **DOLPHIN AMULET. 2nd Century B.C.-4th Century A.D.** Egypt. Glass amulet of fish in green color with yellow fin and nose. 2.1 cm long, 1 cm wide, 5 mm thick. Cf. Cambridge, *Glass at the Fitzwilliam Museum*, #85b. ......**CHOICE 150.00**

JEWELRY
917. **GOLD EARRING. 18th Dynasty. 1567-1304 B.C.** Thick earring of thin sheet gold. Removable cutout section. Diameter 2.6 cm. Cf. Aegiptisches Museum Berlin #678-691. Simple and plain, but nice workmanship. Some holes. Filled with sand. ....**CHOICE 250.00**

918. **PAIR OF ELECTRUM GOLD EARRINGS. 18th-19th Dynasty. 1567-1205 B.C.** Heavy hoop earrings, broken by slit. Produced from sheet electrum. 25 mm diameter. Williams, N.Y. Historical Society, *Catalogue of Egyptian Antiquities, Gold and Silver Jewelry and Related Objects*, #44. Chipping to ends of one earring. ....**CHOICE 500.00**

919. **AMENHOTEP IV (Akenaten), 1379-1362 B.C. RING FRAGMENT.** Bright blue faience ring fragment with design of cartouche of Amenhotep IV. Measures 22 x 14 mm. Cf. Petrie, *Historical Scarabs*, Pl. 43; BM 1713 i and j var. This is the famous pharaoh Akenaten who worshipped Aten and who established the new capital at Tel-el-Amarna. Most of cartouche of pharaoh present but the rest of the ring is missing. ....**CHOICE 135.00**

920. **GOLD CYLINDER BEADS. 1200 B.C.** Three beads with faience beads. Sheet gold folded into cylinders, inscribed with horizontal bands. 15 cm. Re-strung into a bracelet with modern clasp. Cf. Park Hurst, Oberlin College, Gutman Collection, #146b....................................**CHOICE 125.00**

921. **GOLD HATHOR HEAD–REPOUSSÉ. 21st Dynasty. 1085-935 B.C.** On the back, commemorative cartouche of Sesostris II, issued by Psussennes 1, 21st dynasty. 35 mm. Hathor was one of the goddesses of ancient Egypt and was preeminently the sky-goddess. She also was the female counterpart of the sun god Ra. Hayes, *Scepter of Egypt*, Vol. II, fig. 225. Cf. *Annual des Service des Antiquities d l'Egypte* LIV, Cairo, Pl. Xvf. ....**CHOICE 1000.00**

922. **GOLD SCARAB REPOUSSÉ. 22nd-26th Dynasty. 935-525 B.C.** 29 x 25 mm. Finely detailed scarab with back attached with dual spiral symbol. Cf. Park Hurst, Oberlin College, Gutman 146g. ....**CHOICE 800.00**

923. **FAIENCE NECKLACE. 26th Dynasty.** Multi-colored faience bead necklace. Length 39 cm. Re-strung. ....**CHOICE 75.00**

924. **FAIENCE NECKLACE. Late Period-Ptolemaic.** Unusual faience necklace of rust, black, and beige/yellow small beads. One strand at top joining into four strands for the rest of the necklace. Length 30 cm. Bold colors. Modern re-stringing and clasp. ....**SUPERB 300.00**

925. **BEADED FUNERAL ORNAMENT. Ptolemaic Period. 304-30 B.C.** Outspread winged figure of Horus Falcon composed of yellow, black, maroon, white, turquoise and dark blue beads faience beads. 16.5 x 20.5 cm. Cf. Malloy Sale, Summer 1977, #17...........................**SUPERB 1500.00**

926. **GLASS NECKLACE. Roman Period. 1st-3rd Century A.D.** Necklace made of tubular, rectangular and small round iridescent glass beads. Colors range from light green to gold with shades of blue. Slightly graduated in size with larger rectangular beads in center. Restrung with modern clasp. 34.5 cm long. Cf. for similar style, Dubin, *History of Beads*, p. 56. Gold glass. ....**CHOICE 175.00**

927. **GLASS AND FAIENCE NECKLACE. Roman Period. 2nd-3rd Century A.D.** Necklace constructed of iridescent, rectangular green glass beads with blue and white faience beads. Glass beads graduating to one large deep green bead at center. Re-strung with a modern clasp. 34 cm. long. Cf. for similar style, Dubin, *History of Beads*, p. 56. Some nice color and iridescence. ....**CHOICE 200.00**

WRITING

928. **LINEN FRAGMENT. New Kingdom. 1567-1085 B.C.** Hieratic script painted in black. Some material discolored at end. Measures 9.5 cm x 15.5 cm. Three lines of hieratic with a portion of the Book of the Dead. ....**CHOICE 200.00**

929. **LINEN SHROUD FRAGMENT. New Kingdom. 1567-1085 B.C.** Weave. Tabby linen cloth. Very fine. Painted on cloth are stylized floral designs. Extremely rare. 14 cm x 8.5 cm. ....**CHOICE 200.00**

930. **PAPYRUS FRAGMENT. c. 19th Dynasty.** Buff papyrus with hieroglyphic inscription in red and black. Two vertical columns, one in each color. Measures 42 x 42 mm. A fragment. ....**CHOICE 200.00**

931. **OSTRACON. 1320-935 B.C.** Triangular shape with hieroglyphics. Small piece, but good example. Three lines, 22 characters. 4.5 cm x 4.5 cm x 5.5 cm. Hieratic writing was the less formal everyday writing used by Egyptian priests. This writing was not so difficult as hieroglyphics to read or write. This form of writing was also popular until the more cursive demotic script came about in around 700 B.C. Cf. The British Museum, *Introductory Guide to the Egyptian Collections*. p. 76, fig. 25. ....**CHOICE 250.00**

932. **FUNERAL CONE. 26th Dynasty. 750-656 B.C.** Terracotta. Hieroglyphs on top. Good condition. Other side has center of black colored stone. Lacks tip of body. 8 cm diameter, 4.5 cm deep. Fourth prophet of Amun, called Monthemhat, who was mayor of Thebes 11. These cones represented the ends of beams above the entrance of a tomb. Cf. Charles Ede Ltd. Catalogue, 37 Brook Street, London. ....**CHOICE 450.00**

933. **PAPYRUS. 700-200 B.C.** Demotic script on papyrus. 6 lines, 20 characters. 5.7 cm, 2.4 cm. The type of demotic script seemed to have originated in Lower Egypt and during the 26th dynasty took over from the popular hieratic script. For a further example of demotic script, see *Introductory Guide to Egyptian Collections*, The British Museum, p. 80, fig. 29. ....**CHOICE 250.00**

934. **MUMMY BANDAGE. Egyptian. 30th Dynasty to Ptolemaic.** Fragment of a linen mummy bandage containing hieratic text from the Book of the Dead. Measures 9 x 7.1 cm. ....**CHOICE 300.00**

935. **LINEN BANDAGE. Ptolemaic Period. 343-30 B.C.** A piece of linen wrap removed from a mummy at the British Museum in the 19th century. The piece depicts a priest before an altar with the goddess, Sekmet, before from the Book of the Dead. Sixteen lines of hieratic script. 20 cm long x 6.6 cm wide. Ex. M.F. Petrie Collection. Fine drawing. ....**RARE 3000.00**

SCARABS

936. **MYCERINUS (MENDAURA). 2613-2494 B.C. 4th Dynasty.** Green paste glass scarab. 9 mm x 7 mm. Traces of gold where it was once in a mount. Nice color. Cf. Petrie, HS 33. Mycerinus was one of three kings who built his pyramid at Giza. He built the third and smallest pyramid. During his reign the Book of the Dead was revised. His remains are in the British Museum. ....**CHOICE 225.00**

937. **MYCERINUS (MENDAURA). 2613-2494 B.C. 4th Dynasty.** Blue glass paste scarab. Commemorative of the 26th dynasty. Winged lion before cartouche of Men-Ka-Ra. 19 mm x 13 mm. Nice light blue color. Cf. Cartouch-Hall, 13mc, Vol. 1, 35. ....**CHOICE 200.00**

938. **USERKARE. 2345-2181 B.C. 6th Dynasty.** 17 mm x 12 mm. This pharaoh is mentioned in a cylinder by Petrie as Vazra the Great. Cf. Hall, *BMC* Vol. 1, 233. According to a popular story of the Egyptian Middle Kingdom, Userkare was one of the kings of the 5th-6th dynasty who believed he was a child of Re, thus he was called son of Re. Many of the kings of 5th and 6th dynasties built elaborate sun temples at Abu Gurab in commemoration of Re. ....**SUPERB 200.00**

939. **NEFER-RA. 2345-2181 B.C. 6th Dynasty.** Carved steatite scarab, grey. Ra-Nefer, Deshert. Commemorative of the 26th dynasty. Petrie, *Scarabs* X var. ....**CHOICE 175.00**

940. **GLAZED STEATITE BUTTON SEAL. 9th Dynasty. 2160-2050 B.C.** Light brown. Lotus plant with ribs at side. Measures 1.1 cm x 0.9 cm. For style, Cf. Petrie, *Buttons* #393; Matouk 2011. Cf. Petrie, *Buttons* 410, 417. An early button seal. Chip at top. ....**SUPERB 150.00**

941. **MIDDLE KINGDOM. 2050-1786 B.C.** Carved steatite scarab with red color in various areas. Horus-Ra kneeling, holding two feathers. Solar disc with two uraei above, nub below. 17 mm x 12 mm. Represented as the falcon-headed human figure, the falcon was the favorite emblem of Horus-Ra. Hall, Style D-8. Matouk-. Cf. Petrie, *Buttons* 101 I var. Chip at base to edge of bottom. ....**CHOICE 125.00**

942. **MIDDLE KINGDOM. 2050-1786 B.C.** Carved steatite cowroid, tan. Thouris, the hippopotamus-headed goddess of childbirth, standing before Nefer sign meaning good luck. 17 mm x 10 mm. Cf. Matouk 338. ....**CHOICE 80.00**

943. **MIDDLE KINGDOM. 2050-1786 B.C.** Glazed carved steatite, gray. Amen-Tat-Neb-Nith. Lily bud. Signifies the substance of Amen. 15 mm x 11 mm. Newberry-. Ward-. Petrie-. Hall-. Chip at wings. ....**CHOICE 75.00**

944. **MIDDLE KINGDOM. 2050-1786 B.C.** Carved steatite, beige. Beloved Sobek advancing holding lotus and ankh. 16 mm x 11 mm. Cf. Matouk 323. ....**CHOICE 80.00**

945. **CARVED STEATITE PLAQUE. Middle Kingdom. 2050-1786 B.C.** Standing figure. Horus standing advancing. Reverse: Hare seated. right. Ex. Collection of N.E. Homsy, April 12, 1911. Note says "Came from Syria 20 d(ays) ago, (March 23, 1911) EJN? Cut of man std. 3 cm B.C. other side, Isis or bird. Purchased it for 50 cents." Ex. E. J. Burgess. R: Matouk 830-4. O: Matouk 157 var. ....**CHOICE 80.00**

946. **STEATITE PLAQUE. Middle Kingdom. 2050-1786 B.C.** Glazed carved plaque gone brown. Amen-Ra on obverse. Lion walking. Lotus above. 16 mm x 11 mm. Nice carving. Petrie, *Buttons* 1134. Frazer 471. ....**CHOICE 85.00**

947. **MIDDLE KINGDOM. 2050-1786 B.C.** Dark green glass paste scarab. Crude carving. Man standing before antelope. "The Antelope Hunt." 14 mm x 8 mm. Matouk 747-748. ....**CHOICE 100.00**

948. **MIDDLE KINGDOM. 2050-1786 B.C.** Faience scarab gone beige. Private name scarab. Peda-Neter-Her. Measures 15 mm x 10 mm. Matouk-. Petrie, *Scarabs*. Hall-. Crude. ....**CHOICE 125.00**

949. **MIDDLE KINGDOM. 2050-1786 B.C.** Glazed carved steatite scarab gone white. Ka-Nefer-Kau. Lotus above. 16 mm x 13 mm. Cf. Petrie, *Scarabs* A.S. Chip at bottom end. ....**CHOICE 60.00**

950. **MIDDLE KINGDOM. 2050-1786 B.C.** Heart scarab uninscribed. Blue-green feldspar. 35 mm x 45 mm. The heart scarab functioned as a replacement of the heart organ and represented the person or spirit of the deceased individual. Cf. Riefstahl, *Ancient Egyptian Glass and Glazes*, 44. ....**SUPERB 1000.00**

951. **MIDDLE KINGDOM. 2050-1786 B.C.** Black steatite carved scarab. Blank base, suspension hole through middle. 12 mm x 9 mm. Used as jewelry inset. .....**CHOICE 100.00**

952. **MIDDLE KINGDOM.** Glazed white steatite scarab. Head of Hathor facing. Measures .9 x .6 cm. Hall, *BMC* Type Cl. Matouk II, 138 ....**CHOICE-SUPERB 150.00**

953. **BUFF STEATITE BUTTON SEAL. Late Middle Kingdom.** With design symbolizing the union of the two lands. Diameter 1.5 cm. Cf. Petrie, *Buttons* 386a. Ex. Malloy, Sale Summer 1980, #268. Small chip in side, some surface wear. A superb example of the button seals which were so popular in the Middle Kingdom.. ....**CHOICE 150.00**

954. **LATE MIDDLE KINGDOM.** Glazed steatite design scarab, gone buff. Five blossoms of papyrus. Style *BMC* Fl. Cf. Matouk II, 2022 var. ....**CHOICE 150.00**

955. **EARLY DYNASTIC. 12th Dynasty. 1991-1786 B.C.** Ornamental scarab. Five circles. 13 mm x 9 mm. Ex. Thomas Elder, Feb. 21, 1910. Matouk 269...**CHOICE 75.00**

956. **AMEN-RA. 12th Dynasty-Hyksos Period. 1991-1542 B.C.** Buff carved steatite scarab. Amen-Ra. Measures 12 x 9 mm. *BMC* Hall, style #1. Cf. Petrie SC XXV 19 rev. ....**CHOICE 100.00**

957. **12TH DYNASTY-HYKSOS PERIOD. 1991-1542 B.C.** Dark buff carved steatite scarab. Two uraeus facing palm branch. 12 x 10 mm. *BMC* Hall, Style H1. **CHOICE 100.00**

958. **12TH-18TH DYNASTY. 1991-1320 B.C.** Decorative, carved steatite scarab gone white. Scroll quartered pattern terminating in central knot. Length 20 mm. Cf. Newberry, XVIII, 15. Chip on left wing. Superb design. ....**CHOICE 150.00**

959. **12TH-18TH DYNASTY.** Decorative scarab, beige carved steatite, with leaf pattern each side of central scroll. Length 19 mm. Newberry, XIX, no. 4....................**CHOICE 175.00**

960. **12TH-18TH DYNASTY.** Before and after Hyksos. Carved steatite scarab, glaze gone grey-buff. Four uraeus ending in central rope pattern. Length 18 mm. Newberry-. Wear to edge. ....**CHOICE 135.00**

961. **12TH-18TH DYNASTY.** Buff carved steatite scarab. Intertwined rope design emanating from center, resulting in "woven" pattern. Measures 18 x 13 mm. *BMC* style C1; Newberry XVIII, 5-17 var. ....**SUPERB 150.00**

962. **SESOSTRIS I (NEFER-KHEPER-KA). 1971-1928 B.C. 12th Dynasty.** Glazed carved steatite, now turned white. Nefer-Kheper-Ka imprinted twice on scarab. 24 mm x 13 mm. Cf. Hall, *BMC* Vol. 78 (User & SenI). For cartouche, Petrie *Scarabs* 17 (Senusert I). Chip at base. Sesostris I took control over a unified Egypt after his father died while he was on campaign in the Western Desert. He transferred the seat of administration from Thebes to Hj-towy. This enabled the pharaohs more control over the whole country. ....**CHOICE 150.00**

963. **USERTSEN III . (KHA-KA-RA). 1878-1843 B.C. 12th Dynasty.** Carved grey steatite scarab. Cartouche of Usertsen, uraeus to left. Measures 1.8 x 1.2 cm. Cf. Hall, *BMC* 135 var. Chip at side. ....**CHOICE 225.00**

964. **LATE MIDDLE KINGDOM. 19th Dynasty. 1800-1200 B.C.** Buff carved steatite scarab. Ankh between rope and Neb signs. Measures 16 x 11 mm. Cf. *BMC* Hall, for style G2; Ward-; Newberry-; Petrie *SC*; Petrie *HS*-; Matouk-; Rowe -. Chip on top.................**CHOICE 110.00**

965. **LATE MIDDLE KINGDOM. 19th Dynasty. 1800-1200 B.C.** Buff carved steatite lion scarab. Lion advancing, tree above, trap before. 16 x 12 mm. *BMC*, style G2; for lion scarabs, Cf. Matouk 383, 516-548. ....**CHOICE 125.00**

966. **12th-15th (HYKSOS) DYNASTY. Ra-Ne-Ka (?).** Glazed steatite scarab. Brown-beige. Ne-Ka-Ra-Anka-Iri, uraei each side. Long life to Nekara. Commemorative from the Levant. The Ra-Kha refers to king. Cf. Rowe 21. Cf. Petrie, *Scarabs* X, 7 (VII-VIII Dynasty). ....**CHOICE 200.00**

967. **13th DYNASTY. 1786-1720 B.C.** Green glazed, carved steatite cowroid. Neb-Desres-Ankh. 12 mm x 7 mm. Good color. Petrie, *Buttons* 1120. ....**SUPERB 75.00**

968. **MAA-AB-[RA]-AMEN. 12th-16th Dynasty.** Buff carved steatite scarab with inscription Son of Sun, Maa-Ab-Ra. Measures 15 x 10 mm. For scarab style, *BMC* G2; Cf. *BMC* 253 for name..**SUPERB 175.00**

969. **EBEHETOP III. 1786-1633 B.C. 13th Dynasty.** Carved glazed steatite gone beige with hawk and wat eyes, ankh at sides. 17 mm x 13 mm. Cf. Ward 435. Petrie HS 103-4. Petrie described the type as a king Neferkara of 7th-8th dynasty. The name, however, is used by Sebek Hetep III in the 13th dynasty. Cf. Hall. ....**CHOICE 175.00**

970. **NEFER-DED-RA (DEDU-MES). 1786-1633 B.C. 13th-14th Dynasty.** Carved steatite glazed gone white. Nomen in center with Upper and Lower Egypt including symbols of kingship. 21 mm x 14 mm. Chip on front. Cf. Newberry, Pl. X, 29. For the nomen of this king, see a stone slab in the Cairo Museum, 20533. Not much is known about these rulers because this dynasty marks the beginning of the Hyksos Period, the rise to power of the "shepherd kings." ....**CHOICE 175.00**

971. **13th DYNASTY. 1788-1633 B.C.** Decorative carved steatite scarab with white to beige glaze. Ten concentric circles around center circle on base. Length 19 mm. Rowe 11, 79. Matouk, 2186. Newberry-. Chip at base. ....**SUPERB 135.00**

972. **13th DYNASTY HYKSOS. 1786-1567 B.C.** Decorative beige scarab with rope pattern scroll. Length 25 mm. Cf. Rowe, no. 89. Small chip, nice large size...**CHOICE 300.00**

973. **13th DYNASTY HYKSOS. 1786-1567 B.C.** Carved steatite scarab with hieroglyphs translated - "Great is Ra" (ava). Length 13 mm. Cf. Rowe, 256. ....**CHOICE 125.00**

974. **13th DYNASTY HYKSOS. 1786-1567 B.C.** Faience scarab gone buff. Egyptian standing right in bag wig holding lotus. Length 19 mm. Newberry, XXV, 1 var.......**CHOICE 200.00**

975. **SEBEKHOTEP I. 13th Dynasty.** Faience scarab with traces of green. Royal name of Sebekhotep I. Measures 1.2 x 0.8 cm. Petrie, *HS*, 283. ....**CHOICE 250.00**

976. **13th-26th DYNASTY.** Buff steatite scarab, with traces of green glaze. Tall date palm with two baboons below looking inward. Measures 12 x 9 mm. *BMC* style J1; w/palm tree. Cf. Ward 24; Cf. Matouk Pl. 7.........................**CHOICE 130.00**

977. **14th DYNASTY.** Beige carved steatite scarab. Two Djed pillars (stability) on each side of Nub-Nub-Nub (Nub refers to gold). Measures 19 x 14 mm. Rowe-, Petrie *HS*-, *BMC*-, Matouk-, Petrie-. Nice carving. Base; hole in central design. ....**CHOICE 125.00**

978. **RA-NEFER. 14th Dynasty-Hyksos Period.** White-buff carved steatite scarab. Papyrus for Lower Egypt above and below RE-NEFER with h-h- between. Measures 10 x 10 mm. For Ra-Nefer scarabs, Cf. Rowe 114-132. ...**SUPERB 175.00**

979. **14th-15th DYNASTY. 1786-1567 B.C.** Large carved scarab. Two baboons facing each other with palm leaf in middle. Two lotus flowers beneath apes. Rather crudely carved back. Measures 3.1 x 2.2 cm. Cf. Petrie, *Buttons*, Pl. XII:839-846. ....**CHOICE 400.00**

980. **SECOND INTERMEDIATE PERIOD. 1786-1567 B.C.** Carved steatite beige scarab. Private name: Sa-Maat. Priest of the Temple of Horus. 16 mm x 10 mm. Petrie, *Historical-*. *BMC*-. Petrie, *Scarabs*-. Chip on top of wing. ....**CHOICE 120.00**

981. **SECOND INTERMEDIATE PERIOD. 1786-1567 B.C.** Glazed carved steatite scarab gone beige. Two ankhs with Neb-Het. 26 mm x 17 mm. Nice, large forepart of lion depicted. Nice size. Newberry 29. Petrie, *Buttons* 510 var. ....**CHOICE 300.00**

982. **HYKSOS PERIOD.** Carved steatite scarab, buff colored. Lion seated left, behind kneeling male with bag wig and kilt. Gazelle above. Fine linear and cross-hatching design. Length 23 mm. Cf. Newberry, Pl. XXV, 34 var. Bold design. ....**CHOICE 300.00**

983. **HYKSOS PERIOD.** White carved steatite scarab. Crude ΔΔΔ with Neb Kara. Rowe identified ΔΔΔ as a corruption of Ka. (Rowe 223) 12 x 9 mm. Rowe-; For style, Cf. Rowe XXXV 34; Matouk-; Petrie *SC*. ....**SUPERB 150.00**

984. **HYKSOS PERIOD.** Light buff carved steatite scarab. Papyrus plants emblematic of Lower Egypt, around fourfold protection. Measures 17 x 12 mm. Cf. Rowe 349-50 var. ....**SUPERB 150.00**

985. **HYKSOS PERIOD.** Buff carved steatite scarab. Central twisted rope, rope to each side. Measures 17 x 10 mm. *BMC* shape F1; Cf. Newberry XIX, 1 var............**CHOICE 130.00**

986. **HYKSOS PERIOD.** Buff carved steatite scarab. Kneeling man dressed in tunic, holding lotus and ankh. Measures 14 x 9 mm. The ankh means life. Cf. Rowe 285. A gem. ....**SUPERB 175.00**

987. **HYKSOS PERIOD. 1786-1567 B.C.** Carved steatite scarab. Deshert-Wah-Deshert. Endurance of red crown of Lower Egypt. Cf. Rowe 251 var. ....**CHOICE 150.00**

988. **HYKSOS PERIOD. 1786-1567 B.C.** Buff carved steatite scarab.. Two tied plants each side. Cf Nesew. Cf. Rowe 362 var. ....**CHOICE 125.00**

989. **HYKSOS PERIOD. 1674-1567 B.C.** Buff carved steatite scarab. Khnum, ram-headed deity advancing. Matouk 88. Very rare. ....**SUPERB 300.00**

990. **CARVED STEATITE COWROID. Hyksos. 1720-1570 B.C.** Geometric design. Measures 1.6 x 1.3 cm. Matouk 2231 var. ....**CHOICE 135.00**

991. **CIVIC SCARAB OF MEMPHIS. Hyksos Period. 1674-1567 B.C.** Glazed steatite cowroid, beige. Ra-Aa-Em-Neter. 17 mm x 13 mm. Cartouche between two red crowns. Read "Satisfaction of heart living at Memphis." Rare. Petrie, *Buttons* 612. Hall, *BMC* Vol. 1, 2563........**CHOICE 250.00**

992. **APEPA I. 15th Dynasty. 1674-1567 B.C.** Glazed carved steatite scarab. Nesut Bat, O-Seuser-Deshert-Wah-Deshert. Measures 1.9 x 1.2 cm. Cf. Petrie, XXI, 9 var. Some repair. ....**CHOICE 225.00**

993. **15th DYNASTY. 1674-1567 B.C.** Carved steatite scarab, glazed but gone white. RA-KHEPER, a king. Length 11 mm. Cf. Rowe, 156. ....**CHOICE 125.00**

994. **HYKSOS PERIOD. 1674-1567 B.C.** Imitation cartouches. Glazed steatite scarab gone buff. Kha. *BMC* type D6. Cf. Newberry XXIV, 15 var. Cf. Matouk 2349-72. ....**CHOICE 50.00**

995. **LATE MIDDLE KINGDOM. 15th-16th Dynasty.** "Nub" type. Carved steatite scarab gone beige. Nub Nefer Nefer. Petrie, *HS* Pl. 23......................................**CHOICE 150.00**

996. **HYKSOS PERIOD. 16th Dynasty. 1674-1567 B.C.** Carved steatite scarab, white. Ra-Ne-Ra. "He who belongs to the god." The Rowe scarab was found at Jericho. Rowe 231 var. Large chip at head. ....**CHOICE 75.00**

997. **SE-KHO-NE-RA. 1674-1567 B.C. 16th Dynasty. Hyksos Period.** Sekha-N-Ra meaning Good God. 17 mm x 12 mm. Wear to base edge. Cf. Petrie, *Scarabs* 7. Budge, *Hist. Eg.* ii, 166. Cf. Hall, *BMC* 277 and 279. ....**CHOICE 175.00**

998. **16TH DYNASTY. Hyksos Period.** Beige steatite scarab with lengthwise twist design, with borders described by Petrie as typical of the Hyksos period. Crude but effective design on top. Length 15 mm. Cf. Petrie, *Buttons and Design Scarabs*, #225 and similar. ....**CHOICE 85.00**

999. **RA-NE-RA GROUP. 16th Dynasty.** White carved steatite scarab. Ra-Ne-Ra-Ne. Measures 14 x 10 mm. Cf. Rowe 220 var. A little gem.....................................**SUPERB 175.00**

1000. **RA-NE-RA GROUP. 16th Dynasty.** Buff carved steatite scarab. N-RA N-RA. Measures 13 x 10 mm. Cf. Rowe 224 var. Chipped at nose. ....**CHOICE 100.00**

1001. **NETER-HOR-NUB-RA. 1674-1567 B.C. 16th Dynasty.** Carved steatite scarab, glaze gone white. Wings are not glazed. Two uraei above and below falcon. 18 mm x 12 mm. Some small chips. Petrie. *HS*, 713 var. Rowe 175. ....**CHOICE 125.00**

1002. **NEB-NE-NEB. 16th Dynasty.** Buff carved steatite scarab. Cartouche of Neb-Ne-Neb surrounded by S-shaped scroll design. Measures 20 x 13 mm. Petrie *HS*-; *BMC*-, Cf. for variant Ra-Ne-Ra, Rowe 231; Cf. 216. Superb quality. ....**SUPERB 250.00**

1003. **NE-KA-RA. Uncertain king. Perhaps 17th Dynasty.** Ra-Kheper-Neb in scroll border. 19 mm x 14 mm. Chip at right wing. Petrie *Scarabs* AY ....**CHOICE-SUPERB 140.00**

1004. **INYOTEF VII. NUB-KHEPER-RA. 1650-1567 B.C. 17th Dynasty.** Carved steatite gone white. 17 mm x 11 mm. Small chip. Cf. Hall, *BMC* Vol. 1, 220. ....**CHOICE 150.00**

1005. **HYKSOS PERIOD. 1624-1567 B.C.** Glazed carved steatite gone white. Design scarab. On scarab wings, spirals with crowns, NEB. 17 mm x 11 mm. For style, Cf. Rowe 333, 345, 346, 349. ....**SUPERB 125.00**

1006. **HYKSOS PERIOD. 1624-1567 B.C.** Carved steatite glaze gone white. Design scarab. Red crowns of Lower Egypt with WAH (endurance). 16 mm x 11 mm. Cf. Rowe 343. ....**CHOICE-SUPERB 125.00**

1007. **HYKSOS PERIOD. 1624-1567 B.C.** Glazed, carved steatite scarab gone white. Hotep-Wah-Neb. Crown of Lower Egypt. 14 mm x 10 mm. Rowe 345 var. ......**SUPERB 125.00**

1008. **HYKSOS PERIOD. 1624-1567 B.C.** Carved white steatite. Uraei before Horus right. The god Horus. 16 mm x 13 mm. Nicely defined realistic legs. Chip at base. Cf. Hall, *BMC* Vol. 2575 var. ....**CHOICE 80.00**

1009. **HYKSOS PERIOD. 1624-1567 B.C.** Glazed steatite scarab gone white. Sphinx in form of lion. Uraeus before. 17 mm x 11 mm. Rowe 300. ....**CHOICE 85.00**

1010. **HYKSOS PERIOD. 1585-1542 B.C.** Buff carved steatite scarab. Two standing figures in kilts and bag wigs holding hands. Uraeus each side, blossom above. Measures 20 x 14 mm. *BMC*-; Newberry-; Cf. Matouk 1611 var.; Petrie-; Rowe-. Chips to back of base. ....**CHOICE 160.00**

1011. **MENKUARE (Mycerinus). Commemorative Scarab of the 18th Dynasty.** Blue glass paste. Contains cartouche of MEN-KA-RA and uraeus. Length 19 mm. Menkaure ruled during the 4th dynasty; his is the smallest pyramid at Giza. For cartouche, Cf. Hall, *British Museum Collection of Scarabs*, Vol. 1, no. 35. Nice light blue color. ....**CHOICE 350.00**

1012. **18th-19th DYNASTY. 1567-1200 B.C.** Design cowroid. Turquoise glazed carved steatite. Cross with four uraei. 15 mm x 6 mm. Nice color. Matouk 2242. .....**CHOICE 100.00**

1013. **18th-19th DYNASTY. 1567-1200 B.C.** Heart scarab. Black carved steatite. Seven lines of chapter of the heart abbreviated. With name Mat-Nefer-Men-T-An. 7 mm x 4.3 mm. Finely carved scarab with hieroglyphs. Crude traces of bitumen in crevices. For types, Cf. Petrie, *Scarabs* XLVIII, 9...................................**SUPERB 3,500.00**

1014. **NEW KINGDOM. 1567-1085 B.C.** Good luck scarab. Glazed carved steatite gone beige. Inscribed on base IKHT-NEB-NEFER, meaning "all good things." Measures 11 x 9 mm. Cf. Ward 126. Two minor chips at edge of base. A finely carved scarab. ....**SUPERB 125.00**

1015. **NEW KINGDOM. 1567-1085 B.C.** Lapis lazuli carved scarab. 16 mm. Blank base scarabs were used as jewelry in gold mountings ....**SUPERB 200.00**

1016. **NEW KINGDOM. 1567-1085 B.C.** Green durite carved scarab. Blank base. 14 mm x 10 mm.........**SUPERB 175.00**

1017. **NEW KINGDOM. 1567-1085 B.C.** Light blue glass paste scarab. Spiral S with Nebs. 15 mm x 10 mm. Cf. Matouk 2095..**CHOICE 80.00**

1018. **NEW KINGDOM. 1567-1085 B.C.** Bright turquoise cowroid. 10 mm x 7 mm. Neb-Hen-Nefer. Praise and Beauty. Superb color..............................**CHOICE 100.00**

1019. **NEW KINGDOM. 1567-1085 B.C.** Buff carved steatite scarab. Pharaoh advancing wearing crown of Upper and Lower Egypt. Uraeus in crown, holding flail and sceptre. 17 mm x 12 mm. Style, Hall E-4. Superb style. Chip at base of wings. Matouk-. Petrie, *Buttons* . ...**CHOICE 125.00**

1020. **NEW KINGDOM. 1567-1085 B.C.** Green glazed steatite scarab. Crosslet with ureai at each corner. Looped uraei. 9 mm x 13 mm. Chip at side. Matouk 1185 var. Petrie, *Buttons* 280....................................**CHOICE 65.00**

1021. **NEW KINGDOM. 1567-1085 B.C.** Hedgehog. Blue-green glazed carved steatite. Ra standing with wing raised. Uraeus before. Solar disc with Uraeus above. 15 mm x 9 mm. Chip at head. Superb color. Matouk 287. Matouk 861 var. ....**CHOICE 135.00**

1022. **AGATE SCARAB. New Kingdom. 1567-1085 B.C.** Suspension hole at either side of scarab. Measures 1.3 x 9 cm. Chip at back. Beautiful color..............**CHOICE 80.00**

1023. **GOOD WISH SCARAB. New Kingdom.** Carved glazed scaraboid, brown-green. Inscription. Measures 1.2 x .8 cm. Newberry, XL 15 var. ....**CHOICE 75.00**

1024. **ROUND FAIENCE AMULET. New Kingdom.** Eye of Horus on one side and head of Bes on other. Suspension hole through middle. Diameter 1.5 cm. Cf. Ayed, *Egyptian Antiquities* #2036. ....**AVERAGE 35.00**

1025. **GREEN DIORITE SCARAB. New Kingdom.** Blank base. Measures 1.4 x 1 cm. ....**SUPERB 175.00**

1026. **GREEN SCHIST SCARAB. New Kingdom.** Blank base. Measures 1.6 by 1.1 cm. These hard stone scarabs were usually mounted in gold jewelry and worn as rings or pendants. ....**SUPERB 200.00**

1027. **NEW KINGDOM.** Carved grey limestone scarab. Naturalistic. Measures 2.5 x 2.0 cm. Used in jewelry or ornamentation. ....**CHOICE 150.00**

1028. **AMENHOTEP I. 1546-1536 B.C. 18th Dynasty.** Buff carved steatite uzat (eye of Horus) scaraboid. Base depicts elements of Amenhotep I's name. Length 10 mm. Cf. Hall, *Egyptian Scarabs in the British Museum*, #365 var. Small chip at base.............................**CHOICE 250.00**

1029. **THOTHMES III. 1504-1450 B.C.** Steatite scarab. Gone grey. Measures 1.5 cm x 1.1 cm. Thothmes III, a vigorous pharaoh, extended the Egyptians' control far throughout the known world of the ancients. ....**CHOICE 150.00**

1030. **THOTHMES III. 1504-1450 B.C. 18th Dynasty.** Glazed steatite scarab, grey. Royal name of Thothmes III. Cf. Hall, *BMC* 564..**CHOICE 100.00**

1031. **THOTHMES III. 1504-1450 B.C.** White steatite scarab with cartouche of Thothmes III in rope border. Suspension hole. Rather good carving. 1.3 cm x 2·cm. Petrie, *Scarabs and Cylinders*, Pl. XXVI, 18.6 var. ....**CHOICE 150.00**

1032. **THOTHMES III. 1504-1450 B.C.** Gray faience scarab with traces of green. Royal cartouche of Thothmes III. Cf. Hall, *BMC* #1235.........................**CHOICE 75.00**

1033. **THOTHMES III. 1504-1450 B.C. 18th Dynasty. 1567-1320 B.C.** Carved steatite plaque, cream. Prenomen of Thothmes III-Loved by Amen. 18 mm x 11 mm. Cf. Petrie, *Scarabs* 32. ....**CHOICE 75.00**

1034. **THOTHMES III. 1504-1450 B.C.** Scrolls on each side of cartouche of Men-Kaeper-ra. Measures 14 mm x 9 mm. ....**CHOICE 80.00**

1035. **THOTHMES III. 1504-1450 B.C.** Glazed faience scarab with traces of green and red ochre in crevices. 16 mm x 12 mm. ....**CHOICE 85.00**

1036. **THOTHMES III. 1504-1450 B.C.** God Ra standing before cartouche of Thothmes III. The symbol of Neith is substituted here for the Scarabaeus in the magical name. 17 mm x 12 mm. Somewhat crude. Cf. Petrie 4.5 985. Hall, *BMC* Vol. I, 1123 var. ....**CHOICE 60.00**

1037. **THOTHMES III. 1504-1450 B.C.** Prenomen of Thothmes III in cartouche. Two uraei at sides. 18 mm x 13 mm. Large chip to base. ....**CHOICE 50.00**

1038. **THOTHMES III. 1504-1450 B.C.** God Set standing before prenomen of Thothmes III. 17 mm x 13 mm. Large chip at base of set. Petrie *HS* 986. Hall, *BMC* Vol. 1, 1142 ....**CHOICE 50.00**

1039. **THOTHMES III. 1504-1450 B.C.** Prenomen of Thothmes III with two uraei. 14 mm x 9 mm. Cf. Hall, *BMC* Vol 1, 1563...**CHOICE 75.00**

1040. **THOTHMES III. 1504-1450 B.C.** Carved steatite, glaze gone white, ring. 26 mm in diameter. Scarab 13 mm x 10 mm. Imitation prenomen of Thothmes III. For ring style, Cf. Hall, *BMC*, p. XV, Pl. #2. Base mount with silver band, ring of bronze. Chip on silver base. Hall identifies a similar type as a corrupt form of Thothmes. This scarab has the addition of two signs of truth used by Thothmes. Cf. Hall, *BMC*,. Vol. 1, 1348 var. ....**CHOICE 350.00**

1041. **THOTHMES III. 1504-1450 B.C.** Green glazed carved steatite scarab. Amen-Ra, lord of two lands, gold sign below, wings above. Cartouche of Thothmes III to right. 18 mm x 14 mm. Ex. R. H. Blanchard Collection, Cairo, Egypt. On Blanchard card written in his own handwriting, "Fine royal scarab, one of the finest scarabs in my collection. Bought of Abdul Mohannud. Very clear cartouche of Thothmes III, March 1929." Cf. Hall, *BMC* 649, Petrie, *H.S.* ....**SUPERB 350.00**

1042. **THOTHMES III. 1504-1450 B.C.** Buff carved steatite scarab. Cartouche of Thothmes III. RA-MEN-KHEPER. Measures 14 x 11 mm. Petrie, *SC* XXIX, 144. Crude inscription...**CHOICE 125.00**

1043. **THOTHMES III.** Buff carved steatite scarab. Cartouche of RA-MEN-KHEPER AMEN-RA-TAT. Measures 16 x 13 mm. Cf. Petrie *SC*, XXVII, 28. Part of base is restored. ....**CHOICE 100.00**

1044. **AMEN-HETEP II. 1450-1425 B.C. 18th Dynasty.** Carved steatite scarab. Buff. Prenomen of Amen-Hetep II with truth, goodness and ankh. Measures 1.5 x 1 cm. Cf. Hall, *BMC* 1681 var. Wing cases broken off. ....**CHOICE 225.00**

1045. **18th DYNASTY. 1425-1417 B.C.** Glazed steatite cowroid, tan. Facing head of Hathor with uraei each side below, representing the Sistum. Made during the reign of Thothmes IV. 14 mm x 8 mm. The Sisturm was the emblem of Hathor, one of the chief goddesses of Egypt. The sky goddess was intimately associated with the sun god Ra. Cf. Petrie, *Buttons* 550. ....**SUPERB 125.00**

1046. **18th DYNASTY. 1425-1417 B.C.** Light green glazed carved steatite scarab. Amen-Ra before lion. Made during the reign of Thothmes IV. Passent. 15 mm x 12 mm. Matouk. ....**CHOICE 125.00**

1047. **THOTHMES IV. 1425-1417 B.C. 18th Dynasty. 1567-1320 B.C.** Light blue faience scarab cartouche of Thothmes IV. Also signs of goodness and hard. 17 mm x 13 mm. Cf. Hall, *BMC* Vol 1, 1688 var. ....**SUPERB 250.00**

1048. **THOTHMES IV. 1425-1417 B.C.** Buff carved alabaster scarab, once glazed. Beautiful son of Amen-Ra. 15 mm x 11 mm. This type is prevalent on Thothmes IV type scarabs. Cf. Hall, *BMC*-. 1698, 1699, 1760, 1706. Petrie, *Scarabs*. ....**CHOICE 150.00**

1049. **AMEN-HETEP III. 1417-1379 B.C. 18th Dynasty.** Carved steatite with light green glaze. Lion before prenomen of Amenhotep III. 16 mm x 10 mm. Petrie-. Ward-. *BMC*-. Chip at end of wings................................**CHOICE 135.00**

1050. **AMEN-HETEP III. 1417-1379 B.C. 18th Dynasty.** Glazed carved steatite scarab, tan with green in crevice. Maot-Ra-Nefer-Sebek = Amenhetep, beloved of Sebek. Ra is represented in a boat. Superbly carved scarab with fine open work. For relationship with Sebek and Amenhetep see Hall Cylinder 2647 and the Tradition of Sebek in the XII Dynasty. 16 mm x 11 mm. Nice open work scarab. Chip on base and foreleg. Petrie, *Scarabs*. Ex. Collection Maurice Nalima, Cairo. Ex. Azeez Khayat, New York, c. 1930. Ex. E.S. Burgess, given to his wife by Khayat with card from him. ....**SUPERB 200.00**

1051. **AMEN-HETEP III. 1417-1379 B.C. 18th Dynasty.** Sphinx couchant right wearing Atef crown, holding figure of the god, Ra. Winged Uraeus behind. Length 21 mm x 15 mm. Cf. Hall, *British Museum Collection of Scarabs*, Vol. 1: no. 1857. Most of wings chipped off. Nice base design. ....**CHOICE 90.00**

1052. **AMEN-HETEP III. 1417-1379 B.C. 18th Dynasty.** Light blue faience cowroid. Cartouche of the prenomen of Amen-Hetep III. Measures 22 by 12 mm. *BMC*, Hall 1763 and 1754. ....**CHOICE 350.00**

1053. **QUEEN THII. Wife of Amen-Hetep III.** Green faience scarab inscribed "Great King's Wife Thii" in two lines. Measures 17 x 11 mm. Petrie *HS* 42. BM var. ....**CHOICE 400.00**

1054. **18th DYNASTY.** Cream-white glazed carved steatite scarab. Four petals as cross, with petals in angles. Measures 15 x 10 mm. Rowe 620 var. Attractive. ....**CHOICE 80.00**

1055. **AMEN-RA. 18th Dynasty.** Buff carved steatite scarab. Hieroglyphic inscription of Amen-Ra, flower bud with long stalk. Measures 13 x 9 mm. Rowe 606; *BMC* style A3. ....**SUPERB 150.00**

1056. **AMARNA PERIOD. 1417-1362 B.C.** Turquoise faience ring intaglio. Lotus sprigs. 19 mm x 12 mm. Lovely color. ....**SUPERB 125.00**

1057. **QUEEN NEZEMT. Wife of Herembeb. 1349-1320 B.C. 18th Dynasty.**   Queen seated, green and brown faience cowroid.   Traces of green. 20 mm x 11 mm. Very rare. Cf. Petrie, *Scarabs* 28. ....**AVERAGE-CHOICE 200.00**

1058. **RAMESSES I. 1320-1318 B.C. 19th Dynasty.** Carved steatite scarab glazed white. Cartouche of Pharaoh with NEB below. 18 mm long. Cf. Petrie, *H.S.*, 45. Superbly carved scarab, chip at base.......................**CHOICE 350.00**

1059. **MEN-SA-PTAH-SA-PTAH.   19th Dynasty. 1320-1200 B.C.** Black carved steatite hedgehog. Not much is known about this pharaoh because at the end of this dynasty, according to the Great Harris Papyrus, Egypt fell into a decline. For a similar hedgehog see Hornong and Staehelim, *Scarabaen und Andere Siegelamulette*, Taf. 116, c7. Cf. Hedgehog, Matouk 853-4. Hall, *BMC*-. Petrie, *Scarabs*-. Petrie, *H.S.*-. Very rare. ....**CHOICE 500.00**

1060. **19th DYNASTY. 1320-1200 B.C.**   Carved steatite, beige. Ra standing holding sceptre. 13 mm x 9 mm. Rowe 706. For shape, Cf. Petrie, *Scarabs* R, 36. Matouk 278. ....**CHOICE 60.00**

1061. **19th DYNASTY. 1320-1200 B.C.**   Glazed carved steatite scarab gone white. Hapi kneeling wearing headdress of lotus. Before, lidded vessel. 13 mm x 8 mm. Hapi represents the spirit of the Nile. Ex. R.H. Blanchard Collection, Cairo, Egypt, #1951 with card written in his handwriting. Cf. Matouk 93 var. ....**CHOICE 175.00**

1062. **19th DYNASTY. 1320-1200 B.C.**   Carved steatite plaque. O: Maat (feathers). R: Solar deity in the form of man with falcon head wearing kilt. Uraeus before. Suspension hole through length of plaque. Length 16 mm. Rowe, 704 var. ....**CHOICE 120.00**

1063. **PRIVATE NAME SCARAB. 19th Dynasty. 1320-1200 B.C.** Blue lentoid scarab with some brown on top and green at edges. Band of short vertical lines around lower edge of top. Imprint of hawk (Horus) on underside. Measures 2.0 x 1.0 cm. Cf. Petrie, *Scarabs* Pl. LXXI, fig. 235. ....**CHOICE 150.00**

1064. **SETI I. 1318-1304 B.C.   19th Dynasty. 1320-1200 B.C.** Nomen of Seti I. 15 mm x 10 mm. Cf. Hall, *BMC* 2057. ....**CHOICE 135.00**

1065. **SETI I. 1318-1304 B.C.   19th Dynasty.** Carved steatite glaze gone white. Contains prenomen of Seti I. Measures 1.5 x 1.0 cm. Seti I was the father of the famous Rameses, whom many believe to be the pharaoh of the Exodus. Cf. Matouk 598. ....**CHOICE 200.00**

1066. **RAMESES II. 1304-1237 B.C.   19th Dynasty. 1320-1200 B.C.** Carved steatite glaze gone white. Cartouche of Rameses II on back of beatie. Ptah seated before figure of pharaoh standing before with libation. 18 mm x 13 mm. Cf. Hill, *BMC* Vol. 1, 2196. Cf. Petrie, *Historical Scarabs* 1596. Wear to bottom. ....**AVERAGE 100.00**

1067. **RAMESES II. 1304-1237 B.C.   19th Dynasty. 1320-1200 B.C.** Faience scarab. Brownish beige. Ra-User-Maot-Neb. 25 mm x 17 mm. Cf. Petrie, *Scarabs* 97. ....**AVERAGE 125.00**

1068. **RAMESES II. 1304-1237 B.C.   19th Dynasty. 1320-1200 B.C.** Carved steatite gray-beige, Uraeus falcon before prenomen of Rameses II. 15 mm x 10 mm. Rowe 747 var. ....**CHOICE 150.00**

1069. **RAMESES II. 1304-1237 B.C.   19th Dynasty. 1320-1200 B.C.** Carved steatite scarab. Glaze mostly white with traces of green. User-Maat-Ra-Setep-En-Ra beloved of Amen Ra. 22 mm x 13 mm. Fine style scarab. Minor chip in base. Hall, *BMC* Vol. 1, 2108 var. Newberry XXXV, 11. ....**SUPERB 250.00**

1070. **RAMESES II. 1304-1237 B.C.   19th Dynasty. 1320-1200 B.C.** Carved, glazed steatite plaque. Figure of king slaying animal with prenomen of Rameses II. Sphinx advancing right, uraeus before. 19 mm x 13 mm. Chip to reverse. Cf. Hall, *BMC* Vol. I, 2217. ....**CHOICE 125.00**

1071. **RAMESES II. 1304-1237 B.C.   19th Dynasty. 1320-1200 B.C.** Carved dark gray steatite glaze gone beige. Commemorative of Thutmoses III. Prenomen before couchant. Figure of ram-headed sphinx wearing Atef crown. Cartouche of Thutmoses III. 21 mm x 15 mm. Shows wear. Cf. Hall, *BMC* Vol. I, 2228. ....**CHOICE 125.00**

1072. **RAMESES II. 1304-1237 B.C. 19th Dynasty.**   Glazed carved steatite scarab, buff. Inscription of prenomen of Ramses II. Rameses II was the Biblical pharaoh of the Exodus. Cf. Hall, *BMC* 2251 var. ....**SUPERB 250.00**

1073. **RAMESES II. 1304-1237 B.C.** Glazed steatite scarab, light green-yellow. Prenomen of Rameses II. Rameses II was the pharaoh of the exodus where Moses led the people of Israel out of bondage. Petrie, *HS* 1502 var. Chip to base on each side. ....**CHOICE 125.00**

1074. **RAMESES II, 1304-1237 B.C.** Black and white diorite carved scarab. RA-USER-MAOT-, SETEP-NE-RA. Size is 19 x 14 mm. Petrie *SC* SLI 66; Petrie *HS* XIX, G. Considered to be the pharaoh of the Exodus. Hard stone scarabs are rare, and this one is a gem! ....**SUPERB 650.00**

1075. **CARVED YELLOW-JASPER SCARABOID PLAQUE. 19th Dynasty.** Column with hippopotamus advancing right. Measures 1.4 x 1.1 cm. Rowe-; Frazer-; Petrie, *HS*-; Ward-; Petrie, *Scarabs*-; Hall-; Newberry-............**CHOICE 250.00**

1076. **HER-USER-RA. 19th-26th Dynasty.** Buff carved steatite scarab. HER-USER-RA with uraeus behind. Measures 19 x 11 mm. Cf. Petrie HS 68, 217. ....**SUPERB 175.00**

1077. **HA-MEN-HEH. Priest of Maat. 19th-26th Dynasty.** Buff carved steatite scarab. Mot-Hes/Ha-Men-Heh. 20 x 10 mm. Rowe-; Petrie *SC*-; Petrie *HS*-. ....**NEAR SUPERB 150.00**

1078. **20th DYNASTY. 1200-1085 B.C.** Lion hunt scarab. Carved steatite scarab with glaze gone white. Portrays a lion with mane to right, lioness below to right, hunter before wielding weapon. Length 13 mm. Cf. Rowe, 851 for lions. ....**CHOICE 250.00**

1079. **20th DYNASTY. 1200-1085 B.C.** Carved steatite cowroid. Amen-Ra. Neb, Ra, the good god, Lord of Upper and Lower Egypt. 19 mm x 13 mm. Rowe 844. ....**CHOICE 75.00**

1080. **20th DYNASTY. 1200-1085 B.C.** Carved steatite scarab, beige. Two monkeys seated, arms raised to obelisk, before, partial prenomen of Rameses. 15 mm x 11 mm. Cf. for cartouche Prazler 323. Cf. Cartouche of Rowe 833. Chip at base. ....**CHOICE 135.00**

1081. **LATE PERIOD. 1085-343 B.C.** Carved steatite plaque in buff color, two men standing. Suspension hole through length. Length 17 mm. Cf. Matouk, 1552. Traces of blue and yellow color around carving. ....**CHOICE 150.00**

1082. **LATE PERIOD. 1085-332 B.C.** Dark green glazed pottery. Large baboon seated. 19 mm. Crude glazing. Petrie, *Buttons*-. Matouk. ....**CHOICE 75.00**

1083. **USARKEN II. 883-855 B.C.** Buff carved steatite scarab. RA-KHEPER-NEB, within uraeus and Maot feather. Measures 13 x 9 mm. Cf. Petrie *SC* C1, 4 var. ....**CHOICE 225.00**

1084. **PETABASTET. 817-730 B.C. 23rd Dynasty.** Carved steatite scaraboid. Grey. Royal name of Petabastet. Measures 1.2 x 0.8 cm. Cf. Hall, *BMC* 2475-7. Very rare royal scarab. Petrie index, 152. ....**CHOICE 400.00**

1085. **SHASHANQ IV. 765-725 B.C.** Buff carved steatite scarab. Prenomen of Shashanq IV in hieroglyphics. Measures 1.2 x 0.7 cm. Cf. *BMC* 2471. ....**CHOICE 225.00**

1086. **NEFER-HOR-RA. Vassal of Shashanq IV. 22nd Dynasty.** Carved buff steatite scarab. Cartouch of Nefer-Hor-Ra. Measures 12 x 9 mm. Cf. Petrie, HS 57, 1815. ....**SUPERB 175.00**

1087. **SHASHANQ IV. 765-725 B.C. 22nd Dynasty. 935-730 B.C.** Libyan. Uraeus before the nomen of Shashanq V (IV). Below, large crocodile (Sebek). 22 mm x 16 mm. Cf. Cartouche Hall *BMC* 2461. Cf. Matouk, 306 var for cartouche...**CHOICE 150.00**

1088. **SHASHANQ IV. 765-725 B.C. 22nd Dynasty.** Carved brown steatite. Name of Amon Ra. 15 mm x 10 mm. Cf. for design, Petrie Pl. XLIX. for scarab, Petrie, Pl LXVI. Petrie P and S, 666 var. ....**CHOICE 60.00**

1089. **NUB-TET-HEB-KEP. 22nd-27th Dynasty. 945-404 B.C.** Black hematite carved scarab. Inscription in finely carved hieroglyphics. Measures 15 x 11 mm. Newberry -; Ward -; Petrie *SC* -; Petrie *HS* -; *BMC* -; Matouk -; Rowe -. Superbly carved scarab. Chip at left wing and small flaking to base. A similar finely carved hard stone cowroid in the NFA 12/11/91 sale brought $880. ....**CHOICE 600.00**

1090. **RAMENHER. Vassal of Khmeny. 750-656 B.C. 25th Dynasty.** Glazed, carved steatite scarab. Gone buff. Measures 1.7 x 1.1 cm. Ramenher was a vassal during the Ethiopian dynasty. Cf. Petrie, *Scarabs*, LIII, 9 var. Chip at base. Scarce. ....**CHOICE 275.00**

1091. **TAHARQA. 690-664 B.C. 25th Dynasty. 750-656 B.C.** Nubian. "Beautiful, Shu son of Ra." 15 mm x 10 mm. Top of scarab chipped off. Cf. Ward, *Sacred Beetle*, 129. ....**SUPERB 150.00**

1092. **NUB SCARAB. 25th-26th Dynasty. 750-525 B.C.** Kingship of Upper and Lower Egypt. Over gold (Nub). Uzats and red crowns at sides. 15 mm x 11 mm. Big chip at top. Petrie, *H.S.* Matouk 2409 var. ....**CHOICE 65.00**

1093. **MEN AB RA. 26th Dynasty.** Opaque carved chalcedony scarab with traces of black. Cartouch of Menabra. Measures 29 x 20 mm. Cf. Petrie *HS* XXVI G var. Menabra was not known to Petrie. Hard stone scarab, crude design. ....**CHOICE 175.00**

1094. **PSEMTHEK I. 664-610 B.C.** Buff steatite scarab. RAH-UAH-AB, NEFER. Measures 13 x 10 mm. Cf. Petrie *HS* 60j; Cf. Petrie *SC* 20 var. Chip at nose. ....**CHOICE 175.00**

1095. **PSEMTHER. 664-610 B.C. 26th Dynasty. 664-525 B.C.** Depicts Horus. 14 mm x 8 mm. Cf. Hall *BMC*, Vol. 1, 2575. ....**CHOICE 150.00**

1096. **SAITE PERIOD. 26th Dynasty. 664-525 B.C.** Black and white diorite carved scarab. Detailed legs on base and hole for mounting. 13 mm x 11 mm. This type was sewn on garments. For similar diorite scarab, Cf. Hornung-Staehelin, *Skarabaen*, Taf. 108, Bii. ....**SUPERB 150.00**

1097. **26th DYNASTY. 664-525 B.C.** Carved steatite scarab. Cobra before neb. Measures 1.2 x 0.8 cm. Hall, *BMC* Type A8. Saleh, Zagreb 292. Matouk 1131. Finely carved naturalistic scarab. Chip at base. ....**SUPERB 125.00**

1098. **26th DYNASTY. 664-525 B.C.** Light green faience scarab. Four blooming flowers on plant. Measures 19 mm x 11 mm. Cf. *BMC*, Hall Style A-8; Ward 415. ....**CHOICE 125.00**

1099. **26th DYNASTY**. Buff steatite Bes scarab. Facing figure of Bes, arms at sides. Measures 11 x 9 mm. *BMC* Style A8; Matouk 374-84. ....**CHOICE 135.00**

1100. **26th DYNASTY** Buff carved steatite scarab. Ra-Neb-Maot, above sphinx seated right. Measures 15 x 11 mm. Rowe -; *BMC* -; Petrie *SC* -; Petrie *HS* -. ....**CHOICE 125.00**

1101. **PTOLEMAIC PERIOD. 304-30 B.C.** Private seal. Bronze seal of ring. Priest of Ptah. 16 mm x 13 mm. Cf. Petrie, *Scarabs* AV. ....**AVERAGE-CHOICE 85.00**

1102. **PTOLEMAIC PERIOD. 3rd-2nd Century B.C.** Glass multi-color scarab. Design scarab. Black-yellow and brown. Measures 2.4 x 1.8 cm. Used as an inlay in jewelry. Petrie, *Scarabs*-. Rare. Colorful. ....**CHOICE 300.00**

1103. **PTOLEMAIC PERIOD.** Bright blue faience scarab. Small hieroglyph carved on bottom. Suspension hole through middle. Measures 0.9 x 0.6 cm. Cf. Petrie #226. A lovely, vividly colored piece. ....**CHOICE 90.00**

1104. **ROMAN PERIOD 1st-3rd Century A.D.** Light blue faience scarab. Ornamental. Petrie, *Amulets*, 89, J,K,L. ....**CHOICE 80.00**

FAIENCE

1105. **PLAQUE OF SEKMET. 18th Dynasty**?. Multi-colored faience. Very unusual. The plaque is very detailed, especially braided hair and necklace. Solar disk and serpent uraeus missing. Maybe used for a name plaque or pendant. 50 mm x 38 mm. Cf. *Catalogue General des Antiquities Egyptiennes* 12721, 12716.....................**SUPERB 1000.00**

1106. **USHABTI. 18th Dynasty. 1561-1320 B.C.** Red-buff terracotta ushabti with bag wig and crossed arms. Traces of blue and white wash. Height 4.8 cm.............**CHOICE 65.00**

1107. **USHABTI. New Kingdom. 19th Dynasty. 1320-1200 B.C.** Light green and black faience. Represented in mummiform, with collar. Features molded instead of carved. Solid black wig, folded arms holding implements, basket on back. Hieroglyphs on panel down front. Color slightly faded. Measures 13.5 x 4 cm. Cf. Petrie, *Shabtis*, p. 35, 223; Hans Schneider, *Shabtis*, 3.3.31, 13, 3.3, 2.4, p. 39 and 41. ....**CHOICE 750.00**

1108. **USHABTI. 19th-20th Dynasty. 1320-1085 B.C.** Green faience gone beige. Black wig, but crude modeling and no facial features. 10.7 cm long, 3.8 cm wide. Chips on surface. Cf. Hans D. Schneider, Part III, 3.3.2.4 ....**CHOICE 150.00**

1109. **STATUETTE. 19th-20th Dynasty**. Turquoise glaze faience statuette. Base with two heads of bound captives by stairs. One head Asiatic. Ex. Christie's London, 1988, Lot 257. Extremely rare. Christie's estimate £1500...**CHOICE 800.00**

1110. **USHABTI. Third Intermediate Period. 1085-935 B.C.** Crude faience ushabti, mummiform in shape. Wears a plain lappet wig with long strips in front. Hands crossed holding two hoes. Evidence of light green colored faience. Carved from back to soles of feet. Height 13.5 cm. Cf. Catalogue of the Egyptian Museum in Berlin, no. 900-909 for similar shapes. Ex. Harry Houdini/Joseph Dunninger Collection. Rather worn. ....**CHOICE 1200.00**

1111. **USHABTI. 21st-22nd Dynasty. 1085-730 B.C.** Light blue glazed mummiform ushabti, originally bright blue. Crude modeling with features and one band of hieroglyphs down center in purple black color. Hieroglyphs quite clear. Ushabti carries two hoes with basket on back. 10.7 cm high. Ex. Harry Houdini/Joseph Dunninger Collection. Cf. Schneider, *Shabtis*, 4.3.1.89. ....**CHOICE 800.00**

1112. **USHABTI. 21st-22nd Dynasty. 1085-730 B.C.** Green faience ushabti partly toned brown holding two hoes. Wears a plain wig with fillet painted black. Basket on back. Hieroglyphs on panel center front. 10 cm high. Cf. Schneider, *Shabtis*, pp. 49, 50, *52*. Some chipping. Crude modeling and style typical of the period. ...**CHOICE 500.00**

1113. **USHABTI. 21st-22nd Dynasty. 1085-730 B.C.** Faience of bright green color. Short. Right arm crossed over left, both holding hoes. Wears wig with folded fillet painted black. Writing on front, bottom half of ushabti but cannot be deciphered because of corrosion. Vivid color but some chipping. Crudely modeled which is typical of this period. 10 cm long, 4.3 cm wide. Cf. Schneider, *Shabtis*, pp. 49, 50, 52 ....**CHOICE 425.00**

1114. **USHABTI. Late Period. 1085-730 B.C.** Small faience. Very worn. Green color turned sandy white. Figure holds simple implements with rope over his left shoulder holding basket or pot. Features are rather obscured. No hieroglyphs on front or back. Feet standing on plinth. Mummiform in shape. 9 cm long, 3.3 cm wide. Intact. Face worn. Cf. Hans D. Schneider, Part III, 5,3, 4, 1. ....**CHOICE 150.00**

1115. **USHABTI. 21st-22nd Dynasty. 1085-730 B.C.** Blue-green faience ushabti with crude modeling. Holding two hoes, with basket over both shoulders. Hands crossed and band of hieroglyphs down center front in black. Height is 8.7 cm. Cf. Schneider, *Shabtis*, 4.3.1.66, 71, 72. Good condition. ....**CHOICE 400.00**

1116. **USHABTI. Probably 21st Dynasty. 1085-730 B.C**. Bright blue ushabti turned blue-green and beige. Black painted features. Wearing plain bag wig. Mediocre carving. One band of hieroglyphs in center panel. 8.7 cm high. Cf. Schneider, *Shabtis*, 4.3.166, 71, 72. ....**CHOICE 350.00**

1117. **USHABTI BUST FRAGMENT. New Kingdom. 18th Dynasty.** Terracotta fragment of bust and upper portion of ushabti, cut off at waist. Surface wear, but what remains is intact. Measures 45 mm by 85 mm. Cf. Schneider, *Shabtis*, 3.4.2.3. A nice fragment of the typical terracotta ushabti of the New Kingdom......................................**CHOICE 125.00**

1118. **STATUETTE. Probably 21st-22nd Dynasty.** Limestone. Two figures kneeling side-by-side on base, naked, holding legs of third figure which faces them; feet of third figure do not touch the base. Statuette is broken off at the necks of the kneeling figures and at the knees of the third. Petrie-, Steindorf-, Michelowski-. ....**CHOICE 500.00**

1119. **USHABTI. Third Intermediate Period. 1085-715 B.C.** Faience reis-shabti who was an overseer of one subdivision of the shabti gang. Overseer was one in twenty, out of four hundred. Worn and now a bright green with brown paint depicting eyes, whip and seshed-band. Also painted panel of hieroglyphs down front of shabti. Overseer shabti wears skirt and holds whip in left hand, right hand by side. 11.5 cm x 3.2 cm. Ex. Harry Houdini/Joseph Dunniger Collection. Schneider-*Shabtis*, Parts 1, II, III for type see 4.5.5.1.1. Intact. ....**CHOICE 800.00**

1120. **FRAGMENT OF STATUETTE OF PTAH. Late Period. 1085-332 B.C.** Bottom half of light green faience statue shows Ptah-Seker standing on two crocodiles facing each other and winding around back of statue. The remains of the goddesses Isis and Nephthys at side of Ptah-Seker. At back of goddess Isis stands with outstretched wings to protect Ptah-Seker. Measures 50 mm x 35 mm. This little statuette was used in the house to protect it from wild animals. Broken off at waist. Blanchard Pl. XL, 222 var. Petrie, *Amulets* Pl. XXXI 176h. Steindorf, Walter's Art Gallery, Pl. XCV, 626. ....**CHOICE 250.00**

1121. **NEFERTUM AMULET FRAGMENT. Late Period. 1085-332 B.C.** Light green faience fragment of an amulet showing the legs of the god Nefertum, standing on the back of a crouching lion. Measures 20 x 34 mm. Cf. Blanchard, 157 for a complete figure. Nefertum missing above knees. Some chips. Good color. ....**CHOICE 150.00**

1122. **STATUETTE OF A PRIEST. 22nd-23rd Dynasty. 935-730 B.C.** Green and black faience. Only upper torso. Very detailed face which also has character. Wears plain wig, originally dark black now faded to blackish-brown. Right arm bent over front of body. Very clean-cut lines. 4.3 cm long, 2.4 cm wide. Green and black faience statuettes were made during these dynasties. A rare representation of a priest. ....**SUPERB 800.00**

1123. **BEAD NECKLACE. Saite Period. 26th Dynasty. 664-525 B.C.** Faience. Good condition with some particularly bright beads included. Modern clasp. 52 cm long. Quality vivid colors. ....**SUPERB 100.00**

1124. **USHABTI. Late Period. 26th Dynasty. 664-525 B.C.** Greenish blue faience ushabti in mummiform with mediocre, worn modeling. Wears false beard and lappet wig. One band of hieroglyphs center vertical and one center horizontal. 9.6 cm x 3.1 cm. Ex. Harry Houdini/Joseph Dunninger Collection. Cf. Schneider, *Shabtis* Parts, I, II, and III, see 5.3.1.184. Cracked. Nice color. ....**CHOICE 2000.00**

1125. **USHABTI. Saite Period. 26th Dynasty. 664-525 B.C.** Light green for Her-M-Heb. Beautiful condition. Crack on bottom half. This piece follows exactly the style of the Saite Period. 14 cm long, 4.5 cm wide. The hieroglyphics, one reads from right to left in horizontal lines. The first line contains the name of the tomb owner, and it also contains his titles and parentage. The remainders of the hieroglyphics consist of Chapter VI of the Book of the Dead, which is an Egyptian religious text: "Her-M-Heb son to Tau Isis be illuminated .. Hail Ushebt figure! If the Osiris, Her-M-Heb is ordered to do any of the work which is to be done in the after life, let everything which stands in the way to be removed from him- whether it is to plough the fields or to fill the channels with water, or to carry sand from east to west." The ushabti's function in the tomb was to do agricultural works for the deceased. The ushabti was modeled in the style of Osiris, thus shown mummified with arms crossed over chest. A lovely work of Egyptian art. Broken at ankles. Cf. Schneider, *Shabtis* p. 26, 5.3.4.1. Budge, *The Mummy*, pp. 211-213. ....**SUPERB 1250.00**

1126. **USHABTI. Late Period. 26th-27th Dynasty. 664-404 B.C.** Green glazed faience ushabti with fine modeling. Slender shape with hieroglyphic down center front. Ushabti wears a beard and plain wig, holding two hoes and carries basket over left shoulder. 14 cm high. Ex. Harry Houdini/Joseph Dunninger Collection. Cf. Schneider, *Shabtis*, 5.3.1.139-145. Good condition. Slightly discolored in places. ....**SUPERB 3500.00**

1127. **STATUETTE OF THOTH. 26th-30th Dynasty. 664-343 B.C.** Light blue faience. Good detail. Two hairline cracks in back. Stands upright with hands closely by sides. Height 45 mm. Thoth was god of writing and knowledge. This god would be in the main row of gods which decorate the chest of a mummy in burial. Cf. Petrie, *Amulets* Pl. XXXVI 202i, B. ....**CHOICE 125.00**

1128. **FAIENCE HEAD OF BES. Ptolemaic Period. 4th-3rd Century B.C.** Head of Bes, upper part with eyes, ears, nose and large plumed crown of five feathers. Back is stylized seated rabbit looking up on pedestal. Daressy, Statues de Divinities II, XL, 38, 730. Cf. Staatliche, Sammlung Agyptische Kunst 4279. Ex. Harry Houdini/ Joseph Dunninger Collection. ....**CHOICE 450.00**

1129. **USHABTI. Late Period. 30th Dynasty. 380-343 B.C.** Blue-turquoise faience. Of Nes-Hen-Kh. Quite detailed. Hands and mouth chipped. Standing on plinth and frame supporting at back. Holding implements and basket. Unplaited beard level with wig. 11 cm long, 3.5 cm wide. Nice color. Hieroglyphics read vertically, right to left with the name Nes-Hen-Kh mentioned twice in the ushabti formula. Schneider, *Shabtis* p. 72, 5.3.1.184 and 5.3.1.197. ....**CHOICE 275.00**

1130. **USHABTI. Late Period. 30th Dynasty.** Blue-green faience with chips on face and hands. Plain wig with plain beard. Hands holding implements and basket which is over back. Firing cracks in feet. Hieroglyphs down front panel not deciphered. Faded somewhat. 8.6 cm long, 2.5 cm wide. Cf. Hans D. Schneider Part III, 5,3,1,197. ......**CHOICE 150.00**

1131. **USHABTI. 30th Dynasty. 380-343 B.C.** Blue-green glazed ushabti with plain wig and false beard. Hands crossed, holding two hoes. Slender body with back column, base beneath feet. Color formally bright blue. Mediocre modeling. 8.4 cm high. Ex. Houdini/ Dunninger Collection. Little restoration and repaired. Petrie, *Shabtis*, nos. 643-645 for similar style.......................................**CHOICE 500.00**

1132. **USHABTI. 30th Dynasty. 380-343 B.C.** Buff colored ushabti with glaze worn off. Mummiform in shape. Slender form with back column and small base. Plain wig and false beard. 9.4 cm high. Petrie, *Shabtis*, 643, 644, 645, 649. Features are a little worn, with crack on top of head. ....**CHOICE 200.00**

1133. **USHABTI. 30th Dynasty. 380-343 B.C.** Glazed ushabti gone buff-white in colour. Plain wig with false beard. Crossed hands holding two hoes. Mediocre modeling, but facial features rather comical. Slender form with back column and short base. Repaired around midriff. 10.8 cm high. Cf. Schneider, *Shabtis*, nos. 5.3.1.150 var. ....**CHOICE 275.00**

1134. **USHABTI. 30th Dynasty.** Buff colored faience ushabti in plain wig and false beard. Crossed hands holding two hoes. Slender form with back column and base. Cf. Schneider, *Shabtis* no. 5.3.1.150 var. Length 120 mm. Re-attached at midsection. ....**CHOICE 275.00**

1135. **USHABTI. 30th Dynasty. 380-343 B.C.** Green faience with good modeling. Mummiform with hands holding crook, flail, and basket. Lower body with incised hieroglyphs in horizontal registers to back pillar. Small rectangular plinth. Facial features clear, rather Archaic in style. Mounted. Height 15.9 cm. (not including base). Schneider, *Shabtis*, no. 5.3.1.263. Repaired at the knees and right side of head. ....**CHOICE 500.00**

1136. **FAIENCE PTAH SEKER. Ptolemaic Period. 304-30 B.C.** Blue faience Ptah Seker, good color but legs missing. Two hieroglyphs on back column. Black faience band around head. Suspension hole in neck. Worn as decoration. Length 5.4 cm. Petrie *Amulets*, Pl. XXXI, #176, f,g,k. Nice color. ....**CHOICE 250.00**

1137. **BUST OF FIGURE. Ptolemaic Period. 304-30 B.C.** Faience bust of figure, probably Aphrodite. She has her arms up to her face or head. Moderately crude carvings and artwork. She wears diadem. 5 cm high. Mounted. Hayes-; Petrie-..**CHOICE 275.00**

1138. **USHABTI. Ptolemaic. 300-100 B.C.** Blue faience ushabti with bag wig and crossed arms. Height 5.5 cm. Cf. Petrie, *Shabtis*, 649. Repaired. ....**CHOICE 55.00**

1139. **FAIENCE VESSEL. Late Ptolemaic-Early Roman.** Faience hanging vessel. Bright blue/green color with black "necklace"-like pattern around shoulder and collar of neck. Incised line just below rim. Straight sides, rounded bottom. Pierced lug on either side to allow hanging. Probably used for perfumes or oils. Height 7.8 cm. Very rare. Some faience discoloration but bright original color still visible. Chip to rim, otherwise no cracking and intact. ......**SUPERB 1500.00**

1140. **GLAZED LION. Early Roman Period. 1st Century B.C.-1st Century A.D.** Faience. Yellow-beige with olive-green color in crevices. Seated with head turned. This lion was used as an appliqué on the rim of bowls. Cf. Riefstahl, *Ancient Egyptian Glass and Glazes in the Brooklyn Museum* #87. Chip at forelegs. Rare ....**CHOICE 400.00**

1141. **FRAGMENT OF VENUS. Early Roman Period. 1st Century A.D.** Faience. Bright blue bust with breasts. Green glaze necklace. 55 mm high. Venus or Hathor was goddess of love. For style, Cf. Brooklyn Museum, *Late Egyptian Art and Coptic Art*. Pl.. 24. Cf. Brooklyn #88. Superb color. Rare. ....**CHOICE 300.00**

1142. **FAIENCE BUST. 3rd-4th Centuries A.D.** Very crude, bright blue faience bust of goddess Aphrodite. Top of headdress missing. Both arms raised to head. Crude facial features. 5.2 cm high, 4.7 cm wide. Petrie-; Blanchard-; Hayes-. Bold color. ....**CHOICE 350.00**

1143. **TERRACOTTA HEAD. 3rd-4th Centuries A.D.** Red clay terracotta head of Parthian soldier. Wearing Phrygia helmet with hair showing from underneath. Features worn with some evidence of paint. 8.5 cm.................**CHOICE 100.00**

AMULETS

1144. **ORANGE CARNELIAN AMULET. 6th Dynasty. 2345-2181 B.C.** Amulet of Khep which means "determinative in action." Lovely color with intact suspension hole. Measures 1.8 cm x 1.1 cm. Petrie, *Amulets*, Pl. 1, #12a, b and c. ....**CHOICE 150.00**

1145. **ORANGE CARNELIAN AMULET. 6th Dynasty. 2345-2181 B.C.** Jackal head amulet meant to find the way in the future world. Very stylized. Suspension hole in center. 1 cm long. Petrie, *Amulets*, no 22 var. Chip. ......**CHOICE 100.00**

1146. **ORANGE CARNELIAN AMULET. 6th Dynasty. 2345-2181 B.C.** Hippopotamus head. Very stylized with suspension hole in back. 1 cm long. Petrie, *Amulets* #237, h and l..................**CHOICE 125.00**

1147. **AMULET OF A BABOON. 6th Dynasty-Ptolemaic. 2345-30 B.C.** Green faience. Very good color. Chipped at back, base of amulet missing. Very detailed eyes and face. Ape of Thoth. 26 mm high. All apes of Thoth were helpers to the god Thoth, who was the decider of the balance at the weighing of the heart against a feather of truth. Thoth was usually looked upon as having even more power than Ra or Osiris. Blanchard Pl. XLIII, 245, 247. Petrie, *Amulets*, Pl. XXXVII, 206a..................**CHOICE 125.00**

1148. **DUAL PLUME PLAQUE. New Kingdom. 1650-1085 B.C.** Carved steatite glazed buff. Design of two uraeus facing outward, Sa between (protection), solar disk above for Ra. Matouk I, 1159..................**SUPERB 250.00**

1149. **SEKMET PLAQUE. XVIII Dynasty. 1567-1320 B.C.** Multicolored faience. Highly detailed upper portion of a plaque depicting the lion-headed goddess Sekmet. Solar disk and uraeus missing. Measures 50 x 38 mm. For style, Cf. *Catalogue General des Antiquities Egyptiennes* 12721, 12716..................**SUPERB 1000.00**

1150. **FAIENCE EMBROYEN. New Kingdom. 1567-1085 B.C.** Light green-blue faience embroyen of Ptah. Height 2.8 cm. Cf. Blanchard 219. Broken off at knees, some chipping. ....**CHOICE 150.00**

1151. **LAPIS LAZULI BUTTON. New Kingdom.** Beautifully carved button with square flat beveled head. Carved suspension hole in back with three lines as decoration. Head measures 1.0 x 1.1 cm. Executed in the style of the New Kingdom. Petrie-; Hayes-. Lovely color and intact. ....**SUPERB 150.00**

1152. **COW AMULET. New Kingdom. 18th-20th Dynasty. c. 1567-1085 B.C.** Bound cow in red glass paste. Length 25 mm. Cf. Petrie, *Amulets* 63a. Chip on head and tail. Traces of bitumen. ....**AVERAGE 45.00**

1153. **KHNOUN AMULET. New Kingdom. 1567-1085 B.C.** Light green faience. Ram-headed, human body, walking. 27 mm. Khnoun was the sculptor who made mankind and the "Creator" in the period of the animal gods. At Elephantine he was regarded as parallel to Amen at Thebes. Good color. Cf. Walters 583. Cf. Blanchard, *Handbook of Egyptian Gods and Mummy Amulets*, Pl. XXVII 137, 138....**CHOICE 85.00**

1154. **AMULET. New Kingdom. 1567-1085 B.C.** Light green faience. Lion reclining. 25 mm. Small chips at base. Blanchard 150..................**CHOICE 125.00**

1155. **AMULET OF PTAH. New Kingdom. 1567-1085 B.C.** White-green faience. Embryon. Broken at waist. 22 mm. Petrie, *Amulets*, Pl. XXI 176 h, k. Blanchard, 219. ....**CHOICE 80.00**

1156. **EYE OF HORUS AMULET. New Kingdom. 1567-1085 B.C.** Diorite. 13 mm. For shape, Cf. Petrie, *Amulets* Pl. XXIV, 138 var. ....**SUPERB 50.00**

1157. **APPLE GREEN FAIENCE AMULET. Late New Kingdom to Late Period.** The god Thoth walking, left foot advancing. Suspension hole in the middle of the back column. Height 24 mm. Petrie, *Amulets*, #202 var. Headdress missing, otherwise intact. ....**CHOICE 125.00**

1158. **HEAD OF PTAH. 18th Dynasty to Ptolemaic. 1567-30 B.C.** Embryon. Faience, light greenish-blue. Some chipping on the back of the neck. Beautifully carved features. 32 mm high. Ptah was the main god in the "Triad of Memphis" along with Sekhmet, his consort, and his son Nefertum. Blanchard Pl. XL 222. Petrie, *Amulets*, Pl. XXXI 176 h,k ....**CHOICE 150.00**

1159. **AMULET OF MAU. 18th Dynasty to Roman. 1567 B.C.-1st Century B.C.** Faience gone white. Mau was an emblem of the goddess Bastet. Finely carved with tail going to right, detail on face with suspension hole on cat's back. 25 mm high. Stands mounted on wooden plaque. Mau was sacred to Bastet and was often thought of as her incarnation. These amulets were very common on necklaces of 22nd and 23rd dynasties. Blanchard, Pl. XIII, 50, 59. Petrie, *Amulets* Pl. XXXIX 224e ....**CHOICE 300.00**

1160. **AMULET OF BES. 18th Dynasty to Roman. 1567 B.C.-1st Century A.D.** Lapis lazuli. Worn with chip at base. Nicely carved face. Evidence of suspension hole on top of head. 27 mm. Unusual form and shape. Worn to right of figure. Chip at loop and broken at knees. Petrie, *Amulets*, Pl. XXXIII, 188 var. ....**AVERAGE-CHOICE 125.00**

1161. **AMULET OF BES. Amarna Period. 1379-1362 B.C.** Brilliant yellow and bright greenish-blue faience. Some encrustation on one side. 23 mm long. Bes was a household god, god of dance and games. Petrie, *Amulets*, Pl. XXXIII, 188. ....**CHOICE 75.00**

1162. **FAIENCE HEAD. Late Period. 1085-334 B.C.** Green-blue faience head of Ptah Seker (Patek) with snake across mouth and scarab on the head. Height 1.7 cm. The snake on the face is an unusual feature. Cf. Steindorff #634. Broken off below neck and back of head. ....**CHOICE 90.00**

1163. **FAIENCE EYE OF HORUS. Late Period.** Light green faience uzat, or eye of Horus. Incised detail. Length 1.2 cm. Petrie 138..................**SUPERB 85.00**

1164. **FAIENCE EYE OF HORUS. Late Period.** Blue and green faience uzat, or eye of Horus. Detailed eye. 1.9 x 1.5 cm. Petrie 138. Suspension loop missing. ....**SUPERB 125.00**

1165. **AMULET OF BES. Late Period. 1085-332 B.C**. Light green faience. Very crude style but nice. 20 mm x 10 mm. ....**CHOICE 20.00**

1166. **AMULET OF ANUBIS. Late Period. 1085-332 B.C**. Blue greenish. Break just above knees. Anubis, arms at sides, walking wearing kilt, top of head chipped. Nice color. Suspension hole in back. 45 mm. Anubis was the god of the underworld. He was very influential in the ceremony of the mummy being received into the afterworld. He was also the son of Nephthys and Osiris or Seb, or even Ra. R.H. Blanchard, Pl. VIII, 22, 24. ....**CHOICE 150.00**

1167. **FAIENCE AMULET OF SHU. 1085-332 B.C**. Green faience. Shu holding up the sky. Chipped arm, subdued color. 2 cm high. Cf. Petrie, *Amulets*, Pl. XXX 167, a and d. Some pitting to faience..............................**NEAR CHOICE 75.00**

1168. **FAIENCE AMULET OF NEFERTUM. 1085-332 B.C**. Light green faience. Small chip at base. Measures 4 x 8 cm. Cf. Blanchard, 155. Excavated at Saqqara by the Egyptian Exploration Society. De-accessed by Oberlin College Museum. ....**CHOICE 150.00**

1169. **AMULET OF HATHOR. Late Period. 1085-332 B.C**. Bright blue faience head. Suspension loop missing. Very good color. 19 mm x 13 mm. ....**CHOICE 55.00**

1170. **AMULET OF ISIS. Late Period. 1085-332 B.C**. Light green faience. The goddess stands with hands to her sides and wears the step crown. Fine facial detail. Recomposed and missing lower legs. 10 mm x 52 mm. This is a finely detailed large amulet of the most important female deity in the Egyptian pantheon. Some minor chips. Cf. Blanchard 118. Petrie, *Amulets* Pl. XXVI 149 b,c. .....**CHOICE 200.00**

1171. **AMULET OF DUATMUTEF. Late Period. 1085-332 B.C**. Green faience. Jackal-headed son of Ra or Horus. Fading color. Intact. 10 mm x 60 mm. Duatmutef protected the lungs and heart. This amulet probably was part of a bead shroud. Cf. Petrie, *Amulets*, 182e. ....**CHOICE 80.00**

1172. **AMULET FRAGMENT OF NEFERTUN. Late Period. 1085-332 B.C**. Light green faience. Crouching lion beneath the legs (partial) of the god who stands upon the lion's back. Some chips but good color. Measures 20 mm x 34 mm. Nefertun, the god of vegetation, was often depicted standing on the back of a lion. Cf. Blanchard, 157 for a complete figure. ....**CHOICE 200.00**

1173. **AMULET OF NEFERTUM. Late Period. 1085-332 B.C**. Faience. Good color, but feet missing. Large, thus unusual size. Suspension hole in back of head. Some chipping of face. 8.7 cm long. Nefertum is a member of the Memphis triad. He stood alongside Ptah and Sekhemt as their son, however, I-em-hetep was their eldest son. Neferium's symbol is the lotus. He is a human-headed god who was "Protector of the two worlds." Blanchard, PL XXX 157, 158. ....**CHOICE 150.00**

1174. **AMULET OF SEKHMET. Late Period**. Vivid blue faience amulet of Sekhmet. The goddess stands with arms to sides. Lion head. Feet missing. Excellent color. Measures 5 mm x 30 mm. Cf. Blanchardd, 49. Sekhmet was the sister of Bastet and mother of Nefertum. She represented the crop-destroying rays of the sun. ....**CHOICE 225.00**

1175. **AMULET OF SHU. Late Dynastic Period. 1085-332 B.C**. Light blue faience. He is shown kneeling, holding up the sky. Intact, but minor flaking. Good color. 15 mm x 30 mm. Suspension hole at back. Shu was "the god of light and of the space which is filled with the atmosphere, the sky-bearer, par excellence." Lovely color faience. Cf. Blanchard 225. ....**CHOICE 150.00**

1176. **AMULET OF SHU. Late Period. 1085-332 B.C**. Green faience. Unusual because artwork is crude. 15 mm. Petrie, *Amulets* 167e. ....**CHOICE 25.00**

1177. **AMULET OF SHU. Late Period. 1085-332 B.C**. Green faience. Shu holding up the sky. Chipped arm. Not much color. Height 20 mm. Interesting. Chip at left arm. Some pitting to faience. Petrie, *Amulets* Pl. XXX 167, c.d. ....**NEAR CHOICE 75.00**

1178. **AMULET OF THOTH. Late Period. 1085-332 B.C**. Light green faience. Thoth walking, left foot forward, arms at side. Wearing kilt and wig, but no headdress. End of face missing. Greenish tinge to color. Suspension hole in back of amulet. 45 mm high. Thoth was the scribe of the gods and inventor of the arts and sciences. Very powerful god. Chip at tip of muzzle. Blanchard, Pl. XLIII. 239,238. Steindorf, *Egyptian Sculpture in the Walters Art Gallery*, Pl. LXXXVIII, 592. ....**CHOICE 150.00**

1179. **AMULET OF THOTH. Late Period. 1085-332 B.C**. Dark green faience. Thoth holding Eye of Horus. The head is chipped and the feet are missing. 20 mm x 50 mm. Good workmanship. Dark variegated color. Lovely style and nice size...**CHOICE 250.00**

1180. **DJED AMULET. Late Period. 1085-332 B.C**. Blue. Broken at 3rd horizontal line. Glass made to look like lapis lazuli. 23 mm x 11 mm. The Djed amulet is the symbol of Osiris and as an amulet, represents eternal strength and permanence. Sacred tradition orders that the Djed amulet should be hung on the neck of the deceased. Chapter CLV of the Book of the Dead. Cf. *Egyptian Antiquities*, Dr. Abd El Hamid Zayed, p. 56, fig. 68. Cf. Petrie, *Amulets* Pl. III 35 var. ....**CHOICE 150.00**

1181. **FAIENCE AMULET. Late Period. 1085-334 B.C**. Light green faience amulet of Thoth walking with left foot forward. Wears kilt and wig but no headdress. Suspension hole behind figure. Length 45 mm. Thoth was the scribe of the gods, the inventor of arts and sciences. Steindorf XXXVIII 592, Blanchard Pl. XLII, 238, 239. Chip at tip of nose. ....**CHOICE 165.00**

1182. **CARVED HEMATITE AMULET OF TAUERT. New Kingdom. 18th Dynasty.** Tauert depicted as a hippopotamus walking upright, left leg advancing, arms to sides. Very rounded stomach indicating pregnancy. Length 25 mm. Cf. Petrie, *Amulets*, fig. 236d. Some red oxide and splitting to rear. ....**AVERAGE-CHOICE 80.00**

1183. **BRIGHT BLUE FAIENCE SEED VESSEL AMULET. 18th-19th Dynasty. 1567-1200 B.C.** Flat on one side with wear to glaze. Measures 16 by 9 mm. Cf. Knight, p. 219. Very popular on necklaces of the 18th and 19th dynasties. ....**CHOICE 85.00**

1184. **FAIENCE BES AMULET. 18th Dynasty to Roman.** Light green faience amulet of Bes seated. Bes was the god of children, dance, and games. Height 1.5 cm. Petrie 188y. ....**CHOICE 85.00**

1185. **FAIENCE BES AMULET. 18th Dynasty to Roman.** Light green faience amulet of Bes. Height 1.0 cm. Cf. Petrie 188o. ....**CHOICE 50.00**

1186. **LAPIS EYE OF HORUS. 18th Dynasty to Roman.** Dark blue lapis lazuli uzat, or Eye of Horus. Contains no incised decoration. Length 1.6 cm. Petrie 138. Suspension loop broken. ....**CHOICE 150.00**

1187. **GREEN BES AMULET. 18th Dynasty to Roman.** Green amulet with suspension hole. Measures 26 x 15 mm. Petrie, *Amulets* Pl. XXXIIIVI, fig. 188 var., p. 40; Knight pp. 32-33. ....**CHOICE 85.00**

1188 **FAIENCE BES AMULET. 20th Dynasty.** Light green faience. Highly stylized. Two suspension holes in back. Height 1.9 cm. Cf. Petrie, *Amulets* #188r. ..**CHOICE 85.00**

1189. **AMULET OF BES. 23rd Dynasty to Roman. 935 B.C.-1st Century A.D.** Green faience head and shoulders of Bes with black faience moustache and eyebrows. Two holes in ears to attach to necklace. Very detailed features. Right arm missing. 40 mm x 35 mm. Top missing from head. Bes, a popular god, was god of the toilet and is frequently seen adorning the mirrors of Egyptian women. Bes was also the god of dancing. He later became a war god. Nice color. Cf. Petrie, *Amulets*. Pl. XXXIV 190d, c. ....**CHOICE 225.00**

1190. **EYE OF HORUS AMULET. 23rd Dynasty. c. 817-730 B.C.** Green and black faience amulet. Black eye with black along top as if a black eyebrow. Suspension hole through sides. 18 cm long. Petrie reports "138 a and b came from XXIII," although this eye of Horus is slightly different because it is greenish-blue faience instead of just blue. Good color. Petrie, *Amulets*, Pl. XXV, Tanas Cf. 138. ....**CHOICE 30.00**

1191. **KHESES AMULET. 26th Dynasty. c. 664-525 B.C.** Black hematite kheses (square) amulet. Large right-angled L. Length 23 mm. This amulet bestowed the power of rectitude. Cf. Petrie, *Amulets* 36a. ....**SUPERB 150.00**

1192. **SOW AMULET. 26th Dynasty.** Blue green-glazed amulet depicting grazing sow. Measures 12 x 10 mm. Petrie, *Amulets*, 234b. ....**CHOICE 75.00**

1193. **FAIENCE KHNUMU AMULET. 26th Dynasty.** Reddish-grey faience amulet of Khnumu, the Creator. Suspension hole behind. Height 2.0 cm. Cf. Petrie, *Amulets* 187 e-g. ....**CHOICE 85.00**

1194. **RED CROWN FAIENCE AMULET. 26th Dynasty.** Also known as Tesher or Deshert. Powder blue. Suspension hole. 31 x 19 mm. Cf. Knight, p. 225. Petrie, Pl. IV, fig. 49 var., p. 18. The royal crown of Lower Egypt. Small chip at top. ....**CHOICE 85.00**

1195. **BRIGHT BLUE GLASS INLAY OF COW'S HEAD. 26th Dynasty.** Measures 30 x 30 mm. The cow was sacred to Hathor. Unusual and very bright color. Rare and nice. ....**CHOICE 500.00**

1196. **AMULET OF HATHOR. 26th Dynasty. 664-525 B.C.** Saite Period. Turquoise blue glazed pottery sistrum head. Good color. Minor ear chip. 30 mm in length. Sistrum meant joy, and was an emblem of Hathor. Sistra was a kind of musical instrument used by Egyptian high women or priestesses in religious festivals. Sistrum was a smaller version of this. Rare. Petrie, *Amulets* Pl. III, 32a. ....**CHOICE 100.00**

1197. **FAIENCE AMULET. Late Period. 26th-30th Dynasty. 664-343 B.C.** Blue green faience papyrus scepter amulet with suspension loop. VAZ "flourishing youth." 3.2 cm long. Cf. Petrie, *Amulets*, 20d-e. ....**CHOICE 90.00**

1198. **"BROWN MARBLE" SEQEQ AMULET. 26th Dynasty to Roman.** Brown amulet of a plummet, worn to impart an evenly balanced mind. Measures 1.4 x 2.5 cm. Cf. Petrie 37. ....**CHOICE 100.00**

1199. **FAIENCE ANUBIS AMULET. 26th Dynasty to Roman.** Light green faience amulet. Anubis, the protector of the dead, stands with hands at sides, striding with left leg forward. Suspension hole through back. Height 2.1 cm. Cf. Petrie 197h. Left ear broken off. ....**CHOICE 100.00**

1200. **FAIENCE EYE OF HORUS AMULET. Ptolemaic Period.** Blue faience amulet in quadruple form, which was believed to allow the deceased to see in the four houses of the other world. Measures 2.0 x 2.0 cm. Cf. Blanchard #261. ....**AVERAGE 50.00**

1201. **BES AMULET. Ptolemaic Period. 304-30 B.C.** Green faience bust of Bes in openwork oval. Length 18 mm. Cf. Petrie 190t. Crude workmanship. ....**CHOICE 40.00**

1202. **AMULET OF BES.   304-30 B.C.** Green faience head. Some chips and color faded to brown. 38 mm x 31 mm. The Bes head amulet was very much in vogue in the Ptolemaic Period. Such amulets were very popular with children since Bes was the protector of children. Cf. Petrie, Pl. XXXIV 190k var. Cf. Blanchard, 29. ....**CHOICE 85.00**

1203. **FAIENCE SMA AMULET. Ptolemaic Period.** Light green faience amulet showing two plumes, disc, and two horns. Signifies the union of different powers. Two suspension holes through sides. Height 1.9 cm. Cf. Petrie, *Amulets* 40c. ....**CHOICE 75.00**

1204. **FAIENCE BABOON AMULET. Ptolemaic Period.** Turquoise faience amulet. Shows baboon seated on base. Suspension hole through back. Height 1.3 cm. Cf. Petrie, *Amulets*, #206j...........................**CHOICE 125.00**

1205. **PLAQUE AMULET. Ptolemaic.** Green faience amulet of a plaque, showing the triad of Isis, Horus, and Nebhat (Isis' sister). They stand side-by-side holding hands with left foot advancing. Very finely executed with original pale blue faience color on the back. Suspension hole in back. Measures 2.0 x 2.2 cm. Cf. Blanchard, p. 212; Petrie 152a. ....**SUPERB 1500.00**

1206. **HEAD OF PTAH SEKER. Ptolemaic Period.** Light blue faience head of Ptah Seker, shown with dwarf-like features. Ptah was worshipped at Memphis, Seker at Saqqara. Height 2.2 cm, width 1.7 cm. For style of head, Cf. Petrie, *Amulets* Pl. XXI #176 h, k. Right ear missing, face very slightly cracked. ....**CHOICE 85.00**

1207. **FAIENCE FALCON AMULET. Ptolemaic.** Green-blue. Aegis, a falcon head with broad collar and solar disk. Serpent winding around disk. Lovely color. 10 x 15 mm. Perhaps of Ra as a falcon-headed god. Petrie, *Amulets* 181 for style of face and shoulder. ....**CHOICE 80.00**

1208. **AMULET OF BES. Ptolemaic to Roman.** Bright blue faience. Rather nice expression on face. Feathers chipped from head. Rather crude in design. 45 mm x 22 mm. Chip on headdress and at base. For facial expression, see Petrie. ....**CHOICE 50.00**

1209. **AMULET MOLD. 2nd Century B.C.-2nd Century A.D.** Reddish-brown terracotta mold for uzat (Eye of Horus). Feathers below eye. 30 x 29 mm. ....**SUPERB 150.00**

1210. **FAIENCE USHABTI AMULET. Graeco-Roman Period.** Buff faience mummiform amulet. Suspension hole runs vertically through length of body. Length 2.4 cm. Cf. Petrie, *Amulets*, 86 a, b...**CHOICE 60.00**

1211. **FAIENCE FIGURE. Roman Period. 1st-2nd Century A.D.** Green-glazed figure of Harpocrates wearing the lock of youth, holding a large cylindrical object with circular head. Linear design on back. Suspension hole through center, wider at back. Measures 4.6 x 2.5 cm. Cf. Petrie, *Amulets*, 145, 4-2. Chip at side of head and right leg area. ....**CHOICE 165.00**

1212. **STATUETTE OF HARPOCRATES. Roman Period. 1st-2nd century A.D.** Faience. Greenish-blue with black lines which emphasize contours of Harpocrates' body. He is sitting with right hand near face and with left arm on left knee. Hole in back. Wearing the lock of youth. Height 43 mm. Harpocrates was the form of Horus as a young boy or youth. ....**CHOICE 125.00**

1213. **STATUETTE OF HARPOCRATES. Roman Period. 2nd-4th Century A.D.** Greenish-blue faience. Wearing the lock of youth, which identifies the youthful form of Horus. Seated, holding his thumb to mouth. Left arm rests on left knee. Rather crude design.   4.2 cm high..   Mounted. ....**CHOICE 125.00**

1214. **FAIENCE DJED AMULET. Roman Period. 2nd-4th Century A.D.** Grey-green faience amulet of the tree of Osiris. Suspension hole in back. Length 2.8 cm. Cf. Blanchard 328...**CHOICE 85.00**

TERRACOTTA

1215. **LION PLAQUE. Late Period. 1085-332 B.C.** Terracotta. Votive. Grey. Cast from mold. Clear facial features of cat or lion. 5 cm high, 3.7 cm wide. The goddess, Bast, was a very popular goddess in the Late Dynastic Period.   In fact, Sheshonq's seat of power was at the city of Babastis, which was the Bast's chief seat of worship. Bast was a member of the triad of Babastis which consisted of Osiris, Bast and Nefer-Tem. This plaque was a votive sold at the shrine of Bast to be given as a votive to her. Mounted on black lucite base. Rare. Cf. Malloy Auction Sale, XXV, #389. ....**CHOICE 300.00**

1216. **FEMALE FIGURE. Late Period. 1085-30 B.C.** Red pottery figure of woman who probably represents a mother-goddess. Woman standing, arms by side, wearing wig. Very shapely figure with crude modeled facial features. 7 cm high. Mounted. Cf. Petrie, Gerar; Petrie, Roman Esnasya, Pl. XLIX, 87. Broken. Missing below hips. An early and rare example..**CHOICE 450.00**

1217. **MOLD OF SEATED BABOON. Late Period. 1085-332 B.C.** Buff-brown terracotta with impression of baboon amulet, solar disc top, rectangular body, seated baboon. Measures 35 x 24 mm.   Impression 8 x 17 mm. ....**CHOICE 125.00**

1218. **UZAT MOLD. Late Period.** Red-beige terracotta uzat (Eye of Horus) casting mold. Eye finely designed with white slip in mold casting area. Feathers below eye. Measures 29 x 27 mm. ....**SUPERB 150.00**

1219. TERRACOTTA STATUETTE. Ptolemaic Period. 304-30 B.C. Almost intact terracotta statuette of enthroned Amsu (Min) assimilating Horus. Horus is shown with right hand raised and wearing lock of youth. Extended phallus. Throne has decorations either side of Horus's legs. 18 cm high. Ex. Harry Houdini-Joseph Dunninger Collection. Cf. Knight, Amentet. Kaufmann, *Agyptische Terrakotten* pp. 46-49. Cf. *Agyptische Terrakotten* (Philip), no. 5 1. Excellent carving. ....**SUPERB 2000.00**

1220. MINIATURE STATUETTE. Ptolemaic Period. 3rd Century B.C. Upper and lower torso of a nude young female in red/brown terracotta. Hands to sides. Locks of hair visible on shoulders. Left leg advancing. Crudely molded in places, back left flat and unmolded. Typical Hellenistic style. Height 7.8 cm. Cf. German Exhibition Catalogue of "Götter Pharaonen" 1978/9, #88. Some chipping. Rather charming. ....**CHOICE 300.00**

1221. SEAL IMPRESSION. Ptolemaic Period. 3rd Century B.C. Buff terracotta seal of a Ptolemaic queen (possibly Berenike II). Shows queen facing left, with long hair falling over before and behind shoulder. Braided hair at front. Very youthful portrait. Diameter 1.7 cm. Cf. Petrie, Odci 238. Chipped around edges. ....**CHOICE 200.00**

1222. VOTIVE FEMALE HEAD. Hellenistic Period. 3rd-2nd Century B.C. Light orange brown terracotta. Rather large, stern features with hint of double chin. Plain hair, parted in middle, curling to just below the ear. Left side of face missing. 5 cm high. Cf. Kaufmann.............**CHOICE 125.00**

1223. FIGURE OF MAN. Ptolemaic. 3rd-1st Century B.C. Pale beige terracotta figure of man standing, contrapostal. Wears a polos and himation which drapes well, with left hand on thigh. Details on undergarment around neck. Provenance-Israel. 4.8 cm high. Chip on base. Head missing. Nice molding. Cf. Higgins, *Greek Terracotta Figures.* ....**CHOICE 80.00**

1224. HEAD OF A SLAVE. Ptolemaic/Early Roman. Very small buff/brown solid terracotta head of a slave wearing a pointed hat. Hat is similar in shape to a Phrygian helmet. Facial features pronounced, particularly lips. Height 3.2 cm. Mounted. Cf. Kaufmann, *Aegyptische Terrakotten*, fig. 107 var. Nose missing. ....**CHOICE 125.00**

1225. MOLD FOR TERRACOTTA SCARAB BEETLE. Ptolemaic to Roman Period. Upper portion depicting head and wings of scarab. A theory is that these circulated in Lower Egypt as currency. 35 mm. ....**CHOICE 75.00**

1226. HEAD OF HARPOCRATES. Ptolemaic/Roman. 304 B.C.-1st Century A.D. Terracotta. He has the characteristic hair lock of youth on right side of face, and his finger is near his mouth. Nice facial features, but top of head missing. 4.3 cm long, 3.2 cm wide. Harpocrates was known as a late form of Horus. Horus was the first god worshipped throughout Egypt. Cf. *Aegyptische Terrakotten*, Carl Maria Kaufman, fig. 28, 29, 31. ....**CHOICE 75.00**

1227. HEAD OF HARPOCRATES. Ptolemaic/Roman. 304 B.C.-1st Century A.D. Terracotta. Wears shallow wreath around his head, on top of which are horns. Nice facial features, but nose chipped. Head tilted toward right shoulder. Hair lock on right side of head. 4.5 cm long, 3.3 cm wide. Harpocrates was known as a late form of the god Horus. Cf. *Aegyptische Terrakotten*, Carl Maria Kaufman p. 54, 56, fig. 51 for style of head. ....**CHOICE 70.00**

1228. FINIAL. Late Ptolemaic/Early Roman. Triangular orange terracotta finial from an oil lamp. Termination or handle shows bust of Zeus Serapis in relief. Red/brown slip. Height 6 cm. Rather scarce...................................**CHOICE 100.00**

1229. HEAD OF A SLAVE. Late Ptolemaic/Roman. Dark orange/brown fragment of a terracotta head of a slave. Facial features contorted into a grimace. Height 4.3 cm. Cf. Kaufmann, *Aegyptische Terrakotten*, fig. 107 var. Mounted. ....**CHOICE 100.00**

1230. HEAD OF PRIEST. Ptolemaic. 2nd Century B.C. Orange buff terracotta. Strangely shaped, bald head with very unique features. One ear missing. Provenance-Alexandria. 4.6 cm high without mount. Ex. Michael Abe Mayor. Some minor cracking. Mounted. Cf. Philipp, *Terrakotten aus Aegypten*, fig. 5, cat. no. 7. Bold powerful style. ....**CHOICE 350.00**

1231. FIGURE OF SLAVE. 2nd-1st Century B.C. Orange-red terracotta. Left arm is raised to head to carry basket or water jug which is missing. Right arm placed on hip. Facial features look unhappy and strained. 5.5 cm high. Cf. Philipp, *Terrakotten aus Agypten*, cat. no. 9. Slightly worn. Missing beneath hips. ....**CHOICE 200.00**

1232. HEAD OF HELLENISTIC WOMAN. Hellenistic. 2nd-1st Century B.C. Attractive head with hair braided around her crown. 3.6 cm high. Features a little worn but nicely molded. Typically Hellenistic, probably a head from a Tanagra statuette. Kaufmann......................**CHOICE 85.00**

1233. CARICATURE HEAD. 2nd Century B.C.-1st Century A.D. Alexandrian-Hellenistic caricature-type portrait head fragment in terracotta of a man with grinning mouth and small moustache. What remains is intact. 9.0 x 6.5 cm. Such caricature portraits in terracotta were very popular in the area around Alexandria during the Hellenistic period. Cf. Kaufmann, fig. 112....................................**SUPERB 400.00**

1234. **HEAD OF YOUNG GOD OR PHARAOH.** Ptolemaic. **2nd Century-30 B.C.** Light brown terracotta head. Wears Egyptian headdress. 3.8 cm high. Worn features...**CHOICE 75.00**

1235. **HEAD OF YOUNG HARPOCRATES.** **2nd Century B.C.-1st Century A.D.** Small Hellenistic type terracotta head. Left-hand finger to mouth. Elaborate hairstyle wearing the horn and sun disc headdress. 4.7 cm high. Cf. Kaufmann, fig. 28. Nice molding, but missing below neck. ....**SUPERB 40.00**

1236. **HEAD OF HARPOCRATES.** **2nd Century B.C.-1st Century A.D.** Red terracotta head. Hellenistic style with elaborate hairstyle and horn and sun disc headdress. Below chin missing. 4 cm high. Cf. Kaufmann, fig. 35. ....**CHOICE 85.00**

1237. **HEAD OF HARPOCRATES.** **2nd Century B.C.-1st Century A.D.** Terracotta fragment of head in Hellenistic style. Wears striated lappet wig, lock of youth, and probably had finger to mouth. Light brown-beige clay. Left side of face missing. 3 cm high. Kaufmann, fig. 28. A rare type. ....**CHOICE 80.00**

1238. **HEAD OF WOMAN.** **2nd Century B.C.-1st Century A.D.** Hellenistic-type head with elaborate headdress with stylized curls underneath. Detailed facial features. Moderate molding with remains of cream paint or slip. 3 cm high. Cf. Kaufmann, fig. 108 for similar types. Bold rendering...................................**CHOICE 100.00**

1239. **PORTRAIT OF HEAD FRAGMENT.** **2nd Century B.C.-1st Century A.D.** Hellenistic caricature-type fragment. Moderate molding, but with strange representation of eyes. Stylized curls of hair surrounding face. Brown-red terracotta. 5.5 cm x 4.5 cm. Cf. Kaufmann, fig. 112. ..**CHOICE 125.00**

1240. **FRAGMENT OF SISTRUM HANDLE.** Greco-Roman. **2nd Century B.C.-1st Century A.D.** Terracotta fragment. Orange handle depicting face and underneath bunch of grapes. Late Hellenistic style. 7 cm high. Kaufmann, fig. 102. ....**CHOICE 75.00**

1241. **BUST OF HORUS HARPOCRATES.** Roman Period. **1st Century B.C.-1st Century A.D.** Orange clay terracotta bust with red slip. Although worn, good artwork. Harpocrates is seen with hand or finger to mouth with elaborate hairstyle and headdress. Isis crown missing. Missing below waist. 4 cm high. Cf. Kaufmann, fig. 28. Bold. ....**CHOICE 85.00**

1242. **BUST OF YOUNG HARPOCRATES.** **1st Century B.C.-1st Century A.D.** Small Hellenistic-type bust. Right-handed finger to mouth. Head tilted slightly to one side. Wearing horns and sun disc headdress. Rather rough molding. 4.5 cm high. Cf. Kaufmann, fig. 35 and 36. Bold. ....**CHOICE 85.00**

1243. **HEAD OF HARPOCRATES.** Hellenistic. **1st Century B.C.-1st Century A.D.** Light orange terracotta head with finger to mouth and lock of youth. Elaborate hairstyle with Isis crown missing. Left part of head missing. 4.5 cm high. Cf. Kaufmann, fig. 29. ....**CHOICE 65.00**

1244. **HEAD OF GOD BES.** Roman Period. **1st Century B.C.-2nd Century A.D.** Light orange-buff terracotta. Good facial features looking particularly fierce. Elaborate hairstyle with headdress missing. Missing below neck. 6.8 cm high. Cf. Kaufmann for similar Bes figures. ....**CHOICE 100.00**

1245. **BUST OF CYBELE.** **1st Century B.C.-1st Century A.D.** Light orange terracotta bust with elaborate headdress. Costume and features rather worn. Headdress rather stylized, as is hair which is parted in the middle, underneath headdress. Woman wears a chiton which falls in soft folds. 8.5 cm high. Cf. Kaufmann for similar hairstyles and headdress, fig. 108. ....**CHOICE 125.00**

1246. **FIGURE OF EROS OR HARPOCRATES.** **1st Century B.C.-2nd Century A.D.** Has right-hand finger to mouth. Evidence of elaborate hairstyle points to Hellenistic style. Moderate molding but rather worn. Missing above forehead and below neck. 3 cm high. Kaufmann fig. 35. ....**CHOICE 75.00**

1247. **LIONESS HEAD.** **1st Century B.C.-1st Century A.D.** Brown terracotta head with mouth open and ear flat back against neck. Features portray an Eastern look. Cf. Kaufmann...**CHOICE 125.00**

1248. **HEAD OF GIANT MASTIFF.** **1st Century B.C.-1st Century A.D.** Orange-red terracotta head. Rather unusual with two sides of a detailed mold joined together. The line runs off center making head seem rather lopsided. Dog is snarling with mouth open on right side. Detailed molding showing hair of hound's coat on neck. Left ear broken off. 3 cm high. Kaufmann-. Paul Grunder. ....**SUPERB 175.00**

1249. **FLASK FRAGMENT.** Roman Period. **1st–2nd Century A.D.** Part of an amphora flask. Depiction of two heads side by side just beneath rim of flask. The heads are probably the Dioscuri, Castor and Pollux, who were the sons of Zeus. Probably Memphis ware. For similar types of wares, Cf. *Roman Pottery in the Ontario Museum*, Pl. 21-22. Petrie-. ....**CHOICE 50.00**

EGYPTIAN

816

817

818

819

822

823

824

827

831

839

840

PLATE 14

EGYPTIAN

842

855

849

852

848

851

858

845

861

868

876

862

PLATE 15

EGYPTIAN

864

873

888

895

879

897

884

901

893

878

910

PLATE 16

EGYPTIAN

900

899

921

908

913

935

931

PLATE 17

932

933

936

937

938

939

941

943

942

945

946

962

954

970

989

1032

981

1009

1050

1056

1068

1088

1045

1041

1013

1017

1072

1046

1040

1105

1040

1109

1122

1123

PLATE 18

EGYPTIAN

1107

1125

1129

1113

1139

1164

1180

1144

1169

1179

1178

1170

1171

1189

1174

1205

1175

1202

1173

1212

PLATE 19

EGYPTIAN

1215

1216

1230

1231

1222

1220

1245

1235

1219

1233

1248

1239

PLATE 20

GREEK

GREEK - Large Terracotta from Myrina

Hellenistic female standing on flattened base. Wearing chiton draped over breasts and to the ground and himation draped around waist. Left hand to waist, right hand raised holding object. Hair parted in front and bought to bun; wearing spendone. Ancient colors are partially preserved; reddish brown hair and pink traces on garment. Later 3rd century B.C. Height 11". Superb preservation. Exceptional style and beauty. A masterpiece of Greek Coroplastic.   Sold in 1971 for $1250. Estimated value in 1997 is $5000.

GREEK

The Neolithic Age in Greece resulted in early settlements dating from the 7th millennium B.C. in Macedonia. The earliest pottery dates from 6500-6000 B.C., from Nea Nikomedia. During this early period the evidence of trade with other areas is apparent. Flint and obsidian were widely traded. With the advent of the Bronze Age came the development of metallurgy. These people were illiterate into the 3rd millennium B.C.

The first great emergence of the Greek civilization started in the islands, and specifically in Cnossus in Crete, in the 4th millennium B.C. This was the Greek civilization in its oldest form, before the Hellenistic civilization. This Bronze Age period is divided into three periods: Early Minoan (2800-2000 B.C.), Middle Minoan (2000-1550 B.C.), and Late Minoan (1550-1050 B.C.). By the 3rd millennium B.C., Crete was influencing culture far beyond its borders. The grand palace of Cnossus, along with associated buildings, covered an area of eight acres. The best pottery of the Middle Minoan period has rarely been equaled. Also, Cyclades were produced during this period, c. 2600-2500 B.C., in the form of stylized goddesses carved in marble.

While the influence of Crete was diminishing in the 14th century B.C., Mycenae on mainland Greece was experiencing a wide spread of prosperity. Mycenaean settlements in the East developed trade as far away as Egypt, Palestine, Syria, and Mesopotamia. Areas throughout Asia Minor saw Mycenaean settlements like Miletus, Samos, Halicarnassus, and Ephesus. The Heroic Age sung of by Homer, with the siege of Troy, belongs to the Mycenaean Age. The Mycenaean man was a warrior attesting to weapons and human combat scenes carved in intaglio gems.

By 800 B.C., the Dorian invasion had revolutionized the distribution of population in the Peloponnese. This Geometric period began a new era in Greek history. The Indo-European invaders from the North brought a new religion, a new language, and the use of iron. The people of this period produced no monumental architecture or sculpture, but rather confined their work to pottery, small bronze, terracotta statuettes, and engraved seals. The designs consisted of systematized geometric patterns, and depended on the locality in which they were produced for both technique and ornamentation. This style reached its highest level of development in Attica. From 700-550 B.C. was the period of Orientalizing influence. The geometric style was supplanted everywhere with ever new ideas, in which the Eastern Mediterranean played a major part. The Phoenicians introduced the alphabet. Monumental sculpture was being produced in Cyprus. Corinth was the great center of pottery, and the result was wide distribution in Asia Minor, Egypt, and the Crimea. It was also imitated by the Etruscans.

The Archaic period, in the 6th century B.C., is one of growth in every direction. The artists surpassed the stage of the primitive. Greek art was now heading toward the state of great artistic genius and appreciation of beauty which it would eventually realize. Bronze casting progressed to a high state of artistic expression. Pottery, terracotta, marble sculpture, and glass manufacturing were all expressive of this age.

By the end of the 6th century B.C., most Greek states throughout the Mediterranean world had rejected their tyrants, and accepted the principles of democratic government. For most of the Classical stage in art, Greek history is taken up by the powerful struggles between Sparta and Athens, and then by the Persian invasions. Under these influences the stimulus in art was rapid. In a small stretch of time, less than half a century, every trace of Archaism was discarded. A new concept, idealism, was pursued, along with an expression of spirituality. Each medium of artistic work was transformed. Red figure painted vases reached splendid heights, as did sculpture in stone and bronze. Terracotta figures and engraved gemstones also displayed excellent craftsmanship.

The 4th century B.C. is the epoch of great civic building of theaters, stadiums, gymnasiums, and temples out of stone.

Greece entered a new stage in history with the conquests of Alexander the Great. The extension of Greece was to include the Mediterranean world, Southwestern Asia, and part of Central Asia. This Hellenistic period from the 3rd to the 1st century B.C. saw a new outlook on artistic endeavors. The aim of the artisan was no longer idealism or pure beauty, but realism. The realistic spirit was particularly strong at the new schools in Asia Minor. More attention to scientific and anatomical detail was the artist's goal. A broadened variety of subjects were of interest, such as children and the elderly, as well as caricatures.

Roman art would be the next phase in history, starting at different times as Rome swept down with its conquering legions.

SOUTHERN ITALY

Sicily and Southern Italy prospered with the vast Greek colonizations. The Greek pioneers gave way to new styles developed by the Magna Graecia Greeks. Taras, Metapontum, Poseidonia, Croton, Regium, and Locri, from Southern Italy, along with the great cities of Sicily such as Syracuse, Gela, Aeragas, Segesta, and Leontini, all added to the fineness of Greek civilization and art. Syracuse, an area of great prosperity, drew Greek artists from distant areas. The South Italian pottery was of exceptional quality, second only to Attic vases. Various regions developed their own signature styles. Lucanian, Campanian, and Apulian styles were all in the strong Greek tradition, while Gnatia and Daunia produced more Magna Graecia-style ware.

ETRUSCANS

The Etruscan people settled between the Tiber and Arno Rivers. The Greek influence was very great there at certain periods. Etruscan art is a combination of elements taken from the East and from Greece, with varying degrees of originality. The early Villanovan was initially of strong influence, but gave way to the Greek presence in the south. The pottery can be closely Corinthian in style. Some of the most attractive plainware pottery made was the all-black Bucchero ware. Bronze development was strong, but not on a par with Athens. Jewelry workshops were of the finest quality. Exceptional gold work has come down to us today, and commonly go for high prices when offered. Terracotta figures were made of lovely style, exhibited in large human heads, burial urns, and sarcophagi.

EASTERN GREEKS

The Greek influence coming from Asia Minor was strong. These Eastern Greeks established themselves after the end of the Bronze Age on the coastal areas of Western Asia. Rhodes was a center of pottery terracotta manufacture from the Geometric period on. The sculpture from Asia Minor is magnificent, but can be seen in museums only. One can never forget the sculpture from Pergamon. Cities like Ephesus, Smyrna, Chios, Lesbos, Troy, Samos, Cnidus, Halicarnassus, Antioch on the Orontes, and Ba'albek attest to the greatness of Greek influence in Asia Minor and the Levant. Smaller objects from the Eastern Greek world are very often available in the marketplace.

MAGNA GRAECIA POTTERY		
Lucanian	red-figure	430-330 B.C.
Apulian	red-figure	430-300 B.C.
Campanian	red-figure	430-300 B.C.
Campanian	black-figure	330-300 B.C.
Paestan	red-figure	360-310 B.C.
Paestan	black-figure	340 B.C.
Sicilian	red-figure	330-300 B.C.
Gnathia	Gnathian technique: black glaze	350-275 B.C.
Teano	variation Gnathian technique	310-280 B.C.
Centuripe	fugitive pastel colors	3rd cent. B.C.
Messadian	brown on buff	7th-3rd cent.B.C.
Peycetian	various	700-330 B.C.
Daunian	various	700-330 B.C.
Xenox	red on black glaze	375-350 B.C.
Calenian	black glaze w/relief decor	4th-3rd cent.B.C.
Apulian	black gloss	4th cent. B.C.
Campanian	black gloss	3rd cent. B.C.
Campanian	grey-body	2nd-1st cent.B.C.

CYPRUS

Cyprus was first settled in the 7th millennium B.C., and a stone working culture slowly gave way to the Bronze Age in this area. Weapons and bronze pins were manufactured over a period ranging from 2700 to 1050 B.C. Cypriot artists in the Bronze Age used bold designs in their pottery. Red polished ware, mottled red polished, black polished ware, and drab polished were the dominant wares of the Early Bronze Age. During the Middle Bronze Age, red on black and white painted wares were made, as were the base ring and white slip wares later on. All were exported to the mainland. By the 10th century, Greek colonizers had brought their culture to the island. During the Iron Age, Cyprus was a center for exporting fine wares to the Levant, such as wheel-made bichrome white and red ware. Terracotta fertility figurines were made in human form with unusual simplistic designs and shapes. Animal terracotta figures and vessels were made, representing bulls, deer, cattle, horses, pigs, camels, sheep, goats, dogs, birds, and snakes. The lotus was a favorite painted design on pottery.

POTTERY

The earliest Minoan pottery was incised ware and painted ware with parallel lines and cross-hatching in various patterns. Early Minoan pottery has a beautiful flare spout in its pitchers and juglets. Magnificent stone carved vases are found from the Early and Middle Minoan phases. By the Middle Minoan period, many shapes were used, with butterfly, double axepations, sworls, branches, and various marine designs. In the later part of this period, wonderful polychrome vessels with dolphins, crabs, and stylized octopi appear. The Late Minoan period is distinguished by finer baking. The designs become more complex with an emphasis on floral and marine patterns. A distinct two-handled goblet with a pedestal uses a single self-contained unit for decoration. All of the Cretian pottery is rarely on the market today, and commands strong prices.

The fine Greek pottery can be divided into four main groups. The Geometric wares are dated from 1000-700 B.C. The designs and origins were from many localities and were painted in brown or black monochromes. Trade contact with Egypt, Phoenicia, and inland Western Asia resulted in the Orientalizing phase of Greek pottery. The images as seen on imported textiles, ivory, and metal objects from the East inspired the introduction of human, animal, and plant forms on the new polychrome painting. Corinth was the center of this widely exported ware. Rhodes, Chios, and the Cycladic Islands were also pottery centers. The Athenian potters during the 6th century until 530 B.C. developed the mature black-figure technique. This was an expanded technique from Corinthian ware with details of the black figures incised. Athens was the center, but Chalkidian ware and East Greek wares were also produced. This stage of Greek pottery grew to such an extent that the artists began signing their works. Alongside the black-figure painting, the red-figure phase was invented around 530-520 B.C. This technique used a predominantly black glazed background with figures and designs left in red-orange. The individual artists were rapidly developing skill in human anatomy, and the results are magnificent. Professor Beazley of Oxford was able to identify by style over 500 different painters. The height of this period is in the period from 480-450 B.C., when the generation of artists created a concept of ideal beauty. During this period, different wares also competed for excellence. White-ground ware and the plastic vases were made, but not commonly found. Greek pottery declined during and after the Peloponnesian Wars. Many Attic artists moved their craft to Magna Graecia, where red-figure painting lasted to the 3rd century B.C.

The pottery from Magna Graecia was varied and rich in quality. The red-figure pottery falls into two basic groups. One is Apulian and Lucanian, and the other group is Campanian, Sicilian, and Paestan. The pottery from this area is the most collected today. A.D. Trendall estimates the total number of extant examples of Apulian pottery is more than 10,000, Campanian at over 4000, and less than 1000 each of the other wares. The function of most South Italian vases was to hold water, wine, and oil. The funerary vases were not constrained by their function, but were designed more for visual appeal. Some were so large as to be unusable for holding water. This pottery was primarily used in the locality in which it was manufactured. The black glaze wares were produced with an unbroken lustrous surface. Its fine sheen resembles metal. This classic ware was extensively made, and a large degree of examples are available today on the market. They are often collected for their various elegant shapes.

METAL OBJECTS

Small Greek bronze antiquities are available in many shapes, sizes, and uses. They included utilitarian objects such as vessels, household implements, furniture appliqués, tools, arms and armor, ornaments, horse trappings, mirrors, amulets, and objects used in daily life. Most objects had some decoration. Bronze handles to vessels are attractive, and can be found in many price ranges. Bronze figurines exemplify Greek art and are available in all periods from Minoan down to Late Hellenistic.

TERRACOTTA

Greek terracotta sculptures and figures make up one area of collecting in which fine examples of Greek art can be purchased at very reasonable values. The finest examples of terracottas found are from Tanagra. Made in the first half of the 4th century B.C., they fall into the figurative terracotta category, or statuettes and other small portable objects. The second main category is architectonic terracottas. These were made as decorations for buildings. They are usually found in areas where marble was scarce. Areas where fine examples are found include Magna Graecia and Corinth. The objects can be beam ends, rainspots, friezes, and pediment sculptures. Figurines and reliefs follow, and exemplify the lines of stylistic development of the larger sculptures, e.g. Archaic, Classical, and Hellenistic. This field of collecting can be one of the most rewarding. A fine collection can be put together today.

GREEK TERRACOTTA CHARACTERISTICS			
AREA	COLOR CLAY	TEXTURE	COMMENTS
Attica	orange-yellow brown	fine	small quantity of mica
Corinth	cream: greenish: orange	extremely fine	no mica
Boeotia	yellow ochre: pale orange-brownish	fine before 500 B.C.	mica present
Rhodes	reddish-brown	coarse	mica present
Halicarnassus	orange: cream: purple-brown	coarse	large mica crystals
Ephesus	orange	coarse	much mica
Crete	pale orange cream	very fine	encrusted with chocolate-brown
Tarentum	orange-yellow brown	fine	much mica
Sicily	pale orange-light greenish gray	coarse	some mica
Cyrenaica	most colors except greenish	coarse	small quantity mica

TOOLS AND WEAPONS

Bronze was the main metal in forging Greek tools and weapons. While bronze helmets and greaves appear on the market occasionally, the main objects available are spearheads and arrowheads. Bronze arrowheads are found in all areas once controlled by the Greeks.

STONE

For the most part, marble sculpture is collected by museums and a few private collectors in the world today. However, non-Classical Greek sculpture can still be collected from the Eastern Greek world. Limestone sculptures from Cyprus or Crete will bring in much less than those from Greece or Magna Graecia.

LAMPS

Greek lamps are found in a much simpler form than those manufactured during the time of the Roman Empire. The earlier lamps, dating from the 7th century B.C. on, were open in the center, with closed nozzles. They were usually black glazed. As time progressed, the central portion became more enclosed. Lamps with vertical and strap handles were made. By the Hellenistic and Ptolemaic periods, shoulder decoration began to be produced, and side lugs were often present. Most Greek lamps can be purchased for under $150 apiece.

JEWELRY

Jewelry appeals to a wide area of collectors. While the asking prices of Greek gold jewelry is handsome, some simpler designs can bring in cheaper prices for those with a smaller budget. Even today, just as in ancient times, gold jewelry is coveted for its sheer luxury and beauty. Greek mythology tells of Eriphyle's betrayal of her spouse because of her desires for a fine necklace, Polycrates' defeat for a fine intaglio set into a gold ring.

GLASS

The center for Hellenistic glass workshops was Alexandria, in Egypt. The vessels are all derived from Greek pottery forms. The glass was core-formed, with colorful molded rods of various colors swirling around the shoulders. It is not until the Roman period that glass was made on a large scale.

WRITING

Early writing and lettering is an area of collecting that is increasing in popularity. Greek writing is not frequently found. Usually when it is encountered, it is in the form of an inscription on an object, or a name signed on a Greek vase by its maker. Papyrus fragments with Greek writings can be found, however, and are highly sought after.

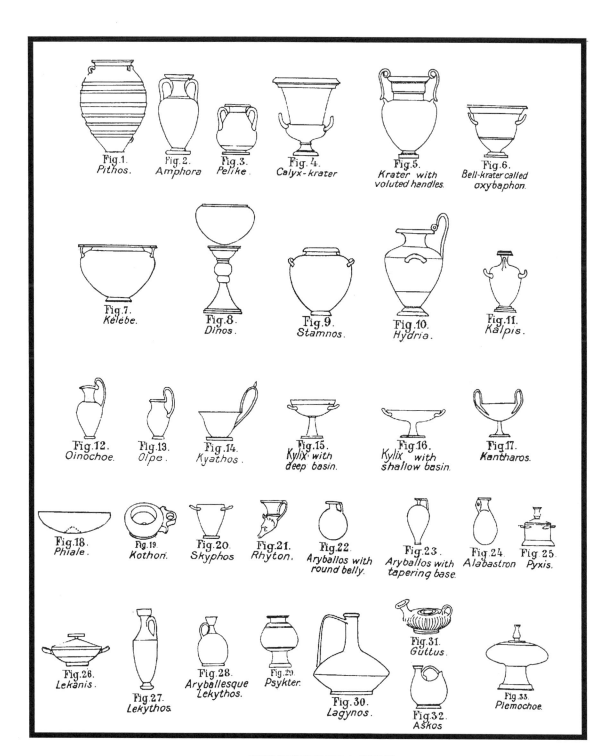

Fig.1.
Pithos.

Fig.2.
Amphora.

Fig.3.
Pelike.

Fig.4.
Calyx-krater

Fig.5.
Krater with
voluted handles.

Fig.6.
Bell-krater called
oxybaphon.

Fig.7.
Kelébe.

Fig.8.
Dinos.

Fig.9.
Stamnos.

Fig.10.
Hydria.

Fig.11.
Kálpis.

Fig.12.
Oinochoe.

Fig.13.
Olpe.

Fig.14.
Kyathos.

Fig.15.
Kylix with
deep basin.

Fig.16.
Kylix with
shallow basin.

Fig.17.
Kantharos.

Fig.18.
Phiale.

Fig.19.
Kothon.

Fig.20.
Skyphos.

Fig.21.
Rhyton.

Fig.22.
Aryballos with
round belly.

Fig.23.
Aryballos with
tapering base.

Fig.24.
Alabastron

Fig.25.
Pyxis.

Fig.26.
Lekanis.

Fig.27.
Lekythos

Fig.28.
Aryballesque
Lekythos.

Fig.29.
Psykter.

Fig.30.
Lagynos.

Fig.31.
Guttus.

Fig.32.
Askos

Fig.33.
Plemochoe.

GREEK VASES

GREECE
c. 1100-332 B.C.

		INTERNAL/ECONOMIC	EXTERNAL/POLITICAL	CULTURAL
D	1100 B.C.	Farming and nomadic tribes, tribal kingdoms	Era of small states Phoenicians, Israelites	
A				
R	1050 B.C.			Protogeometric pottery
K	1000 B.C.		David	
	950 B.C.		Solomon	
A	900 B.C.		Rise of Assyria	Geometric pottery
G	800 B.C.	Revival of eastern trade		Adoption of alphabet
E	750 B.C.	Beginning of colonization		
S				Orientalizing pottery
			Spartan conquest Messenia	
A	700 B.C.		Rise of Lydia	
G		Invention of coinage		
E	650 B.C.			
		Growth of commercial- industrial classes	Second Messenian War Tyranny at Sicyon, Corinth, etc.	
O				
F	600 B.C.		Spartan expansion	
R		Expansion of Athenian trade		Attic black-figure
E	550 B.C.		Western wars with Etruscans, Phoenicians	Attic red-figure
V				
O	500 B.C.		Ionian revolt Themistocles at Athens: fleet	Classic sculpture
L			Persian invasion: Salamis, Plataea,	
U			Mycale	
T			Delian League	
I				
O			Pericles at Athens	Temple of Zeus at Olympia
N	450 B.C.			Writers: Sophocles, Herodotus Philosopher: Socrates
			Athens vs. Sparta	Writers: Sophocles, Euripides, Aristophanes
			Peloponesian War	Decline of red-figure
			Expedition to Syacuse	
			Fall of Athens	
	400 B.C.		Domination by Sparta	Death of Socrates
			Expedition of Cyrus	Philosopher: Plato
			Revival of Athens	Artist: Praxiteles
	350 B.C.		Rise of Macedonia	Mausoleum
			Philip	Philosopher: Aristotle
			Alexander the Great	Writer: Demosthenes
	332 B.C.		**HELLENISTIC AGE**	

GREEK

WEAPONS

Spear and Javelin Points

1250. **BRONZE SPEARHEAD. Troy. Greek Bronze Age. 2200-1500 B.C.** Leaf shaped blade with midrib and twisted tang. Two splits, one each side of mid rib. Length 15 cm. Width 3.7 cm. Similar types are of the early civilization of the Cyclades. This example was found in Western Turkey. The two split holes were known to the Trojans as eye-holes. This type is from Troy II. Cf. *Guide to Greek and Roman Life*, British Museum, fig. 78c. #198. Cf. Hall, Rhind Lectures 1923, fig. 98. Rare. ....**CHOICE 350.00**

Arrowheads

1251. **BRONZE ARROWHEAD. Greek. 1200-800 B.C.** Rhombic head with triangular projection at base. Raised midrib. Length 59 mm. This type was in widespread use in the eastern Mediterranean; it has been found in Egypt, Greece, and Anatolia, and iron examples in Israel. Group A #20. Cf. Petrie, *Egyptian, T and W* #200. ...**SUPERB 125.00**

1252. **BRONZE ARROWHEAD. Greek. 1000-800 B.C.** Head with rhombic sides. Socketed, no shaft. Length 23 mm. Transitional from tanged rhombic style to socketed style. Group A #4. Petrie -; Malloy -......................**CHOICE 50.00**

1253. **BRONZE ARROWHEAD. Greek. 1000-800 B.C.** Rhombic head, socketed, no shaft. Length 25 mm. Similar to the preceding example. Group B #17. Petrie-; Malloy-. ....**CHOICE 65.00**

1254. **BRONZE ARROWHEAD. Greek. 10th-7th Century B.C.** Biblade, flat ribbed, with blade ends at 90° angle. Shortened solid tang. Length 38 mm. Group A #6. Petrie -; Malloy-. ....**CHOICE 50.00**

1255. **BRONZE ARROWHEAD. Greek. 10th-7th Century B.C.** Biblade, flat ribbed head with spur on end of one blade. Socketed. Group A #5. Petrie 134; Malloy -. A rare type. ....**CHOICE 150.00**

1256. **BRONZE ARROWHEAD. Greco-Scythian. 8th Century B.C.** Three blade with long shaft. 4.5 x 1 cm. Cf. Azarpay *Urartian Art and Artifacts* 8. Karmir-Blur-Hermitage Museum, Leningrad.......................**SUPERB 35.00**

1257. **BRONZE ARROWHEAD. Greco-Scythian. 8th-7th Century B.C.** Leaf shape. Short socket. Length 44 mm. Group A #8. ....**CHOICE 60.00**

1258. **BRONZE ARROWHEAD. 8th-7th Century B.C.** Pointed leaf shape with socket. Length 40 mm. Group A #2. ....**CHOICE 55.00**

1259. **BRONZE ARROWHEAD. Greek. 8th-7th Century B.C.** Narrow deltoid head with medium socket. Length 41 mm. Group A #1..................................**CHOICE 45.00**

1260. **BRONZE ARROWHEAD. Greco-Scythian. 8th-6th Century B.C.** Three triangular blades with no shaft. 22 x 8 mm. The Scythians introduced the triblade arrowhead into civilization. They drank the blood of their enemies and made drinking mugs out of their skulls. Cf. Azarpay, *Urartian Arts and Artifacts*, 8. ....**SUPERB 35.00**

1261. **BRONZE ARROWHEAD. Greco-Scythian. 8th-6th Century B.C.** Leaf-shaped head with socket. Length 38 mm. Group A #9...**CHOICE 55.00**

1262. **BRONZE TRIANGULAR BLADE. Greco-Sythian. 8th-6th Century B.C.** No barbs, shaft hole, no shaft. 2.7 cm long, 1.5 cm wide. The Sythians introduced the triblade arrowhead into civilization. These barbarians from the north drank the blood of their enemies and made drinking mugs out of their skulls. ....**SUPERB 35.00**

1263. **BRONZE ARROWHEAD. Greco-Sythian. 8th-6th Century B.C.** Triangular blade with no barbs, short central shaft, and shaft hole. 4 cm long, 1 cm wide. End of wooden arrow shaft still present. A gem. The Sythians were instrumental in Nineveh's fall in 612 B.C. Herodotus commented that the Sythians "flay the right arms of their dead enemies and make of the skin, which is stripped off with nail hanging to it, a covering for their quivers." Cf. Azarpay, *Urartian Art and Artifacts* 8, Karmir-Blur-Hermitage Museum, Leningrad. ....**SUPERB 35.00**

1264. **BRONZE ARROWHEAD. Greco-Sythian. 8th-6th Century B.C.** Similar to the preceding example. Cf. Azarpay, *Urartian Art and Artifacts* 8, Karmir-Blur Hermitage Museum, Leningrad. ....**SUPERB 30.00**

1265. **ROUNDED ARROWHEAD. Greek. 8th-4th Century B.C.** Flat blade, short, central shaft, encrusted. Bronze spur on side of shaft. 3.5 cm long, 1.3 cm wide. Petrie 35. ....**CHOICE 50.00**

1266. **BRONZE ARROWHEAD. Greek. 8th-4th Century B.C.** Flat blade with short central shaft, spur on side of shaft. 3.5 x 1 cm. Encrusted. ....**CHOICE 55.00**

1267. **BRONZE ARROWHEAD. Greek. 6th-3rd Century B.C.** Biblade, flat ribbed, leaf shape. Spur on socket shaft. Length 36 mm. Group A #3a. Petrie-; Malloy-. Scarce. ....**CHOICE 75.00**

1268. **BRONZE ARROWHEAD. 6th-3rd Century B.C.** Biblade flat ribbed with spur on long socket shaft. Length 37 mm. Group A #3. Cf. Petrie 136. ....**CHOICE 65.00**

1269. **BRONZE ARROWHEAD. Greek. 6th-3rd Century B.C.** Biblade flat ribbed with spur on socket. Length 45 mm. Group A #7. Petrie 135; Malloy 113. ..**CHOICE-SUP 75.00**

1270. **BRONZE ARROWHEAD. Greek. 5th-3rd Century B.C.** Trilobate head with long socket shaft. Length 37 mm. Group A #13. Petrie; Malloy ....**CHOICE 65.00**

1271. **BRONZE ARROWHEAD. Greek. 5th-3rd Century B.C.** Trilobate head with long socket shaft with spur. Length 41 mm. Group A #12. Petrie-; Malloy-. A scarce type. ....**CHOICE 100.00**

1272. **BRONZE ARROWHEAD. Macedonian. 350-330 B.C.** Trilobate, barbed and socketed. Sharp blades. Length 33 mm. N. Yalouris, *Treasures of Ancient Macedonia* #359. From the time of Philip II and Alexander the Great. ....**SUPERB 150.00**

1273. **BRONZE ARROWHEAD. Macedonian. c. 350-330 B.C.** Trilobate, barbed, socketed. Sharp blades. Length 27 mm. Cf. N. Yalouris 359 var. ....**CHOICE 75.00**

1274. **BRONZE ARROWHEAD. Macedonian. c. 350-330 B.C.** Trilobate, barbed, socketed. Sharp blades. Length 33 mm. N. Yalouris #359 var. One barb chipped off ....**SUPERB 100.00**

1275. **BRONZE ARROWHEAD. Macedonian. c. 350-330 B.C.** Trilobate with deep barbs. Socketed. Sharp blades. Length 36 mm. N. Yalouris 359. 3 mm. chip in one blade. Still a gem arrowhead. ....**SUPERB 125.00**

1276. **BRONZE ARROWHEAD. Macedonian. c. 350-330 B.C.** Trilobate with sharp blades. Slight barbs, medium socket. Length 30 mm. N. Yalouris 359 var. Yalouris shows arrowhead inscribed ΦΙΛΛΙΠΟΥ. ....**SUPERB 150.00**

1277. **BRONZE ARROWHEAD. Macedonian. c. 350-330 B.C.** Trilobate, with deep barbs. Socketed. Sharp blades. Length 33 mm. N. Yalouris 359. ....**CHOICE-SUPERB 100.00**

1278. **BRONZE TRIANGULAR ARROWHEAD. Greek. 3rd-2nd Century B.C..** Central shaft. Each of three planes divided by central line, with slight barbs. 3 cm long, 1 cm wide. Scarce. ....**SUPERB 60.00**

1279. **BRONZE ARROWHEAD. Greek. Hellenistic: 3rd-1st Century B.C.** Trilobate head with socket, bladed. Length 22 mm. Group A #10. Petrie -; Malloy -............**CHOICE 65.00**

1280. **BRONZE ARROWHEAD. Greek. Hellenistic: 3rd-1st Century B.C.** Trilobate head, socketed, bladed. Length 22 mm. Group B #10a. Petrie -; Malloy -. More pointed example than the preceding. ....**CHOICE-SUPERB 85.00**

1281. **BRONZE ARROWHEAD. Greek. Hellenistic: 3rd-1st Century B.C.** Trilobate head with barbs, rounded blades. Medium socket shaft. Length 28 mm. Group B #11. Petrie 11; Malloy -. Three-quarters of one blade and one barb broken. ....**CHOICE 40.00**

1282. **BRONZE ARROWHEAD. Greek. Hellenistic: 3rd-1st Century B.C.** Trilobate head. Straight blades, no barbs but high-angle ends. Socketed. Length 29 mm. Group A #11. Petrie 69-71 var.; Malloy 116 var. (Parthian). Tip missing. ....**CHOICE 50.00**

1283. **BRONZE ARROWHEAD. Greek. 3rd-1st Century B.C.** Elongated trilobate head, bladed with socket. Barbed. Length 36 mm. Group B #19. Petrie -; Malloy -. Tiny chip off one blade. Rare type and a gem. ....**SUPERB 150.00**

1284. **BRONZE TRIANGULAR BLADE. Sicily. 2nd-1st Century B.C.** Barbs, hole shaft. 2.4 cm long, 6 cm wide. Similar to Achaemenid period. Cf. Petrie. ....**CHOICE 30.00**

POTTERY

1285. **JUG/BOTTLE. Cypriot. Early Bronze Age. 2700-2075 B.C.** Black and red mottled ware with incised design including rows of bands, with rows of semicircles and chevrons between bands on body. Rounded base, body large in relation to neck. Neck slightly flared to shoulder and wide flaring rim. Plain handle from rim to body. Handmade. Mottled polished effect overall. Black has some purplish tint. Height 14 cm. Cf. Desmond Morris, *The Art of Ancient Cyprus*, type 19, p. 334. Chip to rim, some scouring and pitting to body. Two holes in body restored. ....**CHOICE 500.00**

1286. **JUG. Cypriot. Middle Bronze Age. c. 1750-1600 B.C.** White painted ware with spout and handle. Decorated with cross-hatched diamonds in vertical rows. 20 cm high, 12.5 cm wide. Cf. CVA, Leipzig, Pl. 3/1-4 ....**CHOICE 750.00**

1287. **LARGE VESSEL. Cypriot. Iron Age.** Large vessel of white painted ware; wheel made. Hydna-shaped type with straight neck, small slightly flaring rim. Handle curved upwards set on either side in center of body. Small flat base. Vase tilted to the right. Concentric circles around middle. Thick and thin circles around top; thicker circles around bottom. Cross-hatched rectangular designs around neck; three vertical stripes around shoulder. Height 24.3 cm. Cf. Desmond Morris, *The Art of Ancient Cyprus*, Pl. 111. ....**SUPERB 800.00**

1288. **BICHROME JUGLET. Cypriot. Iron Age.** Bi-chrome wheel-spun juglet, buff-colored with a pinched spout. Banded design in brown around the outside of the handle and the body. Single brown band around the neck and lip. High molded handle. Height 10 cm. Cf. Morris Pl. 74, fig. c. Intact with no chipping. ....**SUPERB 350.00**

1289. **SMALL FOOTED BOWL. South Italy. Second half of 7th Century B.C.** Dull light brown clay, somewhat porous. Wide rim with folding lip, trumpet-shaped foot with curved rim and concave base. Decorated with light brown bands both inside and outside. 6.7 cm high, 11.8 cm dia. rim, 4.8 cm dia. foot. Cf. Hayes, *ROM*, #A54.........**CHOICE 150.00**

1290. **ARYBALLOS. Etrusco-Corinthian. 600 B.C.** Piriform aryballos, buff with decoration of two reddish-brown concentric bands. Flare rim, small thumb-pinch handles. Height 8.5 cm. Chip at rim. Potter's thumbprint still visible.
....**CHOICE 175.00**

1291. **LEKYTHOS. Attic. 6th Century B.C.** Large vessel, pedestal foot, ovular body and strap handle. Neck and rim broken off. Frieze on red-orange field of warrior holding shield advancing right with head turned back. Draped figures standing, one behind, two in front, one facing left, the other facing right with head turned back to left. Scrolling and tendrils in field, palmettes on shoulder. 15 cm high. Bottom half broken off as well as neck and rim. Cf. CVA Lyon, Pl. 23 #7. ....**CHOICE 1500.00**

1292. **BLACKWARE BUCCERO. Etruscan. 6th Century B.C.** Black wide-mouth cup with three concentric incised bands around side. Small pedestal base. Diameter 13.5 cm, height 5.7 cm. Intact...**CHOICE 500.00**

1293. **STORAGE JAR SHARDS. 6th Century B.C.** Red slip. Part of shoulder stamp frieze of coninuous rectangular panel, with winged sphinx advancing. Two large fragments. Cf. Sotheby Fortuna Sale, 1970, #98. Cf. Hornbostel, Hamburg, 132, 133. ....**CHOICE 150.00**

1294. **UNGUENT POT. Greek. c. 6th-4th Century B.C.** Wheel-made unguent pot with high-bellied rounded body and slightly concave cylindrical neck. Wide flared mouth with flat top. Flared ring base. Bands of black gloss cover upper portion of body, solid black gloss covers lower portion of body as well as interior and exterior of mouth. Pink-orange ware. *ROM-*. *Athenian Agora* (39:1162 shape). Farwell-. Merzagora, *Milano-*. RISD-. Part of mouth reconstructed. Some gloss flaking. ....**CHOICE 285.00**

1295. **LARGE ALABASTRON. Corinth. 580-560 B.C.** Black and red glazed vessel, full body, narrow neck and flat, large rim. Two registers of panthers, birds, lions and a deer. Full rosettes with crosses. Red and black bands between registers. Hercle painters. 25.5 cm high, 6.1 cm diameter rim. Cf. *Kunstwerk der Antike*, #44 for subject matter. Cf. Hamay pp. 114-115. Repaired and some restoration.
....**CHOICE 4000.00**

1296. **COTHON. Corinth. 575-550 B.C.** Flanged base, spurred strap handle. Linear design in black glaze. 13.5 cm dia., 16 cm with handles. Cf. CVA, Cambridge Fasc. 1, IV/39. Cf. CVA, Limoges, Pl. 3878-64. Intact. Weathered surface.
....**CHOICE 300.00**

1297. **BLACK GLAZED KYLIX. South Italy. c. 560 B.C.** Kylix with strap handles at side on long pedestal base. Bowl diameter 12.1 cm, width including handles 17 cm, height 5.9 cm. For dating and type (Attic) Cf. *Athenian Agora* 404. Reconstructed: missing piece in center of cup. Very attractive. ....**CHOICE 300.00**

1298. **BLACK FIGURE KYLIX FRAGMENT FROM RIM. Attic. 540-530 B.C.** Male figure in himation standing right, wearing cap. 45 mm x 45 mm. ....**CHOICE 165.00**

1299. **BLACK FIGURE FRAGMENT. Attic. 540-530 B.C.** Black figure vase fragment of rim of kylix with wide black rim. Red background depicting black horseman and horse galloping right. Fine style. Horse's mane and tail in red. Measures 74 x 50 mm. Cf. Buitron, #7. .....**CHOICE 250.00**

1300. **BLACK FIGURE FRAGMENT. Attic. 540-530 B.C.** Fragment of the rim of a blackware kylix. Lion prancing right with his foreleg raised, head looking back, tail curled over his back. The decorated band has a red background; the sections above and below are black. Measures 93 x 76 mm. Fragment reconstructed from six shards. ...**CHOICE 250.00**

1301. **BLACK FIGURE FRAGMENT. Attic. 540-520 B.C.** Black figure vase fragment of shoulder of amphora. Depicts the head and shoulder of a warrior left in a crested Athenian helmet. Measures 100 x 43 mm. ....**CHOICE 250.00**

1302. **BLACK FIGURE PARTIAL VASE. Attic. 540-520 B.C.** Partial black figure lekythos, nude red-headed athlete running left, male figures to each side draped in himations. Height 10.8 cm. Cf. CVA Fogg Pl. XI, #9 var.; Cf. CVA Midelaon Pl. 14, 3 and 4. The back portion, handle, neck and rim are missing. The rest is reconstructed. Fragments.
....**CHOICE 275.00**

1303. **BLACK OINOCHOE BUCCHERO. Late 6th Century B.C.** Circular body with small flaring pedestal base. Flaring neck into trefoil mouth with small handle. 21.6 cm high. Buccheros like this are commonly found in pit graves mostly found in the Villanuova region near Bologna. Lovely style. Cf. Massimo, *Etruskernas Konst och Kultur*, 40FF. Ex. Malloy Catalogue, Summer 1977 #34. Cf. Fairbanks, Museum of Fine Arts, Boston, Catalogue of Greek and Etruscan Vases, #644, Pl. LXXXV. ....**CHOICE 750.00**

1304. **BLACK FIGURE LEKYTHOS. Attic. Last Quarter of the 6th Century B.C.** Hoplite warrior holding spear and shield, wearing crested helmet, standing left, to each side are two males in himations holding spears facing warrior. On shoulder above are two males with himations facing black and red palmette. Similar to group of "Hoplite Leaving Home." Phanyllis Group. Restored and reconstructed. Beazle, *ABV* p. 464. Cf. CVA, Lyon. 1, Pl. 14, 5.
....**AVERAGE-CHOICE 500.00**

1305. **BLACK FIGURE FRAGMENT. Attic. 520 B.C.** Black figure vase fragment of lower portion of neck amphora. Two panel decorations: left meander pattern with lotus bud wreath pattern above. Measures 105 x 82 mm. ....**CHOICE 80.00**

1306. **BLACK FIGURE AMPHORA FRAGMENT. Attic. 520-510 B.C.** Satyr head and arm in profile with mouth open. Black face, red hair and long red beard flowing down arm. Two flutes being played before. A fragment from a Dionysiac dance. 35 mm x 45 mm. Cf. Moon, *Greek Vase Painting in Midwestern Collections*, 64. ....**CHOICE 275.00**

1307. **STEMLESS CUP. South Italy. 520-290 B.C.** Light grey-buff clay stemless cup. Light orange slip with black handles. Flat bottom, horizontal rolled handles. Width 14.5 cm. Nice but reglued handle. ....**CHOICE 225.00**

1308. **KYATHOS. Attic. 515-500 B.C.** Black figure with high handle, decorated with pointed knob. Palmette on handle. Satyr dancing. Maenads on both sides, ivy sprigs around with three palmette patterns. Cf. Kyathos in Oxford, Seated Deities ABV 614.3. Repaired. ....**CHOICE 4000.00**

1309. **BLACK FIGURE FRAGMENTS. Attic. 510-500 B.C.** Three black figure vase fragments from a kylix. Eye motif. Two Maenads dancing gracefully with garlands of grape vines. Women's drapery black with red bands. Seated figure to left. Measures 90 x 70 mm. Cf. CVA Lyon 1, Pl. 3 #7. Fragments ....**SUPERB 1000.00**

1310. **BLACK FIGURE KYLIX FRAGMENTS. Attic. 510-500 B.C.** Three fragments from the same cup depicting eye motif and women dancing with garland. Women's drapery black with red bands. Women move gracefully with arms on thighs or shoulders. On far left, a seated figure. Black figures with white limbs and faces. Fragment (3). 4 in. x 3 in. CVA Lyon, 1, p. 23 #7. ....**SUPERB 900.00**

1311. **BLACK FIGURE LEKYTHOS. Attic. Very late 6th-Early 5th Century B.C.** Large vessel of orange clay. Black lip, top reserved. On shoulder, pattern of palmettes. Scene of three women seated playing lyres for a male figure reclining on a couch, two to his left, one to his right. The women's faces and hands, as well as some decoration, are white; drapery is indicated by incised lines. Two rows of black dots above the scene, black band below. Lower portion of foot reserved. Handle black, underside reserved. Height 21 cm. Cf. CVA Fitzwilliam, Pl. XXII #22 for shape and palmettes; Cf. CVA Fogg, Pl. XII #3 for similar subject; Cf. CVA Lyon, Pl. 17 #9, 10 for subject. Surface chipping; upper portion of rightmost woman in scene missing. Hole below handle. Handle reglued. Salt encrustation. Otherwise intact. ....**CHOICE 2000.00**

1312. **BLACK FIGURE LEKYTHOS. Attic. 500-450 B.C** Black lip, unpainted top, painted within. Plain neck with dashes on shoulder. Triple palmette and lotus design on front, back plain. One, then two reserved lines below. Simple, painted foot, slightly depressed in center. 12.1 cm. Restoration at neck. Cf. CVA (29), Pl. 23.9. Cf. Christie's, The Castle Ashby Vases, 73ii. ....**CHOICE 350.00**

1313. **LEKYTHOS. Attic. 500-490 B.C.** Combat of two hoplite warriors facing and brandishing spears, between which is red bearded man in white chiton holding staff. Youth at each end, standing watching. This scene has been interpreted as the combat of Ajax and Ulysses by Agamemnon. Cf. Munich Amphora #141 1. Cf. CVA Lyon, Pl. 13, 2. CVA Munich 1, p. 29. Reassembled. ....**CHOICE 3000.00**

1314. **PYLEX/OINOCHOE. Magna Graecia. 5th Century B.C.** Round-mouthed oinochoe with globular body and ring base. Narrow aperture at offset neck-ring. Neck and handle have been removed to form a pyxis by the addition of a cover. Black glaze over buff ware, reserved on place near base where evidence remains of potter's fingers during the dipping process. With cover consisting of disc, hollow plug with prong below, knob within concentric circle above. Dark non-metallic black glaze over buffware, underside reserved. Base: height 6.3 cm, diameter 8 cm. Cover height and diameter 3 cm. Cf. RISD 15. Covers such as this are rare. ....**CHOICE 375.00**

1315. **PYXIS LID. Attic. 5th Century B.C.** Top decorated with seven compartmentalized ananthus leaves which surround the center where a handle is missing. Two scenes of a woman receiving gifts depicted at sides. Main female figure is delineated by a border of curlicue scroll pattern. In one scene, she receives pearls and gifts from two Eroi. Leading up to next scene is a procession of seven maids passing on boxes and draperies. 6.5 cm high, 17.5 cm dia. Cf. Malloy, Winter 1978, #23. ....**CHOICE 6000.00**

1316. **WHITE GROUND LEKYTHOS. Attic. 2nd Quarter of the 5th Century B.C.** The Tymbos Painter. On shoulder, lotus chain, above, figure scene is simple meander with key running right. Scene depicts woman presenting large designed dish before a grave relief. 22.5 cm high. A basic feature of the Tymbos workshop of lekythoi is the figure on the side of the tomb. Reconstructed. Cf. Kurtz, *Athenian White Lekythoi*, Pl. 21, 4, Pl. 22, 1. ....**AVERAGE 800.00**

1317. **BLACK FIGURE FRAGMENT. Attic. c. 480 B.C.** Black figure vase fragment of rim of kylix. Two horses to right with grape vine above. Measures 46 x 33 mm. Cf. CVA Lyon Pl. 23.6, Groupe du pientre de Haimon............**SUPERB 150.00**

1318. **RED FIGURE FRAGMENT. Attic. 460-450 B.C.** Red figure vase fragment of central portion of kylix. In tondo a figure of a nude youth kneeling on left knee, back showing. Head turned back to left. Right arm holding rod, cloak over extended left arm. Measures 137 x 118 mm. Two ancient repair holes. ....**CHOICE 575.00**

1319. **BLACK GLAZED LEKANIS. Attic. 460 B.C.** Black-glazed one-handled lekanis with lid. Heavy foot ring; heavy skyphos handle; disk top with depressed center. White concentric bands on shoulder of lid. Height 13 cm, width 17 cm. Cf. *Athenian Agora* 1251. Intact. ....**CHOICE 450.00**

1320. **BLACK GLAZED LEKANIS. Attic. Late 5th Century B.C.** Black-glazed lekanis with ribbon handle. Lidless. Flat bowl with horizontal handles. Small pedestal base. Bowl has two inner and two outer circle bands. Width (incl. handles) 20.5 cm. Height 4.6 cm. Cf. *Athenian Agora* 1216. Intact. Thin flaking to glaze. ....**CHOICE 400.00**

1321. **OINOCHOE. Corinth. c. 425 B.C.** Red ware with black glaze. Flat base, rounded handle and lip. Full, rounded body. 6.2 cm high, 2.4 cm dia. rim, 4 cm dia. with handle. Cf. Ede, Charles, *Corinthian and East Greek Pottery*, 111, #13 for shape. ....**CHOICE 350.00**

1322. **RED FIGURE LEKYTHOS. Attic. 400 B.C.** Squat red-figure lekythos showing a seated boy, nude but for drapery over shoulder. He holds sprigs to left and right. Tongue-and-dot pattern below. Height 6.7 cm. Cf. CVA Deutschland Tf. 29:10. Some repair. ....**CHOICE 600.00**

1323. **BELL KRATER. Attic Red Figure. 4th Century B.C.** Laurel band below rim, alternating checkerboard and triple meander band below scenes, panel A seated maiden in white chiton playing tambourine. Ithyphallic satyr standing each side, holding thyrsos, Maenad in chiton dancing behind playing tambourine, panel B, three draped youths standing. Cf. Christie's, London, June 1988. ....**CHOICE 5000.00**

1324. **GREY-BLACK GLAZED PLATE. South Italy. 4th Century B.C.** Grey-black glazed plate with pedestal foot. Spiral construction evident in base. Diameter 24 cm. Nice size. Intact. Wear to edges. Stress crack in center. ....**CHOICE 250.00**

1325. **OINOCHOE. Campania. 4th Century B.C.** Trefoil mouth and drop handle. Obverse shows scene of warrior standing before seated woman. He wears short tunic, sandals, fillet in short hair, holding in right hand shield and spear. In left holding mirror. Woman draped from head to foot. Eyes, wide open, express surprise. Scene bordered top and bottom by a row of parallel rectangles. Reverse, decorated with palmettes. 31.5 cm high, 14 cm wide. Cf. Trendall, *Red Figure Vases of Lucania, Campania and Sicily*, Vol. II, Pl. 162, 1 and 4. Paint worn in small area on reverse exposing red pottery. Repaired. ....**CHOICE 4000.00**

1326. **SMALL JUG. South Italy. 4th Century B.C.** One-handled jug, full body and flaring neck. Handle attached from mid neck to midbody. Black glaze over body, reserved ring base. Only upper portion of rim with black glaze. 9.3 cm high, 5.3 cm dia. Cf. Merzagora, *I Vasia Vernice Nera Della Collezione*, H.A. di Milano, #55, Pl. LIV....**SUPERB 350.00**

1327. **KRATER FRAGMENT. Apulian. 4th Century B.C.** Fragment shows two men in conversation. Laurel pattern above. Measures 9.9 cm x 9.2 cm. Mounted. ....**CHOICE 275.00**

1328. **KRATER FRAGMENT. Apulian. 4th Century B.C.** Krater fragment with heads of two men in conversation. Laurel pattern above. 9 cm high. ....**CHOICE 225.00**

1329. **BLACK GLAZE GLOBULAR OINOCHOE. South Italy. 4th Century B.C.** Oinochoe with wheel-made spherical body, no neck, sharply everted rim, and flat base. Single strap handle from midpoint to rim, forming loop above rim. Dull black paint over exterior and inside rim, except base and low, irregular band thereto. Height 6.5 cm to rim, 8.5 cm to handle. Cf. Farwell Coll. XXI5, Z5. .....**CHOICE 125.00**

1330. **BLACK GLAZE KANTHAROS. South Italy. c. 4th Century B.C.** Wheel-made sessile kantharos with rounded convex shoulder above base. Wide strap handles from shoulder to rim. At midpoint stamped band of tongue and ray motif divides upper and lower bands of palmettes, also stamped. Base bears two incised circles around rim, and three concentric circles underneath. Pink-orange clay with glossy black glaze to entire surface. 9.8 cm high. Restored and reconstructed. Cf. Farwell Coll. XIII:7-8. Cf. Attic Type CVA Fitzwilliam XLI, 40. ....**CHOICE 225.00**

1331. **KYLIX. South Italy. c. 4th Century B.C.** Wheel-made kylix with stemmed foot, and rim everted above slight shoulder. Pink-beige clay with red paint on handles, interior, foot, shoulder line, and lower portion of body. 13.1 cm diam., 18.5 cm with handles. For similar ware Cf. Farwell, fig. 64-69. Very small chip to rim. ....**SUPERB 150.00**

1332. **BLACKWARE BOWL. South Italy. 4th Century B.C.** Bowl with curved body offset below midpoint from concave ring base. Inverted rim thinning near lip. Faint rouletted stroke design around interior, surrounding five spiral-in-square stamp impressions in cruciform. Metallic black glaze applied throughout, except under base, over red-beige core. Slight depression at edge of base as made. 11.6 cm diam. CVA Limogeslvannes (France 24)-15.2. Merzagora, *Milano* 75.var. ....**SUPERB 150.00**

1333. **BLACKWARE BOWL. South Italy. 4th-3rd Century B.C.** Small blackware bowl with fluted body offset at midpoint from concave ring base. Eight-petal rosette stamp impression in center of bowl. Black glaze applied throughout except for underside within base and edge of base. Red-beige core. Diam. 7.5 cm. Merzagora, *Milano* 72..**CHOICE 75.00**

1334. **HANDLELESS KYLIX. Magna Graecia. 4th-3rd Century B.C.** Small bowl with rounded sides and interior, curved rim thickening into an exterior ridge. Cylindrical pedestal gradually widening to splayed foot with wide resting area and recessed center. Black glaze over orange-buff ware. Diameter 8.3 cm. *ROM-*; Merzagora, *Milano -*; RISD -. ....**CHOICE 150.00**

1335. **OINOCHOE. South Italy. 4th-3rd Century B.C.** Buff oinochoe with ovoid body with cylindrical neck and trefoil mount. Strap handle. Height 10.5 cm.........**SUPERB 175.00**

1336. **RED FIGURE HYDRIA. Apulia. First Half of the 4th Century B.C.** Trenddall's "Plain style." Woman wearing a peplos, seated on draped mantle with no visible supporting element. She holds a round object divided into quarters, possibly a mirror. Her hair is bound at the nape of her neck. She looks right toward another woman who stands facing, wearing peplos and draped mantle, holding a long-handled fan in her right hand. Meander pattern below, tongue pattern banding neck, vertical line on rim. Height 26.5 cm, width at handles 24 cm. Nice rendering of drapery with long fold lines and short fold ellipses. Handle is mended, one surface chip, some peeling of paint. ....**SUPERB 3500.00**

1337. **OINOCHOE WITH TREFOIL MOUTH. South Italy. 4th Century B.C.** Reddish ware jug with flat footed base, trefoil mouth and strap handle. 11.8 cm high, 6.5 cm diameter rim, 8 cm diameter rim with handle. Heavy salt encrustation. Cf. American School of Classical Studies, *The Athenian Agora*, Pl. 74, #1626 for shape. ..**CHOICE 135.00**

1338. **KYLIX. South Italy. 4th Century B.C.** Pink-beige clay. Wheel-made ware, with a stemmed foot. Everted rim at shoulders. Handles of circular cross section. Brownish, with black glass on outside and inside. 11.6 cm diameter, height 5.8 cm. Cf. Farwell Collection, fig. 64-69. Nice color. ....**CHOICE-SUPERB 500.00**

1339. **SMALL JUG. South Italy. 4th Century B.C.** One-handled jug, full body and flaring neck. Handle attached from mid neck to midbody. Black glaze over body, reserved ring base. Only upper portion of rim with black glaze. 9.3 cm high, 5.3 cm diam. Cf. Merzagora, *I Vasia Vernice Nera Della Collezione*, H.A. di Milano, #55, Pl. LIV.....**SUPERB 350.00**

1340. **SMALL SALT CELLAR. South Italy. 4th Century B.C.** Orange-buff clay with glossy black glaze, almost metallic. Convex upper wall, tapering incurved lip, vertical base with slight carination. Rounded interior. 4.5 cm high, 5.9 cm diam. Cf. Hayes, *ROM, Greek and Italian Black Gloss Wares and Related Wares*, #138. ....**SUPERB 250.00**

1341. **SALT CELLAR. Magna Graecia. 4th Century B.C.** Orange-buff clay miniature salt cellar with black glaze (probably with lead base). Convex upper wall, vertical raised base. Diam. 4.6 cm, height 2.5 cm. Cf. Hayes, *ROM, Greek and Italian Black Gloss and Related Wares*, #138. Some wear to black glaze, otherwise intact. ....**CHOICE 100.00**

1342. **VASE. Attic. 4th Century B.C.** Amphora. black body glaze with black row of grape leaves at neck. Two handles with three straps. Height 21 cm. Some glaze flaking at shoulder. Reconstructed. Lovely shape. ....**CHOICE 800.00**

1343. **JUGLET. South Italy. Late 4th Century B.C.** Orange clay with black glaze juglet. Low-bellied form curving up in "S" curve to form a flaring rim. Flat handle connected to rim and shoulder. Very slight concave base. 7.7 cm high, 8.7 cm diam. Cf. Hayes, *ROM*, #94 ....**CHOICE 350.00**

1344. **OINOCHOE. Magna Graecia. 4th-3rd Century B.C.** Buff oinochoe with orange glaze to rim handle. Three rows on body and wavy line between two straight on neck. Pinched trefoil mouth. Pedestal base. Height 11.5 cm. A gem. ....**SUPERB 250.00**

1345. **MINIATURE SKYPHOS. Sicily. 4th-3rd Century B.C.** Porous orange clay. Blunt foot with strap handles attached at rim. 3.5 cm high, 4.7 diam., 7.5 cm diam. with handles. Cf. American School of Classical Studies, *The Athenian Agora-*. Cf. Hayes, *ROM*. ....**CHOICE 75.00**

1346. **OINOCHOE. South Italy. 4th-3rd Century B.C.** Buff oinochoe with ovoid body, wide cylindrical neck and wide mouth. Slightly flared rim pinched in slightly at joint with handle. Slight chip in the base, but otherwise intact. ....**CHOICE 150.00**

1347. **PHANTOM WARE. Etruscan. Mid 4th-3rd Century B.C.** Blackware oinochoe with futive cream design of dancing satyr with patera and tambourine with tail, palmette design, at shoulder spray of lines. Cf. Hayes, *ROM*, pp. 126-8, #207. Intact. ....**CHOICE 2200.00**

1348. **BLACKWARE SKYPHOS. South Italy. Late 4th-Early 3rd Century B.C.** Wheel-turned skyphos with two horizontal loop handles. Ring base. Some iridescence to glaze. Height 8 cm, diam. 11 cm, width including handles 17 cm. Cf. Merzagora, *Milano* 15; Cf. Lullies, *Vergddete Terrakotta-Apliken aus Tarent*, Taf. 22:9. Chip to rim, restoration. ....**CHOICE 225.00**

1349. **BLACKWARE SKYPHOS. South Italy. Late 4th-Early 3rd Century B.C.** Wheel-turned skyphos with two horizontal loop handles, body cylindrical at handle area, receding concave to ring base. Brown-black glaze applied throughout except under foot. Pale red-tan core. This receding body form evolved from earlier rounded types of the 5th century. Merzagora, *Milano* 15. Cf. Lullies, *Vergddete Terrakotta-Apliken aus Tarent*. Taf. 22, 9. Some restoration, one handle broken and partially restored. ....**CHOICE 200.00**

1350. **LUCANIAN RED FIGURE FRAGMENT. South Italy c. 390-370 B.C.** Red figure vase fragment of bell krater. Profile of person looking up. Measures 65 x 61 mm. ....**CHOICE 150.00**

1351. **RED FIGURE SHARD. South Italy. c. 380-370 B.C.** Part of the neck of a large krater. Scene includes head and shoulders of a girl wearing a chiton, her hair falling to her shoulders. Semicircle, possibly the moon, above to the right. Floral decoration above and below rim. Style of Ilinpersis Group. Measures 15 x 9.3 cm. ....**CHOICE 250.00**

1352. **BLACK GLAZED OINOCHOE. Xenon Group. 375-350 B.C.** Decorated in red-pink with laurel leaves band as a wreath on shoulder. The Xenon ware group from central Magna Graecia was first named for the Kantharos in Frankfurt with the inscription "Xenon." It is neither Greek nor native ware but unique in itself. Scarce. Intact. Some paint wear. *Cf.* Beazley, *Etruscan Vase Paintings*, 33-6, p.220. Hayes, *ROM*, #194. Cf. Mayo, *Vases from Magna Graecia*, #158. ....**SUPERB 400.00**

1353. **RED FIGURE FRAGMENT. South Italy. Apulian. 350-320 B.C.** Red figure vase fragment of hydria with Eros facing right, hair rolled up, wings behind with white decorations. With reversed palmette. Measures 146 x 60 mm. ....**CHOICE 225.00**

1354. **KNOB-HANDLED PATERA. 2nd Half of 4th Century B.C.** Circle of Ganymede Painter. A white wreath of ivy leaves with tendrils around a wave pattern-around tondo scene. The tondo is large bust of Nike facing three-quarters left decorated with thick white paint and delineated with red-ochre with hair bound in a kekryphalos. Open wing to each side. She rises from a flower. Knobs on rim decorated as mushroom caps. Restored and reconstructed. Cf. Mayo, *Vases from Magna Graecia*, #52 for outer interior design. Cf. Oberleitner, Kunsthistorishces Museum, Wien, #171 ....**CHOICE 1600.00**

1355. **BLACK GLAZE BOWL. Campanian. 350-300 B.C.** Small black-glaze bowl "salt cellar" with pedestal base. Diameter 10.5 cm. Part of glaze turning to brown-red glaze. Some salt deposits. Intact ....**SUPERB 185.00**

1356. **RED FIGURE PROCHOUS. Apulian. South Italy. c. 340-330 B.C.** Red figure ware with graceful handle, spout and relief heads on neck. Female seated on rocks left, holding mirror and wreath. Fine drapery and floral design on back. Wheel-made base. 18.4 cm. ....**SUPERB 3000.00**

1357. **GNATHIA SKYPHOS. Apulian. South Italy. c. 340-320 B.C.** Black ware skyphos with horizontal bands, dots and pendants in red, white and cream color. 9.5 cm high, 7.2 cm dia. mouth, 13.2 cm dia. with handles, 3.2 cm dia. base. ....**CHOICE 400.00**

1358. **FRAGMENT. Apulian. 330-300 B.C.** Red figure fragment portraying Castor drawing two horses of quadriga right. His head is turned right, advancing left. Lion-headed spout. Plastic in center. Cf. Mayo, *Vases from Magna Grecia*, #79 for similar design and other plastic spout. This scene is part of the story of the rape of the Levcippidae by Castor and Polydeucer, the twin sons of Zeus. Very rare. ....**CHOICE 500.00**

1359. **GNATHIA WARE OINOCHOE. Magna Graecia. c. 300 B.C.** High-bellied ovoid body with wide cylindrical neck and broad everted mouth. Double handle rising from shoulder to lip at which it separates at opposite right angles. Slightly recessed base offset by low groove. Black glaze over entire exterior, buff ware. Eight simple flower designs around neck, rays on body below neck, below which eight curving leaf-bands. Designs white with "gold" detail. Height 15.5 cm. CVA Fogg.-. CVA BM I-. *ROM* 261 for leaf-bands; *ROM* p. 139. The "gold," actually yellow-orange in appearance, is actually a diluted black glaze applied over white. It is particularly characteristic of Gnathia ware. Restoration at lip. ....**SUPERB 750.00**

1360. **DISH. South Italy. c. 300 B.C. or later.** Light brown clay washed in a black glaze. Sloping floor with vertical lip and sloping foot. Five small ovoid stamps at center. Ring base reserved. 16.8 cm dia. 5.1 cm high. Cf. Hayes, *ROM* #1, 19 for stamps. Cf. Falwell, fig. 77 of stamps...**CHOICE 300.00**

1361. **MASTOID BOWL. South Italy. 3rd Century B.C.** Black glaze mastoid bowl. Deep black glaze over entire body. Diameter 16 cm, height 8 cm. Reglued. Otherwise superb. ....**SUPERB 350.00**

1362. **BLACKWARE JUG. South Italy. Campanian. 3rd Century B.C.** Blackware jug, stemmed. Height 16.5 cm. Restored rim. ....**CHOICE 250.00**

1363. **BLACKWARE OINOCHOE. South Italy. 3rd–2nd Century B.C.** Ovoid wheel-turned body, cylindrical neck with pinched trefoil mouth, strap handle from mouth to shoulder, slightly recessed disc base. Grey beige clay with black paint over exterior, except below midpoint, and within lip. 12.5 cm. Sicilian manufacture. Contemp. RISD-81, BK4 Oinochoe shape 2. Paint worn and tiny chip to base. ....**CHOICE 150.00**

1364. **SKYPHOS. South Italy. Campania. 3rd-2nd Century B.C.** Black ware with handles which are blunt and joined to the rim. Angular foot. Mottled grey glaze covering body, ring base reserved. 8.3 cm high, 10.5 cm diam. Cf. Rhode Island School of Design, Classical Vases, #80, Pl.122. ....**CHOICE 225.00**

1365. **BOWL. Corinthian. 1st Century A.D.** Buff pottery bowl with black matte slip. Groove inside rim, two grooves on inside base. Base is indented circle. Diam. 15 cm, height 5.5 cm. *ROM* -; Cf. *Athenian Agora* G76 for date. This vessel was intended to replicate the Attic blackware and was found with other Corinthian painted vessels. It would have been in use during the time when St. Paul was in Corinth. Intact. ....**CHOICE 300.00**

TERRACOTTA

1366. **HEAD. Neolithic. 6th-4th Millennium.** Thessaly, Greece. Terracotta head with squared, dome-like top, coffee bean eye, and beak-like nose. Left side smooth, no features. 5.9 cm high, 3.3 cm wide. Cf. Barrelet, Pl. IV #39. Very rare. ....**CHOICE 1500.00**

1367. **TERRACOTTA HEAD. Late Bronze Age. 1650-1050 B.C.** Grey terracotta head of a female with hair tufts at side. Beak-like nose, button eyes with ring around. Measures 3.6 x 3.8 cm. Mounted. Cf. Morris, *Cyprus*, fig. 269-72 var. without hair tufts. Similar to the pubic triangle figures. ....**CHOICE 150.00**

1368. **TERRACOTTA HORSE. Late Bronze Age. 1500-1000 B.C.** Red-buff terracotta horse with incised mane. Eye defined as circle containing X. Four pellets on back for rider to sit. Measures 19 cm x 12.5 cm. (7½" x 5"). Cf. Morris, *The Art of Ancient Cyprus*, fig. 330 var. Nice size. Very rare. ....**CHOICE 650.00**

1369. **FIGURE OF A MAN. Cypriot. 750-600 B.C.** Terracotta figure of a man wearing a pointed cap. Prominent nose. Hands held out before. No bottom: probably was a horseman; hands would have been grasping reins or mane. The clay is very coarse with small holes. Remains of white slip can be seen. Solid. Height 9.6 cm. Cf. Desmond Morris, *The Art of Ancient Cyprus*, Pl. 263 and figs. 335, 338. Broken below hips. Although crude, this figure is charming. Rare. ....**CHOICE 600.00**

1370. **FIGURE. Rhodes. 7th Century B.C.** Terracotta figure of ram. Simple legs and body with slight modeling of mane. Long tail and chin appendage. Snout and horns missing. Orange-white slip over orange clay with grey-brown core. Some restoration. *BM*. ....**AVERAGE 350.00**

1371. **TERRACOTTA WOMAN. Rhodes. 7th-6th Century B.C.** Woman seated, wearing tall headdress. Hole at base, primitive in style. 8.6 cm x 4.8 cm. Cf. Malloy Catalogue, Fall 1973 #47b. During this time Rhodes was one of the center cities for this style terracotta. Other cities included Corinth, Argos and Samos. Crude. ....**CHOICE 250.00**

1372. **CYPRIOT SNOWMAN. Cyprus. 7th-6th Century B.C.** Terracotta torso of male. Flat body with perpendicular flat head, of simple primitive form. Orange-brown ware. 4.3 cm. Chin, arms and legs absent. Nicholson 45. Pottier 11:31-32. Sometimes called "snowmen," these figures were votive in nature. Rare. ....**CHOICE 1200.00**

1373. **BUST OF A WOMAN. Early 6th Century B.C.** Grey terracotta bust with pale orange surface and some mica. Has an unusually long neck with long oval face. Worn archaic features. Curls surrounding forehead. Separate decorations (added after molding) of earrings and necklace with four pendants. Missing below breast. Front molded, back crude and unfinished. Height 8.5 cm. Probably came from Tegea, where nearly all work showed added decoration. Cf. for type Higgins, *Terracottas in the British Museum*, fig. 989-999. Very unusual. Rare piece. ....**CHOICE 300.00**

1374. **FIGURE OF A WOMAN. Corinthian. 530-500 B.C.** Cream terracotta statuette of a standing woman. Solid with molded front and flat back. Set on a rectangular base. Left arm straight down at side, right folded across body. Wears polos, chiton, and himation with left shoulder and breast bare. Himation decorated with red slip. Hair curled across forehead, falls to shoulders. Height 14 cm. Right foot and part of base chipped off; otherwise intact. Cf. Higgins #903. ....**CHOICE 1000.00**

1375. **SPHINX PLAQUE FRAGMENT. Corinth. 525-500 B.C.** Orange terracotta fragment of the forepart of a sphinx. Facial features archaic in style. Wearing a polos with hair in curls surrounding her forehead and on either side to the shoulder. Decorated wing curls over her back to touch her ear. Measures 8.5 x 5.7 cm. Cf. von Bothmer, *Ancient Art from N.Y.* #177; Robinson, *Olynthus* 333-4. Back of body broken off. Lovely style. ....**CHOICE 250.00**

1376. **FEMALE FIGURE. Rhodes. Late 6th Century B.C.** 16 cm high, 5 cm wide. Orange terracotta. Figure standing on base, wearing headband with two strands of hair falling over her shoulders. She wears a chiton and himation. Right hand holding a dove to her breast. Cf. British Museum, *Terracottas in the British Museum* Vol. 1, #58, Pl. 12, p. 48. ....**CHOICE 500.00**

1377. **FIGURE OF SEATED WOMAN. Rhodes. Late 6th Century B.C.** Sits on throne with foot stool, hands on knees. Wears high polos, covered by symmetrical himation and chiton. Vent hole in base. Tan over orange ware. Shallow detail. *BM* 68-72. Intact. ....**CHOICE 500.00**

1378. **HEAD OF WOMAN. Rhodes. Late 6th Century B.C.** Terracotta head with flat smiling face and pointed nose. Symmetrical himation over head, locks visible above forehead. Spout with thick lip and flat top and sides emerge from top of head. Traces of red slip over orange ware. 4.5 cm. *BM* 57, 60. ....**CHOICE 250.00**

1379. **FEMALE PROTOME HEAD. Rhodes. Late 6th Century B.C.** Orange-buff terracotta female protome head, wearing a low headband and stephane. Measures 55 x 38 mm. Mounted. Cf. *BMC* 108 var. Full face but broken off at neck and part of left ear. Chip on nose and cut on cheek. Soft archaic style. ....**CHOICE 175.00**

1380. **HORSE. Boeotian. Late 6th-Early 5th Century B.C.** Light orange terracotta horse. solid and handmade. Crude modeling. Crosshatch decoration on shoulder and hindquarters of near side. Incised mouth and reins. Molding on head. Four clay dots on back, probably for placement of rider. Remains of black and red paint. Very elongated body. Roached mane. Length 21 cm, height 15 cm. Cf. Higgins, figs. 772, 787, 788, 804, 805. Tail and part of foreleg missing. ....**CHOICE 1500.00**

1381. **HEAD OF MAN. Rhodes. Late 6th-Early 4th Century B.C.** Terracotta head wearing beard as well as polos-like stephane with symmetrical himation over top. Orange-red ware. Traces of white slip. 5.4 cm. *BM* 79, 486-8. ....**CHOICE 300.00**

1382. **FIGURE OF STANDING WOMAN. Corinth. c. 500 B.C.** Cream terracotta statuette of a woman standing and holding a pomegranate in each hand. She wears a polos, chiton, and striated skirt. Hair in a curl across her forehead and long curls to each side. Flat back. Height 10.6 cm. Cf. Higgin, *Terracottas in the British Museum* #905. Features rather worn, but intact. ....**CHOICE 300.00**

1383. **DANCING DOLL. Corinth. Early 5th Century B.C.** Cream terracotta bust of dancing doll, polos pierced. Hair at brow and sides defined. Front molded, back blank. Measures 85 by 50 mm. Mounted. Cf. *BMC* 912 var. Only head and bust portion still present. ....**CHOICE 200.00**

1384. **FRAGMENT OF SPHINX PLAQUE. Corinthian. Early 5th Century B.C.** Orange terracotta fragment of a plaque of a sphinx. Female head wearing polos with curls on forehead. Wing with molded decoration curls around to touch ear. Archaic facial features, slightly worn. Cf. Helga Herdesingen, Pl. 44, #24. Broken off below waist. ....**CHOICE 500.00**

1385. **HEAD OF A WOMAN. Early 5th Century B.C.** Brown terracotta head with hair in curls, swept back, wearing polos with projecting rim around top. Back not molded. Height 3.2 cm. Mounted. Cf. *BM* 1089 bis for rim. .....**CHOICE 135.00**

1386. **TERRACOTTA FEMALE PROTOME. Rhodes. Early 5th Century B.C.** Red-brown. Late Archaic style. Hair parted in center and wearing stephane and himation draped over head. Face with finely modeled archaic features. Hole at top for suspension. 10.5 cm high, 7.5 cm wide. Chip at base. Cf. Higgins, 148. Cf. Sotheby, Fortuna Sale, 1970, #93. ....**CHOICE 350.00**

1387. **FIGURE OF WOMAN. Western Asia Minor. Early 5th Century B.C.** Right hand holding unidentified object to breast, left rests on left hip. Wearing polos, chiton and symmetrical himation going over polos. Pale orange ware with white slip. 6.6 cm. *BM* 324-29. Broken off below elbows. ....**CHOICE 300.00**

1388. **PROTOME HEAD OF WOMAN. Rhodes. Early 5th Century B.C.** Wears stephane pierced by vent hole. Hair pulled back. Eyes show strong Archaic inspirations. Stern, dignified features. Back unmolded. Traces of white slip over red-orange ware. 6.3 cm. Contemp. *BM* 111. Nice Archaic style. ....**CHOICE 350.00**

1389. **HEAD OF WOMAN. Early 5th Century B.C.** Hair in curls, swept back, wearing polos with projecting rim around top. Back not molded. Drab brown clay. *BM* 1089 bis (rim). ....**CHOICE 135.00**

1390. **TERRACOTTA HEAD. Early 5th Century B.C.** Buff terracotta head in a pointed cap. Red band at rim, geometric rendering of hair as oval in oval. Archaic eyes, traces of red on face. Height 7.5 cm. Cf. *BMC* 566 for male head style from Troy. Cesnola-. Very fine craftsmanship and a haunting archaic smile. Chip on nose. ....**CHOICE 600.00**

1391. **TERRACOTTA RAM. Corinth. Early 5th Century B.C.** Standing figure of a ram with grey clay and white and dark grey slip. Height 7 cm, length 12 cm. *Walters* B95; *BMC* 920. Intact. A charming figure. ....**CHOICE 300.00**

1392. **HEAD OF FEMALE. 5th Century B.C.** Hair swept back under symmetrical himation. Distinct nose. Black slip over orange ware. 4 cm. *BM* 115. Bold.............**CHOICE 200.00**

1393. **LEG OF DOLL. Corinthian. 5th Century B.C.** Pale orange terracotta leg of a dancing doll. Shows ankles and foot shaped like a clog with upturned toes. Four holes at top of leg for fastening to body. Some white slip remains. Height 7.8 cm. Cf. Higgins 909, 913, 924, 929, 930 for dolls with similar legs. ....**CHOICE 75.00**

1394. **FEMALE PROTOME. Sicily. 490-470 B.C.** Very pale orange clay with mica, surface cream. Large protone of woman's head broken from figure. Wears a short polos, her hair curls around forehead and drops to her shoulders. Facial features archaic (now faded). Nose chipped. Hollow with back left unmolded. Height 9.8 cm. Cf. R.A. Higgins, *Terracottas in the British Museum,* figs. 1105, 1099. Repaired at back. Nice size for display. .....**CHOICE 350.00**

1395. **STATUETTE OF ATHENA. Athens or Corinth. 480-460 B.C.** Pale orange statuette of Athena seated on a throne, wearing chiton and polos. Traces of white and red slip. Features between Archaic and Classical. Flat back, hole in base. Height 8.7 cm. Higgins, *Greek Terracotta Figures*, p. 17, Pl. 5. Typical worn state. ....**CHOICE 275.00**

1396. **DOVE. Attic. Mid 5th Century B.C.** Terracotta dove seated on stand. Mold-made orange clay. White slip intact. Bird perched on geometrically designed open flower on base. 12 cm high. Cf. *Terracottas in the BMC*, Pl. 692-3. Some restoration. ....**CHOICE 500.00**

1397. **GROTESQUE FIGURE. Corinth. Mid 5th Century B.C.** Creamy terracotta figure wearing a female mask with a band of rosettes. Higgins defines this type of figure as a satyr "wearing female or grotesque mask." Height 8.3 cm. Mounted. *BMC* 937 var. The head is a grotesque. Limbs are all broken off. ....**CHOICE 250.00**

1398. **FIGURE OF EROS. Mid 5th Century B.C.** Orange terracotta of nude squatting boy (Eros). Head facing, right knee up, left knee down. Back not molded; open bottom. White slip over all front. Height 9 cm. Cf. *BMC*. Probably manufactured in Gela. In the earlier part of the 5th century these squat boy (Eros) terracottas were exported from Rhodes to the Greek cities; by the mid-century local manufacture had begun. ....**CHOICE-SUPERB 350.00**

1399. **TERRACOTTA DOLL. Late 5th Century B.C.** 7.5 cm high. Orange-light cream colored clay with brown encrustation. Small naked female seated figure without feet and arms. Very archaic in style like the British Museum example #941, but seated like #703. Cf. British Museum, *Catalogue of the Terracottas*, Higgins. Vol. I. #702, 941. Rare type ....**AVERAGE-CHOICE 225.00**

1400. **FIGURE OF A WOMAN. Late 5th-Mid 4th Century B.C.** Seated figure of a woman, hands on lap. Wearing a chiton and himation; the end going over her left shoulder. Hair swept back, polos on head. Back plain. White slip over tan clay with pale orange core. Hair painted black. Height 15 cm. Mounted. *BM* 288-93, 1337, 1343. Ex. Magruder Collection. Ex: Smithsonian Institution, Loan #170449. Full figure intact ....**CHOICE 750.00**

1401. **FIGURE OF LION. Rhodes. End of 5th-4th Century B.C.** Orange/red terracotta fragment showing the hindquarters of a lion. Stands with legs bent, tail under left leg. Paws and claws visible. On thin base. Molded in two parts and crudely joined together. Height 7.4 cm. For style of tail and paws, Cf. Higgins, figs. 171-173. This fragment is later than the solid ones in Higgins. ....**CHOICE 65.00**

1402. **TERRACOTTA HEAD. Early 4th Century B.C.** 3.7 cm long. Small head with a crudely styled coiffure. Cf. Higgins, *British Museum, Catalogue of the Terracottas*, Vol. 1, #1 185. Coiffure style like #108 Kaufman, *Agyptische Terrakotten der Griechisch-Romischen und Koptischen Epoche*, Pl. # 108 ....**CHOICE 80.00**

1403. **COMIC HEAD. Attic. Early-Mid 4th Century B.C.** Terracotta head of comic actor in female role. Hair hanging on forehead and at sides; hair gathered at back. Orange and white slip, grey core. Height 42 mm. Mounted. Contemp. *BM* 724, 737. ....**CHOICE 500.00**

1404. **COMIC HEAD. Attic. Early-Mid 4th Century B.C.** Terracotta head of comic actress. Large nose (broken), bulging eyes, and bold chin. Thick locks hanging on forehead and at sides; hair gathered at back. Orange and white slip over grey core. 4.3 cm. Contemp. *BM* 724, 737. *Rare and desirable*....................**CHOICE 700.00**

1405. **FIGURE OF EROS. 4th Century B.C.** Terracotta figure of Eros, head towards viewer, body fully to viewer's right. Wearing himation held out by left hand. Shoulder position indicates right arm slightly forward. Hair rises to peak over forehead. Round face. Back plain. Brown ware. 4.2 cm. Broken below shoulder. Contemp. *BM* 878. Lovely. ....**CHOICE 250.00**

1406. **FEMALE HEAD. Southern Italian. 4th-3rd Century B.C.** Buff terracotta female head. Hair to side. Wearing tall stephane. Height 3.2 cm. Mounted on walnut base. This piece is part of a hoard which was found in the vicinity of Sybans in southern Italy in 1969; part of a study by B. Kingsley in a Getty Museum publication. Sybans Hoard #30. Nose slightly chipped. ....**CHOICE-SUPERB 135.00**

1407. **FEMALE HEAD. Southern Italian. 4th-3rd Century B.C.** Buff terracotta female head. Hair pulled back and garlanded. From Sybans Hoard (see above). Height 3.5 cm. Mounted on walnut base. Sybans Hoard #228..............**CHOICE 125.00**

1408. **FEMALE HEAD. Southern Italian. 4th-3rd Century B.C.** Buff terracotta female head. Hair in high coiffure. From the Sybans Hoard (see above). Height 3.8 cm. Mounted on a walnut base. Sybans Hoard #273. Slight trace of white slip. ....**CHOICE 135.00**

1409. **FEMALE HEAD. Southern Italian. 4th-3rd Century B.C.** Buff terracotta female head. One-sided. Hair to sides with band above and wreath of ivy. From the Sybans Hoard (see above). Height 3.3 cm. Mounted on a walnut base. Sybans Hoard #334. Slight trace of white slip. ....**SUPERB 150.00**

1410. **HEAD OF A WOMAN. Southern Italian. 4th-3rd Century B.C.** Grey terracotta female head with long curling hair and headdress. Some orange and white slip showing. Height 6.1 cm. Fine Hellenistic style. ....**CHOICE 200.00**

1411. **FEMALE HEAD. 4th-3rd Century B.C.** Orange terracotta head. Hair curled at sides, band above. Fine eye detail. Height 37 mm. *BMC* -; Bell -; Loeb -. Lovely Classical look. ....**CHOICE 165.00**

1412. **HEAD OF WOMAN. Mid 4th Century B.C.** Hair in tight curls in neat rows, pulled together at back. Wearing large wreath. Top of an ornamental phiale at left. Expression of sadness in eyes. Grey slip over orange ware. *BM* 729 bis. ....**CHOICE 150.00**

1413. **HELLENISTIC MALE HEAD. 350-250 B.C.** Buff-brown head of male with long hair, large wreath at top. Traces of red ochre to face. Modeled only in front. Appears to be an athlete. Height 50 mm. Lovely style. ....**CHOICE 225.00**

1414. **HELLENISTIC FEMALE HEAD. 350-250 B.C.** Buff head of female playing flute. Hair drawn back and tied at back. Drapery drawn up to sides of face. Head is turned to the side. Modeling all around. Height 45 mm. Face worn. ....**CHOICE 150.00**

1415. **HEAD OF KYBELE. 330-200 B.C**. Grey terracotta. Wearing polos; hair drawn back into bun at nape of neck. Hollow. Traces of white slip to face. Cf. Thompson, *Troy*, #35-37. Rather worn. ....**AVERAGE-CHOICE 90.00**

1416. **FIGURE OF A FEMALE COMIC ACTOR. Late 4th Century B.C.** Cap on head, simple features and wearing mask. Putting something in waist-high basket. Height 8.9 cm. Cf. Morgantina Studies, *The Terracottas I*, pl. 117, fig. 742, p. 214. Bottom chipped off. Rather worn....**CHOICE 125.00**

1417. **STATUETTE OF A BOY. c. 300 B.C.** Terracotta statuette of a young boy, looking downward, grasping his woolen cloak to his chest with his left hand; right hand down to side. Cloak ends below knees. Wears boots and beret. Hollow figurine with rectangular vent hole in back. Height 18.7 cm. Cf. Thompson, *Terracotta Figurines of the Hellenistic Period - Troy*, pp. 53-55, Pl. LXI. The vent hole probably denotes a Tanagra type rather than Asia Minor or Seleucia. Relatively rare. ....**CHOICE 600.00**

1418. **HELLENISTIC PERSEPHONE HEAD. 300-200 B.C.** Light orange-buff head of Persephone. Hair is somewhat short. Protruding ears. Finely defined face. Modeled in the round. Height 28 mm. Cf. *Troy* 237; Cf. Bell fig. 14. ....**SUPERB 250.00**

1419. **HELLENISTIC FEMALE HEAD. 300-200 B.C.** Orange buff head of a veiled woman. White paint on part of face. Hair partly rolled back. Pellet earrings. Traces of red ochre for hair. Modeled in the round. Height 38 mm. Cf. Morgantino, *Terracottas*, Bell 627 and 630. Lovely style. ....**CHOICE 175.00**

1420. **HEAD OF A WOMAN. 3rd Century B.C.** Orange terracotta head of a woman with hair in curls surrounding her face, then gathered in a very large mass in back and coiled above. Wears earrings. Features crude and blurred. Joint of front and back molds visible. Height 4.7 cm. Mounted. *BM* -. Broken off below neck. ....**AVERAGE-CHOICE 150.00**

1421. **HEAD OF A WOMAN. 3rd Century B.C.** Grey terracotta female head with ornate curls pulled back and up. Traces of white slip remaining. Height 4.6 cm..........**CHOICE 125.00**

1422. **FEMALE HEAD. Possibly Rhodian manufacture. 3rd Century B.C.** Orange-red terracotta of woman's head. Hair in stephane. Modeled completely around. Height 3.3 cm. ....**CHOICE 125.00**

1423. **STANDING TERRACOTTA FIGURE. 3rd Century B.C.** Height 12.3 cm. Nude figure standing of Dionysos, with right knee slightly bent. He is wearing polos, holding thyrsus in right hand, holding vessel in left hand. Traces of white slip. Cf. British Museum. *Catalogue of the Terracottas*, # 1260. Thompson, *Troy: The Terracotta Figurines of the Hellenistic*. Van Ingen, *Figurines from Seleucia in the Tigris.-.* Sieveking, *Die Terrakotten der Sammlung Loeb-.* ....**AVERAGE-CHOICE 125.00**

1424. **SMALL SEATED FIGURE. 3rd Century B.C.** Height 4.5 cm. Orange with traces of brown color. Small figure of woman with right hand on breast, probably a mother goddess. Left hand on leg. Modeled in the round. Higgins, *British Museum: Catalogue of the Terracottas*, Vol. I.-. Thompson, *Troy: The Terracotta Figurines of the Hellenistic Period-.* Van Ingen, *Figurines from Seleucia on the Tigris-.* Sieveking, *Die Terrakotten der Sammlung Loeb.* Vol. I and II.- ....**CHOICE 150.00**

1425. **HEAD OF WOMAN. 3rd Century B.C.** Terracotta head with hair in rows in front, gathered in very large mass in back and tightly coiled at top. Himation over back. Wearing earrings and leaning slightly to left. Slight traces of red paint. Orange ware. 5 cm. *BM..* ....**AVERAGE-CHOICE 85.00**

1426. **HEAD OF SILENUS. 3rd Century B.C.** Terracotta head with large nose, thick eyebrows and lips. Bald head with slight wrinkle to forehead. Bearded, with neck folds. Cf. *Troy* 8-9. ....**CHOICE 150.00**

1427. **FEMALE HEAD. 3rd Century B.C.** Light brown terracotta head, traces of white slip. Hair at side. Wearing sphendone. Head turned slightly to the right. Height 48 mm. Cf. Bell, *Morgantina, Terracottas* 654, 662 var. Eyes not well defined, but charming. ....**CHOICE 85.00**

1428. **HEAD OF SILENUS. 3rd Century B.C.** Buff terracotta head of Silenus. Bearded, with two flute pipes to mouth. Goat ears. Height 40 mm. *BMC.* Cf. Loeb Pl. 26 var.; Cf. Bonhams 4/29/91, #55. Rare. ....**CHOICE 165.00**

1429. **FEMALE HEAD. Egypt. 3rd-2nd Century B.C.** Orange terracotta head with traces of light brown slip. Large, stern face with double chin. Straight hair parted in the middle. Height 5 cm. Mounted on plexiglass. Missing hair and forehead on her left side, hole at edge of hair on her right. ....**CHOICE 125.00**

1430. **FIGURE OF EROS. 3rd-2nd Century B.C.** Well-proportioned figure, wearing wreath, locks descending at side of head. Right arm crosses before body, slightly bent. Wing with smooth surface extends behind right shoulder. Red brown ware. Broken below arm. *BM* 970 (antecedent). ....**CHOICE 150.00**

1431. **HEAD OF HIERODOULOS. 3rd-2nd Century B.C.** Terracotta head of a female temple slave. Hair in curls around head, high stephane ornamented in relief with rays at top. Plain back. Grey-black ware. 8 cm. *Troy* 71 (descendant). ....**CHOICE 250.00**

1432. **HEAD OF DANCER. 3rd-2nd Century B.C.** Wearing himation over entire head including forehead and neck. Squinting eyes. Head tilted slightly right. Peach-brown ware. 4 cm. *Troy* 178. Pottier XVII: 273. ....**CHOICE 175.00**

1433. **HEAD OF YOUTH. 3rd-2nd Century B.C.** Terracotta head with plump face, recessed eyes and curly hair distinguished by "feather" coil from forehead to back of head. Hair curls incised after molding. Cf. Kaufmann fig. 4. Fine details. ....**CHOICE 150.00**

1434. **HEAD OF WOMAN. 3rd-2nd Century B.C.** Terracotta head with himation over entire head except face, with two rows of curls above. Knot at back, also within himation. Fine style. Red-brown ware. 2.9 cm. *Troy* 173, 180, 184-5. Lovely, delicate Tanagra style. ....**CHOICE 150.00**

1435. **HEAD OF WOMAN. 3rd-2nd Century B.C.** Terracotta head with hair in melon style, bound at back. Stern features. Cream slip over orange ware. 2.3 cm. Cf. *Troy* 245-50. ....**CHOICE 100.00**

1436. **FIGURE OF MAN. 3rd-2nd Century B.C.** Terracotta figure in dignified gesture with right arm extended. Himation over left shoulder and right arm. Tan-beige ware. 4.8 cm. *BM.* ....**AVERAGE 75.00**

1437. **BUST. 3rd-2nd Century B.C.** Terracotta bust wearing sphendone with curls protruding slightly from front, long neck. Rear portion of shoulders are present and, as evidenced by internal construction, are from independent mold. 4.5 cm. Lovely long neck. *BM..* .....**AVERAGE 75.00**

1438. **HEAD OF CHILD. 3rd-2nd Century B.C.** Terracotta head wearing wreath which was added after head was removed from mold. Plump face with low relief details. Brown ware. 3.1 cm. Cf. Van Ingen 336 (707). ....**CHOICE 125.00**

1439. **FIGURE OF EROS. 3rd-2nd Century B.C.** Well-proportioned figure, wearing wreath, locks descending at side of head. Right arm crosses before body, slightly bent. Wing with smooth surface extends behind right shoulder. Red-brown ware. Cf. *BM* 970 (antecedent). Broken below arm. ....**CHOICE 150.00**

1440. **TANAGRA FLUTIST. Boeotia. 330-200 B.C.** Exquisitely detailed flutist, wearing a wreath on his head, and with his hair parted in the middle. Overlapping draperies with some pink and white paint remaining. Repaired. Part of base missing. Charming. Height 11.3 cm. ....**CHOICE 285.00**

1441. **HEAD OF A WOMAN. 3rd Century B.C.** Grey terracotta female head with ornate curls pulled up and back. Traces of white slip remaining. Height 4.6 cm. ....**CHOICE 150.00**

1442. **TERRACOTTA HEAD. 3rd-2nd Century B.C.** 3.5 cm high. Young maiden head with hair braided in center from forehead to back of head. Slightly bent to left. Cf. Sieveking, *Die Terrakotten der Sammlung Loeb*, Pl. 7504. ....**SUPERB 135.00**

1443. **TERRACOTTA APPLIQUÉ. 3rd-2nd Century B.C.** 7 x 3.5 cm. Rosette design appliqué with eight petals. Cf. *Die Tarentinischen Terrakotten des 6 bis 4, Jahrhanderts v. Chr. im Antikenmuseum, Basel* #74. *Vergoblete Terrakotta-Appliken aus Tarent* #4, Pl. 22. ....**CHOICE 35.00**

1444. **HEAD OF A WOMAN. Hellenistic. 3rd-2nd Century B.C.** Wearing headdress, has a small face. Back and front both intact. 3 cm high. Cf. James Chesterman, *Classical Terracotta Figures*, fig. 91, pp. 73, 75. ....**CHOICE 60.00**

1445. **ROSETTE DESIGN APPLIQUÉ. 3rd-2nd Century B.C.** Orange clay. Design of eight petals. Measures 7 x 3.5 cm. Cf. *Die Tarantinischen Terrakotten in Antikemuseum Basel*, #74. ....**CHOICE 35.00**

1446. **SELEUCID-SYRIAN. Hellenistic Period. 3rd-2nd Century B.C.** Bone goddess figure with arms at breast wearing long chiton. Hair tied up in bow on top of head. Chip to left of lower drapery. Repaired at neck and knees. ....**CHOICE 150.00**

1447. **HERM. 3rd-1st Century B.C.** Terracotta portion of herm, from shoulders up, wearing long straight beard. Curls below modius-like hat. Brown ware with white slip. 5.4 cm. Cf. *Greek and Roman Sculpture (in the) Fitzwilliam Museum*, 48. Cf. *Troy* 300. ....**CHOICE 250.00**

1448. **TERRACOTTA HEAD. Ptolemaic Egypt. Late 3rd Century B.C.** 3.5 cm high. Head slightly bent to right, veiled. Hair tied in small knot. Long neck. Cf. *Troy: The Terracotta Figurines of the Hellenistic Period*, #177. ....**CHOICE 80.00**

1449. **HEAD OF WOMAN. Late 3rd Century B.C.** Terracotta head with himation drawn over melon-coiffure, tied in projecting knot at back. Head leaning slightly left. Pained expression. Grey-brown over drab orange ware. 4.7 cm. *Troy*, Suppl. monographs 3:186. ....**CHOICE 150.00**

1450. **FEMALE HEAD. c. 200 B.C.** Terracotta head of a woman, with cloak over head. Head bent slightly to left. Sweet expression, features only slightly worn. Nice style, probably Tanagra type. Height 4 cm. Mounted. Cf. Higgins, *Tanagra and the Figurines*, fig. 162. ....**CHOICE 125.00**

1451. **HEAD OF MUSICIAN. c. 200 B.C.** Terracotta grotesque head. Protruding eyebrows and nose bridge. Brown ware with traces of white slip. Some chipping to nose. Philipp 41 (musician). ....**CHOICE 150.00**

1452. **HEAD OF KYBELE. 2nd Century B.C.** Terracotta head wearing high ornamented stephane, hair pulled back. Head angled slightly left. Orange slip over pale red ware with light grey core. 5.5 cm. Cf. *Troy* 39 (type). A finer and earlier example than the Troy example cited. Large chip at chin. ....**CHOICE 160.00**

1453. **HEAD OF HIERODOULOS. 2nd Century B.C.** Terracotta head of a temple slave. Hair in melon style. Sharp nose and shallow eyes. Grey ware. 3.9 cm. *Troy* 66-69. ....**CHOICE 200.00**

1454. **FEMALE HEAD. 2nd Century B.C.** Terracotta head with hair in curls, drawn up in bushy mass at back. Wears sphendone. Grey-brown ware. 2.8 cm. Contemp. *Troy* 204-7. Lovely style. ....**CHOICE 125.00**

1455. **HEAD OF WOMAN. 2nd Century B.C.** Terracotta head wearing sakkos with some hair protruding from front. Wearing ring-shaped earrings. Fine features and slender neck. Peach-buff ware. 2.3 cm. *Troy* 191 (Sakkos). Attractive style. ....**CHOICE 125.00**

1456. **HEAD OF WOMAN. c. 2nd Century B.C.** Terracotta head with hair in loose waves pulled back. Rear unmolded. Traces of stephane. Head angled to right and slightly upwards. Slight flaws above right eyebrow. Fine mild orange ware. Contemp. *Troy* 223. Nice style but worn...**AVERAGE 65.00**

1457. **HEAD OF WOMAN. 2nd Century B.C.** Terracotta head, inclined to right, wearing hair in loose waves drawn back in knot at back (absent). Low stephane. Dull features. Long, solid neck with two rings. Vent hole at top. Grey ware with traces of brown slip. 5.6 cm. *Troy* 219. Chips on face. The two rings, a goiter condition, was a symbol of beauty in Roman times. .... **CHOICE 75.00**

1458. **TERRACOTTA HEAD. Early 2nd Century B.C.** 3.9 cm high. Female head with hair in melon style with flat waves tied in coil at back, with wreath. Holes at ears for earrings. This can be identified as a female because of the traces of pink paint over a white slip of paint. Cf. Thompson, *Troy: The Terracotta Figurines of the Hellenistic Period*, #254. ....**CHOICE 85.00**

1459. **FEMALE HEAD. 2nd Century B.C.** Cream terracotta woman's head. Draped, turned slightly to the right. Height 4.5 cm..**CHOICE 100.00**

1460. **CHILD'S HEAD. 2nd Century B.C.** Cream terracotta head of a child. Fully modeled. Height 2.5 cm. Van Ingen, *Figurines from Seleucia*, Pl. LXX, 5 var.....**CHOICE 100.00**

1461. **TERRACOTTA HEAD, VEILED. 2nd Century B.C.** 2.6 cm. Female head with hair arranged in two rows of curls, tied in knot in back, covered with himation. One ring around neck. Cf. *Troy: The Terracotta Figurines of the Hellenistic Period*, #185. ....**CHOICE 100.00**

1462. **HEAD OF DIONYSOS. 2nd Century B.C.** 8.7 cm high. Terracotta head of Dionysos with three rosettes on top of head. Low relief. Some features worn. Nice size. This piece is dated later than the high relief heads as the quality of workmanship started to decline. Cf. British Museum, *Catalogue of the Terracottas*, #1288. ....**CHOICE 125.00**

1463. **WOMAN'S HEAD. 2nd Century B.C.** Cream draped woman's head. Slightly turned to the right. Wearing a polos and earrings, hair at forehead and down sides of head. Height 4.5 cm. ....**CHOICE 100.00**

1464. **TERRACOTTA HEAD. 2nd Century B.C.** Light orange-beige terracotta head of a fertility goddess with four slender "pearl locks" on each side of her head. Diademed. Measures 3.2 x 3.3 cm. Cf. Van Buren 189. ....**CHOICE 125.00**

1465. **TERRACOTTA HEAD. Mid 2nd Century B.C.** 5.7 cm high. Female head leaning to left. Hair in curls, tied in back. Fillet around head. Narrow eyes with heavy eyelids. Long neck with two rings around. Traces of white slip and pink. Chip to cheek and left forehead. Similar to *Troy: The Terracotta Figurines of the Hellenistic Period*, #207. ....**CHOICE 75.00**

1466. **TERRACOTTA HEAD. Mid 2nd Century B.C.** 3.6 cm high. Pinkish buff clay. Female head with hair drawn together in two masses of curls at crown. Long neck. Traces of white slip. Chip to nose and mouth. Cf. *Troy: The Terracotta Figurines of the Hellenistic Period*, #204. ....**CHOICE 75.00**

1467. **FEMALE HEAD. Mid 2nd Century B.C.** Terracotta head leaning to left. Hair in curls, drawn up to bushy double mass at crown. Narrow eyes with heavy eyelids. Long neck. White slip over grey-brown ware. Pink paint to hair mass. *Troy:* Suppl. Monographs 3-204-5 (hair), 207 (face). Lovely style. ....**CHOICE 100.00**

1468. **HEAD OF HEMCIES. 2nd-1st Century B.C.** Terracotta head with thick parted beard, bare head. Brown ware with traces of lighter slip. Crude face depicting the expression of a tired Hellenistic fighter or wrestler. Cf. Pottier XIX:404. Good detail. ....**CHOICE 175.00**

1469. **HEAD OF KYBELE. c. 2nd-1st Century B.C.** Terracotta head wearing high plain stephane. Hair parted in middle from front to back, at which hair is tied in low knot. White slip traces over orange ware. *Troy* 39.....**AVERAGE 100.00**

1470. **DOG. 2nd-1st Century B.C.** Terracotta dog (toy breed). Fragment depicting entire head and much of back. Hair indicated by incision after molding. Pointed, canine snout. Protruding eyes as in toy breeds. Brown ware. 2.5 cm high at head, 4 cm long. Kaufmann, 118. Rare. ....**CHOICE 150.00**

1471. **HEAD OF WOMAN. 2nd-1st Century B.C.** Terracotta head with calm expression, tilted slightly to right. Wears wreath (partially absent), hair visible at front and sides and earrings. Red-beige wares. Possibly the head of Hierodoulos. 6 cm. Cf. *Troy* 274. Large chip to the headdress. ....**CHOICE 80.00**

1472. TERRACOTTA MEDALLION. 2nd-1st Century B.C. 4.5 cm diameter. Medallion with a female head, Gorgon with long locks of hair. Used as an appliqué. Cf. *Figurines from Seleucia on the Tigris*, Van Ingen, #890. ....**AVERAGE-CHOICE 60.00**

1473. FIGURE OF NIKE. Seleucid-Parthian. 2nd-1st Century B.C. Pink-buff terracotta figure of winged Nike wearing a chiton with each side tied at shoulders. Belt tied at waist. Wings open. Right hand to breast, left arm outstretched down, holding cornucopiae. Part of double mold. Height 11 cm, width 8.3 cm. Cf. Levi, *Napoli*, fig. 138 for expression. Cf. Van Ingen, *Figurines from Seleucia on the Tigris* #40 for detailed head and work from Level III, 143-43 B.C. Similar style and Nike figures are found in the Seleucid west. Left forepart of top wing missing from thighs down. Chip at bottom of right wing. Reconstructed from five pieces. A magnificent terracotta fragment ....**SUPERB 600.00**

1474. GORGON MEDALLION. 2nd-1st Century B.C. Medallion with female head, Gorgon with long locks of hair. Used as an appliqué. Diam. 4.5 cm. Cf. Van Ingen, *Figurines from Seleucia on the Tigris.* #890. ....**CHOICE 75.00**

1475. SELEUCID. Hellenistic. 2nd-1st Century B.C. Terracotta figure of man. Slightly seated man with old, wrinkled face and very slight emaciated body with ribs showing. 8.6 cm. high, 3.2 cm wide. Nice workmanship......**CHOICE 300.00**

1476. TERRACOTTA HEAD OF YOUTH. 1st Century B.C. 2.7 cm high. Head with braided locks of hair rolled to a crown, attached in knot at forehead. Delicate features. Worn to right side of face. Cf. *Athenian Agora*, Vol. 5, Robinson, Pl. 48g5. ....**CHOICE 80.00**

1477. HEAD OF WOMAN. c. 1st Century B.C.-1st Century A.D. Terracotta head with hair drawn back, wearing thick wreath with smooth surface aside from vertical incisions to indicate front panel. Wreath added after molding. Pale orange ware. 32 cm. Van Ingen 409 (898i). Crude workmanship. ....**CHOICE 75.00**

1478. LEDA AND SWAN PLAQUE. Hellenistic/Early Roman. 1st Century B.C.-1st A.D. Light cream terracotta plaque with grey slip. In relief a swan with wings outstretched stands in front of Leda with her arms outstretched, robes on bottom half of body. Two suspension holes, one on either side of Leda's head. Flat back. 7.5-8 cm in diam. Cf. According to mythology, Zeus, in the form of a swan, ravished Leda. The union resulted in Helen of Troy. For similar but earlier plaques see Higgins, *Terracottas in British Museum*, no. 613-623, and later terracotta appliqués, Reinherd Lullies, *Vergoldete Terracotta Appliken Aus Tarent*, Tafel 19, 1-5. Some chipping to head and neck of swan and face of Leda, Very rare indeed. ....**CHOICE 500.00**

1479. MALE HEAD. 1st-2nd Century A.D. Terracotta head of male, wearing crown of six points and circular bosses, angled slightly right. Van Ingen 486 (1191 a). Hellenistic style during the Roman Period. ....**CHOICE 150.00**

1480. MALE HEAD. 1st-2nd Century A.D. Terracotta head of male, possibly youth. Chubby proportion and indistinct eyes. Light brown ware. 3.3 cm. Cf. Van Ingen 1227, 1280, 1269. ....**CHOICE 125.00**

1481. GREY TERRACOTTA FEMALE HEAD. Mid 1st Century A.D. 7.2 cm long. Head slightly leaning left with hair in two rows of curls in Flavian style. Traces of white slip on left cheek. Two rings around neck. The rings probably represent goiter which in ancient times, symbolized beauty. Charming style. Chip at right of chin. Thompson, *Troy: The Terracotta Figurines of the Hellenistic Period*, #281. ....**CHOICE 135.00**

METAL

1482. BRONZE LION. 7th-6th Century B.C. Bronze figure of a standing lion with mane incised. Tail curled around back right leg. Mouth open. Measures 45 x 48 mm. Cf. Kimmig-Heu 110. This lion figure was probably used as an ornamental lid cover or furniture finial. Light green patina. ....**CHOICE 600.00**

1483. BRONZE BULL FIGURINE. c. 6th Century B.C. Bronze figurine of a bull with humps on neck and rear. Fairly geometric. Intact. 2.2 x 2 cm. Cf. Museum of Fine Arts, Boston, *Greek, Etruscan, and Roman Bronzes.* p. 19, fig. 18. A lovely charming piece. ....**SUPERB 500.00**

1484. BRONZE WARRIOR AMULET. 5th Century B.C. Stylized amulet in the shape of the figure of Mars. Length 29 mm. Comstock & Vermeule #206; Cf. Reine Margot 1990-91 #75f. Leg broken at knee. Rare. ....**CHOICE 65.00**

1485. LEAD SLING BULLET. Magna Graecia. 4th Century B.C. Lead sling bullet with pointed ends and bulbous body, flattened by image stamp. The obverse shows a horse galloping left with a star above, all in shallow incuse circle. The reverse shows a large figure of Athena standing facing left, holding a spear and shield. Length 3.5 cm., width 2.5 cm. Cf. SNG ANS, 631. in Apulia. A most unusual military antiquity with a numismatic connection. ....**CHOICE 250.00**

1486. BRONZE LEKYTHOS. Macedonian. Second half of 4th Century B.C. Squat bronze lekythos. Ovate body, pedestal base. Concentric lines at shoulder, narrow neck, rim flaring out and up. Shoulder handle with incised lines. Winged putti above, facing Medusa head below. Height 10 cm. N. Yalouris, *Treasures of Ancient Macedonia*, p. 14, #279. Used as a perfume container. Shoulder has many indentations. ....**CHOICE 750.00**

1487. **BRONZE FEMALE HEAD FROM A BALSAMARIUM.**
3rd Century B.C. A portion of a bronze balsamarium, in the
shape of a female head. She has a band in her hair and finely
delineated features. Only the face and part of the
balsamarium's rim are still present. Yellow-green patina.
Charming style and attractive patina. ....**CHOICE 675.00**

STONE

1488. **LIMESTONE HEAD OF FEMALE. 3rd Century B.C.**
Veiled and in high headdress. Short locks at forehead. Most
of the examples of heads found by Cesnola were found at the
Temple at Golgoi.   Mounted on Lucite. Cf. *Cesnola
Collection of Cypriot Antiquities in the Metropolitan
Museum of Art, NY*...................................**CHOICE 600.00**

1489. **ALABASTER JAR. 3rd-1st Century B.C.** Long alabaster
jar (alabastron) with flaring rim, two small lug handles.
Height 23 cm. Large size. Broken and repaired rim, and
restored. ....**AVERAGE-CHOICE 275.00**

GLASS

1490. **GLASS PASTE SCARAB. 6th-5th Century B.C.** Light
blue glass paste scarab. Pictures Herakles carrying Apollo's
tripod, star behind. 11 x 14 mm. Cf. Hague, 35 for subject
matter. This Eastern manufacture scarab is probably from
Phoenicia or Israel but obviously has a Greek motif. The
tripod is not apparent due to weathering. A rare example.
....**CHOICE 375.00**

1491. **GOLD HELIOS APPLIQUÉ. 5th-3rd Century B.C.**
Small rectangular gold appliqué plaque with a relief portrait
of Helios facing with curly hair around. Beaded circle
around. Hole in each corner for attachment. Measures 11 x 9
mm. Cf. *Catalogue of Jewelry in the British Museum* Pl. XL,
#2068; Cf. Rhodes coin types. Top left corner missing.
....**SUPERB 250.00**

LAMPS

1492. **OIL LAMP. 6th-5th Century B.C.** Wheel-made lamp
with central tube and inverted concave rim.   Large nozzle
with large filling hole. Orange buff ware with red slip. Ring
around shoulder and red detail around wick hole. 10.6 cm.
Cf. *BM* Q 642 (Sicily). ....**SUPERB 200.00**

1493. **GREEK OIL LAMP. 5th Century B.C.** Boeotian
manufacture. Buff clay lamp. Open bowl with nozzle. Length
7.5 cm. *BMC-, Schl.-, ROM-.* Chip at nozzle; handle off.
Rare. ....**AVERAGE 75.00**

1494. **OIL LAMP. 5th-4th Century B.C.** Wheel-made oil lamp
with rounded body, extremely wide filling hole and rounded
sides. Nozzle with rounded end and slightly rounded top.
Horizontal ribbon handle thicker at bottom. Flat base. Grey-
black glaze over orange ware. 10.2 cm. *BM* Q 622 (Eastern
Libya). Contemp. *Athenian Agora* 171-176. Some flaking to
glaze. ....**CHOICE 225.00**

1495. **GREEK OIL LAMP. c. 575-450 B.C.** Wheel-made lamp
with central tube and wide slightly concave shoulder. Large
wick hole in short beak nozzle. Black slip over shoulder and
nozzle. Orange buff ware. Flat bottom. Length 10 cm.
Contemp. Schl. 3-6; contemp. *Ath. Agora.* 76, 98; contemp.
BM Q 13-27 (Athens).   Some salt deposits.
....**CHOICE 150.00**

1496. **GREEK OIL LAMP. c. 525-450 B.C.** Wheel-made lamp
with central tube and wide flat shoulder. Large wick hole in
beak nozzle. Orange ware with dark red slip to nozzle, dark
brown to shoulder. Length 10 cm. *Ath. Agora* 76, 98; *BM* Q
13-27 (Athens) ....**SUPERB 200.00**

1497. **WHEEL-MADE LAMP Late 5th Century B.C.** Magna
Graecia.   Rounded wall and incurved rim, no base, blunt
nozzle with horizontal band handle at rear.   Glossy black
glaze over entirety, over beige clay. Some encrustation and
chipping of glaze. *ROM* IIj, Bailey, *BM* 662; Schloessinger
Coll. 7. ....**CHOICE 125.00**

1498. **GREEK OIL LAMP. 4th Century B.C.** Wheel-made lamp
with open bowl and squared nozzle. Flat shoulder and
straight sides. String-cut base. Orange-buff ware. Length 8.2
cm. Cf. *BM* 661, 671-72 (Sicily). ....**CHOICE 85.00**

1499. **GREEK OIL LAMP. 4th Century B.C.** Possibly Athenian
manufacture. Buff clay lamp with groove and raised nozzle.
Length 8.5 cm. Cf. *BMC* Q 77 for style. ....**CHOICE 100.00**

1500. **WHEEL-MADE OIL LAMP. 4th Century B.C.** Sicily.
Buff terracotta, open bowl, short nozzle, no central tube, with
no evidence of having been glazed. 6.6 cm. Votive deposits
of these lamps were found at the sanctuary of the Chthonic
dieties at Agrigentum in Sicily. Cf. *Arch. Classica*, IX 1957
(Pl. XXVI. 1). Cf. Bailey, *BM*-0661. ....**CHOICE 95.00**

1501. **LAMP. 4th Century B.C.** Sicily. Rounded sides, large
filling hole with two rims separated by groove. Pierced lug
on left side. Raised deeply concave base, long narrow
nozzle. Black glaze on tan-brown clay. 8.7 cm. Some glaze
flaking. Cf. Bailey *BM* 669 (form), 673 (ware). Found at
Gela. ....**CHOICE 100.00**

1502. **WHEEL-MADE LAMP. 4th Century B.C.** Open bowl and
short nozzle. Concave rim. Rounded sides. String cut base.
6.8 cm. White-buff ware. *BM* 661, 671-2 (Sicily).
....**CHOICE 75.00**

1503. **TERRACOTTA LAMP FILLER. 4th-3rd Century B.C.**
Beige clay with brown-orange slip. Rim and ovoid shape
with pedestal base. High strap handle, pointed spout.
Western Asia minor manufacture. Heavy wear to slip on one
side.   Intact.   Szentleleky-. Cf. Schloessinger 688ff.
....**CHOICE 250.00**

1504. WHEEL-MADE LAMP. Late 4th-Early 3rd Century B.C. Athens. With high bulging sides curving in at top. Flat rim, slightly recessed, surrounding large filling hole. Vertically pierced knob applied to side. Deep flat-topped nozzle. Heavy raised base, concave, with interior rim. Dark red glaze on orange clay with appreciable mica present. 8.8 cm. Encrustation. Cf. Bailey, *BM*, Pl. 19:96 et alii. ....**CHOICE 125.00**

1505. GREEK OIL LAMP. First Half of 3rd Century B.C. Rhodian manufacture. Orange buff clay with red-brown slip. Side nozzle turned slightly up. Side lug. Length 8.5 cm. *BMC* Q 391. Chip at nozzle. ....**CHOICE 125.00**

1506. GREEK OIL LAMP. 3rd century B.C. Wheel-made lamp with biconical body and small lug handle to left side. Concave rim around medium filling hole. Long round-topped nozzle. Thick concave disc base. Blackening at wick hole. Orange self slip. Length 8.3 cm. *BM* Q380-382 ....**CHOICE 150.00**

1507. HELLENISTIC OIL LAMP. 3rd Century B.C. Manufactured in Western Turkey. Wheel-made lamp with long flat-topped nozzle. Dolphin-form handle. Knob at side. Dark buff clay with dark brown slip. Length 8.5 cm. *ROM* 77-82; Cf. *BMC* Q 447. The British Museum sample was made at Calyma. ....**SUPERB 150.00**

1508. WHEEL-MADE LAMP. 3rd Century B.C. Western Asia Minor. With double convex body. Concave rim surrounding large filling hole. Small lug at side. Flat-topped nozzle, slightly splayed. Shallow concave base. Red to black glaze over pink-orange clay. 8 cm. Cf. Bailey, *BM*, Pl. 80 (Rhodes), 84 (Calymna). ....**CHOICE 85.00**

1509. WHEEL-MADE LAMP. 3rd Century B.C. Egyptian manufacture. Red clay. Raised concave base, rounded body. Large filling hole surrounded by one incised circle. Pierced lug at left. Long nozzle with flat top and thick neck, leading to rounded bottom. Some red slip remaining. Measures 10.5 x 7.5 cm. Cf. Bailey, Q526. Small chips to base. Large lamp. ....**CHOICE 200.00**

1510. GREEK OIL LAMP. 3rd-2nd Century B.C. Wheel-made lamp with circular bowl-shaped body and added flat-topped nozzle. Medium filling hole with projecting neck, five vent holes around. Base of handle remains behind filling hole. Recessed disc base. Pale orange ware with black slip. Base and lower third reserved. Length 10.6 cm. *ROM*-; *Athenian Agora*-; Schl.-; *BMC*-. Dura, IV, Ill-; Tushingham-; Szentleleky-. Reportedly Jordanian provenance. Rare. ....**CHOICE 225.00**

1511. GREEK OIL LAMP. 3rd-2nd Century B.C. Wheel-made oil lamp with bi-conical body with very low underside. Small lug to left. Concave rim around medium filling hole. Long flat topped nozzle. Concave disc base. Black to black-red slip over buff ware. Length 9.2 cm. Cf. *BM* Q 447-8, 499. Surface dirt. ....**CHOICE 150.00**

1512. GREEK OIL LAMP. 3rd-2nd Century B.C. Eastern Levant manufacture. Orange-buff clay with black slip. Rim with radiating lines in relief. Large bowl-type nozzle. Large high handle with two points and incised decoration. Length 11.2 cm. Szent.-; *BMC*-; *ROM*-; Schl.-; Warschaw-; Corinth-; Athens-; Menzel-. Rare type. ....**CHOICE 165.00**

1513. OIL LAMP. 3rd Century B.C. Egyptian manufacture. Red slip over brown clay. Nozzle blackened from use. Lug at left chipped. Incised ring around filling hole. Raised base. Measures 7.9 x 5.7 cm. Cf. Qedem 8.26. .....**CHOICE 85.00**

1514. MINIATURE OIL LAMP. 200-30 B.C. Egyptian manufacture. Mold-made lamp of drab brown Nile Valley ware. Piriform body with wide band carination. Filling hole off-center as a result of misalignment of upper and lower molds. 4.5 cm x 2.6 cm. Cf. *ROM* 199, Petrie, *Roman Ehnasya* LX 90. Miniature lamps were used in house-shaped shrines. ....**CHOICE 50.00**

1515. LATE HELLENISTIC OIL LAMP. 225-125 B.C. Probably Corinthian manufacture. Orange clay with traces of black glaze. Relief lamp. Oval nozzle and grooved sides. Loop handle. Length 11.2 cm. Corinth Class type XVIII; *BMC* 620-634. Glaze flaking to top. ....**CHOICE 100.00**

1516. LAMP. 2nd Century B.C. Asia Minor. Wheel-made body of double convex shape with rounded low-placed carination. Wide discus, with large filling hole, set off by very shallow groove. Unpierced lug on left side. Wide concave disc base. Wide nozzle with flat top, rounding at end. Orange-brown slip over pale orange clay. Found in Northern Turkey. A lovely Greek Hellenistic lamp. Cf. Bailey, *BM*, Q156 (ware), 157 (shape). ....**SUPERB 150.00**

1517. LAMP. c. 125 B.C.-25 A.D. Ephesos. Circular body merging with long deep nozzle. High circular ridge surrounding wide flat discus with filling hole but no drain holes. Low rim on nozzle spraying to form lozenge end. Sharp carination above which leaf design. Oval base. 11.8 cm. This type of lamp would still have been in common use during Paul's visit to Ephesus. Handle chip. Scarce. Cf. *Athenian Agora* Vol. IV, 651. ....**CHOICE 150.00**

JEWELRY

1518. BRONZE FIBULA. 1400-1230 B.C. Bronze fibula of an early, crude design. Small stem, broken, with spring then large lion. Made from one piece of metal. 10.3 cm long. Ex. MacGruder Collection on loan to the Smithsonian Institution. Cf. Comstock and Vermuele, Greek, *Etruscan and Roman Bronze in the Museum of Boston*, #249. Encrusted patina. Unusual piece. ....**CHOICE 75.00**

1519. BRONZE FIBULA. 8th Century B.C. Semi-elliptical bow, decorated with two bead moldings. 2.5 cm. Pin missing. Ex. Villa Julia Collection De-Accession. Cf. Marshall, *BMC* 1038. Green patina.....................................**CHOICE 50.00**

1520. **BRONZE BROOCH. Magna Graecia. 8th Century B.C.** Bronze brooch of a bow decorated with bead molding. Nice green patina. Pin missing. ....**CHOICE 50.00**

1521. **GOLD FIBULA. Geometric Period. 8th-6th Century B.C.** Solid gold leach-style fibula decorated with ten bands of incised angular parallel lines. Probably of Italian manufacture. 20 mm. Tip of pin missing. Cf. Ball Auction, Nov. 1929, Sammlung Marc Rosenberg, 17. For shape, Cf. Hackens, Rhode Island School of Design, p. 32. Cf. Marshall, *BMC* 1379 var. ....**SUPERB 1250.00**

1522. **ROSETTE APPLIQUÉ. Cypriot. 8th-7th Century B.C.** 13 mm diameter. Gold rosette with six petals. Very thin. Four holes for application. Appliqués like this were sewn onto garments or diadems. Similar rosettes were found at Kythrea Sardis and throughout the Levant and the East. Some breaks to edge. Cf. Curtis, Sardis Pl. II, fig. 3, #12. Cf. Peirides, *Jewelry in the Cyprus Museum*, Pl. XIII, 11. Maxwell-Hyslop, *Western Asiatic Jewelry c. 3000-612 B.C.*, fig. 179, p. 212. ....**CHOICE 100.00**

1523. **GOLD DISC APPLIQUÉ. 800-600 B.C.** Gold disc appliqué which is stamped with a rosette of six petals. Three holes for attachment. Beaded edge to disc. Possible Cypriot manufacture. 1.3 cm in diameter. Cf. *Catalogue of the Jewelry, Greek Etruscan and Roman in the Department of Antiquities*, British Museum, #873. Cf. Maxwell-Hyslop, *Western Asiatic Jewelry c. 3000-612 B.C.*, fig. 179, p. 212. Broken in half. ....**CHOICE 125.00**

1524. **BRONZE RING. Geometric Period. 7th-6th Century B.C.** Ring with oval intaglio section on top with image of ram seated looking back. Band diameter 2 cm, intaglio measures 1.5 x .8 cm. Cf. *BMC* Pl. I, 36. Lovely style similar to Mycenean work. One-fourth of the band is missing. ....**CHOICE 200.00**

1525. **GOLD BEAD. 7th-5th Century B.C.** Oval hollow bead with banded ends. 10 mm. Some cracks. Cf. Curtis, Sardis, Pl. II, fig. 9, #22. ....**CHOICE 50.00**

1526. **BRONZE PIN. 600-500 B.C.** Bronze pin, curved over like a shepherd's crook. Stem broken off. Four pairs of nodules, two pairs above and two pairs below following curve of pin head produces wavy line effect ending with flattened disc. 5.1 cm long. Cf. Comstock and Vermuele, #331. A very unusual piece. Pin missing. ....**CHOICE 150.00**

1527. **BRONZE RING. Archaic Style. 5th Century B.C.** Bronze ring with long oval bezel depicting hippocamp swimming. Bezel measures 1.5 cm x .8 cm, ring diameter 2.2 cm. Cf. Boardman, *Greek Gems and Finger Rings* H, no. 429, ring type II. Ring is completely intact. ....**AVERAGE 125.00**

1528. **SILVER BEZEL RING WITH GOLD PELLET. 5th Century B.C.** Archaic. Pellet to right. Intaglio of Herakles standing nude holding a club and lion's skin. 15 x 10 mm. Sicily manufacture. Part of band missing. This style is Archaic but most probably manufactured later in Classical times. Boardman, *Greek Gems and Finger Rings*, #44 ....**CHOICE 300.00**

1529. **BRONZE RING WITH OVAL BEZEL. 5th Century B.C.** Herakles standing nude holding club and lion's skin. Undetermined inscription to edge. 20 x 13 mm. Cf. Florange, Duval Collection, Geneve, Pl. IV, 13. Cf. Boardman, *Greek Gems and Finger Rings*, #222. Cf. Boardman, *GGFR*, p. 217, type II, ring style. Intact. ....**AVERAGE 225.00**

1530. **BRONZE RING WITH OVAL BEZEL. 5th Century B.C.** Hero, Othryades, kneeling, head back, facing bearded, nude figure behind. 22 x 12 mm. The scene, recounted by Herodotus, is the death of the hero Othryades. The second figure is the Spartan Comyrad, the last survivor of 300 warriors, who committed suicide rather than face the shame of returning alive to Sparta. Intact. Cf. Boardman, *Greek Gems and Finger Rings*, p. 217, type II, for Classical ring shape. Cf. Richter, *EGR*, 6 (Republic) for similar type. Cf. Hague, #20 var. ....**CHOICE 300.00**

1531. **BRONZE RING. 5th-4th Century B.C.** Ring with oval intaglio with head of male with close cropped hair. Cf. *BMC*, CX for shape. Cf. Boardman, *Greek Gems and Finger Rings*, 416 for head. ....**CHOICE 175.00**

1532. **BRONZE RING. 5th-4th Century B.C.** Diademed female bust, hair bound in back, facing the forepart of a stylized lion head. 17 x 12 mm. Anatolian manufacture. Nice impression. Band missing. Cf. Boardman, *Greek Gems and Finger Rings*, p. 217, Type V11, for Classical ring style...**CHOICE 150.00**

1533. **BRONZE RING WITH INTAGLIO. 5th or 4th Century B.C.** Ring with oval intaglio with image of Herakles seated on a rock. Band diameter 2.2 cm, intaglio measures 1.4 x .7 cm. For shape, Cf. *BMC* CXV. Munchen-. Boardman-. Berlin-. Drill style. ....**CHOICE 150.00**

1534. **BRONZE RING. Eastern Greek. 5th or 4th Century B.C.** Bronze ring with impression of Greek female and lion's head. Length 2 cm. Band missing. ....**CHOICE 150.00**

1535. **GOLD APPLIQUÉ PLAQUE. 5th-3rd Century B.C.** Small gold appliqué plaque. Portrait of Helios in relief, facing with curly hair. Circle of molded beading surrounding. Four holes in corners for attachment. Measures 1.1 x .9 cm. Cf. Rhodus coins types. Cf. *Catalogue of Jewelry in the British Museum*, Pl. XL, #2068. Top left corner missing. ....**SUPERB 300.00**

1536. **BRONZE RING WITH ROUNDED BEZEL. 4th Century B.C.** Standing cult figure of Samos with traces of Greek inscription behind. The figure in long chiton with arms extended with fillets, wearing modius is the cult statue of Samian Hera. Cf. SNG. Cop. 1725. 13 x 11 mm. Intact. Boardman, *Greek Gems and Finger Rings*, p. 217, type VI, for ring style. ....**ABOUT CHOICE 125.00**

1537. **BRONZE RING WITH ROUND BEZEL. 4th Century B.C.** Poppy plant with two branches of leaves, central with buds. 16 x 12 mm. Some green patination. Intact. Cf. Boardman, *Greek Gems and Finger Rings*, p. 217, Type VII, for ring style. ....**CHOICE 150.00**

1538. **GOLD BAY LEAF WREATH PETAL. 4th Century B.C.** Sheet gold bay leaf petal that was part of a large wreath with straight creases to ends. 32 x 20 mm. Traces of reddish patination. Cf. Hoffman and Claer, *Antiker Gold und Silberschmuck*, 32 var. Breglia, *Catalogo delle Oreficerie del Museo Nazionale di Napoli*, XVI. Cf. Park Hurst, Oberlin College, Gutman Collection, 27.....**CHOICE 100.00**

1539. **GOLD JEWELRY IMITATION IN TERRACOTTA. 4th-2nd Century B.C.** Pendant head of a woman, surmounted by a palmette. Hair rolled to front of head. Bronze loop for suspension. 33 mm high. Gilded parts remain. Rare. Marshall, *BMC*, 2169. ....**CHOICE 200.00**

1540. **GILDED TERRACOTTA PLAQUE IMITATION. 4th-2nd Century B.C.** Terracotta gold-plated plaque; an imitation of pure gold jewelry. Bust of Athena wearing triple-crested helmet and necklaces. Tendril pattern in the background. Beaded border. Diameter 1.5 cm. Cf. *Catalogue of Jewelry in the British Museum* #2136. Nice molding of facial features. Traces of gilt still visible. A lovely example of the plated terracotta worn by the middle class. Rare. ....**CHOICE 250.00**

1541. **PAIR OF GOLD HOOP EARRINGS. Hellenistic. 3rd Century B.C.** 3 cm diameter. Two gold lynx head earrings with two red garnets and one green emerald stone bead with collars of granulated dog teeth ending in gold fluted horn. The lynx are inlaid with enamel. Traces of enamel seen from lynx's ear to tips of cheeks. The Sotheby earrings brought $6,800 in 1987. Sotheby's, London, July 13, 1987, #87. Cf. Hoffman & Claer, *Antiker Gold und Silberschnuck*, 77. Cf. Marchall, *BMC Jewelry*, 2443 var. Cf. Hackens, Rhode Island School of Design, #28 var. Cf. Hoffman Davidson, *Greek Gold*, fig. 31....................**SUPERB 5500.00**

1542. **GOLD PAIR OF SATYR HEAD EARRINGS. 2nd Century B.C.** Sheet gold repoussé. Facing heads of satyr, bearded, attached to band. Bars shaped as a diamond with coiled ends. Loop at each end in back. Modern gold loop for wearing. 21 x 11 mm. For repoussé types, Cf. Appliqué Masks, Hoffmann and Davidson, *Greek Gold*, #133. ....**SUPERB 1500.00**

1543. **GOLD GENIE PENDANT. 2nd-1st Century B.C.** 1 cm high, 1.5 cm long. Solid gold Genie seated leaning on left arm with right hand resting on bent right knee on platform. For similar style, Cf. Hoffmann and Davidson, *Greek Gold*, fig. 50b-c, p. 141. ....**SUPERB 1500.00**

1544. **GOLD CLUB OF HERAKLES PENDANT. 1st Century B.C.-2nd Century A.D.** Gold club decorated with three rows of leaves outlined in wire. Beads between, loop above. 30 mm. Greek Asia minor manufacture, probably the Black Sea region. Park Hurst dates this much earlier to the 3rd Century B.C. End of club damaged. Cf. Marshall, *BMC Jewelry*, 2412. Cf. Park Hurst, Oberlin College, Gutman Collection, 5. ....**CHOICE 350.00**

WRITING

1545. **GREEK PAPYRUS FRAGMENT. 2nd-3rd Century A.D.** Part of a private letter. Written on both sides. Measures 2.3 x 2 cm. Written in a fine hand. ....**CHOICE 150.00**

1546. **GREEK PAPYRUS FRAGMENT. 3rd Century A.D.** Part of an official correspondence. Possible reference to the Prefect of Egypt. Contains the end of one letter, the writer's valediction, and the beginning of a second letter. Measures 20 x 8 cm. Elegant hand. Nice large fragment. ....**CHOICE 300.00**

1547. **TERRACOTTA AMPHORA HANDLE.** Maker's name stamped on handle. ΝΙΚΑΓΙΔΟΣ-Nikagidos. 8.6 mm high, 6 cm wide. These handles were part of a very large amphora used to ship wine. The regions of Rhodes and Knidos were major shippers. Name not listed in Grace, *Stamped Amphora Handles* ....**CHOICE 75.00**

1548. **BRONZE BOX COVER. During Roman Period.** Four lines of inscription. 55 x 25 mm. ΤΡΕΦΗΜΙC ΝΟΥΥΙCΤΡΕ ΒΗΜΕΙC ΠΡΕFΙΑCΕΥC. Very rare. ....**CHOICE 350.00**

GREEK

1250   1256   1266   1260   1275   1276   1288

1287   1320   1313

1308   1301   1304

PLATE 21

GREEK

1304

1306

1303

1346

1339

1328

1351

1356

PLATE 22

GREEK

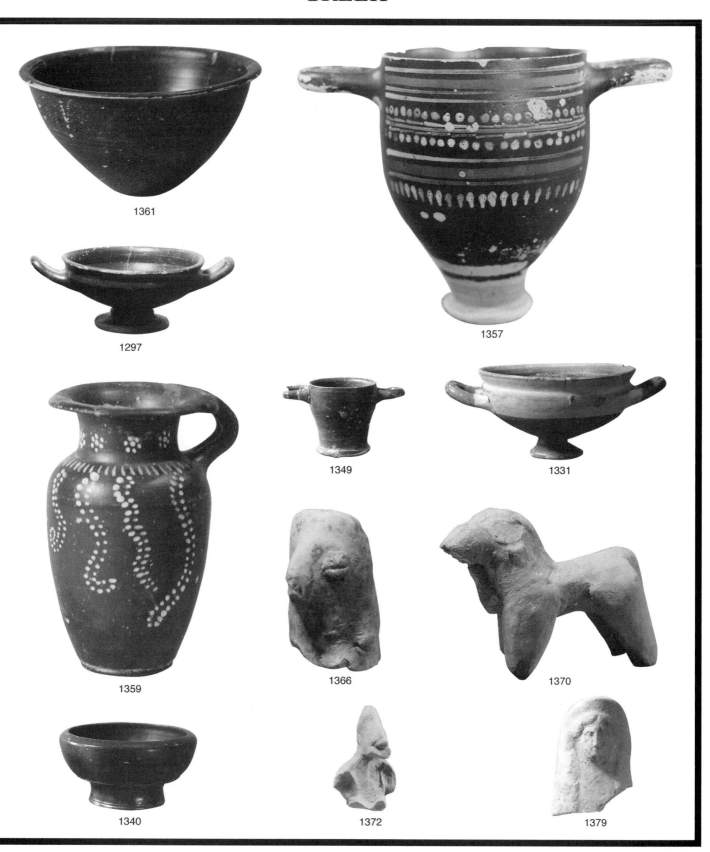

1361

1357

1297

1349

1331

1359

1366

1370

1340

1372

1379

PLATE 23

GREEK

1376   1390   1399

1406   1409   1410

1471   1389

1430

1396

1438

1431   1447   1473

PLATE 24

1482

1492

1493

1496

1486

1497

1498

1499

1506

1507

1510

1515

1516

1517

1521

1522

1535

1538

1542

1540

1539

1543

1544

1548

PLATE 25

ROMAN

ROMAN- Marble Statuette of Bacchus

Second century A.D. This representation of the adolescent god is nude with the exception of a mantle over his left shoulder, which falls in folds down his back. The mantle is used in the front to form a depression which is filled with various fruits, such as grapes, pomegranates, and a melon. His long hair falls into seven corkscrew curls. Smooth polished marble with some dark discoloration. Height 8 ½". Restoration to neck.

Sold in the winter of 1974 for $1500.   Estimated value in 1997 is $5000.

ROMAN

Say the name Rome and you invoke many responses, for Rome has been and is many things to many people in the course of its long history. It is Rome, the Eternal City and Rome, the Great Empire. It is the Rome of Myth and the Rome of History. It is Rome, the Fallen City lying in dust and ruins, and Rome the Mighty served by its invincible legions. It is the Rome of the poet Cicero and the Rome of the degenerate Emperor Caligula. It is the Rome of the "Noble" Julius Caesar and the Rome of Brutus, who, in the words of Marc Antony as presented by Shakespeare, was an "Honorable" man. It is the Rome of Law, the Roman civil law, which reached its peak under the emperors. It was a law which, as many legal authorities have pointed out, excelled in precision of formulation and logic of thought, but it was a law of inequality and social prejudice, a law whose major purpose was to preserve the power of the Roman state. It was a Rome which created great works of public art and whose common artisans created objects of daily use prized by collectors today. To understand this art we must first understand something of Roman history and culture. Rome, pronounced Roma in Latin, was once the seat of a vast empire stretching from the British Isles in the west to Parthia in the east. It is now the capital of Italy and the seat of the supreme pontiff of the Roman Catholic Church (at Vatican City, a sovereign state within Rome). The city is also the capital of Italy's Rome province and Latium region. Located in central Italy on both sides of the Tiber River between the Apennine Mountains and the Tyrrhenian Sea, the city was originally situated here because it is the first easy crossing of the Tiber upstream from the sea. Although the earliest remains found in Rome date to the Bronze Age, about 1500 B.C., continuous settlements probably began about 1000 B.C. on Rome's future site – around the fording point of the Tiber and in the surrounding hills. These early settlers probably lived in small clan type encampments and practiced a modified hunter-gatherer culture with some agriculture typical of the European Bronze Age.

According to one legend, Rome was founded by Aeneas, a Trojan who fled to Italy after the fall of Troy. The most popular of the legends of the founding of Rome involves two individuals who may have been descendants of Aeneas, Romulus and Remus, twin brothers who were abandoned at birth and suckled by a female wolf. The brothers being suckled by the wolf is a popular theme in Roman art often found on the coins of the Republic and the later Empire. The brothers founded a town on the Palatine, one of the seven hills of Rome, and ruled it jointly for a while. They eventually quarreled, and Romulus killed his brother, becoming the sole ruler. According to tradition, Rome was founded on April 21, 753 B.C. The ancient Romans celebrated the anniversary of that day, and it is still a national holiday in Italy.

Recent archaeological excavations on the Palatine hill have revealed remains of village cultures from the 8th and 7th centuries B.C. That evidence indicates the coexistence of groups of Latins and Sabines, two different but closely related peoples. Although the Sabines spoke Oscan, Latin appears to have been the language of Rome from its earliest beginnings.

These remains included post holes for huts and clay funerary vessels in the shape of these huts. In the 7th century the Latin and Sabine villages coalesced to form a unified city on the eastern, or left, bank of the Tiber. It was protected by strongholds on its hills, and was in a strategic position because it controlled the Tiber ford and the trade route to the central uplands. For this and other reasons it is not surprising to learn that Rome soon outstripped other towns in Latium in wealth and power. This period is known to history as the reign of the Latin Kings.

By the late 7th century B.C., the Etruscans, an advanced people from Eturia to the northwest, had extended their rule to Rome. The Etruscans are generally credited with expanding the power and influence of Rome. Under their rule a large part of Latium was brought under Rome, and the Capitoline temple was built among other well-known sites in the city. Etruscan art was characterized by a certain Eastern influence, not surprisingly, as they are supposed to have originally emigrated to Italy from the East. The art of the 7th century B.C., executed in the local Villanovan style or in the Greek Orientalizing style current in the Mediterranean, exhibits contemporary Greek as well as Near Eastern influence. The Etruscans were noted for their skill as builders. Their roads, bridges, canals, and temples were famous in Roman times but regrettably few have been excavated since they mostly lie under modern cities. Their art is, however, well known from the funerary remains in their extensive necropolises. Their art is also characterized by painted and sculpted works intended for religious and funerary purposes, particularly pottery vases which were often of elaborate form and decoration. They were masters of bronze work and Etruscan bronze objects are among the most highly prized of all Etruscan antiquities. Subsequent artistic development in the emerging Roman sphere of influence more or less closely followed the stylistic phases of Greek art, although the general phases of Greek art were followed and Greek art was much admired and even copied. The art itself took on a genuinely Roman character for this was the period of the Roman Republic. This Republican art is characterized by a realism often lacking in the idealized Greek art of the time.

The Roman Republic, founded, according to tradition, in the 6th century B.C., was at its heart an aristocratic form of government rather than a republic as we know it today. It was headed by the Senate and by magistrates, later called Consuls – usually two in number – who were elected annually by the Senate.

The Senate was deviled by class and the lower class citizens were effectively frozen out of government. Even when the lower classes obtained a modicum of power the real power remained in the hands of a small noble class.

Despite internal conflict between the various classes in society and external threat from the Gauls and the Carthaginians, among others, the Republican period was one of growing expansion of the emerging Roman political entity. Rome's numerous foreign wars brought great new wealth and this wealth is reflected in the art.

One of the great Roman contributions to art in general is portrait sculpture. Its roots lie both in the Roman custom of keeping ancestor masks in the home and in the practice of erecting honorary statues in public places. Although the extensive Etruscan and Greek Hellenistic portrait art contemporary with the Republican period also contributed substantially to the development of Roman portrait sculpture, few cultures to this day have rivaled the realism and expression found in Republican portrait sculpture. Surviving examples are mainly marble copies, especially busts, a typically Roman, abbreviated portrait form that flourished from the late Republic onward. Other materials such as bronze and terracotta were also used. The 1st century B.C. was a period of great creativity in which the images of patricians became so realistic they seem almost ready to arise from their long sleep. This tradition persisted into the Imperial Age but with diminished strength.

The history, sociology, politics, art and archaeology of the civil war period, the Triumvirate, and certainly the succeeding Empire is extremely complex and the following should be considered only the briefest of introductions. Suffice it to say that it is replete with events and personalities whose influence resound into the modern era. Obviously an intense study of this complex subject should be a priority for any collector of Roman art.

The economic changes of the Republican period also brought forth genuine reformers. The best known were the Gracchi but the deaths of the Gracchi in the 2nd century B.C. opened a century of anarchy and civil wars. In 91 B.C., Rome's allies in Italy rose in a great revolt called the Social War. Under this pressure the Romans granted the franchise to all Italians and mercilessly crushed those who did not submit. Civil war followed (88-82 B.C.). Sulla became dictator but his rule was short-lived. The resulting political instability led to the rise of Julius Caesar. With Caesar we begin the period of the 12 Caesars. He set about reforming the laws and reorganizing the administration of the colonies. Under Caesar, Rome controlled all of Italy, Gaul, Spain, Numidia, Macedonia, Greece, Palestine, Egypt, and virtually all of the Mediterranean islands. Greek art and philosophy had permeated Roman culture, and Rome perceived itself as the civilizer of the barbarians. Caesar, however, was moving toward a monarchical form of government and in an effort to stop him and restore the Republic, Brutus and the other conspirators stabbed him in the senate on the Ides of March, 44 B.C.

Caesar's opponents had underestimated the allegiance of Caesar's partisans. However, they were now galvanized into action by Mark Antony. Antony, Octavian, and Marcus Aemilius Lepidus formed a triumvirate – sometimes called the Second Triumvirate – and forced the Senate to accept their rule. They instituted a reign of terror, and at the Battle of Philippi in 42 B.C. they defeated the forces of Brutus and Cassius, both of whom committed suicide. By 31 B.C. the new imperial government was established, ending the Republic, although sympathy for it continued for many generations to come.

Octavian, who assumed the title and name Imperator Caesar Augustus, established a system of government called the principate that endured for two centuries. The principate was a monarchy disguised as a republic. The princeps (the emperor) ostensibly ruled by commission from the Senate and the people. There was no automatic system of succession. Normally an emperor succeeded to the throne by virtue of connection with a predecessor by blood, adoption, or affinity, or one could seize power by force and inaugurate a new dynasty. During Augustus' reign, the Roman Empire was at its height, and it had no rivals. Thus began the 200 years of peace known as the Pax Roma. Augustus died in A.D. 14 and was succeeded by his stepson Tiberius. Thus the Julio-Claudian dynasty was established, which ruled during the 1st century A.D., the height of the Roman Imperial Period. Tiberius, the son of the second wife of Augustus, Lucilla, continued the policies of Augustus. The later years of his reign, however, were marked by court intrigue, mostly concerning the succession.

His great-nephew Caligula followed him. The latter's reign became a virtual synonym for cruelty and debauchery. Almost certainly insane during much of his reign, he was assassinated in A.D. 41 by a cabal of the Praetorian guard, an elite body of the emperor's personal bodyguards that constituted an increasingly powerful institution. The officers of the guard named Caligula's uncle, Claudius I, as emperor. Claudius was generally an efficient administrator. He wrote a famous history of his family which was adapted into a famous television miniseries in recent years often shown on public television ("I Claudius"). Claudius passed over his own son, Britannicus (41-55 A.D.), for the succession in favor of his wife Agrippina's son, Nero. Agrippina probably poisoned Claudius once she was assured that Nero would succeed him.

Nero, the last emperor in the Julio-Claudian dynasty, assumed the throne in 54. He governed well in his early years. Gradually, however, the influence of his mother and of his second wife, Poppaea, triumphed, and Nero's reign deteriorated into a reign of terror similar to Caligula's. He poisoned Britannicus, his mother, and Burrus, and legend says that he kicked Poppaea to death. Nero was accused of burning Rome in 64 A.D. He in turn blamed a new sect, the Christians, for the fire and began the first Roman persecution of them; Saint Peter and Saint Paul were among its victims. Nero committed suicide in 68 A.D.

when he saw that a revolution against him was succeeding. He was followed by Galba and, in 69 A.D. (the year of the four emperors), by Otho, Vitellius, and Vespasian.

Vespasian (69-79 A.D.), founder of the Flavian dynasty, declared emperor by his soldiers in the East, brought order and efficiency to the administration of Rome's affairs. He built the Colosseum and other important public works. Although he was popular among Romans he was much hated in other parts of the empire, particularly in Judea where the First Jewish Revolt succeeded in ousting Roman rule for a brief period. He was succeeded by two sons, Titus (79-81 A.D.), and Domitian (81-96 A.D.). They were followed in the 2nd century A.D. by the Antonines, the next six emperors. They ruled for nearly a century, and the period is sometimes called the Golden Age of the Roman Empire. The first Antonine, Nerva (96-98 A.D.), was elected by the Senate in an effort to assert its power over the military. An elderly, well-respected statesman, he was opposed by the Praetorian guard. He adopted, as his successor, the great soldier Trajan (a Spaniard, the first non-Italian to serve as emperor). Trajan (98-117 A.D.), is considered one of the greatest emperors. He was succeeded by Hadrian (117-138 A.D.). He brutally put down the Second Jewish Revolt in Jerusalem under Bar Kochba (A.D. 132-35), and instituted the period of the Hadrianic persecutions. Antoninus Pius had a long and prosperous reign (138-161 A.D.), and was succeeded by joint emperors, the philosopher Marcus Aurelius and Lucius Verus.

Marcus Aurelius, although a philosopher and historian, brutally persecuted the Christians. The reign of his son, Commodus, is generally regarded as the beginning of Rome's long decline. In the 3rd century the Roman world plunged into a prolonged crisis. Sharp divisions between the notables in the cities and the poor peasants created tensions. The wars and increased taxation destroyed the prosperity of the empire. To meet rising military costs and to pay the bureaucracy, the emperors debased the coinage, and the resulting inflation contributed to the decline. The defenses of the empire on the Rhine and Danube collapsed under the attack of various Germanic and other tribes, and the eastern provinces were invaded by the Persians. In the fifty years from 235 to 284 A.D. more than two dozen emperors ruled, all but one of whom suffered a violent death. Out of the turmoil of the 3rd century a new totalitarian Rome emerged. The emperor, Diocletian (284-305 A.D.), adopted the title dominus (master) and transformed the principate into the dominate and citizens into subjects. He adopted an elaborate court ceremonial with many oriental elements. The requisitions and forced labor to which the emperors of the 3rd century had resorted in order to save the state were transformed into a lasting system. The average citizen lost many of the rights he had heretofore enjoyed.

Constantine I (306-337 A.D.), is sometimes regarded as the second founder of the empire. He successfully fought off his numerous opponents and, once firmly in power, reorganized the entire system of local government. Most importantly, however, he converted the entire empire to Christianity. He even moved the capital from Rome to Byzantium, which he had rebuilt and renamed Constantinople. Constantine's reforms were not enough, however, to halt the slide of the Western Empire into ruin and final conquest. The Eastern Empire, often referred to as the Byzantine Empire, survived its demise and lasted for almost another millennium, but that is another story.

In general, we should note that unlike Egyptian art, which showed a distinct chronological development, Roman art progressed along no single, easily traceable course of development. A number of disparate artistic currents and traditions coexisted and influenced one another, not infrequently within the same genre, as in the portraiture, noted above. Spurts of great inventiveness vied with the generally retrospective trend toward following Greek prototypes. In addition to the major arts represented by painting, architecture, and sculpture, many minor arts and crafts flourished throughout the Empire. Small gems were engraved with scenes ranging from the sublime to the simple, and elegant pottery vessels were manufactured for domestic and public use. Pottery was also in wide use for utilitarian and votive objects such as lamps and statuary. Vessels of silver and bronze were cast with or without engraved or relief decoration. The more common bronze was also used for a wide variety of small objects ranging from simple household fixtures and utensils to fine statuettes. Although glass was in use earlier, after glassblowing was invented in the 1st century B.C. this material also became relatively low in cost. A thriving industry developed in the later empire, and Roman glass is among the most prized of collectibles. Coins, first minted in the 3rd century B.C., were made mainly of gold, silver, bronze and their alloys. They usually showed the portrait of the reigning ruler. In addition to the vast amount of art produced in Italy itself, the art of Rome's provinces exhibited an almost endless variety, which is one of the reasons that ancient Roman art is so popular among collectors today.

TOOLS AND WEAPONS

Many tools and weapons in iron, bronze and even precious metals are found in Roman period excavations. While scarce and precious items such as helmets and full breast plates are beyond the scope of this work, many more mundane items such as arrowheads, spearheads, agricultural and domestic tools of various kinds, personal implements such as tweezers, forks, spoons, knives, cosmetic applicators and the like, and even medical implements, to name only a few, are fairly readily available to the collector. Nice arrowheads and tools are readily available to the collector for under $100 from most dealers.

POTTERY

Pottery is perhaps the most readily available of all Roman antiquities to the modern collector. Roman pottery ranges from the simple to the elaborate. Often it is mold decorated with interesting designs in relief – for example, the Samian luxuryware – or etched with various patterns such as those found on North African redware. Some Roman pottery, particularly in peripheral parts of the empire such as Egypt, is painted. Types of pottery include domestic vessels of various wares, oil lamps often with relief decoration, some ritual vessels, architectural elements such as tiles, and various types of pottery used in funerary rituals, such as cineary urns. Many fine examples of the various types of Roman pottery can often be purchased by the astute collector for modest sums.

TERRACOTTA

Terracotta is a type of hard-baked clay, produced by means of a single firing. Usually rendered brownish red in color after firing, terracotta may be glazed (covered with a layer of molten glass) but is most often left in its natural state, sometimes called "buff" pottery. It was used extensively in the Roman Empire, particularly for the production of sculptures of various sizes. The term terracotta has often come to be loosely applied to any sculpture in pottery, whatever type of clay was actually used. Pottery sculpture on a monumental scale and, even more importantly for the average collector, on a small scale – statuettes, effigy vessels, figurines, and the like – was an important part of Roman daily life. Pottery sculpture representing deities, animals, objects, people, and even toys is found in large quantities throughout the Empire. Because of this, such sculpture is relatively cheap on the antiquities market. A somewhat worn head from a statuette, for example, might be purchased for as little as $10, while a superb example might go for several hundred.

METAL OBJECTS

Much Roman metalwork has survived from antiquity. Ranging from simple cooking pots to elaborate oil lamps cast in the lost wax process, these objects can often be of great artistic merit. Mirrors, for example, often had elaborately sculpted decoration. Perhaps the most popular of all Roman metalwork among modern collectors are the numerous bronze sculptures which frequently appear on the market. These sculptures were often for religious use representing the various deities of the Greco-Roman pantheon, such as Aphrodite, Zeus, Apollo, Mercury, etc. Many sculptures were made for political use and/or public display – portraits of the reigning emperor, funerary busts and the like – but small sculptures of animals and people often used to decorate other metal objects such as handles are also quite common. While a full-sized bust of one of the twelve Caesars might fetch tens of thousands of dollars in a major auction of antiquities, a handle finial with a man's bust can be had for under $100 from many dealers.

STONE

Collectable stone objects from the Roman world can be divided into two classes. Utilitarian objects and stone vessels such as cosmetic pallets, weights and the like form one class, stone sculpture the other. Sculpture can further be divided into sculpture in the round and bas relief. Sculpture in stone had its beginnings in the Etrusco-Italic funerary tradition of tombstones and grave statues. As interest in Greek art increased, marble copies of Greek masterpieces, as well as eclectic works in the Greek manner, were commissioned by wealthy Romans to decorate their residences. Marble ornamental works of a purely decorative nature as well as funerary furniture such as tombstones and sarcophagi were also quite common. Portrait sculpture saw perhaps its finest expression in the Roman world. Relief sculpture was also quite important from the Republican period onward, reaching its height in the great historical reliefs of the Imperial period. Many collectors feel that Roman stone objects are beyond their financial reach. This, however, is a mistaken impression. While a monumental Roman statue in the finest style can bring hundreds of thousands of dollars, nice stone vessels and interesting fragments of relief, even some poorer quality sculpture in the round, can be had under $300.

GLASS

Prior to the 1st century B. C. there were only four methods of glass manufacture known in the ancient world: 1) applying molten glass to a pre-formed core, the oldest method and one still in use in the early Roman period, 2) arranging sections of pre-formed glass rods around a pre-formed core; a good example of this technique is the highly desirable mosaic glass of the early Empire, 3) grinding from a block of glass, a technique more akin to stone carving or sculpture than glass making and usually confined to luxury wares in the Roman period, and 4) casting in open or closed molds, a method much used in the Eastern or Sidonian workshops. In the 1st century B.C. a revolution occurred in Roman glassmaking. This was the invention of glass blowing, which formed the basis of the mass production of glass vessels, which distinguished the Roman period from earlier periods. The introduction of blown glass made it a widespread commodity in the Roman Empire and accounts for the large quantity of Roman glass on the antiquities market today. While good examples of rarer types of glass are rather pricey, a nice perfume vessel can still be purchased for under $200.

LAMPS

Lighting in the Roman world was provided by torches, candles, and oil lamps. Although oil lamps were made in metal, glass, and stone, the vast majority were manufactured in pottery. The pottery lamps were usually manufactured in small workshops which specialized in their manufacture or which, while they might also produce other objects, considered the manufacture of lamps to be one of their major lines of endeavor. Although a variety of techniques were in use, most were mold made. So common were these lamps in the Roman period that archaeologists can often date a site by the style of the lamps or lamp fragments found. The lamps are often decorated either in relief or by incising the mold. Sometimes the whole lamp was formed into the effigy of an object or person. Some of the molds and archetypes used in their manufacture also survive. Since lamps were so common and were often provided in large numbers in tombs, they are often found among the less expensive Roman antiquities. Despite this they can be among some of the most interesting due to the creative nature of their decoration. For this reason many collections have been formed exclusively devoted to these lamps.

JEWELRY

Ancient Roman jewelry can be of precious metal or base metal. Personal ornament was widespread among both men and women in the Roman period. Much jewelry has survived and pins, rings, bracelets, earrings and necklaces in gold, silver and bronze are readily available to the collector. Intaglio and cameo gems carved with scenes ranging from depictions of animals to depictions of the Roman deities, in various stones and glass, were also in wide use and can form an interesting class of objects to collect. One of the most common objects of personal adornment was the fibula, a type of metal safety pin used to fasten clothing. These come in a wide variety of shapes, sizes, and decorations and can usually be purchased rather inexpensively today, good specimens often fetching less than $50 in dealers' lists.

WRITING

Written records in the Roman period were usually in Greek or Latin although other languages and scripts such as Hebrew, Aramaic, hieroglyphic, and demotic were in use in various parts of the Empire. Inscriptions often appear on objects of metal, pottery, and even glass. For example, short inscriptions were often written on pottery shards called ostraca or stamped into clay objects such as lamps and tiles. Coins almost always bore some inscription and much study has gone into its meaning by numismatists. Some of the written records were on wax tablets, few of which have survived. Many more were on papyrus which, at least in dry parts of the empire such as Egypt, have survived in some quantity. Many public and private inscriptions were carved in stone, much of which has survived. For example, Roman stone funerary monuments are quite common and are almost always inscribed. It would not be hard to form an interesting collection devoted to Roman writing.

ROMAN REPUBLIC
c. 500-50 B.C.

	INTERNAL	EXTERNAL	CULTURAL	GREEK WORLD
	ROMAN REPUBLIC	WARS IN ITALY		CLASSICAL
500 B.C.	Patricians vs. Plebians Centuriate and tribal assemblies	Alliance with Latin league Wars with Aequi, Volsci, Etruscans	Loss of links to Greek world	
450 B.C.	Twelve Tables			Peloponnesian War
400 B.C.	Licinian-Sextian reforms	Destruction of Veii Gallic invasion		Philip of Macedonia
350 B.C.		Conquest of Central Italy War with Latin league Samnite wars begin		Alexander the Great HELLENISTIC AGE
300 B.C.	Ogulnian law Hortensian law Development of senatorial aristocracy	Sentinum War with Pyrrhus OVERSEAS WARS First Punic War	Livius Andronicus	Political division: Ptolemies, Seleucids, Antigonids Writers: Menander, Callimachus, Eratosthenes, Apolionius
250 B.C.		Acquisition of Sardinia-Corsica Adriatic sphere War	Hellenistic education introduced	Rhodius, Herodas, Theocritus Philosophers: Epicurus, Zeno Cleanthes, Chrysippus, Pyrrhon
	C. Flaminius Centuriate assembly reorganized Claudian law	in Po Valley Second Punic war	Q. Fabius Pictor Plautus, Naevius	Scientists: Theophrastus, Strato, Herophilus, Erasistratus, Euclid, Archimedes, Aristarchus, Eratosthenes
200 B.C.	Conflict of "isolationists" and "internationalists"	Second Macedonian war War with Antiochus	Ennius, Cato, Pacuvius	Revolt of Maccabees
150 B.C.		Third Macedonian war Revolts in Spain Annexation of Macedonia	Aebutian law: formulary system Terence, Lucilius	Writer: Polybius Philosophers: Carneades, Panaetius Scientist: Hipparchus Parthian conquest of Mesopotamia
	Ti. Gracchus C. Gracchus Marius: new army	Third Punic war Jugurthine war		
100 B.C.		Cimbri-Teutones		
	Italian revolt Civil War Sulla dictator Pompey-Crassus cos. Cicero cos.	Mithridatic war Sertorius' revolt	Lucretius, Catullus, Cicero, Sallust, Caesar, Varro	Posidonius
50 B.C.	Civil War Dictatorship of Caesar	Pompey in east Caesar in Gaul		

ROMAN EMPERORS
c. 14-491 A.D.

	EMPERORS AND *CO-EMPERORS 14-238 B.C.			EMPERORS AND *CO-EMPERORS 238-364 B.C.	
14 A.D.	Augustus				
	Tiberius	14-37 A.D.		Pupienus Maximus	238-238 A.D.
	Caligula	37-41 A.D.		*Balbinus	238-238 A.D.
	Claudius	41-54 A.D.		Gordiantis III	238-244 A.D.
50 A.D.	Nero	54-68 A.D.		Philippus	244-249 A.D.
	Galba	68-69 A.D.	250 A.D.	Decius	249-251 A.D.
	Otho	69-69 A.D.		Trebonianus Gallus	251-254 A.D.
	Vitellius	69-69 A.D.		Aemilianus	253-253 A.D.
	Vespasian	69-79 A.D.		Valerian	253-260 A.D.
	Titus	79-81 A.D.		*Gallienus	253-268 A.D.
	Domitian	81-96 A.D.		Claudius II	268-270 A.D.
100 A.D.	Nerva	96-98 A.D.		Aurelian	270-275 A.D.
	Trajan	98-117 A.D.		Tacitus	275-276 A.D.
	Hadrian	117-138 A.D.		Florianus	276-276 A.D.
	Antoninus Pius	138-161 A.D.		Probus	276-282 A.D.
150 A.D.				Carus	282-283 A.D.
	M. Aurelius	161-180 A.D.		Carinus	283-284 A.D.
	*L. Verus	161-169 A.D.		*Numerianus	283-284 A.D.
	Commodus	180-192 A.D.		Diocletian	284-305 A.D.
	Pertinax	193-193 A.D.		*Maximian	286-305 A.D.
	Julianus	193-193 A.D.	300 A.D.	Constantius I	305-306 A.D.
200 A.D.	Septimius Severus	193-211 A.D.		Chlorus	
	Caracalla	211-217 A.D.		Galerius	305-311 A.D.
	*Geta	211-212 A.D.		*Constantine I	306-337 A.D.
	Macrinus	217-218 A.D.		(the Great)	
	Elagabalus	218-222 A.D.		*Licinius	307-323 A.D.
	Alexander Severna	222-235 A.D.		Constantine II	337-340 A.D.
	Maximinus	235-238 A.D.		*Constantius II	337-361 A.D.
	Gordianus I	238-238 A.D.		*Constans I	337-350 A.D.
	*Gordianus II	238-238 A.D.		Julian	361-363 A.D.
				Jovian	363-364 A.D.

AFTER 364 A.D.

	WESTERN EMPIRE			EASTERN EMPIRE	
364 A.D.	Valentinian I	364-375 A.D.		Valens	364-378 A.D.
	Gratian	367-383 A.D.			
	Valentinian II	375-392 A.D.		Theodosius I	378-395 A.D.
	Theodosius I	392-395 A.D.			
	(Emperor of both East and West)				
	Honorius	395-423 A.D.		Arcadius	395-408 A.D.
400 A.D.					
				Theodosius II	408-450 A.D.
	Theodosius II	423-425 A.D.			
	(Emperor of both East and West)				
	Valentinian III	425-455 A.D.			
450 A.D.				Marcian	450-457 A.D.
	Petronius Maximus	455-455 A.D.			
	Avitus	455-456 A.D.			
	Majorian	457-461 A.D.		Leo I Thrax	457-474 A.D.
	Libius Severus	461-465 A.D.			
	Anthemius	467-472 A.D.			
	Olybrius	472-472 A.D.			
	Glycerius	473-474 A.D.			
	Julius Nepos	474-475 A.D.		Leo II	474-474 A.D.
	Romulus Augustulus	475-476 A.D.		Zeno	474-491 A.D.
491 A.D.					

ROMAN

WEAPONS
Metal
Swords, Daggers, and Blades

1549. **IRON DAGGER BLADE. 1st Century B.C.-2nd Century A.D.** Iron blade with single edge and crude, wide tang. Thick outer (non-blade) edge. Length 17 cm, width 2.1 cm. Cf. British Museum, *Guide to Greek and Roman Life,* fig. 180c. ....**CHOICE 100.00**

1550. **IRON DAGGER BLADE. Roman. 1st Century B.C.-2nd Century A.D.** Single edge blade. 12.7 cm long, 2 cm wide. Found in the Holy Land. Cf. *Guide to Greek and Roman Life in the British Museum,* fig. 180c. ....**CHOICE 150.00**

1551. **IRON KNIFE BLADE. Roman. 1st-3rd Century A.D.** Blade with one sharp edge, tang for fitting into handle. Total length 4.5 cm. Malloy #67a; Petrie, *Tools and Weapons,* XXV:71. Cf. Smith, fig. 180c. Some corrosion on sharp edge. ....**CHOICE 125.00**

1552. **IRON KNIFE BLADE. Roman. 1st-3rd Century A.D.** Blade with one sharp edge, short tang for fitting into handle. Total length 8.9 cm. Petrie, *Tools and Weapons,* XXV:71. Cf. Smith, fig. 180c. Cf. Malloy, *Weapons,* #67a. Corrosion. ....**CHOICE 125.00**

1553. **IRON KNIFE BLADE. 1st-3rd Century A.D.** One straight sharp edge. Tang flat, curved inward at one point. Total length 11.5 cm. Petrie, *T&W* XXV:71; Cf. Smith, fig. 180. ....**CHOICE 150.00**

1554. **BRONZE DAGGER BLADE. 1st Century B.C.-3rd Century A.D.** Double edged. Iron pin at tine. Minor traces of wooden handle remain. 12.7 cm long, 2.5 cm wide. Italian manufacture. Scarce. Ex. Villa Julia Collection. ....**SUPERB 250.00**

1555. **IRON BLADE. Roman. 1st-4th Century A.D.** Double edged blade, curved, with back-chopper for cutting hard stems. Has tang which is surrounded by socket held together by iron pin. Some remains of wooden handle in socket. Length 12 cm, width 10.2 cm. Cf. Petrie 13,14. This type found mainly in the Mediterranean, used for the vine. ....**CHOICE 150.00**

Spear and Javelin Points

1556. **IRON JAVELIN HEAD. Roman. 1st Century B.C.-3rd Century A.D.** Square head, pointed, with tang. Length 3.8 cm. Petrie 157, James p. 11, Cf. Malloy #137a. ....**CHOICE 50.00**

1557. **IRON JAVELIN HEAD. Roman. 1st Century B.C.-3rd Century A.D.** Square head, pointed, with tang. Length 4.9 cm. Malloy 137a; Petrie 157; James p. 11. ..**CHOICE 35.00**

1558. **IRON SPEARHEAD. 1st Century B.C.-3rd Century A.D.** Leaf blade with folded socket. The pilum was the Roman throwing spear with wooden shaft and long slender iron forepart terminating in a small head. Iron oxide. Pinched shaft. Cf. Brailsford, *Antiquities of Roman Britain,* fig. 36, 4. ....**CHOICE 80.00**

Axe, Adze, and Mace Heads

1559. **LEAD AXE HEAD. 1st Century A.D.** Ceremonial axe head. Blade widens at end. Has hole for handle. Length 5.7 cm, blade width 2.6 cm. Cf. Petrie 30; Pompeii #31, 32. Ex. Villa Julia Collection. Similar designs have been found at Pompeii. ....**CHOICE 100.00**

Arrowheads

1560. **BRONZE ARROWHEAD. Roman Republic (Spain). 300-100 B.C.** Biblade head with long socket and extended spur. Length 3.8 cm. Petrie-, Savory-. Cf. Malloy 119. Found in the Cordoba area of Spain. Spur is chipped. ......**CHOICE 60.00**

1561. **BRONZE ARROWHEAD. Roman (Italian). 3rd-1st Century B.C.** Socketed triblade head with lung. Length 3.1 cm. Ex. Villa Julia Collection. ....**CHOICE 125.00**

1562. **BRONZE ARROWHEAD. Roman Republic (Italian). 3rd-1st Century B.C.** Socketed biblade head with one spur-barb. Length 2 cm. Malloy #120; Tushingham -, Petrie -. Ex. Villa Julia Collection.................................**CHOICE 60.00**

1563. **BRONZE ARROWHEAD. Roman Republic (Sicily). 3rd-1st Century B.C.** Trilobate head with depressions at each side of the shaft, creating three barbs. Length 1.9 cm. Malloy #122; Tushingham -, Petrie -.......................**CHOICE 45.00**

1564. **BRONZE ARROWHEAD. Roman (Sicily). 2nd-1st Century B.C.** Triblade head, flat sides, shaft very short. Small hole on one side. Length 1.7 cm. Tushingham-, Petrie-. ....**CHOICE 60.00**

1565. **BRONZE ARROWHEAD. Roman Republic (Spain). 200-100 B.C.** Biblade arrowhead, with trace of spur. Socketed. Length 34 mm. Petrie-; Savory-. Found in the Carmona area of Spain. ....**CHOICE 50.00**

1566. **BRONZE ARROWHEAD. Roman (Italian). 1st Century B.C.-1st Century A.D.** Triblade head, indents at sides. Length 1.9 cm. Tushingham -, Petrie -, Cf. Malloy #125. Ex. Villa Julia Collection. ....**SUPERB 75.00**

1567. **BRONZE ARROWHEAD. Roman. 1st Century B.C.-1st Century A.D.** Trilobate head, flat sides but half grooved at socket end. Slight barbs. Length 24 mm. Petrie-; Group A #14. Malloy 126 var. ....**CHOICE 50.00**

1568. **BRONZE ARROWHEAD. Roman. 1st Century B.C.-1st Century A.D.** Trilobate head with upper portion flat-bladed to grooved socketed shaft. Length 18 mm. Petrie-; Group B #14a. Malloy-. ....**CHOICE 60.00**

1569. **BRONZE ARROWHEAD. Roman. 1st Century B.C.-1st Century A.D.** Trilobate head with flat upper and blades to base socket. Pronounced barbs. Length 29 mm. Group B #18. Malloy -; Petrie -. Tip off. Chip on one blade. Superb surface. ....**CHOICE 75.00**

1570. **BRONZE ARROWHEAD. Roman (Italian). 1st Century B.C.-1st Century A.D.** Triblade head with defined shaft. Length 1.7 cm. Malloy #123; Tushingham-; Petrie-. Ex. Villa Julia Collection. ....**CHOICE 35.00**

1571. **BRONZE ARROWHEAD. Roman (Italian). 1st Century B.C.-1st Century A.D.** Triblade head with small barbs to shaft. Length 1.3 cm. Malloy #124; Tushingham -; Petrie -. Ex. Villa Julia Collection. ....**CHOICE 30.00**

1572. **BRONZE ARROWHEAD. Roman (Italian). 1st Century B.C.-1st Century A.D.** Triblade head, indents at sides. Length 1.8 cm. Malloy #125; Tushingham-; Petrie-. Ex. Villa Julia Collection. ....**CHOICE 40.00**

1573. **BRONZE ARROWHEAD. Roman. 1st Century B.C.-2nd Century A.D.** Trilobate head, straight flat edge with medium socket shaft. Barbed. Length 28 mm. Group A #15. Petrie -; Malloy -. Scarce. ....**CHOICE 75.00**

1574. **IRON ARROWHEAD. 1st Century B.C.-2nd Century A.D.** Rhombic head with long tapering rhombic tang. Length 3.5 cm, width 1 cm. Cf. Petrie, *The Arrow*, p. 35 var. A rare type. ....**SUPERB 125.00**

1575. **IRON ARROWHEAD. 1st-2nd Century A.D.** Rhombic head with tine. Length 3 cm, width 1 cm. Cf. Petrie. *The Arrow*, p. 35 var. ....**SUPERB 125.00**

1576. **BRONZE ARROWHEAD. Roman. 1st-3rd Century A.D.** Bronze triangular arrowhead. No shaft, but hole for shaft. Italian manufacture. Length 2 cm, width .4 cm. Ex. Villa Julia Collection. ....**AVERAGE 30.00**

1577. **BRONZE ARROWHEAD. 1st-3rd Century A.D.** Triangled without shaft, hole for shaft. Italian manufacture. Length 2 cm, width .6 cm. Ex. Villa Julia Collection. ....**CHOICE 50.00**

1578. **BRONZE ARROWHEAD. Roman (Egyptian). 1st-3rd Century A.D.** Triangular blades with shaft hole. Length 2.3 cm. Malloy #128; Petrie-. Found in Egypt; of local manufacture. Scarce.. ....**CHOICE 70.00**

1579. **BRONZE ARROWHEAD. 1st-4th Century A.D.** Bronze deltoid blade arrowhead with socketed shaft. Measures 2.4 x .5 cm. Ex. Villa Julia Coll. One barb worn and some corrosion. Scarce type. ....**CHOICE 70.00**

1580. **BRONZE ARROWHEAD. Roman. 1st-4th Century A.D.** Long triangular head without shaft. Length 18 mm. Ex. Villa Julia Collection. Chip at base. ....**CHOICE 40.00**

1581. **BRONZE ARROWHEAD. Roman (Italian). 1st-4th Century A.D.** Bronze tip blade head with indentation to sides. No shaft. Length 14 mm. Malloy 127 var. Ex. Villa Julia Collection. Tip off. ....**CHOICE 45.00**

1582. **BRONZE ARROWHEAD. Roman. 1st-4th Century A.D.** Triangular head without shaft. 15 x 8 mm. Ex. Villa Julia Collection. Dura Europus. ....**CHOICE-SUPERB 65.00**

1583. **BRONZE ARROWHEAD. 2nd-3rd Century A.D.** Bronze trilobed arrowhead with socketed shaft. Measures 2.1 x .7 cm. Similar arrowheads were found at the Dura Europus excavations in 1932. Cf. Yale, Dura Europus 1932 #159. ....**CHOICE 60.00**

Bullets

1584. **SLING BULLET. Roman Republic. 4th-2nd Century B.C.** Pointed at each end, with bulbous center. Italian manufacture. Length 3 cm. Cf. Petrie CLIV 15-16, Cf. Malloy, *Weapons* #138. Ex. Villa Julia Collection. ....**CHOICE 75.00**

1585. **LEAD SLING BULLET (Glans). Roman Republic. 4th-2nd Century B.C.** Large, mold-cast, almond-shaped. Length 5 cm. Malloy #139; Petrie XLIV 15-23. Found in Spain. Larger and heavier than later examples. Lead glandes were found at the Battle of Marathon and throughout the Hellenistic period. ....**CHOICE 35.00**

1586. **SLING BULLET. Late Roman Republic. 1st Century B.C.** Two sharp-pointed ends. Length 4.5 cm. Petrie -, Cf. Malloy #140. Found at the site of the Battle of Munde. ....**CHOICE 60.00**

1587. **SLING BULLET. Late Roman Republic. 1st Century B.C.** Short and stubby, pointed at each end. Length 3.6 cm. Petrie -, Cf. Malloy # 142. From the Battle of Munde, fought between the armies of Pompey and Caesar...**CHOICE 50.00**

1588. **LEAD SLING BULLET. Roman. 1st Century B.C.** Round ball flattened at one end. Diameter 1.6 cm. Malloy #143. Ex. Villa Julia Collection..................**CHOICE 40.00**

1589. **LEAD SLING BULLET. Republic. 1st Century B.C.-45 B.C.** From the Civil Wars. Long pointed shot with round raised waist. Incised L...VI. (Legion VI). Length 4.3 cm. Found at the site of the Battle of Munda. Legion VI Victrix was one of Caesar's legions, stationed in Spain. ....**CHOICE 175.00**

1590. **LEAD SLING BULLET. Roman. 1st Century B.C.-1st Century A.D.** Medium size, mold cast, almond shape. Length 3 cm. Malloy #144; Cf. Petrie XLIV 15-23. Found in Spain. These smaller examples were used in battle by the late Republican and very early Principate slingers. The glandes were used primarily during the Roman Republican period. ....**CHOICE 30.00**

1591. **LEAD SLING BULLET. Roman. 1st Century B.C.-1st Century A.D.** Medium size, mold cast, almond shape with casting knob. Length 4.5 cm. Malloy #145; Cf. Petrie XLIV 15-23. Found in Spain. This interesting sling bullet shows the casting knob used in making the bullet...**CHOICE 35.00**

1592. **LEAD SLING BULLET. Roman. 1st Century A.D.** One end pointed, the other blunt. Inscribed "[LE](XXI." Length 4.9 cm. Malloy #147. Ex. Villa Julia Collection. Legion XXI Rapax was raised by Augustus, and remained in Germany through the later part of the first century. ....**CHOICE (IMAGE VG) 100.00**

1593. **LEAD SLING BULLET. Roman. 1st Century A.D.** One end pointed, the other blunt. Inscribed "[LE](," with legion name obscured. Length 4 cm. Malloy #148. ....**CHOICE (IMAGE VG) 50.00**

1594 **LEAD SLING BULLET. 1st-3rd Century A.D.** Very elongated, pointed ends. Length 9.4 cm. The Latin name for the sling bullet, glans, translates literally as "acorn." Petrie-. ....**CHOICE 75.00**

Tools

1595. **IRON BORING TOOL. Roman. 1st Century B.C.-1st Century A.D.** Four-sided bit widening at midpoint. Length 8.5 cm, width 1 cm. Cf. Petrie 18, Pompeii N.71832 Iron. ....**CHOICE 65.00**

1596. **IRON BILL HOOK OR PRUNING HOOK. Roman. 1st Century B.C.-1st Century A.D..** One-sided blade, curved tip, no handle but pin hole at base. Length 17.5 cm, width 4.5 cm. Cf. Petrie, Pl. LVII. 41,42. Found in the Phoenicia-Judaea area. "And they shall beat their swords into plowshares, and their spears into pruning hooks." Isaiah 2:4. A rare item. ....**CHOICE-SUPERB 250.00**

1597. **IRON SPADE. Roman. 1st Century B.C.-2nd Century A.D.** Pointed, of triangular form with central ridge. Length 29 cm, width 11.5 cm. Cf. Petrie, p. 55. Both pointed and square spades were in use at Pompeii. This heavy example was from the Roman Antioch region. A rare item. ....**CHOICE 400.00**

1598. **BRONZE RAZOR. Roman. 1st-3rd Century A.D.** Small knife. 95 mm. This type was used for food, not as a weapon. Ex. Villa Julia Collection. ....**CHOICE 75.00**

POTTERY

1599. **UNGUENTARIUM. 1st Century B.C.-1st Century A.D.** Cream unguentarium with red slip at rim. Height 15 cm. Albright 48/15. ....**CHOICE 125.00**

1600. **PLATE. 1st Century B.C.-1st Century A.D.** Buff plate with dull red-orange slip on the edge; some slip runs into the central portion. Diameter 16.5 cm. Intact...**CHOICE 200.00**

1601. **BOWL. Cyprus. Roman Period. 100 A.D.** Brown ware with slightly concave base. One small handle. Decorated in bands of geometric design with a dark brown glaze. Criss-cross design in dark glaze on base of bowl. 22.4 cm diam., 5.4 cm high. Cf. Hayes, *ROM-*. Cf. Cesnola Collection of Cypriot Antiquities-. A rare Roman vessel...**CHOICE 700.00**

1602. **SIGLATA FRAGMENT. 1st Century A.D.** Fragment with floral decoration. Measures 5.5 x 7 cm. Some chipping of slip to left. ....**CHOICE 35.00**

1603. **PILGRIM FLASK. 1st-2nd Century A.D.** Egyptian manufacture. Buff pottery pilgrim flask with traces of pink. Plastic design of tied rim. Stamping of four men in a boat with oars below and two fish. Stamped inscription: AZANETH. The reverse side shows a grotto. Height 6 cm. Chip at rim. Rare and unusual. ....**CHOICE 150.00**

1604. **MEGARIAN WARE. Roman. 1st-3rd Century A.D.** Orange-red clay with metallic black gloss (sepia color). Round basin, slightly concave base and very slight indentation before rim. Outturned lip. On base is eight-petalled rosette surrounded by palmette, leaves, and curly stems. Beaded line above, and rosettes with two small dolphins between. Beaded lines above that, then wavy spiral decoration with plain line and groove. 16.2 cm diam., 9 cm high. Cf. *ROM* #185-187. Restored. ....**CHOICE 900.00**

1605. **JUG PORTION. 2nd Century A.D.** Barbotine ware. Buff clay, lower portion of a jug with an ovoid ribbed body. Barbotine decoration applied in lines of horizontal zig-zag. Height 8.2 cm. This ware is from the Greek mainland; this example was found near Corinth and is certainly related to the Egyptian Barbotine ware. *Athenian Agora-*; *ROM-*. Recomposed. Very rare. ....**CHOICE 150.00**

1606. **UNGUENTARIUM. 3rd Century A.D.** Buff unguentarium; a large elongated vessel with ridges at the ovoid section, and a flare rim. Height 20 cm. Mounted. Intact and nice size. ....**CHOICE 150.00**

1607. **TWO-HANDLED JAR. 3rd-4th Century A.D** Buff two-handled jar. Light orange slip, ovoid body with knob at base. Ribbing over body. Strap handle at each side. Cf. *ROM* 300. Height 9.8 cm. Small chip at rim...............**CHOICE 125.00**

1608. **POTTERY JUGLET FRAGMENT. Late 3rd-4th Century A.D.** Red clay. Molding showing eagle standing right with wings outstretched. Garland to right. Fairly thick coarse clay with occasional dark or black inclusions. 6.5 cm x 6.5 cm. For similar molding of clay, Cf. *ROM* #170 (Late Roman Pottery). Mounted. ....**CHOICE 125.00**

1609. **POTTERY SHARD: BOWL FRAGMENT. 4th Century A.D.** Roman Carthaginian-Early Christian. Red terra siglatta from North Africa. Shows the mummified figure of Lazarus in a temple. Measures 6.9 x 4.8 cm. Mounted. An early symbol of the Christian resurrection. ....**CHOICE 200.00**

1610. **FIGURINE. 4th-5th Century A.D.** Figurine of warrior executed in crude provincial style. Probably North African. Appears to be a finial from a round bowl or vessel. Height 64 mm. Crude style. ....**CHOICE 80.00**

1611. **FLAGON. Late Roman. 5th Century A.D.** Egyptian manufacture. Red slip ware. Narrow-neck flagon with orange-red slip. Molded rim, handle slightly flared. Pedestal base. Height 8 cm. Cf. *ROM*, Hayes 116 var. ....**SUPERB 250.00**

1612. **FRAGMENT OF RED SLIP WARE. 5th Century A.D.** Roman Africa. Part of the rim of a plate, showing a flying male figure with arms and legs outstretched. Measures 6.5 by 5.3 cm. Cf. Hayes, *ROM* 99/100. Interesting piece. ....**CHOICE 100.00**

1613. **FRAGMENT OF RED SLIP WARE. 5th Century A.D.** Roman Africa. Part of a shallow bowl, showing a leopard in relief with an ornate dagger in front of his open mouth. Animal has patterned body. Fragment measures 10.1 x 7.2 cm. Cf. Hayes, *ROM* 99. Nice detail and decoration. ....**CHOICE 125.00**

TERRACOTTA

1614. **FIGURE OF SILENUS.   Roman Republic. 3rd-1st Century B.C.** Seated figure with knees drawn up, on which he rests hands. Protruding belly. Bald with beard, head and shoulders against back rest. Coarse pale orange ware with much grit. 11 cm high. Possibly from an architectural pediment. *BM*-. Seleucia-. Nice size. ....**CHOICE 350.00**

1615. **FEMALE HEAD. 1st Century B.C.-1st Century A.D.** Buff clay head, possibly Aphrodite. Hair rolled up; wearing large earrings. Height 2.5 cm. Very similar to Aphrodites found in Egypt. For style, Cf. Van Ingen #214. Bold detail. ....**CHOICE-SUPERB 125.00**

1616. **HEAD OF A DOG. Roman Egypt. 1st Century B.C.-1st Century A.D.** Perked ears and rough hair. 6.8 cm high. Cf. Kaufmann, *Agyptische Terrakotten*, fig. 118 var, p. 135. Probably from Faijum. These types of dogs are still seen in modern Egypt ....**AVERAGE-CHOICE 50.00**

1617. **MASK OF BES. Roman Rule. 30 B.C.-641 A.D.** Face nicely carved. Chipped on right side and top of face. Could have been used as a hanging amulet. 5 cm long, 4.5 cm wide. Bes was the god of children and of the household. He was not of Egyptian origin, but rather from the land of Punt on the African coast. Shows wear to face. Cf. Kaufmann, *Agyptische Terrakotten*, p. 74, fig. 41-43 var and p. 71, fig. 40 var. ....**CHOICE 65.00**

1618. **HEAD OF YOUNG MALE. Roman Period. 1st Century A.D.** Beautiful facial features. Lovely workmanship. Left ear remaining. 4.2 cm long, 3.4 cm wide. Possibly Harpocrates as an older youth. Cf. Kaufmann, *Agyptische Terrakotten*, fig. 189, 112. ....**SUPERB 125.00**

1619. **ARRETINE POTTERY SHERD. 1st Century A.D.** Orange-brown pottery sherd with hare. 5.4 cm high, 5 cm wide. For design, Cf Pl. XXXVI.33, for shape, Cf. Pl. XIX.2, Oswald, *An Introduction to the Study of Terra Sigillata*. Mounted ....**CHOICE 40.00**

1620. **FIGURE. 1st Century A.D.** Fragment of reclining figure. Terracotta painted with traces of blue and cream remaining. Decoration around neck, crown which resembles horns. Face has severe expression. Roman Egyptian. Length 83 mm. Cf. for type *Agyptische Terrakotten*, fig. 107. Superb fragment. ....**SUPERB 140.00**

1621. **NEGROID HUMAN HEAD. 1st Century A.D.** Orange terracotta siglatta handle with African head terminal; handle with palmettes. Head height 23 mm, total length 55 mm. Oswald-Price-, *ROM*-, Brown *BMC*-, Chase Boston-. This handle came from a skyphos. ....**CHOICE 135.00**

1622. **HARPOKRATES BUST Roman Egypt. 1st-2nd Century A.D.** Finger to mouth. Above head and below waist chipped off. 4.5 cm high, 4 cm wide. Cf. Kaufmann, *Agyptische Terrakotten*, fig. 28-38 var, pp. 46-69. Sammlung Loeb, *Terrakotten II*, Pl. 109, fig. 1, p. 50. ....**CHOICE 85.00**

1623. **SEALING. 1st-2nd Century A.D.** Round sealing showing Hercules standing facing, holding a club and lion's skin. Diameter 13 mm. Cf. Hague 603. ....**CHOICE 100.00**

1624. **FIGURE OF APHRODITE. 1st-2nd Century A.D.** Terracotta figure of Aphrodite . Nude, arms raised, legs bent at sides. Hair bound up, rosette at forehead, wearing necklace. Height 13 cm. Broken at knee of right leg, otherwise intact. Bold features. ....**CHOICE 375.00**

1625. **HEAD OF SERAPIS. Greco-Roman. 1st-2nd Century A.D.** Brown terracotta. Wearing beard and Isis crown of horns and sun disc. Worn features. 5 cm high. Mounted. Cf. Kaufmann, fig. 16-17. ....**CHOICE 80.00**

1626. **HEAD OF A MAN. 1st-2nd Century A.D.** Orange terracotta head of a man, probably a slave. Wearing a cloth headdress. Stern expression. Features rather worn. Height 3.5 cm. Mounted. Kaufmann fig. 107. Bold. Scarce. ....**CHOICE 135.00**

1627. **YOUTH'S HEAD. 1st-2nd Century A.D.** Cream terracotta head of a young male with short hair. Height 3.4 cm. ....**CHOICE 75.00**

1628. **HEAD OF SERAPIS. Egyptian (Greco/Roman). 1st-2nd Century A.D.** Light orange terracotta head wearing beard and modius. Features worn. 4.5 cm high. Cf. Kaufmann, figs. 16-17 ....**AVERAGE 50.00**

1629. **HEAD OF SERAPIS. Egyptian (Greco/Roman). 1st-2nd Century A.D.** Brown terracotta. Wearing beard and Isis crown of horns and sun disc. Worn features. 5 cm high. Cf. Kaufmann, fig. 16-17................................**CHOICE 100.00**

1630. **HEAD OF A CHILD. Egyptian. 1st-2nd Century A.D.** Red-brown terracotta head. Stylized curls underneath tall semi-pointed hat. Nice molding. Left side of face is missing. 3.5 cm high. Cf. Kaufmann, fig. 103. Lovely style. ....**CHOICE 125.00**

1631. **HEAD OF YOUNG CHILD. Egyptian. 1st-2nd Century A.D.** Small orange-brown terracotta head wearing what looks like a cloth cap with a band across forehead. Features clear and the child is frowning. 2.5 cm high. Kaufmann-. Philipp-. Charming style. ....**CHOICE 125.00**

1632. **HEAD OF MAN. Egyptian. 1st-2nd Century A.D.** Orange terracotta head, probably a slave. Wearing a cloth headdress. Although features rather worn, he has a long face with a stern look. 3.5 cm high. Kaufmann, fig. 107. Bold. Scarce. ....**CHOICE 125.00**

1633. **HEAD OF NEGRO SLAVE. Egyptian/Roman. 1st-2nd Century A.D.** Orange-brown terracotta head. Face shows worry lines and a certain sadness. Moderate carving but worn. 4 cm high. Kaufmann-. Bold style. Some wear to lower face. ....**CHOICE 150.00**

1634. **HEAD OF HORSE. Egyptian/Roman. 1st-2nd Century A.D.** Orange-brown terracotta head with snarling features and ears missing. Moderately well molded with quite a lot of detail. Missing behind ears. 5.7 cm long. Kaufmann, fig. 115. ....**SUPERB 150.00**

1635. **HEAD OF FOREIGNER. Egyptian/Roman. 1st-2nd Century A.D.** Orange terracotta head. Heavy jowled face with moustache. Scrinched eyes and frown. Hair surrounding face is curly. Left side of head missing. 3.7 cm long. Kaufmann, fig. 107. Very rare. ....**CHOICE 200.00**

1636. **HEAD OF DEMETER. 1st-2nd Century A.D.** Grey-brown terracotta. Veiled head with hair pulled back. Veil to right missing and above enlongated ears. Eastern manufacture. Height 9.7 cm. Cf. Cesnola, IX, 69; Van Ingen-. Traces of white slip. Nice size. ....**SUPERB 275.00**

1637. **HEAD OF GENIE FIGURE. Roman Egyptian. 1st-3rd Century A.D.** Terracotta. Cone-shaped hat is worn along with a garland. Detail quite good, but face chipped on right side. Good expression on face. Faiyum type. 5.7 cm long, 4.6 cm wide. Traces of original white paint remaining. Cf. Kaufmann, *Agyptische Terrakotten*, p. 141, fig. 103 var. ....**CHOICE 100.00**

1638. **HEAD OF ISIS. Roman Egyptian. 1st-3rd Century A.D.** Terracotta head. Wears a head ornament which may represent the step-crown or the horns and sun disk. Facial features are slightly chipped. Nice detail of hair surrounding the face. 5.2 cm long, 4.1 cm wide. Isis was the most famous goddess of Egypt. She had many names given to her according to different times of the year. Cf. Kaufmann, *Agyptische Terrakotten*, p. 45, fig. 26. ....**CHOICE 65.00**

1639. **NEGROID HEAD. 1st-3rd Century A.D.** Terracotta. Chip at top of nose. 45 mm. Scarce...................**CHOICE 65.00**

1640. **TERRACOTTA HEAD OF TYCHE. Roman Egyptian. 1st-3rd Century A.D.** Head of Tyche, slightly tilted to right, wearing polos. 45 mm. Chip in left of chin, crack in polos, nose worn...................................**ABOUT CHOICE 35.00**

1641. **WOMAN'S HEAD. Hellenistic style, found in Syria. 115-200 A.D.** Large buff clay female head with white slip to face. Hair at sides. Height 9.6 cm. Van Ingen, *Seleucia*, #868. Nice size. ....**CHOICE $250.00**

1642. **HEAD OF APHRODITE(?). Roman Egyptian. 2nd Century A.D.** Brown-red terracotta head fragment. Missing above eyes. Moderate molding. Part of suspension loops for earrings. Measures 6.0 x 5.1 cm. Mounted. Cf. Kaufmann, fig. 112. Bold style. ....**CHOICE 150.00**

1643. **FEMALE HEAD VESSEL FRAGMENT. Roman Egyptian. 2nd Century A.D.** Female head with two rings around neck. 5.3 cm high. Kaufmann, *Agyptische Terrakotten*, fig. 4, p. 16. Fragment, broken at hairline. ....**SUPERB 100.00**

1644. **TERM SIGILETTA MOLD. 2nd Century A.D.** Facing male at center with design above oval and below are two entwined diving dolphins, below which is fruit in basket. 7 x 4.6 cm. Cf. for mold, MFA, Boston, Catalog of Arretine Pottery. ....**CHOICE 150.00**

1645. **HEAD OF HORSE. Roman Egyptian. 2nd Century A.D.** Orange buff terracotta. Rather delicate artwork. The horse wears a diadem. Interesting, nice horse head. Probably from the Faiyum. 4.6 cm long. Kaufmann, fig. 115. Charming style. ....**CHOICE 150.00**

1646. **HEAD OF A GOD. Roman Egyptian. 2nd-3rd Century A.D.** Orange terracotta head of a god, probably Horus. Wearing pharaoh's plain lappet wig with elaborate headdress of horns, feathers, and sun disc. Height 9.3 cm. Mounted. Cf. Kaufmann, fig 59. Rather worn but good detail. ....**CHOICE 100.00**

1647. **HEAD OF HARPOCRATES/HORUS. Roman Egyptian. 2nd-3rd Century A.D.** Orange terracotta head with hand raised to ear. Childlike features; wearing pointed hat or headdress. 6.4 cm high. Mounted. Kaufmann, fig. 38. Features worn. ....**CHOICE 125.00**

1648. **HEAD OF A SLAVE. Roman Egyptian. 2nd-3rd Century A.D.** Orange-red terracotta. Plain hairstyle. 4.5 cm high. Mounted. Gainder #76. Features worn. Missing below neck. Interesting piece. A rare type. ....**CHOICE 100.00**

1649. **HEAD OF HERCULES. Roman Egyptian. 2nd-3rd Century A.D.** Brown terracotta head, probably enthroned. Features worn, but wears a beard and stylized hairstyle. Height 5.5 cm. Mounted. Kaufmann.........**CHOICE 125.00**

1650. **FRAGMENT OF SERAPIS. Egyptian/Roman. 2nd-3rd Century A.D.** Orange terracotta with enthroned figure, missing beneath neck. Wears beard and abundant hair with a modius. Throne behind head on either side. Length 7.5 cm, height 5.5 cm. Mounted. Kaufmann, fig. 16-17. Features worn. ....**CHOICE 75.00**

1651. **HEAD OF A DOG. Roman Egyptian. 2nd-3rd Century A.D.** Orange terracotta head with fierce expression. Has only right ear, which is laid back. Wearing two decorated collars. Height 7 cm. Mounted. Cf. Kaufmann, *Ägyptische Terrakotten,* fig. 119-120. ....**CHOICE 125.00**

1652. **HEAD OF YOUNG HARPOCRATES. Roman Egyptian. 2nd-3rd Century A.D.** Orange-red terracotta head, face crudely carved. Wears Isis crown of horns and sun disc. Also wears lock of youth. 6.8 cm high. Cf. Kaufmann, *Agyptische Terrakotten,* fig. 28. Charming smile. ....**CHOICE 75.00**

1653. **BUST OF HARPOCRATES. Egyptian. 2nd-3rd Century A.D.** Orange-brown terracotta. He wears an elaborate hairstyle and Isis crown of horns and sun disc. Finger to mouth in typical pose. Also has water jug held up over his left arm. 6.3 cm high, 5.5 cm wide. Kaufmann, fig. 29 var. ....**CHOICE 75.00**

1654. **VOTIVE PLAQUE WITH TYCHE. Egyptian. 2nd-3rd Century A.D.** Orange terracotta with Tyche standing inside. Bottom of plaque missing and molding worn. 5.5 cm high. Kaufmann-. Philipp-. Unusual piece. ....**CHOICE 65.00**

1655. **HEAD OF CHILD POPPET STATUE. Egyptian. 2nd-3rd Century A.D.** Orange terracotta head with stylized curls underneath long pointed hat similar to Phrygian helmet. High points of features. 5 cm high. Kaufmann, fig. 103 and 107. Worn. Mounted. ....**CHOICE 75.00**

1656. **FACE OF BES. Roman Period. 2nd-3rd Century A.D.** Small terracotta face. Measures 2.8 x 2.3 cm. Cf. Kaufmann, pp. 49-57. Although slightly worn, has good molding of face. ....**CHOICE 65.00**

1657-1665. No entries.

1666. **HEAD OF RAM. Egyptian/Roman. 2nd-3rd Century A.D.** Light orange terracotta. Details of ram's face, horns and coat which is somewhat worn. 5 cm long, 5 cm high. Cf. Kaufmann, fig. 120. Missing below neck....**CHOICE 135.00**

1667. **POTTERY FRAGMENT. Roman Egyptian. Alexandria. 2nd-3rd Century A.D.** Fragment of a large pottery vase with polychrome male bust. Upper portion of body, head facing, turned right. Right arm raised. Black paint outlining head and eyes, red, orange, beige and yellow decorating body and face. Ex. French Collection. Fine style. Lovely painting. ....**CHOICE 1600.00**

1668. **TERRACOTTA HEAD OF HORUS. Roman Egyptian. 2nd-3rd Century A.D.** Orange terracotta head of god. Wearing pharaoh's plain lappet wig with elaborate headdress of horns, feathers, and sun disc. Height 9.3 cm. Mounted. Cf. Kaufmann, fig. 59. Rather worn but good detail ....**CHOICE 100.00**

1669. **FIGURE OF VICTORY. 2nd-3rd Century A.D.** Brown terracotta standing figure, wings visible behind shoulders. Height 5.3 cm. Missing right arm and lower legs. Rather worn. ....**CHOICE 100.00**

1670. **FIGURE OF HARPOCRATES/HORUS. Roman Egyptian. 2nd-4th Century A.D.** Orange terracotta. Right hand raised, left hand holding water jug. Stylized hair and headdress. Molding slightly worn. Lower left of body broken off. 7 cm high. Mounted. Kaufmann, fig. 38. ....**CHOICE 125.00**

1671. **FIGURE OF HARPOCRATES. Roman Period. 2nd-4th Century A.D.** Light orange terracotta. Young child wearing horns and lock of youth. Also wears long flowing robes with small figure of Horus/Harpocrates (?) on breast. 12 cm high. Mounted. Kaufmann, fig. 28 var. Very unusual type with the small figure. Features worn. ....**CHOICE 125.00**

1672. **HEAD OF A SATYR. Egyptian/Roman. 2nd-4th Century A.D.** Light orange-brown terracotta head of a satyr wearing a beard. Bold forehead and fierce eyes. Tuft of hair at top of head. Height 4.5 cm. Mounted. Kaufmann-; Philipp-. ....**CHOICE 100.00**

1673. **VOTIVE STATUE HEAD OF APHRODITE. Egyptian. 2nd-4th Century A.D.** Light orange terracotta with moderate carving. Hair parted in center, either side of head. Suspension holes in ears. One ear missing. 3.6 cm high. Cf. Kaufmann. Bold. ....**CHOICE 100.00**

1674. **HANDLE OF SISTRUM. Egyptian. 2nd-4th Century A.D.** Orange terracotta. Goddess (Hathor?) with long tresses either side of face. Rather large elaborate headdress. Cylindrical in shape. 6.5 cm high. Moderate molding with artwork pointing toward Roman style. For similar votive figs., Cf. Kaufmann var. ....**CHOICE 100.00**

1675. **HEAD OF APIS BULL. Egyptian. 2nd-4th Century A.D.** Terracotta. Holy cow of Hathor. Wearing collar and head-dress of feathers. Right ear missing. 7 cm high. Kaufmann, fig. 60. ....**CHOICE 85.00**

1676. **TERRACOTTA BUST OF APHRODITE.** Roman Egyptian. 2nd half of 2nd Century A.D. Aphrodite with arm raised to ornate headdress with Uraeus. Three strands of hair falling to shoulder. Upper right portion. 9 cm high. Hornborstel, Kunstder Antika, Hamburg #153. Kaufmann, *Agyptische Terrakotten*, fig. 50, p. 81. ......**CHOICE 125.00**

1677. **BUST OF WOMAN.** Egyptian/Roman. c. 3rd Century A.D. Terracotta. Wearing her hair tied back under a plain headdress. Surrounding forehead, stylized curls. Wearing necklace and dress. 7 cm high. Features are clear but not delicate. Body missing below breast. Philipp-. Kaufmann. ....**CHOICE 125.00**

1678. **PALMYRAN TERRERA.** 3rd Century A.D. Obverse: Rosette motif. Reverse: Human figure seated on the back of two panthers facing. Measures 1.5 x 1.0 cm. Some chipping. Scarce. ....**CHOICE 100.00**

1679. **HEAD OF A CHILD.** Roman Egyptian. 3rd-4th Century A.D. Light buff-orange terracotta. Very crude features. Crude decoration of hair and remains of cap. Clear details of face and hair. Height 4.3 cm. Mounted. Cf. Kaufmann. Bold. ....**CHOICE 80.00**

1680. **BUST OF WOMAN (Isis).** Egyptian/Roman. 3rd-4th Century A.D. Orange terracotta. Facial features late Roman, early Coptic style. Headdress has red slip on it. 10 cm high. Cf. Hanna, Philipp, Pl. 27 for similar shape of bust. ....**CHOICE 100.00**

1681. **TERRACOTTA COIN MOLD.** Roman 4th Century A.D. Dark grey coin mold with an impression of a follis-type coin from Egypt and Judaea. 2.8 cm. diam. These were circulated in Southern Egypt probably as emergency coinage. ....**CHOICE 75.00**

1682. **RED TERM SIGILATTA PLAQUE FRAGMENT.** Roman Carthaginian. 4th Century A.D. Figure of gladiator in combat, holding spear. Triangular in shape, squared corner, perhaps a plaque or a plate. ....**CHOICE 125.00**

1683. **POTTERY SHERD BOWL FRAGMENT.** Roman Carthaginian-Early Christian. 4th Century A.D. Red terra sigilatta from North Africa. Mummified figure of Lazarus in a temple. Has a Christian connotation. 6.9 x 4.8 cm. An early symbol of the Christian resurrection with the mummiform figure of Lazarus, here represented in an early church. ....**CHOICE 200.00**

1684. **COIN MOLD.** 4th Century A.D. Mold of the obverse and reverse of a follis of Maximinus II from the Alexandria mint. Diameter 27 mm. These were circulated in southern Egypt as emergency coinage. Impressions are sharp. ....**CHOICE 85.00**

1685. **TERRACOTTA HEAD OF SATYR.** Roman Egyptian. 4th Century A.D. Light orange/brown head, bearded. Bold forehead and fierce eyes. Also remains of tuft of hair at top of head. Length 4.5 cm. Mounted. Kaufmann-; Philipp. ....**CHOICE 100.00**

1686. **HEAD OF A WOMAN.** Roman Egyptian. 4th-5th Century A.D. Orange terracotta. Large head with staring eyes and hair held back by a decorative diadem. Height 6.3 cm. Mounted. Kaufmann-; Philipp-. Slight crack in center. ....**CHOICE 125.00**

1687. **HARPOCRATES FIGURINE.** Roman Egyptian. 4th-5th Century A.D. Complete orange-brown terracotta figure of Harpocrates sitting, wearing a crown and sun disk. Wearing lock of youth on right side. Vent hole in back. Traces of white slip and black paint remaining. Height 12 cm. Mounted. Cf. Kaufmann, fig. 29, 30. ....**SUPERB 450.00**

1688. **FIGURINE OF VICTORY.** Roman Egyptian. 4th-5th Century A.D. Brown terracotta standing female figure, wings visisible behind shoulders. Flat back. Height 5.3 cm. Missing right arm and lower legs. Rather worn. ....**CHOICE 100.00**

1689. **FIGURE OF WOMAN.** Egyptian. 4th-5th Century A.D. Orange terracotta. Large, staring eyes with hair held back by a decorative diadem. 6.3 cm high. Kaufmann-. Philipp. Only face left with slight crack in center. ....**CHOICE 125.00**

1690. **HEAD OF COCKEREL.** Egyptian. Late 4th Century A.D. Fragment of small jug in beige terracotta. Fine detailing of band showing crown. Beak like that of a bird of prey. Spout of jug above. Remains of handle on crest of bird. 4 cm high. Cf. P. Grannidor, Pl. 1, no. 2 for similar artwork. ....**CHOICE 100.00**

METAL

1691. **BRONZE HANDLE.** Etruscan/Roman Republic. c. 300 B.C. Bronze patera (dish) handle in cast bronze. Fixed handle below. Handle midpoint has concave and convex bead molding. Escutcheon shows relief with volutes above. 10.3 cm wide x 12 cm high. Surface with olive green patina. Nice size. ....**CHOICE 350.00**

1692. **BRONZE BALSAMARIUM HEAD.** Etruscan-Roman 3rd Century B.C. Bronze balsamarium in the shape of a female head with a band in her hair. Finely delineated features. Yellow-green patina. Only the face and part of the rim are still present. ....**CHOICE 550.00**

1693. **BRONZE FISH HOOK.** 2nd Century B.C.-3rd Century A.D. 3 cm long. Found in Roman excavations. Cf. Petrie, *Tools and Weapons*, XLIV, 78. ....**CHOICE 25.00**

1694. **BRONZE NETTING NEEDLE. 2nd Century B.C.-3rd Century A.D.** Dual prongs to each end. 11.5 cm long. Ex. MacGruder Collection #X I 6l2. Scarce. Cf. Petrie, *Tools and Weapons*, LXV, 100. Cf. BMC, *Greek and Roman Life*, fig. 168. Cf. Boucher, *Vienne Bronzes Antiques*, #474. Cf. Robinson, Olynthus, #1763. ....**CHOICE 100.00**

1695. **BRONZE DOLPHIN FORM ASKOS. Roman Republic. 1st Century B.C.** Askos in dolphin form with trefoil rim forming wide flaring spout. Handle has three pointed leaf decorations at each end. Mounted. 9.5 cm high. Cf. *Vienne* #252. This askos style was adopted from the Etruscans. ....**CHOICE 1000.00**

1696. **BRONZE CHAIN. Roman. 1st Century B.C.-1st Century A.D.** Chain of necklace. Each link has a double ring of bronze. 11.9 cm long. Ex. Villa Julia Collection. Cf. *Vienne* #99. Some erosion. ....**CHOICE 75.00**

1697. **LEAD SARCOPHAGUS PLAQUE FRAGMENT. 1st Century B.C.-1st Century A.D.** Shows relief of an eagle standing right. Manufactured in Phoenicia. 16.3 cm wide, 8.2 cm high. *Vienne-*. An unusual piece. ....**CHOICE 100.00**

1698. **LEAD SARCOPHAGUS PLAQUE FRAGMENT. 1st Century B.C.-1st Century A.D.** Shows relief of a two-handled crater. Manufactured in Phoenicia. 6.7 cm high x 9 cm wide. *Vienne -*.....................................**CHOICE 90.00**

1699. **BRONZE BROOCH. 1st Century A.D.** Diamond-shaped brooch with traces of original enamel. Two perforations off-center from design. Pin remains, but end of catch missing. ....**CHOICE 50.00**

1700. **BRONZE STRYGIL HANDLE. 1st Century A.D.** 6.5 inches long. The Romans, after the bath, would use this as a scraper to remove oil and water from their skin. Green patina. Ex. Villa Julia Collection. Cf. BM, *Antiquities of Roman Britain*, fig. 5/12. ....**CHOICE 80.00**

1701. **BRONZE NAIL. 1st Century A.D.** Used in the making of ships. 2.5 cm diameter head, 3.5 cm. shaft. Found at Nemi. This nail was part of Caligula's barge, which measured 71 meters x 20 meters! For excavations of Nemi, Cf. Moretti-Caprino, *Il Museo delle Navi Romane de Nemi*. ....**CHOICE 65.00**

1702. **BRONZE CHEST FITTING. 1st Century A.D.** Bronze fitting, hasp in strip form. Hole in top and square pierced projection on bottom back form catch. Cross-shaped element at top with a concentric circle design. Disc element in center also with concentric circle design. Slender tapering toe with short outward curl at tip. 6.3 cm. Cf. *ROM* 310. ....**CHOICE 75.00**

1703. **BRONZE HANDLE. 1st Century A.D.** Bronze handle from a large vessel. Circular with ends turned down. Ends ornamented. Width 9 cm. Ex. Villa Julia Collection. *Vienne* 349. ....**CHOICE 175.00**

1704. **FAIENCE APPLIQUÉ. 1st Century A.D.** Green faience appliqué of Zeus. Length 5 cm. Egyptian manufacture. ....**CHOICE 150.00**

1705. **BRONZE FINGER CYMBAL. Roman. 1st Century A.D.** Small finger cymbal, circular disc, concave with broad flange. Ex. Villa Julia Collection. *Pompeii, A.D. 79*, Vol. II, 188 (Pompeii). Daremberg/Sagid, Cymbalum. A.S. A. E. Hickman 1949, 451. Cymbals were portrayed in conjunction with tambourines and pipes and were commonly played at religious and social functions. ....**CHOICE 75.00**

1706. **CHEST FITTING. Roman. 1st Century A.D.** Bronze chest fitting of a hasp in strip form. Hole in top and a square pierced projection on back at bottom forming the catch. Cross-shaped element at top with a concentric circle design. Disc element in center also with concentric circle design. Slender tapering toe with short outward curl at tip. 6.3 cm. Cf. *ROM* #310. ....**CHOICE 75.00**

1707. **BRONZE ARM. 1st Century A.D.** Left forearm with clasping hand. Length 3 cm. This arm was cast in the lost wax process. It was common for metalworkers to cast parts of a statue to be assembled later: this piece shows working for insertion into the upper arm. Cf. Vermeule Comstock, *Bronzes in the Boston Museum of Fine Arts*. ....**CHOICE 75.00**

1708. **BRONZE BELT APPLIQUÉ. 1st Century A.D.** Round disk with stamped-out (repoussé) design. Diademed head facing right, with a floral branch before. Diameter 19 mm. Cf. Mills, *Roman Artifacts found in Britain*, p. 10-M116. London manufacture. Half edge chipped off. Full portrait in high relief. ....**CHOICE 200.00**

1709. **IRON NAIL. 1st-2nd Century A.D.** Iron nail with expanded round head. Length 6.4 cm. *Vienne*, 76. Similar nails were found at Caligula's barge in Remi, Italy. Chip on side of head. ....**CHOICE 35.00**

1710. **LEAD FEMALE HEAD. 1st-2nd Century A.D.** Head with hair rolled up, wearing tiara. Open back. Height 4 cm. Ex. Villa Julia Collection. Indentation to side of face. ....**AVERAGE 100.00**

1711. **BRONZE APPLIQUÉ. 1st-2nd Century A.D.** Bronze vase handle appliqué with a facing mask of a child or Eros. Height 44 mm. Cut at forehead and cheek. Variegated green and brown patina. Fine style. ....**CHOICE 175.00**

1712. **BRONZE ARM. Roman. 1st-2nd Century A.D.** Detailed bronze handle from a small jug or askos. Arm from a togate figure. The arm is bent and is in the attitude of one holding a spear. 4.6 cm long. Ex. Villa Julia Collection. For similar positioning of arm, Cf. *Vienne #*I. Lovely patina. ....**CHOICE 150.00**

1713. **BRONZE HANDLE OF JUG OR ASKOS. Roman 1st-2nd Century A.D.** Detailed bronze handle from a small jug or askos. Two branches form ends in the shape of leaves with a central leaf or stem in center curling outwards. Near top, stylized Herakles knot. Cast slightly misshapen. 9 cm high. Cf. *Vienne* #287 for similar style. Cf. *ROM* # 102-109 for very similar shape. Ex. Villa Julia Collection. The style of the handle is Hellenistic; however, the workmanship points to early Roman askos handle. Green patina. Delicate style. ....**CHOICE 300.00**

1714. **BRONZE FISHHOOK. Roman. c. 1st-2nd Century A.D.** Very small fishhook in delicate and fine style with tiny arrow at one end and flat spatula-shaped end. Height 3.2 cm. *Vienne*-. *ROM.* ....**CHOICE 35.00**

1715. **LEAD GLANDES OR SLING SHOT. Roman. 1st-2nd Century A.D.** Winged thunderbolt each side. 3.5 cm. The winged thunderbolt was thrown by Jupiter, thus depicting the thunderbolt on the glandes would make it divinely inspired. ....**CHOICE 120.00**

1716. **HANDLE TERMINAL OF PANTOMIME MASK. Roman. Late 1st-2nd Century A.D.** Hollow cast. Mask wears wide cap (tricone) and row of curls underneath. Double screw curls down either side of face. Beautiful face with parted mouth. Small palmette below chin. 5.8 cm long x 4.8 cm wide. This handle terminal comes from a bronze oil lamp. Cf. *ROM* #211 (almost exactly the same). Magnificent style. Nice pine green patina. ....**SUPERB 1000.00**

1717. **BRONZE NAIL. 1st-2nd Century A.D.** Small rounded head with long shaft. 9 cm long shaft, 1.7 cm diam. head. Cf. Excavations in Yugoslavia, Plesnicar-Gec, *Severno Emonsko Grobisce*, Pl. VI 27.4 ....**CHOICE 50.00**

1718. **BRONZE HANDLE FROM FOOTED BOWL OR KRATER. 1st-2nd Century A.D.** Very ornate bronze handle. Both arms end in griffin heads. Molded and turned decoration covering entire handle. 10.3 cm in length. *ROM* 134 and 133. Ex. Villa Julia Collection. Superb metalwork with lovely green patina. ....**SUPERB 400.00**

1719. **BRONZE ORNAMENT TO TRIPOD. 1st-2nd Century A.D.** Spiral leaf patterns. 14 cm long. Cf. Tarbell, *Catalogue of Bronzes in the Field Museum of Natural History*, Pl. XLIV, 23. Green patina. ....**CHOICE 165.00**

1720. **IVORY SPOON. 1st-2nd Century A.D.** Ivory spoon of "cochlear type," reportedly used for eating eggs and shellfish. Length 9 cm. Cf. Mills, *Roman Artifacts*, Pic. M161. End of handle chipped. ....**CHOICE 200.00**

1721. **IVORY SPOON. 1st-2nd Century A.D.** Ivory ligula, a tiny spoon used for extracting cosmetics from a container. Length 9 cm. BMC *Roman Britain*, fig. 5-3. End of handle chipped off. ....**CHOICE 175.00**

1722. **BRONZE SPOON. 1st-2nd Century A.D.** Bronze ligula with one round flattened end. Length 12.5 cm. Cf. BMC *Roman Britain*, fig. 5-3; *Vienne* 448. ....**CHOICE 150.00**

1723. **BRONZE FIGURE OF GENIUS. 1st-2nd Century A.D.** Diademed figure of nude Genius standing with left leg to front. Height 6.9 cm. Mounted. Cf. D.T. Hill, *Classical Bronze*, Pl. 34 #157 for pose. Left arm and right hand missing. Red oxide corrosion. Heavy green patina. Heavy encrustation. ....**AVERAGE 200.00**

1724. **BRONZE FINGER RING KEY. 1st-2nd Century A.D.** Ring with key attached at right angle. Ring diameter 18 mm. Key measures 10 x 12 mm. Mills, pic. M137b var. Nice green patina. Wearable on small hand. ....**CHOICE 80.00**

1725. **BRONZE RAZOR. 1st-3rd Century A.D.** Bronze razor with curved end terminal with a loop. Length 11 cm. Ex. Villa Julia Collection. Cf. Petrie X: 86-93 for loops; Cf. Petrie XIII for shape of knife; LXIII 44-47. Only part of loop present. Rare. ....**CHOICE 300.00**

1726. **BRONZE STRAIGHT PIN. 1st-3rd Century A.D.** Turned pattern around. Length 11 cm. *Vienne*, p. 183, Pl. 1, #30 ....**CHOICE 100.00**

1727. **BRONZE STRAIGHT PIN. 1st-3rd Century A.D.** Spiral pattern. Suspension hole at end. Length 13 mm. ....**CHOICE 100.00**

1728. **BRONZE LIGULA. 1st-3rd Century A.D.** Spoon with enlongated narrow bowl for extracting cosmetics from a narrow glass phial. Thin stem, probe worn away. Length 9.5 mm. Mills p. 59, pic. 164. ....**CHOICE 100.00**

1729. **BRONZE SPOON/SPATULA. 1st-3rd Century A.D.** Flattened blade with triangular design below, ending with an olive-shaped probe. Length 14 mm. Cf. Mills, p. 60 pic. M170. ....**CHOICE 100.00**

1730. **BRONZE EAR SCOOP. 1st-3rd Century A.D.** Small circular bowl at end of bronze pin. Scoop was used to remove ear wax. Would be part of a toiletry set. Length 11 mm. Mills, p. 59, pic. M165. ....**CHOICE 100.00**

1731. **BRONZE NAIL. 1st-3rd Century A.D.** Slightly bent bronze nail with dome-shaped head. Corrosion around head. 8.2 cm long. Head 1.4 cm diameter. Ex. Villa Julia Collection. Cf. Boucher, *Vienne Bronze Antiques,* fig. 710-735...**CHOICE 75.00**

1732. **BRONZE SPOON. 1st-3rd Century A.D.** Pointed spoon with curved shaft and rounded end. 14 cm long. Bowl of spoon has minor holes of corrosion. Cf. Boucher, *Vienne* 385; Schumacher, *Karlsruhe*, Pl. XII, #30; Hayes, *ROM* #6. Mounted. ....**CHOICE 225.00**

1733. **BRONZE SEWING NEEDLE.   1st-3rd Century A.D.** Needle with two holes to end. 14.5 cm long. Ex. Villa Julia Collection. Cf. Excavations in Yugoslavia, Plesnicar-Gec, *Severno Emonsko Grobisce*, Pl. XC, 341, 12 var. Cf. BMC, *Greek and Roman Life*, fig. 167. ....**CHOICE 80.00**

1734. **BRONZE LIGULA. 1st-3rd Century A.D.** Long stemmed with small cup-shaped end. 12.3 cm long. The ligula was used for extracting cosmetics and liquids from narrow glass vials in which they were kept. Green patina. Cf. Boucher, *Vienne*, #447. Cf. Tonnochy, *Antiquities of Roman Britain*, 1966, fig. 5135. ....**CHOICE 75.00**

1735. **BRONZE HANDLE OF OINOCHOE. 1st-3rd Century A.D.** Ornamented end with palmette with head of female with long hair to sides, other end with palms at side of comic mask with open mouth. 12.5 cm long. Green patina. Cf. Boucher, *Vienne, Bronzes Antiques* #280. ...**CHOICE 350.00**

1736. **LEAD STEEL YARDWEIGHT. 1st-3rd Century A.D.** In the shape of an amphora. Loop for suspension. 4 inches high. Rare. Ex. Villa Julia Collection De-accession. ....**CHOICE 140.00**

1737. **BRONZE SEWING PIN. Roman. 1st-3rd Century A.D.** Cast with two holes at the base. 13 cm long. Ex. Villa Julia Collection. Cf.-*Vienne* #563-78. Ex. MacGruder Collection #XI599. ....**CHOICE 150.00**

1738. **BRONZE MEAT HOOK. 1st-3rd Century A.D.** Small hook with thick stem ending in curved hook with flat spur protruding behind. Suspension hole in top. Measures 6.5 x 2.8 cm. ....**CHOICE 85.00**

1739. **BRONZE NAIL. 1st-3rd Century A.D.** Domed round head, square shaft. Twist at end of shaft. Found in Cordoba. Length 53 mm. ....**CHOICE 145.00**

1740. **LEAD WEIGHT. 1st-3rd Century A.D.** Heavy weight in the shape of a two-handled amphora. Suspension hole at top, another hole in the base. Length 109 mm, width 33 mm. Weight 11.6 oz. Rare. ....**CHOICE 135.00**

1741. **LARGE BRONZE NEEDLE. 1st-3rd Century A.D.** Large needle with one end slightly flattened for eye. Found in Cordoba. Length 103 mm. ....**CHOICE 100.00**

1742. **IRON KEY. 1st-3rd Century A.D.** Iron key with loop finial. Length 10 cm. Heavy flaking, as usual with iron. ....**CHOICE 75.00**

1743. **BRONZE NAIL. 1st-3rd Century A.D.** Round slightly domed head, square shaft, slightly twisted. Length 62 mm. Found at Rome.   Encrustation   at   top   of   shaft. ....**CHOICE 75.00**

1744. **THREE BRONZE CHAIN LINKS. 1st-3rd Century A.D.** Two complete "figure 8" links, half of third. Length 43 mm. No encrustation - links are not molded together and move freely. Green patina. ....**CHOICE 18.00**

1745. **Bronze Plating. 1st-3rd Century A.D.** Plate of bronze from armor or shield. Straight edge lined with very small rivet holes. Four large rivet holes, remains of two others in body. Ragged edges. Encrusted, much wear and chipping, one crack. 20.3 cm. x 9 cm.............................**AVERAGE 75.00**

1746. **BRONZE TWEEZERS. 1st-4th Century A.D.** Cotter-pin type tweezers. Found in Cordoba. Length 65 mm. ....**CHOICE 85.00**

1747. **BRONZE SPIKE.   1st-4th Century A.D.** Large bronze nail with round head slightly off-center from round shaft. Length 183 mm. Large size suggests that it was used in boat-building. Cf. *Vienne* #710-735, but this example is larger than those referenced. Ex. Villa Julia Collection. ....**CHOICE 125.00**

1748. **BRONZE THIMBLE.   1st-4th Century A.D.** Standard thimble with tiny punch holes throughout surface. 2 cm high, 1.8 cm opening. Cf. Boucher, *Vienne, Bronzes Antiques*, 559-562. Cf. Gusman, Pompei, *La Ville-Les Moeurs-Les Arts*, p. 302. Musee de Naples. ....**CHOICE 75.00**

1749. **BRONZE FINGER.   1st-4th Century A.D.** Finger with nail finely delineated from an outstretched hand. 4 cm long. Dark patina. For hands, Cf. Boucher, *Bronzes Romans*, Lyon, #217-9. ....**CHOICE 80.00**

1750. **BRASS SCALES. Roman. 1st-4th Century A.D.** Scales with brass weight hook at one end. Suspension hole at the center and only a ring where probably another hook was placed. Balance rod 16.2 cm long. Hook 4 cm long x 6.8 cm wide. Ex. Villa Julia Collection. Cf. Vienne #500. Very interesting piece in fine condition. Was probably used as a portable scale for soldiers on campaigns. ....**CHOICE 500.00**

1751. **BRONZE TWEEZERS. Roman. 1st-4th Century A.D.** Small, delicate pair of tweezers. Two arms joined together by circle at top. 5.5 cm long. Ex. Villa Julia Collection. Cf. *Vienne* #556. Minor corrosion, but lovely workmanship. These tweezers still work. ....**CHOICE 175.00**

1752. **IRON COMPASS. Roman. 1st-4th Century A.D.** Compass with two arms joined at the center by a rather large hinge fused together. 12.7 cm long. Ex. Villa Julia Collection. Cf. *Vienne* #553-555. Corrosion and left arm broken at bottom. ....**CHOICE 100.00**

1753. **BRONZE STYLUS OR ERASER ROD. Roman. 1st-4th Century A.D.** Pointed at one end and hammered flat into a disc on the other end. 11.3 cm long. Ex. Villa Julia Collection. Cf. *Vienne*, #446-459. Green patina with some dirt adhering...**CHOICE 100.00**

1754. BRONZE BRACELET. Roman. 1st-4th Century A.D. Very delicate, thin bands of bronze with ends of bracelet made with a wavy line decoration which doubles up on itself. 5 cm diam. Ex. Villa Julia Collection. Cf. *Vienne* #100-126 var. Would go around child's arm several times. One end broken off. Green patina. ....**CHOICE 100.00**

1755. BRONZE LEATHER STUD. Roman. 1st-4th Century A.D. Stud which probably was either in a breastplate for a soldier or horse's harness. Two convex discs either side of a short thick stem. 1 cm high, 1.8 cm dia. Ex. Villa Julia Collection. *Vienne-. ROM.* ....**CHOICE 50.00**

1756. BRONZE ZOOMORPHIC AMULET. Roman. 1st-4th Century A.D. Dog lying, ears alert and tail carved out from beneath him. Suspension hole behind dog's head. 2.4 cm long. Ex. Villa Julia Collection. Cf. for similar zoomorphic amulets, *Vienne* #66-68. Rather worn, but intact. Rare. In the style of Egyptian magical amulets. ....**CHOICE 125.00**

1757. DOUBLE-HEADED BRASS FLESH HOOK. Roman. 1st-4th Century A.D. Right hook missing. Rather thick molded metal with sharp flat arrow at end of carve. 4.6 cm high. *Vienne-. ROM-.* Used for handling meat in the market. End chip. ....**CHOICE 100.00**

1758. BRONZE HAIRPIN. Roman. 1st-4th Century A.D. Delicate style with decorative bauble on the top. Beneath, two bands of beadwork. 10.3 cm long. Ex. Villa Julia Collection. End is slightly bent. ....**CHOICE 100.00**

1759. BRONZE WIRE CHAIN. Roman. 1st-4th Century A.D. Length of bronze wire chain which was probably used for a pendant necklace. Each section has small loop. One end the wire twisted in spiral form ending in a small loop other end. Six sections of chain. 16.5 cm long. Ex. Villa Julia Collection. Vienne-. *ROM-.* Some twisting and erosion. ....**CHOICE 75.00**

1760. BRONZE NAIL. Roman. 1st-4th Century A.D. Long nail with convex. circular head. Cylindrical stem. 18 cm. Probably used in boat building because of length. Ex. Villa Julia Collection. Cf. *Vienne* #710-735 only larger than references given.......................................**CHOICE 125.00**

1761. BRONZE HANDLE OF SITULA. Roman. 1st-4th Century A.D. Deep semi-circle with ends turned down with lovely decoration. Attachment to situla still left on one side. 5.6 cm long. Ex. Villa Julia Collection. Cf. *Vienne* #337-346. Very good workmanship. Intact. ....**SUPERB 150.00**

1762. BRONZE BOWL HANDLE. Roman. 1st-4th Century A.D. Square-shaped cast bronze handle from large bowl. Spiral molding on handle itself. Attachment hooks are U turned then looped once more. 12.3 cm high, 10 cm wide. Ex. Villa Julia Collection. Tarbell, *Catalogue of Bronzes in Field Museum of Natural History*, Nos. 197-200. Intact, but surface encrustation. ....**CHOICE 150.00**

1763. BRONZE POT HANDLE. Roman 1st-4th Century A.D. Very plain sizable pot handle which is attached to bowl by soldering. Inverted stem with circular end with core hole and three small protrusions on the outward side of circle. Cast bronze. 14.5 cm long. Ex. Villa Julia Collection. *Vienne-. ROM.* Intact handle, bowl or pan missing. ...**CHOICE 75.00**

1764. MIRROR FRAGMENT. Roman. 1st-4th Century A.D. Fragment which came from a square-shaped frame. Metal material with evidence of a highly polished surface. 4.6 cm. x 3 cm. Ex. Villa Julia Collection. Cf. *Vienne* #94-97. Erosion. Rare. ....**CHOICE 50.00**

1765. BRONZE NAIL. 1st-4th Century A.D. Square shaft, slightly rounded flat head. Length 8.1 cm. Found in Rome. Partial green patina. ....**CHOICE 75.00**

1766. LARGE IRON NAIL. 1st-4th Century A.D. Iron nail with umbrella-shaped head. Square-sided shaft. End turned. 9.5 cm long. *Vienne* 693 var. Large size. ....**CHOICE 75.00**

1767. BRONZE SPOON. 1st-5th Century A.D. Pointed spoon with curved shaft, ending in globe. 14 cm long. Bowl shows minor holes of corrosion. Cf. Perkins and Claridge, *Pompeii A.D. 79*, #317. Cf. Boucher, *Vienne, Bronze Antiquities*, 385. Cf. Schumacher, Karlsruhe, Pl. XII, #30. Cf. Hayes, *ROM*, #6. ....**CHOICE 250.00**

1768. BRONZE HANDLE. c. 2nd Century A.D. Solid cast bronze handle of a small cauldron or chest. U-shaped ends with points. Central part contains a spiral decoration. 17.7 cm wide. Ex. Villa Julia Collection. Cf. Hayes, *ROM* #268. Intact with no corrosion. ....**CHOICE 150.00**

1769. BRONZE FURNITURE FOOT. 2nd Century A.D. Bronze foot in the form of a lion's paw. Height 5.2 cm, width 3.2 cm, depth 3.4 cm. Ex. Villa Julia Collection. *Vienne* 411 and 415. ....**CHOICE 100.00**

1770. BRONZE SLEEPING LION APPLIQUÉ. 2nd Century A.D. Relief plaque with sleeping lion with tail curved. Iron pin to 1.6 x 4.3 cm. This lightweight bronze lion appliqué was probably applied to a military breastplate. For similar thin bronze sheet work, Cf. Tarbell, *Field Museum of Natural History*, Chicago, Vol VII, cl. 224-6. ....**CHOICE 175.00**

1771. IRON KEY. 2nd Century A.D. 7.5 cm long. Highly encrusted as usual with iron. Cf. Excavations in Yugoslavia, Plesnicar-Gec, Pl. CXVI 504, 2. Cf. Petrie, *Tools & Weapons*, LXXVI, 156-64..........................**CHOICE 75.00**

1772. **BRONZE JUGLET. Roman. 2nd Century A.D.** Small bronze juglet with a red-oxide patina. Squat round body with small base. Convex underneath with incised lines. Inverted neck with flat rim. Amphora-type handles either side of rim. Incised lines (three) on shoulder. 5.6 cm high. Cf. Valenti, Natural Museum of Zaray (Il Museo Nazionale de Zara), Pl. 34. A lovely example of small bronze Roman vases ....**CHOICE 500.00**

1773. **BRONZE HANDLE. Roman. c. 2nd Century A.D.** Solid cast bronze of a small cauldron or chest. U-shaped ends with points central part a spiral decoration. 17.7 cm wide. Ex. Villa Julia Collection. Cf. *Greek, Roman and Related Metalwork in the Ontario Museum* #268. Intact with no corrosion. ....**CHOICE 200.00**

1774. **BRONZE CAULDRON HANDLE. c. 2nd Century A.D.** Solid cast bronze handle from a small cauldron or chest. Bent to a bow shape with upturned ends. Twisted to form a spiral design. Measures 17.7 x 8 cm. Cf. *Greek, Roman and Related Metalwork in the Ontario Museum* #268. Ex. Villa Julia Coll. Intact and no corrosion. ....**CHOICE 200.00**

1775. **BRONZE TWEEZERS. 2nd-3rd Century A.D.** One-piece construction, turned in cotter-pin shape. The ends are wider than the head. Length 4.7 cm., width at tip .8 cm. ....**CHOICE 125.00**

1776. **BRONZE FINIAL. 2nd-3rd Century A.D.** In the shape of a wolf's head, with the ears and mouth shown in detail. Length 3.5 cm. Ex. Villa Julia Collection. Ex. Malloy Auction XX, July 1984. Broken at curve of neck. Green patina. ....**CHOICE 80.00**

1777. **PAIR OF BRONZE MINIATURE SHEEP BELLS. 2nd-3rd Century A.D.** Round/oval shape with loop for suspension. Slit to insert the ball extends half the diameter. Ball remains inside. Length 1.5-2 cm. Cf. Petrie, *Objects of Daily Use*, Pl. L, fig. 3. ....**CHOICE 75.00**

1778. **APPLIQUÉ FRAGMENT. Roman. 2nd-3rd Century A.D.** Fragment of a handle of an oinochoe. Small head of a lion handle. Cf. *Vienne* #256-258, 274-280 for similar handle. ....**AVERAGE-CHOICE 100.00**

1779. **BRONZE HANDLE FROM CAULDRON. Roman. 2nd-3rd Century A.D.** Straight bronze bar handle which has either end appliqué for soldering onto a cauldron or some such large vessel or box. Handle has bead molding center and either side, straight molding between. Appliqué is in two simple volutes. Other appliqué is missing. 12.7 cm long. Ex. Villa Julia Collection. Cf. *Vienne* #296-302. Rather unusual handle. ....**CHOICE 150.00**

1780. **BRONZE BRAIDED CHAIN. 2nd-3rd Century A.D.** 12 cm long. Ex. Villa Julia Collection. This chain was used for the suspension of hanging lamps and vessels. Cf. Excavations in Yugoslavia, Plesnicar-Gex, Pl. CXIX, 517, 10. ....**CHOICE 35.00**

1781. **BRONZE HANDLE DECORATION. 2nd-3rd Century A.D.** Fragment of an appliqué for the handle of an oinochoe. Small head of a lion; broken off just above the head. Height 3 cm. Ex. Villa Julia Coll. Cf. *Vienne* 256-258, 274-280 for similar handle decoration. Green patina, features rather worn.......................................**AVERAGE-CHOICE 65.00**

1782. **BRONZE HANDLE FROM CAULDRON. 2nd-3rd Century A.D.** Straight bronze bar handle which has either end appliqué for soldering onto a cauldron, large vessel, or box. Handle has bead molding center and either side. Length 12.5 cm. Ex. Villa Julia Collection. ....**CHOICE 75.00**

1783. **BRONZE BRACELET. 2nd-3rd Century A.D.** Child's bracelet with evenly spaced sections of incised lines. 5 cm in diameter, 7 mm thick. Cf. Boucher, *Vienne*, fig. 111-126. ....**CHOICE 65.00**

1784. **BRONZE BRACELET. 2nd-3rd Century A.D.** Bracelet with a design of intermittent incised lines. 5.5 cm diam. Ex. Villa Julia Collection. Cf. Excavations in Yugoslavia, Plesnicar-Gec, *Sevemo Emonsko Grobisce*, Pl. LX, 214, 14. The Plesnicar-Gec example comes from the time of Trajan Decius. Green patina.................................**CHOICE 60.00**

1785. **BRONZE FINIAL. 2nd-3rd Century A.D.** 2.5 cm long, 2 cm diam. head. Used as an end to a dagger or Roman tool. ....**CHOICE 35.00**

1786. **BRONZE SPOON. 2nd-3rd Century A.D.** Handle broken in two pieces. Nice patina. Encrustation with shell and other minute objects to bowl of spoon. Length 17.2 cm. Cf. *Vienne* #385. Broken at midpoint of handle. ....**CHOICE 175.00**

1787. **MIRROR FRAGMENT. 2nd-3rd Century A.D.** Fragment of billon mirror; highly polished on one side. Roman mirrors, or even fragments, are rarely found. Some verdegris. Edges 7.2 x 6.4 cm. Ex. Villa Julia Collection. ....**CHOICE 75.00**

1788. **LEAD FIGURINE OF ROMA. 2nd-3rd Century A.D.** Figure of Roma, holding a shield. Length 3.6 cm. Ex. Villa Julia Collection. Fragment. Head missing. ...**CHOICE 75.00**

1789. **BRONZE MALE HEAD. 2nd-3rd Century A.D.** Full face, part of hair present, eye pupils defined. Height 36 mm. Mounted. Berciu, *Daco-Romana* 48. Olive-green patina. ....**CHOICE 250.00**

1790. **BRONZE FIGURINE OF GENIUS. 2nd-3rd Century A.D.** Figure of Genius, arms outstretched, right knee slightly bent. A guardian spirit; each household had a genius watching over its members. 6.4 cm long. Cf. for style Boucher, *Bronzes Antiques*, p.71. Worn. Green patina. ....**AVERAGE 250.00**

1791. **IRON KEY. 2nd Century A.D.** Long spreading flat pedestal with large ring at end. Shank to cleft at right angle. Length 8.2 cm. Cf. Price, VII, 3. Very nice large example. ....**CHOICE 100.00**

1792. **IRON KEY. 2nd Century A.D.** Key with short shaft and large ring. Cleft at right angle. Length 4.3 cm. Cf. Plesnicar-Gel, *Excavations Yugoslavia*, Pl. CXVI, 504, 2. Encrusted. Attractive. ....**CHOICE 50.00**

1793. **BRONZE KEY. 2nd-3rd Century A.D.** Short pedestal to shank and ring. Designs on shaft and pedestal, cleft plain. Length 5.5 cm. Cf. Mills, pic M128 var. .....**CHOICE 55.00**

1794. **IRON NAIL. 2nd-3rd Century A.D.** Iron nail with rectangular head, long square-sided shaft. Length 9.5 cm. ....**CHOICE 35.00**

1795. **IRON NAIL. 2nd-3rd Century A.D.** Iron nail with irregular globular head, square-sided shaft. Length 6 cm. *Vienne* 710. Shaft slightly turned. ....**CHOICE 25.00**

1796. **BRONZE NAIL. 2nd-3rd Century A.D.** Bronze nail with hollow domed head, short shaft. Length 3.4 cm. *Vienne* 715. Used for furniture or other decoration. Green patina. ....**CHOICE 40.00**

1797. **FINIAL. 2nd-3rd Century A.D.** Bronze finial used as an end to a dagger, or perhaps to a Roman tool. 2.5 cm long, 2 cm head diameter. ....**CHOICE 50.00**

1798. **BRONZE NAIL. 2nd-4th Century A.D.** Bronze nail with flat-round head, irregular round shaft. Length 3.8 cm. *Vienne* 718. Shaft slightly turned. ....**CHOICE 35.00**

1799. **BRONZE NAIL. 2nd-4th Century A.D.** Bronze nail with round head, long rounded shaft. Length 7.8 cm. *Vienne* 716. End of shaft slightly turned. ....**CHOICE 45.00**

1800. **LEAD SEAL. 2nd-4th Century A.D.** Lead seal for a jar or bottle. Triangular symbol in center on bottom. 2 cm in diam. Ex. Villa Julia Collection. An equilateral triangle is one of the most commonly used symbols to represent the Holy Trinity, signifying the equality of the Father, the Son, and the Holy Ghost as stated in the Athanasian Creed. ....**CHOICE 75.00**

1801. **BRONZE TWEEZERS. 2nd-4th Century A.D.** Tiny holes to tip of each pincher. 6.1 cm long. Cf. Boucher, *Vienne, Bronzes Antiques*, 558..................................**CHOICE 50.00**

1802. **BRONZE BELL. 2nd-4th Century A.D.** Bronze bell with rounded body, loop at top. Four small legs. No clapper. Height 6 cm. *Vienne* 612. Nice size. ....**CHOICE 85.00**

1803. **BRONZE BELL. 2nd-4th Century A.D.** Bronze bell with rounded body and two flat sides. Loop handle. Slight protruding legs. No clapper. Height 4.2 cm. *Vienne* 617. ....**CHOICE 75.00**

1804. **DECORATED BRONZE NAIL. 3rd Century A.D.** Female head on the head of a nail. Facing with hair on both sides, bunched at top. Dark brown patina............**CHOICE 150.00**

1805. **BRONZE CLOTHING APPLIQUÉ. 3rd-4th Century A.D.** Square with scalloped edge. Central circle with male bust right, bareheaded and cuirassed. Two dolphins at each corner. Mounting pins at back. Measures 2.5 cm. square. Ex. Villa Julia Collection. ....**CHOICE 150.00**

1806. **BRONZE CLOTHING APPLIQUÉ. 3rd-4th Century A.D.** Square appliqué with two joining pins to back. Two dolphins at each corner. 3/4 facing bust cuirassed bare headed male. 3.5 x 3 cm. Ex. Villa Julia Collection De-accession. An unusual bas relief possibly depicting a 3rd-4th century Caesar. .... **CHOICE 150.00**

1807. **BRONZE NAIL. Roman. 3rd-4th Century A.D.** Large nail with four-sides barrel or stem ending in point and head with a convex carved cap. 7 cm long. Ex. Villa Julia Collection. *Vienne* #710-733. Bent into a curve. Some dirt adhering. ....**CHOICE 75.00**

1808. **BRONZE BELL. 3rd-5th Century A.D.** Bronze bell with four sloping sides. Four round legs. Loop handle. Height 3 cm. Cf. *Vienne* 613. ....**CHOICE 65.00**

1809. **BRONZE BELL. Romano-Byzantine. 3rd-5th Century A.D.** Bronze bell with bulbous body and loop handle. Five incised spoon designs over five concentric lines. Height 28 mm. *Vienne* -. Nice ornamented bell. ....**CHOICE 100.00**

1810. **LEAD APPLIQUÉ. Roman. c. 4th Century A.D.** Cast lead appliqué in form of a disc with round central port and protruding rim denticles. At top, busts of couple within wreath supported by Victories. Below, two winged Genii holding torches. At bottom, two lions support amphora. Rectangular prongue at bottom. 10.3 cm. Ex. Villa Julia Collection. Probably used either as a mirror border or on the surface of a wooden casket. *ROM-*. Brilliant, *Roman Art* #ii.15. Cf. Municipal Collection of Rome, Jones, Pl. 68-13 for appliqués in lead................................**CHOICE 400.00**

1811. **BRONZE HANDLE. 4th Century A.D.** Volute handle with two prongs extending out and slightly curving inwards. Body of handle ends in upside-down pear-shaped disc. Extending from bottom are three spikes, pointing to sides and downward. Length 11 cm. Cf. *Vienne, Bronzes Antiques*, #273. ....**CHOICE 150.00**

1812. **IRON KEY. Roman-Byzantine. 4th-6th Century A.D.** Iron key with five pellets at end. Length 8.5 cm. Cf. Petrie 156-63 ....**CHOICE 125.00**

STONE

1813. **ROMAN WALL PAINTING. Roman. 1st Century A.D.** Wall painting fragment with bearded head of Jupiter facing in the Fourth Style wall. Beige background with trace of red strip to left and maroon strip to right. The head is rendered in bold strokes of maroon, orange and white. Highly stylized. Cf. *Pompeii, AD 79*, Vol. II, #140 (from Herculaneum). Cf. Curtius, *Die Wand Malieri Pompeius*. Cf. Herbig, *Nugae Pompeianorum* ....**CHOICE 1250.00**

1814. **MARBLE HEAD OF MINERVA. Roman. 1st Century A.D.** Bust of Minerva who, along with Jupiter and Juno, made up the Capitoline triad as the most important Roman deities. She wears a low crown decorated with Etruscan ivy leaves. Her hair, in high relief, forms waves around head and then flows down over shoulders. May have originally worn earrings. Intact except for fractoral repairs and the missing lower right portion, not affecting the appeal of the piece. Vermeule, *Roman Art: Early Republican to Late Empire-*, Bunacasca-, Fitzwilliam-. For various herms, Cf. 88, 95, 103. Cf. Museo Capitolino, Pl. 55, #54 var. and Pl. 34, 14 var. ....**CHOICE 8000.00**

1815. **IVORY HAIR PIN. 1st Century A.D.** Pin terminating in pointed knob with swirl pattern. Length 6 cm. Cf. Petrie XIX 40 var. End broken. ....**CHOICE 85.00**

1816. **BONE FIGURE OF HARPOCRATES. Roman-Egyptian. 1st-2nd Century A.D.** Carved bone figure of nude Harpocrates. Striding with left arm at side, right arm to face. Pierced at back for suspension. Length 22 mm. Cf. Bonhams 12/6/94 #126 (est. £300-400, identified as Cupid). ....**CHOICE 175.00**

1817. **BONE DOLL. 1st-2nd Century A.D.** Bone doll of child standing nude. Arm holes with traces of iron pin. 5.5 cm long. Finely detailed face ....**CHOICE 250.00**

1818. **BONE STYLUS. 1st-2nd Century A.D.** Short stylus with a bulbous end. Length 67 mm. ....**SUPERB 45.00**

1819. **PAIR OF CUBICAL DICE. 1st-3rd Century A.D.** Dice with circle and dot pattern with normal numberings on opposites: 6 and 1, 5 and 2, 4 and 3. Measures 9 mm on each side. Cf. Petrie, *Objects of Daily Use*, XLIX, 261. A lovely pair ....**SUPERB 150.00**

1820. **WHITE-BROWN IVORY CLUB FRAGMENT. 1st-3rd Century A.D.** This piece was associated with Hercules. 10 cm long. ....**CHOICE 60.00**

1821. **MARBLE UPPER TORSO. Roman. 1st-3rd Century A.D.** Torso of nude female figure. Evidence of contraposto stance as torso tilted to left side. Moderate carving. Arms missing. Traces of black paint around neck and breasts. 5.8 cm high. Cf. *Vienne #1* I for similar shape. This is probably a torso of Venus. Chipping of marble. ....**CHOICE 300.00**

1822. **LIMESTONE HEAD OF WOMAN. Roman Egyptian. 1st-4th Century A.D.** Unusual head of figure of a woman. Elaborate headdress and hair. Features now worn. Broken beneath neck. 6.5 cm high. Cf. Hanna Philipp, *Terrakotten aus Agypten*, fig. 23, cat. no. 25. Features worn. ....**CHOICE 275.00**

1823. **MARBLE JEWELRY/PENDANT MOLD. Roman Period. 1st-4th Century A.D.** Marble mold of a bird, probably a cockerel, standing on a plinth. Above bird is an oval ring, probably for attachment to necklace. Appears to have been used for making plaques from thin sheet metal, like gold or silver. Makes a very good impression. Height 4.9 cm, width 3.6 cm, depth 2.1 cm. Petrie-; Hayes-. Very unusual. ....**CHOICE 250.00**

1824. **MARBLE SARCOPHAGUS LID FRAGMENT. 2nd Century A.D.** Portion of two panels with border. Left panel shows a man wearing a toga facing, with straight hair and a light beard. Background drapery to the right. The right panel portrays a male mask, turned slightly to the right, with loose hair. Drill marks are added to the hair to indicate curling, to the eye and mouth to indicate depth. Measures 12.5 x 17.5 cm; depth 3.4 cm. Cf. Strong, *Roman Imperial Art*, Pl. 143 for similar style; Cf. Baratte et Metzger, #7 and 8 for type of mask...**CHOICE 2000.00**

1825. **MARBLE ARM AND CLUB. 2nd Century A.D.** Portion of a statue, probably of Hercules. The lower part of an arm, with the hand clutching a knobby club. Stub of a support piece at top of hand. Length of arm 15 cm, length of club 18 cm. Cf. Vermeule, *Greek and Roman Sculpture in America,* #174 ....**CHOICE 650.00**

1826. **MARBLE HEAD AND TORSO OF GENIUS. 2nd-3rd Century A.D.** White marble head and torso of Genius with hands flattened before. The figure was probably attached to a larger marble figure. Height 3.3 cm, width 3.3 cm, depth 2 cm. ....**CHOICE 250.00**

1827. **MARBLE STATUE OF AESCULAPIUS. c. 225-250 A.D.** Aesculapius, the Roman god of medicine, standing bearded and wearing a diadem. Himation draped over his shoulder. Right hand and shoulder present, with hand to waist. Left forearm missing. Traces of serpent entwined on left side. Sculptured in the round, with yellowish grey patina. Drill points present in forepart of hair and beard. Aesculapius, a cult god of healing, was honored by a temple dedicated to him on January 1, 291. Height 23.4 cm. (9.5"). Mounted. Cf. Sotheby's NY 11/29/1989, #111. A rare representation of the god of medicine and healing. ....**CHOICE 8500.00**

1828. **SCULPTURE HEAD. Tetrarchy. 285-337 A.D.** Grey-black basalt portrait of Roman emperor during the Tetrarchy: Diocletian, Maximianus, Constantius, or Galerius. The carving shows the short forehead, short hair not delineated; the expressive eyes are large and high relief with double eyelids. The nose is missing. Traces of red ochre around eyes along with an azure blue. Height of head 12 cm, width 9.5 cm. Height including mounting stand 20.5 cm. The portraiture exemplifies the militaristic period with the brutal strength of the sculpture. Cf. Vermeule, *Roman Imperial Art in Greece and Asia Minor*. 178 from Gortyna. Terrace and Fischer, Cairo Museum Exhibition 1970-1, #7257. Bold and powerful sculpture of the period of the Roman Tetrarchy. Rarely offered.......................................**CHOICE 1500.00**

1829. **BONE DOLL. 4th-6th Century A.D.** Doll with stylized features and arms. Two suspension holes at sides of arms. Length 7 cm. Mogensen, Carlsberg LXXX A629-31; Cf. Petrie, *Objects of Daily Use*, Pl. LV, nos. 592-598. Crude but charming doll. It is broken off below the waist. ....**CHOICE 150.00**

GLASS

1830. **BEAD. Roman, Eastern Roman Empire. 1st Century B.C.-Mid 1st Century A.D.** Opaque red, blue and black bead with stylized face in black on white opaque glass. 11 cm diameter, 6 mm thick. Cf. Goldstein, #820. ....**CHOICE 400.00**

1831. **MILLEFIORI BEAD. 1st Century B.C.-1st Century A.D.** Round millefiori eye bead, transparent aqua with opaque white, red, and yellow eyes. Some corrosion. The millefiori technique of glassmaking is still being used today. ....**CHOICE 50.00**

1832. **BRACELET. Roman. 1st Century B.C.-1st Century A.D.** Blue glass bracelet with orange, yellow and green striped design in six sections. 6.6 cm diameter, 8 mm thick. Cf. Goldstein, #259 for glass bracelet. Chip and some encrustation. ....**CHOICE 200.00**

1833. **GLASS BRACELET. 1st Century B.C.-1st Century A.D.** Blue glass bracelet. Contains five sections of yellow, orange, and green opaque glass design set in. Diameter 6.4 cm. Cf. Goldstein #259 for bracelet. Chips and some encrustation. Very bold colors...................................**CHOICE 225.00**

1834. **GLASS BEAD. 1st Century A.D.** Multicolored glass millefiori bead with checkered, diamond-patterned squares. Large suspension hole through center. Black, red, white, green, and yellow. Diameter 1.4 cm. Cf. Dubin, *The History of Beads*, pp. 60-61....................................**CHOICE 55.00**

1835. **GLASS BEAD. 1st Century A.D.** Round glass bead with millefiori pattern. Green and yellow with "eyes" in red and white. Large suspension hole through. Diameter 1 cm. Cf. Dubin pp. 60-61...**CHOICE 50.00**

1836. **SMALL BOWL. 1st Century A.D.** Small translucent amber glass bowl. Stands on slightly flanged hollowed self base. Has convex sides and flanged rim. Height 4.3 cm, diameter 9.8 cm, base diameter 5.3 cm. Cf. Constable-Maxwell Collection., Sotheby's June 4, 1979, #60. Some iridescence is remaining. Piece is intact. Nice amber color. ....**CHOICE 650.00**

1837. **SMALL FLASK OR MEDICINE BOTTLE. 1st Century A.D.** 5 cm high. Thick blue-green appearing black matrix flask with spots of turquoise-blue, yellow and white. Octagonal in shape. Neck and part of shoulder broken off. Two chips in body. The "splash" decoration is very rare. It was found mostly in the 1st century A.D. This technique was used in both eastern and western glass centers. The "splashes" of multicolored glass were achieved by adding bits of glass to a partially blown bubble while still on the end of a blowpipe. As it becomes full blown, the bits of glass expand causing a blotchy, "splash" effect. For design, Cf. Matheson, *Ancient Glass in the Yale University Gallery*, #109, p. 39. Cf. Von Saldern, *Glass 500 B.C. to A.D. 1900*. The Hans Cohn Collection #34, p. 44. Cf. Oppenlander, *Glaser der Antike*, p. 141, #'s 392, 394. Rim and part of shoulder missing. Very rare. ....**CHOICE 275.00**

1838. **RIBBED BOWL. 1st Century A.D.** 9 cm diameter, 4.5 cm high. Thick, pale green bowl with twenty ribs which run from the rim to base. Smooth interior. These ribbed bowls were of the most common types of early Roman glass found in cemeteries, military camps, and towns throughout Italy, Switzerland, and Germany. Cf. Auth, *Ancient Glass at the Newark Museum*. #40 (50:1327), p. 49, like #300 (50:1325). Cf. Hayes, *Roman and Pre-Roman Glass in the ROM*, #46, Pl. 3. Cf. Glass at the Fitzwilliam Museum, 32a, p. 23. Repaired.......................................**CHOICE 380.00**

1839. **SMALL UNGUENTARIUM. 1st Century A.D.** 6 cm high, 1.8 cm diameter rim. Blue green with slightly constricted neck and large lip. Cf. Auth, *Ancient Glass at the Newark Museum*, #206, p. 154..................................**SUPERB 60.00**

1840. **FLASK. 1st Century A.D.** Opaque aqua-blue glass flask. Rough textured glass with some pitting. Well-rounded body with flattened concave base and pontil mark. Short, tubular neck, broken off. No rim. Constriction at shoulder. 4.8 cm high, 1 cm diameter rim, 1.3 cm diameter base. Repaired. Cf. Hayes, *ROM*, #543. Nice bold color......**CHOICE 500.00**

1841. **UNGUENTARIUM. Roman. 1st Century A.D.** Aqua colored "tear vial" with long slender body, slight constriction at half section. Small, rounded rim, rounded base. 9 cm high, 1.5 cm diam. base, 1.5 cm diam. rim. Hayes, *ROM* #570. Some iridescence. Intact ....**CHOICE 150.00**

1842. **UNGUENTARIUM. Roman. 1st Century A.D.** Pale aqua-greenish tear vial with constriction at midpoint. Tubular neck, flat base and small folded rim. 9.9 cm high, 2 cm diameter rim, 2 cm diameter base. Some nice iridescence. Intact. ....**CHOICE 250.00**

1843. **MINIATURE FLASK. Cyprus. 1st Century A.D.** Pale green-blue transparent glass. Slender piriform body, tubular neck and flaring rim folded in. 4.8 cm high, 16 cm diameter rim, 1.6 cm diameter base. Cf. Hayes, *ROM* #251. Intact. ....**CHOICE 150.00**

1844. **RIBBED BOWL. 1st Century A.D.** Light green transparent bowl. Rather thin, bulbous body with constricted neck and flaring rim, smooth inside, 9 ribs outside bowl. Cream surface deposits. Flattened bottom. 9.4 cm. Cf. Hayes, *Roman and Pre-Roman Glass in the Ontario Museum*, nos. 50-54 var. Probably of Syrian manufacture. Repaired. ....**CHOICE 275.00**

1845. **SMALL FLASK OR MEDICINE BOTTLE. 1st Century A.D.** Thick blue-green with spots of blue, yellow and white. Octagonal in shape. Height 5.3 cm. Cf. Matheson, #109, p. 39. Von Saldem, #34, p. 44. Oppenlander, *Glaser der Antike*, p.141, #392, 394. The "splash" decoration is very rare and found mostly during 1st Century A.D. This technique was used in both east and west Roman glass manufacturing centers. The "splashes" of multi-colored glass were achieved by adding lists of glass to a partially blown bubble while still on end of blowpipe. As it then becomes full blown, the bits of glass expand causing a blotchy "splash" effect. Rare. ....**CHOICE 275.00**

1846. **MILLEFIORI GLASS BEAD. 1st Century A.D.** Round with flattened top and bottom, suspension hole through center. White, black, and yellow stripes and dots millifiori pattern. Diam. .9 cm. Cf. Lois Sherr Dubil, *The History of Beads,* pp. 60-61, var. ....**CHOICE 40.00**

1847. **GLASS MEDUSA APPLIQUÉ. 1st-2nd Century A.D.** Blue glass with head of Medusa. Fragment of off-white/green glass on back. Probably part of a vase or bottle. Diam. 3.5 cm. Eisen, *Glass*, Vol. I fig. 45, p. 41. These appliqués were used on other glassware and pottery as decorations. Upper portion chipped off. Some dirt and encrustation, and minute amounts of iridescence. ....**CHOICE 100.00**

1848. **APPLIQUÉ DISK. 1st-2nd Century A.D.** Blue glass disk showing the head of Medusa or a youth. Fragment of off-white/green glass on rear. Probably part of a vase or bottle. Applied as a decoration on a piece of glassware or pottery. Diameter 3.4 cm. Eisen, *Glass,* Vol. I, fig. 45, p. 41. A trace of iridescence remaining. Some dirt encrustation. ....**CHOICE 100.00**

1849. **AQUA GLASS KNUCKLEBONE. 1st-2nd Century A.D.** Astragalus-gaming piece. The Greek historian Herodotus tells a story about the Lydians inventing dice and knucklebones to help them forget the pangs of hunger in time of famine. The emperor Claudius was an avid knucklebone player. Cf. BMC, *Greek and Roman Life*, fig. 204. ....**CHOICE 80.00**

1850. **APPLIQUÉ DISK. 1st-2nd Century A.D.** 3.5 cm diameter. Blue glass with head of Medusa or youth. These appliqués were used on other glassware and pottery as decoration. Upper portion chipped off. Dirt encrustation. Cf. Eisen, *Glass*, Vol. I, fig. 45, p. 41. ....**CHOICE 100.00**

1851. **UNGUENTARIUM. Roman. 1st-2nd Century A.D.** Slender yellow-green-blue tear bottle with constriction at midsection. Flat base and folded rim. 12.2 cm high, 6.7 cm diameter rim, 2.2 cm diameter base. The tear bottle was the most common glass item in Roman times. They were cheap and carelessly made, being used for cosmetics and perfumes. Auth, # 1 34 (50.1781). Intact.. ....**CHOICE 175.00**

1852. **GLASS BEAD. 1st-3rd Century A.D.** Round glass bead with free form millefiori pattern in black, red, and white. Suspension hole through. Diam. 1 cm. ....**CHOICE 50.00**

1853. **UNGUENTARIUM. Roman. Mid 1st Century A.D.** Light green-blue tear vial with constricted neck. Wide, flat rim. 6.9 cm high, 2.3 cm diameter rim, 1.5 cm diameter base. Some nice iridescence. Intact. ....**CHOICE 250.00**

1854. **BEAKER. Roman. Mid 1st Century A.D.** Brownish-yellow beaker with fat body, tapering at the rim. Thick disc base. 7.5 cm high, 6 cm diameter rim, 4 cm diameter base. Cf. Hayes, *ROM* #132. Intact except for stress cracks. Small chips at rim. ....**CHOICE 700.00**

1855. **RIBBED JAR. Roman. Mid 1st Century A.D.** Pale aqua blue jar with straight neck and folded rim. Flat base. Seven long pinches on body. 4.5 cm high, 1.6 cm diameter rim, 3.5 cm diameter body. Hayes, *ROM*, #223. Slight iridescence. Intact ....**SUPERB 700.00.**

1856. **FLASK. Syria. Mid 1st Century A.D.** 9.2 cm high, 4.5 cm diameter rim. Pale green with spotty iridescence. Flat base with body tapering to neck. Seven pinched ribs around body. Wide rim and short neck. Hole crack in body. Very narrow mouth opening. Cf. Hayes, *Roman and Pre-Roman Glass in the ROM*, #223, Pl. 16. Cf. *Glass at the Fitzwilliam Museum*, #58c, p. 34. ....**CHOICE 300.00**

1857. **BEAKER. Mid 1st Century A.D.** Brownish-yellow beaker with fat body, tapering at the rim. Thick disc base. Height 7.5 cm, diam. 6 cm at rim, 4 cm at base. Cf. Hayes, *ROM* 132. Intact. Stress cracks. Small chips at rim. ....**CHOICE 700.00**

1858. **UNGUENTARIUM. Eastern Mediterranean. Mid to Late 1st Century A.D.** 10.6 cm high. Greenish-blue with constricted neck near the base. Rounded rim. Flat bottom. Free blown method. Unguentaria or "tear bottles" were the most common form of Roman glass. They usually contained cosmetics or perfumes and were given to the dead as gifts. Iridescence. Cf. Hayes, *Roman and Pre-Roman Glass at the ROM*, #234, Pl. 17. Cf. Auth, *Ancient Glass at the Newark Museum*, #134 (50:1781) p. 114. Cf. Matheson, *Ancient Glass at the Yale University Art Gallery*, #79, p. 29. ....**SUPERB 125.00**

1859. **UNGUENTARIUM. Eastern Mediterranean. Mid to Late 1st Century A.D.** 10.5 cm high. Light green with constricted neck near the base which is slightly flared and flat at bottom. Rounded rim. Free blown method. Cf. Hayes, *Roman and Pre-Roman Glass at the ROM*, #234, Pl. 17. Cf. Auth, *Ancient Glass at the Newark Museum*, #134 (50:1781), p. 114. Cf. Matheson, *Ancient Glass at the Yale University Art Gallery*, #79, p. 29. ....**SUPERB 75.00**

1860. **UNGUENTARIUM. Roman. Late 1st-Early 2nd Century A.D.** Slender light blue-green glass tear vial, widening at base and rim. Small, folded rim. 9.9 cm high, 1.9 diameter rim, 1 cm diameter base. Cf. Hayes, *ROM.* #235. Some bold silver iridescence. Intact except for chipped rim. ....**CHOICE 150.00**

1861. **UNGUENTARIUM. Roman. Late 1st-Early 2nd Century A.D.** Slender blue-green tear bottle with flat base and slightly flaring rim. 12.2 cm high, 1.8 cm diameter rim, 1.5 cm diameter base. Cf. Auth, #134 (50.1781). Intact. ....**CHOICE 150.00**

1862. **UNGUENTARIUM. Roman. Early 2nd Century A.D.** Aqua blue-green glass of medium thickness. Small bell-shaped body, slightly concave base, tubular neck with large flaring rim. Hayes, *ROM* 246. Nice iridescence. ....**CHOICE 250.00**

1863. **DROPPER FLASK. 200-250 A.D.** 8.2 cm high. Transparent pale green flask. Globular body, short broad neck with flaring mouth, which is closed off at diaphragm for a smaller opening. Body has diagonal net pattern. The name "dropper flask" along with the narrow opening indicates that the perfume or oil which it contained was meant to be poured out slowly. Cf. Auth, *Ancient Glass at the Newark Museum*, #8 1, p. 78. Cf. Hayes, *Roman and Pre-Roman Glass in the ROM*, #280, pl. 7, p. 193. Some iridescence. Restored. Small hole. Mold-blown technique: the glass was blown into a reusable wood or terracotta mold. Matheson, p. XV. ....**CHOICE 400.00**

1864. **MINIATURE "TEST TUBE" UNGUENTARIUM. Roman. 2nd Century A.D.** Slender colorless tear bottle with widening base and neck. Pointed base with pontil mark. Flaring rim. 6.7 cm high, 1.2 cm diameter rim, 9 mm diameter base. Some encrustation. Cf. Auth, #508 (50.1817). ....**CHOICE 150.00**

1865. **UNGUENTARIUM. Roman. 2nd Century A.D.** Light blue-green tear vial with long, slender neck, small globular body and flat, flaring rim. 14.5 cm high, 2.5 cm diameter rim, 3 cm diameter base. Hayes, *ROM* #238. Rim chip. ....**CHOICE 170.00**

1866. **SQUAT UNGUENTARIUM. Roman. 2nd Century A.D.** Greenish-blue colored glass with full, squat body and sloping shoulders. Flat, base. Tubular neck leaning to one side with fat folded lip. Cf. Auth, #408 (50.1769). Bold silvering iridescence..............................**CHOICE-SUPERB 750.00**

1867. **JUG. Roman. 2nd Century A.D.** Pale green bubbly glass. Rounded body with flat base. Neck evolving to large flat rim with slight constriction at midpoint. Handle coming from body to below lip. 9.6 cm high, 5.6 cm diameter rim, 4.8 cm diameter base. Cf. Bergman, #80. Some nice iridescence. Bold and intact. ....**CHOICE 1500.00**

1868. **MINIATURE "TEST TUBE" UNGUENTARIUM. 2nd Century A.D.** Slender transluscent green tear bottle with slightly widening base and neck. Pointed base with pontil mark. Flaring rim. Height 6.2 cm. Cf. Auth, #508 (50.1817). Slight encrustation. Rim chip. ...**CHOICE 75.00**

1869. **UNGUENTARIUM. 2nd Century A.D.** Light aqua-green tear vial with long, slender neck, small globular body and flat, flaring rim. 12 cm high, 2 cm diameter rim, 3 cm diameter base. Hayes, *Roman and Pre-Roman Glass at the ROM* #238. ....**CHOICE 125.00**

1870. **SQUAT UNGUENTARIUM. 2nd Century A.D.** Aqua-blue glass with full, squat body and sloping shoulders. Flat. base. Tubular neck. Cf. Auth, #408 (50.1769). Much iridescence remains. Intact. ....**CHOICE 450.00**

1871. **JUG. 2nd Century A.D.** Light green glass. Rounded body with flat base. Neck evolving to large flat rim with slight constriction at midpoint. Handle from body to below lip. 7 cm high, 4.5 cm diameter rim, 4 cm diameter base. Cf. Bergman, #80. Has been broken and repaired. ....**CHOICE 300.00**

1872. **INDENTED BEAKER. 2nd Century A.D.** Thin colorless translucent glass. Slender conical shape. Short bulging rim. Hollowed base. Cf. Hayes, *Roman and Pre-Roman Glass at the ROM* #187. Repaired. Some iridescence remaining. ....**CHOICE 275.00**

1873. **TALL NECK UNGUENTARIUM. Roman-Cyprus. Eastern Mediterranean. 2nd Century A.D.** 11 cm high, 2.3 cm diameter at rim, 4.2 cm diameter at base. Small bulbous body with flat base. Tall, narrow neck widening at rim. Lopsided rim with bevelled fold. Some iridescence is remaining at the base. Cf. Hayes, *Roman and Pre-Roman Glass in the ROM*, #498, Pl. 32, #231, Pl. 16. ....**SUPERB 150.00**

1874. **TALL NECK UNGUENTERIUM. 2nd-3rd Century A.D.** 14.8 cm high. Exaggerated neck with constricted base. Flattened rim. The long neck is typical of this period, most likely from the eastern part of the Roman Empire. Cf. Auth, *Ancient Glass at the Newark Museum*, #137, p. 114, #425, p. 215. ....**SUPERB 200.00**

1875. **FLASK. 2nd-3rd Century A.D.** Clear yellow-green glass flask with well-rounded body, flattened concave base, and pontil mark. Tubular neck with folded rim. Eleven horizontal rings around neck in same tone as body. 6.3 cm high, 1.5 cm diameter rim, 1.3 cm diameter base. Cf. Hayes, *ROM*, #459 for neck style, #561 for body shape. Intact. Some encrustation. Small chip on rim. A lovely vessel with a nice example of threaded neck. ....**SUPERB 750.00**

,1876. **LONG NECK UNGUENTARIUM. 2nd-3rd Century A.D.** Colorless tear bottle with small globular body and flat base. Long, narrow neck with flaring rim, folded in. 14 cm high, 1.5 cm diameter rim, 1 cm diameter base. Cf. Hayes, *ROM*, #666. Intact. ....**CHOICE 175.00**

1877. **SMALL UNGUENTARIUM. 2nd-3rd Century A.D.** Light transparent green glass bottle with bulbous body and tapering neck. Large folded rim. Rounded base. Cf. Hayes, *ROM* #611 for body shape. 8.2 cm high, 1.7 cm diameter rim. Some iridescence and encrustation. Intact. Tiny chip to rim. ....**CHOICE 125.00**

1878. **LOPSIDED UNGUENTARIUM. 2nd-3rd Century A.D.** Light blue, thick glass tear bottle with globular, flat base, two constrictions near base and long neck with folded rim. 10.5 cm high, 1.7 cm diameter rim, 3.4 cm diameter base. Some attractive iridescence. Auth, #405 (50.1682). Interesting shape. ....**CHOICE-SUPERB 200.00**

1879. **SQUAT BODIED UNGUENTARIUM. 2nd-3rd Century A.D.** Yellow-green bottle with fat, squat body and indented base. Long neck, tapered at midsection, folded rim. Auth, #424 (50.1752). Nice iridescence. Intact. ...**CHOICE 150.00**

1880. **BEAKER. 2nd-3rd Century A.D.** Clear glass with four elongated indentations. Above body, four fine wheel incisions. Rim flaring outwards. Rounded base has thick glass with an indented bottom. 8.2 cm high. Cf. for similar types Hayes, *ROM* Pl. 171, #157-191. Early example of incising. Repaired. ....**CHOICE 300.00**

1881. **MINIATURE UNGUENTARIUM. Roman. 2nd-3rd Century A.D.** Thin, light green glass with fat body, concave flat base and short neck. Large lip. Pontil mark at base. 2.8 cm high, 1.4 cm diameter rim, 2.1 cm diameter base. Cf. Auth, #504 (50.1797). Intact. A lovely little vessel. ....**SUPERB 200.00**

1882. **SMALL PHIAL. Roman. 2nd-3rd Century A.D.** Thick glass in light blue color. Short broad form, bulging at bottom with flat base. Wide, flat rim. 3.7 cm high, 3.4 cm diameter rim, 1.9 cm diameter base. Possibly from the Fayoum. Hayes, *ROM* #583. Vivid and bold aqua color. Intact. ....**CHOICE 200.00**

1883. **FLASK. Roman. 2nd-3rd Century A.D.** Clear yellow-green glass flask with well-rounded body, flattened concave base and pontil mark. Tubular neck with folded rim. Eleven horizontal rings around neck in same tone as body. 6.3 cm high, 1.5 cm diameter rim, 1.3 cm diameter base. Cf. Hayes, *ROM*, #459 for neck style, #561 for body shape. Intact. Some encrustation. Small chip on rim. A lovely vessel with a nice example of threaded neck. ....**SUPERB 800.00**

1884. **LENTOID FLASK. Roman. 2nd-3rd Century A.D.** Greenish-blue flask with full, round body, concave base and cylindrical neck. Constriction at base of neck. Slightly flaring rim. 7.5 cm high, 1.6 diameter rim, 5 cm diameter base. Some encrustation and iridescence. Hayes, *ROM* #199. Intact. ....**CHOICE 350.00**

1885. **LONG NECK UNGUENTARIUM Roman. 2nd-3rd Century A.D.** Aqua tear bottle with small globular body and flat base. Long, narrow neck with flaring rim, folded in. 12 cm high, 1.3 cm diameter rim, 1 cm diameter base. Cf. Hayes, *ROM*, #666. Intact. ....**CHOICE 150.00**

1886. **TALL NECK UNGUENTARIUM. Roman. 2nd-3rd Century A.D.** Tear vial with bulbous base, flattened and long neck. Small, folded rim. 10.7 cm high, 1.8 cm diameter rim, 4.4 cm base. The tear bottle with the long neck was the most common glass type of this period. Auth, # 1 37-145. Some attractive iridescence. Intact. ....**CHOICE 250.00**

1887. **CANDLESTICK UNGUENTARIUM. Roman. 2nd-3rd Century A.D.** Light aqua blue-green candlestick unguentaria with bell-shaped body and concave base. Long neck with large flat rim. 6.9 cm high, 3.7 cm diameter, 4 cm diameter base. Matheson, # 171. Some iridescence. Nice color. Intact. ....**SUPERB 250.00**

1888. **SMALL UNGUENTARIUM. Roman. 2nd-3rd Century A.D.** Light blue-green glass bottle with bulbous body and tapering neck. Large folded rim. Rounded base. Cf. Hayes, *ROM* #611 for body shape. Measures 8 cm high, 1.5 cm in diameter at the rim. Some iridescence. Intact. Chip to rim. ....**CHOICE 150.00**

1889. **UNGUENTARIUM. Roman. 2nd-3rd Century A.D.** Light aqua, thick glass tear bottle with globular, flat base, two constrictions near base and long neck with folded rim. 11 cm high, 1.9 cm diameter rim, 3.8 cm diameter base. Some iridescence. Auth, #405 (50.1682). ....**CHOICE 175.00**

1890. **SQUAT UNGUENTARIUM. Roman. 2nd-3rd Century A.D.** Aqua bottle with fat, squat body and indented base. Long neck, tapered at mid section, folded rim. Auth, #424 (50.1752). Intact. ....**CHOICE 225.00**

1891. **SPOOL-SHAPED UNGUENTARIUM. Egyptian. 2nd-3rd Century A.D.** Spool shaped with wide flat base and rim. Rim folded and flattened. Very thick glass in light green color. 4.5 cm high, 4.8 cm diameter base, 5 cm diameter rim. This type of glass was particular to Roman Egypt. Cf. Auth, #139 (50.1836). Reconstructed. Iridescent. Bold aqua color.
....**CHOICE 250.00**

1892. **UNGUENTARIUM.   Eastern Mediterranean. 2nd-3rd Century A.D.** Pale blue tear bottle with small body. Two constrictions from base to neck. Long slender neck broken at top. 12 cm high, 1.2 cm diameter rim, 3 cm diameter base. Some iridescence. Cf. Hayes, *ROM*, #416. Cf. Matheson, #169. Nice shape. Broken off at rim. ....**CHOICE 150.00**

1893. **FLASK WITH THREADED NECK. 2nd-3rd Century A.D.** Clear greenish glass flask with well-rounded body and flattened, concave base. Pontil mark. Tubular neck with folded rim. Threading in same color as body goes eleven times around neck. Height 6.3 cm, diam. 3.5 cm. Cf. Hayes, *ROM* #459 for neck style, #561 for body shape. Slight encrustation. Intact except for small chip on rim. A lovely vessel with a nice example of the threaded neck.
....**SUPERB 800.00**

1894. **MINIATURE FLASK. 2nd-3rd Century A.D.** Grey-green with a globular body, short neck with flaring rim, lip folded inward. Base rounded, weathered, with some iridescence. Two tiny hairline cracks at base of body. 5.8 cm high. Cf. *Excavations at Dura-Europus*, Part V, #7LP. Intact.
....**CHOICE 175.00**

1895. **TALL NECK UNGUENTARIUM. Cyprus. Mid 2nd Century A.D.** Pale blue tear bottle with flat bell-shaped body and tall, slender neck. Concave base. 12 cm high, 1.2 cm diameter rim, 4.2 cm diameter base. Cf. Hayes, *ROM* #508.   Reassembled.   Nice silver-blue iridescence.
....**CHOICE 150.00**

1896. **UNGUENTARIUM. Roman. Mid 2nd Century A.D.** Pale blue, almost colorless tear bottle. Bell-shaped body with flat base. Long, narrow neck with faint constriction at bottom, flaring neck at top with folded rim. 14.2 cm high, 2.1 cm diameter rim, 4.5 cm diameter base. Cf. Hayes, *ROM* #508. Flaking iridescence. ....**CHOICE 200.00**

1897. **TALL NECK UNGUENTARIUM. Cyprus. Late 2nd-Early 3rd Century A.D.** Pale turquoise tear bottle with flat, broad base and tall, tubular neck. Rim folded in. 15.8 cm high, 2.6 cm diameter rim, 6.2 cm diameter base. Some iridescence. Cf. Hayes, *ROM* #518. Nice variegated iridescence. Chip at rim. ....**CHOICE 300.00**

1898. **TALL NECK UNGUENTARIUM. Roman. Late 2nd-Early 3rd Century A.D.** Light blue glass tear bottle with fat body and flat base. Constriction at neck. Long tapering neck with large, flat, folded rim. 23.8 cm high, 4 cm diameter rim, 5.8 cm diameter base. The exaggerated shape of this tear bottle was common during this time. This probably comes from Eastern Roman empire, possibly Cyprus. Cf. Auth, # 1 37 (50.1753). Iridescence. Reassembled. Very large vessel.
....**CHOICE 500.00**

1899. **SMALL PHIAL. Egypt. Late 2nd-3rd Century A.D.** Light blue phial with squat body. Neck with large flaring rim. Hayes, *ROM*, #584. 3 cm high, 2.5 cm diameter rim, 1.9 cm diameter base.   Iridescence and intact.
....**CHOICE 150.00**

1900. **FLASK. 3rd Century A.D.** Light green-brown flask with long slender neck. Globular body with small flattened base. 9 cm high, 1.8 cm diameter rim, 4.8 cm diameter base. Hayes, *ROM* #288.   Some slight iridescence. Intact.
....**CHOICE 250.00**

1901. **MINIATURE FISH FLASK. Roman. 3rd Century A.D.** Stylized fish in thick light green glass with brown fins and mouth. Tail fin broken off. Opening at mouth. 6.8 cm long, 1.9 cm wide. Cf. for similar style Bergman, #149. Cf. for style, von Saldern, #113. Very rare. ....**CHOICE 1500.00**

1902. **FLASK. Roman. 3rd Century A.D.** Light green-brown flask with long slender neck. Globular body with small flattened base. 9 cm high, 1.8 cm diameter rim, 4.8 cm diameter base. Some slight iridescence. Hayes, *ROM* #288. Intact. ....**CHOICE 400.00**

1903. **JAR. Roman. 3rd Century A.D.** Light yellow-white jar with bulbous body and folded, flaring rim. Concave base. 4.8 cm high, 3.5 cm diameter rim. This particular piece, being too fragile for use as a child's toy, was probably either used as a sample for grave use or made with "left over glass batch" at the end of the day. Some iridescence. Cf. Hayes, *ROM* #271. Auth, #203 (50.1816). Intact. ....**SUPERB 300.00**

1904. **SMALL FLASK. Roman-Egypt. From the Fayoum. 3rd Century A.D.** Colorless glass.   Piriform, rounded body curving up to short neck with wide, flat rim. Lip folded in. 6.4 cm high, 2 cm diameter rim, 3.5 cm diameter base. Some nice iridescence. ....**CHOICE 250.00**

1905. **FLASK. Roman. 3rd Century A.D.** Brownish-clear glass flask with well-rounded globular body and slightly concave base. Tubular neck, no rim, constriction at shoulder. 9 cm high, 1.5 cm diameter rim, 2 cm diameter base. Lovely blue iridescence. Cf. Hayes *ROM*, #288 for style. Intact.
....**CHOICE 300.00**

1906. **LARGE FLASK. Roman. 3rd Century A.D.** Large globular body, well rounded, made from thin light greenish-brown glass. Constriction at shoulder, short tubular neck. No rim, perhaps broken off. Concave base. 10.8 cm high, 1.8 cm diameter rim, 2.6 cm diameter base. Cf. Hayes, *ROM* #288 for style. Reassembled with chips at rim. ....**CHOICE 350.00**

1907. **JUG. 3rd Century A.D.** 9 cm high, 2.6 cm diameter rim, 3 cm diameter flat base. Green-brown jug speckled with iridescence. Globular body with narrow neck. Folded lip and flat base. Handle, from lip, slightly tapering to mid-body. Restored handle. Cf. Hayes, *Roman and Pre-Roman Glass in the ROM*, #283, Pl. 19. ....**CHOICE 300.00**

1908. **INDENTED CUP. Eastern Mediterranean. 3rd-4th Century A.D.** 8 cm high, 7.4 cm diameter rim. Cream colored cup with four indents and rim. Flat base. Chip on rim. Salt encrustation. Free-blown. The free-blown method was a technique in which the vessel was inflated from molten glass through a hollow rod. It was then shaped with pinchers while on a pontil rod. This rod usually left a mark at the base of the object known as a punty mark. Cf. Matheson, p. XV. Chip at edge. Cf. Matheson, *Ancient Glass at the Yale University Art Gallery*, #250, p. 93. ....**CHOICE 175.00**

1909. **FLASK. 3rd-4th Century A.D.** Colorless glass flask with long body. Four deep vertical indentations. Tubular neck and flaring rim. 11.8 cm high, 2 cm diameter rim, 2.5 cm diameter base. Cf. Ede, 99, #38. Interesting shaped vessel. ....**SUPERB 400.00**

1910. **SMALL JAR. 3rd-4th Century A.D.** Thick light aqua-blue glass jar with globular body. One row of six pinches around body, one row of five pinches around base. Straight tubular neck, no lip. 6.8 cm high, 2 cm diameter rim, 3.5 cm diameter Cf. for shape, Auth, #468. Cf. for pinched design, Auth, #175. Slight iridescence and encrustation. Interesting shoulder design. ....**CHOICE 275.00**

1911. No entry.

1912. **SMALL SQUARE BOTTLE. Eastern Mediterranean. 3rd-4th Century A.D.** Thick green glass bottle with square body, tapering at base. Short neck with flaring rim. 6.3 cm high. 2.4 cm diameter rim, 1.6 cm diameter base. A lovely pattern of iridescence covering the entire body. This style bottle was more common in the Western Empire. Cf. Matheson, #220. Intact. Variegated light and dark iridescence. ....**CHOICE 350.00**

1913. **SMALL FLASK. Roman. 3rd-4th Century A.D.** Light blue-aqua flask of moderately thick glass. Conical body with flat base. Cylindrical neck with wide flaring rim. Hayes, *ROM* #585. Some encrustation and iridescence present. ....**CHOICE 200.00**

1914. **SMALL JAR. Roman. 3rd-4th Century A.D.** Thick light aqua-blue glass jar with globular body. One row of six pinches around body, one row of five pinches around base. Straight tubular neck, no lip. 6.8 cm high, 2 cm diameter rim, 3.5 cm diameter Cf. for shape, Auth, #468. Cf. for pinched design, Auth. #175. Slight iridescence and encrustation. Interesting shoulder design. ....**CHOICE 500.00**

1915. **FLASK. Roman. 3rd-4th Century A.D.** Colorless glass flask with long body. Four deep vertical indentations. Tubular neck and flaring rim. 11.8 cm high, 2 cm diameter rim, 2.5 cm diameter base. Cf. Ede, 99, #38. Interesting shaped vessel. ....**SUPERB 700.00**

1916. **SPINDLE-SHAPED UNGUENTARIUM. Roman 3rd-4th Century A.D..** Spindle shaped with flat, squat base and tapering neck. Large folded rim. Light green thick glass. 8.7 cm high, 3.5 cm diameter rim, 4 cm diameter base. Auth, #426 (50.1677). Some iridescence. Bold yellow-green color. Intact. ....**CHOICE-SUPERB 350.00**

1917. **JAR. Roman. Late 3rd Century A.D.** Yellowish-green, medium-thin glass. Low, broad body of globular form with narrow flat shoulder. Short, concave neck with rounded rim, folded in. Pontil mark in concave base. Protrusion from base broken off what may have been a decoration or support in dark blue, thicker glass. 4.1 cm high, 3.2 cm diameter rim, 2 cm diameter base. Cf. Hayes, *ROM* #323. Superb green iridescence. ....**CHOICE-SUPERB 450.00**

1918. **FLASK. Cyprus. 4th Century A.D.** Green glass, somewhat thick and bubbly. Rounded body with five circular indentations and round base. Tubular neck with flat lip. Cf. Hayes, *ROM*, #669. Bold yellow-green color. Intact. ....**SUPERB 300.00**

1919. **FLASK. 4th Century A.D.** Green glass with thin body, slightly thicker base. Body has seven vertical ribs, tapers to neck. Neck constricted. Rounded rim with outward fold beneath. Height 9.7 cm. Cf. Bergman #180 for ribbing; Cf. Bergman #188 for rim shape. Iridescence. Large chips out of body. ....**CHOICE 300.00**

1920. **AMULET DISK PENDANT. 4th Century A.D.** 15 mm long. Blue, iridescent glass. Relief of a turtle. Cuff at top for suspension. These amulets were very prominent as pendants on necklaces. The turtle symbolizes longevity. Top of loop missing. Some pitting and iridescence. CF. Eisen, *Glass*, Vol. II, fig. 230, p. 533....................**CHOICE 50.00**

1921. **BEAKER. 4th Century A.D.** 9.5 cm high, 8.5 cm diameter rim, 3 cm diameter base. Green-blue beaker on base. Two lines around top for decoration. Three loop handles. Similar to larger beakers from Tyre. Reconstructed. Cf. Auth, *Ancient Glass at the Newark Museum*, #112, p. 101. ....**CHOICE 500.00**

1922. **FLASK. Roman. 4th Century A.D.** Pale greenish flask with rounded body. Straight vertical neck with small rounded rim. Five small circular indentations in body. Hayes, *ROM* #669. Traces of iridescence. Nice pinched body vessel. Intact. ....**CHOICE-SUPERB 300.00**

1923. **FLASK. Roman. 4th Century A.D.** Green-blue glass. Rounded body with seven circular indentations and round base. Tubular neck with flat lip, slightly flair rim. Cf. Hayes, *ROM*, #669. Nice blue-green color. Has been reconstructed. ....**SUPERB 225.00**

1924. **MINIATURE JAR. Roman. 4th Century A.D.** Thick yellow glass, heavily encrusted. Squat body with flat base and straight neck. 3.8 cm high, 2 cm diameter rim, 2.8 cm diameter base. Cf. Auth, #514 (50.1800). Heavy patina. Intact. ....**CHOICE 175.00**

1925. **BALSAMONIUM. 4th Century A.D.** Multiple flask in green glass, rather thick at bottom. Thin threads of blue glass wrapped around middle part of body (10 lines). One handle at side, other and high arch missing. Cream crust covering part of flask - iridescence all over. 10.4 cm high. Cf. Hayes, *Roman and Pre-Roman Glass in Royal Ontario Museum (ROM)*, nos. 360-361. ....**CHOICE 450.00**

1926. **BEAKER. 4th Century A.D.** Green-blue vessel on pedestal base, two trailing lines around side, three loop handles. Height 9.5 cm, diameter 8.5 cm. Auth, Newark #112, p.101. Reconstructed but no restoration. A rare vessel with attractive loops. Charming. ....**CHOICE 350.00**

1927. **MEDUSA HEAD AMULET APPLIQUÉ. Asia Minor. c. 4th-5th Century A.D.** Dark brownish-blue stamped Medusa head appliqué with two horizontal suspension holes. Cf. Frank Sternberg, Zurich, Jewish, Early Christian and Byzantine Antiquities, Auction XXIII, Nov. 1989, #295. Intact. ....**CHOICE 150.00**

1928. **SMALL JAR. Roman. 4th-5th Century A.D.** Light green jar with round body and concave base. Short, flaring neck. 5.1 cm high, 2.5 cm diameter rim, 3.8 cm diameter base. Cf. *Yale University Art Gallery Catalogue*, #289. Intact. ....**CHOICE 250.00**

1929. **FLASK. Roman. 4th-5th Century A.D.** Deep maroon flask with tall, slender body and slight bulge at bottom. Conical foot with tubular edge. Pontil mark under base. Zig-zag openwork around rim, fused to lip at five points. Four threads of glass wound around body. 9.5 cm high, 2.3 cm dia rim, 3.5 cm diameter base. Hayes, *ROM* #353. Lovely color and shape with attractive thread work. Intact except for part of base missing. ....**SUPERB 1500.00**

1930. **FLASK. 4th or 5th Century A.D.** 9.5 cm high, 3.2 cm diameter rim, 3.5 cm diameter base. Yellowish-brown transparent flask. Bulbous body with short neck and wide rim. Intact. Cf. similar to Hayes, *Roman and Pre-Roman Glass in the ROM*, Pl. 20, #290. ....**CHOICE 250.00**

1931. **SMALL JAR. 4th-5th Century A.D.** Light green jar with round body and concave base. Short, flaring neck. 5.1 cm high, 2.5 cm diameter rim, 3.8 cm diameter base. Cf. *Yale University Art Gallery Catalogue*, #289. Intact. Good color. ....**CHOICE 250.00**

1932. **FLASK. 4th-5th Century A.D.** Aqua glass flask, bulbous body with neck and wide rim. Height 10.8 cm, diameter 10 cm. Manufacture imperfection to part of rim. Constable-Maxwell 6/79 315, Hayes *ROM*, Plate 20, #290. Intact. Nice size. ....**CHOICE 275.00**

1933. **GLASS PENDANT. 4th-5th Century A.D.** Lime green glass medallion, with remains of a suspension hole at the top. Depicts a lion walking left with a star in crescent above. Egyptian manufacture. Height 2.4 cm, pendant 1.8 cm in diam. Cf. for similar glass pendants Frank Sternberg Auction XXIII, 1989 #264-291. Some iridescence. ....**CHOICE 75.00**

1934. **GLASS PENDANT/EARRING. 4th-5th Century A.D.** Small pale green glass pendant with large suspension hole at top. Amphora motif stamped slightly off-center. Beautiful blue and rainbow-colored iridescence covering entire pendant. Height 1.9 cm, pendant 1.3 cm in diam. Cf. Sternberg Auction XXIII, 264-291. Lovely iridescence. ....**SUPERB 85.00**

1935. **JUGLET WITH TREFOIL MOUTH. Roman. Mid 4th Century A.D.** Light blue-green body. Ovoid body, curving at bottom, slender neck narrowing to trefoil mouth. Handle, rim and seven horizontal lines around neck in dark blue glass. Handle and base broken off. 7.2 cm high (without base), 4.2 x 3.6 cm diameter mouth. Cf. Hayes, *ROM* #345 and #346 for style. Part of handle missing, otherwise intact. Nice polychrome vessel. ....**SUPERB 1600.00**

1936. **JAR. 5th Century A.D.** 9 cm high, 2.8 cm diameter rim, 4.5 cm diameter base. Thick brownish clear jar with spots of iridescence. Fat, globular body with vertical tooled ribs. Straight neck without lip. Pontil mark at base. Cf. Auth, *Ancient Glass at the Newark Museum*, #538, p. 232. ....**SUPERB 350.00**

LAMPS

1937. **MOLD-MADE LAMP. 1st Century B.C.** Piriform body and beak nozzle. Flat top with small filling hole piercing slightly concave discus. Slightly curved sides with flat base extending forward along contour of body. Dark red-brown slip over buff ware. 8.5 cm. Deneauve 693 (rare) 6. Probably of North African manufacture...................**CHOICE 125.00**

1938. **OIL LAMP. 1st Century B.C.-1st Century A.D. Roman.** Probably Antioch manufacture. Buff clay with orange slip. Volute nozzle, knob handle. Cornucopiae on each shoulder, rosette in center of base. Length 9.5 cm. Cf. Dura fig. 5 for similar style. Sharp shoulder design. ....**CHOICE 200.00**

1939. OIL LAMP. 1st Century B.C.-1st Century A.D. Roman Egyptian. Mold-made lamp with ovoid body and long nozzle with mildly spade-type end. Small filling hole with ridge. Shoulder decorated by three outward-facing series of small semicircles. Flat base. Blackening at wick hole. Dark red slip over brown ware. Length 8.5 cm. Cf. *BM* Q570.
....**CHOICE 100.00**

1940. MOLD-MADE LAMP. Late 1st Century B.C.-1st Century A.D. Oil lamp with ovoid body and long nozzle with mildly spade-type end. Small filling hole with ridge. Shoulder decorated by seven outward facing series of semicircles. Flat base. Blackening at wick hole. Brown ware. 8.5 cm. Cf. *BM*: Q570. Similar to above. ....**CHOICE 125.00**

1941. OIL LAMP. 1st Century A.D. Roman. Mold-made lamp with piriform body and beak nozzle. Flat top with small filling hole piercing slightly concave discus. Slightly curved sides with flat base extending forward along contour of body. Dark red-brown slip over buff ware. Length 8.5 cm. Deneauve 693 (rare). Probably of North African manufacture.
....**CHOICE 100.00**

1942. OIL LAMP. 1st Century A.D. Roman. Orange clay lamp with red-orange slip. Volute nozzle. Large Skylla in discus. Length 10 cm. Schl.-; *ROM*-; *BMC*-. Nice color.
....**CHOICE 250.00**

1943. VOLUTE LAMP. 1st Century A.D. Mold-made with flat top and curved sides receding to slightly raised base ring. Voluted nozzle with angular tip. On concave discus, a rosette with thirteen petals surrounded by double ridged rim. Light buff clay with brown-black slip. 8.5 cm. Italy manufacture. Cf. Schloessinger Collection, 73-74. Bailey, *BM* 83 1. Italian manufacture. ....**CHOICE 175.00**

1944. MOLD-MADE LAMP. 1st Century A.D. Broad body with curved shoulder and rounded side, short deep round nozzle and high pierced handle with double groove at top. Two circular grooves surround concave discus depicting Pegasus leaping right, filling hole below. Large vent hole at edge. Egg and dot border. Flat bottom with shallow incised pseudo ring base. Buff slip over clay varying from brick-red to greenish-grey. North African manufacture. Deneauve, *Lampes de Carthage*, 819 (motif), 825-33 (type). Menzel, *ABB* 32, 14. ....**CHOICE 165.00**

1945. MOLD-MADE LAMP. 1st Century A.D. Orange-red clay, watch-shaped body with protruding nozzle with flattened tip. Large filling hole through very narrow discus set off by thick ridge. Radiating grooves around upper body, squat column motif on nozzle, small knob to one side. 7.8 cm. Cf. Bailey, *BM* Q586 and 588. Cf. *ROM*, 61-69, 76.
....**CHOICE 80.00**

1946. MOLD-MADE OIL LAMP. 1st Century A.D. With round body and pointed nozzle offset by two semi-volutes. Depressed discus depicting woman left before lighted altar. Ring base. Cream ware. 9 cm. *ROM* 307 (contemp.)
....**CHOICE 200.00**

1947. MINIATURE LAMP. 1st Century A.D. Mold made with oval body and large wide nozzle. Small filling hole within rim. Egg and ray border. Ring base inscription A. Drab brown ware. 5.5 cm. Cf. *ROM* 205-6. For use in contemporary "lamp houses."......................**CHOICE 75.00**

1948. MOLD-MADE VOLUTE LAMP. 1st Century A.D. Roman Italian. Light buff clay with brown-black slip. With flat top and curved sides receding to slightly raised base ring. Voluted nozzle with angular tip. Concave discus with thirteen-petalled rosette surrounded by double-ridged rim. Length 8.5 cm. Cf. Schloessinger Collection 73-74.
....**CHOICE 175.00**

1949. MINIATURE LAMP. 1st-Early 2nd Century A.D. Roman. Red-beige slip over red buff clay. Mold made: deep circular body, short rounded nozzle, and high pierced handle with groove. Raised rim, depressed discus containing rosette petals. Large filling hole. Flat base, central circle set off by rim. Length 6.8 cm. Cf. Bailey, *BM* 1241. Chip to inner ring.
....**ABOUT CHOICE 75.00**

1950. MINIATURE LAMP. 1st-Early 2nd Century A.D. Mold made with deep circular body, short rounded nozzle, and high pierced handle with groove. Raised rim within ovolo surrounds depressed discus containing rosette petals. Large filling hole. Flat base with central filling hole. Flat base with central circle set off by rim. Raised border delineates underside of nozzle. Red-beige slip over red buff clay. 6.8 cm. Chip to inner ring. Cf. Bailey, *BM* 1241.
....**ABOUT CHOICE 75.00**

1951. VOLUTE LAMP. 1st-Early 2nd Century A.D. Mold made with curved shoulder and rounded sides. Ridge, within ovolo, surrounds discus depicting dolphin, downward, entwined around trident, with head of lion left with tongue extended covering tail, small filling hole in field. Double semi-volutes separate wick hole from discus. Flat base marked by groove. Orange-buff clay with traces of dark-red glaze. 9.2 cm. For form, Cf. Schloessinger Collection 116. For motif, Cf. *BM*-. Schloessinger-. *ROM*-. Szentleleky-. Some repairs and restoration to end of nozzle.
....**CHOICE 85.00**

1952. MOLD-MADE LAMP. 1st-2nd Century A.D. Oil lamp with round body and biconical cross section. Small filling hole within recessed, double bordered discus. Rosette on each shoulder. Angular "rope" pattern sets off long flat-topped nozzle. Flat, base with impressed planta pedis. Red to black slip over buff ware. Schl. 80, 85 (planta pedis). Variegated orange to brown. ......**CHOICE-SUPERB 150.00**

1953. **MOLD-MADE LAMP. 1st-2nd Century A.D.** Oil lamp with round body with large scoop nozzle. Medium filling hole "butterfly" on each shoulder. Volutes forward of filling hole border offset nozzle. Disc base with impressed planta pedis. Red-orange slip over light orange buff ware. *ROM* 353-4 (butterfly). Schl. 80, 85 (planta pedis). Small shoulder hole. Nice color. ....**CHOICE 120.00**

1954. **MOLD-MADE LAMP. 1st-2nd Century A.D.** With round body and slightly broad blunt end nozzle. Round discus depicting two lovers on a bed. The man kneels to right approaching woman, lying, from front. Woman rests back on pillow, her left leg is held up by man's right hand. Medium filling hole below. Flat, base. Buff ware. 8.6 cm. A most unusual scene for a Roman erotic lamp, depicting a position more in keeping with modern western practice than those typically depicted on this series. Contemp. *ROM* 378 [or later]. Deneauve 889 (discus). Some encrustation. ....**CHOICE 500.00**

1955. **MOLD-MADE LAMP. 1st-2nd Century A.D.** With round body and wide bow end nozzle of set by semi-volutes. Medium filling hole and short handle. Low relief wreath on shoulder. Ring base. Red orange slip over buff ware. Contemp. Schl. 344-5..............**AVERAGE-CHOICE 95.00**

1956. **MOLD-MADE LAMP. 1st-2nd Century A.D.** Circular body, sloping shoulders, and beak-type nozzle. Concave disc depicting cock right with palm over shoulder. High pierced handle. Flat base with incuse initials CCV. Beige ware. 10 cm. Deneauve 779. Encrusted. ....**SUPERB 165.00**

1957. **MOLD-MADE LAMP. 1st-2nd Century A.D.** Virtually round body merging with round end nozzle offset by two semi-volutes. Round concave discus depicting cuttle fish. High pierced handle. Flat base with vestigal ring. Black to red-purple slip over cream ware. 11.5 cm. Cf. *ROM* 323 (form). Cf. *ROM* 270 (design). ....**CHOICE 95.00**

1958. **MOLD-MADE LAMP. 1st-2nd Century A.D.** Deep circular body with short rounded nozzle. Undecorated, deeply hollowed discus surrounded by two grooves, flat base. Brown glaze on greyish clay. 8.5 cm. While this undecorated type is more frequently encountered with a thin handle, one handleless example was excavated at the Synagogue of Delos. Cf. Delos XXVI, *Les Lampes*, 4653. Reconstructed but complete. ....**CHOICE 65.00**

1959. **MOLD-MADE LAMP. 1st-2nd Century A.D.** With sloping shoulder, sharply carinated midpoint and convex base, set off by subtle ring, and continuing with rounded underside of body. Shallow ridge underneath. Flat topped semi-volute nozzle. Shallow rosette design on shoulder, pierced raised handle. Large filling hole. Irregular red glaze over thin buff clay. Of Cilician or Cypriot manufacture. 9.2 cm. For motif, Cf. Schloessinger Collection. 345. For fabric and ware, Cf. *ROM*, p. 72. ....**AVERAGE 60.00**

1960. **OIL LAMP. 1st-2nd Century A.D. Roman.** Mold-made lamp with round body and high pierced handle. Round beak-type nozzle. Concave discus depicting a shrine with pine cones atop. Figure seated at right playing lyre. Two figures in the foreground are playing with a garland, Cupid at upper left. Shoulder ornamented by wreath. Ring base with incised inner rings. Nozzle offset on underside by row of grooves. Variegated brown slip over brown-buff ware. Length 9.7 cm. Schl. 174 and 176 (contemporary). Very rare. ....**CHOICE 450.00**

1961. **OIL LAMP. 1st-2nd Century A.D. Roman.** Mold-made oil lamp with round body and biconical cross section. Small filling hole within recessed, double bordered discus. Rosette on each shoulder. Angular "rope" pattern setting off long flat-topped nozzle. Flat base with impressed planta pedis. Red to black slip over buff ware. Length 8.6 cm. Cf. Schl. 80, 85 (planta pedis). Variegated color of orange to brown. ....**CHOICE-SUPERB 150.00**

1962. **MOLD-MADE OIL LAMP. 1st-2nd Century A.D.** With round body and wide flaring nozzle with bowed end. Small filling hole piercing concave discus surrounded by wide border. Egg band around shoulder. Large pierced handle with three grooves on top edge. Flat, base. Blackening at wick hole. Possibly of Italian manufacture. *ROM* 229. With early antiquity tag. ....**CHOICE-SUPERB 125.00**

1963. **MOLD-MADE LAMP. 1st-2nd Century A.D.** With round body and large bow-end nozzle offset by volutes. Plain concave discus with small filling hole and vent hole, plain shoulder. High pierced handle. Crude disc base. Maroon black slip over pink-peach ware. 13 cm. Contemp. *ROM* 436. Nice size. ....**CHOICE 80.00**

1964. **MOLD-MADE LAMP. 1st-2nd Century A.D.** Oil lamp with ovoid body and bow end nozzle offset by semi-volutes. Recessed discus with rough filling hole, surrounded by ring. Small "conical" handle attached at back. Pronounced ring base. Drab red-buff ware. 7.9 cm. *ROM*-. Schl.-. Said to be of North Levantine manufacture. ....**CHOICE 75.00**

1965. **MOLD-MADE LAMP. 1st-2nd Century A.D. Roman.** Red glaze over buff clay. Wide with curving shoulder and body. Double ridge sets off flat, recessed discus around medium filling hole. Small rosette at each side of shoulder. Angled border sets off nozzle with flat top and small raised protuberances by wick hole replacing volute design. Impressed planta pedis on circular base. Length 8.5 cm. Cf. Schloessinger Coll. 80ff for planta pedis. Broneer XXIII derived. A very nice example. ....**CHOICE 150.00**

1966. **VOLUTE LAMP. c. 25-100 A.D.** With double convex body. Shoulder sloping more gradually than lower portion. Pierced handle with large aperture and two grooves on top edge only. Concave discus with small filling hole between two cornucopiae. Large flat-topped nozzle with pair of single volutes and vent at intersection with body. Round base, set off by groove, with incised C*L potter's mark. Mottled red glaze on grey-brown clay for form and signature. North African manufacture. Cf. *ROM* 226. For motif, Cf. Schlessinger Collection 72. Small chip at base. ....**SUPERB 200.00**

1967. **MOLD-MADE LAMP. Late 1st-2nd Century A.D.** Wide with curving shoulder and body. Double ridge sets off flat recessed discus around medium filling hole. Rosette at each side of shoulder. Angled border sets off nozzle with flat top. Wick hole. Orange glaze over buff clay. 8 cm. Cf. Schloessinger Collection, 80ff. Broneer XXIII derived. A very nice example. Excellent type. ....**CHOICE 150.00**

1968. **VOLUTE LAMP. Late 1st-2nd Century A.D.** Mold made with curved shoulder and rounded sides receding to slightly raised circular base ring containing potter's mark. Ridge surrounds concave discus depicting an amphora with bunches of grapes and vine leaves emerging. Small filling hole in field and raised dot, replacing vent, at ridge. Double volutes set off nozzle. Red-brown slip over buff clay. 8.6 cm. Cf. Schloessinger Collection 101 (form), 105 (motif). Cf. Menzel, *ABB*, 34, 3. ....**CHOICE 150.00**

1969. **MOLD-MADE LAMP. Late 1st Century A.D.** With round body and flat topped round nozzle. Concave discus depicting facing Medusa head. Egg design on shoulder. Flat base. Traces of brick-red slip over pink-buff slip. 9 cm. Contemp. *ROM* 382. ....**CHOICE 175.00**

1970. **MOLD MADE LAMP. Late 1st-Early 2nd Century A.D.** Broad body with curved shoulder and rounded side, short deep round nozzle and high pierced handle with double groove at top. Two circular grooves surround concave discus depicting bird standing right on myrtle branch, pecking at berry. Filling hole in field. Flat base, set off by groove, inscribed LMADIEC. Black to brown glaze over buff clay. 10.5 cm. Italian manufacture. Bailey, *BM* Q984 (potter's mark), Q1277. ....**CHOICE 150.00**

1971. **LAMP. Late 1st-Early 2nd Century A.D.** Broad body with curved shoulder and rounded side, short deep round nozzle and high pierced handle with double groove at top. Two grooves surround concave discus depicting star over crescent. Filling hole between. Short palm separates nozzle from discus. Flat base marked by groove. IVNC I potter's mark. Buff slip over brown-red to black clay. 10.5 cm. North African manufacture. Reconstructed. Cf. Deneauve, *Lampes de Carthage*, 739. ....**SUPERB 175.00**

1972. **MOLD-MADE DISCUS. Late 1st-2nd Century A.D.** Depicting helmeted head of Athena left, two filling holes. Egg border. Tan ware. 5.7 cm. Schl. 167 (contemp.) Szentleleky 94a (design)............**CHOICE-SUPERB 100.00**

1973. **OIL LAMP. Late 1st-2nd Century A.D. Roman.** Syrian style. Buff clay with orange slip. Stamped palmetted shoulder design. Discus shows the bust of a hornless satyr left, with a himation on his left shoulder. Length 9 cm. Kennedy type 5; Cf. *ROM* 351 for type. Schlossinger 351 (same mold?). Sharp design in discus. ....**CHOICE-SUPERB 275.00**

1974. **OIL LAMP. Beginning of 2nd Century A.D. Roman.** Light buff clay with light grey slip. Spatulated nozzle with projections near base. Flat palmette handle. Discus shows two rings of ornamented globules. Made in the easternmost regions of the Roman Empire. Similar lamps were found at Dura-Europus, Palmyra, and Damascus. Length 11.8 cm. *Dura-Europus* 26-31. Encrusted and flaking to handle. ....**CHOICE 125.00**

1975. **OIL LAMP. Early 2nd Century A.D. Roman.** Mold-made lamp with round body and short round nozzle. Depressed discus depicting Pan left, pedum over shoulder. Border of rays on shoulder. Ring base. Thin orange slip over buff ware. Length 8.7 cm. Cf. for topic: Deneauve 1018-9; Contemp. ROM 351-353. Interesting depiction of Pan. ....**CHOICE 175.00**

1976. **MOLD-MADE LAMP. Early 2nd Century A.D.** With round body and short nozzle. Depressed discus depicting bust of Sol facing over crescent. Border of demi-fleurs on shoulder. Double ring base. Black slip over cream ware. 8.7 cm. *ROM* 353 (contemp.). ....**CHOICE 150.00**

1977. **MOLD-MADE LAMP. Early 2nd Century A.D.** Round body and short round nozzle. Depressed discus depicting ram walking right. Border of rays on shoulder. Ring base. Thin orange slip over buff ware. 8.2 cm. Cf. *ROM* 351-353. Bold depiction of ram. ....**CHOICE 150.00**

1978. **MOLD-MADE LAMP. 2nd Century A.D.** Circular body and rounded biconical cross section. Rounded nozzle tip. Small unpierced handle. Flat discus within three recessed borders. Groove sets off wick hole with another leading back towards filling hole rim. Flat, base with several incised "rings." Traces of red slip over buff ware. 9 cm. Probably of Syrian manufacture. *ROM* 357. Small lower side hole. ....**CHOICE-SUPERB 150.00**

1979. **MOLD-MADE LAMP. 2nd Century A.D.** Broad body with curved shoulder and rounded side, short deep nozzle and high, holed rounded handle. Narrow wreath surrounds concave discus depicting bear walking left. Filling hole and vent in field. Decoration of close rays on shoulder. Slightly concave base set off by groove. Drab tan-buff ware. 12.5 cm. This lamp is actually a second generation product made using a lamp of earlier decades to form a new mold. Potter's mark: IVC PC[?]/IVRI... North African provenance. Deneauve, mark.-. Deneauve, *Lampes de Carthage*, 839 (prototype). ....**CHOICE 200.00**

1980. **OIL LAMP. 2nd Century A.D. Roman.** Mold-made lamp with a circular body. Rounded nozzle tip. Small handle. Flat, discus. Groove sets off wick hole with another leading back towards filling hole rim. Flat base with several incised "rings." Traces of orange slip over buff ware. Length 9 cm. Syrian manufacture. *ROM* 357. Scarce type. ....**CHOICE 125.00**

1981. **OIL LAMP. 2nd Century A.D. Roman.** Mold-made lamp, with a broad body with curved shoulder and rounded side. Short deep nozzle and high, holed rounded handle. A narrow wreath surrounds concave discus depicting a cock standing right. Filling hole and vent in field. Traces of iron at filling hole. Carbon deposits at spout. Decoration of close rays on shoulder. Slightly concave base set off by groove. Buff ware. Length 12.3 cm. North African provenance. Deneauve, *Lampes de Carthage*, 839 (prototype). ....**CHOICE 175.00**

1982. **OIL LAMP. 2nd Century A.D. Roman.** North African manufacture. Buff lamp with volute nozzle. Wreath design on shoulder; horse galloping left in tondo. Length 11 cm. Schl.-; *ROM* -...**CHOICE 175.00**

1983. **MOLD-MADE LAMP. 2nd Century A.D.** Broad body with curved shoulder and rounded side, short deep nozzle and high solid handle. Narrow wreath surrounds concave discus depicting a bear walking left. Filling hole and vent in field. Decoration of close rays on shoulder. Slightly concave base set off by groove. Traces of black slip over grey clay. Length 12.6 cm. This lamp is actually a second generation product made using a lamp of earlier decades to form a new mold. The place of the intended handle hole from the original can still be seen on this specimen. North African manufacture. Deneauve, *Lampes de Carthage*, 839 (prototype). ....**CHOICE 100.00**

1984. **MOLD-MADE LAMP. c. 2nd Century A.D. Roman. North Africa.** Light brown slip over brownish clay. Wide body with curved shoulder and crudely angled sides receding to flat base with three concentric circles. Double groove surrounds recessed discus with pattern of rays around small filling hole. Small knob handle with incised grooves, leaning to side. Small ridge separates wick hole from discus. Length 8.7 cm. This form and ware bears strong similarities to Egyptian products. Cf. Szentleky, *Ancient Lamps.* 166; Cf. Petrie, *Roman Ehnasya*, LVI:40..................**CHOICE 65.00**

1985. **MOLD-MADE LAMP. c. 2nd Century A.D.** Wide body with curved shoulder and crudely angled sides receding to flat base inscribed with three concentric circles. Double groove surrounds recessed discus with pattern of rays around small filling hole. Small knob handle with incised grooves, leaning to side. Small ridge separates wick hole from discus. Light brown slip over brownish clay. 8.7 cm. This form and ware bears strong similarities to Egyptian products. North African manufacture. Cf. Szentleleky, *Ancient Lamps*, 166. Cf. Petrie, *Roman Ehnasya*, LVI:40. ....**CHOICE 65.00**

1986. **FROG LAMP. 2nd-3rd Century A.D.** With deep ovoid body with frog depicted with body pierced by filling hole. No separate nozzle but large wick hole. Flat base. Red-brown clay with yellow-buff slip. 6.6 cm. The frog, being a symbol of resurrection in Egyptian religion, was adopted as an early Christian symbol as well. Cf. Petrie, *Roman Ehnasya*, LXIII:58, 60, 62. Cf. Schloessinger Collection, 243. Egyptian manufacture. ....**AVERAGE 25.00**

1987. **OIL LAMP. 2nd-3rd Century A.D. Roman.** Mold-made lamp with round body and beak-type nozzle. High pierced handle. Concave discus with small filling hole, decorated with Capricorn left, shoulder ornamented with wreath. Ring base. Red-brown slip over buff ware. Length 10.2 cm. *ROM* 174-6, and 277. Some encrustation. Handle repaired. ....**CHOICE 185.00**

1988. **OIL LAMP. 2nd-3rd Century A.D. Roman.** Mold-made lamp with round body and short beak-type nozzle. High pierced handle. Wide discus depicting Hercules and the Nemean lion. Wreath on shoulder. Two filling holes, one with possible filling rod remnant. Grey-black slip over cream ware. The scene on the discus portrays one of the Labors of Hercules. Length 11.2 cm. Contemp. *ROM* 277 and Schl. 174-6. ....**AVERAGE-CHOICE 150.00**

1989. **OIL LAMP. 2nd-3rd Century A.D. Roman. North Africa.** Mold-made lamp with round body and beak-type nozzle with medium wick hole. Concave discus ornamented with confronted busts of Isis and Serapis, small filling hole between. High handle. Wide, slightly concave base. Beige slip over ivory ware. Length 11.5 cm. Deneauve 913 var. ....**AVERAGE 100.00**

1990. **MOLD-MADE LAMP. 2nd-3rd Century A.D.** With round body and beak type nozzle. High pierced handle. Concave discus, small filling hole and vent hole, decorated with bust of Jupiter left. Shoulder ornamented with wreath. Ornament design on underside separates nozzle. Ring base with potter's monogram in form of mountain. Black slip over buff slip. Cf. Schl. 176. Cf. Deneauve XV:956-9 for form of mark, 926 (design). Contemp. *ROM* 277. North African manufacture. ....**CHOICE 175.00**

1991. MOLD-MADE LAMP. 2nd-3rd Century A.D. With round body and beak-type nozzle. Pierced handle. Concave discus, with small filling hole. Decorated with Pegasus to right. Shoulder ornamented with wreath. Ring base. Orange-brown slip over buff ware. Contemp. Schloessinger. 174-6 and *ROM* 277. Nice surface. ....**CHOICE 175.00**

1992. MOLD-MADE LAMP. 2nd-3rd Century A.D. North Africa. With round body and beak-type nozzle with medium wick hole. Concave discus ornamented with confronted busts of Isis and Serapis, small filling hole between. High handle. Wide, slightly concave base. Beige slip over ivory ware. 11.5 cm. Deneauve 913 var. Very similar to #1989 but sharp details of Isis and Serapis. ....**CHOICE 225.00**

1993. MOLD-MADE LAMP. 2nd-3rd Century A.D. With round body and wide nozzle. Concave disc depicting bull in harness left. Two filling holes. Floral ornamentation on shoulder, rounded handle. Concave disc base. Brick red slip over tan-red ware. Schl. 362 (discus). *ROM* 458-60 (contemp.). ....**CHOICE 200.00**

1994. MOLD-MADE LAMP. 2nd-3rd Century A.D. With round body and high pierced handle. Short squared nozzle. Concave discus with rosette of ten petals. Small filling hole and vent hole. Rope design around. Seep ring base. Orange-buff ware. *ROM* 369 (contemp.). ...**CHOICE 150.00**

1995. MOLD-MADE LAMP. 2nd-3rd Century A.D. With round body and short beak-type nozzle. High pierced handle. Wide discus depicting Diana standing right carrying bow and arrow. Wreath on shoulder. Two filling holes. Grey slip over cream ware. Cf. Schloessinger Collection 174-6. ....**CHOICE 225.00**

1996. MOLD-MADE LAMP. 3rd Century A.D. With slightly elongated body merging into long nozzle decorated with two semi-volutes. Circular discus with house lying right, short rays around. Ring base containing rosette of four petals. Handle missing. Contemp. to Dura IV, Pt. III, Pl. IX:346. Scarce type...**CHOICE 150.00**

1997. MOLD-MADE LAMP. 3rd Century A.D. With round body and short nozzle. High pierced handle. Concave discus, with small filling hole and vent hole, depicting Hercules and the Cretan bull. Short rays to shoulder. Flat offset base. Buff ware. 11.5 cm. A Labor of Hercules. Contemp. Schl. 213. ....**AVERAGE 85.00**

1998. FROG LAMP. 3rd Century A.D. Piriform body with triangular nozzle, integral and not offset. Small filling hole within small sloping discus, stylized frog around. Shallow ring base, A within. Heavy red brown ware. 8.8 cm. Petrie, *Roman Ehnasya*, LXIII:69 (type) and LXXIII: 136 (potter's mark)..**CHOICE 125.00**

1999. OIL LAMP. 3rd Century A.D. Roman. Mold-made lamp with round body and short nozzle. Pierced handle. Concave discus, with small filling hole and vent hole, depicting a lion walking right. Short rays to shoulder. Flat offset base. Buff ware. Length 12 cm. Contemp. Schloessinger Collection, 213. ....**CHOICE 165.00**

2000. FROG LAMP. 3rd Century A.D. Roman/Egyptian. Oil lamp with piriform body with triangular nozzle, integral and not offset. Small filling hole within small sloping discus, stylized frog around. Shallow base ring, Δ within. Heavy red-brown ware. Length 8.8 cm. Petrie, *Roman Ehnasya*, LXIV #65 and LXXIII #136 (for potter's mark)...**CHOICE $150.00**

2001. MOLD-MADE LAMP. 3rd Century A.D With incised details. Oval body with integral nozzle. Small filling hole with large border forming top on ankh, on the cross-bar of which is the inscription APHCIC. Stylized arm design extending around shoulder from short knob handle. Simplified palm ornament at sides of ankh. Wick hole faces front and is offset by double ridge. Plain base with tan cross dividing two potter's marks. Traces of yellow-green slip over grey white clay. The ankh remained a common symbol among early Christians in Egypt, having connotations of the Nile, even water itself. The inscription also bears Christian connections and can be rendered in English as "remission." This word, NAPHCIC, is used by St. Paul in Romans 3:25: "Whom God has set forth to be a propitiation through Faith in his blood to declare his righteousness for the remission of sins that are passed through the forbearance of God." For ankh, Cf. Eisen, *Glass* 11, pp. 510-15. For potter's mark, Cf. Petrie, *Roman Ehnasya*, LXV:299. For ankh lamp, Cf. Petrie, *Roman Ehnasya*, LXVIII, 15. Cf. Petrie, LXVI. *ROM*-. Petrie-. Baur, *Dura-Europos Final Report* IV, Pt. III-. Szentleleky, *Ancient Lamps.*- Schloessinger Collection.- Small handle damage. Very rare. ....**CHOICE 400.00**

2002. MOLD-MADE LAMP. c. 300-450 A.D. With incised detail. Ovoid body with sloping shoulder. Large concave discus connected by channel to nozzle. Double ridge around discus with petal design containing two concentric circles. Two filling holes. Stump handle with pinched sides. Engraved double ring base connected by engraved grooves to handle, and by line and wreath motif to nozzle. "Target" potters mark at back of body. Red slip over red clay. 12 cm. North African manufacture. Cf. Schloessinger Collection 278 var. ....**SUPERB 150.00**

2003. MOLD-MADE LAMP. c. 300-450 A.D. Ovoid body with sloping shoulder on which is half-wreath motif. Concave discus connected by channel to nozzle. Two filling holes to either side of lion right. Mold-made pierced handle with central groove. Slightly concave base with potter's mark and double ridge to handle. Orange-red slip over orange-red clay. 12.3 cm. Schloessinger Collection 279 (form), *ROM* 287 (motif). North African manufacture. ....**CHOICE 125.00**

2004. **WREATH LAMP. 3rd-Early 4th Century A.D.** Red-buff clay with buff wash. Deep piriform body with short tapering nozzle. Degenerate but recognizable wreath design, narrow raised discus around filling hole. Incised double-stroke design on underside mark off nozzle. Flat bottom with pine-leaf potter's mark. Egyptian manufacture. Petrie, *Roman Ehnasya* LVIII, 70. Cf. Schloessinger Collection 255. ....**CHOICE-SUPERB 60.00**

2005. **FROG LAMP. 3rd-4th Century A.D.** Wide ovoid body with offset nozzle, small recessed discus surrounded by ridge. Shallow ring base with "B" potter's mark. Stylized frog design. Light brown ware with yellow-cream slip. 8.8 mm. Egyptian manufacture. Cf. Petrie, *Roman Ehnasya*, LXIV:63. ....**SUPERB 75.00**

2006. **FROG LAMP. 3rd-4th Century A.D.** Piriform body with triangular nozzle set off by two shoulder grooves on underside. Stylized frog design. Flat base with potter's mark. Pink-brown ware with buff slip. 7 cm. Cf. Petrie, *Roman Ehnasya*, LXIV. 84, 94. *ROM*, p. 13, 1. Egyptian manufacture...**CHOICE 35.00**

2007. **BOSS LAMP. 3rd-4th Century A.D. Roman.** Piriform body and short triangular nozzle offset by two shallow grooves to underside. Small filling hole within small sloping discus offset by groove. Three bosses with dimples around. Wick hole offset by groove. Flat base incised with "B". Ivory-green slip over red-buff core. Length 8 cm. Petrie, *Roman Ehnasya*, LXVII:94-96. ....**CHOICE 55.00**

2008. **"CORN AND PALM" OIL LAMP. 3rd-4th Century A.D. Roman.** Circular body, short tapering nozzle. Corn pattern, degenerated to the appearance of palms, around filling hole piercing small concave discus. Two grooves to underside set off nozzle. Flat base shows crescent within incised circle. Grey-buff ware, top blackened. Length 8.4 cm. Petrie, *Roman Ehnasya*, LXV: 82 var. ....**CHOICE-SUPERB 65.00**

2009. **"ARM" OIL LAMP. 3rd-4th Century A.D. Roman.** Piriform body with triangular nozzle offset by two shallow grooves to underside. Small filling hole within medium sloping discus. Degenerate arm design around. Wick hole offset from body by two grooves and row of rays. Degenerate incised ring base; "A" within. Drab brown ware. Length 8.5 cm. Petrie, *Roman Ehnasya*, LXVI:34. Light splitting about seam. ....**CHOICE 50.00**

2010. **FROG LAMP. 3rd-4th Century A.D.** Wide ovoid body with short nozzle offset by two grooves to underside. Small recessed discus. Stylized frog design around. Shallow ring base. Ware varying from grey to pale orange-buff. Petrie, Roman Ehnasya, LXIV:65. One edge chip...**CHOICE 75.00**

2011. **LAMP. 3rd-4th Century A.D.** Circular body with short tapering nozzle. Corn pattern around filling hole piercing small concave discus. Two grooves to underside set off nozzle. Flat, base with crescent. Within incised circle. Grey-buff ware, top blackened. 8.2 cm. Petrie, *Roman Ehnasya*, LXV: 82 var. ....**CHOICE-SUPERB 70.00**

2012. **BOSS LAMP. 3rd-4th Century A.D.** Piriform body with short triangular nozzle offset by two shallow grooves to underside. Small filling hole within small sloping discus offset by groove. Three bosses with dimples around. Wick hole offset by groove. Flat base incised with dark ware. Ivory-green slip over red-buff core. 8.2 cm. Petrie, *Roman Ehnasya*, LXVII:94-96. ....**CHOICE 55.00**

2013. **MOLD-MADE LAMP. c. 350-450 A.D.** Ovoid body with sloping shoulder on which is wreath motif. Concave discus depicting rooster right between two filling holes. Stump handle with pinched sides and central groove. Slightly concave ring base with double ridge to handle. Pale red slip over red clay. 11.4 cm. North African manufacture . Cf. Schloessinger Collection, 278 (form), *ROM* 284 (motif). ....**CHOICE 125.00**

2014. **OIL LAMP. 350-450 A.D. North African. Roman.** Red slip wear lamp with herringbone shoulder design. Discus shows Eros standing facing holding a bow. Length 11 cm. Cf. *ROM* 281 for type. Handle missing, otherwise intact. ....**CHOICE 175.00**

2015. **MOLD-MADE LAMP. c. 350-450 A.D Roman. North Africa.** Pale orange slip over red clay. Ovoid body with sloping shoulder with wreath motif. Concave discus depicting rabbit between two filling holes. Stump handle with pinched sides and central groove. Concave ring base with double ridge to handle. Length 12 cm. Cf. Schloessinger Co.. 278 (form). ....**CHOICE 125.00**

2016. **OIL LAMP. 4th Century A.D. Roman Judaean.** Bow-shaped nozzle type, mold-made. Piriform body, pyramidal handle and large filling hole. Integral bow nozzle, "pinched" at sides. Herringbone pattern to shoulder, two pine cones at intersection with nozzle. Ring base with central pellet. Traces of red slip over orange-tan ware. Length 7.5 cm. Schl. 436-7, 439. Scarce. ....**CHOICE-SUPERB 135.00**

2017. **OIL LAMP. 4th Century A.D. Roman.** Mold-made lamp with watch-shaped body and nozzle offset by two incised volutes. Shoulder with radial ornaments. Flat base with incised "B" within ring. Reddish-buff ware. Eastern manufacture. Length 7.4 cm. Petrie, *Roman Ehnasya*, LXI:44. ....**CHOICE 75.00**

2018. **MOLD-MADE LAMP. 4th Century A.D.** With watch-shaped body and nozzle offset by two incised volutes. Shoulder with radial ornaments. Flat. base with incised "B" within ring. Reddish buff ware. Of Eastern manufacture. *Roman Ehnasya* LXI:44. ....**CHOICE 75.00**

2019. **OIL LAMP. 4th-5th Century A.D. Roman Judaean.** Bow-shaped nozzle type. Mold-made lamp with ovoid body, large filling hole with thick border, and pyramidal handle. Bow-shaped nozzle decorated with inverted amphora between two bunches of grapes. Herringbone to shoulder. Flat base. Dark buff ware. Length 9.2 cm. Schl. 439. Scarce type ....**AVERAGE 75.00**

2020. **JONAH AND THE WHALE LAMP. 4th-5th Century A.D. Roman. North Africa.** Red-orange slip over red-orange clay. In tondo is grotesque whale to left, looking right. Jonah lies on mat, two doves with other symbols on shoulder. Two small filling holes. Pattern of birds, fish, squares, and hearts around. Pinched handle. Ring base with ridge to handle. Length 12.4 cm. Cf. BMC *Byzantine and Christian*, p. 337, fig. 20; Ennabli, p. 48, Pl. 11 #53; Cf. Sternberg Sale XXIII, Nov. 1989 #82; Cf. Jonah 1:17. "And the Lord appointed a great fish to swallow up Jonah; and Jonah was in the belly of the fish three days and three nights." Nozzle chipped off. Very rare. ....**CHOICE 750.00**

2021. **BUFF CLAY LAMP. 4th-5th Century. Roman.** Wide flat rim with eight raised rosettes. Cross at wick hole. Length 9 cm. Cf. Waage Pl. X, 814 (4th cent.); Cf. Rosenthal-Sivan, *Qedem* 575. Scarce. ....**CHOICE 75.00**

2022. **OIL LAMP. 4th-6th Century A.D. Roman.** Mold-made lamp with piriform body and nozzle with rounded top. Sharp radial ridges on both shoulder and nozzle. Two small semi-circles forward of large filling hole. Ridges from filling hole to wick hole. Ring base. Spur handle. Sharp carination. Pink-buff ware. Length 9.5 cm. *Dura IV*, Pt. III, Pl. XIII: 411; Schl. 574 (descendant). Handle broken. Chips from base. ....**SUPERB 85.00**

2023. **MOLD-MADE LAMP. 4th-6th Century A.D.** With piriform body and nozzle with rounded top. Fine radial lines on back shoulder and nozzle. Small circles forward of large filling hole. Ridges from filling hole to wick hole. Ring base. Spur handle. Sharp carination. Pink-buff ware. 9.5 cm. *Dura* IV, Pt. III, Pl. XIII: 411. Schl. 574 (descendant). Similar lamps are found at the Dura Europa site. ....**SUPERB 85.00**

2024. **MOLD-MADE LAMP. Late 4th-5th Century A.D. North Africa/Tunisia.** With piriform body merging with broad deep nozzle with large wick hole. Deep bodied with rounded sides and concave discus, merging with broad channel on top of nozzle. High grooved handle. Discus decorated with lion facing right, two filling holes. Shoulder ornamented with wreath. Ring base interrupted by dashes towards nozzle. Incised cross within, grooved ridge to back. Brick red slip over similar ware. 11.7 cm. Cf. Schl. 279. *ROM* 285-6. Bold orange color. ....**CHOICE 250.00**

2025. **MOLD-MADE LAMP. Late 4th-5th Century A.D. North Africa/Tunisia.** With near circular body merging with broad deep nozzle with large wick hole. Deep bodied with rounded sides and concave discus, merging with broad channel on top of nozzle. High handle. Discus decorated with rayed bearded bust of Serapis left wearing modius, two small filling holes. Shoulder plain except for edge groove. Concave ring base with grooved ridge to handle. Ridge offset by two additional grooves. Brick red over similar ware. Deneauve-. *Lampes Chretiennes-. ROM* 285-6 (contemp.) Bold orange color. ....**CHOICE 250.00**

2026. **OIL LAMP. 5th Century A.D. Late Roman. North Africa/Tunisia.** Mold-made lamp with near circular body, merging with broad deep nozzle with large wick hole. Deep bodied with rounded sides and concave discus, merging with broad channel on top of nozzle. High handle. Discus decorated with female comic mask three-quartered facing. Shoulder ornamented with wreath. Two small filling holes. Ring base with ridge to handle. Brick red slip over similar ware. Some blackening to wick hole. Length 13.5 cm. This lamp was probably used as theatre lighting. Deneauve-; *Lampes Chretienne-*; ROM 289-92 (contemp.) ....**CHOICE 250.00**

2027. **MOLD-MADE LAMP. 5th Century A.D.** Oval body and short integral nozzle. Wide flat discus with high rim and floral star pattern pierced by small filling hole. Zig-zag and circle design on shoulder. Wide looped handle (missing) and traces of wick hole with protruding lip. Red-orange clay with tan slip. Eastern manufacture. Chip at the nozzle. Cf. *ROM* 468 (form), 476-82 (nozzle), 529 (design affinities). ....**CHOICE 80.00**

JEWELRY AND INTAGLIOS

2028. **GLASS PASTE INTAGLIO. Italic-Roman Republic. 3rd-2nd Century B.C.** Amber glass paste intaglio. Portrays Hercules Musagetes seated nude on diphros, playing kithara. On stool is lion skin. Measures 1.4 x 1.1 cm. Cf. Richter, *Roman*, 279. Cf. Munchen, Band 1, Teil 2, 1495-7 var. Some chips. ....**CHOICE 150.00**

2029. **SILVER RING. 3rd-2nd Century B.C.** Ring with coin inlaid at center of Ephesus, reverse: forepart of kneeling stag right, with head turned back, Astragalus in field. Coin dates from 288-280 B.C. Silver bezel with silver rope pattern. Cf. Henkel, taf. XXIV, 461 (for side work). Cf. BMC Ionia, 74, for coin. ....**CHOICE 250.00**

2030. **AMBER GLASS PASTE INTAGLIO. 3rd-2nd Century B.C.** Hercules Musagetes seated nude on diphros, playing kithara. On the stool is a lion's skin. Cf. Richter, *Roman*, 279. Cf. München, Band I, Teil 2, 1495-7 var. Some chips. ....**CHOICE 135.00**

2031. **YELLOW GLASS INTAGLIO. 3rd-1st Century B.C.** Hercules standing holding club and lion skin, right arm raised. Cf. München, Band I, Teil 2, 1229 and 1237 var. ....**CHOICE-SUPERB 175.00**

2032. **YELLOW AMBER GLASS INTAGLIO. 3rd-1st Century B.C.** Nude figure with wings of Ganymede standing, facing head, looking up, vase below. Cf. München, Band I, #3225-6 var. ....**AVERAGE-CHOICE 85.00**

2033. **YELLOW GLASS INTAGLIO. 3rd-1st Century B.C.** Seated horse, with its head down. Cf. München, Band I, Teil 2, 1954 for style. Iridescence. Contains some pitting. ....**CHOICE 65.00**

2034. **YELLOW GLASS INTAGLIO. 3rd-1st Century B.C.** Young male hero standing nude holding a spear and looking at a helmet in his hand. Cf. München, Band I, Teil 2, #1578 var. Cf. Hague, 556. ....**CHOICE 150.00**

2035. **BRONZE RING WITH AMBER GLASS INTAGLIO. 3rd-1st Century B.C.** Neptune standing nude holding dolphin and trident. Prow of ship before. 15 x 12 mm. Lovely style. Cf. AGDS, Staatliche, München, 1039-45. For ring style, Cf. Henkel, *Die Rom. Fingerringe der Rheinlande*, taf. 411, 1097. ....**NEAR SUPERB 350.00**

2036. **YELLOW-AMBER GLASS PASTE INTAGLIO. 3rd-1st Century B.C.** Winged, helmeted head of Perseus, sword behind. 14 x 12 mm. Perseus was the great hero, son of Zeus and Dianae. His exploits are numerous in mythology. The most notable is the cutting off the head of Medusa while looking in a mirror so as not to turn to stone. Rare. Superb style. Cf. Brandt and Schmidt, *AGDS*, Band I, Staatliche Munzammlung, 1418................................**CHOICE 250.00**

2037. **KELLY GREEN GLASS INTAGLIO. 3rd-1st Century B.C.** Heifer standing. 13 x 10 mm. This style represents the Republican wheel style. Lovely intaglio. Cf. Maaskant-Kleibrink, *Royal Coin Cabinet, The Hague*, 280. Cf. *AGDS*, Staatliche, 1958. ....**SUPERB 300.00**

2038. **AMBER GLASS INTAGLIO. 3rd-1st Century B.C.** Hercules strangling lion. 10 x 8 mm. Cf. *AGDS*, Staatliche, 1251. ....**AVERAGE 75.00**

2039. **YELLOW-AMBER GLASS INTAGLIO. 3rd-1st Century B.C.** Actor's mask of male head, bearded. 8 mm in diameter. The actors comic and tragic mask can be distinguished from other heads as these have no necks. Variegated color. Cf. *AGDS*, Staatliche, 1841. ....**CHOICE 135.00**

2040. **AMBER GLASS INTAGLIO. 3rd-1st Century B.C.** Helmeted head in Corinthian helmet. 9 x 8 mm. Cf. *AGDS*, Staatliche, 1707. ....**AVERAGE 50.00**

2041. **GREEN GLASS PASTE INTAGLIO. 3rd-1st Century B.C.** White and blue stripe. Upper portion of a ring portraying a female mask. 10 mm. Cf. *AGDS*, Staatliche, 1862. ....**AVERAGE 75.00**

2042. **GLASS INTAGLIO. Italic-Roman Republic. 3rd-1st Century B.C.** Sea-green glass intaglio depicting a heifer standing right. Measures 1.3 x 1 cm. Cf. Maaskank #280, Cf. *AGDS* Staatliche 1958. ....**SUPERB 250.00**

2043. **GLASS INTAGLIO. Italic-Roman Republic. 3rd-1st Century B.C.** Yellow glass intaglio of Hercules standing holding a club and lion's skin, his left arm raised. Measures 1.1 x 0.9 cm. Cf. München, Band I, Teil 2: 1229 and 1237 var. ....**CHOICE-SUPERB 175.00**

2044. **GLASS INTAGLIO. Italic-Roman Republic. 3rd-1st Century B.C.** Yellow glass intaglio depicting a grazing horse. Measures .9 x .8 cm. Cf. München, Band I, Teil 2, 1954 b (for style). Iridescence. Some pitting. ....**CHOICE 65.00**

2045. **GLASS INTAGLIO. Italic-Roman Republic. 3rd-1st Century B.C.** Amber glass intaglio depicting Hercules struggling with the Nemean lion. Measures 1 x .8 cm. *AGDS* 1251. Small chip on back. ....**AVERAGE 75.00**

2046. **GLASS INTAGLIO SET IN RING. Republic. 3rd-1st Century B.C.** Amber glass intaglio set in a ring, showing the head of Janus in profile with long beards. Janus had two heads, one looking into the past, the other the future. Intaglio measures 1.2 x .9 cm. Cf. München *AGDS*, Ta. 170:1893 (appears to be the same die). Lower portion of ring band missing. ....**CHOICE 200.00**

2047. **AMBER GLASS INTAGLIO. 2nd Century B.C.** Apollo, nude, seated before Marsyas. 12 x 10 mm Cf. Maaskant-Kleibrink, *Royal Coin Cabinet, The Hague*, #205. ....**ABOUT CHOICE 80.00**

2048. **GLASS PASTE INTAGLIO. Republic. 2nd Century B.C.** Amber glass paste intaglio showing Hercules standing nude, holding a club and lion skin. Measures 1.2 x .9 cm. Cf. München, Band I, Teil 2, 1257. Lovely iridescence. ....**SUPERB 175.00**

2049. **AMBER GLASS PASTE INTAGLIO. 2nd Century B.C.** Hercules standing nude holding club and lion's skin. Cf München, Band I, Teil 2, #1257. Lovely iridescence. ....**CHOICE-SUPERB 175.00**

2050. **AMBER GLASS INTAGLIO. 2nd-1st Century B.C.** Set in bronze ring. Depicts a garlanded oinochoe. Cf. Henkel, taf. XLIV, 1104 for ring shape. München, *Antike Gemmen in Deutschen Sammlungen*, Band I, Teil 184, 2122. Intact ring and intaglio. ....**CHOICE 200.00**

2051. **AMBER GLASS INTAGLIO. 2nd-1st Century B.C.** Bearded male head right in profile. München, taf. 166, 1839. Lovely style. ....**CHOICE-SUPERB 350.00**

2052. **GREEN GLASS INTAGLIO. 2nd-1st Century B.C.** White and blue stripe down center. Nude Apollo seated on rock, before Marsyas nude with arm raised. 16 x 14 mm. For ring style, Cf. Henkel, *Die Rom Fingerringe der Rheinlande*, taf XLIII, 1095. Cf. Gramatopol, *Les Pierre Gravees du Cabinet Numasmatique de l' Academie, Roumaine*, #78. ....**CHOICE 125.00**

2053. **BRONZE RING WITH GLASS STRIPED RING INTAGLIO. 2nd-1st Century B.C.** Green matrix with white and black stripe. Garlanded modius with two corn-ears at sides. Scales suspended. 12 x 10 mm. Small repair to ring. For intaglio, Cf. Henig, *Corpus of Engraved Gemstones from British Sites*, Pt. ii, #404. For ring style, Cf. Henkel, taf XLIII, 1099. ....**CHOICE 125.00**

2054. **AMBER GLASS INTAGLIO. 1st Century B.C.** Set in bronze ring. Head of Octavia? in profile. Cf Henkel, taf. XLIV, 1109 for ring shape. Cf. Duval Collection, Florange, 85. Cf. Richter, *Romans*, 489. Lovely Hellenistic style. Part of band missing. ....**CHOICE 250.00**

2055. **AMBER GLASS INTAGLIO. 1st Century B.C.** Portrays Hercules struggling with the Nemean lion. Measures 10 x 8 mm. *AGDS* Staatliche Museum Preussischen Kulturbesitz Berlin #1251. ....**AVERAGE 75.00**

2056. **SKY BLUE NICOLO PASTE GLASS INTAGLIO. 1st Century B.C.-1st Century A.D.** Victory advancing. Henig, Bar 8, 310. ....**CHOICE 125.00**

2057. **YELLOW AMBER GLASS INTAGLIO. 1st Century B.C.-1st Century A.D.** Bronze ring with intaglio. Bust of Africa in elephant headdress. München, Band I, Teil 2, 1774. *Hague* 317. One third of band missing. .....**CHOICE 150.00**

2058. **SKY BLUE NICOLO PASTE GLASS INTAGLIO. 1st Century B.C.-1st Century A.D.** Boar advancing with dog biting at legs. For boar, Cf. München, Teil 3, taf., 321, 3398. München, Teil 2, taf. 176 1985. ......**CHOICE 135.00**

2059. **GREEN GLASS PASTE INTAGLIO. 1st Century B.C.-1st Century A.D.** Intaglio with blue and white stripe through center. Medusa head facing, mounted in bronze ring. Cf. München, Teil 2, 1436. Gold gilding to incuse image. Repair to band. ....**CHOICE 300.00**

2060. **GLASS PASTE INTAGLIO. 1st Century B.C.-1st Century A.D.** Sky-blue Nicolo glass paste intaglio showing Victory advancing. Measures 1.2 x .9 cm. Henig, Bar 8: 310. ....**CHOICE 125.00**

2061. **GLASS PASTE INTAGLIO SET IN RING. 1st Century B.C.-1st Century A.D.** Green glass paste intaglio with blue and white stripe through the center, portraying a medusa head facing. Set in bronze ring. Band diam. 2.2 cm, intaglio measures 1.3 x 1.1 cm. Cf. München T2: 1436. Gilding to incuse image. Repair to band. ....**CHOICE 300.00**

2062. **BRONZE RING. 1st Century B.C.-2nd Century A.D.** Intaglio depression. Griffon seated with wings up. 8 x 6 mm. Marshel, *BMC Rings*, 126 var. for ring style. ....**CHOICE 125.00**

2063. **PAIR OF GOLD EARRINGS. 1st Century B.C.-2nd Century A.D.** Hellenistic-style gold earrings. Circles of varying thickness of gold. The fastenings are called Herakles knobs. Each approx.1.4 cm in diam. Cf. Staatliche Kunstsammlungen Kassel, Antiker Schmuck, katalog no. 74 var. Neat workmanship. Minute amount of red discoloration of the gold. ....**SUPERB 325.00**

2064. **GOLD EARRING. 1st Century B.C.-2nd Century A.D.** In the form of a club. The bottom filled with a bunch of grapes. The knots are represented by wires and globules. Suspension hole in top which is then held by a bigger gold circle with gold stud attached. 2.5 cm long Cf. Park Hurst, Oberlin College, Gutman #5. Cf. *Catalogue of Jewelry in the British Museum*, #2412. Represents the club of Hercules. Lovely delicate workmanship. ....**SUPERB 400.00**

2065. **GOLD RING WITH GARNET INTAGLIO. 1st Century A.D.** Gold ring with garnet intaglio depicting a mask of the bald and bearded head of Silenus. Intaglio measures .9 x .7 cm. For intaglio variation, Cf. Maaskant-Kleibrink # 320; for ring style, Cf. Ricci 391 and Henkel Tf. VIII:141-152. Partly restored band present. ....**CHOICE 400.00**

2066. **YELLOW-AMBER GLASS INTAGLIO. 1st Century A.D.** Seated figure of Erotes with hand to mouth. 6 mm in diameter. Cf. Richter, *EGR*, #15 var. ....**CHOICE 150.00**

2067. **AMBER GLASS INTAGLIO. 1st Century A.D.** Nude figure of Aesclapius standing. before Salus, who stands facing him. 12 x 10 mm. These were the gods of healing Cf. Maaskant-Kleibrink, *Royal Coin Cabinet, The Hague*, 664 var. ....**CHOICE 125.00**

2068. **CAMEO SARDONYX FRAGMENT. 1st Century A.D.** White on yellowish-brown, on ivory back. Poseidon in biga of Hippocampus traveling over waves. 20 x 12 mm. Numerous chips but central design totally intact. Cf. Richter, *EGR*, 69-70 var. For style, Cf. Boardman, *Ionides Collection* #56. ....**CHOICE 500.00**

2069. **RED GARNET INTAGLIO. 1st Century A.D.** Intaglio set into ring. Profile bust of Dionysus, hair wreathed in grape wreath, draped. Henkel, taf. LXXVII, 231. Cf. München, Band I, Teil 2, 1073. Some oxide corrosion to band. ....**CHOICE-SUPERB 700.00**

2070. **ONYX CAMEO GEM. 1st Century A.D.** Head of Socrates right with long beard and bald head. Cf. Glypothek, Munich for similar Socrates head in bronze and Villa Albani, Rome for marble head. Cf. Bieber, *Sculpture of the Hellenistic Age*, fig. 126. Cf. Berrh Collection, 47. Small chip to back. A very lovely piece with a stunning portrait. ....**CHOICE 600.00**

2071. **AMBER GLASS INTAGLIO. 1st-2nd Century A.D.** Actor wearing grotesque mask and baggy trousers. Cf. Henig, Bar 8, 623. Irregular oval. ....**CHOICE 85.00**

2072. **GLASS INTAGLIO. 1st-2nd Century A.D.** Amber glass intaglio depicting bull, set in a bronze, bezel-type ring. Measures 1.9 x .9 cm. Cf. *The Royal Coin Cabinet, the Hague* #414, 415. Very interesting, but only mount area of ring remains. Some oxidation. ....**FINE 125.00**

2073. **GLASS INTAGLIO. 1st-2nd Century A.D.** Amber glass intaglio showing an actor wearing a grotesque mask. Measures .9 x .6 cm. Cf. Henig, Bar 8:623. Irregular shape. ....**CHOICE 85.00**

2074. **SILVER EARRING. 1st-2nd Century A.D.** Silver earring with plain ring of varying thickness. Blue glass bead set in simple setting, soldered onto ring. The glass bead set by vertical rod running through it. At base of bead, two rows of molded beadwork. 2 cm in diam. Cf. for similar setting of bead, *Allen Memorial Museum Bulletin*, Vol. XVIII, #107. Some iridescence on bead. Intact and in good condition ....**CHOICE 50.00**

2075. **GOLD EARRING. 1st-3rd Century A.D.** Gold earring with plain wire with loop fastening. Square setting soldered on for a stone (missing). Loose pendant rod with incised lines on wire hanging from earring. Pendant missing. 1.4 cm long. Cf. *Catalogue of Jewelry, British Museum*, Pl. LIII, #2535. Slightly misshapen. ....**SUPERB 150.00**

2076. **SOLID GOLD EARRING. 1st-3rd Century A.D.** Rather thick wire gold earring with interesting pin clasp. Decoration of encircling wire twice on ring. Small loose piece of wire, maybe end of pendant rod remaining. 1.9 cm in diam. *Catalogue of Jewelry in the British Museum*-. Clasp and pin still working. ....**SUPERB 160.00**

2077. **FRAME OF INTAGLIO PENDANT. 1st-3rd Century A.D.** Gold frame of intaglio pendant. Oval or pear drop with loop for suspension hole. Twisted wire decoration on frame. 1.7 cm long. Cf. Staatliche Kunstsammlungen Kassel, Antiken Schmuck, Katalogue, No. 18. Lovely piece. Could still be used. Suspension hole broken. .....**CHOICE 150.00**

2078. **GOLD EARRING. 1st-3rd Century A.D.** Small gold earring with bunch of grapes decoration at bottom. Center in the form of bead globules. Clasp with disc decoration, also with globule in center to one side. Ring thicker metal at bottom than top. 1.4 cm diam. Cf. *Catalogue of Jewelry in the British Museum*, Pl. LII, #2501. Intact. ....**SUPERB 150.00**

2079. **GOLD EARRING. 1st-3rd Century A.D.** Reddish gold earring. Ring is plain wire and hollow, raised shield with a border of beaded wire and a globule in the center. Incised line decoration of ring. Part of earring. 1.3 cm long. Cf. *Catalogue of Jewelry in the British Museum*, Pl. LIII, #2516. Intact. Superb red oxide patina. ....**SUPERB 175.00**

2080. **PAIR OF SILVER EARRINGS. 1st-3rd Century A.D.** Pair of silver earrings in the form of amphorae. Globular bodies, bunch of grapes at base. Very little decoration. 1.9 cm high each. Similar to the pendant amphora which are influenced by the Eastern Roman Empire. Otherwise no parallel found. Some minor encrustation and holes to centre of body. Marshall-. Rather unusual. No loops for suspension present. ....**CHOICE 150.00**

2081. **GOLD EARRING. 1st-3rd Century A.D.** Small gold earring with "bunch of grapes" decoration formed by bead globules. Clasp with disk decoration, also with globule. 1.4 cm diam. Cf. *BM* Pl. LIII # 2501. Intact. ...**SUPERB 150.00**

2082. **GOLD FRAME OF INTAGLIO PENDANT. 1st-3rd Century A.D.** Pear-shaped drop with suspension loop. Twisted wire decoration on frame. Length 1.7 cm. Cf. Staatliche Kunstsammlungen Kassel, #18. Lovely piece. Suspension loop broken. ....**CHOICE 150.00**

2083. **CARNELIAN INTAGLIO. 2nd Century A.D.** Orange carnelian intaglio depicting Mars standing holding a spear, with a shield at his feet. Victory stands behind crowning him; Fortuna stands facing him, holding rudder and cornucopiae. Measures 1.6 x 1.4 cm. Cf. Hague #969 for style. Some chips to edge. ....**CHOICE 350.00**

2084. **AMBER GLASS INTAGLIO. 2nd Century A.D.** Nude figure of Mars standing holding spear and shield. 15 x 11 mm. Cf. Maaskant-Kleibrink, *Royal Coin Cabinet, The Hague*, 1030 var. ....**CHOICE 150.00**

2085. **RED-BROWN SARD OVAL INTAGLIO. 2nd Century A.D.** Fortuna standing in long chiton, turreted, holding rudder and cornucopiae. 14 x 11 mm. Chip at top. Cf *AGDS*, Staatliche, #2604. Cf. Gramatopol, *Academie Roumaine*, #298. ....**CHOICE 160.00**

2086. **AMBER GLASS INTAGLIO. 2nd Century A.D.** Lion rampant on pedestal. 12 x 9 mm. Cf. Maaskant-Kleibrink, *Royal Coin Cabinet, The Hague*, 719. ....**AVERAGE 75.00**

2087. **ORANGE CARNELIAN INTAGLIO. 2nd Century A.D.** Depicts a centaur standing. Measures 11 x 9 mm. Cf. Righetti, *Gemme e Cammei delle Collezioni Comonail*, Tafi, #14. ....**CHOICE 200.00**

2088. **RED AND MILKY CHALCEDONY. 2nd Century A.D.** Lion fighting serpent. 14 x 11 mm. Cf. Florange, Duval Collection, Geneve, Pl. XVIII, 86. Cf. Maaskant-Kleibrink, 1063 var. ....**CHOICE 200.00**

2089. **RED CARNELIAN. 2nd Century A.D.** Upper portion of Tyche standing holding caduceus. 9 x 6 mm. Reshaped. *AGDS*, Staatliche, 2608-9. ....**CHOICE 75.00**

2090. **ORANGE CARNELIAN INTAGLIO. 2nd Century A.D.** Ant as seen from above. 9 x 7 mm. *AGDS*, Berlin, 505. ....**CHOICE 85.00**

2091. **CARNELIAN CAMEO. 2nd Century A.D.** High relief full-face portrait of putto or Eros. 11 mm diam. Cf. Park Hurst, Oberlin College, #112 for cameo. Cf. Henig, *Lewis Collection*, #284. ....**SUPERB 600.00**

2092. **REDDISH-WHITE ONYX CAMEO. 2nd Century A.D.** Head of bearded Hercules left in lion skin. 16 x 10 mm. ....**CHOICE 350.00**

2093. **ONYX CAMEO GEM. 2nd Century A.D.** Head of Medusa, two snakes from top. Cf. Henig, bar 1974, 728. ....**CHOICE 200.00**

2094. **DARK RED CARNELIAN INTAGLIO. 2nd Century A.D.** Spes walking left, holding skirt, holding flower. Walters, *BM* 1760. Henig, Bar 8, 340-1.....**CHOICE 175.00**

2095. **ORANGE CARNELIAN INTAGLIO. 2nd Century A.D.** Mars standing holding spear and shield at feet, Victory standing behind crowning him, Fortuna standing facing him, holding rudder and cornucopiae. Cf. *Hague* #969 for style. Some chips to edge. ....**CHOICE 350.00**

2096. **YELLOW AMBER GLASS INTAGLIO. 2nd Century A.D.** Bust of Fortuna with turreted headdress, in profile. Attractive. ....**CHOICE 125.00**

2097. **SARD FISH INTAGLIO. 2nd Century A.D.** Octagonal red sard intaglio. Design of two fish hanging on stand. Measures 9 x 8 mm. ....**SUPERB 150.00**

2098. **CARNELIAN CUPID ON BIRD INTAGLIO. 2nd Century A.D.** Orange carnelian intaglio. Complex design of Cupid standing holding whip and reigns, on back of bird with horse's head. Hidden mask of bald Silenus at end of bird's body. The bird stands on an eagle which is eating a hare. Measures 17 x 13 mm. Munich 2, 1899; Cf. *Hague* 1093. Chip in field. ....**SUPERB 500.00**

2099. **GLASS INTAGLIO. 2nd Century A.D.** Yellow-amber glass intaglio. Bust of Faustina Sr. in profile. Measures 11 x 9 mm. Richter, *Engraved Gems of the Romans* 554. A nice representation of Faustina, the wife of Antonius Pius. ....**CHOICE 165.00**

2100. **CARVED AMBER HEAD AMULET. 2nd Century A.D.** Opaque mottled orange-red carved amulet of female goddess. Hair in groups at side of face and above forehead. Eyes are pellets, mouth is worn smooth. Pierced in the upper center at sides for suspension. Measures 21 x 18 mm. Amber was prized by the ancients because it was attractive and pleasant to the smell and touch, and was felt to have magical powers. It was an object of luxury; Pliny mentions it as highly valuable. Its greatest use was during the Flavian and Antonine periods; Aquileia was the main center of carving at this time. Cf. Strong, *Catalogue of the Carved Amber*, for eyes Cf. 110, for amulet Cf. 125. Nose and mouth worn smooth. Surface patina in orange. ....**CHOICE 500.00**

2101. **NICOLO PASTE INTAGLIO. 2nd-3rd Century A.D.** Sky blue nicolo paste intaglio. Depicts an eagle standing with its head back and wings open, holding a thunderbolt. Measures 11 x 8 mm. Cf. München, Band I, T3, taf. 322, 3408. ....**CHOICE 100.00**

2102. **CARNELIAN FORTUNA INTAGLIO. 2nd-3rd Century A.D.** Light orange carnelian intaglio. Design of Fortuna standing, head back. Rudder at feet. Measures 8 x 6 mm. ....**SUPERB 135.00**

2103. **SKY BLUE NICOLO PASTE GLASS INTAGLIO. 2nd-3rd Century A.D.** Fortuna standing. Cf. for type, München, Band I, Teil 3, taf. 322, 3408. ....**CHOICE 125.00**

2104. **YELLOW AMBER GLASS INTAGLIO. 2nd-3rd Century A.D.** Eagle standing on garland round altar, head looking back. *Hague* 267. Cf. München, Band I, Teil 3, 3439-40. ....**CHOICE 125.00**

2105. **AMBER GLASS INTAGLIO. 2nd-3rd Century A.D.** Rooster standing. Cf München, Band I, Teil 2, 2036 var. ....**AVG-CH 65.00**

2106. **ORANGE CARNELIAN INTAGLIO. 2nd-3rd Century A.D.** Roma standing holding scepter, shield at feet. *Hague* 973. ....**CHOICE 150.00**

2107. **BRONZE RING WITH INTAGLIO. 2nd-3rd Century A.D.** Design of Nike advancing holding garland wreath before altar. Cf. Henkel, taf. LXVII, 1783 for ring shape. Cf. München, Band I, #2631-7. ....**CHOICE 200.00**

2108. **RED CARNELIAN INTAGLIO. 2nd-3rd Century A.D.** Two-handled kantharos. Cf. Walters, *BM* 3410. Henig, Bar 8, 423. ....**CHOICE 85.00**

2109. **BRONZE RING. 2nd-3rd Century A.D.** Central domed incised pattern, band flattened with molded shoulders, all enameled blue. Henkel, taf. LXXX, 8. Intact. ....**CHOICE 125.00**

2110. **CARNELIAN INTAGLIO. 2nd-3rd Century A.D.** Red carnelian intaglio depicting Victory crowing a figure, Fortuna to left. Palm above, inscription R COC below. Measures 1.8 x 1.5 cm. Cf. *Royal Coin Cabinet* #676. Many chips to face. ....**AVERAGE 75.00**

2111. **GLASS PASTE INTAGLIO. 2nd-3rd Century A.D.** Sky-blue Nicolo glass paste intaglio showing clasped hands with cornucopiaea behind. Measures 1.5 x 1.0 cm. Attractive. ....**CHOICE 125.00**

2112. **CARNELIAN INTAGLIO. 2nd-3rd Century A.D.** Orange carnelian intaglio showing Roma standing holding a sceptre, with a shield at her feet. Measures 1.1 x .8 cm, .6 cm thick. *Hague* 973. Fracture through top of stone. ....**CHOICE 150.00**

2113. **AMULET. Found in Syria. 2nd-3rd Century A.D.** Blue-green faience phallic amulet. Measures 1.7 x 1.2 cm. Suspension hole at top. Similar amulets were excavated at Dura Europa. Petrie, *Amulets* #16. ....**CHOICE 500.00**

2114. **RED CARNELIAN INTAGLIO. 2nd-3rd Century A.D.** Two clasping hands, poppy plant between. 8 x 6 mm. This intaglio is done in the small grooves style. Maaskant-Kleibrink, *The Hague*, #463, for type, 730 for style. ....**CHOICE 75.00**

2115. **LEAD RING WITH BAS RELIEF. 2nd-3rd Century A.D.** Cast with veiled standing female to right. 18 x 12 mm. Ex. Villa Julia Collection Deacession. Impression off center. For ring style, Cf. Henkel, 1783. ....**CHOICE 150.00**

2116. **BRONZE FIBULA. c. 2nd-3rd Century A.D.** Bow-shaped fibula with coiled top continuing to form the pin. Square at center of bow. Length 3.8 cm. Price, *Roman Antiquities*, Pl. VIII, fig. 8. ....**CHOICE 115.00**

2117. **BRONZE FINIAL OR APPLIQUÉ. 2nd-4th Century A.D.** Two serpents, their heads bending to touch the central circle formed by their intertwined bodies. Measures 2.5 x .9 cm. *Vienne-*. ....**CHOICE 75.00**

2118. **BRONZE KEY RING. 2nd-4th Century A.D.** Key protruding from top of ring. Cf. Henkel, *Romischen Fingerringe der Rheinlande*, taf LXXII, 1941 for key rings. Intact. ....**CHOICE 150.00**

2119. **GLASS INTAGLIO. Mid to Late 2nd Century A.D.** Yellow-amber glass intaglio showing a profile bust of Faustina Senior. Measures 1.1 x .9 cm. Richter, *Engraved Gems of the Romans*, 554. A nice representation of Faustina. ....**CHOICE 165.00**

2120. **YELLOW AMBER GLASS INTAGLIO. Late 2nd-early 3rd Century A.D.** Facing vis-a-vis heads of young male and female. Cf. München, Band I, Teil 2, #1741. Similar to types of Elagabalus and Julia Maesa. Heads small. ....**CHOICE 75.00**

2121. **CHILD'S GOLD RING. 3rd Century A.D.** Small gold ring with palm intaglio design; palm has small fruit (dates below). Gold loop at top center of taped design. Diameter 1.2 cm. Cf. Haehens, *Rhode Island School of Design* 68 var. for type. Parkhurst Oberlin 114. Cf. Siviero, *GLI Oriene* Tf. 235c, 237d. ....**CHOICE 300.00**

2122. **CARNELIAN INTAGLIO. 3rd Century A.D.** Red carnelian intaglio depicting standing figure. Length .8 cm. Some minor chips along base. Miniature and fine style. ....**SUPERB 80.00**

2123. **FAIENCE AMULET. 3rd Century A.D.** Green-blue faience amulet depicting Eros facing, wings behind, on a circular disk. Measures 2 x 2.4 cm. Chip at top of amulet. ....**CHOICE 85.00**

2124. **CHALCEDONY INTAGLIO. 3rd Century A.D.** Creamy chalcedony intaglio of a reclining lion. .....**CHOICE 125.00**

2125. **CHALCEDONY CAMEO. 3rd Century A.D.** Nicolo chalcedony cameo. Dark behind, carved face of Medusa lighter. Curls surrounding entire head. 1.2 x 1.1 cm. Cf. Boardman, *Iodenes Collection* #73. ....**CHOICE 135.00**

2126. **CHALCEDONY INTAGLIO. 3rd Century A.D.** Amber chalcedony intaglio depicting a large powerful dog with curled tail standing in alert pose on patch of grass. 1.7 x 1.4 cm. For style, Cf. Munich *Coin Cabinet* Tf. 43, #202, 203. Chip at top. Sharp image. ....**CHOICE 150.00**

2127. **IRON RING BEZEL. 3rd Century A.D.** Bezel with pseudo inscription on its face. Measures 2.3 x 1.5 cm. Slightly chipped. Some red oxidation. ....**CHOICE 65.00**

2128. **GOLD COIN RING. 3rd Century A.D.** Gold ring containing a gold semissis of Constantine the Great. The obverse of the coin, visible when the ring is worn, shows a bust of Constantine facing right, cuirassed and laureate. The inscription reads DNCONSTANTINUS PF AVG. The coin's reverse shows Victory seated facing right on a cuirass with shield beside, holding a shield inscribed VOT/XX, which is supported by Genios. The inscription reads VICTORIA CONSTANTINI AVG. The esergue reads SIRM, indicating the Sirmium mint. Ring diam. 2.1 cm. The first issue of the semissis, this rare denomination was issued on the occasion of Constantine's stay of two months in Sirmium during his travel to Italy in the spring of 326. For ring style, Cf. Marshall, *BMC*, fig. 265 and 269, Pl. VII, page 47. For coin ring, Cf. Ricci Grilhon Coll. #812. Some pitting on chin. ....**SUPERB 2200.00**

2129. **BRONZE RING WITH LARGE CIRCULAR BEZEL. 3rd Century A.D.** 3rd-century emperor standing in military dress holding short sceptre, sacrificing over tripod altar. 19 x 13 mm. For similar depiction, Cf. Richter, *EGR*, 583. For style ring, Cf. Marshall, *BMC Rings*, 95. Some encrustation. ....**CHOICE 200.00**

2130. **RED CARNELIAN. 3rd Century A.D.** Helios standing left, nude, holding sceptre, with his arm raised. 14 x 11 mm. Chips at base. Cf. *AGDS*, Staatliche München, 2646. ....**CHOICE 85.00**

2131. **RED CARNELIAN INTAGLIO. 3rd Century A.D.** Palm in wreath. 6 x 5 mm. Small, reshaped. ....**CHOICE 65.00**

2132. **BRONZE FLAT BAND RING. 3rd Century A.D.** Decorated with three rosettes. 20 mm diameter band. Eastern manufacture. Cf. Genfer Museum, #1274. Cf. Ricci, *Guilhov Collection*, 629. ....**CHOICE 80.00**

2133. **YELLOW CARNELIAN INTAGLIO. 3rd Century A.D.** Fortuna standing holding rudder and cornucopiae. München 2603. ....**CHOICE 65.00**

2134. **AMBER GLASS PASTE INTAGLIO.** 3rd Century A.D. Fortuna Nemesis standing holding palm and rudder. Cf. München 2616. ....**CHOICE 75.00**

2135. **RED CARNELIAN INTAGLIO.** 3rd Century A.D. Frog. Chip at head. ....**AVERAGE 60.00**

2136. **AMBER GLASS INTAGLIO.** 3rd Century A.D. Forepart of Kerberos, two-headed dogs. Cf. München, Band I, Teil 2, 792 var. ....**CHOICE 80.00**

2137. **CREAMY CHALCEDONY INTAGLIO.** 3rd Century A.D. Lion reclining. ....**CHOICE 125.00**

2138. **NICOLO INTAGLIO.** 3rd Century A.D. Grey-black nicolo intaglio depicts an eagle looking back. Measures 12 x 10 mm. ....**CHOICE 85.00**

2139. **BRONZE RING.** 3rd-4th Century A.D. Stylized head of man in oval. Eastern manufacture. Cf. Henkel, taf. XXXIV, 892 for style and ring shape. Crude stylized design. ....**CHOICE 125.00**

2140. **BRONZE RING WITH INTAGLIO.** 3rd-4th Century A.D. Design of stylized head. Cf. Henkel, XXXIX, 1008 for style and shape. Crude stylized design. ....**CHOICE 125.00**

2141. **WHITE CHALCEDONY INTAGLIO.** 3rd-4th Century A.D. Bust of bearded male in cap. Palm to left and right. 10 x 8 mm. ....**CHOICE 150.00**

2142. **CLEAR CRYSTAL INTAGLIO.** 4th Century A.D. Depiction of a bird. ....**CHOICE 150.00**

2143. **GLASS PENDANT.** 4th-5th Century A.D. Probably Egyptian manufacture. Lime green glass medallion, with remains of suspension loop at top. Stamped in the center is the depiction of a lion walking left with a star in a crescent above. Measures 2.4 x 1.8 cm. For similar glass pendants, Cf. Frank Sternberg Auction XXIII 1989, # 264-291. Some iridescence. ....**CHOICE 125.00**

2144. **GLASS PENDANT.** 4th-5th Century A.D. Small pale green glass pendant with large suspension loop at top. Amphora vase motif stamped slightly off-center. Beautiful blue and rainbow-colored iridescence over the entire pendant. Measures 1.9 x 1.3 cm. Cf. Frank Sternberg Auction XXIII 1989 # 264-291 var. Suspension loop broken. ....**SUPERB 125.00**

FIBULAS

2144A **BRONZE ELABORATE FIBULA. Roman Republic. 1st Century B.C.-1st Century A.D.** Bronze fibula known as the thistle or rosette fibula. Round-shaped center with short arch curving backwards to a tubular wing. Fantail leg ending bluntly. Fantail and arch have fluted decor and tubular wing and round center incised decor. At back, square plaque with two stamped holes. Ex. Villa Julia Collection. Cf. *Vienne* #199-201. Hattat, #71. Pin missing, otherwise very lovely condition with elegant workmanship-shape. Most of pin missing. ....**CHOICE 250.00**

2145. **BRONZE FIBULA.** 1st Century A.D. Round bronze fibula with plain bow and twisted spring with wire to front. Diameter 26 mm. Ettlinger-; Mills-; *Guide to BM-*. Pin intact. ....**CHOICE 150.00**

2146. **BRONZE FIBULA.** 1st-2nd Century A.D. Curved bow with doubled bar. Wing foot has shed decoration. Catch plate slightly eroded. A line of tine-punched indentations along spine of bow. 578 cm long. Ex. MacGruder Collection on loan to Smithsonian, no. X1591. Cf. *Vienne*, Nos. 203-210. Pin and spring missing. ....**CHOICE 125.00**

2147. **BRONZE FIBULA.** 1st-2nd Century A.D. Fibula with three bands in relief on bow. Iron pin set in hinge. End of foot a simple boss. Traces of original silvering. 5.3 cm. Ex. Frence Coll. Cf. *Vienne*, Nos. 203-10. Yellow-green patina. ....**CHOICE 350.00**

2148. **BRONZE FIBULA.** 1st-3rd Century A.D. Arched body with rounded ends. Length 6.2 cm. Ex. Villa Julia Collection; Ex. Malloy Auction XX, July 1984. Cf. *Vienne*, #219. Pin missing. Green patina. ....**CHOICE 100.00**

2149. **BRONZE RING.** 1st-3rd Century A.D. Plain wide adjustable band. Diameter 2.5 cm. Ex. Villa Julia Collection. Ex. Malloy Auction XX, July 1984. Some green patina. ....**CHOICE 105.00**

2150. **BRONZE FIBULA.** 1st-3rd Century A.D. Roped top fibula with plain bowed front. Cf. Ettlinger, taf. 1:17. Intact. ....**CHOICE 110.00**

2151. **BRONZE FIBULA.** 1st-3rd Century A.D. Simple crossbow-type fibula. Length 6 cm. Cf. Hattatt, *Ancient and Romano-British Brooches*, p. 211, fig. 90, #101. Latch piece worn away. ....**CHOICE 125.00**

2152. **BRONZE FIBULA.** 1st-3rd Century A.D. Buckle style, with separate pin, no spring. Raised ridge on bow, knob at end. Length 5.0 cm. Cf. Ettlinger 9:6. Pin broken. ....**CHOICE 135.00**

2153. **BRONZE FIBULA.** 1st-4th Century A.D. Sharply bowed spring-type fibula. Central design on bow, knob, then straighter undecorated section to catch. Length 5.0 cm. Cf. Ettlinger, taf. 4:14. Pin broken. ....**CHOICE 110.00**

2154. **BRONZE DISK FIBULA. Mid 1st-Late 2nd Century A.D.** Shield-style fibula with central ball and incised circle around. Diameter 3 cm. Cf. Ettlinger, *Die Römischen Fibeln in der Schweiz*, taf. 12: 10. ....**CHOICE 135.00**

2155. **BRONZE FIBULA. 2nd Century A.D.** Bow type. 3.5 cm. Rhein border manufacturer. Light green patina. Complete and intact. Riha, 84f, taf 12, 291f. ....**CHOICE 125.00**

2156. **BRONZE FIBULA.** 4.5 cm. No pin. Cf. Ottlinger, Schweiz, taf. 5, 4. ....**AVERAGE 65.00**

2157. **BRONZE BROOCH. Roman-British. 2nd Century A.D.** Diamond-form yellow-green enamel decorated with traces of red bronzed enamel as outer decoration with bronze circular projections at ends. 4.5 x 3.5 cm. Pin intact. Some chips to top of pin. Cf. BMC, *Guide to Antiquities of Roman Britain*, fig. II /37. Cf. Boucher, *Vienne, Bronze Antiques*, 234 var. ....**CHOICE 100.00**

2158. **BRONZE FIBULA. 2nd-3rd Century A.D.** Intact with pin which is plain with no incised makings. 5 cm long. Ex. MacGruder Collection on loan to Smithsonian with no. X1583. Encrusted patina. ....**CHOICE 250.00**

2159. **ENAMELED BRONZE BROOCH. 2nd-3rd Century A.D.** Bronze disc with central knob. White with blue stripes. Enamel with pin at back. 2 cm diameter. Enameling was a lively art in Britain and Gaul during this time. Cf. Strong Brown, *Roman Crafts*, #50. ....**CHOICE 200.00**

2160. **BRONZE BRACELET. 2nd-3rd Century A.D.** Bracelet with intermittent incised lines. 5.5 cm diameter. The Plesnilar-Gec example comes from the time of Trajan Decius. Green patina. Ex. Villa Julia Collection. Cf. Excavations Yugoslavia, Grobisce, Pl. LX, 214, 14. Plesnicar-Gex, *Severno Emonsko*. ....**CHOICE 60.00**

2161. **BRONZE FIBULA. 2nd-3rd Century A.D.** Delicate fibula with roped spring at top. Knobs at middle and tip of bow. Length 3.5 cm, width 1.5 cm. Cf. Ettlinger, taf. 5:7. Catch broken, pin free. ....**CHOICE 100.00**

2162. **ENAMELLED BRONZE BROOCH. 2nd-3rd Century A.D.** Enamelled bronze brooch, in the shape of a disc with central knob. Enamel has blue stripes. Brooch has pin at the back. 1.9 cm diam. Cf. Strong-Brown, *Roman Crafts*, #50. ....**CHOICE 200.00**

2163. **BRONZE FIBULA. 2nd-3rd Century A.D.** Coiled top with an extreme turn to the bow-shaped fibula. Front is banded within the coil and above a long tapered front. Length 5 cm, width 2.5 cm. Ettlinger, taf. 5: 4. Pin broken. ....**CHOICE 100.00**

2164. **BRONZE FIBULA. 2nd-3rd Century A.D.** "Knee" fibula, a type which originated in the Rhineland and circulated into Britain in the 2nd century. Semi-circular head tapering to a sharply turned bow. Length 3.6 cm. Cf. British Museum, *Guide to the Antiquities of Roman Britain*, fig. II #32. Quite a stumpy piece. ....**CHOICE 110.00**

2165. **BRONZE FIBULA. 2nd-3rd Century A.D.** Roped band across top of bowed-out banded fibula. Length 3.3 cm., crossbar 3 cm. Ettlinger, taf. 5:7. Pin frozen in place. ....**CHOICE 150.00**

2166. **MILITARY REPOUSSÉ BROOCH. Mid 2nd Century A.D.** Probably Hadrianic. Disc-type brooch composed of pewter repoussé medallion welded to bronze-alloy backplate with traces of latch and pin. On medallion, horseman (Hadrian) faces his troops right. Denticulated border inset from rim. 29 mm diameter. Derived from a similar sestertius of Hadrian, c. 134 A.D. BMC 1672. This specimen is perhaps one of the finest known. Hattatt, *Ancient and Romano-British Brooches*, No. 138-40. .....**CHOICE 300.00**

2167. **MILITARY PEWTER KNEE BROOCH. Mid 2nd-Mid 3rd Century A.D.** Curved rectangular bar ending at square foot at left. Barrel-housing for iron spring at right, hook to back of foot. Within two recessed squares, the inscription VITA VINI, within blue enamel. Pin gone but traces of bronze-iron spring mechanism remain. 37 mm. This brooch was used primarily for military cloaks. Hattatt, *Ancient and Romano-British Brooches*, No. 92. ....**SUPERB 400.00**

2168. **BRONZE BROOCH FROM ROMAN BRITAIN. 3rd Century A.D.** Crossbow brooch. Two groups of four indented circles on bow. A circular knob to each end of the head; there may have been a third knob which broke off. Length 7.7 cm. Cf. Hattatt, *Ancient and Romano-British Brooches,* p. 122, fig. 103. A nice example of the crossbow fibula. ....**CHOICE 150.00**

2169. **BRONZE CROSSBOW FIBULA. 3rd Century A.D.** Fibula with three bulb-shaped bosses with small and large concentric circles. 8.7 cm. Light green patina. Intact. Sotheby's, 1960, 40. Bouchier, *Vienne, Bronzes Antiques* #219. ....**SUPERB 150.00**

2170. **BRONZE CROSSBOW FIBULA. 3rd Century A.D.** Circle and dot pattern with open filigree work to cross bow. 8 cm. Green patina. Intact. For similar open work, Cf. Ettlinger *Die Romischen Fibeln in der Schweiz*, taf, 29, 5. ....**CHOICE 150.00**

2171. **BRONZE FIBULA. 3rd-4th Century A.D.** Length 3.7 cm. Found at the Carnuntum site. Slightly crushed. ....**AVERAGE 35.00**

WRITING
2172. **COPTIC PAPYRUS FRAGMENT. 5th Century A.D.** Part of a contract, referring to "the son of Philem." Seven lines of script. Measures 8.7 x 3.3 cm. ....**CHOICE 500.00**

2173. **COPTIC PAPYRUS FRAGMENT. 7th-8th Century A.D.** Part of a contract, reading in part "Give one measure of salt to Apa Shenoute and a pitcher of fish." Eight lines. Measures 5 x 6.6 cm. Written in pure Sahidic Coptic in an elegant hand. ....**CHOICE 400.00**

TEXTILES

2174. **LATE ROMAN/EARLY COPTIC. To Early 4th Century A.D.** Brown wool on natural linen, round medallion with crenellated border, surrounded by square border. Scene of Hercules, holding a club, fighting the Nemean lion. Total measurement 9 x 9 cm.; medallion measures 5 x 5.2 cm. Cf. Victoria and Albert Museum, *Catalogue of Textiles from Burying-Grounds in Egypt*, Vol. I, p. 54. Cf. Kybalova, p. 65. ....**CHOICE 250.00**

2175. **EARLY COPTIC. 3rd-4th Century A.D.** Tapestry woven square of red and natural wool. Wave border, inner rounded medallion depicting group of dancing figures. Measures 8.8 x 9.5 cm. Cf. Thomson, *Textiles in the Brooklyn Museum*, #1; Cf. Kybalova #46 for style. ....**CHOICE 250.00**

2176. **EARLY COPTIC. 3rd-4th Century A.D.** Border decoration from a tunic, in linen. Stylized red pomegranate in center, pattern in red and two shades of green. Outer border of red. Measures 10.2 x 8 cm. Cf. Mayer Inst. #11. Nice colors. ....**CHOICE 175.00**

2177. **COPTIC. 4th Century A.D.** Square design in dark green wool on natural linen. Outer square contains border of four vases, one on each side. Inner square contains owl facing. Measures 12.5 x 11.2 cm. The border pattern of four vases is a recurring motif in Coptic art, representing the four Evangelists and the four rivers. Cf. Kybalova #31; Cf. *Brooklyn Museum* #207 for square and vases. ....**CHOICE 200.00**

2178. **COPTIC. 4th Century A.D.** Dark brown on natural wool. Part of a horizontal band from a tunic, containing the upper portion of two panels. Left panel: only the arched border, containing a double twist pattern, remains. The right panel has an arched border of brown dots on a natural background. Below is the upper portion of a draped dancing female figure. To her right is the shield of a male dancer (missing). Floral design between arches. Measures 13 x 4.7 cm. Cf. Shurinova, *Coptic Textiles*, fig. 3; Cf. Kybalova, *Coptic Textiles*, #13. ....**CHOICE 200.00**

2179. **ROMAN PERIOD. 4th Century A.D.** Brown wool square tapestry insert with linen beige geometric design, border of beige linen. Measures 11 cm x 9 cm. Cf. Carrol, p. 86. Mounted in card frame. Half of square present. ....**CHOICE 85.00**

2180. **COPTIC. 4th-5th Century A.D.** Portion of a tunic band with repeating pattern of amphorae and vines. Dark green wool on natural linen. Narrow dark green border to each side. Measures 24.5 x 6 cm. Cf. Kybalova 31; Cf. Shurinova #69 and #121-2 for subject, #125 for border style. ....**CHOICE 225.00**

2181. **COPTIC. 4th-5th Century A.D.** Decoration from a tunic, of dark brown wool on natural linen. Dark brown medallion containing natural-color rosette with red center. False hatching outside medallion in one corner. Measures 7.5 x 8 cm. Cf. Kybalova #23. ....**CHOICE 150.00**

2182. **COPTIC. 4th-5th Century A.D.** Portion of a vertical tunic band with a pattern of a dancing female figure, draped and with her head up, above a large floral motif. Tendril inner border, straight outside border. Dark green-brown wool on natural linen. Total measurement 14 x 21 cm, band measures 8 x 21 cm. Cf. Kybalova #19, 20 for style; Cf. Shurinova #6 for similar figure. ....**CHOICE 300.00**

2183. **COPTIC. 4th-5th Century A.D.** Linen and wool fragment, probably from a horizontal tunic band. Central motif shows a large flower with butterfly or petal detail. Red fruit below. Border and vine to either side. One blue bud to right, one red bud to left. Measures 7.0 x 6.1 cm. Mounted in mat. Cf. Kybalova p. 107. ....**CHOICE 150.00**

2184. **COPTIC. 4th-5th Century A.D.** Fragment of a woolen band, sewn onto natural linen tunic. Band shows a pattern of flowers colored in red, white, and green, alternating with dark brown and white roundels. The border consists of a plain dark-brown stripe on each side. Measures 11 x 5 cm. Cf. Kybalova #63, Victoria and Albert, Vol. II, #434. ....**CHOICE 150.00**

2185. **COPTIC. 4th-5th Century A.D.** Wool and linen portion of a tunic band. Brown on natural. Roundel shows a dog crouching left with its head turned back. Border of thick dashes. Measures 9.2 x 9 cm. Mounted in mat. Cf. Shurinova #4; Cf. Kybalova #33. ....**CHOICE 150.00**

2186. **COPTIC. 4th-7th Century A.D.** Linen fragment. Natural with two dark brown bands. Top band: alternating putti and birds. Lower band: cable pattern. Ornamental border. Measures 13.5 x 8.6 cm. Cf. Errera, *Collection d'anciennes étoffes égyptiennes*, #242..........................**CHOICE 150.00**

2187. **COPTIC. 4th-7th Century A.D.** Tunic decoration of reddish-brown on natural wool. Round fragment containing oval design of hare running right. Embroidered outer border in wave pattern. Total measurement: 8.6 cm diameter; medallion measures 5.3 x 5.5 cm. Cf. Errera #162. ....**CHOICE 250.00**

ROMAN

1556 1560 1564 1582 1583 1561 1586 1587 1596 1609

1554 1604 1608

1599 1605

PLATE 26

ROMAN

1643

1650

1627

1641

1636

1687

1691

1695

1789

1803

1707

PLATE 27

1772

1718

1756

1736

1794

1801

1766

1757

1759

1792

1758

1734

1733

1706

1732

1713

1810

PLATE 28

ROMAN

1813

1822

1821

1843

1826

1827

1824

1850

1830

1927

1855

1840

1841

1842

1864

PLATE 29

ROMAN

1862

1896

1866

1867

1938

1943

1944

1883

1951

1958

1960

1967

1968

1971

1929

1973

1980

1982

1985

2001

PLATE 30

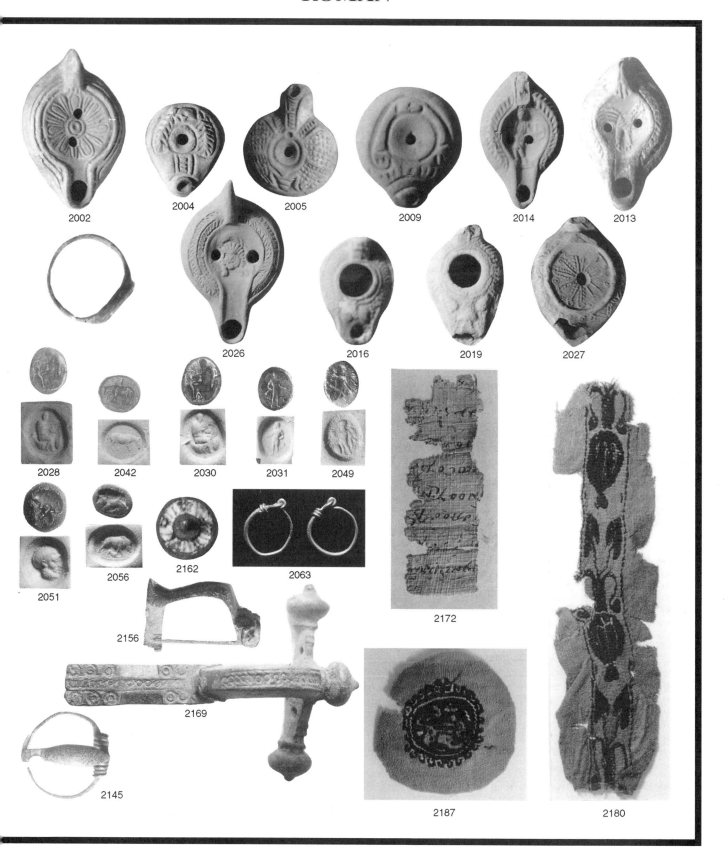

2002

2004

2005

2009

2014

2013

2026

2016

2019

2027

2028

2042

2030

2031

2049

2051

2056

2162

2063

2172

2156

2169

2145

2187

2180

PLATE 31

PRE-COLUMBIAN CULTURE

The Pre-Columbian cultures of the Americas were many and varied, ranging from the Eskimo cultures of the far north to the Indian tribes of Tierra del Fuego in the far south. Most were isolated, although there is some evidence of widespread trade. The Pre-Columbian Indian cultures reached their highest cultural achievements in the 4000-mile-long strip of Pacific coastal land stretching from Mexico to Peru. Although there is some evidence of Pre-Columbian contacts with other parts of the world (the Viking colonies are but one example), it was the arrival of Christopher Columbus in 1492 which changed these cultures forever. The impact the European colonization which followed had on the native civilizations was so devastating that the region's history has been divided into the Pre-Columbian and Post-Conquest periods. Two civilizations stand out in Pre-Columbian America. One was centered in Mesoamerica, the valley of Mexico south of Honduras and parts of Nicaragua. The other was centered in the region of the central Andes which is mostly in what is now Peru. They were divided by intermediate areas, peopled by tribes and chiefdoms stretching from Nicaragua south to Ecuador. Pre-Columbian cultures are divided into chronological periods. Mesoamerican cultures have three chronological periods: Pre-Classic from roughly 2000 B.C.-300 A.D., Classic from 300-900 A.D., and Post-Classic from 900-1540 A.D., based on the dating of the Maya area. Although other Mesoamerican cultures do not fit as well within this dating scheme, the same terms are often used with their chronologies. The central Andean region has its own time divisions based on the seven cultures, such as the Chavin (c. 900-200 B.C.), that spread over the entire region. The tribal cultures of the intermediate areas are dated in "Phases" based on archaeological evidence: for example, the Jama-Coaque phase in Ecuador, which reached its height c. 300 B.C. to 300 A.D.

The Pre-Classic period in Mesoamerica is dominated by the Olmec culture. Often considered the mother culture of Mesoamerica, it arose in about the 12th century B.C. and spread through the region. The Olmecs introduced a civilization with kings, professional specialization, and writing into the area, which up to that time had been dominated by local village-centered societies. Olmec culture transformed the individual village-centered cultures of Mesoamerica into a network dominated by advanced centers where masses of people were organized to produce monumental art and architecture for the benefit of the King and his priests and officials. This laid the groundwork for succeeding cultures in the area. Between 100 B.C. and 300 A.D., Olmec innovations were developed in distinctively varying ways in the different regions of Mesoamerica. In central Mexico, the local Nahuatl-speakers focused on architecture, developing the precursors of the famous pyramids of a later date. In the Maya speaking southeast, the Izapa culture of the Pre-Classic stressed the stela cult, which laid the groundwork for the most advanced system of writing in Pre-Columbian America: the Mayan Hieroglyphs.

In central Mexico around the 1st century A.D., the lords of Teotihuacan erected what was to be the largest pyramidal structure for more than a millennium. Teotihuacan motifs spread widely through Mesoamerica during the early Classic period. The art of the Teotihuacan culture has a severe geometric form. In the south, the Maya developed their highest culture in the Classic period, building the great stone cities which were later reclaimed by the jungle.

Early in the Post-Classic era, drastic movements of people dramatically altered the face of Mesoamerica. The Toltec, formerly a nomadic people, settled at Tula, northwest of Teotihuacan, and soon extended their control over long-settled peoples, such as those of Veracruz, and even the Maya according to some theories. They brought with them their own unique forms of art which emphasized new motifs, such as the serpent and the human skull. The Maya themselves had recently abandoned their older cities in the central jungles in a process whose causes have been hotly debated by historians and archaeologists alike, and increased the population of their northern Yucatan centers where they continued to prosper until the Spanish conquest.

Such movements brought the peoples of Mesoamerica in closer contact with each other. This increased contact was ultimately reflected in a greater similarity of their art forms. The Aztec, the dominant political power in Mesoamerica when the Spaniards arrived in 1519, had been northern nomads like the Toltec, whose culture they copied. Although all the Conquistadors wanted to see was the bloody sacrificial rituals and pagan pomp in order to justify their own superiority, the Aztec culture was in many ways more advanced than their own. Contemporary accounts show the European conquerors had to admit the technical skill of the New World artists, even as they melted down priceless artifacts into gold bullion for transport back home. The art which has survived from the various Mesoamerican cultures is among the most highly desired of all Pre-Columbian art.

South of Mesoamerica, the Intermediate Area was populated by Indian tribes whose archaeological remains are primarily noted for small objects made of gold or tumbaga, an alloy of gold with copper, and ceramics, some of which, such as those found in Panama and Columbia, are highly decorative, with occasional ornamental objects in fine stone and bone. With few exceptions, the monumental art for which the cultures of Mesoamerica to the north and Peru to the south were noted was absent. Although lacking in sculpture, the artifacts produced in this area are still eminently collectable.

In the Andes region of South America, civilization began at an early date, perhaps prior to the 4th millennium B.C. The earliest artistic traditions appeared along the coast and foothills of the northern Andes. The Indians of Ecuador manufactured containers of clay, often decorated with small figures of men and animals and fired at high temperatures, as well as crude stone and clay figures in the round. Their culture is known as the Valdivia culture. In villages along the north coast of Peru, the earliest art, dating from before 2000 B.C., resembled the art of the neighboring Valdivia culture of Ecuador, but lacked ceramics. The first ceramic making culture in Peru was the Chavin, and by 900 B.C., the Chavin art style had become the first widespread art style in the Andes. In the south around 100 B.C., the Paracas culture was also noted for its ceramics and textiles.

Perhaps the two most important styles of art in Pre-Columbian Peru were the Nazca (c. 200 B.C.-600 A.D.) and Mochica (100 B.C.-700 A.D.) styles. Nazca is the name given to the culture that flourished from about 200 B.C. until about 600 A.D. on the southern coast of present-day Peru. It is centered in the Nazca Valley, an almost rainless desert region broken by rivers from the Andean highlands to the east. It was characterized by exquisite painted pottery which almost looks glazed, although the Indians of Peru never achieved a true glaze. It is also known for its beautiful textiles and feather work, much of which was preserved by the dry climate. During the same period on the north coast, the culture known as Mochica created the most humanistic statements in art found south of Mesoamerica. Most central Andean art up to this time was concerned with geometric forms, and even where animals and humans were depicted they were somewhat stylized. Mochica ceramicists, on the other hand, building on Chavin motifs, modeled remarkably realistic animals and human figures shown in the myriad activities of daily life, and portrayed with powerful realism. The Mochica also excelled in gold work and other arts. They were succeeded by the Huari (c. 600-900 A.D.) and Chimu (c. 1000-1450 A.D.), whose artistic styles built on their predecessors.

The last great culture in Peru was the Inca culture (c. 1450-1540 A.D.). Although its pottery was rather uninspired, tending toward geometric decoration, it was very advanced in civil engineering and architecture. The art of ancient Peru is avidly sought by collectors today.

POTTERY AND TERRACOTTA

In Pre-Columbian America, pottery was used for the production of domestic and ritual vessels, as well as for sculptures in many of the cultures. Much of the pottery is decorated, usually with geometric patterns. Some of the most desirable pottery is painted with elaborate scenes of ritual life, as in the Maya area, or modeled with relief art, as in Peru and Panama. A wide variety of animal and human subjects are found. Often the artwork is somewhat stylized, but sometimes, as in the Mochica culture, it can be highly realistic. Some Mochica effigy heads are believed to be actual portraits. This realism is reflected in many pottery sculptures from Mesoamerica, particularly those of the village culture of Colima. Because much of it was buried in protected graves, Pre-Columbian pottery is perhaps the most abundant form of Pre-Columbian art on the market today. Small heads can be had for a few dollars, but a fine statue or decorated vessel can go for many thousands.

STONE

Many of the important buildings in Mesoamerica and Peru were decorated, and in cultural areas, such as the Maya and Olmec, large stele and other stone sculptures played an important part in the rituals of the people. Stone carving was also widely used for the production of jewelry and small items such as figurines. Due to export controls in many countries, large stone items are extremely expensive when available at all, but some smaller examples, such as Guerero figurines, can be had from time to time for a reasonable price.

METAL

Precious metals, such as gold and silver and alloys such as tumbaga, were in widespread use in Pre-Columbian America, as was copper. Indeed, it was the presence of large quantities of precious metals in the societies of Mexico and Peru which attracted the European conquerors to the area. Needless to say, much of this art was wantonly destroyed, or hidden by the Indians to protect it, giving rise to many a lost treasure legend. Some items do appear on the market from time to time, though, and are eagerly sought after.

THE CENTRAL ANDES

	PERU					OTHER COUNTRIES	
	NORTH COAST	**CENTRAL COAST**	**SOUTH COAST**	**NORTH/SOUTH HIGHLANDS**		**ECUADOR/NW ARGENTINA AND N CHILE**	
PRE CERAMIC 3000 B.C.	Pre-ceramic	Pre-ceramic	Pre-ceramic			**FORMATIVE**	
FORMATIVE 1000 B.C.	Chavín (Cupinsnique)	Chavín		Chavín	↑		
	Salinar		Paracas	Pucára	Chiripa	**REGIONAL DEVELOPMENTS** Bahía, Guangala, etc.	
1 B.C. 1 A.D.	Virú			↕	↓		
Teotihuacán →		→	→	→			
CLASSIC	Mohica	Interlocking	Nasca	Recuay	Tiahuanaco	**INTEGRATION**	Aguada
Xochicalo →		→	→	→			
POST-CLASSIC 1000 A.D.	← The Tiahuanico Spread →					Manteño, Milagro, etc.	
				Decadent Tiahuanaco			Chilean Diaguite
	Chimú	Chancay	Ica				Santa Maria Belén
1500 A.D.	← The Inca Conquests →						

MESOAMERICA

		CENTRAL MEXICO	OAXACA	GULF COAST	MAYA
P R E – C L A S S I C	1500 B.C. —				
	1000 B.C. —	El Arbolillo Zacatenco Tlatico			
			Monte Albán I	Olmec (La Venta)	
			Monte Albán II	Izapa style	
	1 B.C.	Cuicuilco			Proto-Classic and
	1 A.D.			Husatec begins	Formative Maya
C L A S S I C	Teotihuacán →		Mixtec begins →	→	→
			Monte Albán III		
					Classic Maya
				Classic Veracruz	
	Xochicalo →		→	→	→
P O S T – C L A S S I C					Toltec Maya begins
	1000 A.D. —				
		Toltec			
			Monte Albán IV		Toltec Maya
		Chichimec		Husatec ends	ends
		Aztec	Mixtec ends		Post-Classic Maya
	1500 A.D. —				

PRE-COLUMBIAN

MESOAMERICA

NAYARIT

2188. **NAYARIT FIGURE.** An intact musician playing a tortoise-shell drum and wearing headband. c. 100 B.C.-200 A.D., red slipped terracotta, 3 3/8" to 4"H ....**CHOICE 200.00**

2189. **NAYARIT SEATED FIGURE WITH FAN.** Ixtlan del Rio redware figure rendered with wide-eyed expression and mouth held open baring the delineated teeth. Left hand raises fan/blade. Black striped facial paint, headband with beads, ears covered in rings, nose ring, arm cuffs, and loin protector, make up adornments. 300 A.D. 10 5/8"H., light surface wear and nicks, else intact. ....**CHOICE 300.00**

2190. **NAYARIT IXTLAN DEL RIO FIGURE.** Seated female covered in profuse red, black, and cream painted detail. Her legs are stretched out in front, and are covered by a striped skirt, and stripes and dots decorate upper body; nose ring around nose. 5 3/4"H. Exceptionally painted. c. 300 A.D. ....**SUPERB 300.00**

2191. **NAYARIT FIGURE.** Archaic Chinesco seated figure. Height 3 1/4". Flattened curved head and pinprick features. Fine cream clay. c. 100 B.C.-200 A.D. ....**CHOICE 300.00**

JALISCO

2192. **SEVEN JALISCO MINIATURES ON A NECKLACE.** Great little grouping of standing Jalisco figures, six in redware, the seventh in buff, each with double perforation through chest and strung on a necklace, 23"L., of buff terracotta, conical beads. Two figures with heads reattached, another missing arms. c. 300 A.D. ....**CHOICE 250.00**

2193. **JALISCO HUNCHBACK.** He is seated, with hands resting upon swollen knees, and phallus bared. He carries a pouch across his deformed distended back. Long applied coils of hair, a vertical spout, and disc earrings adorn head characterized by a quite prominent nose. Few hair coils gone and chipped, else exc. cond. 7"H. c. 100 B.C.-200 A.D. ....**SUPERB 500.00**

2194. **JALISCO FEMALE FIGURE.** Red-slipped 8"H. figure with distinctive large breasts, nodes upon shoulders, and applied necklace and ring adornments; repaired. 7 1/8"H. c. 200 A.D. ....**CHOICE 200.00**

2195. **JALISCO FIGURINE.** 7" freestanding female figure with red and black chapapote accents, intact. c. 300 A.D. ....**CHOICE 250.00**

2196. **JALISCO FAMILY (2).** Rare group of cream slipped terracotta figurines, clearly sculpted by the same artist. A seated father, and a nude standing mother with black striped legs. Seated male's arm reglued. Each fig. modeled with squared long hair, long pointed nose, and earrings. c. 300 A.D. 4 1/4" to 6 3/8"H. ....**CHOICE 500.00**

2197. **WEST MEXICO JALISCO DOG.** Chunky blackware dog with paws splayed and open mouth with wagging tongue; reglued, chipped. With a Nayarit snake whistle, tail reglued. 4 3/4" to 6 7/8"L., c. 100 B.C.-200 A.D. ..**CHOICE 250.00**

2198. **JALISCO FEMALE.** A cream-slipped bare-breasted female with conical bowl. Intact. 6 1/2"H. c. 300 A.D. ....**CHOICE 250.00**

2199. **JALISCO SEATED WOMAN.** Buff terracotta lady. Thick torso, hands raised, and wearing elaborate fringed earrings. Also armlets, headband, and red painted detail. 10"H. Legs reattached, else intact. c. 300 A.D. ....**CHOICE 300.00**

2200. **TZIN TZUN TZAN "TEAPOT" VESSEL.** West Mexican terracotta vessel with stirrup and elongated pouring spout. Body painted brick-red with white star, serpentine border and "S" shaped geometric patterns. Repaired break on stirrup, else exc. c. 300 A.D. ....**CHOICE 550.00**

COLIMA

2201. **COLIMA MOTHER AND CHILD WITH METATE.** A seated mother with hands full holds her child in right arm while preparing food with mano and metate in left. Mother wears headband, earrings, necklace, appliqués on shoulders, and skirt. Wonderful! 4 1/4"H., repaired at metate and mother's bottom. c. 300 A.D. ....**CHOICE 295.00**

2202. **COLIMA WOMAN.** Wonderful nude figure of a possibly pregnant female, with bulging stomach, and large genitals. Band across forehead with conch shell ornament, pageboy plaits hang at sides, long plait down back. Also bears prominent nose, applied brows, eyes, and tiny mouth. c. 200 A.D. 6 1/4"H. Stable age crack along belly, else exc. with surface deposits ....**CHOICE 250.00**

2203. **COLIMA FEMALE.** Lovely figure adorned in crosshatched turban, fastening hair in long plait down back, large beaded necklace, armcuffs, and incise-detailed loincloth, wrapped along back. Body enriched by faded black pigment. 6 3/4"H. Exc., c. 300 A.D. Custom mount. Finer than average type usually encountered. ....**CHOICE 400.00**

2204. **COLIMA DOG.** In pink-brownware, standing foursquare, a heavy belly hanging beneath. Also huge incised toothy grin, diamond eyes, and overall quite pleasant expression. Shard reglued to nose, else intact. 11"L., 8 1/2"H. at tip of ears. c. 100 B.C-300 A.D..................................**CHOICE 1100.00**

2205. **COLIMA SHELL AMULET.** A 3"H. flattened profile fig. with one arm raised, other at waist. Intact, drilled and carved. c. 200 A.D. ....**CHOICE 175.00**

CHUPICUARO

2206. **CHUPICUARO POLYCHROME BOWL.** The wide-bodied vessel slightly askew on pointed tripod legs is geometrically decorated with echoing diamonds in red and black against tan clay. 5 1/2"H. 9 1/2"D. Rim chipped. Mexico, c. 400 B.C. ....**SUPERB 225.00**

2207. **CHUPICUARO "SISTERS."** Two exceptional figurines. Each delicately and carefully detailed, the larger one with particularly fine face. Both have lovely do's, pendant necklaces hanging between nippled full breasts, and paunch bellies. Nice proportions. 3 1/4" and 2 1/2"H. Choice. c. 400 B.C. ....**CHOICE 300.00**

2208. **CHUPICUARO SKIRTED FIGURE.** Female skirted figure adorned with decorative bands encircling forehead, thick necklace, applied bracelets, and bare breasts. 6 7/8"H. Intact with dangling earrings. Shows traces of black pigment along slab-like skirt. c. 400 B.C. ....**CHOICE 250.00**

MICHOACÁN

2209. **MICHOACÁN "PRETTY LADY."** A lovely terracotta. Her hair is wonderfully decorated with small birds along sides of the linear incised band, and fastened in back by a layered fringe. Her hair gathered between shoulders. These rich details, a collar necklace, and bracelets are the only elements adorning her nude body. One breast and legs reglued. 6 3/4"H. c. 200 B.C. ....**CHOICE 400.00**

2210. **MICHOACÁN OLLA.** Particularly fine, round-bodied terracotta vessel, covered in tan slip, richly and skillfully painted with swirl and ticked designs directly upon striped horizontal layers. White, brown, and black paint. 4 1/8"H. Gorgeous, in choice condition, with light root structure. c. 100 B.C. ....**CHOICE 300.00**

2211. **PRE-CLASSIC MINIATURE.** 3"H. Valley of Mexico female with coiffure, crescentic eyes, and broad shoulders, reglued. c. 400 B.C. ....**CHOICE 100.00**

2212. **MICHOACÁN "PRETTY LADY."** A nice-sized nude, pregnant female in buff terracotta. Centrally parted hair wrapped in fillet, large cross encircled earrings, choker, and fruitful body. 4 1/2"H. One earring and legs reattached, nose nicked, else intact. c. 100 B.C. Custom stand. ....**CHOICE 125.00**

2213. **MICHOACÁN MACE HEAD.** Stone weapon, carved with pineapple texture, horizontal notched blade, and grenade texture. With vertical shafthole. 2 1/2"H. c. 300 B.C. ....**CHOICE 100.00**

GUERRERO

2214. **MEZCALA MONKEY.** Green hardstone with carved and string-cut features. Standing figure with arms indicated by incised lines, slightly jutting, oval-shaped head with heavy brow ridge, thin neck, and long tail extending to head height and curving at the tip. Perforated at base of the tail. Finely polished finish. 3 5/8"H. c. 300 B.C. ....**SUPERB 750.00**

2215. **MEZCALA GREENSTONE FIGURE.** Slender figure with rectangular hairdo, multipunctate eyes, relief nose, and slit mouth. Arms held tight to body. Green soft stone with brown inclusions, surface worn, root marks. 5 1/2"H. c. 300 B.C. Custom base.................................**CHOICE 300.00**

2216. **GUERRERO STONE FIGURE.** Sensitively carved blue-green stone figure rendered in the Mezcala manner, and developed from the highly stylized Celt prototype. The face is well detailed with relief brows and nose, inset eyes, and grooved hair and displays considerable Teotihuacan influence. The body is also naturalistic with rounded shoulders, and hands at waist. Right leg gone, and surface weathered. 7 1/2"H. c. 100-600 A.D. Custom stand. ....**CHOICE 300.00**

2217. **MEZCALA FIGURE, MEXICO.** Pointed beak face, forehead band and small cap, arms indicated, perforated through neck, blade on base. c. 300 B.C....**SUPERB 300.00**

TLATILCO

2218. **TLATILCO PRE-CLASSIC FIGURE** Standing buff terracotta figure wearing simple loin wrap, with short, nubbin arms, wide hips and simple headwrap. Minor chip on very top of head. Middle Pre-Classic, c. 1100-5500 B.C., 5 1/4"H. ....**CHOICE 275.00**

2219. **TLATILCO "PRETTY LADY."** 4 1/2"H. with hair in long plaits, her head and one arm reglued. 1100-550 B.C. ....**CHOICE 300.00**

2220. **TLATILCO PRE-CLASSIC FIGURE.** Nude terracotta female, her hair in plaits falling beside breasts, and applied headband with roundels. Open mouth with punctate detail, and sharp relief nose with angular eyes. 5 5/8"H. Covered in traces of red pigment. 1100-550 B.C. Custom stand. ....**CHOICE 300.00**

2221. **TLATILCO FRAGMENTED FIGURE.** A rare 5 1/4"H. hollow wide-bodied female, seated with her genitals visible. Face is painted red, while body is carbonized black. Reglued from fragments, and some losses. 100 B.C.-200 A.D. ....**CHOICE 200.00**

TEOTIHUACAN

2222. **TEOTIHUACAN HEAD.** Excellent head with headdress detail, including featherwork and chin straps. 2 1/4"H. 450-750 A.D. ....**CHOICE 50.00**

2223. **TEOTIHUACAN LIMESTONE MASK.** An exceptional almost life-sized stone mask. Crisply modeled on typical flat plane, with oval eyes, linear nose with slight incised nostrils, subtle rounded cheeks, and open lipped mouth. Back flat with side flanges drilled for attachment. Right ear chipped, earth deposits, some wear of surface, otherwise excellent. 6"H. c. 800 A.D. Fine piece. ....**CHOICE 1500.00**

2224. **ENGRAVED RELIEF MAYAN CUP, Teotihuacan.** Small greyware terracotta urn standing on three rounded legs and with two wide, diagonal bands engraved on body, each bearing an intricate network of hieroglyphics. A few minor rim nicks, else exc. cond. Mayan. 4 5/8"H. 4 3/8"D. c. 600 A.D. Nice! ....**SUPERB 400.00**

AZTEC

2225. **AZTEC KNIFE.** Aztec obsidian knife, 3 3/4", c. 1400 A.D. ....**CHOICE 100.00**

VERACRUZ

2226. **TERRACOTTA HEAD.** Modeled with deep groove eyes and applied pupils, high arched brows, tightly pursed lips. Also wearing layered headdress, disk earrings, and a rope choker. Encrustation on pinched nose, minor chips, else intact. 8"H. Remojadas, 600-900 A.D. ....**CHOICE 300.00**

2227. **REMOJADAS SONRIENTE FIGURE.** Molded 13 3/4"H. terracotta in wide stance with arms akimbo. His broad toothy grinning face in amusing scrunched expression, with pendant earrings, and broad cap with black border. Also wearing beaded necklace, and breechcloth with geometric pattern. Head, left arm and legs reattached. 600-900 A.D. ....**CHOICE 1500.00**

2228. **VERACRUZ HEAD.** Remojadas style, with deep engraving representing facial paint or scarification, a finely formed nose, and slits in forehead probably for feather head-dress attachment. 5"H. 600-900 A.D. ....**CHOICE 295.00**

2229. **FINE VERACRUZ SONRIENTE HEAD.** Charming, well-detailed face, smiling with mouth open to reveal two teeth. Wearing a squared turban with scroll incised design. Face covered with yellow slip and black painted tattoos. One leaf earring other gone, and bell pendant collar intact. Minor repair to side of hat, and separated from larger figure, else excellent. 5 1/2"H. 100-600 A.D. Custom stand. ....**CHOICE 300.00**

2230. **NOPILOA FIGURAL RATTLE.** Hollow molded figure attired in crescentic ribbed headdress, earrings necklace, and tunic with relief glyphic design and geometric patterns. Fine white applied slip intact. 6 1/2"H. Veracruz, 600-900 A.D. ....**CHOICE 250.00**

2231. **HUASTEC SPOUTED FACE VESSEL.** Rare and unusual pouring vessel with squat body bearing a relief human face with slit, half-moon eyes, relief nose and ovular mouth. Slight indication of chin and relief ears. Brown filler paint in geometric patterns on rest of body, up-pointed spout in rear and flared rim with basket handle above. Restoration to strap handle, else intact and nice. c. 600-900 A.D. 7"H. ....**CHOICE 800.00**

MIXTEC

2232. **EXCEPTIONAL JADE PINOTE.** Mixtec squatting figure in grey-green jadeite, the crouching male incised to indicate hands crossed over chest, coffee-bean shaped eyes, hollow drilled ear flares and navel, incised hair in rear, and all accentuated with red cinnabar in the low spots. Beautifully polished and in choice cond. c. 900-1200 A.D. 3 3/8"H. Double perforation in rear. ....**SUPERB 600.00**

2233. **MIXTEC COPPER ORNAMENT.** Monkey head with openwork and applied wire details, with a bell dangling from the chin loop. About 2 1/4" length. c. 1200-1500 A.D. ....**CHOICE 200.00**

2234. **OBSIDIAN EAR SPOOL.** Mixtec grey-black translucent obsidian ear spool. Beautifully polished, extremely delicate. About 1 1/2" D. c. 1200-1500 A.D. ....**SUPERB 300.00**

2235. **MIXTEC FIGURE.** Mixtec pinote, string-cut figure depicted squatting. Grey jadeite, 1 7/8"H.; c. 800-1200 A.D.. ....**CHOICE 200.00**

2236. **OBSIDIAN EAR FLARE.** Translucent black ornament in spool form with beautifully polished face and recessed area beneath. 1 1/4"D. Mixtec, c. 800-1200 A.D. Mexico. ....**SUPERB 250.00**

PUEBLA

2237. **PUEBLA FEMALE FIGURE.** Pre-classic female figure wearing only forelock or headband hair, and earspools. She is rendered with double punctate or raised node eyes, thick open lips, and blocky outlines. With hands over breasts. Reglued breaks, minor nicks. 6 5/8" to 3 1/4"H. Cream terracotta. c. 550 B.C. Custom mounted. ..**CHOICE 600.00**

OAXACA

2238. **OAXACAN JAGUAR DEITY.** Crouching on hind legs, the fierce jaguar forming a vessel, extends his rotund head with open fanged jaws, protruding tongue, and tiny snout in air while eyes are closed. Suspended from a rope collar around neck, hang two bells. Rim extends from back. Head repaired, stable age crack in body, else intact. 8 5/8"H. 600-1200 A.D. ....**CHOICE 800.00**

2239. **ZAPOTEC EFFIGY URN.** Greyware terracotta cylinder of tapered form with relief facial detail of a god. Bears incised decoration on front and rear, relief nose with ring and open mouth. 8 1/4"H. Choice condition. c. 300-100 B.C. ....**SUPERB 550.00**

2240. **ZAPOTEC FIGURAL URN.** Grey terracotta with brown slip and traces of red, seated figure, cross-legged wearing elaborate headdress, ear spools, wide collar and loin cloth, with cylindrical vessel on back. Intact but with several chips and a wing of the headdress reattached. 8"H. Monte Alban, Oaxaca. c. 800 A.D. ....**CHOICE 800.00**

2241. **MONTE ALBAN SEATED FIGURAL VESSEL.** Zapotec urn in the form of a seated god with hands on knees of crossed legs. He wears a loin apron, necklace, ear spools, and high headdress. Greyware terracotta, 9 1/4"H. Some restoration including ears and headdress may be a replacement from another piece. Still attractive. Oaxaca, c. 800 A.D. ....**CHOICE 450.00**

OLMEC

2242. **SEATED OLMEC FEMALE.** Solid buff terracotta with traces of red pigment. Sits with one leg crossed, the other with knee up, hand to knee, other to navel. Nude figure has a long braid down back. Intact. 2 1/4"H. c. 1150-550 B.C. Xalitla, West Mexico. ....**CHOICE 500.00**

2243. **OLMECOID "PRETTY LADY."** Buff terracotta fertility figure with wide hips, short nubbin arms, relief nose, slit eyes and mouth and turbaned headdress. Chipped on crown and eyebrow, else intact. 6 1/8"H. Tlapacoya, middle Pre-classic, c. 1100-550 B.C. ....**CHOICE 295.00**

2244. **OLMECOID FEMALE.** Pre-classic lady with wide bloated hips and thighs, and displaying slight pregnancy. She wears only a crosshatched and punctured skirt, and a collar necklace. Distinctive face with asymmetrical coiffure, broad narrow eyes, and grimace with deep corners. 7 1/2"H. In cream clay, one hand chipped, else exc. 400 B.C. ....**CHOICE 300.00**

2245. **OLMECOID FIGURE.** Overall cream-slipped and bearing the distinctive punctate eyes and full-lipped mouth, with a bulbous nose. Nodes are applied to thighs, body modeled with sunken chest and paunch belly. 6 5/8"H. Mayan area. c. 300 B.C. ....**CHOICE 225.00**

2246. **PRE-MAYAN HEAD POT, Olmecoid.** Life-size head of an elderly man forming bowl of pink-brown terracotta. Modeled with sunken cheeks, narrow perforated eyes, ridged slender nose, and protruding tongue. Stylized ears extended at sides are pierced, and turban knotted in front. Minor chip on tongue, gouge in back, else intact. 6 1/4"H. 4 3/8" rim diam. c. 200 B.C.-200 A.D. Rare. ....**CHOICE 850.00**

2247. **OLMEC BLUE JADE SPOON PENDANT.** Beautiful translucent stone triangular pendant with circular concavity. Two angular drilled suspension holes covered with cinnabar. Edges subtly curved and tapered underneath, and on the whole exquisitely carved, but possibly repolished. 3 1/2"L. c. 400 B.C. ....**CHOICE 300.00**

2248. **PRE-CLASSIC HEAD.** Olmec, probably from Tlatilco with drilled pupils, wide nose, and well formed lips and mouth. Linear hairdo and small ear spools. 1 1/4"H., some traces of red pigment. c. 500-100 B.C. ....**CHOICE 200.00**

MAYAN

2249. **SPEARHEAD.** 500-800 A.D. Grey metamorphic stone spearhead with barbs and flat grooved tang. Length 85 mm. ....**CHOICE 50.00**

2250. **ARROWHEAD.** 500-800 A.D. Metamorphic grey stone arrowhead. Leaf shape. Length 50 mm. ....**CHOICE 40.00**

2251. **ARROWHEAD.** 500-800 A.D. Black chalcedony arrowhead, straight back. Length 38 mm...**CHOICE 50.00**

2252. **MAYAN SEAL.** 500-800 A.D. Buff terracotta seal representing a palm branch. Measures 42 by 12 by 30 mm. ....**CHOICE 50.00**

2253. **A MAYA AVIAN EFFIGY VESSEL.** Of cylindrical form with slightly flaring walls, interior with tree roots, exterior with orange pigmentation on ceramic, a vertical relief of bird head and linear design, an upper horizontal band with similar bird forms, slight crack on rim, 8"H, c. 600-900 A.D. ....**CHOICE 600.00**

2254. **MAYAN CYLINDER.** Buff terracotta painted orange on the exterior and with a band of relief glyphs at the slightly flared rim. 6"D. 6"H. Minor crack at rim, else exc. save for minor paint loss. c. 600-900 A.D. ....**CHOICE 350.00**

2255. **MAYAN POLYCHROMED CYLINDER.** Terracotta urn standing on four small rounded legs and intricately painted with a seated human figure amidst well-detailed filler, a band of glyphs above, black line border at rim and base. Scene is repeated on reverse. 7 3/4"H., 6"D. c. 650 A.D. Intact, light retouching of scene. ....**CHOICE 2500.00**

2256. **MAYAN CODEX PLATE.** Small terracotta plate with red rim and black painted, fine line details of a profile human face entwined in swirls, tentacles and other supernatural treatments. 7 1/2"D. "Kill" hole in center and stable crack radiating from center to rim. Some encrustation remains and light pocking. Rim retouched, else intact. c. 600 A.D. ....**CHOICE 1250.00**

2257. **MAYAN CYLINDER VASE.** Tall slender vessel covered in a rich pattern of petaled circles, long ovals with dotted borders, and swirled dots. Painted in deep orange and black. The whole pattern simulating a stylized jaguar pelt. Cracks radiating from rim are stable, rim repainted, and minor paint loss, else intact. 8 3/4"H. c. 600 A.D. .....**CHOICE 1500.00**

2258. **MAYAN COPADOR-TYPE BOWL.** Large red painted glyphs outlined in black around exterior, one glyph containing a kan cross, and band of fine glyphs encircling the rim. Interior painted with two hummingbirds around tondo. Pale orange slip. Interior worn. 7"D. c. 600-900 A.D. ....**CHOICE 600.00**

2259. **COPADOR BOWL.** Large shallow bowl painted with simple glyph forms encircling interior and repeating around rim of exterior. Petals encircle base, and linear bands encircle torso. 8 1/2"D. Red, black, and orange pigment; repaired from several shards, repainting in cracks only. c. 600-900 A.D. ....**CHOICE 550.00**

2260. **MAYAN COPADOR BOWL.** Well-preserved painted design of three running monkeys, and a border of repeating facial glyphs. Red, orange, and black on yellow-orange ground. 3 1/8"H. 7 1/8"D. Intact. 600-900 A.D. ....**CHOICE 500.00**

2261. **CLASSIC MAYAN PLATE.** The large plate, painted with a fish in the center, and covered in orange slip. The fish with thick lips, and wavy undulating black outline. Repaired break, fish outline touched up. 12 1/2"D. 600-900 A.D. ....**CHOICE 450.00**

2262. **MAYAN BOWL.** 7 1/2"D. Encircled by birds around concave neck. Intact. Late Classic period, 600-900 A.D. ....**CHOICE 250.00**

2263. **MAYAN CYLINDER.** Engraved with band of dotted steps and "Greek key" motifs, diagonal lines along body; orange slipped. 5 3/4"H. Intact. 600-900 A.D. ...**CHOICE 400.00**

2264. **MAYAN FIGURE.** Standing crowned figure with perforated chest, 5 3/4"H., unburnished, intact. Late Pre-Mayan, c. 100 A.D. ....**CHOICE 200.00**

2265. **MAYAN JADE EAR SPOOLS.** Lovely medium jade green ear ornaments, square in shape with short hollow shaft in rear, each double perforated. Face decorated with incised channels forming a square pattern. Exc. cond. 2"W. c. 600 A.D. ....**CHOICE 500.00**

2266. **JADE CONDOR CELT.** The axe god formed with round plumes atop head. Long pointed beak incised upon tapered celt body. Perforated through neck. Pale green color. Exc. cond, minor abrasion. 3"H. Custom stand. c. 600 A.D. ....**CHOICE 275.00**

2267. **MAYAN DOUBLE-MOTIF JADE.** Small pale blue-green jade, the flat surface in image of a face incised with plumed hair, almond lidded eyes, circular drilled earspools, and swirls issuing from chin. The smooth convex reverse, in the form of a fish with rounded bifurcated fins. Pierced on sides. 2"H., exc. cond. Honduras, c. 600 A.D. Custom mount. ....**CHOICE 800.00**

2268. **MAYAN BACKWARE TRIPOD VASE.** Slightly flared body with flange around base decorated with incised crescents and relief nodes. The legs with punched decoration simulating open work. Traces of red ochre pigment. Displays strong Teotihuacan influence. Excellent condition, only minor chips. 4 3/4"H. Early Classic, 250-600 A.D. ....**SUPERB 275.00**

2269. **EL QUICHE FRAGMENT.** From a large El Quiche urn, the enormous grotesque face of a deity modeled with large inset eyes painted white, large beak nose, and fierce projecting lips with fangs and wall of white teeth. Modeled over the curve of the cylinder vessel. Repaired from large fragments with minor restoration over cracks. 10 1/2"H. 12"W. Custom mount. Impressive! ....**CHOICE 3000.00**

2270. **MAYAN WARRIOR WHISTLE.** Free-standing terracotta warrior attired in a tall crown with feathers, a necklace with spiked ornament, and a ballplayer-type yoke around his waist. Also holds club in arm, tubular earrings extending from ears, lip plug from chin, and a bead on forehead. Right arm reglued, some facial detail eroded, and one spike gone, else excellent condition, with areas of Maya blue pigment remaining and root marks. 9 3/4"H. c. 600-900 A.D. ....**CHOICE 300.00**

2271. **MAYAN FIGURAL VASE.** Jaguar forms this ovoid vase with crude broad incised limbs and tail, the paws in serrated relief. Head is fully modeled with relief pendant necklace. Red-brown specular hematite paint on cream slip. Exc., only hairline crack. 7 1/2"H. Late to Post-Classic period, 600-1500 A.D..**CHOICE 275.00**

2272. **JAINA MOLDED FIGURAL WHISTLE.** Seated dignitary bearing fine dwarf-like facial features, surmounted by wrapped textured headdress with white fugitive slip, and large ear flares. Thickset body with arms held to sides, and applied bead at center of chest. A fine detailed fig. 4"H. End of headdress chipped. 600 A.D. ....**CHOICE 325.00**

2273. **JAINA TLALOC FIGURE.** A superb hollow molded figure of a priest of Tlaloc, with distinctive raised rings around lidded eyes and covered mouth. He is extraordinarily adorned, crowned by a tall helmet with a fantastic central bird head, feathered deity eyes, relief decorative ornaments, and horizontal flanges. He also wears a beaded collar over another tripartite crosshatched collar, a beaded belt, and hanging loincloth. A cuff bracelet, beaded ear flares, and knotted sandals complete his finery. He wields a royal sceptre in right hand, and a shield incised with a face of Tlaloc in left. Well done. Traces of Maya blue and white pigment and red cinnabar. Intact. 6 1/8"H. Late Classic, 600-900 A.D. ....**SUPERB 2700.00**

2274. **MAYAN HEAD RATTLE.** Creamware terracotta hollow molded rattle in the form of an aged human head with wrinkled cheeks, pointed nose with large ornament beneath, ear flares and a ridged bib beneath bearing some traces of Maya blue. Missing shard off base (not visible), and rattling stones, else intact. 4 3/4"H. c. 600 A.D. Custom mount. ....**CHOICE 300.00**

SOUTH AMERICA

COSTA RICA

2275. NICOYA JAGUAR TRIPOD VASE. A rattling three-dimensional jaguar head with pointed ears, and bulging eyes extends from vessel. A decorative band of demon serpents encircles neck, and patch of dotted pelt at chest of vessel. Well-painted in chocolate and red-brown upon cream slip. Unnoticeable repair to tip of rim and ears. 9 1/8"H. 800-1000 A.D. ....**CHOICE 750.00**

2276. COSTA RICAN VESSEL. Small tripod vessel, particularly fine with crab-like painting in red on brown slip. Intact. From the Nicoya region. 2 1/4"-3 3/4"H. 800-1200 A.D. ....**CHOICE 250.00**

2277. FINE COSTA RICAN STONE METATE. Superbly carved from single unit, each quadrupled leg in the form of a female with soft rounded features. They stand with parallel legs slightly bent, hands supporting breasts, and wear linear headdresses. The crushing surface is in oval concave form with a smooth finish, and a small relief semicircle on two ends. Forty-five tiny trophy heads line the border beneath an encircling groove. 14"L., 8 1/4" H. c. 1000-1200 A.D. Stable age crack in one figure, else excellent condition. ....**SUPERB 2500.00**

2278. COSTA RICAN MACE HEAD. Green hard stone in the form of a male face with sunken eye orbits, relief nose, incised mouth and forehead, and crest on top of head. Boat-shaped body with central hollow shaft for hafting. Branch design on rear. 5"L. c.100-500 A.D. .....**CHOICE 2500.00**

2279. DIQUIS GOLD DISC. High karat gleaming yellow gold roundel with two perforations near top and a double border of punched node designs. A bend or two and a tiny tear, else exc. Costa Rica, 3 1/2" D. 19.5 grams.......**SUPERB 300.00**

2280. COSTA RICAN AXE GOD. A long blue-green jade chisel form, with rectangular head carved in angular geometrics along three sides. Blade nicked, else intact. 800-1000 A.D. 3 5/8"H. ....**CHOICE 150.00**

2281. COSTA RICAN AXE-GOD AVIAN PENDANT. A dark greenstone bird with hair tuft and crescentic blade body. Perforated through neck for wear, and intact. 800-1000 A.D. Approx. 3 1/2"H. ....**CHOICE 100.00**

2282. COSTA RICAN AXE GOD. Nicoya. Turquoise-green serpentine deity rendered with drilled eyes and corners of mouth, horned and brimmed cap, and relief linear hands at waist. Crescentic blade torso. 3 7/8"H. Split down center and reglued, else intact. 800-1200 A.D. ...**CHOICE 275.00**

2283. COSTA RICAN STONE SEATED FIGURE. Carved of coarse volcanic stone, seated upon small ledge, his arms crossed and resting upon bent knees, and phallus displayed. Head with long perforated ears, large angular nose, bean-shaped eyes and mouth. 6 1/2"H. Exc. cond. c. 800-1200 A.D. ....**SUPERB 300.00**

2284. COSTA RICAN FELINE STONE HEAD. Brunkas or Huetares. Long feline head carved of grey volcanic stone, and separated from a ceremonial metate. Grinning jaws reveal crossed fangs. Well-carved. 7 1/2"L. Losses to surface on one side, else exc. cond. Break at neck smoothed. Middle Period 800-1300 A.D. Custom stand. ....**CHOICE 500.00**

2285. COSTA RICAN JADE PARROT HEAD. Nicoya. A marbled blue-green and amber translucent jade carved as a parrot's profile. Drill hole forms eye. Drilled and string cut slits form open mouth of bent beak, with tufts around bridge of beak, and grooves above vertical neck. 2 3/8"H. Exc. cond. c. 800 A.D. ....**SUPERB 300.00**

PANAMA

2286. GOLD TRIPLE BIRD PENDANT. High karat yellow gold figural pendant of three birds in a row, each with splayed tail, wings present only on two end birds, and with double "snakes" held in each mouth and terminating in opposing spirals. Suspension loops on reverse under two end birds. Veraguas, Panama, c. 500-1500 A.D. 48.5 grams. ....**SUPERB 5000.00**

2287. MINIATURE COCLE BOWLS. Superb pair. The 1"H. footed bowl painted in browns and black with beast bearing long claws, target body, and humorous grin. Nick on rim. Exterior of rounded bowl with bands of abstract design, in purple, red, cream, and black. Stable age crack at rim. Panama. 2 3/8"D. 800-1000 A.D. ....**CHOICE 295.00**

2288. GOLD AVIAN. Panama. Exquisite miniature with fine sharp detail. Splayed wings and tail, double spiral earrings, curved beak, beady eyes, and tall ringed neck. Loop behind neck. Just shy of 1"H. Veraguas style. .....**SUPERB 500.00**

COLUMBIA

2289. TUMBAGA JAGUAR FINIAL. Cast jaguar crouching upon horizontal shaft, with tiny claws clutching sides. Wonderful scrollwork forms eyes, nostrils, and tail curled up over rear of body. Strips of ropework cover the spine and open lips, baring top and bottom teeth. Well done. 43.5 grams. 2 3/4" L., gold surface corroded, small casting flaws. Sinu, Columbia. 500-1000 A.D. ....**CHOICE 500.00**

2290. TAIRONA TUMBAGA FINIAL BELL. High copper content gold ornament with central depiction of a feline with head leaning on front paws, seated upon a pedestal base and with bud-shaped bell atop. Exc. cond. Still contains rattling balls, a few minute casting holes, and a slight bend to the shaft. 3 1/4 " H. c. 1000-1500 A.D. ......**SUPERB 2200.00**

2291. TAIRONA STONE PEG FIGURE. Grey-brown igneous stone carving with rounded base and flat back somewhat similar to a mano. Figural depiction on front is of a grimacing figure holding hands to chest, with splayed nose, linear hair, and textured trunks. 8 1/4"L. Exc. cond. Columbia, c. 500-1500 A.D. ....**SUPERB 2000.00**

2292. **TAIRONA NECKLACE.** Fine necklace, composed of carnelian beads in long and short tubes, discs, and few tear-shaped beads. Also strung with some black veined red jasper beads, and crystal cylinders. Approximately 25"L. Colombia, 800-1500 A.D. ....**CHOICE 300.00**

2293. **BLACKWARE BAT VESSEL.** Fine vessel with detailed bat's head wearing rectangular crown, baring crossed fangs and toothy grin. Crescent body with noded detail at corner and serrated sides. Exc. cond. 7 1/2"H. c. 500 A.D. Tairona. ....**CHOICE 295.00**

2294. **TAIRONA ANTHROPOMORPHIC JAR.** Grey terracotta, wide-mouthed jar on ring base with relief arms and legs forming loops on the body. Facial details in relief on the neck beneath banded rim. Intact, 10"H. Colombia, c. 500 A.D. ....**CHOICE 600.00**

2295. **NARIFIO VESSEL.** Black resist painted. Globular olla, with crosses within fringed diamond forms. With nubbin suspension loops flanking rim; black against pink-brown slip. 4 1/4"H. Displaying own unique lovely pattern. Colombia, 1000-1400 A.D.....................**CHOICE 300.00**

2296. **SINU TUMBAGA FINIAL.** Charming cast ornament of three hummingbirds with long beaks, bead eyes, and relief folded wings. The three birds perched upon T-shaped hollow terminal, base open. Shaft perforated laterally. Exc. cond. with small areas of black and green patina. 1 3/4"L. Colombia c. 500-1500 A.D. ....**SUPERB 1500.00**

2297. **QUIMBAYA GOLD NOSE RING.** Fine U-shaped tubular ring with flattened terminals. A high 20+ karat gold. 800-1500 A.D. Columbia. 7/8"W. Wearable as a lovely ring or pendant. ....**SUPERB 295.00**

2298. **GOLD FROG PENDANT.** Stylized frog with legs bent behind, triangular body, beady eyes and nostrils. The head detailed with braided rope around eyes and neck. Suspension hole at chest. Cast of high copper content gold. Exc. cond. Tairona, 1000-1500 A.D. ....**SUPERB 800.00**

2299. **QUIMBAYA "FLAT" FIGURE.** Solid, buff terracotta figure with squared, slab body, perforated numerously for feather attachment and with slit eyes, mouth, and realistic relief nose. Arms and legs each bear a bracelet indicated by indentation and there is a small penis visible. Just over 8"H. Arms reattached, else exc., and better than usually found. Columbia, 500-1000 A.D. ....**CHOICE 600.00**

2300. **TAMALAMEQUE BURIAL URN.** Buff terracotta miniature urn with human-form lid. The base bears two relief birds on the body interspersed with two perforated lugs and the rim is tapered to fit the lid. Lid with high relief, triangular with coffee-bean eyes, relief nose, small mouth and perforated ears. Arms and navel in low relief on base of lid. Minor chipping and minor repair, as usual on this fragile type of clay. Rio Magdalena, Colombia, c. 1000 A.D. 13"H. ....**CHOICE 800.00**

2301. **FINE TUMACO HEAD.** Greyware terracotta head off a full figure with puffy cheeks, possibly a coca chewer, semi-smile, wide, well-formed nose and a relief headband over rounded pate. Relief and engraved eyes and ears; earrings hanging beneath. 4 1/8" H., about fist-sized. Colombia, c. 1000 A.D. Custom mount. ....**CHOICE 300.00**

2302. **LARGE LA TOLITA FIGURAL HEAD.** Greyware terracotta, 9 1/2"H. with relief eyes, nose with ornament beneath, slit mouth and round ear spools. Four pieces reattached to crown, nose reglued, face intact. Ecuador-Colombia. c. 1000 A.D. Custom mount. ...**CHOICE 275.00**

2303. **CARNELIAN ARROWHEAD BEAD. Tairona.** Unusual bead in the form of an arrow point, with serrated edges, two flat faces and large central hole for stringing. 1". Colombia, c. 1000-1500 A.D. ....**SUPERB 35.00**

ECUADOR

2304. **CARCHI ABSTRACT BIRD PENDANT.** Hammered, high karat yellow gold with spread wings, splayed tail and tiny bird head, suspension loop behind. 4 5/8"W., 4 1/4"H. Excellent condition. c. 500-1000 A.D. Ecuador. 18.3 grams. ....**CHOICE 800.00**

2305. **VALDIVIA FIGURE.** Fine example of the most ancient of Ecuadorian figurines dating 3500-2700 B.C. Portrayed with thick incised hair falling below shoulders, and framing her tiny face. Hands below pointed breasts, squared bare buttocks behind. Legs reglued but intact. 3 1/4"H. ....**CHOICE 200.00**

2306. **NARINO AMPHORA.** A tall slender vase with round tapered base and trumpeting spout is painted in a black resist pattern of crosshatching and geometrics. Red outlining accentuates the design. Exc. cond., some paint loss. 28"H. 700-1200 A.D. Elegant! ....**CHOICE 1000.00**

2307. **ECUADORIAN FIGURE.** Standing figure with textured rayed headdress. ....**CHOICE 250.00**

2308. **CHORRERA DIAMONDBACK SNAKE JAR.** Speckled brown stone, probably breccia, with flat base, hollowed on the interior and with a relief snake head extending from the jar. Body incised with diamond pattern, drilled eyes and linear differentiation of the body coiling around the jar. Possibly a poison jar. 3"L. Exc. cond. Chorrera, Ecuador, c. 500 A.D. ....**CHOICE 900.00**

2309. **SOUTH AMERICAN FIGURAL ITEMS (2).** La Tolita or Jamacoaque, Ecuador mask with fanged grimace, rough on edges, mostly there, 4"W. Nice. Also, molded flat twins figure, missing legs, each with hand to other's belly, 4 1/2". c. 500-1000 A.D. ....**SUPERB 300.00**

PERU

Chimu

2310. **CHIMU BLACKWARE VESSEL.** Seated monkey clutching a nut to chest, with another tiny monkey at nape of stirrup spout. Displays Moche Chimu transitional style. Arms are reglued. Rim nicked. Choice. 8 1/2"H. c. 800-1200 A.D. ....**CHOICE 450.00**

2311. **CHIMU BLACKWARE VESSEL.** A human figure seated upon a stepped rectangular platform, with prominent nose, and cap with chinstrap. 6 3/4"H. Small hole in belly. Rim nicked, else exc. c. 800-1200 A.D. ....**CHOICE 300.00**

2312. **CHIMU ELECTRUM DEPILATORY TWEEZER.** A gold and silver alloyed tweezer decorated with a relief face, dot border, and crescentic blades functioning as a tweezer. Exc. cond. 1 3/4"H. c. 800 A.D. ....**SUPERB 150.00**

2313. **CHIMU GOLD ROUNDEL.** Hammered disc decorations with engraved "unca" designs, energetic avian motifs, encircling the raised central boss. Two perforations along rim for attachment. 3 1/8"D. Deposits and small hairline crack c. 800-1200 A.D. ....**CHOICE 500.00**

2314. **PERUVIAN BRONZE AXE. Chimu.** Heavy cast and has curved blade, flat, hammer base and perforation hole in body for hafting. 5" blade with green patina. c. 800-1200 A.D. Mounted on black base. ....**SUPERB 250.00**

Moche

2315. **MOCHE I STIRRUP VESSEL.** Low angular body painted in iron red with stepped triangles against ground of tiny circles. Tan slipped body. 7"H., minor paint touch up. Moche I period, c. 200 A.D. ....**CHOICE 600.00**

2316. **MOCHE PORTRAIT HEAD VESSEL.** Sensitive, lifelike rendering of a mature dignified male. Lidded inset almond eyes with large pupils, high cheekbones, prominent pierced nose, and pursed thin lips. He wears striped facial paint in red and tan, a turban with bands of seabirds, and three dangling flaps behind with stepped border. Turban in red-brown over tan ground. Spout restored, and on back of head with light repainting but not extensive. An excellent piece. 10 1/2"H. 400-700 A.D. ....**CHOICE 2500.00**

2317. **MOCHE PRISONER STIRRUP VESSEL.** Noble-looking seated prisoner with lovely swirl black tattooing around nude orange slipped body, including a monkey head emitting swirls on back. A rope extends from his neck, body robustly modeled, and bare phallus visible. He stares forward with dignified face, high cheekbones, prominent nose, and pursed lips. Face of brown hue with white detailed eyes, and black long hair. Top of the head repaired, else intact. 8 1/8"H. Moche IV, 400-700 A.D. An exceptional sculpture. ....**SUPERB 4000.00**

2318. **MOCHE TURQUOISE NECKLACE.** Centered with a brilliant blue turquoise squared bead, and flanked with turquoise and chrysocolla pebbles. The ends strung with tiny tubular chrysocolla beads, and terminating with five or six pink coral beads. Modern clasp. 9 1/2"D. c. 400-700 A.D. Exc. cond. and stunning! ....**CHOICE 1800.00**

Chavin

2319. **CHAVIN SHELL AMULET.** Cream and orange colored spondilus shell amulet, in humanoid form with incised fierce, grimacing face and reclining body. 1 1/4-1 1/2" each. c. 100 B.C. Peru. ....**SUPERB 1200.00**

2320. **FINGER RING.** A Chavin gold circle bezel and soldered simple band. 2.3 grams, size 9. Sturdy and wearable. c. 100 B.C.-500 A.D. ....**SUPERB 250.00**

2321. **CHAVIN STONE CINNABAR CUP.** Engraved with an abstract geometric motif, squared swirl with triangular rays. Repeated four times around sides. The lines highlighted with cinnabar against the tan stone with faint black inclusions. 2 1/2"H. Excellent cond. c. 400 B.C. ....**SUPERB 1500.00**

Salinar

2322. **SALINAR NODED VESSEL.** A fine, early, small creamware vessel, the hemispherical body divided by relief sharp ridge, one half covered with spiked nodes and brown slip, other plain. 7 1/4"H. Spout lightly repaired, two nodes chipped, and paint worn. 300-100 B.C....**CHOICE 1000.00**

2323. **SALINAR FANGED PORTRAIT HEAD VESSEL.** Human head transforming to jaguar with large, relief fangs over incised teeth, jutting, triangular nose and incised almond-shaped eyes with tiny drilled pupils pigmented with red cinnabar. Face with matte finish, head ears burnished. Stirrup spout above with ridged rim. Intact and just about choice cond. 8"H. c. 400-100 B.C. ....**SUPERB 2500.00**

Mochica

2324. **MOCHICA I LOBSTER VESSEL.** A lovely tan slipped vessel, the squat body adorned with a realistic schematic of two lobsters, their feelers fluidly coiled into spotted background. Painted in red-brown, very light paint loss and scratch on same side, tiny nick on rim. Lovely burnished surface. 7"H. c. 100-400 A.D. ....**CHOICE 700.00**

2325. **JAGUAR "CORNPOPPER" VESSEL.** Lentoid-shaped terracotta vessel with small opening at top, slender handle with relief jaguar head bearing fanged snarl, red details over the cream ground. Reverse bears red painted images of two striding jaguars. Well done, intact but with some light paint fading and minor wear. 11 1/4"L. Mochica, c. 500-700 A.D. ....**CHOICE 600.00**

2326. **MOCHICA DRUMMER.** Seated figure wearing cloak and hood in cream color over the buff ground, other areas painted in red. Phase IV stirrup spout extends from rear. Exc. cond. save for light paint loss. 8 5/8"H. c. 500-700 A.D., Peru.
....**SUPERB 600.00**

Huari

2327. **HUARI CUP.** Painted band around rim composed of triangles containing stepped fret, and motifs; in beige, grey, black, white, and brown. Lower body covered in grey slip, and interior in brown slip. 3 7/8"H. 3"D. rim. Only minor paint loss. c. 800 A.D. ....**SUPERB 550.00**

2328. **HUARI PAINTED CUP.** Pink-buff terracotta, slightly flared cup of simple form, painted with two polychromed, beaked profile faces with large crests. Separating the face is a double band in cream, another as the base border. Intact. 4 1/2"H. Peru, c. 700 A.D. ....**CHOICE 400.00**

2329. **HUARI CROSS-EYED FELINE BOWL.** Humorous, round-bodied vessel with relief short snout and ears. Painted with rest of facial detail and spots in black, red, and white over tan-ochre ground. 7 1/4"H. Small area of rim restored, nick on ear, minor paint loss, else intact. c. 800-1200 A.D.
....**CHOICE 600.00**

Wari

2330. **WARI POLYCHROME COUPLE.** A seated couple, the woman with facial tattoos wraps her arms around the man, who wearing a patterned shirt, places one hand on her knee, and holds a black disc, probably a mirror. The colorful couple formed the front part of a double chambered bottle. Visible Nazca influence. One hole where other chamber was attached has been filled and repainted, else intact with light wear and excellent preserved paint. 5 1/4"H.   South or Central Coast, 750-1000 A.D. ....**SUPERB 600.00**

Inca

2331. **INCA WOOD MASK.** Striking mask of pale brown wood. Well carved with inlaid eyes, painted large black pupils, realistic aquiline nose, high cheekbones, accentuated philtrum, and relief lips and chin. 7 3/8"H. Pigment of one eye smeared, tiny nick beside nose, otherwise in well preserved exc. cond. 800-1000 A.D.   Custom mount.
....**SUPERB 1500.00**

2332. **INCA GLAZED ARYBALLOS.** An evenly covered, luminous yellow-green glazed vessel. The sides bearing relief crawling lizards, and slithering snakes. On rounded base, with two loop handles flanking long spout and flared rim. 7"H. Lovely, and a fine example. The method of this glaze was introduced by the conquistadors and incorporated into existing Inca vessel types. Aside from being among the first of the New World glazes, it can be dated to almost exactly the period of the conquest.   c. 1530 A.D.
....**SUPERB 1200.00**

2333. **MOQUEQUA VESSEL.** An Inca aryballos richly painted with red-brown slip. The domed top painted with two layers of rich geometric pattern with stepped design around an oval center. Patterns in cream, deep brown, and light brown. Rim repaired, small pocking of surface, else intact and excellent. Chile. 11 1/4"H. c. 1200-1400 A.D.   Gorgeous vessel!
....**SUPERB 3700.00**

Cajamarca

2334. **CAJAMARCA SERPENT BOWL.** Two serpents with spiral patterned bodies, and rectangular mouths slither along sides. Stars in fields. Black-brown paint. Minor repair at rim. c. 800-1200 A.D. ....**CHOICE 275.00**

2335. **CAJAMARCA TRIPOD CRAB BOWL.** A mirror image of two crabs in center encircled by petal border, concentric circles along sides, and repeating serrated border rim. c. 800-1200 A.D. ....**CHOICE 275.00**

2336. **CAJAMARCA ABSTRACT PAINTED BOWL.** Central cartouche with scrolls, step designs extending from center, and pointed triangles around rim. Repaired crack in side. c. 800-1200 A.D. ....**CHOICE 275.00**

Vicus°

2337. **VICUS TUMBAGA MEDALLION.** Thick, sturdy sheet centered around a repoussé heart-shaped face, with perforated nostrils, and cut-out jagged tooth mouth. Double-perforated at top and bottom for attachment to apparel. Tear in border, hole in chin, else intact. 4"D. c. 100-500 A.D. A rare item. ....**CHOICE 400.00**

2338. **VICUS WARRIOR VESSEL.** Double globular vessel with pointed spout and double bridged handle. Warrior wielding spear and shield stands on frontal globe, wearing beanie cap, ear spools, necklace and resist-painted mantle, both globes also decorated in black negative-resist paint over red terracotta. 9 3/4"L. Repaired at handle attachment with restoration over the cracks. Peru, c. 200 A.D. An unusually fine example. ....**SUPERB 1200.00**

2339. **VICUS VESSEL.** A round-bodied face vessel with relief nose and ears, tiny relief eyes and a slit mouth. Tapered to slightly flared spout with loop handle (repaired). 8"H. encrusted but body intact.   Peru, c. 200 A.D.
....**CHOICE 275.00**

Paracas

2340. **PARACAS SNAKE VESSEL.** The domed top engraved with pattern of a thick mythical double headed snake with relief eyes and snout. Scales of the snake rendered as dot-circles, and heads with intricate linear pattern and toothy grin. Red resin paint fills in incised areas. Blackware. Nick on rim. 5 1/2"H. c. 400-100 B.C. ....**SUPERB 2500.00**

2341. **PARACAS BOWL.** Small blackware bowl, portion of the slightly curved walls decorated with an engraved band of abstract geometrics, each area painted red, olive-green, or black. Remains of painted resin dots adorn part of rim. Stable age crack, erosion on interior, else intact. 3"H. c. 200 B.C. ....**CHOICE 350.00**

Recuay

2342. **RECUAY POURING VESSEL.** A globular figural vessel, with spout extending from headdress. Ridge forms waist, and relief feet beneath. Negative resist painted design of a face with open toothed mouth on back. The red and black paint on brown slipped clay. Restoration to body. 7 1/4"H. c. 100-500 A.D. ....**CHOICE 300.00**

2343. **RECUAY PEDESTALED BOWL.** Resist technique painted with geometric toothy faces, in pink and black on cream slip. Choice condition. 2 1/4"H. 4 3/4"D. ....**CHOICE 300.00**

2344. **RECUAY BOUND PRISONER.** Vessel with bridge handle and spout, in the form of a human figure squatting on his haunches and with hands tied behind back. Figure wears elaborately decorated garment with horizontal stripe bands, a small beanie type cap and triangular pectoral. Has bulging eyes, perforated ears and relief nose. 7 3/4"H., Peru, c. 200 A.D. ....**CHOICE 450.00**

Chancay

2345. **CHANCAY/HUACHO POLYCHROMED FIGURE.** The flat-form terracotta figure still retaining the extensively painted surface. Portrayed with striped cap, relief dot eyes, and nose. The arms painted at chest, and stripes and dots detail body with triangular genital area. On flat feet and custom stand. Figure 7"H. c. 800-1200 A.D. Brown and cream on red-brown clay. ....**CHOICE 300.00**

2346. **BONE TUPUS.** Cloak pin, of extended triangular form and with a carved finial, human head. The human wears ear spools, a decorated yoke and a knee-length tunic. About 7"L. Chancay, Peru, c. 800-1200 A.D.........**SUPERB 250.00**

2347. **WOODEN MUMMY MASK.** Grave marker in the form of a human face painted deep red with white eyes, black pupils, slit mouth, high cheekbones and relief nose. Numerous age cracks and border chips only give the piece more character. Generally exc. cond. Just over 7". Small section reattached at far right with restoration over the cracks and a minor amount of retouching of the red. Chancay, Peru, c. 800-1200 A.D. ....**CHOICE 300.00**

2348. **CHANCAY CUP.** A flared cup on footed base with three-color geometric detail. Reassembled from fragments but complete, with rim chips. 6 3/8"H. 800-1200 A.D. ....**CHOICE 300.00**

Nazca

2349. **NAZCA POLYCHROME GLOBULAR VESSEL.** Decorated with a mythical beast wearing feline mouth mask, crescent headdress, and serpent body dangling trophy heads along all sides. Surface repainted following original design. 8 1/4"H. Spouts repaired. c. 200 A.D. .....**CHOICE 295.00**

2350. **FLARED NAZCA VESSEL.** 4"H., vigorously painted with overlapping borders containing sea animals, trophy heads, and partial cacti tongues, all against dot backgrounds. c. 100-400 A.D. Repaired. ....**CHOICE 300.00**

2351. **FLARED NAZCA VESSEL.** 5 1/2"H., with trophy heads bordering curved base, and slanted weapons. Repaired. c. 100-400 A.D. ....**CHOICE 300.00**

2352. **SMALL NAZCA BOWL.** Round-bottomed dish with flared walls decorated by frieze of hanging chile peppers. Each pepper painted different color, separated into panels, and stem suspended from rim. Yellow, maroon, purple, and red against white ground. 2 1/4"H. 5 3/4"D. Excellent condition. c. 200 A.D. ....**CHOICE 350.00**

2353. **NAZCA BOWL.** The flare-rimmed bowl adorned on overall exterior with two crossed mythical serpents. Each bearing dotted, scaled, and spiked body. Zoomorphic heads terminate each end, with paws in front, and long slippery tongues. Repaired from three large shards, repainted over breaks, but intact. 3 1/8"H. In bright polychrome paint over red-brown slip. c. 400 A.D. ....**SUPERB 500.00**

PRE-COLUMBIAN

2189

2193

2195

2199

2201

2202

2206

2218

2222

2209

2215

2227

PLATE 32

PRE-COLUMBIAN

2230

2232

2237

2238

2243

2249

2269

2272

2275

2282

2287

2311

2291

PLATE 33

2308

2319

2316

2322

2330

2326

2335

2329

2331

2339

2340

2351

2345

PLATE 34

GLOSSARY

Achaemenids: Persian dynasty ruled from 6th century B.C. to 331 B.C.

Acheulean Age: Second period of the Paleolithic Age, named for the archaeological site of Saint Acheul in France.

Adze: Flat cutting tool.

Aegis: Greek breastplate worn by Athena, decorated with a Gorgon's head.

Agate: Irregular colored chalcedony with bands or laurels of reddish brown and greyish white.

Agora: An open area serving as a market or meeting place in a Greek city.

Akkad: Babylonian city, capitol during the Akkadian Dynasty.

Alabaster: White or cream calcite. It is translucent, and often streaked.

Alabastron: Greek long, slim vessel with narrow neck.

Alexandria: Egyptian city founded in 332 B.C.

Amarna Period: High state of Egyptian art during the reign of Akhnaton or Amenophis IV, 1369-1353 B.C.

Amber: Fossilized pine resin.

Amethyst: Violet to deep violet transparent quartz rock.

Amphora: Large Greek two-handled vessel.

Amulet: Object believed to have magical powers.

Anatolia: An ancient region that is now modern Turkey.

Antefix: A decorative facing on the junction between roof and ridge of tiles.

Antiquities: Objects made or fashioned by man in ancient times.

Anubis: Egyptian god with jackal head.

Apollo: Greek sun god.

Appliqué: Ornament or object that can be attached to base material.

Ares: Greek god of war.

Arretine ware: Relief-molded Roman pottery.

Artemis: Greek moon goddess.

Aryans: Indo-Europeans of Central Asia.

Aryballos: Greek bottle with narrow neck.

Astarte: Canaanite goddess of fertility, love, sex, and war.

Aterian Points: North African tool industry dating 75,000-100,000 years ago, noted for squared-off tang from base.

Attica: Easternmost region of Central Greece.

Aurignacian: Stone industry dating 40,000-28,000 years ago, during the Upper Paleolithic period.

Azilian culture: Mesolithic culture in Europe.

Baal: Canaanite deity of storm, lightning, and rain.

Bas-relief: Low relief sculpture.

Basalt: Black igneous rock with small glittering particles.

Blowpipe Process: Glass-making process in which hot glass is gathered at the end of a hollow tube, through which air is blown. This process is still used today.

Boeotia: Region in central Greece.

Bronze: The discovery of smelting was accidental. Bronze was copper alloyed with 5-15% tin.

Bronze Disease: An oxide that eats into a bronze piece and causes the surface to deteriorate. It can be spotted by its light green powder appearance, starting with little pinhead spots and growing to cover the entire object.

Bucchero Ware: Etruscan black pottery, 7th-6th century B.C.

Cameo Glass: Type of glass made by a process in which one white, opaque color layers a design on another opaque surface. The artisan would then cut away the upper portion to create a design.

Canaanites: Semitic people of Eastern Mediterranean in Israel and Syria, 2000-1200 B.C.

Canodic Jars: Egyptian containers for holding human organs.

Cappadocia: Mountainous region in Eastern Turkey.

Carnelian: Red-brown to orange translucent chalcedony rock. Sometimes found with red color.

Cartoche: Egyptian oval containing a royal name in hieroglyphics.

Celts: The Celts were the first Europeans of note in the Temperate Zone lying north of the Alps. In Greek, Keltoi.

Chalcedony: Translucent, creamy white quartz rock with a waxy look.

Chatel Perronian: Stone industry during the Upper Paleolithic named for French cave excavations at Chatel Perron.

Chert: Quartz similar to flint.

Chibcha Culture: Pre-Columbian culture in Columbia and Peru.

Chimu: Peruvian empire.

Chiton: Greek linen dress, shaped to figure.

Chlamys: Greek cloak or mantle fastened on right, and draped over left side of pottery.

Colima: West Mexican culture.

Condition: The degree to which an antiquity has withstood the test of time and weathering.

Copper Age: Beginning 7000 B.C. in Southeastern Turkey, at Diyar Bakr.

Core Vessel: Glass vessel produced by a process which involved pouring melted glass into a clay core, which was in the shape of the desired vessel.

Corinth: Central Greek city.

Coroplats: Greek word for a terracotta craftsman, from the word meaning "dollmaker."

Cro-Magnon: Homo Sapiens of the Aurignacian and Magdalenian periods.

Cuneiform: Earliest system of writing from Mesopotamia.

Cupisnique: Culture variation of Chavin culture in Peru.

Cut Design: Design produced on cooling glass vessels by cutting designs into the still pliable glass. Only master craftsmen could perform this difficult process.

Cycladic: Neolithic culture in the Aegean Sea.

Demeter: Greek goddess of agriculture.

Dionysus: Greek god of wine and fertility.

Diorite: Black and white speckled igneous rock found in Aswan, Egypt.

Dorians: Last of the Northern peoples to enter Greece c. 1100 B.C.

Drehem: City in power during the Third Dynasty of Ur.

Dura-Europus: Major caravan center in Syrian Desert, founded in 300 B.C.

Electrum: A natural alloy of gold and silver.

Enamel: Glassy substance joined to metal.

Ephesus: Large Greek port city in Western Asia Minor.

Eros: Greek god of love.

Faience: A powdered quartz mixed with an adhesive of native soda, fired and glazed. Mainly used on pendants and jewelry.

Feldspar: Green to blue-green opaque potassium aluminum silicate rock.

Fibula: Ancient pin similar in use to a safety pin, although often used for decorative purposes.

Field: Background, or undecorated area.

Filigree: Wires soldered in patterns on a background.

Fortuna: Roman goddess of good luck.

Gandhara: Greco-Buddhist school of art in Afganistan and Pakistan.

Gauls: Celtic tribes.

Gilgamesh: Sumerian-Akkadian hero.

Glaze: Glassy coating on porous pottery.

Granulation: A gold jewelry technique of soldering fine grain gold balls onto gold surfaces in a decoration.

Gravettian: Stone industry dating 28,000-22,000 years ago, during the Upper Paleolithic period.

Gupta: Classical period in Indian art.

Hacilar: Site in Southwest Turkey dating from the 7th millennium B.C.

Halicarnasus: Greek city in Asia Minor, near island of Cos.

Hallstatt Culture: Iron Age culture dating from 1100-500 B.C.

Harran: Upper Mesopotamian city mentioned in the Old Testament during the time of Abraham.

Hattusa: Capital of the Hittite Empire.

Hematite: Solid black iron-oxide rock with metallic sheen.

Hera: Greek sister and wife of Zeus.

Herakles: Greek hero.

Herm: Four-sided marble or bronze pillar with head with extended phallus.

Hermes: Messenger and herald of the gods.

Hieroglyphs: Picture writing of ancient Egypt.

Himation: Greek rectangular-shaped mantle draped over body, worn by both men and women.

Homo Erectus: Early erect man that emerged from Africa 1.8 million years ago or later.

Homo Habilis: Early man dating from 1.9 million years ago that never left Africa.

Homo Neanderthalensis: Known as Neanderthal man, left Africa during the same period as Homo Sapiens.

Homo Sapiens: Modern man.

Huastec: Culture in Veracruz.

Hydria: Tall Greek water jar.

Hyksos: Egyptian period during succession of complex migrations, and conquests of Egypt.

Intaglio: Design incised or engraved into stone gems or metals.

Ionians: Indo-European Greeks who entered Peloponnesus c. 2500 B.C.

Isin: City in Central Lower Mesopotamia.

Isis: Egyptian goddess of the moon, and wife of Osiris.

Jade: Hard, semi-precious mineral found in Turkestan and Middle America.

Jaguar God: Pre-Columbian god of unifying themes.

Jasper: Red, green, or yellow quartz stone sometimes found mottled.

Jericho: One of the oldest cities, first occupied in 8000 B.C.

Jerusalem: One of the world's holiest cities.

Keltoi: Greek word for Celts.

Kish: Sumerian city-state near Babylon.

Kouros: A type of Greek statue depicting a male nude in a frontal pose. Also called an "Apollo" in some older reference books.

Kushan: Kingdom in Afganistan, Pakistan, and Northern India during the 1st-3rd century A.D.

La Tène: Celtic culture in Central and Northern Europe, 5th-1st century B.C.

Lapis Lazuli: Dark blue opaque rock of sodium-aluminum silicate, streaked with white and freckled gold rock.

Larsa: Southern Babylonian city.

Levallois: A stone technology of the Mousterian era, involving the production of flakes with a long, rectangular edge from a highly prepared core.

Limestone: Opaque calcium carbonate rock. Colors range from cream-yellow or pink, to black.

Lost Wax Process: Metal casting method in which a wax model of the object would be made and coated in moist clay. This was baked in a kiln, and as the clay hardened, the wax would melt and pour out through vents in the clay. The wax would then be replaced with molten metal. When the metal cooled and hardened, the clay would be chipped away to reveal the finished product. This method was later also used for making glass objects.

Luristan: Bronze-working culture in the Zagros Mountains between Iraq and Iran, 1100-700 B.C.

Lycia: Ancient kingdom in Southwestern Asia Minor, conquered by Alexander the Great.

Lydia: Kingdom in West-Central Asia Minor.

Magdalenian: Stone industry dating 18,000-12,000 years ago, during the Upper Paleolithic period.

Magna Graecia: Greek colonies of South Italy and Sicily from late 5th century B.C. to 3rd century B.C.

Malachite: Green carbonate of copper used as a pigment in Egypt.

Marduk: Chief god of Babylon.

Milleform and Mosaic Glass Process: Glassmaking process which is accomplished by pounding long threads of glass of contrasting design and color, creating a cross-section design, often with floral, geometric, or animal motifs. After heating, this bundle is called a cane. It is then sliced and used as inlays. These could be used in outer designs of vessels, beads, or inlays.

Mitanni: Kingdom extending to Upper Mesopotamia and Northern Syria.

Mithra: Persian god of light and truth.

Mixtec: Civilization of Mexico.

Mochica: Peruvian culture, 1st century B.C. to 8th century A.D.

Mohenjo-Daro: A main city of Indus Valley civilization.

Mold-Blown Glass: Type of glass manufactured by heating glass, and blowing it into a mold with a pipe.

Molded Vessel: Glass vessel made by a process which involved pouring hot glass into a mold, or a procedure called the lost wax process.

Mousterian Age: This industry overlapped with the Acheulean Age, appearing 200,000 years ago until 40,000 years ago.

Nasca: Coastal Peruvian culture of Inca and Nasca Valley from 200 to 600 A.D.

Natufian: Palestinian Neolithic culture, 9th-5th millennium B.C.

Nayarit: Pre-Columbian Western Mexican culture, 300-900 A.D.

Nike: Greek goddess of victory.

Nimrud: One of the great capitals of the Assyrian Empire.

Nineveh: Capital of Neo-Assyrian Empire.

Nippur: City of Central Babylonia.

Obsidian: Natural translucent, shiny, black volcanic glass.

Oldowan Age: Earliest period of the Paleolithic Age, dating 2.5 million years ago.

Olmec: Oldest civilization of New World.

Osiris: Major Egyptian God identified with death and resurrection.

Palmette: Palm leaf motif.

Papyrus: Egyptian Nile reed used in making ancient paper.

Parian Marble: Very fine creamy white marble quarried on the Greek island of Paros.

Patina: Green or blue film found on ancient bronze.

Pectoral: Ornament worn on the breast.

Pella: Macedonian Greek city capital.

Petasos: Greek wide-brimmed felt hat.

Plastic: Molded or modeled three-dimensional decoration on vases.

Polos: Tall Greek cylindrical headdress worn by goddesses.

Porphyry: Term used for igneous rocks with a solid-colored matrix with scattered colored crystals.

Poseidon: Greek god of sea, water, and earthquakes.

Pottery: Originated in Central Asia around 8200 B.C. at Ulan Bator.

Protome: Decorative device attached to vessels.

Ptolemies: Hellenistic dynasty who ruled Egypt.

Quality: The original fineness of craftsmanship with which an antiquity was made.

Ra: Egyptian sun god.

Reconstruction: The act of taking a broken antiquity and putting the pieces back together, usually without adding any new ones.

Recuay: Northern Peruvian culture.

Reserve: Unpainted area on vase.

Restoration: The act of enhancing the look and value of an antiquity by replacing or adding missing parts.

Rhyton: Greek drinking cup with body in form of animal's head.

Rock Crystal: Hard, translucent, glass-like, colorless quartz rock.

Saccos: Greek cloth covering for women's hair.

Sard: Red-brown translucent chalcedony. Darker than carnelian.

Sargon: Founder and ruler of the city of Akkad.

Schist: A hard, crystalline sedimentary rock colored in shades of grey.

Scythians: Mounted warlike peoples from the Russian steppes.

Seleucids: Greek dynasty, based in Syria, from 312-64 B.C.

Serpentine: Dark green to black opaque to semi-translucent magnesium silicate rock.

Sin: Moon god of Babylonia and Assyria.

Soapstone: See steatite.

Solutrean: Stone industry dating 21,000-19,000 years ago, during the Upper Paleolithic period.

Steatite (Soapstone): Grey to black opaque magnesium silicate rock.

Stele: Upright stone slab sometimes used as grave marker.

Sthendone: Greek women's headband.

Strigil: Curved blade used to scrape oil and grime from skin.

Stylus: Sharp instrument for writing on wax tablet.

Toltec: Mexican civilization from 10th-12th century A.D.

Tondo: Circular decorative field in interior of cup or plate.

Turquoise: Sky blue or blue-green opaque aluminum phosphate rock.

Tyre: Phoenician island city.

Ugarit: Canaanite city-state in coastal Northern Syria.

Upper Paleolithic: The last Paleolithic era, 40,000-12,000 years ago.

Urartu: Kingdom centered around Lake Uan.

Villanovan: North Central Italy culture in transition from Bronze Age to Iron Age, 1000-750 B.C.

Volute: Scroll-like ornamental motif.

Votive Figures: Terracottas offered to a deity in a temple or a shrine.

Ware: A group of vases decorated in a certain technique.

Zapotec: Civilization in Mexican state of Oaxaca.

Zeus: Greek supreme god of Heaven.

SELECT
BIBLIOGRAPHY

GENERAL ANTIQUITIES

Cesnola, Louis P.D. *Cesnola Collection of Cypriote Antiquities.* 3 Volumes. Boston: 1885.

Ede. *Collecting Antiquities, an Introductory Guide.* London: 1975.

Encyclopedia Italiana. *Encyclopedia Dell'arte Antica Classica e Orientale.* 12 Volumes. Roma: 1958.

Herbert, Kevin. *Ancient Art in Bowdoin College.* Cambridge, MA: 1964.

Kurtz, Seymour. *The World Guide to Antiquities.* London: 1975.

Winkelmann, J. *Histoire de l'Art Chez les Anciens.* 3 Volumes. Paris.

TOOLS AND WEAPONS

Aharoni, Y. *Investigations at Lachish, The Sanctuary and the Residency, Lachish V.* Tel Aviv: 1975.

Azarday, G. *Urartian Art and Artifacts, A Chronological Study.* Berkeley: 1968.

Besancon, J. *Tableaux de Prehistoric L. Bandar in Pdlorient.*

Boisgiarard-Heechern. *The Boisgiarard-Heechern Auction- Collection X.* 1980.

Ceram, C.W. *The Secret of the Hittites.* New York: 1955.

DeShayes. *Les Qurils de Bronze, de Indus au Danube.*

Giarod & Bate. *The Stonage of Mt. Carmel.*

Goddard, Andre. *Les Bronzes du Luristan.* Paris: 1931.

Hamilton, F.W. *Exhibition of Ancient Persian Bronzes, Bumford Collection.* Oxford: 1966.

Hancock, P.S.P. *The Archaeology of the Holy Land.* London: 1916.

Hayes, William C. *The Sceptre of Egypt.* Greenwich, CT: 1953.

Johnson & Shreeve. *Lucy's Child.*

Kenyon Kathleen M. *Archaeology in the Holy Land.* London: 1960.

Koldewey, Robert. *Das Wieder Ersthende Babylon.* Liepzig: 1913.

Kozloff, Arielle. *The First 4000 Years: Ratner Collection of Judaean Antiquities.* Cleveland: 1978.

MacGregor, A. *Antiquities from Europe and the Near East in the Collection of the Lord McAlpine of West Green.* 1987.

MacKenzie, Duncan. *Palestine Exploration Fund 1912-1913. Excavations at Beth Shemesh.*

Malloy. A. *Weapons.* South Salem, NY: 1993.

Minns. *Scythians and Greeks.* Cambridge, England: 1913.

Moorey, P.R.S. *Catalogue of the Ancient Persian Bronzes in the Ashmolean Museum.* Oxford: 1971.

Muscarella, O.W. *Bronze and Iron, Ancient Near Eastern Artifacts in the Metropolitan Museum of Art.* New York.

Petrie, Sir W.M.F. *Tools and Weapons.* London: 1917.

___. *Prehistoric Egypt.* British School of Archaeology in Egypt. London: 1921.

Phillips, E.D. *The Mongols.* 1969.

Read, Cecil. *British Museum Guide of Antiquities of the Stone Age.* London: 1911.

Rostbvtzoff, M.I. *The Excavations at Dura-Europus.* Fifth Season Work, Oct. 1931-Mar. 1932, New Haven: 1934.

Savory, H.N. *Spain and Portugal.* 1968.

Smith. Cecil. *British Museum Guide to Greek and Roman Life.* London: 1908.

Watson, G.R. *The Roman Soldier.* 1969.

Wheeler, R.E.M. *Medieval Catalogue.* London Museum, London: 1940.

Wilkes, J. *The Roman Army.* 1972.

ANCIENT GLASS

Auth, Susan H. *Ancient Glass at the Newark Museum.* New Jersey: 1976.

Cambridge University. *Glass at the FitzWilliam Museum.* Cambridge University Press: 1978.

Goldstein, S. *Pre-Roman and Early Roman Glass in the Corning Museum of Glass.* Corning: 1979.

Hayes, John W. *Roman and Pre-Roman Glass in the Royal Ontario Museum.* 1975.

Matheson, Susan B. *Ancient Glass in the Yale University Art Gallery.* New Haven: 1980.

Neuberg, Fredric. *Ancient Glass.* Toronto: 1962.

Oliver, Andrew. *Ancient Glass in the Carnegie Museum of Natural History.* Pittsburgh: 1980.

Sothby Parke-Bernet & Co. *The Constable-Maxwell Collection of Ancient Glass.* London: 1979.

LAMPS

Bailey, D.M. *A Catalogue of the Lamps in the British Museum I, Greek, Hellenistic, Roman Pottery Lamps.* London: 1975.
___. *A Catalogue of the Lamps in the British Museum, II, Roman Lamps Made in Italy.* London: 1980.
Baur, P.V.C. *Excavations at Dura-Europus, Final Report IV, Part III, The Lamps.* New Haven.
Breneau, P. *Exploration Arceologique de Delos.* Paris: 1965.
Hayes, J.W. *Ancient Lamps in the Royal Ontario Museum.* Toronto: 1980.
Howland, R. *The Athenian Agora, Vol. IV, Greek Lamps and Their Survivals.* Princeton.
Perlzwig, J. *The Athenian Agora, Vol. VII, Lamps of the Roman Period.* Princeton: 1961.
Petrie, Sir W.M.F. *Roman Ehnasya.* London: 1905.
Rosenthal, R. & Swan, R. *Ancient Lamps in the Schloessinger Collection.* Jerusalem: 1978.
Szentleleky, T. *Ancient Lamps.* Cairo: 1969.
Tushingham, A.D. *Excavations in Jerusalem 1961-67, Vol. I.* Toronto: 1985.

ANCIENT JEWELRY

Boardman, John. *Greek Gems and Finger Rings.* New York.
___. *Ionides Collection.*
Brandt, Elfriede & Schmidt, Evamaria. *Antike Gemmen in Deutschen Sammlungen. Staatliche.* Munchen: 1970.
Briglia, Laura. *Catalogo della Oreficierie de la Museo Nazionale di Napoli.* Roma: 1941.
Florange, Jules. *Gemmes Antiques de la Collection Duval.* Geneve: 1925.
Giselam, Richter. *Engraved Gems of the Romans.* London: 1971.
Gramatopol, Mihai. *Les Pierre Gravees du Cabinet Numismatique de I' Academie, Romanine.* Bruxelles: 1974.
Greifenhagen, A. *Schmuckarbeiten in Edelmetall.* Museen Berlin: 1975.
Hackens, Tony. *Rhode Island School of Design: Classical Jewelry.* Providence: 1976.
Hayes, William C. *The Sceptre of Egypt, Vol. II.* Greenwich, CT: 1959.
Henig, Martin. *Corpus of Engraved Gemstones from British Sites, Part II.* Oxford: 1974.
___. *Lewis Collection of Gemstones.* Oxford: 1975.
Henkel, Dr. Friedrich. *Die Rom. Fingerringe dier Rhienlande.* Berlin: 1913.
Hoffman, Herbert, and Davidson, Patricia. *Greek Gold.* Boston: 1965.
Maaskant-Kleinbrindt, Marianne. *Royal Coin Cabinet, the Hague.* Netherlands: 1978.
Marshel, F.H. *Catalogue of Finer Rings in the British Museum.* Oxford: 1968.
Maxwell-Hyslop, K.R. *Western Asiatic Jewelry c. 3000-612 B.C.* London: 1971.
Park Hurst Collection. Oberlin College, Guttman.
Peirides. *Jewelry in the Cyprus Museum.*
Ricci, Seymour de. *Guilhov Collection.* Paris: 1912.
Righetti, Romolo. *Gemme e Cammei delle Collezione Comonali.* Roma: 1955.
Rudolph, Burton Y. *Ancient Jewelry from the Collection of B.Y. Berry.* Bloomington, IN: 1965.
Siviero. *Gli Ori e Le Ambre del Museo Nazionale di Napoli.*
Spink, M. *Islamic Jewelry.* London: 1986.
Williams. *Catalogue of Egyptian Antiquities, Gold and Silver Jewelry and Related Objects.* New York Historical Society.

ANCIENT BRONZE FIBULAE

Bouchier, S. *Vienne Bronzes Antiques.* Paris: 1971.
Ettinger, E. *Die Romischen Fibelin in Der Schwiez.* Bern: 1973.
Hattatt, R. *Ancient and Romano-British Brooches.* Dorset: 1982.
Sotheby. *Various Auction Sale Catalogues.*
Sundwall. *Die Alteren Italischen Fibelin.*

EARLY MAN

Arribas, Antonio. *The Iberians.* NY: 1964.
Barfield, Lawrence. *Northern Italy Before Rome.* NY: 1971.
Beitz, Berthold. *Historische Schätze aus der Sowjet Union.* Essen: 1967.
Berciu, Dumitru. *Ancient Peoples and Places.* Romania/NY: 1967.
Bordes, François. *The Old Stone Age.* trans. Weidenfeld, Hampshire: 1968.
Chadwick, Nora K. *Celtic Britain.* NY: 1963.

EARLY MAN (cont.)

Dannheimer, Herman. *Prähistorische Staatssammlung.* München: 1976.

Forman, W. & B., & Poulik, Josef. *Prehistoric Art.* trans. Samsour, R.F. London.

Gibson, Alex. *Neolithic and Early Bronze Age Pottery.* Aylesbury: 1986.

Hall, H.R. *The Civilization of Greece in the Bronze Age.* New York: 1923.

Hencken, Hugh. *Tarquinia and Etruscan Origins.* 1968: NY.

Hoernes, Moritz. *Urgeschichte der Bildenden Kunst in Europa.* Wien: 1925.

Isaksson, Olou. *Ori Uichinghi.* Roma: 1969.

Jazdzewski, Konrad. *Ancient Peoples and Places.* Poland/NY: 1965.

Joffroy, R. *The Gauls.* British Museum, London.

Johanson, Donald, & Edgar, Blake. *From Lucy to Language.* NY: 1996.

__. *Lucy's Child: The Discovery of a Human Ancestor.* NY: 1989.

Kimmig, Von Wolfgang. *Vorzeit an Rhein und Donau.* Lindau: 1958.

Laing, Lloyd. *Later Celtic Art in Britain and Ireland.* Aylesbury: 1987.

Leakey, Mary D. *Olduvai Gorge: Excavations in Beds I and II.* Cambridge: 1960-63.

MacGregor, Arthur, ed. *Antiquities from Europe and the Near East in the Collection of Lord McAlpine of West Green.* Oxford: 1987.

McBurney. *The Stone Age of Northern Africa.* London: 1960.

Megaw, J.V.S. *Art of the European Iron Age.* NY: 1970.

Megaw, Ruth & Vincent. *Early Celtic Art in Britain and Ireland.* Aylesbury: 1986.

Merriman, Nick. *Early Humans.* London: 1989.

Neustupny, E. & J. *Ancient Peoples and Places.* Czechoslovakia/NY: 1961.

Nicholson, Susan M. *Catalogue of the Prehistoric Metalwork in Merseyside County Museums.* Liverpool: 1980.

Piggott, Stuart. *Ancient Europe.* Chicago: 1965.

__. *The Druids.* NY: 1968.

Powell, T.G.E. *The Celts.* NY: 1958.

__. *Prehistoric Art.* NY: 1966.

Pryor, Francis. *A Catalogue of British and Irish Prehistoric Bronzes in the R.O.M.* Royal Ontario Museum, Ontario: 1980.

Read, Charles. *A Guide to the Antiquities of the Stone Age.* 2nd edition. British Museum, London: 1911.

__. *A Guide to the Antiquities of the Early Iron Age.* British Museum, London: 1905.

__. *A Guide to the Antiquities of the Bronze Age.* British Museum, London: 1920.

Ross, Ann. *Pagan Celtic Britain.* London: 1967.

Savory, H.N. *Guide Catalogue of the Bronze Age Collections.* National Museum of Wages, Cardiff: 1980.

__. *Guide Catalogue of the Early Iron Age Collections.* National Museum of Wages, Cardiff: 1976.

__. *Spain and Portugal, the Prehistory of the Iberian Peninsula.* NY: 1968.

Smith, Rev. Frederick. *The Stone Ages in North Britain and Ireland.* London: 1909.

Stern, Philip van Doren. *Prehistoric Europe.* NY: 1969.

Trump, David H. *Central and Southern Italy Before Rome.* NY: 1965.

Tyler, John M. *The New Stone Age in Northern Europe.* NY: 1921.

Wheeler, R.E.M. *Prehistoric and Roman Wales.* Oxford: 1925.

Wilson, Thomas. *Prehistoric Art; or the Origin of Art as Manifested in the Works of Prehistoric Man.* Smithsonian Institution, Washington: 1898.

WESTERN ASIATIC ART

Albright, W.F. *The Archaeology of Palestine.* 1949, rev. 1960.

Amiet, P. *Art of the Ancient Near East.* New York: 1980.

__. *Elam.* Auver-sur-Oise: 1966.

Barrelet, M.T. *Figurines et Reliefs en Terre Cuite de la Mesopotamie Antique.* Paris.

Colledge, M.A.R. *The Parthians.* New York: 1967.

Goff, B.L. *Symbols of Ancient Mesopotamia.* New Haven: 1963.

Kozloff, A. *Animals in Ancient Art from the Leo Mildenberg Collection.* Cleveland: 1981.

Legrain. *Terracottas from Nippur.* University of Penn., The University Museum, Babylonian Section, Vol. XVI.

Mackay, E. *Sumerian Palace and the "A" Cemetery at Kish, Part II.* Field Museum of Natural History, Chicago: 1931.

__. *Reports of Excavations at Jemdet Nasr, Iraq.* Field Museum of Natural History, Chicago: 1931.

Maxwell-Hyslop, K.R. *Western Asiatic Jewelry, c. 300-612 B.C.* London: 1971.

Moorey P.R.S. *Catalogue of the Ancient Persian Bronzes in the Ashmolean Museum.* Oxford: 1971.

Muscarella, O.W. *Ladders to Heaven.* Toronto: 1981.

WESTERN ASIATIC ART (cont.)

__. *Bronze and Iron, Ancient Near Eastern Artifacts in the Metropolitan Museum of Art*. New York: 1988.

Oppenheim, A. Leo. *Ancient Mesopotamia, Portrait of a Dead Civilization*. Chicago: 1964.

Parrot, A. *Tello-Vingt Campagnes de Fouilles 1877-1933*. Paris: 1948.

Pope, A.V. & Ackerman, P. *A Survey of Persian Art*. London: 1958.

Schmandt-Besserat, D. *Reckoning Before Writing*. Archaeology Magazine, May/June. 1979.

Schmidt, E.F. *Alishar Mound, 1927-1929*.

__. *Excavations at Tepe Hissar, Iran 1931-1933*. Philadelphia: 1937.

Sotheby & Co. *Catalogue of Ancient Iranian Bronzes*. November, 1975.

Terrace. *Art of Ancient Near East*. Museum of Fine Arts, Boston.

Van Buren, E.D. *Clay Figurines of Babylonia and Assyria, Vol. 16*. New York: 1930.

Volk, J.G. *Iranian Art from the 5th Millennium B.C. to the 7th Century A.D.* Habib Anavian Collection.

WESTERN ASIATIC SEALS

Amiet, P. *La Glyptique Mesopotamienne Archaique*. Paris: 1980.

__. *Glyptische Susienne*. Paris: 1972.

Bismachi, F. *Iraq Museum*. Baghdad: 1976.

Borowski, Elie. *Cylindres et Cachets Orientaux, Tome I*. Ascona, Mésopotamie: 1947.

Buchanan, Briggs. *Seals in the Ashmolean Museum, Vol. I*. Oxford: 1966.

__. *Catalogue of Ancient Near Eastern Seals in the Ashmolean Museum II, The Prehistoric Stamp Seals*. Oxford: 1984.

__. *Seals in the Yale Babylonian Collection*. New Haven: 1981.

Collon, Dominique. *Catalogue of the Western Asiatic Seals in the British Museum, Vol. II*. London: 1982.

__. *First Impressions: Cylinder Seals in the Ancient Near East*. Chicago: 1987.

__. *Catalogue of the Western Asiatic Seals in the British Museum, Cylinder Seals III, Isin-Larsa and Old Babylonian Periods*. London: 1986.

DeLaporte, Louis. *Catalogue des Cylindres Orientaux et des Cachets Assyro-Babyloniens, Perses et Syro-Cappadociens de la Bibliothèqué Nationale*. Paris: 1910.

Eisen, Gustavus A. *Ancient Oriental Cylinder and Other Seals with a Description of the Collection of Mrs. William H. Moore*. Chicago: 1940.

Forte, Elizabeth Williams. *Ancient Near Eastern Seals, Mrs. William H. Moore*. NY: 1976.

Frankfurt, H. *Cylinder Seals*. 1939.

__. *Stratfield Cylinder Seals from the Diyala Region*. University of Chicago Oriental Inst., Vol. LXXII, Chicago: 1955.

Goff, Beatrice Laura. *Symbols of Prehistoric Mesopotamia*. Yale: 1963.

Homès-Fredericq, H. *Le Cachets Mésopotamiens Proto Historiques*. Leiden: 1970.

Kjaerum, Poul. *Kailaka/Dilmun, Vol I:I The Stamp and Cylinder Seals*. Aarhus: 1983.

Kohl, Philip. *Bronze Age Civilization of Central Asia*. New York: 1981.

Legrian, Leon. *The Culture of the Babylonians from Their Seals in the Collections of the Museum*. University of Pennsylvania, Philadelphia: 1925.

__. *Gem Cutters in Ancient Ur, Museum Journal*. Philadelphia: 1929.

__. *Ur Excavations, Vol. III, Archaic Seal-Impressions*. NY: 1936.

Marcus, Michelle I. *Emblems of Identity and Prestige: the Seals and Sealings from Hasanlu, Iran*. Philadelphia: 1996.

Masson, M. & Kiiatkina, T.P. *Man at the Dawn of Civilization: The Bronze Age Civilization of Central Asia*. New York: 1981.

Menant, M. Joachim. *Recherches sur la Glyptique Orientale, I Cylinders de la Chaldée II, Cylinders de l'Assyrie*. 2 vols. Paris: 1883 and 1886.

Muscarella, O.W. *Ladders to Heaven*. Toronto: 1981.

Nougayrol, J. *Les Palais Royal d'Ugarit*. Paris: 1955-56.

Novack, M. *Mark of Ancient Man*. Brooklyn Museum, New York: 1975.

Pitman, H. *Ancient Art in Miniature*. Metropolitan Museum of Art, New York: 1984.

Porada, Edith. *Corpus of Ancient Near Eastern Seals in North American Collections*. Washington, D.C.: 1948.

__. *Seal Impressions of Nuzi, American Schools of Oriental Research, Vol. XXIV*. Baltimore: 1947.

__., ed. *Ancient Art in Seals*. Princeton: 1980.

Ravn, O.E. *Cylinder Seals and Impressions in the Danish National Museum*. Copenhagen: 1960.

Rowe, A. *Catalogue of Egyptian Scarabs*. Cairo: 1936.

Schaeffer-Forrer, Claude F.A. *Corpus I des Cylindres - Sceaux de Ras Shamra - Ugarit et d'Enkomi - Alash*. Paris: 1983.

Teissier, B. *Ancient Near Eastern Cylinder Seals: Marcopoli Collection*. Beverly Hills, CA.

von der Osten, H.H. *Altorientalische Siegelsteine der Sammlung Hans Silvius von Aulock*. Uppsala: 1957.

__. *Ancient Oriental Seals in the Collection of Mr. Edward T. Newell*. Chicago.

WESTERN ASIATIC SEALS (cont.)

Ward, William Hayes. *The Seal Cylinders of Western Asia.* Washington: 1916.

Wiseman, D.J. *Catalogue of the Western Asiatic Seals in the British Museum.* London: 1962.

HOLY LAND

Ackerman, A. & Braunstein, S. *Israel in Antiquity.* Jewish Museum, New York: 1982.

Aharoni, Yohanan. *Investigations at Lachish.* Tel Aviv: 1975.

Albright, William Foxwell. *From the Lands of the Bible: Art and Artifacts.* NY: 1968.

Amiran, R. *Ancient Pottery of the Holy Land.* Camden, NY: 1970.

Ben-Tor, Ammon. *Archaeology of Ancient Israel.* Israel: 1992.

__. *Two Burial Caves...* Jerusalem: 1975.

Diringer, D. *The Alphabet.* New York: 1948.

__. *Writing.* New York: 1967.

Douglas, J.D., et al., eds. *The Illustrated Bible Dictionary.* Leicestger, UK: 1980.

Finegan, Jack. *The Archaeology of the New Testament.* Princeton: 1972.

Grant, E. *Beth Shemesh.* Haverford: 1929.

Hayes, J.W. *Roman Pottery in the Royal Ontario Museum.* Toronto: 1976.

Hestrin, Ruth. *The Philistines and Other Sea Peoples.* Jerusalem: 1970.

Horn, H.G. & Ruger, C. *Die Numider.* Köln: 1979.

James, F. *The Iron Age at Beth Shan.* Philadelphia: 1966.

Kenyon, K. *Archaeology in the Holy Land.* London: 1979.

MacKenzie, D. *Palestine Exploration Fund Annual 1912-1913.* London: 1913.

Negev, A. *Archaeological Encyclopedia of the Holy Land.* New York: 1972.

Ornan, Tallay. *A Man and His Land, Highlights from the Moshe Dayan Collection.* Jerusalem: 1980.

Petrie, W.M. Flinders. *Researches in Sinai.* London: 1906.

Pritchard, J. *Tell es-Sa'idihey: Excavations on the Tell, 1964-1966.* Philadelphia: 1985.

Rosenthal, R., and Sivan, R. *Ancient Lamps in the Schloessinger Collection.* Jerusalem: 1978.

Skupinska-Lovset, I. *The Ustinov Collection: The Palestinian Pottery.* Oslo: 1976.

Tushingham, A.D. *The Excavations at Dibon (Dhibân) in Moab: The Third Campaign, 1952-3.* Cambridge: 1972.

__. *Excavations in Jerusalem, 1961-67, Vol I.* Toronto: 1985.

Wright, G. Ernest. *Biblical Archaeology.* Philadelphia: 1962.

Yadin, Y. *Hazor.* New York: 1975.

CENTRAL ASIA

Hambly, Gavin. *Central Asia.* NY: 1966.

Jettmar, K. *Art of the Steppes.* Baden-Baden: 1967.

Kohl, Philip L., ed. *Bronze Age Civilization of Central Asia.* Armonk, NY: 1946.

Musée, Guimet. *L' art du Gandhâra et de l'Asa Centrale.* Paris: 1958-59.

Rice, Tamara Talbot. *Ancient Arts of Central Asia.* NY: 1965.

Starr, Richard F.S. *Indus Valley Painted Pottery.* Princeton, 1941.

EGYPT

Andrews, Carol. *Amulets of Ancient Egypt.* London, 1994.

Blanchard, R.H. *Handbook of Egyptian Gods and Mummy Amulets.* Cairo: 1909.

Breasted, James Henry Jr. *Egyptian Servant Statues.* Washington: 1948.

British Museum. *Introductory Guide to Egyptian Collections in the British Museum.* London: 1964.

Budge, E.A. Wallis. *Collection of Egyptian Antiquities.* Lady Meux, London: 1896.

__. *The Mummy.* Cambridge: 1894.

Burlington Fine Arts Club. *Catalogue of an Exhibition of Ancient Egyptian Art.* London: 1922.

Carlsberg. *La Glyptothèque NY, La Collection Égyptienne par Maria Mongeasen.* Copenhague: 1930.

Cooney, J.D. *Five Years Collecting Egyptian Art, 1951-1956.* Brooklyn: Rep. 1969.

__. *Late Egyptian Art and Coptic Art.* Brooklyn Museum, New York: 1943.

Ede, C. *Various Sale Catalogues.*

El-Khouli, Ali. *Egyptian Stone Vessels: Predynastic Period to Dynasty III, 3 Vol..* Mainz am Rhein: 1978.

Emery, Walter B. *Nubian Treasure.* London: 1948.

EGYPT (cont.)

Graindor, Paul. *Terre Cuites de l'Egypte Gréco-Romaine.* Antwerpen, 1939.
Hall, H.R. *Catalogue of Egyptian Scarabs in the British Museum.* London: 1943.
Hayes, W. *Sceptre of Egypt, Vol. II.* Greenwich: 1959.
Heick, *Agyptens Aufstieg fur Weltmacht.*
Hilton Price, F.G. *A Catalogue of the Egyptian Collection.* London: 1897.
Hornemann, Bodil. *Types of Ancient Egyptian Statuary.* Denmark, 1951.
Hornung, E. & Staehelin, E. *Skarabaen und Andere Seigel Amulette aus Basler Sammlungen.*
Kaufmann, C.M. *Agyptische Terrakotten.* Cairo: 1913.
Kelley, Allyn L. *The Pottery of Ancient Egypt.* Toronto: 1976.
Louvre, Au Musée du. *Les Objets de Toilette Egyptiens, Par J. Vandier d'Abbadie.* Paris: 1972.
Malloy, A. *Auction Catalogue.* Summer, 1980.
Matouk, F.S. *Corpus de Scarabee.* Beyrouth: 1971.
Museum of Fine Arts, Boston. *Egypt's Golden Age: The Art of Living in the New Kingdom 1558-1085 B.C.* Boston.
NFA Classical Auctions, Inc. *Scarabs and Design Amulets.* NY: 1991.
Noblecourt. *Un Siede Defouilles Francaeses Egypte 1880-1890.*
Petrie, Sir W.M.F. *Amulets.* London: 1914.
__. *Buttons and Design Scarabs.* London: 1925.
__. *Glass Stamps and Weights: Ancient Weights and Measures.* Egypt: 1926.
__. *Historical Scarabs.* London: 1889.
__. *Prehistoric Egypt.* London: 1921.
__. *Scarabs and Cylinders.* London: 1917.
__. *Shabtis.* London, 1935.
__. *Stone and Metal Vases.* London: 1925.
Pier, Garrett Chatfield. *Egyptian Antiquities in the Pier Collection.* Chicago: 1906.
Raphael, Max. *Prehistoric Pottery and Civilization in Egypt.* Washington: 1947.
Reisner, M.G.A. *Catalogue Génerál des Antiquités Égyptiennes du Musée du Caire.* Caire: 1958.
Riefstahl, E. *Ancient Egyptian Glass and Glazes in the Brooklyn Museum.* Brooklyn: 1968.
Rowe, Alan. *A Catalogue of Egyptian Scarabs, Scaraboids, Seals, and Amulets in the Palestine Archaeological Museum.* Cairo: 1936.
Schneider, H. *Shabtis.* Netherlands: 1977.
Scott, Gerry D., III. *Ancient Egyptian Art at Yale.* New Haven: 1986.
Sotheby, Wilkinson and Hodge. *Catalogue of the MacGregor Collection of Egyptian Antiquities.* London: Sale 6-26-1972.
Steindorff, G. *Catalogue of the Egyptian Sculpture in the Walters Art Gallery.* Baltimore.
Ward, John. 77ie *Sacred Beetle.* San Diego: 1902.
Williams. *Catalogue of Egyptian Antiquities, Gold and Silver Jewelry and Related Objects.* New York Historical Soc.
Zayed, Abd El Hamid. *Egyptian Antiquities.* Cairo: 1962.

GREEK

American School of Classical Studies. *Black and Plain Pottery, Vol. XII.* Princeton. (Athenian Agora)
Beazley, J.D. *Attic Black Figure Vases, Vol. I.* Oxford: 1963.
__. *Etruscan Vase Painting.* Oxford: 1974.
Boardman, J. *Greek Gems and Finger Rings.* New York.
__. *Ionides Collection.*
Brandt, E. & Schmidt, E. *Antike Gemmen In Deutschen Sammlungen.* Munich: 1970.
Briglia, L. *Catalogo della Oreficiere-de Museo Nazionale di Napoli.* Rome: 1941.
Cesnola, L.P. *Cesnola Collection of Cypriot Art in the Metropolitan Museum of Art.* New York: 1984.
Christie's. *Greek, Etruscan, and South Italian Vases: The Castle Ashby Vases.* London: 1980.
Corpus Vasorum Antiquorum. Various museums.
Ede, C. Various price lists.
Florange, J. *Gemmes Antiques de la Collection Duval.* Geneva: 1925.
Hackens, Tony. *Rhode Island School of Design: Classical Jewelry.* Providence: 1976.
Henig, M. *Lewis Collection of Gemstones.* Oxford: 1975.
Hayes, J.W. *Etruscan and Italic Pottery in the Royal Ontario Museum.* Toronto: 1985. (ROM)
__. *Greek and Italian Pottery in the Royal Ontario Museum.* Toronto: 1984. (ROM)
Higgins, R.A. *Terracottas in the British Museum.* Oxford: 1954.
Hoffman, Herbert. *Collecting Greek Antiquities.* NY: 1971.
Hoffman, H. & Davidson, P. *Greek Gold.* Boston: 1965.

GREEK (cont.)

Hornbostel, W. *Aus Grabern und Heiligtumern.* Hamburg: 1980.

Johnson, F.P. *Farwell Collection.* Massachusetts: 1953.

Kaufman, C.M. *Agyptische Terrakotten der Griechisch-Romischen und Koplischen Epoch.* Cairo: 1913.

Kurtz, D.C. *Athenian White Lekythoi.* Oxford: 1975.

Luilles. *Vergdette Terrakotta-Apliken aus Tarent.*

Malloy. *Auction Catalogue.* Summer 1977.

Marshall, F.H. *Catalogue of Finer Rings in the British Museum.* Oxford: 1968.

Mayo. *Vases from Magna Graecia.*

Mergazora, L. *I Vasi a Vernice Nera Della Collezione H.A. Di Milano.* Milan: 1971.

Moon. *Greek Vase Painting in Midwestern Collections.*

Oberleitner. *Kunshistorisches Museum.* Vienna.

Oberlin College. *Parkhurst Collection.* Oberlin, Guttman.

Peirides. *Jewelry in the Cyprus Museum.*

Richter, Gisela M.A. *The Metropolitan Museum of Art: Handbook of the Classical Collection.* NY: 1927.

Robinson, H.S. *Atheidan Agora Vol. I.* Princeton: 1959.

Rudolph, B.Y. *Ancient Jewelry from the Collection of B.Y. Berry.* Bloomington: 1965.

Sieveking, J. *Die Terrakotta der Sammlung Loeb Vol. I and II.* Munich: 1916.

Siviero, G. *Li Ori e le Ambre del Museo Nazionale di Napoli.*

Sotheby & Co. *Fortuna Sale.* 1970.

Thomson, D.B. *The Terracotta Figurines of the Hellenistic Period.* Princeton: 1963.

Trendall, A.D. *Red Figure Vases of Lucania, Campania and Sicily.* Oxford: 1967.

Van Ingen. *Figurines from Seleucia in the Tigris.* Ann Arbor: 1939.

GREEK TERRACOTTA

Higgins, R.A. *Terracottas in the British Museum.* Oxford: 1954.

Kaufman, Carl Maria. *Agyptische Terrakotten der Griechisch-Romischen und Koptischen Epoch.* Cairo: 1913.

Robinson, Henry S. *Athenian Agora Vol I.* Princeton: 1959.

Sieveking, Johannes. *Die Terrakotta der Sammlung Loeb Vol. I and II.* Munchen: 1916.

Thompson, Dorothy Burr. *The Terracotta Figurines of the Hellenistic Period.* Princeton: 1963.

Van Ingen, Whilelmina. *Figurines from Seleucia in the Tigris.* Ann Arbor: 1939.

ROMAN

Auth, S.H. *Ancient Glass at the Newark Museum.* New Jersey: 1976.

British Museum. *Guide to Antiquities of Roman Britain.* London: 1964.

__. *A Guide to the Exhibition Illustrating Greek and Roman Life.* British Museum, London: 1908.

Boardman, John. *Ionides Collection.*

Boucher, S. *Vienne Bronzes Antiques.* Paris: 1971.

__. *Bronzes Ronains.* Lyon: 1973.

Brandt, E. & Schmidt, E. *Antike Gemmen In Deutschen Sammlungen.* Munich: 1970.

Briglia, L. *Catalogo delle Oreficierie-de Museo Nazionale di Napoli.* Rome: 1941.

Cambridge University. *Glass at the FitzWilliam Museum.* Cambridge: 1978.

Chase, G. *Arreline Pottery.* Museum of Fine Arts, Boston: 1916.

DeRicci, S. *Guilhov Collection.* Paris: 1912.

Ettinger, E. *Die Romischen Fibelin in der Schweiz.* Beni: 1973.

Florange, J. *Gemmes Antiques de la Collection Duval.* Geneva: 1925.

Giselam, R. *Engraved Gems of the Romans.* London 1971.

Goldstein, S. *Pre-Roman and Early Roman Glass in the Corning Museum of Glass.* Corning: 1979.

Greifenhagen, A. *Schmuckarbeiten in Edelimetall, Museen Berlin.* 1975.

Grematopol, N. *Les Pierre Gravees du Cabinet Numismatique de I'Academie Romanine.* Brussels: 1974.

Gusman. *Pompeii, La- Ville-Les Moeur-Les Arts.*

Hackens, Tony. *Rhode Island School of Design: Classical Jewelry.* Providence: 1976.

Hattatt, R. *Ancient and Romano-British Brooches.* Dorset: 1982.

Hayes, J.W. *Greek, Roman and Related Metalwork in the Royal Ontario Museum.* Toronto: 1994. (ROM)

__. *Roman and Pre-Roman Glass in the Royal Ontario Museum.* Toronto: 1975. (ROM)

ROMAN (cont.)

Henig, M. *Corpus of Engraved Gemstones from British Sites, Part II.* Oxford: 1974.

__. *Lewis Collection of Gemstones.* Oxford: 1975.

Henkel. *Die Rom. Fingerring der Rheinlande.* Berlin: 1913.

Higgins, R.A. *Terracottas in the British Museum.* Oxford: 1954.

Kaufmann, C.M. *Agyptische Terrakotten.* Cairo: 1913.

Maakant-Kleinbrindt, M. *Royal Coin Cabinet, the Hague.* Netherlands: 1978.

Marshall, F.H. *Catalogue of Finer Rings in the British Museum.* Oxford: 1968.

__. *Catalogue of Jewelry in the Departments of Antiquities.* British Museum, London: 1911.

Matheson, S.B. *Ancient Glass in the Yale University Art Gallery.* New Haven: 1980.

Moretti, G. & Caprino, C. *Il Museo delle Navi Romane de Nemi.* Rome: 1957.

Neuburg, F. *Ancient Glass.* Toronto: 1962.

Oberlin College. *Parkhurst Collection.* Oberlin, Guttman.

Oliver, A. *Ancient Glass in the Carnegie Museum of Natural History.* Pittsburgh: 1980.

Oswald, F. *An Introduction to the Study of Terra Sigiliala.* London: 1920.

Perkins, J.W. & Claridge, A. *Pompeii A.D. 79, Vol. II.* Boston: 1978.

Petrie, Sir W.M.F. *Objects of Daily Use.* London: 1927.

__. *Tools and Weapons.* London: 1917.

Plesnicar-Gec, L. *Severna Emonsko Grobisce: Excavations in Yugoslavia.* Ljubljana.

Righetti, R. *Gemme e Cammei delle Colleqione Comonali.* Rome: 1955.

Rudolph, B.Y. *Ancient Jewelry from the Collection of B.Y. Berry.* Bloomington: 1965.

Sieveking, J. *Die Terrakotta der Sammlung Loeb Vol. I and II.* Munich: 1916.

Siviero, G. *Li Ori e le Ambre del Museo Nazionale di Napoli.*

Sotheby Parke-Bernet & Co. *The Constable-Maxwell Collection of Ancient Glass.* London: 1979.

Sotheby's. Various auction sale catalogues.

Strong, D. & Brown, D. *Roman Crafts.* New York: 1976.

Sundwall, *Die Altern Italische Fibelin.*

Tarbell, F. B. *Catalogue of Bronzes in the Field Museum of Natural History, Vol. VII.* Chicago: 1909.

PRE-COLUMBIAN

Abbate, F., ed. *Pre-Columbian Art of North America and Mexico.* London: 1972.

Abel-Vidor, Suzanne, and Bakker, Dirk. *Pre-Columbian Art of Costa Rica.* NY: 1981.

Bennett, W.C. *Ancient Art of the Andes.* NY: 1954.

Benson, E.P., and Boone, E.H. *Falsifications and Misreconstructions of Pre-Columbian Art.* Washington: 1982.

Brinckerhoff, Deborah. *A Cosmic View: Pre-Columbian Art from the John Platt Collection.*

Bushnell, G.H.S. *Peru.* 2nd printing, NY: 1966.

Cervantes, Maria Antonieta. *National Anthropological Museum.* Mexico: 1978.

Coe, Michael D. *The Maya.* NY: 1966.

Meggers, Betty J. *Ecuador.* NY: 1966.

Montreal Museum of Fine Arts. *Man-Eaters and Pretty Ladies.* Montreal: 1971.

Reichel-Dolmatoff, G. *Columbia.* NY: 1965.

Stone, Doris. *Pre-Columbian Man in Costa Rica.* Cambridge, Mass.: 1977.

Winning, Hasso von. *The John Platt Collection of Pre-Columbian Art.* Charlottesville, VA: 1986.

__. *The Shaft Tomb Figures of West Mexico.* Southwest Museum, Los Angeles: 1974.

Wuthenau, Alexander von. *Terracotta Pottery in Pre-Columbian Central and South America.* Holland: 1969.

INDEX